VOLUME · THREE

DEMOCRACY

IN DEVELOPING COUNTRIES

ASIA

Also Available:

Volume 1, Persistence, Failure, and Renewal

Volume 2, Africa

Volume 4, Latin America

VOLUME•THREE

DEMOCRACY
IN DEVELOPING COUNTRIES

ASIA

Edited by
Larry Diamond
Juan J. Linz
Seymour Martin Lipset

Lynne Rienner Publishers •
Boulder, Colorado

Adamantine Press Limited •
London, England

Published in the United States of America in 1989 by
Lynne Rienner Publishers, Inc.
1800 30th Street, Boulder, Colorado 80301

Published in the United Kingdom by Adamantine Press Limited,
3 Henrietta Street, Covent Garden, London WC2E 8LU

Library of Congress Cataloging-in-Publication Data

Democracy in developing countries.

Bibliography: p.
Includes index.
Contents: —v. 2. Africa. —v. 3. Asia.
1. Developing countries—Politics and government.
2. Democracy. I. Diamond, Larry Jay. II. Linz, Juan J.
(Juan José), 1926–   . III. Lipset, Seymour Martin.
D883.D45   1988   320.917′4   87–23457
ISBN 1–55587–041–4
ISBN 1–55587–042–2 (pbk. v.3)

British Library Cataloguing in Publication Data

Democracy in developing countries.
  - Vol. 3: Asia.
  1. Developing countries. Democracy.
  I. Diamond, Larry   II. Linz, Juan J.
  III. Lipset, Seymour Martin
  321. 8′09172′4

ISBN 0–7449–0008–5
ISBN 0–7449–0009–3 pbk

Printed and bound in the United States of America

The paper used in this publication meets the requirements of the American National
Standard for Permanence of Paper for Printed Library Materials Z39.48–1984.

5 4 3 2

• Contents •

• List of Tables •

· Preface ·

This comparative study of democracy in developing countries—encompassing this and three other volumes—was undertaken at a time of tremendous democratic ferment in the developing world. The movement toward democracy that witnessed, in the mid-1970s, the toppling of Western Europe's last three dictatorships, in Greece, Portugal, and Spain, then moved on through Latin America. In the ensuing decade, most Latin American military dictatorships collapsed or withdrew, defying predictions of a longer reign for the "bureaucratic-authoritarian" regimes. Democratic progress was apparent in East Asia as well, in the Philippines, Korea, and even to some extent Taiwan. In the old British South Asian raj, both the more authoritarian states of Pakistan and Bangladesh and the democratic ones, India and Sri Lanka, were facing recurrent tensions and conflicts that could lead to a restoration or revitalization of democracy, or to deeper crisis.

Among the states of Africa, which found it difficult to establish new nationhood and democratic regimes, there have also been signs of democratic emergence or renewal. Uganda, for example, is struggling to put an end to decades of anarchy, tyranny, and civil strife, in order to fulfill its hopes for democracy and human rights. Despite intense repression, the black and coloured peoples of South Africa continue their struggle for a nonracial democracy through an increasingly powerful trade union movement. In Nigeria and Ghana, debate proceeds under military regimes over the constitutional structure for new attempts at democratic government.

These and similar dramas in Asia, Africa, and Latin America form the backdrop for renewed political and intellectual concern with the conditions for democratic government. To be sure, there is no guarantee that the recent and continuing democratic progress will not be reversed. If the past is any guide, many of the new democratic and semidemocratic regimes are likely to fail. Indeed, a number appear to be perched precariously on the precipice of new breakdowns into one-party or military rule or even chaos.

But the 1980s have seen an unprecedented growth of international concern for human rights—including (prominently) the rights to choose democratically the government under which one lives and to express and organize around one's political principles and views. As torture, disappearances, and other grave human rights violations have become more widespread, but also more systematically exposed and denounced around the world, there has developed a renewed and deeper appreciation for the democratic institutions that, with all their procedural messiness and sluggishness, nevertheless protect the integrity of the person and the freedoms of conscience and expression. The growth of democratic norms throughout the world is strikingly evident in the degree to which authoritarian regimes find it necessary to wrap themselves in the rhetoric and constitutional trappings of democracy, or at least to state as their goal the eventual establishment of democracy.

The great competing ideologies of the twentieth century have largely been discredited. Fascism was destroyed as a vital force in World War II. The appeals of Marxism-Leninism have declined with the harsh repressiveness, glaring economic failures, and loss of revolutionary idealism of the existing communist regimes. More limited quasi-socialist or mass mobilizational models—the Mexican, the Yugoslav, the Nasserite—have also lost their aura. Military regimes almost universally lack ideological justification, and legitimacy beyond a temporary intrusion to correct political and social problems. With the important but still indeterminate exception of the Islamic fundamentalist state—for that large portion of the world from Indonesia to West Africa where Islam is a major or dominant religion—democracy is the only model of government with any broad ideological legitimacy and appeal in the world today.

• STUDIES OF THE CONDITIONS FOR DEMOCRACY: A BRIEF INTELLECTUAL HISTORY •

An important element of this new global *zeitgeist* is the renewed proliferation of intellectual concern with the conditions of the democratic order. Beginning perhaps with the four-volume work on *The Breakdown of Democratic Regimes* in Europe and Latin America, edited by Juan Linz and Alfred Stepan,[1] one can trace a growing efflorscence of academic literature on transitions to and from democracy, and the sources of democratic persistence and failure. Studies have focused on varying themes, such as the means for accommodating ethnic or other sectional cleavages within a democratic framework,[2] the role of political institutions and political violence,[3] and the place of competitive elections in the development of democracy.[4] This outpouring of intellectual interest has recently produced a new four-volume study of transitions to democracy,[5] the most prominent in a rich new harvest of literature on the subject. On the more theoretical level of the definition of democracy and the debate surrounding its concepts, relationships, and forms, a stream of stimulating new work is appearing, of which the recent two-volume contribution of Giovanni Sartori should be considered an essential reference.[6]

Of course, intellectual concern with the social requisites, correlates, or conditions for democracy and other types of political systems has a long tradition, dating back at least to the classical Greek thinkers. Aristotle argued that democracy is more likely to occur where the middle strata are large, oligarchy and tyranny where the population is overwhelmingly poor. The Renaissance political theorist, Machiavelli, also placed an emphasis on class distribution in specifying the sources of political systems. The subsequent writings of Hobbes, Locke, and Montesquieu heavily influenced the founding fathers of the American democratic experience in their emphasis on the restraint of state powers through the institutionalization of checks and balances. Turning to the young American republic for clues to the development of democracy, the rule of law, and personal freedom, Alexis de Tocqueville emphasized in his writings the impact of voluntary associations as mediating institutions and contervailing forces to the central government; the division of powers in a federal system; and the relative socioeconomic equality that fostered political participation. In different ways, the role of the middle class in fostering liberty and democracy was also emphasized by the laissez-faire disciples of Adam Smith and by the Marxists.

However, while democracy slowly took root in much of northern Europe, as well as in North America and Australasia, attempts in Southern, Central, and Eastern Europe and in Latin America were generally less successful. These abortive democratic openings unleashed levels of political and social moblization that alarmed established interests such as the aristocracy, the landed elite, the church, and the military. As these groups, often allied with a weaker bourgeoisie, formed reactionary coalitions, the prospects for democracy dimmed. These various trends culminated during the 1920s and 1930s with the establishment of communist dictatorship in the Soviet Union, fascism in Germany and Italy, a host of other rightist dictatorships throughout Europe, and populist autocracies in Argentina, Brazil, and Mexico.

The pessimism about democracy and free institutions occasioned by the events of this period was inverted by the victory of the Allied powers in World War II. Democracy was imposed on Germany, Italy, and Japan, and surprisingly took hold and endured. Beginning with India in 1947, a host of new nations in Asia, Africa, and the Middle East that had been colonies of the Western democracies were granted independence under constitutions and following election procedures modeled on those of their former colonial rulers. The wave of excitement and optimism about the prospects for democracy and rapid development in these newly independent nations spawned a new generation of scholarly thinking and research.

More extensively than ever before, theory and empirical research in political development examined the world outside the West. Employing a multidimensional, functionalist framework, *The Politics of the Developing Areas* (1960) was (to quote its coeditor, Gabriel Almond) "the first effort to compare the political systems of the 'developing' areas, and to compare them systematically according to a common set of categories."[7] There followed a wealth of case studies of emerging political systems in the new nations, as well as comparative studies. Almond and Verba's *The Civic Culture* was the first scholarly attempt to apply the methods of modern survey analysis to the comparative analysis of political systems, in this case the relationship between democracy and political attitudes and values in five nations (four of them Western, but also including Mexico).[8] With increasing statistical sophistication, a new style of social science analysis examined quantitatively the relationship between democracy and socioeconomic modernization, or political development more broadly, across nations throughout the developed and developing worlds.[9] Some scholars, such as Samuel Huntington, focused a more skeptical eye on the sources of political disorder and breakdown in the new nations.[10] Also in this period came the ambitious and controversial sociological-historical effort of Barrington Moore to account for the emergence of democracy, authoritarianism, and totalitarianism in the world.[11]

Probably the most ambitious and important project of the decade was the work of the Committee on Comparative Politics of the Social Science Research Council (SSRC), which produced a series of nine volumes (mostly during the 1960s) on the relationship between political development and such social and political subsystems as bureaucracy, education, parties, and political culture. Much of this work was synthesized and distilled theoretically in *Crises and Sequences of Political Development,* which argued that patterns of political development, including the chances for stable democracy, could be explained by the way in which countries encountered and dealt with five characteristic problems of state- and nation-building.[12] The publication that same year (1971) of Robert Dahl's classic study, *Polyarchy,* can be seen as the crowning work on democracy of the political development decade.[13] To this day, it remains one of the most important treatments of the historical, social, economic, cultural, and political factors that foster or obstruct the development of stable democracy, and it has much influenced our own work. Although centered on the European historical experience, the work of Stein Rokkan has also been extremely fruitful for our understanding of the conditions under which states and party systems emerged and the variety of coalitions involved.[14]

The study of democracy was to sag through most of the 1970s. By 1970, critiques of pluralist political development studies as ethnocentric and even reflective of U.S. imperialism were in full cry. Although these criticisms were often based on a superficial and ideologically biased reading of these works,[15] they nevertheless pushed the study of comparative political systems into the background. The fields of comparative politics, political development, and international political sociology became dominated by issues relating to economic dependence and by theories of international dependency—often carrying with them the Marxist assumption that political systems were mere superstructures and "bourgeois democracies" largely illusory and epiphenomenal. To the extent they dealt with the political system explicitly, theories of dependency maintained that political exclusion and repression of popular mobilization were inevitable concomitants of dependent economic development and peripheral

status in the world division of labor.[16] Cynicism about political democracy in
the developing countries was reflected and deepened by a new cycle of democratic breakdowns in Latin America into particularly harsh, "bureaucratic-
authoritarian" dictatorships. This development was interpreted as a consequence of the inherent strains and pressures of economic dependence at a
particular, middle stage of development.[17] But the collapse of these and other
dictatorships around the world—beginning with the transitions to democracy in
southern Europe in the mid-1970s—along with the revalorization of political
democracy as an end in itself (partly in response to the extraordinary brutality
of many recent authoritarian experiences), has now refocused the attention of
the scholarly world on the conditions for liberal democracy.

• THE PROJECT ON DEMOCRACY
IN DEVELOPING COUNTRIES •

The growth of political and intellectual interest in democracy in developing
countries provided a propitious climate for the study we wanted to launch. Despite the rich profusion of literature, it seemed to us that there remained huge
gaps in our understanding of the factors that fostered or obstructed the
emergence, instauration, and consolidation of democratic government around
the world. All of the existing studies were limited in important ways: to a particular period of time; to particular regions (usually Europe or Latin America);
to particular moments or segments of the historical record (such as crises and
breakdowns, or transitions); or to a limited range of theoretical variables. While
understanding that any one study would inevitably be bound more or less by
such limits, we undertook to design a comparative historical analysis that
would, nevertheless, reach wider and further than had any previous one.

The resulting four-volume work is, we believe, somewhat unique in several respects. In geographical scope, it is the first study of democracy to compare systematically the historical experiences of individual countries throughout Asia, Africa, and Latin America. In the "developing" world, only the
Middle East (for reasons we will later explain) is excluded. In sheer size, it may
be the largest comparative study of national political systems to date, with chapters on twenty six different countries. Significantly, these chapters are not the
loose collection of varied papers and themes one sometimes encounters. Each
was written specifically for this project, in response to a common set of
guidelines, definitions, and theoretical concerns. Also we as editors took a
broadly inclusive approach theoretically. Rather than pursuing some new, ele-
gant, "parsimonious" model, we deliberately eschewed monocausal and reduc-
tionist interpretations in favor of an exhaustive examination of all the historical,
cultural, social, economic, political, and international factors that might affect
the chances for stable democracy; how they interact; and the conditions that
might mediate their salience or their effects.

The contributions to this work are also distinctive in that they deal with the entire history of a country's experience with democracy. This includes the whole range of phenomena: establishment, breakdown, reequilibration, and consolidation of democratic government; periods of democratic persistence, crisis, authoritarianism, and renewal; and all of the ambivalences and oscillations in between. In the process, we consider each country's early cultural traditions, analyze (where relevant) the colonial experience, consider all of its postindependence history, but give special emphasis to post-World War II developments. Whereas most other works cut horizontally through the history of countries to focus on limited time spans and particular processes (usually ignoring the phenomena of democratic consolidation and stability),[18] our study cuts vertically through historical phases in order to explain the overall path of a country's political development.

While it can be enormously fertile, this historical approach is not without certain methodological problems. In particular, it runs the risk of attributing contemporary political patterns to antecedents far removed in time, without clearly demonstrating that those factors (or characteristics resulting from them) are operating at a later time and account for the failure or success of democracy. The past, to be relevant, must in one way or another be present at the time the realities we want to explain happen. We feel, however, that within the constraints of space, the authors of the case studies have generally avoided accounting for events at time t^{20} by reference to factors that appear only at time t^1 or t^5, although sometimes the link with t^{19} might have been made more explicit.

The result is an eclectic, but also very rich, analysis of the opportunities and obstacles for democracy in the developing world today. Indeed, it is the very richness of our study that presents to us, as perhaps it will to many of our readers, the greatest frustration. As our colleague Robert Dahl remarked at a recent scholarly meeting where our work was discussed, a key problem with the previous generation of work on democracy was the paucity of comparative evidence in relation to the abundance of theorizing; on the other hand, the current generation of work, including this comparative study, appears destined to suffer from an abundance of evidence for which there will be a relative dearth of theory. Readers of Volume 1 in this set will find no shortage of theoretical arguments and lessons drawn from this study. But we concede that these are not integrated into a single, all-encompassing theory, and that it will be some time (if ever) before the field produces one.

We began our study by inviting distinguished comparativists and country specialists to write case studies of individual countries' experiences with democratic and authoritarian government. Each of our authors was given the same broad set of guidelines, flexible enough to permit them to do justice to the uniqueness of the society and its history, but structured enough so that each case study would share a common conceptual orientation, analytical purpose, and framework for organizing the material.

The first section of each chapter was to review the country's political history, describing the major experiences with democratic and nondemocratic government, including the structure, nature, and characteristic conflicts and tensions of each regime. The second section would explain the fate of each regime (especially each democratic one), why it persisted or failed or evolved as it did, and why successive ones emerged as and when they did. Alternatively, authors were given the option of combining these tasks of historical review and analysis, which many did. In a third (or second) section, the author was asked to offer a summary theoretical judgment of the factors that have been most important in determining the country's overall degree of success or failure with democratic government—to abstract across the various regimes and events the most consistently significant and salient factors from among the broad inventory of variables in our project outline (and any others we might have neglected). Finally, each author was asked to consider the future prospects for democratic government in the country, along with any policy implications he or she might wish to derive. In addition, each author was asked to assess (somewhere in the chapter) the country's overall experience with democratic government, using our six-point scale (of ideal types ranging from stable and consolidated democratic rule to the failure or absence of democracy).[19]

The task we gave those who wrote our case studies was an imposing one. What made it even forbidding—and sometimes (especially for countries with long and variegated political histories) nearly impossible—was the space constraint we were forced to impose as a result of the economic realities of contemporary book publishing. Thus, each author was compelled to be selective and often painfully brief, both in the treatment of important historical developments and in the analysis of theoretical variables. Although we have sought to make our case studies readily accessible to readers with little or no prior knowledge of the country—in part to encourage the wide reading across regions we feel is essential—we could not avoid giving many key problems and events little or no attention. Our readers are thus cautioned that the case studies provide no more than capsulized surveys of a country's experience, which will, we hope, inspire wider study from among the many other sources they cite.

The theoretical framework for the study grew out of an extensive review of the previous literature, one which appears in Volume 1. The ten theoretical dimensions in this framework covered the gamut of factors that various theoretical and empirical works have associated with democracy: political culture; regime legitimacy and effectiveness; historical development (in particular the colonial experience); class structure and the degree of inequality; national structure (ethnic, racial, regional, and religious cleavage); state structure, centralization, and strength (including the state's role in the economy, the roles of autonomous voluntary associations and the press, federalism, and the role of the armed forces); political and constitutional structure (parties, electoral systems, the judiciary); political leadership; development performance; and international factors.

These broad dimensions encompassed dozens of specific variables and questions, from which we derived forty nine tentative propositions about the likelihood of stable democratic government. Obviously, it would have been foolish to pretend that our study could have "tested" these propositions. In spite of having twenty six countries, we still had the problem of "too many variables, too few cases" to enable us to reach any definitive conclusions about the effects of these variables. But we did believe that the evidence and conclusions from twenty six carefully selected cases, if structured systematically, could shed much light on how these variables affected the democratic prospect, and how these effects might vary with other conditions.

• CONCEPTS, DEFINITIONS, AND CLASSIFICATIONS •

Depending on the individual, ideology, paradigm, culture, or context, the term "democracy" may mean many different things. In fact, it is reflective of the political climate of our time that the word is used to signify the desirable end-state of so many social, economic, and political pursuits, or else to self-designate and thus presumably legitimate so many existing structures. Hence, it is imperative that we be as precise as possible about exactly what it is we are studying.

We use the term "democracy" in this study to signify a political system, separate and apart from the economic and social system to which it is joined. Indeed, a distinctive aspect of our approach is to insist that issues of so-called economic and social democracy be separated from the question of governmental structure. Otherwise, the definitional criteria of democracy will be broadened and the empirical reality narrowed to a degree that may make study of the phenomena very difficult. In addition, unless the economic and social dimensions are kept conceptually distinct from the political, there is no way to analyze how variation on the political dimension is related to variation on the others. But most of all, as we will argue shortly, we distinguish the concept of political democracy out of a clear and frankly expressed conviction that it is worth valuing—and hence worth studying—as an end in itself.

In this study, then, democracy—or what Robert Dahl terms "polyarchy"—denotes a system of government that meets three essential conditions: meaningful and extensive *competition* among individuals and organized groups (especially political parties) for all effective positions of government power, at regular intervals and excluding the use of force; a highly inclusive level of *political participation* in the selection of leaders and policies, at least through regular and fair elections, such that no major (adult) social group is excluded; and a level of *civil and political liberties*—freedom of expression, freedom of the press, freedom to form and join organizations—sufficient to ensure the integrity of political competition and participation.[20]

While this definition is, in itself, relatively straightforward, it presents a number of problems in application. For one, countries that broadly satisfy these criteria nevertheless do so to different degrees. (In fact, none do so perfectly, which is why Dahl prefers to call them polyarchies). The factors that explain this variation at the democratic end of the spectrum in degrees of popular control and freedom is an important intellectual problem. But it is different from the one that concerns us in these four volumes, and so it is one we have had largely to bypass. This study seeks to determine why countries do or do not evolve, consolidate, maintain, lose, and reestablish more or less democratic systems of government.

Even this limited focus leaves us with conceptual problems. The boundary between democratic and nondemocratic is sometimes a blurred and imperfect one, and beyond it lies a much broader range of variation in political systems. We readily concede the difficulties of classification this variation has repeatedly caused us. Even if we look only at the political, legal, and constitutional structure, several of our cases appear to lie somewhere on the boundary between democratic and something less than democratic. The ambiguity is further complicated by the constraints on free political activity, organization, and expression that may often in practice make the system much less democratic than it appears on paper. In all cases, we have tried to pay serious attention to actual practice in assessing and classifying regimes. But, still, this has left us to make difficult and in some ways arbitrary judgements. For countries such as Turkey, Sri Lanka, Malaysia, Colombia, and Zimbabwe, the decision as to whether these may today be considered full democracies is replete with nuance and ambiguity.

We have alleviated the problem somewhat by recognizing various grades of distinction among less-than-democratic systems. While isolated violations of civil liberties or modest and occasional vote-rigging should not disqualify a country from broad classification as a democracy, there is a need to categorize separately those countries that allow greater political competition and freedom than would be found in a true authoritarian regime but less than could justifiably be termed democratic. Hence, we classify as *semidemocratic* those countries where the effective power of elected officials is so limited, or political party competition is so restricted, or the freedom and fairness of elections so compromised that electoral outcomes, while competitive, still deviate significantly from popular preferences; and/or where civil and political liberties are so limited that some political orientations and interests are unable to organize and express themselves. In different ways and to different degrees, Senegal, Zimbabwe, Malaysia, and Thailand fit in this category. Still more restrictive is a *hegemonic party system,* like that of Mexico, in which opposition parties are legal but denied—through pervasive electoral malpractices and frequent state coercion—any real chance to compete for power. Descending further on the scale of classification, *authoritarian* regimes permit even less pluralism, typically banning political parties (or all but the ruling one) and most forms of political organization and competition, while being more repressive than liberal in their level of civil and political freedom. Paying close attention to actual behavior, one may distinguish a subset of authoritarian regimes that we call *pseudodemocracies,* in that the existence of formally democratic political institutions, such as multiparty electoral competition, masks (often, in part, to legitimate) the reality of authoritarian domination. While this regime type overlaps in some ways with the hegemonic regime, it is less institutionalized and typically more personalized, coercive, and unstable. Nevertheless, we prefer not to ignore the democratic facade, because, as we argue in Volume 1, its coexistence with an authoritarian reality may generate distinctive problems for a transition to democracy.

Democratic trappings aside, authoritarian regimes vary widely in the degree to which they permit independent and critical political expression and organization. By the level of what the regime allows, one can distinguish between what O'Donnell and Schmitter call "dictablandas," or liberalized autocracies, and "dictaduras," harsher dictatorships that allow much less space for individual and group action.[21] By the level of what groups in the society recurrently demand (which may or may not overlap with the above), one can distinguish, as we do in Volume 1, between authoritarian situations with strong democratic pressures and those with weak democratic pressures. In selecting cases for this study, our bias was toward the former. Finally, of course, are the *totalitarian* regimes, which not only repress all forms of autonomous social and political organization, denying completely even the most elementary political and civil liberties, but also demand an active commitment by the citizens to the regime.[22] Because our concern in this study was primarily with democracy, these regimes (mainly now the communist ones, although not all of them are totalitarian) were excluded from our analysis.

The "dependent variable" of our study was concerned not only with democracy, but also stability—the persistence and durability of democratic and other regimes over time, particularly through periods of unusually intense conflict, crisis, and strain. A *stable* regime is one that is deeply institutionalized and consolidated, making it likely therefore to enjoy a high level of popular legitimacy. (As we argue in Volume 1, the relationship between stability and legitimacy is an intimate one.) *Partially stable* regimes are neither fully secure nor in imminent danger of collapse. Their institutions have perhaps acquired some measure of depth, flexibility, and value, but not enough to ensure the regime safe passage through severe challenges. *Unstable* regimes are, by definition, highly vulnerable to breakdown or overthrow in periods of acute uncertainty and stress. New regimes, including those that have recently restored democratic government, tend to fall in this category.

• THE SELECTION OF COUNTRIES •

One of the limitations, as well as one of the values, of our enterprise is the great heterogeneity of the twenty six countries included. The value is that the country studies provide us with insights into the whole range of factors relevant to our study, rather than limiting us to those variables for which there are data for all countries of the world (as with the social and economic statistics of the United Nations and the World Bank) or those factors shared by a relatively homogeneous set of countries. The major disadvantage, however, is that—unless we turn to studies and data not included in our volumes—the lack of statistical representativeness (which is, anyhow, dubious in dealing with states) precludes a statistical approach to testing hypotheses. In fact, our introductory volume contains a substantial quantitative analysis, based on data for over eighty countries, of the relationship between socioeconomic development and democracy, a relationship found to be basically positive.[23] Still, for the most part, we believe that the study of twenty six carefully chosen countries, by scholars familiar with each of them, and guided more or less by the concepts and issues suggested, provides us with a better understanding of the complex problems involved.

The criteria for the selection of countries were complex and, although not ad hoc, do not entirely satisfy our plans and ambitions for the well-known reasons encountered in any such large-scale comparative project. The foremost, perhaps debatable, decision was to exclude Western Europe, the North American democracies, Australia, New Zealand, and the most advanced non-Western industrial democracy, Japan—although their historical experiences are analyzed separately in Volume 1. Essentially, these are the OECD countries, members of the Paris-based Organization for Economic Cooperation and Development.[24] All of these countries have been stable democracies since World War II, if not earlier, with the exceptions of Greece, Portugal, and Spain, which joined the club in the mid-1970s and have been stable democracies for over ten years. The southern European experience, however, enters into our thinking and will occasionally be mentioned (if for no other reason than that it is an area of scholarly interest of one of the editors). All in this first group of countries excluded from our study are advanced industrial, capitalist democracies with higher per capita gross national products than the most developed of the countries we included. (The one exception is Portugal, whose per capita GNP is lower than a few of our developing countries, including Argentina and South Korea).

Another basic decision was not to include any communist countries. One of their distinctive characteristics is that, in those with a more or less democratic past (some in Eastern Europe), the absence of democracy is explained more by the power politics of Soviet hegemony than by any internal historical, social, economic, political, or cultural factors (although these might have been important before 1945). Another crucial distinction is that there is little prospect among them of a transition to democracy, but only of liberalization of communist rule. Outside of Eastern Europe, communist countries have little or no past democratic experience, and the present communist rule excludes, for the forseeable future, any real debate about political democracy in the sense defined by us.

Less justifiable, perhaps, is the exclusion of most of the Islamic world from Morocco to Iran, in particular the Arab world. In part, this stemmed from the limits of our resources, which were stretched thin by the scope of the project.

But it was a decision made also in response to theoretical priorities. With the exception perhaps of Egypt, Lebanon, and certainly Turkey (which appears in our Asia volume), the Islamic countries of the Middle East and North Africa generally lack much previous democratic experience, and most appear to have little prospect of transition even to semidemocracy. However, our study does not completely ignore the Islamic world. In addition to the "secularized" Islamic polity of Turkey, we include Pakistan, which shared, until partition, the history of British India and has tried democracy; Malaysia, a multiethnic, multireligious, but predominantly Muslim polity with significant democratic institutions; Senegal, an African Muslim country whose recently evolved semidemocracy is coming under growing challenge from Islamic fundamentalist thinking; and the farthest outpost of Islam, Indonesia, with its syncretic cultural traditions. These five Islamic countries, with their heterogeneity, clearly are not a sample of the world's Islamic polities and, therefore, will not enable us to explore in sufficient depth the complex relationship between Islamic religion and society and democracy.

Otherwise, our twenty six countries are quite representative of the heterogeneous world of those loosely called "Third World" or "developing" countries. These terms are largely misleading, and we want clearly to disassociate ourselves from assuming that such a category is scientifically useful in cross-national comparisons. Certainly, it seems ridiculous to put Argentina or Uruguay or South Korea in the same classification of countries as Ghana, Papua New Guinea, or even India, in terms of economic development, social structure or cultural traditions, and prospects of socioeconomic development. Nevertheless, all twenty six countries included in this study are less developed economically and less stable politically than the established, industrialized democracies of Europe, North America, Australasia, and Japan. And all share the same pressure from within to "develop" economically and socially, to build stable political institutions, and—as we argue in Volume 1—to become democracies, whatever the probabilities of their success in doing so. In this sense, all of these countries may be considered "less developed," or as we most often term them, for lack of a better common label, "developing."

Some readers might feel that all the countries in our study share one characteristic: that they have capitalist economic systems (although some have tried various socialist experiments), but such a characterization again becomes in its vagueness almost meaningless. To what extent can a dynamic, industrial, export-oriented capitalist economy like South Korea be covered by the same term as Uganda, whose population lives largely from subsistence agriculture, with a small native entrepreneurial class based heavily in the informal sector; or as other African countries in which business class formation entails more the access to and abuse of power to attain wealth than it does productive economic activities (which are subject to interference by the state if not extortion by the rulers)? Certainly the term "capitalist economy" covers too much to be meaningful sociologically when it is used simultaneously to describe advanced, industrial, market-oriented economies; state-dominated economies in which much of private enterprise is relegated to the informal sector; and largely subsistence, peasant, agricultural societies with isolated (and often foreign-owned) capitalist enclaves.

For the sake of argument, we might agree that all our countries have nonsocialist economic systems, which, therefore, allows us to ask questions about how "capitalism" in its very different forms may be related to democracy. We start from two obvious facts. First, all democracies (in our sense) are to some degree capitalist. Some are capitalist welfare states, with extensive public sectors and state regulation of the economy; some are capitalist with social democratic governments and more or less mixed economies. But, in all of the world's political democracies, prices, production and distribution of goods are determined mainly by competition in the market, rather than by the state, and there is significant private ownership of the means of production. Second, there are many capitalist countries with nondemocratic governments. But interestingly, among this latter group, those most advanced in their capitalist development (size of market sector of their economy, autonomy of their entrepreneurial class) are also those that have been most exposed to pressures for democracy, leading, in many cases, to the emergence or return of democratic government. This is despite the forceful arguments of some theories that postulated that the authoritarian regimes they suffered were more congruent or functional for their continued capitalist development. In addition, it is not clear how much certain types of nonsocialist authoritarianisms—particularly sultanism[25]—are compatible with the effective functioning of a capitalist economy.

Certainly, our effort can make a contribution to the continuing debate about the relationship between capitalism and democracy, and the even more lively one on the relationship between dependent, peripheral capitalism and democracy. This we seek to do in our theoretical reflections in Volume 1. In doing so, we emphasize that our study did not begin with any *a priori* assumption equating democracy with capitalism. To reiterate an earlier theme, democracy as a system of government must be kept conceptually distinct from capitalism as a system of production and exchange, and socialism as a system of allocation of resources and income. The fact that (to date) one does not find democracy in the absence of some form of capitalism is for us a matter of great theoretical import, but we do not assume that this empirical association must hold inevitably into the future. In our theoretical volume, we suggest why state socialism (which some would insist is only state or statist capitalism) has been so difficult to reconcile with political democracy, and ponder what alternatives to capitalism might potentially be compatible with democracy.

Culturally, our effort includes the Christian societies of Latin America, India with its mosaic of traditions (including the distinctive Hindu culture), five largely Islamic societies, two Buddhist countries, one a mixture of Buddhism, Confucianism, and Christianity, and several African countries that have experienced what Mazrui calls the "triple heritage" of Christianity, Islam, and traditional African religion and culture. Unfortunately, the limited treatment in our country studies does not enable us to deal adequately with the complex issues of the relation between democracy and religious and cultural traditions, although we are unable to ignore them.

One of the most complex and intractable problems in our world is the tension between the model of ethnically, linguistically, and culturally homogeneous societies that satisfy the ideal of the nation-state and the multiethnic, multilingual societies that face the difficult task of nation- or state-building in the absence of the integration and identification we normally associate with the idea of the nation-state. Certainly, even in Europe, before the massive and forced transfers (if not destruction) of populations, most states did not satisfy that ideal, but outside of Europe and Latin America, even fewer do. In our study, only a few Latin American countries—Costa Rica, Venezuela, Argentina, Uruguay, Chile, perhaps Colombia—seem to satisfy that model. Others, like Brazil, the Dominican Republic, Mexico, and above all Peru, include not only descendants of the *conquistadores* and European immigrants, but also substantial populations (intermixed to varying degrees with the above) of Indians and descendants of black slaves. To the list of the relatively homogeneous countries could be added South Korea, Turkey (with some significant minorities), and Botswana (which still has major subtribal divisions). Our remaining cases confront us with the problem of democracy in ethnically and culturally divided societies, some of them, like Sri Lanka, with populations linked culturally with another, neighboring country.

One experience that almost all of the countries in our study share is a previous history of domination by an outside imperial power. Only Turkey and Thailand have been continuously independent countries, and only in the latter do we find a continuity with a premodern traditional monarchy. Our study, therefore, does not cover a sufficient number of countries to deal with the question: does continuous legitimacy of rule by an indigenous state facilitate both modernization and ultimately democratization, by contrast with the historical trauma of conquest and colonial domination?

For those who have raised the question of the relation between size and democracy,[26] our study includes the largest (most populous) democracy, India, and some of the smallest. In each part of the world it includes the largest country and at least some significant smaller ones: Brazil and Costa Rica, Nigeria and Botswana, India and Sri Lanka. Since the major countries—with their political influence and their capacity to serve as models—occupy a special position in their respective areas, where some speak of subimperialisms, we feel our selection on this account is well justified.

In addition to trying, as much as possible, to maximize variation in our independent variables, we have also sought a richly varied pool of cases with regard to our dependent variable, stable democracy. Save for the deliberate exclusion of countries with no prior democratic or semidemocratic experience, or no prospect of a democratic opening, our study encompasses virtually every type of democratic experience in the developing world. Some of our countries are now democratic, some are semidemocratic, some are authoritarian, and one is a hegemonic regime. Some of the democracies have been relatively stable for some time (such as Costa Rica and, so far at least, Botswana and Papua New Guinea); some have persisted in the face of recurrent crises and lapses (India, and now less democratically, Sri Lanka); and some have been renewed after traumatic and, in some cases, repeated breakdowns (e.g., Brazil, Uruguay, and Argentina). Some countries have experienced recurrent cycles of democratic attempts and military interventions, from which Turkey has managed to emerge with a generally longer and more successful democratic experience than Thailand, Ghana, or Nigeria. We have countries in varying stages of transition to democracy at this writing, from the recently completed but still fragile (the Philippines), to the partial or continuing and still undetermined (South Korea, Uganda, Pakistan), to the prospective (Nigeria), to the obstructed (Chile).[27] And, still, we have at least one case (Indonesia) of a failed democracy that seems to have been consolidating a distinctive form of authoritarian rule.

The sheer number of our case studies compelled us to break them up for publication into several volumes. This presented another editorial dilemma. We have opted for the established mode of division into regional volumes, as this follows the dominant organizational logic of scholarship, instruction, and intellectual discourse in the field. But we hasten to underscore our feeling that this is not the most intellectually fruitful or satisfying way of treating such material. It would perhaps have made more sense to group the cases by the characteristic types of regimes and problems they have experienced. But any method of division inevitably breaks the unity of our twenty six cases and disperses the multitude of different comparisons that spring from them. We know of no solution to this problem other than to invite our readers to read widely across the three regional volumes, and to work back and forth between the theory in our introductory volume and the evidence in our cases, as we ourselves have attempted to do over the past three years.

• THE NORMATIVE QUESTION: WHY STUDY DEMOCRACY? •

Finally, we cannot close this introduction to our work without confronting the question (or critical challenge) that is often put to us: Why study political democracy at all? Some critics suggest it is the wrong problem to be studying. They ask: Are there not more pressing issues of survival and justice facing developing societies? Does the limited question of the form of government not conceal more than it reveals? Others contend our choice of topic betrays a value bias for democracy that is misplaced. They ask (or assert): If in some societies democracy in our (liberal) sense has to work against so many odds, as our research unveils, is it worth striving for and encouraging an opposition that purports to establish it, or are there alternatives to democracy that should be considered and whose stability should be supported?

We wish to state quite clearly here our bias for democracy as a system of government. For any democrat, these questions carry serious implications. The former suggest that economic and social rights should be considered more important than civil and political liberties. The latter implies granting to some forms or cases of authoritarian rule the right to use coercive measures, in the name of some higher good, to suppress an opposition that claims to fight for democracy. For ourselves, neither of these normative suppositions is tenable.

If there were many nondemocratic governments (now and in the past) committed to serving collective goals, rather than the interests of the rulers, and ready to respect human rights (to refrain from torture and indiscriminate violence, to offer due process and fair trial in applying laws which, even if antiliberal, are known in advance, to maintain humane conditions of imprisonment, etc.), we might find these questions more difficult to answer. However, nondemocratic regimes satisfying these two requirements are few, and even those that begin with a strong commitment to the collectivity and sensitivity to human rights often become increasingly narrow, autocratic, and repressive (although these trends, too, are subject to reversal).

We emphasize the service of collective goals to exclude those authoritarian systems in which the rulers blatantly serve their own material interests and those of their family, friends, cronies, and clients; and to exclude as well those systems serving a narrowly defined oligarchy, stratum, or a particular ethnic or racial group (which might even be the majority). But even excluding such transparent cases (the majority, unfortunately), who is to define those collective goals, if we disqualify the majority of citizens from doing so? Inevitably, it means a self-appointed minority—a vanguard party, a charismatic leader and his followers, a bureaucracy, army officers, or perhaps intellectuals or "experts" working with them. But why should their definition of societal goals be better than that of any other group with a different concept of the collective good? Only if we were totally certain that one ideological (or religious) concept is the expression of historical reason—true and necessary—would we be forced to accept such an authoritarian alternative as better than democracy. To do so, as we know, justifies any sacrifices and ultimately terrible costs in freedom and human lives. The option between ultimate value choices would inevitably be resolved by force. Thus, democracy—with its relativism and tolerance (so disturbing to those certain of the truth), and its "faith" in the reasonableness and intelligence of the common men and women, including those uneducated and those with "false consciousness" (a concept that assumes others know better their real interests), deciding freely (and with a chance to change their minds every four or five years) and without the use of force—seems still a better option.

Of course, even committed democrats know that the empirical world, and so the normative issue, is full of variation and ambiguity. But this should not lead to intellectual and political confusion. A few authoritarian regimes that manifest commitment to collective goals and human rights might have redeeming qualities, particularly if they are stable and do not require excessive force to stay in power. But that does not make them democracies. Their supporters should be free to argue the positive aspects of their rule, without ignoring or denying the negative ones, but they should not attempt to claim that they are democracies. Not all nondemocracies are totally bad. Nor are all democracies, and especially unstable democracies, good for the people. But, certainly, non-democracies are not likely to achieve those social and moral goals that require democratic institutions and freedoms. Therefore, from the point of view of a democrat, they will always be undesirable. Moreover, should they turn out to betray the ideals and hopes of their founders (as they have done so repeatedly), there is no easy way to oust them from power by peaceful means. Indeed, the almost law-like inevitability of the abuse and corruption of authoritarian power throughout history constitutes, we believe, one of the most compelling justifications for the institutionalized checks and accountability of a democracy.

For all these reasons, we (along with an increasing proportion of the world's population) value political democracy as an end in itself—without assuming that it is any guarantee of other important values. And we believe that a better understanding of the conditions for it is a worthwhile intellectual endeavor, which does not require us to deny the positive accomplishments of some nondemocratic regimes and the many flaws of democratic governments and societies.

Larry Diamond
Juan J. Linz
Seymour Martin Lipset

• NOTES •

1. Juan J. Linz and Alfred Stepan, eds., *The Breakdown of Democratic Regimes* (Baltimore: Johns Hopkins University Press, 1978).
2. Arend Lijphart, *Democracy in Plural Societies: A Comparative Exploration* (New Haven: Yale University Press, 1977); Donald L. Horowitz, *Ethnic Groups in Conflict* (Berkeley: University of California Press, 1985).
3. G. Bingham Powell, *Contemporary Democracies: Participation, Stability and Violence* (Cambridge: Harvard University Press, 1982).
4. Myron Weiner and Ergun Ozbudun, eds., *Competitive Elections in Developing Countries* (Washington: American Enterprise Institute, 1987).
5. Guillermo O'Donnell, Philippe C. Schmitter, and Laurence Whitehead, eds., *Transitions from Authoritarian Rule* (Baltimore: Johns Hopkins University Press, 1986).
6. Giovanni Sartori, *The Theory of Democracy Revisited* (Chatham, N.J.: Chatham House Publishers, 1987).
7. Gabriel A. Almond and James S. Coleman, eds., *The Politics of the Developing Areas* (Princeton: Princeton University Press, 1960), p. 3.
8. Gabriel A. Almond and Sidney Verba, *The Civic Culture* (Princeton: Princeton University Press, 1963).
9. Notable early works here were Daniel Lerner, *The Passing of Traditional Society* (Glencoe, Ill.: The Free Press, 1958); Seymour Martin Lipset, "Some Social Requisites of Democracy," *American Political Science Review* 53 (1959): pp. 69–105, and *Political Man* (New York: Doubleday & Co., 1960), pp. 27–63; and Karl W. Deutsch, "Social Mobilization and Democracy," *American Political Science Review* 55 (1961): pp. 493–514.

10. Samuel P. Huntington, *Political Order in Changing Societies* (New Haven: Yale University Press, 1968).

11. Barrington Moore, Jr., *Social Origins of Dictatorship and Democracy* (Cambridge: Harvard University Press, 1966).

12. Leonard Binder, James S. Coleman, Joseph La Palombara, Lucian Pye, Sidney Verba, and Myron Weiner, *Crises and Sequences in Political Development* (Princeton: Princeton University Press, 1971). The work of this committee, and the evolution of political development studies from the 1960s to the present, is surveyed in a sweeping and erudite review by Gabriel Almond, "The Development of Political Development," in Myron Weiner and Samuel P. Huntington, eds., *Understanding Political Development* (Boston: Little, Brown and Co., 1987), pp. 437–490.

13. Robert A. Dahl, *Polyarchy: Participation and Opposition* (New Haven: Yale University Press, 1971).

14. See, for example, Stein Rokkan, *Citizens, Elections, Parties: Approaches to the Comparative Study of the Processes of Development* (Oslo: Universitetsforlaget, 1970).

15. Almond, "The Development of Political Development," pp. 444–450.

16. Peter Evans, *Dependent Development* (Princeton: Princeton University Press, 1979), pp. 25–54.

17. Guillermo O'Donnell, *Modernization and Bureaucratic-Authoritarianism: Studies in South American Politics* (Berkeley: Institute of International Studies, University of California, 1973); see, also, David Collier, ed., *The New Authoritarianism in Latin America* (Princeton: Princeton University Press, 1979).

18. This neglect is, to some extent, overcome in Arend Lijphart's creative and enterprising study, *Democracies: Patterns of Majoritarian and Consensus Government in Twenty-One Countries* (New Haven: Yale University Press, 1984). However, the focus is mainly on political structure, and the comparison is limited to the continuous and stable democracies of the advanced, industrial countries.

19. Specifically, the points on this scale were: (1) *High success*—stable and uninterrupted democratic rule, with democracy now deeply institutionalized and stable; (2) *Progressive success*—the consolidation of relatively stable democracy after one or more breakdowns or serious interruptions; (3) *Mixed success—democratic and unstable* (e.g., democracy has returned following a period of breakdown and authoritarian rule, but has not yet been consolidated); (4) *Mixed success—partial or semidemocracy*; (5) *Failure but promise*—democratic rule has broken down, but there are considerable pressures and prospects for its return; (6) *Failure or absence*—democracy has never functioned for any significant period of time and there is little prospect that it will in the coming years.

20. Dahl, *Polyarchy*, pp. 3–20; Joseph Schumpeter, *Capitalism, Socialism and Democracy* (New York: Harper and Row, 1942); Lipset, *Political Man*, p. 27; Juan Linz, *The Breakdown of Democratic Regimes: Crisis, Breakdown and Reequilibration* (Baltimore: Johns Hopkins University Press, 1978), p. 5.

21. Guillermo O'Donnell and Philippe C. Schmitter, *Transitions from Authoritarian Rule: Tentative Conclusions about Uncertain Democracies* (Baltimore: Johns Hopkins University Press, 1986).

22. The distinction between authoritarian and totalitarian regimes has a long intellectual history predating its fashionable (and in some ways confusing) use by Jeanne Kirkpatrick in "Dictatorships and Double Standards," *Commentary* 68 (1979): pp. 34–45. See Juan J. Linz, "Totalitarian and Authoritarian Regimes," in *Handbook of Political Science*, Fred I. Greenstein and Nelson W. Polsby, eds, (Reading, Mass.: Addison-Wesley, 1975), vol. 3, pp. 175–411.

23. For a review of the literature on the subject from 1960 to 1980, see the expanded and updated edition of Lipset's *Political Man* (Baltimore: Johns Hopkins University Press, 1981), pp. 469–476.

24. In point of fact, the twenty-four-member organization also includes Turkey, but its per capita GNP ($1,160 in 1984) clearly places it among the middle ranks of developing countries (at about the level of Costa Rica or Colombia, for example).

25. Linz, "Totalitarianism and Authoritarianism," pp. 259–263.

26. Robert A. Dahl and Edward Tufte, *Size and Democracy* (Stanford: Stanford University Press, 1973).

27. One of the most important countries in the world now struggling (against increasingly forbidding odds, it appears) to develop a full democracy—South Africa—we reluctantly excluded

from our study not only because it has lacked any previous experience with democracy (beyond its limited functioning among the minority white population), but because the context of pervasive, institutionalized racial domination generates a number of quite distinctive obstacles and complexities. Although we feel our theoretical framework has much to contribute to the study of the conditions and prospects for democracy in South Africa, the unique character of that problem may make it more suitable for exploration through monographic studies, of which there is a proliferating literature. See, for example, Arend Lijphart, *Power-Sharing in South Africa* (Berkeley: Institute of International Studies, University of California, 1985), and Heribert Adam and Kogila Moodley, *South Africa Without Apartheid: Dismantling Racial Domination* (Berkeley: University of California Press, 1986).

• Acknowledgments •

This comparative study of democracy, and the conference in December of 1985 to discuss the first drafts of the case studies, were made possible by a generous grant from the National Endowment for Democracy. The Endowment is a private, nonprofit organization which seeks to encourage and strengthen democratic institutions around the world through nongovernmental efforts. Since its creation in 1983, N.E.D. has been an extremely creative and effective institution. The editors and authors gratefully acknowledge the support of the Endowment, and in particular of its President, Carl Gershman, and Director of Program, Marc F. Plattner. The Hoover Institution, with which Diamond and Lipset are affiliated, also contributed in many substantial ways to the project during its more than three years of organization, writing, and production. We wish to thank in particular the Director of the Hoover Institution, W. Glenn Campbell, and the two Principal Associate Directors with whom we have worked, John F. Cogan and John Raisian. The final editing and production of this volume were also assisted by a grant to the Hoover Institution from the MacArthur Foundation for a program of research on democracy in developing countries.

A number of people helped us in arranging the 1985 conference and preparing this volume. We thank in particular Janet Shaw of the Hoover Institution for her excellent editing, typing, and administrative support; Lisa Fuentes, now at UCLA, who was our research and administrative assistant during 1985–1986; Katherine Teghtsoonian, now at the University of Seattle, who produced the proceedings of our conference; Juliet Johnston and Laura Morrow, for their assistance with indexing, proofreading, and library research; Connie L. McNeely, for her statistical support; and Nicole S. Barnes, whose efficient and cheerful assistance with typing, indexing, and production has been instrumental to the completion of this book.

• CHAPTER ONE •

Introduction:
Persistence, Erosion, Breakdown, and Renewal

LARRY DIAMOND

The countries in this volume represent a wide range of experiences with democratic government. India, despite the steady erosion of democratic institutions and the two years of authoritarian emergency rule under Indira Gandhi, and the continuing political strains under her son and successor Rajiv Gandhi, continues to stand as the most surprising and important case of democratic endurance in the developing world. In its much briefer life as an independent nation, Papua New Guinea has manifested a remarkably vibrant and resilient democratic system, albeit highly factionalized and patronage-based.

No other Asian countries—neither in our study nor in that wide, expansive region of the globe—have been as continuously successful in maintaining a democratic system as India and Papua New Guinea. However, Turkey has sustained a liberal democracy through most of the four decades since World War II, and after its second (or more correctly, "second-and-a-half") military intervention, it has revived a competitive (though less liberal) democratic system. Today, Turkey appears on the way to democratic consolidation. Far less certain are the fates of the recent democratic transitions in the Philippines and South Korea. In each case, however, authoritarian rule has been decisively rejected through broad-based mobilization, and popular and elite commitment to democracy has been reaffirmed through recent elections. Facing different challenges to democratic consolidation—(among others) a lack of political order in the one case, and an excess of bureaucratic authoritarian control in the other—these two countries will be important tests of the democratic prospect in Asia.

Although its recent path of democratic transition has been more gradual and controlled, and more vulnerable to interruption by its military president, Pakistan has been moving toward the transfer of power from military rule to elected, civilian politicians. Elsewhere in Asia, outside our ten cases, other movements toward democracy proceed at slower paces or earlier stages, with greater control and institutionalized direction from above in Taiwan, and greater popular mobilization, political polarization, and government resistance and oppression in Bangladesh.

Our four remaining cases present sharply differing profiles of the semidemocratic and authoritarian regimes in Asia. Sri Lanka and Malaysia are an interesting contrast in civilian regimes whose democratic character has been battered, eroded, and diminished by profound ethnic divisions and the reality or potential of ethnic violence. The brief experience and haunting fear of a violent ethnic convulsion led in Malaysia to a political restructuring in which competition was limited and fixed to produce a firm parliamentary majority for the Malays and the broad party alliance they control, and freedom of expression was constricted to rule out the explosive issues of ethnic conflict and hegemony. While this restructuring has leveled parliamentary democracy down to a semidemocratic status, it has also brought considerable ethnic peace, political stability, and socioeconomic prosperity (although these now appear less secure). In Sri Lanka, by contrast, the deterioration of one of the developing world's most successful democracies has occurred amidst a tragic slide into civil war, tearing apart the polity and society and ravaging the economy in ways that will take years, if not decades, to resolve and repair.

Thailand and Indonesia may both be considered centralized, bureaucratic polities, in which the military continues to exercise the dominant authority and to penetrate virtually every significant institutional sector of government and society. But here, too, one finds important contrasts with obvious implications for democracy and democratization. In Thailand, a multiparty, parliamentary system (weakly institutionalized though it is) offers some degree of representation, competition, and check on military-bureaucratic authority, with considerable potential for (gradual) evolution toward fuller democracy. In Indonesia, political parties and electoral competition are much more rigidly controlled, parliamentary institutions appear to be more of a facade for military rule, civil and political liberties are more severely repressed, and the prospect for democratization appears much slimmer and more distant. And yet, Indonesia is hardly comparable to China or Vietnam. There are some real niches of pluralism, and as the economy develops and state control loosens, these will mature and perhaps press for political liberalization.

This enormous variation in democratic statuses and experiences stems in part from the breadth of our grouping of countries (by far the broadest of the three regional volumes in this series). It would perhaps be challenging enough to seek to generalize across the countries of East or Southeast Asia, with their varying Buddhist, Confucian, Muslim, Hindu, and Christian traditions, not to mention the many religious mixes and divisions within these countries. In South Asia, particularly India, we find different cultural and colonial legacies, and for the most part poorer economies and less developed societies. Turkey, of course, can only in the very loosest conception be classified as Asian, and is included in this volume only because we have (as yet) no volume on the Middle East or Southern Europe.

The list of other differences among these ten countries is indeed a very long one, extending also to their structure of ethnicity, class, economy, and state, and to their international threats and insecurities. And yet, this tremendous variation presents us with a great challenge and opportunity of scholarship. For it offers a wealth of data with which to explore (though hardly to resolve) the question with which we began this study: What explains the differing outcomes of democratic experiences in Asia, and throughout the developing world?

• BREAKDOWNS OF DEMOCRACY IN ASIA •

All ten of the countries in this volume have had some experience with liberal democratic government, meeting (at least in a very rough and broad sense) the definitional criteria in our preface. Indeed, this one common historical feature was an important criterion in our selection of cases. Of these ten, only Papua New Guinea has not experienced some interruption or breakdown of democracy. A look at the contexts and processes of democratic breakdown or suspension should give pause to those who take a deterministic view of democratic failures in Asia.

Whether we classify the loss of democracy by the gravity of the phenomenon—from the reduction of civil and political liberties, to the temporary interruption of democratic processes, to the complete displacement of the democratic system—or by its agent, the military or the civilian executive, one thing is clear. As a preceding four-volume study of democratic breakdowns has demonstrated in compelling fashion for Europe and Latin America,[1] the breakdowns of democracy in Asia have not been inevitable occurrences. Rather, the choices, decisions, values, and actions of political and institutional leaders have figured prominently—and in many cases, quite clearly decisively—in the decline or fall of democracy. Moreover, the decisive choices, actions, and decisions have primarily been those of civilian politicians—even when the military was the agent displacing the democratic system.

One should not neglect to begin with the obvious. As has been the case throughout the ages and around the world, the onset of authoritarianism in post-World War II Asia can sometimes be traced to the simple desire of a ruler to remain in power indefinitely, at all costs. Many interpretations can and have been offered for Indira Gandhi's declaration of emergency rule on June 26, 1975. But whatever the credibility of her dubious claims of threat to civil order and developmental progress, or of her call for political discipline and a strong state as the price for rapid development, the threat to her own political power by a judicial decision on her 1971 election and by recent opposition electoral gains must have figured largely. As Jyotirindra Das Gupta argues in his contribution to this volume, she opted for the seemingly sure path of seizing upon the constitution's emergency provisions to repress her opposition, rather than "a patiently drawn institutional strategy to utilize her populist appeal in a manner that would strengthen both her party and her democratic authority." Ironically, her choice backfired resoundingly twenty-one months later.

Perhaps because she did not need to, given the broad emergency powers in the Indian constitution, Indira Gandhi bent and abused but did not overthrow the constitutional system that brought her to power. Similarly, the less dramatic but more enduring erosion of democracy in Sri Lanka has come via the actions and choices of political party leaders, using the letter while violating the spirit of the constitutional process. In her chapter on Sri Lanka, Urmila Phadnis makes clear that the key turning point in the deterioration of democracy in Sri Lanka came with the landslide 1970 election victory of the left-leaning United Front, which then used its overwhelming parliamentary majority to ram through a new constitution in 1972, while conveniently (and undemocratically) extending its term of office two years. At the same time, Mrs. Bandaranaike's UF government was freely invoking emergency regulations to suspend the Bill of Rights and to limit the capacity of the legislature and judiciary to check the executive branch.

This flouting of a previously longstanding democratic tradition—which had seen a regular alternation in power between the two major parties since 1952 (theretofore a unique phenomenon in Asia and Africa)—set a dangerous precedent. When J. R. Jayewardene's United National Party (UNP) swept into power with an even greater landslide in 1977, it returned the favor, pushing through a new constitution of its own (equally unacceptable to the opposition), which again extended the ruling party's parliamentary term (this time by five years) while switching to a presidential system and further eroding the independent power of the legislature and judiciary. As we will see, structural problems and opportunities contributed to these abuses of the democratic system. But to those who would or did argue that such actions were compelled by the imperatives of the situation, in particular the crisis of national integration, it is worth noting that the sense of grievance by the minority Tamil community did not crystallize into antisystemic, separatist sentiment until five years *after* the 1970 election of the UF government, whose sweeping policies of "affirmative action" for the majority Sinhalese pressed the Tamils to the wall.

Malaysia's descent toward semidemocracy contrasts with Sri Lanka's experience in several respects. For one thing, it happened in a single period of deliberate restructuring, through the pursuit (heavy-handed though it was) of consensus, rather than in a piecemeal and intensely partisan fashion over many years. Although deep communal divisions provide an important backdrop in each case, in Malaysia the constriction of the democratic system came more visibly in response to the problem of ethnic polarization and violence, following serious ethnic rioting, and was undertaken in order to preserve the hegemony of an ethnic group—the Malays—rather than a political party per se. However, as Zakaria Haji Ahmad notes in these pages, in a system of ethnic parties, the issues of party and ethnic hegemony are inseparable. It was not just the ethnic rioting that led Malay leaders to change the rules of the game, but the fact that the showing of the ruling party Alliance (dominated by their own United Malays National Organization, or UMNO) in the 1969 elections "served notice that [they] might have to one day face the prospect of an electoral defeat."

Looking back in time from the present, it may seem that no instance of democratic breakdown better illustrates the personal desire to retain and expand power at all costs than the executive coup by Philippine President Ferdinand Marcos. As Karl Jackson indicates here, it was Marcos' inability to win constitutional changes permitting him to remain in office beyond his second term that led him to declare martial law on September 23, 1972. Marcos, too, had all sorts of rationales for his action, wrapped up in his promise of a New Society. Authoritarian rule, he said, was needed to "democratize wealth" and "revolutionize society"; to break the political culture of the corrupt status quo and the crippling power of the landed oligarchs; to defeat the renewed communist insurgency; and to inculcate a new discipline that would foster rapid development. But in contrast to India and Sri Lanka, Marcos' action came in response to a widespread sense—not only in the Philippines, but throughout Southeast Asia—that western-style democratic institutions were not working. As Jackson also demonstrates, the declaration of martial law came at a time when the corrupt, oligarchic Philippine democracy did in fact seem to be breaking down (in part because of Marcos' own abuses), and initially his martial law regime achieved popular support and success.

The Philippine case thus reflects two of the underlying causes of democratic breakdown in Asia: overwhelming personal (or in this case family) ambition, and manifest malfunctioning of the democratic system, particularly with regard to the performance of the politicians. This dual causation has also been apparent in South Korea, though at different points in time. The failure of the First Korean Republic—endowed with high hopes and a democratic constitution in 1948—came through the familiar instrument of a creeping executive coup. As Sung-Joo Han writes in this volume, "Rhee was determined to remain in power—for life—which required several constitutional changes, election rigging, and repression of the opposition." By contrast, the failure of the brief attempt at full liberal democracy in the Second Republic was a failure of democratic functioning. As Han shows, this breakdown was fed by deep divisions and difficulties in the social and political structure, but it was advanced and sealed by the weak, indecisive, ineffectual leadership of Prime Minister Chang Myon and by the rigid, uncompromising, and often undemocratic behavior of civilian politicians and parties. The turn of the subsequent authoritarian regime of Park Chung Hee away from limited political competition and potential democratic evolution, toward a much more authoritarian and repressive structure, owed heavily to Park's determination to remain in power indefinitely, no matter how the constitution had to be rewritten and the opposition crushed.

The repeated failure of democratic experiments in Pakistan merits especially close attention, for Pakistan shared the same colonial administration and heritage as democratically successful India, of which it was a part until the bloody partition of August 1947. From the beginning, democratic politics in Pakistan suffered from major structural problems, but as Leo Rose explains in this volume, Pakistan's political elite was no less culturally committed to democracy than India's, and as Myron Weiner has noted, in its first decade Pakistan did operate a "Westminster parliamentary government characterized by competitive political parties, elections, a free press, an independent judiciary and freedom of association."[2] The breakdown of that system in 1958 revealed major institutional flaws and weaknesses, but it also reflected the failure of democratic leadership to resolve political differences and deliver stable, effective government. It is important to remember that the Army intervened only after President Iskandar Mirza had won his struggle for power with the prime minister through an executive coup that ended democracy. The failure of the second chance at civilian democracy under Zulfikar Bhutto was preordained only in the sense that, in his determination to consolidate, centralize, and perpetuate power in his own hands, Bhutto never gave the system a chance to operate and develop democratically. Again, when the military struck in 1977, it displaced a regime that no longer appeared democratic or legitimate.

The latter point is of great theoretical significance, for it recurs across a number of the Asian cases in this volume. Indeed, in all five of our cases where the military has intervened (sometimes repeatedly) to overthrow civilian regime, democratic malfunctioning was painfully evident and regime legitimacy severely eroded by the time the military struck. In addition to the 1961 coup in South Korea and the 1958 and 1977 coups in Pakistan, this generalization applies to all three military interventions in Turkey (1960, 1971, and 1980), to the 1976 military coup in Thailand, and to the Indonesian army's support of martial law in 1957 and its displacement of Sukarno in 1966. Interestingly, it also explains the unsuccessful military coup plot in Sri Lanka in 1962, when "upheaval seemed to be coming from every quarter," in the form of communal violence, labor strikes, mass protests, militant policies, and emergency provisions that the military was given the distasteful task of enforcing.[3]

As Ulf Sundhaussen writes here in his analysis of the Indonesian case, "The army has not increased its political power by coups against legitimate governments, but rather has stepped in whenever vacuums needed to be filled, especially in 1957 and 1966. It has come to see itself as the savior of the nation from rapacious and incompetent politicians. . . ." As Sundhaussen shows, the military supported or at least tolerated parliamentary democracy through seven years of extremely unstable coalitions, revolving and ineffective governments, recurrent ethnic conflict and revolts, and generally corrupt, inept, and selfish politics. It was only when the parlimentary system finally ceased functioning altogether, unable to piece together one more fragile coalition, that the military acted against it. Hence, it was not the personal, institutional, or ideological ambitions of the military that defeated democracy in Indonesia, nor the lack of mass democratic commitment, but, as Sundhaussen puts it, "the actions and attitudes" of the political elite, "and especially those sections of the elite which purportedly stood for democracy." Ironically, among the most ill-advised of these civilian actions was the attempt by politicians to use the military for their own ends, a lesson reinforced by the experience of Bhutto in Pakistan and the Sri Lankan coup plot as well.

It is not simply public disorder, government immobilism, and political polarization that the military (not to mention society in general) find distasteful, but more especially the need or decision of weak, embattled civilian governments to use the military to restore order. When the military is dragged into the turmoil of civilian politics in this way, its total intervention is often not long in coming. Thus, as Ergun Özbudun observes in his chapter on Turkey, "a harmful side effect of martial law is the seemingly inevitable politicization of the armed forces, or the 'militarization' of political conflict, which may pave the way for full-scale military intervention. Indeed, all three military interventions in recent Turkish history were preceded by martial law regimes instituted by civilian governments."

While there may be alternatives in such periods of crisis, the decision to turn to the military often reflects not so much the wrong choice
on the part of political leaders but their mismanagement of political
conflict, mobilizing it or permitting it to be mobilized out of control.
Underlying each cycle of martial law and military intervention in
Turkey has been a precipitous rise in political polarization, intolerance,
and violence. Other failures of government performance have compounded the sense of crisis: inept and authoritarian handling of opposition and protest; conflict between the politicians and the bureaucrats;
serious economic problems; and by 1980, an alarming growth of terrorism.
One can point, as Özbudun does, to a number of social, cultural, and
structural factors that fostered the polarization, but in none of these
breakdowns can one deny the large measure of responsibility of the
civilian political leaders, who proved unwilling and unable to bridge
their partisan and ideological differences in order to rescue democracy
from the polarization and immobilism that were destroying it.

Chai-Anan Samudavanija's analysis of the breakdown of Thailand's
democratic experiment in 1974–76 shows a similar failure of political
leadership. To be sure, the flood of pent-up demands and the absence
of mature political institutions imposed a difficult challenge on party
leaders. But it is far from clear that these challenges could not have
been met, and democratic institutions and patterns gradually developed, if
political leaders had been able to establish some basis of consensus, or
at least stable and effective patterns of interaction, amongst themselves.
Instead, distrustful of one another and preoccupied with their short-
term and narrow interests, they produced a series of ineffectual and
unstable governments that could not manage the underlying tensions in
the society. The context of growing political polarization, violence, and
indecision provided the familiar, fertile ground for military intervention.

The Role of Leadership

None of the contributors to this volume would advance a "great man"
theory of history to explain the fate of the democratic experiments they
analyze. Nevertheless, the role of political leadership emerges in each
case as an important factor. By leadership we have in mind the actions,
values, choices, and skills of both a country's political elite and its one
or few top government and party leaders. We have already mentioned
the self-aggrandizing ambitions and authoritarian styles of putatively
democratic leaders such as Marcos, Rhee, Bhutto, Bandaranaike, Jayewardene, Sukarno, and Indira Gandhi, all of whom used the democratic
process to erode or destroy democracy. Without denying the cultural
and structural factors underlying their different behaviors, it is worth
noting that Prime Minister Michael Somare, and his successor Julius

Chan, did not attempt to twist the political rules or structures of democracy in Papua New Guinea in order to remain in power indefinitely. When their parliamentary coalitions fell or were defeated, they did something unusual in Asian politics: They simply left office.

As David Lipset demonstrates in his chapter, this difference in the politics of Papua New Guinea is heavily shaped by the traditional culture, which has also given rise to a more consensual and accommodating style of politics among party elites. This pragmatic, compromising leadership style contrasts markedly with the intransigence of the major party leaders, Demirel and Ecevit, that hastened Turkey's democratic breakdown in 1980, and with the fragmentation and inability to forge consensus of Thai political leaders during 1974–76. In this respect, the stubborn unwillingness of South Korea's major opposition leaders, Kim Young Sam and Kim Dae Jung, to compromise with one another or the regime in the electoral transition to democracy was seen by many as unfortunate. Despite its deep ethnic divisions, the more consensual style of political leadership in Malaysia has been a factor in its relative political stability from 1971 until the late 1980s, when a new prime minister upset the balance with his intolerance and drive to accumulate personal power.

Malaysia also stands in contrast to countries such as South Korea and Indonesia for the clear democratic commitment of its founding post-independence leaders. As Zakaria writes, Malaysia's first prime minister at independence, Tunku Abdul Rahman, was committed to parliamentary democracy as a "priority principle," and the workability of democracy in those tense early years had much to do with his consensual style and stance "above communal chauvinism." The democratic orientation of Malaysia's early leaders kept the system from plunging into full authoritarianism during the period of democratic suspension in 1969–71, and helped ensure a return to some kind of competitive, constitutional polity. By contrast, the much less tolerant, more confrontational style of Prime Minister Mahathir Mohammed in recent years has subjected Malaysia's semidemocratic system to the greatest stress it has experienced since 1971 (see below).

India (in the first two decades following independence) may be seen as a classic case of the contribution to democratic consolidation made by forceful but accommodating leaders, who embarked upon a conscious and deliberate strategy of political incorporation and expansion of access to previously excluded groups. Pakistan's leaders, Rose maintains, were no less democratically committed in principle, but circumstances led them to a greater sense of political insecurity, and early choices had a large impact. In particular, the decision of the "Father of Pakistan," Mohammad Ali Jinnah, "to retain the position of Governor-General, with the broad powers concentrated in that office . . .

set the basic trend toward an authoritarian system (just as Jawaharlal Nehru's decision to serve as prime minister in India's first postindependence government set a trend toward democracy)."

No less important is the contrast (though it can be overstated, in that the fatal flaws of the latter were not wholly absent from the former) between the leadership style and choices of Nehru and those of his daughter, Indira Gandhi, who followed him into the prime ministership in 1966, only two years after his death. It is important to appreciate that the emergency she declared in 1975 was only an escalation of a decade-long trend toward the centralization and personalization of political power, which resumed and even quickened with her return to power in 1980. Most contemporary analysts of Indian democracy heavily attribute the decay of the Congress party and of the Indian party system, the spread of mass protest and of ethnic separatism and violence, and the diffuse sense of crisis and strain in which India's political institutions find themselves today to the manipulative, coercive, suspicious, and self-serving character of Indira Gandhi's rule from 1966 to 1977 and again from 1980 until her assassination in 1984.[4] Paul Brass argues that the "relentless centralization and ruthless, unprincipled intervention by the center in state politics have been the primary causes of the troubles in the Punjab and elsewhere in India since Mrs. Gandhi's rise to power."[5] But the trouble also involves the larger circle of political leaders who have been chosen and promoted by Mrs. Gandhi, or at least have taken their cue and borrowed in style from her. Kohli thus suggests that institutional decay in India has resulted "not only from increasing social pressures on the state" but from "the destructive and self-serving actions of leaders who find institutions a constraint on personal power."[6] Indeed, that conclusion is a fitting and valid one for most of the cases in this volume.

• EXPLAINING DEMOCRATIC PROGRESS AND FAILURE •

Historical and Colonial Legacies

To say that leadership, behavior, and choice has contributed to the success or failure of Asian experiments with democracy is not to say that all political elites in Asia inherited equally favorable or imposing challenges. Across our cases, the democratic prospect has varied significantly with the historical and cultural legacies and the structural inducements and constraints these leaders have inherited and passed on to their successors.

Perhaps the most salient historical variable is the nature of the colonial experience. Among our ten Asian countries are four former

British colonies (India, Pakistan, Sri Lanka, and Malaysia), two more (the Philippines and Papua New Guinea) whose preindependence colonial rulers (the United States and Australia) shared in the Anglo-Saxon democratic tradition, one former Dutch colony (Indonesia), and two that were never colonized (Thailand and Turkey).

Several students of democracy have observed recently that the developing countries with the most successful democratic experience since independence are, by and large, former British colonies.[7] Weiner attributes this to "two components of the British model of tutelage": the establishment of the rule of law through effective (and increasingly indigenous) bureaucratic and judicial institutions, and the "provision for some system of representation and election" that gave educated elites some opportunity for and experience with limited governance.[8] The resulting legacy, he (and others) maintains, was not simply the presence of more effective political institutions at independence (both in terms of government administration and political party mobilization and competition), but also an enduring *cultural* orientation: a consensus on and commitment to the procedures of politics and governance, and a "concern with the rule of law as a constraint upon arbitrary government."[9]

India represents the most striking case of institutional development under British colonial rule. Despite the very inadequate and often superficial nature of successive colonial political reforms, the British did begin to draw Indian politicians into the process of electoral competition and democratic organization well in advance of independence, especially at the local and provincial level. Electoral success before independence gave the Congress party valuable experience in democratic competition and governance and advanced the process of its early institutionalization as a nationwide political force. Because of certain accidents of geography and history (see below), this process failed to occur in Pakistan, and had much to do with its democratic failure. But in Malaysia and Sri Lanka as well, and in Papua New Guinea under the Australians, preindependence electoral competition permitted the development of political parties and coalitions and the acquisition of democratic experience, which clearly enhanced the capacity of democratic institutions after independence.

Culturally, indigenous traditions and values may have been the more profound influence, but the British colonial legacy should not be underestimated as a source of popular and especially elite democratic commitments. As Weiner notes, even when democratic leaders have acted in an authoritarian fashion, as with Indira Gandhi's emergency rule, they have felt the need to keep their actions within the letter (however distorted in spirit) of legal and constitutional procedures. Thus the erosion of democracy in Sir Lanka has been, strangely, a constitutional one, and if this concern for constitutionalism has not saved democracy, it may at least have blocked the descent into full authoritarianism. A similar observation could be made for the period of "suspended democracy" in Malaysia, in which the National Operations Council supplanted Parliament "under the rule of law, with the appropriate proclamations by the king as stipulated by the Constitution," and during which the NOC "concentrated its efforts on the restoration of parliamentary democracy."[10] Even in the least democratically successful of our four former British colonies, Pakistan, Rose observes that "the advocacy of democratic principles by most of the political and general public has never wavered." Pakistani authoritarian regimes have generally permitted some considerable space for political, social, and regional organizations with differing views, and have not attempted to "project alternatives to a democratic political system as their ultimate objective."

The reason, Rose suggests, for this enduring cultural legacy of British rule is the powerful and diffuse socialization in democratic values that began under British rule and continued to a considerable extent after independence. The educational system of the British Raj was elitist, but it taught and praised British democratic concepts and values of representative government and popular sovereignty. In all four of the former British colonies studied here, this yielded independence elites with a clear philosophical commitment to democracy, and socialization agents—schools, the media, and democratic political organizations—poised to continue the process of democratic enculturation.

Six decades of Australian colonial rule had a similar effect in Papua New Guinea. Like the British, the Australians permitted some experience with electoral competition (in fact, three general elections) before independence, and avoided the radical deculturation policies of some European powers like the French. Indeed, David Lipset maintains, perhaps Australia's greatest contribution was that it allowed "the democratic features of traditional Melanesian polities to perdure into the postcolonial context." Like the British, and even more explicitly and extensively, American colonial rule in the Philippines schooled the people in democratic citizenship. This left behind some important developmental and institutional legacies—universal education, a high literacy rate, a politically active elite, a feisty press—but the cultural commitment it conveyed had to contend with the longer and more structurally rooted legacy of Spanish colonial rule that preceded it. This, Karl Jackson suggests, may help us to understand the persistence of oligarchical control and corrupt, clientelistic politics beneath the veneer of commitment to democracy. In addition, Lucian Pye argues, because the party politics introduced by the Americans was based on personalities rather than principles, it reinforced "traditional Philippine attitudes of power as patron-client relationships, and hence did not produce so great a change in Filipino thinking as might have been expected."[11]

If the commitment of democratic principles remains strong in Pakistan, the contrast between its democratic experience and India's nevertheless stands as one of the critical comparative issues in this volume. After all, both countries experienced the same British colonial administration. Obviously their different paths cannot be explained by reference to their common colonial legacies—or can they? Here we must appreciate the dualistic nature of the British colonial legacy. British rule—like all colonial rule in the developing world—was highly authoritarian. If it educated elites in democratic values and ways, while permitting quite limited but gradually expanding indigenous representation and competition, its first and most important goal was the preservation of its own authority, which was that of a martial law regime. Indeed, as Rose notes, Pakistan's first martial law regime (1958–1962), like subsequent ones, "borrowed extensively from the British martial law system." Thus, Pakistan and Bangladesh on the one hand, and India on the other, have both built upon the institutional legacy of British colonialism, but on different aspects of it: the former "on those institutions that sustained the imperial state" (the "viceregal" tradition) and India on the competitive and representative institutions "that the British either nurtured or tolerated."[12]

It should therefore not surprise us that those countries whose colonial histories were more uniformly authoritarian fared even more poorly with democracy after independence. Here one may cite the former French colonies, and still more so the former Spanish and Belgian, or in this volume, the former Dutch colony, Indonesia, and the former Japanese colony, Korea. Japanese rule in the twentieth century heightened the highly centralized, autocratic features of traditional authority in Korea, leaving it after World War II with no institutions for checking and countervailing executive power. This helps to explain not only the ease with which Rhee overran democracy but also the persistent "underdevelopment" of political input institutions such as parties and interest groups. In marked contrast to Sri Lanka, Malaysia, and Papua New Guinea, Indonesia's transition to independence was riddled with intense conflict, violence, insurgency, and radical mass mobilization, with relatively little preparation for democracy. Its postindependence politics reflected these features of its colonial experience.

Obviously, where there has been no conquest or colonization, traditional values and political legacies tend to perdure into the present with greater force. In this sense, the centralizing, statist tradition of the Ottoman empire has been an obstacle to stable democracy in Turkey, and centralized state authority has similarly persisted in Thailand with fewer institutional checks and popular demands and interest groups than developed in many former European colonies. One could there-fore argue that where traditional sociopolitical structures were not only autocratic but centralized (in contrast to the feudal arrangements of Europe and Japan), and where these structures were not disrupted and reorganized by colonial intervention, civil society has remained weak in relation to the state. And yet, continuity and gradual evolution have their advantages. In the case of Thailand, they have helped to ensure a greater measure of political order and societal coherence than else-where in Southeast Asia, partly by preserving the most precious source of political legitimacy and mediation in the country, the monarchy. These factors hardly predestine democratization, but they can facilitate it. In Turkey, the democratic, secularizing reforms of Mustafa Kemal probably had more immediate and enduring legitimacy than any that might have been imposed by a colonial power.

Distinctive though their histories have been, the lack of a colonial experience has not entirely insulated Turkey and Thailand from the influence of global political trends and ideologies. The political de-velopment of both countries in this century has been markedly affected by their elites' awareness of and fascination with democratic develop-ments in other countries. The Kemalist regime, for example, was born in the prodemocratic spirit of the post-World War I era. The 1932 coup that ended the system of absolute monarchy in Thailand was executed by young military and civilian commoners, many of whom were "educated in England and France, and inspired with ideas of democracy and progress."[13] Ironically, in the contemporary era of independent states, the power of international ideological diffusion and demonstration effects has significantly increased.

Political Culture

While the concept of political culture has been a controversial one in comparative politics and sociology, our Asian cases demonstrate its utility and salience for the study of democratic experiences and out-comes. In each of the countries examined here, one can discern certain distinctive ways of thinking and feeling about politics, power, authority, and legitimacy as they relate to the modern political system, and the role of the individual citizen in it.[14] These beliefs, ideals, attitudes, values, evaluations, and behavioral orientations have sometimes been heavily influenced by foreign rule and international contact, but typically spring even more profoundly from the political and cultural traditions of each country. We are not inclined to think these elements of political culture are as broadly generalizable across Asia (or even within indi-vidual countries) as some have argued, nor are we comfortable with

Pye's broad assertion that the generally paternalistic nature of Asian political cultures—with their psychology of dependency, distaste for open criticism of authority, and deep fear of disunity—make fully democratic government an unlikely prospect.[15] Nevertheless, if one political leader after another is abusing and usurping constitutional authority in a country, it suggests a pattern that is hardly satisfactorily explained by reference to the values and ambitions of the individual leaders alone. It is hard to deny that many of the difficulties with democracy in Asian countries emanate from their political cultures. At the same time, it is clear that democratic progress in Asia also has cultural roots and supports, and that political culture is subject to influence and evolution over time.

To begin with the positive, Das Gupta attributes India's democratic success since 1947 in part to the consensual, tolerant, and accommodating political style and strategy that evolved during the early phase of Indian nationalism. This feature of political culture owed heavily to the decisive influence of Gandhi in mobilizing mass support through a philosophy of *satyagraha*, emphasizing tolerant, non-violent political activism and the peaceful resolution of conflicts. But as Weiner observes, it also has a significant traditional root, in the pervasive belief in and reliance on arbitration as the appropriate method for the resolution of conflict.[16] And even before Gandhi was born, it was fostered by a long tradition of liberal political thought, which spawned numerous associations devoted to extending political freedom and defending popular interests. After Gandhi's death, the democratic, accommodating culture of elite politics was perpetuated, suggests Das Gupta, by a broad consensus not only on the procedures of political competition and conflict resolution but also on the substance of developmental policies and goals.

In Papua New Guinea, we may find the clearest congruence between democratic success and democratic features of traditional culture. The latter, Lipset argues, include an egalitarian, factionalized, exchange-based traditional ethic; a natural hostility to centralized authority and arbitrary rule; and the "relentless" rise and fall of political leaders, whose authority was limited by a high level of individual autonomy and the "conditional and voluntary" nature of political support. If these traditions have produced a highly factionalized polity dominated by primordial, ethnic appeals and the politics of patronage and personality, they have also checked the concentration of power in individual leaders or the state. In democratic Papua New Guinea, the culturally entrenched "insubordination" of the electorate has produced a striking rate of circulation of elites.

Many of the authors in this volume call attention to the cultural roots of democratic difficulties and strains. Although Turkish political leaders since World War II have agreed on the legitimacy of electoral democracy and a secular, republican state, they have been ambivalent if not actively hostile to the notion of political opposition. In fact, Özbudun argues, this intolerance dates back to the Ottoman empire and is reflected as well in excessive fear of a national split. Thus, he writes: "The line separating opposition from treason is still rather thin. . . . The tendency to see politics in absolutist terms also explains the low capacity of political leaders for compromise and accommodation." Cultural obstacles to political accommodation are even more strikingly apparent in South Korea, where compromise is seen as "a signal of weakness and lack of resolve, not only by one's adversaries but by one's allies as well."[17] The resulting zero-sum nature of the political game makes democratic politics highly unstable, and very nearly derailed the recent transition to democracy there. In addition, the insistence on ideological uniformity, stemming from the traditional Confucian pre-occupation with order, respect, and harmony as well as the modern preoccupation with security in divided Korea, has robbed the party system of meaningful debate and choice.

In the case of Malaysia, Zakaria agrees with Pye that the strong curbs placed on political conflict and dissent may be seen as reflective of Malay cultural values, which appreciate strong authority and fear con-flict and dissention. But the tremendous fear of opposition and division has also been shaped by the country's deep ethnic cleavages, and their traumatic explosion into violence in 1969. In Thailand, the powerful concern for stability and consensus has been the particular preoccupation of military and bureaucratic elites, whose narrow conception of dem-ocracy excludes political conflict and independent interest groups. But these illiberal views have not been static. While they have followed from the autocratic nature of traditional authority in Thailand and the historical weakness of democratic values, they have also been deepened by the chaotic nature of multiparty competition in Thailand (itself partly the result of bureaucratic and military dominance of the polity) and by a threat comparable to the ethnic one in Malaysia, that of communist mobilization and subversion. In the case of Indonesia, it is easy to point to features of Javanese culture and society (e.g., the intolerance of opposition to central authority, the lack of moral basis for authority) that are not conducive to democracy. But there was, at least on the village level, "a developed sense of equality, social justice, and accountability," and, at independence, broad appreciation among political elites (especially of ethnic minorities) of the need for demo-cratic mechanisms to manage ethnic divisions.[18]

Indonesia also raises the question of whether Islam is an obstacle to democratic development. This depends to some extent on the way Islam is interpreted and politically mobilized. While our evidence is hardly generalizable to the Islamic countries of the Middle East, we find in our four predominantly Muslim countries (Indonesia, Malaysia, Pakistan, and Turkey) little evidence of Islam directly obstructing democratic development. In Turkey, this may be due in part to the separation of Islam from politics and the state in the twentieth century. In Indonesia it may owe to the heterogeneity within the predominant Islamic community, which is divided between the fully devout *santri* (who themselves are split into traditional and modernizing wings) and the syncretic *abangan*, who mix Islam with pre-Islamic beliefs but nevertheless identify as Muslims. Moreover, in Indonesia, as well as our other three cases, Islamic parties have not fared well in electoral competition (partly because the political system has been structured to their disadvantage). Pakistan might be considered a particularly crucial test, in that it was founded in 1947 as an Islamic state, with the expectation that Islam would be an integrating force, after the trauma of the partition. And yet, Rose finds that Islam has been largely incidental to politics and policy making in Pakistan over the past four decades, neither helping nor hindering democracy. Again, the separation of religion and politics, along with religious subcleavage, appears significant. Pakistan's founders were modernists who conceded no role in governance to Islamic organizations, and subsequent governments have continued to marginalize them politically. Islamic religious leaders and groups have themselves been divided between "purists" and "populists."

The evidence from our various Asian cases thus cautions against drawing any deterministic linkage between political culture and democratic outcomes. That the latter have multiple and complex sources of causation is beyond question, as we further demonstrate below. And political culture itself is determined not only by the past but by the present, through experience with the political system and socialization by it, so that culture also acts as an intervening and dependent variable in relation to political structure.[19] Thus, during its six decades of nationalist mobilization and political functioning prior to independence, the Indian National Congress played a crucial role in socializing a growing political public in India to democratic values, rules, and norms. Similarly, the experience of operating a democratic system, even with interruptions, through most of the past four decades, has served to socialize new generations of Turks into democratic values, while military and bureaucratic control over the instruments of mobilization and socialization have had something of the reverse effect in Thailand, in Chai-Anan's view. Han finds that the extensive, deliberate efforts at mass "education in democracy" increased democratic consciousness among the Korean public after the Korean War, and rapid urbanization and modernization, with the growth of the mass media and the middle class, has accelerated this trend.

Another complication for cultural explanations of democratic outcomes is that all political cultures are to some degree mixed, and many
if not most of those represented in this volume have some significant
values and orientations that press in a democratic direction and others
that press in an authoritarian one. Thus, the traditional clientelistic,
opportunistic style of Philippine politics—which views public service as
a means for private gain and pursues the struggle for power with
violence, fraud, and procedural abandon—has clearly undermined
democracy; and yet, the widespread popular and elite value commitment to democratic participation made it much more difficult to institutionalize an authoritarian regime in the Philippines than in Thailand
or Indonesia. India's substantial democratic values and norms coexist
with certain traditional values that are not particularly conducive to
democracy, such as "a passion for harmony and synthesis" that devalues
competition and conflict and has bred some intellectual cynicism about
multiparty, parliamentary democracy.[20] Political cultures are also mixed
in that the subcultures of some groups in a country may be less democratic than others (compare, for example, the beliefs of military and
party elites in Thailand). Finally, there is the mixture that comes from
the ongoing process of change. Our cases tend to confirm Gabriel
Almond's observation that "all political systems . . . are transitional
systems, or systems in which cultural change is taking place."[21]

Given this substantial "plasticity" of political culture, we are not
inclined to think that it must necessarily stand in the way of democratic
development in Asia. As Almond has written recently, "Political culture
affects political and government structure and performance—constrains
it, but surely does not determine it."[22] Cultural values and beliefs complicate the task of democratic development and consolidation in many
of our cases, but they do not foreclose the prospect of full democracy,
as we have defined it in this study. As democracy is assimilated in
different cultures, it inevitably is going to look and function differently,
but it does not inevitably have to be less democratic.

Ethnic Cleavage and Conflict

There is no shortage of evidence from our Asian cases to demonstrate
the negative effects for democracy of deep ethnic cleavage. In Sri
Lanka, it has been a primary factor in the deterioration of democracy,
and its explosion into violent insurgency and repression has ravaged the
economy, polarized the polity, embittered all groups, and provided an
excuse for increasingly authoritarian measures. In Malaysia, it has provided the overriding rationale for setting firm limits to democratic
expression and competition. In Pakistan and Indonesia, it has played a

significant role in the instability and failure of previous attempts at democracy.

But the conclusion that democracy therefore is inconsistent with deep ethnic divisions is a specious one. India has one of the most complex ethnic structures in the world, and its politics have been relentlessly divided by and preoccupied with ethnic and linguistic conflicts and demands. Papua New Guinea is an utterly fragmented country ethnically, and, like India, has had to contend with repeated secessionist movements. Yet both of these democracies have survived intact. Indeed, one could argue, as does Rose in this volume, that the tremendous social and ethnic complexity of a country like India makes it "difficult to conceive of any system of government other than participatory democracy that could work for such a heterogeneous society." Moreover, relative national homogeneity has not prevented political polarization and democratic breakdown in Turkey and Thailand. Clearly, what matters is not simply the degree of ethnic division, but how it is structured and managed.

With respect to structure, one of the great advantages of Indian society is the cross-cutting nature of its complexity. As Das Gupta explains, "major religious communities are split into many language communities which in turn are stratified into caste and class formations." As a result of these multiple and cross-cutting identities, various levels of cleavage are in competition with one another, shifting in salience across conflicts and over time. By contrast, in the most ethnically troubled countries in this volume, Sri Lanka and Malaysia, ethnic, religious, regional, and linguistic cleavages cumulate, and the majority group in each country, the Sinhalese and the Malays, also feels disadvantaged socioeconomically. This coincidence of cleavages makes it likely that the same broad ethnic division will be tapped, no matter what the specific issue.

This polarizing tendency is further enhanced by the centralized character of the ethnic structure, a situation in which "a few groups are so large that their interaction is a constant theme of politics at the center."[23] In Sri Lanka, the Sinhalese and Tamils together constitute most of the population (with the Tamils in a distinct minority), while the Malays and Chinese are the main groups in Malaysia, with roughly a half and a third of the population respectively. Thus, any issue regarding the allocation of power and resources, or the status of cultural symbols and media, invokes not only the same line of cleavage but the same division between cleavage groups. By contrast, in a more dispersed or decentralized ethnic system, ethnic alignments are much more fluid. For example, beyond the Hindi speakers, who are about 30 percent of the population, no linguistic group in India accounts for as much as 10 percent. "Because of the large number of scattered groups, it would be preposterous to suggest that politics at the center in India revolves around the rivalry of, say, Gujaratis, Bengalis, Oriyas, and Telugus."[24] The situation in Papua New Guinea represents perhaps the extreme of ethnic fragmentation, with roughly 700 languages (in a population of three and a half million) and "many, many more polities than that," in that the village, lineage, or clan has been the more salient unit of political identity. This incredible ethnic dispersion has had much to do with the fluidity of parliamentary coalitions and the relative absence of polarized conflict in Papua New Guinea.

But India and Papua New Guinea also call attention to the importance of political structures and creative, flexible leadership in managing ethnic conflict. Both countries have been plagued with intense ethnic rivalries and serious secessionist movements. To the extent these have been subdued or managed, it has been not with ethnic chauvinism, resistance, and repression, but through negotiation and substantive accommodation that gave aggrieved groups some sense of cultural/political security and socioeconomic stake in the system. When the issue of the national language polarized into bitter conflict and violence in the 1960s, Indian political leaders forged a compromise that backed away from the imposition of Hindi as the effective national language. When the fears and aspirations of India's smaller ethnic groups have crystallized into separatist and militant regionalist agitation, these have generally been allayed through the creation of new states, which, Das Gupta observes, has not only given groups significant autonomy but has transferred the target of political mobilization from the national to the state centers. It is also noteworthy that Papua New Guinea's most serious secessionist conflict was eventually resolved through the decentralization of power, and, ultimately, the establishment of nineteen provincial governments.

These examples of accommodation and relatively successful ethnic management contrast sharply with the tragic experience of Sri Lanka, where the repeated rejection of moderate Tamil interests and demands in the 1960s and early 1970s transformed the Tamil sense of grievance into a militant and ultimately violent separatist movement. In particular contrast to the Indian experience were the refusal of the Sinhalese ruling parties to enact satisfactory guarantees regarding the use of Tamil language and the refusal to give the minority Tamils regional autonomy. Also telling has been the difference within India between the uncompromising, exclusionary, narrowly and ruthlessly self-serving response of Indira Gandhi to the Assam and Punjab regional movements, which drove them "to explosive proportions" of appalling violence, and the more accommodating strategy of her successor Rajiv, who reached accords that have at least relieved the ethnic crises (especially in Assam).[25] Similarly, the refusal of the majority Javanese politicians to recognize minority ethnic concerns, and to accommodate them within a federal order rather than forcing them into submission, "led to protracted internal warfare for more than a decade" and seriously eroded the potential basis for democracy, Sundhaussen concludes.

Accommodation has also restored ethnic peace in Malaysia, but through the very different framework of a semiconsociational grand alliance in which Malay political hegemony is entrenched beyond challenge. The heavy dependence of this formula on the continued cooperation of ethnic elites and on continued rapid economic growth to soften the impact of educational and economic preferences for Malays are important elements of vulnerability. But the fact that the Malays have sought to secure their dominance not through outright hegemony but within an accommodative, coalitional framework, and through an ethnic division of political rewards, has brought an important degree of ethnic peace.

The Malaysian situation calls attention to the important role of political parties and party systems in structuring ethnic conflict. The early failure of noncommunal parties, and the presence of a dominant party within each ethnic group—along with the inability (at least in the early days) of the leading Malay party (UMNO) to secure a stable parliamentary majority on its own—were conducive to the formation of a broad, multiethnic party alliance. By contrast, the presence of two major Sinhalese parties, each outbidding the other in its appeals to the majority electorate, precluded formation of an enduring multiethnic party alliance in Sri Lanka, and has repeatedly undermined the willingness and/or capacity of the ruling Sinhalese party to reach an ethnic accommodation with the Tamils.[26]

No doubt, one reason why the Congress party has generally been willing and able to accommodate ethnic demands is that its political dominance nationally has (usually) been relatively secure, and through most of its life it has not faced a serious challenger in the Hindi heartland that might force it to fall back upon ethnic chauvinism and intransigence. Moreover, even were that the case, the Hindi speakers are not sufficiently numerous in themselves to provide any party with a national majority. In neighboring Pakistan, the Muslim League lacked the secure electoral base of the Congress in India, in large measure because its leadership and much of its cadre were *muhajirs* (refugees) from sections of the British Raj that became part of India after the partition. Rather than seek to build a broad base of support across all ethnic, social, and regional groups (as the Indian Congress had done, albeit under the more favorable circumstances of decades of nationalist mobilization), the leaders of the Muslim League pursued "antiintegrationist" policies that alienated several major regional groups. In the ensuing years, the continuing failure of a highly fractionalized political leadership to effect the integration of ethnic communities into the national polity led to political instability, the failure of democratic experiments and the disintegration of Pakistan into two countries in 1971.

In brief, then, the cases in this volume point to a powerful generalization, rich with policy implications. As Das Gupta has argued from India's recent history, where the state responds to ethnic mobilization with strategies of inclusion and incorporation, often involving only modest concessions that are "more symbolic than substantial," social peace and political stability can be maintained or restored. But where the state responds with exclusion and repression, violence festers. Underlying this is a simple but profound insight: "When ethnic leaders are allowed to share power, they generally act according to the rules of the regime. . . . Although access and mobility do not necessarily decrease inequality, they can make it more tolerable."[27]

State and Society

The evidence from our Asian cases illuminates in varied and distinctive ways the importance for democracy of the relationship between the state and civil society. As with many other factors, this involves something of a dilemma. If the state is too strong, centralized, and domineering, there will be little to prevent its incumbents from exercising power in an authoritarian and abusive fashion. This is why many theories of democracy emphasize the need for a dense, pluralistic structure of economic, social, and political organizations outside the state. On the other hand, if the state is too weak, it may be unable to deliver the social and economic goods that groups are expecting and demanding, and to maintain order in the face of conflicting group demands. Thus, democracy would seem to require some kind of balance between the "output" institutions of the state—most notably the bureaucracy and the security apparatus—and the "input" institutions (political parties, interest groups, associations) that are competing for state control, attention, and resources. More generally, there is a need for some kind of balance between the state and civil society.

For many Asian countries, the supremacy of the state over civil society has been a major source of difficulty for democracy. The inability of Thailand to develop a stable democracy over the past half century must be understood in light of entrenched bureaucratic domination of the polity and society, with the military in an increasingly ascendant role. The dominance of these central, and highly centralized, state institutions has precluded the development of strong and autonomous interest groups, village associations, and political parties. When these have begun to emerge, they have been coopted or overrun by the military and bureaucracy. Over time, this has become a self-perpetuating cycle. Nascent, weak, and ineffective, emergent civil institutions have been unable to check the consolidation of centralized state power or to resist military-bureaucratic cooptation and repression. This failure only reinforces the institutional gap between state and society, enabling the state to expand its role further and to impose a certain vision of development from above. Similarly, the weakness of political parties has fed upon itself in a vicious cycle: Parties (and the ultimate input institution, the elected legislature) have been weak because repeated military intervention has robbed them of the continuity and experience necessary for institutionalization. A quite similar historical process has been at work in South Korea as well. The failure of civic institutions to perform effectively has heightened both the propensity and the legitimacy of military-bureaucratic intervention, to the point where these elites have come to see it not only as their right but their duty to guard and guide the political process. As the Thai military, in its growing suspicion of democratic pluralism, has expanded its influence over far reaches of civil society—the mass media, rural development, civic education—the challenge of developing truly democratic government has been further complicated. The same authoritarian corporatist impulse of state elites to manage- and contain the autonomy of interest groups and the press is now an obstacle to the consolidation of a fully democratic system in South Korea.

Of course, the highly centralized and militarized nature of the state in South Korea did not prevent the recent transition to democracy. But the preceding failures of attempts at democracy, the ensuing decades of authoritarian domination, and the current steep challenges to democratic consolidation have all been shaped by the supremacy of the state and the militarized nature of South Korean society. As in Thailand, historical and cultural factors (including the absence of autonomous social organizations), and external threats, contributed to the formidable power of the state and especially its coercive apparatus. Especially during the Park years, the increasing "militarization" of society and politicization of the military generated a climate conducive to authoritarian rule. Now that they have been so politicized, it is not clear how the military and state security services will be weaned away from their compulsion to dominate and control domestic politics. But few can doubt that their power must be circumscribed and firmly subjected to civilian control if democracy is to take root in South Korea.

The difficulty of reversing military role expansion is especially apparent in Indonesia, where Sundhaussen sees no civilian elites who are ready and willing to assume power, and hence no alternative to the military at present. With the coming of Soeharto's New Order in the mid-1960s and the "Dual Function" doctrine, the military has pervasively penetrated the state bureaucracy and, to quote Sundhaussen, "the life of autonomous social, occupational, and cultural organizations, trade unions and business associations has been gradually strangled." This pattern becomes resistant to change, because military officers develop an ideological stake in and financial appetite for political and administrative roles, and because the very civic associations and movements that might retrench this military state dominance have instead been enervated and preempted by it. Even where the process has not gone nearly so far, as in Pakistan, the lure of lucrative government positions for incumbent or aspiring military bureaucrats presents an obstacle to military withdrawal from government.

That the movement for redemocratization in Pakistan has gone so far is due in part to the space that the Pakistani military continued to allow for independent organization and expression in civil society. Similar space for associational life and independent organization played a critical role in undermining and ultimately bringing down the dictatorship of Ferdinand Marcos early in 1986, after broad popular mobilization by associations of lawyers, intellectuals, students, businessmen, human rights organizations, and the National Movement for Free Elections (NAMFREL), supported by the Catholic Church.

While military role expansion has been a critical problem for democracy in Asia, it should not be equated with the problem of statism. For the domination of the central state over civil society can impede or occlude democracy even when the state is essentially a civilian, bureaucratic one. In Turkey, this highly centralized, bureaucratic state dominance has prevented democracy from acquiring depth, in that intermediate structures (including those of the state, i.e. local governments) have been weak and lacking in autonomy. But beyond this, statism has contributed heavily to the polarization and violence that have plagued Turkish politics in the past. The enormous power of the Turkish state, including its substantial ownership and extensive control over the economy, has made "the costs of being out of power . . . extremely high," Özbudun argues, thus making opposing parties unwilling to contemplate defeat.

Here again, Papua New Guinea provides a significant contrast with many of our other Asian cases. The traditional value of individual autonomy has served to limit state power in Papua New Guinea. The stakes in controlling the central government have remained limited, as power has been decentralized through provincial governments and private enterprise has continued to provide considerable scope for individuals to accumulate wealth outside the state. Moreover, the bureaucracy has developed a certain autonomy from politics, rather than being manipulated and controlled for the benefit of whichever party might be in power.

In India, the bureaucracy has often been referred to as the "steel frame" of democratic rule, and we have already noted that the presence at independence of such an elaborate, largely indigenized administrative framework—which developed alongside, rather than to the exclusion of, participatory institutions—was a major contribution of the British colonial legacy (although its independence and integrity have seriously eroded over the last two decades). A similarly balanced presence of effective output and input institutions served the early democratic development of Malaysia and Sri Lanka as well.

Beyond this, democracy in India has been fortified by the early development and vigorous presence of a rich array of voluntary associations directed to language reform, legal reform, educational modernization, defense of press freedom, and women's rights. These associations began under colonial rule in the nineteenth century and developed dramatically in strength and sophistication during the the Gandhian phase of nationalist mobilization, with its philosophy of "*satyagraha*," or nonviolent resistance. While strong trade unions, peasant, student, and business associations today often align with political parties, they also act autonomously to pursue their own interests, and this political autonomy has increased as new leadership groups have arisen within them giving greater emphasis to economic issues. Moreover, as Das Gupta observers in this volume, India's sociopolitical scene is also replete with a vast array of issue-oriented movements, "bringing together various parties, groups, and concerned publics" in aggressive campaigns for social and political reform.

A good many of these movements have been ethnic in nature, seeking to advance or defend cultural and symbolic interests such as language and land, along with political interests of autonomy and control, often mixed with or superseded by economic interests of resource allocation, employment, and education.[28] Others (often overlapping with ethnicity) have been caste- or class-based, mobilizing disadvantaged, "backward," or "scheduled" groups to fight oppression by landlords and the state, to raise class or group consciousness, and to struggle for land reform, minimum wages, and other elementary social and economic rights.[29] A more recent and particularly important form of civic movement, which has arisen since the emergency in the 1970s, has been the civil liberties movement. It comprises several non-partisan organizations which struggle to expose and combat human rights violations concerning land, labor, urban housing, suppression of free expression, academic protest, and the mistreatment of women. Such autonomous, nonpartisan movements and organizations serve continually to check the relentless tendency of the state to centralize and expand its power and to evade civic accountability and control. At the same time, they broaden popular participation in the political process by adding to the formal arena a number of informal channels, and they may also through their action strengthen certain formal institutions of democracy, such as the courts. Moreover, by combatting abuses of power and violations of civil liberties, the human rights organizations directly improve the (deteriorating) quality of democracy in India.[30] Thus, if one effect of these various groups and movements is to expose the superficiality of democracy in many areas of India's social and economic life, another is "to open alternative political space outside the usual arenas of party and government, though not outside the state," through which the struggle to deepen and rejuvenate democracy may proceed.[31]

Political Parties and Party Systems

The ten countries analyzed in this volume have had markedly different types of parties and party systems. And while caution is certainly advised in generalizing from their experiences, certain patterns of association emerge with rather striking clarity. In particular, three of those countries which have had the least success with multiparty politics—Pakistan, Thailand, and Indonesia—were all plagued by extremely fragmented and weak party systems. Indonesia had more than 100 parties in the late 1950s; forty-two parties contested the crucial 1975 elections in Thailand, and between 1946 and 1981, 143 parties came and went across the Thai political stage. Pakistan began with a single dominant party, the Muslim League, but as we have noted, the ML leaders, being refugees from India, lacked a strong political base among local and especially rural elites. In pointed contrast to the Congress party of India, the ML failed to incorporate the key elites of the differing social, ethnic, and regional groups, and after the assassination of Prime Minister Liaquat Ali Khan in 1951, the party slowly disintegrated. The resultant factionalization of Pakistani politics produced the same fleeting and weak parliamentary coalitions, and the same lack of strong, stable, and effective government, that heralded the failure of democracy in Thailand and Indonesia as well.

Such extreme multipartyism was perhaps the overriding but not the only common feature of these failed party systems. In addition, most of the parties in these cases failed to articulate and aggregate clear interests. Moreover, they suffered from extremely weak organization, discipline, and coherence, which brought upon them serious problems of internal factionalism. As a result, these parties (with a very few exceptions) were unable to mobilize a significant mass base. In these senses, they were more the electoral vehicles of individuals or narrow, shifting cliques than political parties. And in each case, the fragility and instability of extreme multi-partyism was compounded by the inability of these "parties" to co-operate and work with one another.

One indication of the costs of such political fragmentation is the movement currently under way in all three countries toward a much more streamlined party system. Pakistan's ongoing political transition has revealed an emphasis of both government and opposition on party consolidation. Of course, the task is always easier for a governing group, which has the resources at its disposal to build a party base. But Rose sees Benazir Bhutto's Pakistan People's Party emerging as the major opposition force, with other parties having to coalesce around it or the governing Pakistan Muslim League in what could be becoming a two-party-dominant system. In Thailand and Indonesia, the ruling regimes are seeking to encourage such party consolidation as a matter of deliberate strategy. While the Thai political scene remains fragmented, electoral provisions in the present constitution exert a bias against small parties and a good chance of eliminating many of them over time. In Indonesia, consolidation was accomplished by government mandate, reducing the number of parties to ten in 1960 and to only three (including the government-controlled GOLKAR) in 1973. But as Sundhaussen writes, "Party politicians have been unable to grasp the opportunities a unification of weak parties may afford, and have preferred to continue with the bickering and infighting which had been the hallmark of coalition politics in the 1950s." This has undermined the possibility for evolution of a more genuinely open political system.

A different model of democratic failure in the party system is provided by the case of Turkey. There, the problem (especially in the most recent democratic breakdown) was the extreme polarization of national political life, which was reflected in and exacerbated by the strategic position of small radical right parties in Parliament, and the activism of the extraparliamentary left, which dragged the two major parties toward the extremes. Again it is revealing that, in restructuring the democratic system after the September 1980 coup, the Turkish military adopted several measures (a 10 percent electoral threshold for representation in Parliament, and banning of communist, fascist, religious, and separatist parties) to try to produce a two- or three-party system that would yield stable parliamentary majorities.

With its one-party-dominant but nevertheless democratically competitive system, India has been seen as providing an important model for developing countries. But as Das Gupta makes clear, a key factor in the early consolidation of democracy in India was not simply the electoral dominance of the Congress party, but its continuing strategy of "inclusionary participation," incorporating diverse social groups and preemptively coopting numerous popular movements into a broad, multiclass, multiethnic, multiregional political front.

But this is not the whole story of the party system in India, and increasingly since 1967, it has not been the story at all. Democratic incorporation has also been served by a partially decentralized federal system that has enabled both regional party challengers, such as the AIADMK in Tamil Nadu and the Akali Dal in Punjab, and ideological ones, such as the Communist Party (Marxist) in Kerala and West Bengal, to gain a share of power and a stake in the system by winning control of individual states, most of which are larger than the typical Third World nation (e.g., Tamil Nadu, with its roughly fifty million people). But democratic incorporation in India has been undermined, and decades of laborious institution-building seriously eroded, by the transformation of the party system since the coming to power of Indira Gandhi in 1967.

Although the continuing electoral victories of Mrs. Gandhi's Congress (with the brief interruption of the Janata landslide in the massive 1977 rejection of her emergency rule) may have fostered the superficial perception of continuing one-party dominance in India, virtually all close observers of the Indian party system emphasize the institutional decay that set in after 1967. Mrs. Gandhi's response to the Congress's precipitous decline in the 1967 elections (from 73 to 55 percent of seats in the national parliament, despite a drop of only 4 percent in popular vote) was a growing personalization and central-ization of the party (as well as the state), which fractured its unity, eroded its breadth, and undermined its organizational vitality and depth down to the grassroots. As voters became more assertive and new interest groups increasingly demanding, party politics became more competitive. Unfortunately, Mrs. Gandhi continued to respond—even after returning to power in 1980 supposedly chastened by her 1977 defeat—with a still more determined and manipulative concentration of power, rather than creative institutional adaptation. This only reinforced what Das Gupta terms the "plebiscitarian transformation" from a party-based state to a state-based party. No less disturbing, the post-1980 phase of this plebiscitarian decay has seen the Congress campaign on a fiercely confrontational and intolerant stance toward opposition parties (somewhat but not entirely abated under Rajiv after 1984) and a cynical turn toward mobilization of Hindu chauvinism as the only electoral strategy for an organizationally decrepit party. This institutional decay of the ruling party has been accompanied by a general disintegration of the party system into fragmentation and instability, as not only the Congress-I but other parties as well have become more porous, ill-defined, and yet mutually hostile. It is this general deterioration of the party system, probably more than any other single development, that has experienced students worried about the long-term future of Indian democracy—and with good reason, given the experience of other Asian countries.[32]

The importance of party institutionalization is also underscored, in the negative, by the cases of Thailand and South Korea. As we have already indicated, neither country has been able to develop a coherent and autonomous party system because of repeated and prolonged military intervention. Parties in each country have been weak in their internal organization, shallow in their bases of popular support, and disappointing if not disillusioning in their performance. Thus, military-bureaucratic dominance and party underdevelopment have become intertwined in a vicious cycle. With the emergence of new democratic opportunities (dramatically in South Korea, more subtly and gradually in Thailand), the construction of broad-based, coherent parties—mobilizing and incorporating emerging popular interests, organized effectively down to the local level, and penetrating particularly through the countryside—looms as one of the preeminent challenges of democratization.

The turn of the Congress party toward Hindu chauvinist mobilization may be seen as especially alarming in light of Sri Lanka's experience of two major parties outbidding one another for the electoral support of the majority ethnic community. Malaysia, by contrast, indicates the gains for ethnic peace that can be achieved when a single party is able to maintain electoral dominance within the majority community, while using that base to forge a broad, multiethnic, multiparty alliance. Such a party system is highly dependent on party elites skilled in and committed to the necessary bargaining and accommodation at the top. Much of this semiconsociational function was accomplished within the Congress party during the first two decades of India's independence. But with the emergence of a more competitive electorate and a more fragmented party system, it is not clear that it can ever be reconstructed again.

India, Sri Lanka, and Malaysia also demonstrate the strong link between electoral and party systems. In each case, the dominance of one or two parties has been encouraged, and the strength of the victorious party in each election dramatically magnified, by a single-member-district, "first-past-the-post" electoral system for parliament. It is too often forgotten that in all its years of electoral dominance, the Congress party has *never* won an absolute majority of the vote. With the exception of the 1977 debacle, its share of the national popular vote has ranged from 41 to 49 percent, which has always been sufficient to give it majority control of the Lok Sabha (national parliament), often by two-thirds or three-quarters (see Table 2.1 in the following chapter). The electoral data for Sri Lanka and Malaysia shows a similar pattern:

modest pluralities or majorities of the vote producing massive parliamentary majorities. In Malaysia, this tendency has been reinforced by
the rural weighting of the constituencies, which has benefitted the
major Malay Party, UMNO.

Since India, Malaysia and Sri Lanka all had, at least for many years,
three of the most stable and democratic regimes in Asia, one might
argue that such an electoral system, in favoring the dominance of one or
two parties or party alliances, favors democracy. But there is a fine line
between firm and stable parliamentary majorities on the one hand, and
the abuse of power that often follows on the other (particularly with
two-thirds or three-quarters majorities). In each of the above three
countries, democracy has been diminished by governments endowed
with landslide parliamentary majorities, which left the opposition too
weak to check the expansion and misuse of state power. Thus, it is not
clear if the presumed advantages of the single-member-district system
in terms of stability and simplification of the party system are not
outweighed by this disadvantage of conduciveness to abusive majorities.
In the coming years, Sri Lanka's recent switch to a system of proportional representation (not yet employed in an election) will provide an
interesting test. Certainly, if the goal is a streamlined party system, the
case of Turkey suggests this can be accomplished with proportional
representation and a high minimum threshold for representation.

Political Institutions

What is true for parties is true more generally of the institutional
landscape of democracy: There is a need throughout Asia to develop
and reinforce those institutions that articulate and aggregate popular
interests and that check the power of the state and its tendency to
concentrate in the national executive. The chapters in this volume attest
to the importance for democracy of vigorous legislatures and judiciaries, as
well as such informal institutions as the press and popular interest
groups (see above). The problem of Asian legislatures has been, in one
sense, similar to that faced by parties: In countries such as Thailand,
South Korea, and Pakistan, frequent military intervention has interrupted any sense of institutional continuity, and hence the capacity to
gather strength and depth through experience. In addition, in countries
such as India and Sri Lanka, and even more so in Pakistan under
Bhutto and the Philippines under Marcos, the autonomy and power of
legislatures has been deliberately eroded by executives hungry to amass
unaccountable power. Thus it is not surprising that Chai-Anan
Samudavanija sees the gradual enhancement of the organizational
infrastructure, capacity, and authority of the legislature as a crucial
dimension of the steady, often unglamorous process of political

institutionalization that must lie at the heart of developing democracy in Thailand.

It is interesting that in Asia, as elsewhere in the world, the strength and autonomy of the judiciary is roughly proportional to the condition of democracy. Of course, authoritarian regimes typically do not allow independent and vigorously assertive courts. But those of our cases that seem to have the strongest judiciaries, with the greatest legal and real authority to guard liberty, constitutionalism, and due process, have also had the greatest overall success with democracy. One would cite here India, Turkey, and Papua New Guinea, although our cases do not provide the data to substantiate this generalization. The key, as Özbudun notes for Turkey, is both the constitutional capacity of the judiciary to declare an act of Parliament unconstitutional, and the protection of judicial personnel from pressure or intimidation from the other branches of government. In India, the Supreme Court has used its authority over the years to hold more than 100 center and state acts invalid, even striking down part of a constitutional amendment that sought to bar the Supreme Court from reviewing any constitutional amendment! While the autonomy and credibility of the Court eroded during the 1975–1977 emergency, and have suffered further from the general politicization and deterioration of state institutions in the past two decades, the Court has "taken important steps in public interest litigation and in supporting citizens' rights against arbitrary encroachment by the state."[33] A classic case of judicial enfeeblement accompanying and enabling democratic decay has been Sri Lanka, where the constitution does not permit judicial review of enacted legislation, and even an advance judicial ruling on the constitutionality of a pending bill can be waived by a two-thirds vote of Parliament. This inability of the judiciary to overturn antidemocratic legislation, along with the concerted efforts of the executive to erode judicial autonomy, have been important factors in the deterioration of democracy in Sri Lanka.

Federalism and Decentralization

As we have already repeatedly suggested, democracy does not fit well with a highly centralized structure of power. Not only is centralization inherently in conflict with principles of democratic control, but it appears to be at odds empirically with strong and stable democracy. The experience of India underscores the value, indeed perhaps the necessity, of federalism for managing deep and intensely mobilized ethnic divisions. Real autonomy and devolution of power have been indispensable in the resolution of successive waves of ethnic and separatist agitation in India, just as Indira Gandhi's relentless violation of these principles inflamed ethnic divisions and badly damaged ethnic peace in the Punjab and elsewhere. At a minimum, peaceful ethnic coexistence would seem to require at least the scale of devolution of power of Papua New Guinea's system of provincial governments.

As Urmila Phadnis argues in her chapter on Sri Lanka, the scale of the largest unit to which power will be devolved is crucial. In Sri Lanka, the local district will not suffice, and the violent insurgency of Tamil separatists will probably not be ended (certainly not peacefully) until they are offered at least some form of aautonomous provincial government—short of the fully federal system that would be ideal in principle but unacceptable to the Sinhalese majority. In Indonesia as well, Sundhaussen observes that federalism "would have been the most promising constitutional arrangement to contain the evident anxieties of the ethnic minorities," but it was discredited early on because it was seen to be a Dutch design for weakening and dividing the country, and so is now as unacceptable to the majority group in Indonesia as it is in Sri Lanka. Nevertheless, even within Indonesia's current system of provincial government, there is scope for greater decentralization, by loosening central government control over appointments and finance. Similarly, even within a formal structure of federalism, the degree of autonomy allowed individual states may affect the intensity of ethnic protest and separatist movements. This would appear to be the case now in Pakistan, where the traumatic memory of the Bangladesh secession heightens the fear of further "Balkanization" of the country. In a situation where (as in India) the central government provides about two-thirds of the funding for state budgets, a key issue now is broader state autonomy on revenue collection. It is this type of real power that Pakistani "separatist" movements are seeking, writes Rose, and that would be most likely to assure the integrity of the federation.

But there is more at stake than ethnic peace in decentralizing power. The high degree of centralization of power in Thailand and South Korea was not only a concomitant but also a facilitating factor in the perpetuation of authoritarian, military-bureaucratic domination, and the development of meaningful and autonomous local government— both in the cities and in the villages—will be an important factor in whether democracy can be successfully developed and consolidated in those two countries. Similarly, as we have noted, a primary instrument of the erosion of democracy in India and its destruction in the Philippines under Marcos was the assault on autonomous points of power outside the center. Plural sources of power act as a check on the whims or impulses of power at the center. Local participation and control is an important means for socializing people into democratic values. And, as the case of India attests, the opportunity for parties who lose out at the center to gain a share of power at lower levels strengthens their overall commitment to the democratic system and reduces the stakes in winning national elections. It is for these reasons of the quality of democratic life that Özbudun calls for the strengthening of local governments in Turkey by giving them a greater share of public revenue and effective power.

Socioeconomic Development

Generations of theory have grappled with the relationship between democracy and both the level and the process of socioeconomic development. The evidence from our ten cases cannot settle the spirited theoretical controversies that remain with us. Nevertheless, some important insights do emerge. The most obvious of these is the simple static observation that democracy is not incompatible with a low level of development. India has been a living anomaly in this regard for four decades now, and even if one sees the quality or stability of its democracy to be diminishing, the sources of that regression have been heavily political rather than socioeconomic. Sri Lanka also maintained full democracy at a low level of development for many years (and still has a democratic constitution in place), while Papua New Guinea—the least urbanized, industrialized, and educated of our ten Asian cases—remains a democracy today, thirteen years after independence. Among the countries in this volume, one would be hard-pressed to find any clear pattern of association between the degree of democracy and the level of economic development. In fact, the rank order correlation for our ten cases between (1985) per capita GNP and Gastil's summary measure of civil and political liberties in 1987 shows literally no association between the two measures (or more precisely, an inconsequential −.04)[34]

This is not to deny the general positive correlation between democracy and development in the larger world. Nor is it to ignore the pressures and props for democracy that derive from a higher level of socioeconomic development, with the expansion it yields in income and education, and thus political participation. Particularly instructive in this regard is the recent experience of South Korea, whose extraordinary economic growth rate of the past two decades (averaging 7 per cent annually) has brought profound social changes that have facilitated and hastened the transition to democracy. Among the most important of these changes, writes Sung-joo Han, have been an increase in the size and political consciousness of the middle class; the growth of a more pluralistic, organized, and autonomous civil society; increasing circulation of people, information, and ideas; greater economic involvement with the industrialized democracies, and with it, the recognition that a newly industrializing country cannot win full admittance to their "club" unless it, too, is or becomes democratic.

Although its socioeconomic development has been at a much slower pace, Rose sees the significant socioeconomic changes in Pakistan in the past decade—the emergence (as in northern India) of rural and small-town entrepreneurs, the general improvement of the rural economy, diminishing power of the traditional rural landed elite, rapid urbanization, a better organized and more active trade union movement—exerting a similar type of pressure for democratic transition in the late 1980s. In particular, he anticipates that the movement of a new generation of educated men from rural elite families (replacing the older, narrower, urban elite) will broaden the social and economic base of political parties.

And yet, our cases also attest to the destabilizing consequences—for political order in general, and democracy more specifically—that the process of modernization can have for a country moving from poverty to an intermediate state of development.[35] The key problem is that socioeconomic development tends to loosen or sever traditional ties of deference and obedience to authority. New interests are generated, new consciousness is kindled, and new political and organizational capacities are acquired at the individual and group level. Demands multiply—both for the right to participate and for tangible and symbolic benefits—and political institutions must expand to make room for these new entrants, or risk breaking down. Moreover, with the proliferation of demands and interests, social and ideological cleavages may also multiply or deepen, taxing the conflict-mediating capacities of state institutions. If the institutions are authoritarian, as they have been for the last three decades in South Korea, these changes may profoundly erode the legitimacy of authoritarian rule and press powerfully from below for transition to democracy—while also presenting a new democracy with a daunting agenda of pent-up demands, conflicts, and frustrations. However, if the institutions that are having trouble adapting and incorporating are formally democratic ones, as they have been in Sri Lanka and India, then it may be constitutional democracy that becomes strained and even delegitimated. The Thai experience indicates the special difficulty awaiting a new democracy with weak, fragmented participant institutions and exponentially increasing social demands. As Chai-Anan explains, the lack of effective, coherent, and adaptable party institutions meant that there was no channel in Thailand's short-lived democracy (1974–76) for aggregating and expressing the demands of rapidly enlarging and newly mobilizing student, labor, and farmer groups. "As a result, political participation under the full-fledged democratic rule in the mid-1970s was close to anarchy."

Sri Lanka demonstrates some of the ambivalent consequences of development for democracy. On the one hand, its extraordinary early achievements in improving the physical quality of life—as reflected in its impressive adult literacy and life expectancy rates in the early 1960s (the highest of any of our cases then; see Table 1.1)—gave the democratic system considerable legitimacy and international prestige. And yet, the dramatic improvements in public health also gave birth to a population explosion (given the typical lag between the decline in death rates and that in birth rates). Combined with the high rates of literacy and education, this produced a huge bulk of politicized youth, who were reaching maturity, with high expectations, just as the economy was stagnating. That their frustration exploded violently—in the "JVP" insurgency of extremist, rural, Sinhalese Buddhist youth in 1971, and then in the Tamil separatist insurgency—should not be surprising. As Phadnis writes of that first insurgency and Sri Lankan democracy's subsequent tribulations, "with the processes of social transformation, the more the realization of the socioeconomic assumptions of democracy, the greater is the pressure on the ruling regimes to aggregate popular demands. And the less is the capability of the leadership to aggregate them, the more is the tendency to have recourse to populist slogans and to assume the traits of emergency regimes."

Something of the same process has been occurring in India over the past two decades as well. While the contributors to an important new study of Indian democracy give fresh and welcome emphasis to the autonomous role of political leadership in corroding democratic institutions, it is clear that India's very success in achieving "democratically guided economic development," unleashing as it has "growing political demands by both the privileged and the underprivileged," has also been a major source of democratic strain.[36] Growing political demands and organization by the less advantaged in society may nevertheless on balance be a good thing for democracy, in pressing for both a more just society and a more accountable and responsive state. But such popular mobilization forces the issue of democratic evolution: political leaders must either make institutional room for these new entrants—which, as Kohli notes, requires some sacrifice of their own immediate power—or the whole edifice of democracy could, as a result of the accumulated wear of unaccommodated demands, eventually fall down.

Economic Performance and Legitimacy

It is commonly assumed that a brisk and steady pace of economic development is an important source of regime legitimacy. From the evidence in this volume, there is much to support that assumption, but also much that qualifies it. Democracies do develop popular commitment and legitimacy as a consequence of delivering the goods of development. But we have seen that the process of development may also produce new challenges to legitimacy, and that successful development may spawn expectations difficult to fulfill. Moreover, what is true for

Table 1.1   Selected Development Indicators, 1965–1985

	India 1965	India 1985	Papua New Guinea 1965	Papua New Guinea 1985	Turkey 1965	Turkey 1985	Philippines 1965	Philippines 1985
Civil and Political Liberties, 1975 & 1987[a]	5	5	5	4	5	6	10	4
Population in Millions	483.0	765.1	—	3.5	31.0	50.2	32.3	54.7
Population Growth Rate 1973–1984		2.3		2.6		2.2		2.7
Projected Rate of Population Growth 1985–2000		1.8		2.2		1.9		2.2
GNP per Capita in U.S. Dollars, 1985[b]		270		680		1080		580
Average Annual Growth Rate, GNP per Capita, in Percent, 1965–1985		1.7		0.4		2.6		2.3
Average Annual Rate of Inflation 1965–1980, 1980–1985	7.4	7.8	8.1	5.5	20.8	37.1	11.8	19.3
Average Annual Growth Rate of Agricultural Production 1965–1980, 1980–1985	2.8	2.7	—	—	3.2	2.6	4.6	1.7
Percent of Labor Force in Agriculture (1965–1980)	73	70	87	76	75	58	58	52
Life Expectancy at Birth								
Male	46	57	44	51	52	62	54	61
Female	44	56	44	54	55	67	57	65
Infant Mortality Rate per 1000 Births	151	89	140	68	152	84	72	48
Adult Literacy Rate 1960–1980	28	36	29	32	38	60	72	75
Percent Enrolled in Primary School 1965 & 1984[c]	74	90	44	61	101	113	113	107
Percent Enrolled in Secondary School 1965 & 1984	27	34	4	11	16	38	41	68
Urban Population as Percent of Total	19	25	5	14	32	46	32	39

Sources: World Bank, *World Development Report 1983, 1986, 1987* (New York: Oxford University Press, 1983, 1986, 1987); *U.N. Statistical Yearbook*, 1966; and for civil and political liberties, *Freedom at Issue*, January-February 1976, and Raymond D. Gastil, *Freedom in the World: Political Rights and Civil Liberties, 1987–88* (Lanham, MD: University Press of America, 1988).

[a] Combined score of civil and political liberties, each rated on a 1 to 7 scale with 1 being freest and 7 least free. A score of 5 or less (with a 2 on political rights) is regarded as "free," 6 to 11 as partly free, and 12 to 14 as "not free."

[b] 1965 GNP per capita is expressed in constant 1980 U.S. dollars.

[c] The percentages may exceed 100 because of the enrollment of students outside the standard age group.

Sri Lanka		South Korea		Malaysia		Thailand		Pakistan		Indonesia	
1965	1985	1965	1985	1965	1985	1965	1985	1965	1985	1965	1985
5	7	11	8	6	8	8	6	8	9	10	11
11.2	15.8	28.4	41.1	8.0	15.6	30.5	51.7	—	96.2	104.5	162.2
	1.8		1.5		2.4		2.2		2.9		2.3
	1.6		1.2		1.9		1.6		2.7		1.8
	380		2150		2000		800		380		530
	2.9		6.6		4.4		4.0		2.6		4.8
9.5	14.7	18.7	6.0	4.9	3.1	6.8	3.2	10.2	8.1	34.3	10.7
2.7	4.0	3.0	6.3	—	3.0	4.9	3.4	3.3	2.1	4.3	3.1
56	53	55	36	59	42	82	71	60	55	71	57
63	68	55	65	56	66	54	62	46	52	43	53
64	72	58	72	60	70	58	66	44	50	45	57
63	36	63	27	55	28	88	43	149	115	138	96
75	85	71	93	53	60	68	86	15	24	39	62
93	103	101	99	90	97	78	97	40	42	72	118
35	61	35	91	28	53	14	30	12	15	12	39
20	21	32	64	26	38	13	18	24	29	16	25

democracies may not be true for authoritarian regimes, which may be undone by their economic successes as much as by their failures.

An important theme of Das Gupta's contribution to this volume is the insufficiently appreciated success of India in pursuing and achieving what he terms "combined development." As a result of democratic planning and relatively effective administration, India has made quiet but impressive gains in agricultural production, eliminating famine and dependence on foreign food within a generation. Although statist in-efficiency is an urgent economic and political problem, industrialization in India has reached the point where the country produces most of what it needs and ranks among the top five industrial producers in the developing world. Most importantly, steady and substantial improve-ments have been made in the physical quality of life, so that on such measures as the infant mortality rate, the child death rate, life ex-pectancy, and primary, secondary, and university enrollment ratios, India ranks today with the average for lower-middle-income developing countries, even though its per capita national income places it among the twenty poorest countries in the world.[37] These gains have come through steady, prudent investment, avoiding the economic crisis and crippling international indebtedness that gripped many Third World countries which sought shortcuts to development.

If these achievements have unleashed new expectations, and if some of them have been less dramatic than in China or Sri Lanka, they have nevertheless purchased some considerable popular commitment to the system. Overall, the experience of combined development—what Das Gupta calls the "simultaneous treatment of multiple issues like national cohesion, economic development, social justice, citizen efficacy, and human development"—has done much to legitimate the democratic system, or at least to neutralize challenges to it. While poverty and inequality remain, despite the progress, humiliating in degree and haunting in scale, it is significant that the movements against these are primarily working through rather than challenging the legitimacy of the democratic system.[38]

Something of a similar argument could be made for the early social and economic progress of Sri Lanka. But there is also another lesson to be learned from that case, which is catching up with India as well. This is the costs to economic performance, and ultimately to democratic vitality, of statist economic policies. The sharp economic downturn under the socialist-leaning United Front government (1970–1977) was traceable not only to exogenous shocks (rising oil prices, declining tea prices, fertilizer shortages, drought) but to increasing state control over the economy that was often ill advised (with quotas and controls leading to scarcities and long queues) and badly administered. And while in-creasing social welfare spending helped improve the quality of life, it also contributed to recurrent balance of payments deficits. We have already noted how the consequent economic travails have contributed to Sri Lanka's acute political difficulties since 1970. Unfortunately, the combined effects of internal war and plunging commodity prices appear to obscure now the initially tonic effects of the post-1978 economic liberalization policies.

The delegitimating consequences for democracy of prolonged development stagnation may be seen in the ease with which Ferdinand Marcos was able to sweep aside democratic institutions in the Philippines in 1972. Although it was he himself who had failed, in his second presidential term, to come to grips with the enduring and seemingly unsolvable problems of economic stagnation, agrarian oligarchy and inequality, corruption and dependency, Marcos struck a resonant chord among many (if not most) Filipinos with his call for a revolution from above to inculcate discipline, "democratize wealth," and impose technocratic designs for rapid modernization. While he seemed to deliver the goods in the early years of his dictatorship, the progressive narrowing of his base through years of gross corruption, neglect, stagnation, mounting indebtedness, and finally capital flight and impending economic collapse showed the inherent vulnerability of authoritarian rule. Still, Jackson argues, while declining real income for the population may have eroded Marcos' mass support and fed the communist insurgency, it alone did not undo him. The economic decay only became fatal for Marcos when it began to affect the economic fortunes of the Manila business elite, who finally joined the middle class in actively opposing him. It was in this politically strategic sense that economic crisis "supplied the backdrop for a legitimacy crisis which terminated the Marcos regime."

In his review of regime succession in Pakistan, Rose cautions against the temptation to generalize about the relationship between performance and legitimacy. The lesson of Pakistani history seems to be that a government can suffer from a bad economy but gets little credit for a flourishing one. But this may also speak of the inherent difficulties military regimes face in legitimating themselves. If they do not perform, they lose legitimacy, since performance is their only justification for holding power. But as South Korea has shown, if they do perform socioeconomically, they tend to refocus popular aspirations around political goals for voice and participation that they cannot satisfy without terminating their existence. "Thus, no matter whether they perform well or badly, they, in time, face demands for change."[39]

The "inevitable legitimacy crisis" for military regimes appears to be coming in Indonesia as well, Sundhaussen argues. Although the economic stability, reduction in poverty, and significant improvements in per capita income, life expectancy, and education (see Table 1.1) under

Soeharto's New Order contrast pointedly with the economic failures
and chaos of civilian rule (which, in fact, was a major reason for the loss
of legitimacy of parliamentary democracy and the demise of Sukarno in
the mid-1960s), Indonesia's military regime will, under a new generation of leadership, have to find some way to come to grips with popular
restlessness about its legitimacy.

The International Environment

Economic dependence and vulnerability represent only one type of
international influence on the democratic prospect in Asia. To the
extent these factors complicate the quest for vibrant, balanced, and
consistent economic growth, they may exacerbate the problem of performance for a democratic regime. However, a more direct international
impact upon democracy in Asia appears to come through threats
(perceived or real) to national security.

A perception of serious threat to the country's military security,
from either external invasion or external support for subversion or
insurgency, tends to strengthen the hand of military-bureaucratic forces.
In particular, it legitimates the augmentation and centralization of state
power, the militarization of society, and the restriction of civil and
political liberties as matters of necessity for national security. From the
days of the first Korean Republic under Syngman Rhee, through the
authoritarian regimes of Park and Chun Doo Hwan, this effect has been
most strikingly apparent in South Korea, as one might expect of any
divided country in which military tension and readiness remain acute on
both sides of the border. But it has been visible in Thailand, Indonesia,
Malaysia, and Pakistan as well.

In Thailand, communist insurgency during the 1970s heightened
right-wing anxiety about mass political movements, and military-
bureaucratic dominance was further legitimized by the subsequent
expansionist and threatening posture of Vietnam in the region. More
recently, Pakistani politics have felt the pressure of the Soviet war in
neighboring Afghanistan and the disrupting flow of millions of refugees
into Pakistan. While this has not prevented a partial and gradual transition to democracy, it has complicated and perhaps slowed it. Given
Pakistan's vital geostrategic location, historic vulnerability to invading
forces from the west and northwest, and legacy of previous wars with
India, one might expect the issue of military security to remain a
challenge to the democratic transition, a ready excuse for failing to
complete it, and a serious problem for any future democratic regime.

Pakistan's experience suggests two other lessons about the political
effects of security problems. First, palpable threats can have a unifying
effect on a country's political elite. Rose contends that the Soviet

invasion of Afghanistan may have saved President Zia-ul-Huq from a coup that was planned but then suspended. The external military threat from Indonesia submerged ethnic divisions during Malaysia's general elections in 1964, and the threat from expansionist Vietnam again induced greater internal political consensus and a stronger intercommunal coalition in Malaysia during the mid-1970s (while also inducing greater restrictions on democracy).

Secondly, national security is a preeminent dimension of regime performance. Few things can shake the foundation of a regime more violently than defeat or perceived failure in war, as Pakistan's Ayub Khan discovered after his unsuccessful 1965 war with India. The rapid growth of the communist insurgency in the Philippines contributed to the growing disillusionment with Ferdinand Marcos even within the ranks of the military. By contrast, the success of a previous Philippine president, Ramon Magsaysay, in defeating the even graver challenge of the Huk rebellion in the early 1950s gave vigor and legitimacy to the democratic system.

Of course, that military success was aided with considerable support from the U.S., and ever since Philippine independence the U.S. has had a significant influence on the politics of that country. But external political and military influence can cut both ways. In light of the aggressive U.S. role in pressing Marcos to leave—both officially (finally, at the time of the Enrile/Ramos rebellion, through the threat to cut off all military aid) and unofficially (through media attention, Congressional visitors, electoral observers, etc.)—it is useful to recall that Marcos enjoyed warm (often effusive) and substantial American support during the bulk of his authoritarian rule, as well as tens of billions of dollars in international loans that gave his regime symbolic legitimacy and immense, unprecedented powers of patronage. And even now, as the United States aids the democratic government of Corazon Aquino while she appeals for more economic assistance, some sympathetic and sober observers question whether the (gradual) withdrawal of American military bases from the Philippines might not produce a stronger, more confident, less politically ambivalent and polarized democracy.[40] At least, there may be a case for changes in the structure of the bases agreement "that would make the bases, both symbolically and actually, a manifestation of a more equal Filipino-American partnership."[41] In the same vein, democrats on both sides of the U.S.-South Korean relationship worry that excessive international dependence tends to breed radical, nationalist sentiment in South Korea, and thus to deepen problems of political polarization. And despite the obvious contribution to Papua New Guinea's economic (and democratic) prosperity of unconditional aid from Australia (which still accounts for nearly a third of its annual budget), this dependence may also have, over the long run, certain psychological and political effects.

One can find conflicting effects over time in the close U.S. relationship with South Korea. Years of support for authoritarian rulers yielded more recently to pressure for democracy, and U.S. diplomatic pressure may have played a critical role in dissuading President Chun from ruthlessly repressing the mass mobilization of opposition groups demanding democracy. But the greatest international pressure for democracy may have come from the more diffuse and subtle global pressure to be democratic in order to be accepted by the major capitalist industrialized powers as one of them. Diffusion and demonstration effects also play a role, as the Philippine lesson of "people power" was not lost on those very groups that were mobilizing to demand democracy in Korea (just as the Philippine and especially the Korean transitions affect the more gradual political opening now under way in Taiwan). But diffusion, too, can work both ways, as was indicated in 1972 when Marcos seemed to be promising the same path of authoritarian stability-*cum*-economic progress that many other bureaucratic polities of Southeast Asia were embracing.

To the extent it is possible to generalize across such diverse effects, one might begin with two tentative but relatively safe conclusions. First, international effects on democracy (positive and negative) tend to be greater the smaller and more vulnerable the country. Thus, the determinants of democracy in India appear to be overwhelmingly internal (at least since the end of colonialism), but less so in Sri Lanka or Malaysia. Second, international influence, such as it may exist, is more prodemocratic when the regional or global trend is toward democracy, and when the powerful external actors make the promotion of democracy à more explicit foreign policy goal.

• TOWARD DEMOCRACY IN ASIA •

It is beyond our scope here to offer general conclusions about the prospects or conditions for democracy in Asia, much less some overarching formula for achieving or maintaining democratic government. As the above review indicates, there are many factors at work in shaping political development in Asia, and many possible generalizations, but the weight one would give to different factors varies across the markedly different circumstances of our various cases. We leave to Volume One of this study any effort at grander theoretical synthesis, drawing upon all twenty-six of the cases covered.

Nevertheless, we cannot ignore the question with which we are inevitably left at the end of such a study: How can the pursuit of democratic government be advanced and strengthened in Asia? It is useful to divide this question into the three types of challenges Asian countries now face: the transition to democracy, the consolidation of new or unstable democracies, and the renewal or reequilibration of democracies that have weakened or partially broken down.

The Transition to Democracy

Of our ten cases, the transition to democracy is currently an issue (to one degree or another) in three. In Pakistan the issue is how to complete it; in Thailand, how to advance it; and in Indonesia, how to begin it.

Of course, it always helps to have a leader who is firmly committed to democratization, such as Mustafa Kemal and later President Inonu in Turkey. Failing that, if there is a strong democratic movement from below, it may help to have an authoritarian ruler who is politically inept and unpopular, like Chun of South Korea, or manifestly unable to manage political and economic problems, as became the case with Marcos near the end. At a strategic moment, carefully focused international pressure may serve to hasten the exit of a dictator like Marcos, or at least to limit his options, as may have happened with Chun.

Without question, the political choices and tactics of regime and opposition leaders are of great consequence, as may be their own internal divisions and maneuverings, particularly once the momentum for a transition has begun. Pakistan's transition would not have come this far, Rose argues, were it not for the "careful, sensible tactics adopted by both the government and the opposition parties to avoid violent clashes." The Philippine and especially the South Korean cases would also seem to confirm the general emphasis of O'Donnell and Schmitter on the importance of elite strategies and choices, and of avoiding "widespread and recurrent violence" while seeking a negotiated solution. Moreover, our case studies of Thailand and Indonesia also support their emphasis on "a sequence of piecemeal reforms" as the most likely path of democratic transition, and on the need for democratic oppositions to be willing to play within the initially very restricted games allowed them by authoritarian regimes early in the sequence of democratization.[42]

However, the Philippine and South Korean cases also call attention to the importance for the transition of what O'Donnell and Schmitter call the "resurrection of civil society" through an explosion of autonomous interest group expression and activity, and ultimately its convergence from many points into a "popular upsurge" of mobilization for democratization.[43] In addition, these and other Asian cases suggest the importance of a more enduring expansion of autonomous, vigorous associational life, independent of the state. Such a pluralistic infrastructure not only creates a more promising foundation for democracy, but the resulting organization, political consciousness, and vigilance of the citizenry make the democratic transition much more irreversible, and no less importantly, reduce the prospect that authoritarian forces (old or new) may overthrow or somehow capture the new democracy in its vulnerable early days. All of this is vividly illustrated by the Philippine experience, with the striking success of the citizen-based NAMFREL in increasing the integrity of the electoral process during and after the transition, the crucial role of the Catholic Church and its affiliated organizations and press during Marcos' final years, and the proliferation of diverse forms of democratic popular organization since the fall of Marcos. In a sense, the effect is also visible in the determination of military elites in Thailand and Indonesia who oppose democratization to preempt, coopt, manage, license, and permanently control potentially autonomous forms of popular organization and interest expression.

It would seem that one clue to advancing democracy in Asia lies in the wisdom to discern what is possible and press forward within those constraints. In Pakistan, a transition to full democracy, by the end of President Zia's term in 1990, now appears possible, but probably only within the framework of the system and timetable he has crafted. Political developments—the increasing independence, skill, and assertiveness of the civilian prime minister, Mohammad Khan Junejo, and the heavy popular participation in the November 1987 Local Bodies elections—showed the miscalculation of the opposition in boycotting the 1985 legislative elections and the wisdom of their belated decision to take full advantage of the ongoing political opening. Continuing popular mobilization, party development, and prudent political gamesmanship (including credible guarantees of Zia's freedom from prosecution in exchange for his exit) now seem likely to achieve a full military withdrawal from politics.[44]

But no such development seems plausible in the near term in Thailand or Indonesia, and democratic forces must therefore have a longer-term strategy that takes advantage of the possibilities that exist in the near term. For Thailand, Chai-Anan argues that the major hope for democratic progress lies in political institutionalization of participant structures—civilian political parties and the elected parliament—through the gradual development of their organizational depth, mastery of information, policy innovativeness, and linkages with popular interest groups and support bases. Until and unless parties and legislators improve their capacity, performance, image, and credibility, they will have little hope of reducing, much less eliminating, the current military dominance of political life. However, by pragmatically conceding for a time military preeminence in security matters and participation in politics, committed democrats may find the space to build the infrastructural base for future democratization. In Indonesia, which is considerably less democratic, less appears possible. But Sundhaussen implies that some significant opening of the political system may be achievable, under an emerging new generation of military leadership, if democratic politicians in the opposition are able to forge a more coherent and effective front while giving the military no cause to fear an outbreak of unrest or a surge to the left.

Consolidating New Democracies

Three of our cases face the challenge of consolidating new democratic systems. In each case, the outcome will depend on the capacity of the new political leaders to make the democratic system work in two senses: first, to make it function democratically, in a procedural sense; and second, to make it function effectively in coming to grips with the economic, social, and security problems facing these countries.

The prospects for success are probably most favorable in Turkey, because of its considerable prior experience with democracy, and the fact that it has now operated the new system without crisis for several years. Moreover, the new constitution seems so far to be achieving its aim of producing a more stable, less polarized pattern of politics by eliminating small, extremist parties and pressing toward party consolidation. Its legitimacy—and the overall democratic character of the system—would be increased, however, if the remaining limits on free political activity (e.g. by trade unions) were lifted, civil liberties were strengthened, and military influence on government further reduced. Özbudun argues that the foundation of democracy must be deepened by "establishing a healthier balance between the state and the society." This involves not only the reduction of centralized bureaucratic control over the economy, but also the strengthening of local governments (which now receive more revenue) and the growth of autonomous voluntary associations. At the same time, he warns, the pursuit of a new, export-oriented basis of economic growth must not neglect the need for a more equitable distribution of income.

South Korea and the Philippines face more difficult challenges, but at least South Korea begins its new democracy with a healthy and dynamic economy. However, success in development, as we have noted, breeds its own troubles, and the fate of the new democracy will turn significantly on the ability of democratic leaders to lower the pitch of popular mobilization by groups—in particular the large and growing working class, but also its ideological sympathizers among students and intellectuals—who feel deprived or excluded by the years of military rule. Defusing and preempting such militant popular mobilization— which could unleash a new, destructive cycle of political polarization— will require both the institutionalization of effective channels of interest expression inside the political system, primarily through political parties, and the substantive satisfaction over time of aggrieved popular interests. That is to say, the system must become more inclusive, both politically and socioeconomically. It must also develop, as Sung-joo Han repeatedly argues in his chapter, more effective political parties, which, through their skill in mobilizing and governing and their improving relations with one another, give the military no excuse to intervene anew but rather gradually trim back its influence in government and society.

By contrast with Turkey and South Korea, the gravity and multiplicity of challenges that have faced the new government of Corazon Aquino since its accession to power in February 1986 lead many to marvel that it has survived even two years. The most menacing problems facing the new system were the persistence of armed insurgency, not only by the communist New Peoples Army but by the secessionist Moro National Liberation Front, based in Mindanao; the insubordination of dissident elements within the military, which launched three coup attempts in 1987 (one of which appeared to come close to success); the ravaged and severely indebted state of the economy; enormous inequality (especially in land ownership) and social injustice, with roughly 60 percent of the population below the poverty line; and the lack of adequate democratic institutions. The latter problem has been the least intractable: A new constitution that limits executive power has been drafted and ratified, and elections have been successfully conducted for the national legislature and local governments (a particularly crucial level of authority in the geographically dispersed archipelago). But the party system remains unsettled, Mrs. Aquino's government remains politically divided, and the new constitution will not have been put to the real test until the next presidential election, in 1992. Before then, Mrs. Aquino's government must revive the economy, firmly establish civilian supremacy over the military, and turn the tide against the armed insurgencies.

At this writing, there are signs of progress on all three fronts: the first real growth in per capita income in four years during 1987; a tougher stance toward military indiscipline, coupled with tangible reforms (higher military pay, more professional officers); and a more aggressive military response to insurgency by better trained and equipped units, complemented by a program to rehabilitate returning rebels. On the social agenda—labor, housing, health, education, and the acute demand for land reform—progress has been more elusive, but is no less essential. As Jackson notes, the communist insurgency is not likely to be defeated without coordinated social, economic, and political reforms that address the manifest needs for access to land, social justice, and effective local government, so recreating the bonds of loyalty between the people and their political system. Precisely the same is true for the legitimation of the new democratic system. More than any of our cases, the Philippines illustrates the laborious, painstaking, and often treacherous nature of democratic consolidation.[45]

Renewing, Reviving and Reequilibrating Democracy

Of the four long-standing civilian, constitutional systems examined in this volume, none is free of serious, even grave, challenges to its future viability. This may be seen as a rather sad and telling statement on the difficulty of maintaining democracy in the circumstances of developing countries, but it is not a hopeless one.

The most important test is being played out in India, in the sense that its success with democracy has been to date the longest and most influential in Asia. But as we have seen, India's democratic institutions have been steadily deteriorating for twenty years, and it seems apparent to a growing number of Indians that Prime Minister Rajiv Gandhi has neither the determination nor the vision to rejuvenate them. Little has been done to rebuild the grassroots strength and organizational depth, complexity, and autonomy of the Congress-I party, as was reflected in its electoral defeats during 1987 in Kerala, West Bengal and especially Haryana, which is part of the party's electoral base in the northern Hindi belt. Rather than use the prestige of critics and reformers and the investigative vigor of an autonomous press to begin to purge the government of the spreading cancer of corruption—with all its disillusioning and delegitimating consequences—the prime minister has turned vengefully against these forces of renewal, talking of foreigners and traitors trying to "destabilize" the country, raiding the offices of the crusading daily, *The Indian Express*, and forcing his most effective and respected reforming minister, V. P. Singh, out of government when he moved too aggressively to expose and punish corruption. As Bharat Wariavwalla explains, the problem Singh was attacking goes to the heart of India's decay: It is "the 'license-permit Raj,' an alliance of businessmen, politicians, and bureaucrats which, for the past two decades, had cheated the consumer, stifled incentives and production, kept the economy from growing, and above all, subverted democratic processes."[46] More than ever, democratic renewal in India appears to require political leadership with the skill and commitment to cleanse the system, rebuild political institutions down to the grassroots, and resolve festering ethnic violence (especially in the Punjab) democratically. But increasingly, it appears as well that such leadership will result only from the kind of mass-based, democratic movement of citizens that helped reclaim the country from the vise of Indira Gandhi's authoritarianism in the mid-1970s.

A similar type of decay has been evident more recently in Malaysia, where the divisive and abusive administration of the country by Prime Minister Mahathir Mohammed illustrates again the (potentially lasting) damage that can be done to democratic institutions by undemocratic political leadership. As the decline deepened during 1987, the dominant party in the ruling alliance, UMNO, split amid a turbulent struggle for party control, which Mahathir won only narrowly (and, his opponents alleged, fraudulently). Ethnic relations between the Malays and Chinese also precipitously deteriorated as the tolerance, civility, and striving for consensus that have characterized the political culture visibly declined. These escalating tensions served (even, some believe, were encouraged) to justify an authoritarian crackdown, which began in October 1987 with the arrests of government critics, closure of three newspapers, and a ban on public meetings and rallies. Denounced as "undemocratic" and deplorable by the revered founding father of the country, Tunku Abdul Rahman, these and subsequent actions destroyed the vitality of the party structure and weakened the (already con-strained) infrastructure of democracy. In this light, the arrests of several interest and reform group leaders and Mahathir's warning to the judi-ciary—which has issued a series of recent decisions against the government—to stay out of politics were also significant. With the scope for criticism and opposition increasingly constrained, it is difficult to see the source for reinvigoration of the substantial democratic insti-tutions that existed before Mahathir.[47]

Even much graver is the situation in which semidemocratic Sri Lanka finds itself after several years of ethnic bloodletting, terrorism, and civil war. As the violent struggle has continued, despite the inter-vention of over 20,000 Indian troops, the problem of Tamil insurgency has been compounded by a resurgence of violent Sinhalese ethnic chauvinism, as reflected in the revival of the extremist Janatha Vimukthi Peramuna (JVP). The assassination of moderate Sinhalese politicians by the JVP (emulating the tactic of Tamil extremists), the attempted assassination of President Jayewardene in August 1987, and the latter's warning that he might cancel the 1989 elections if the war did not end soon are only some of the signs of the damage that the civil war is doing to the country's political institutions, economy, and social fabric. Its resolution through some kind of compromise agreement—if that is still possible—is the *sine qua non* for any kind of reequilibration of democ-racy in Sri Lanka. But in a political climate in which the MPs of Jayewardene's ruling UNP "fear for their lives and do not dare return to their homes, many of which have . . . been burned to the ground by angry mobs," it is not likely that a democratic election, even if it is held, will produce a solution. The way out would seem to require some sort of temporary and historic united front of the two major Sinhalese

parties that would negotiate and sell to the Sinhalese majority a peaceful ethnic accommodation, before the formal structures of democracy
come crashing down in an extremist takeover or military coup.[48]

Nothing like the same degree of crisis and danger is apparent in
Papua New Guinea today, but there as well the 1987 election revealed a
serious erosion of the party system into a state of more severe fractionalization. Collectively, the four largest parties lost twenty parliamentary seats, of the 106 contested, as independents increased their
seats from eight to twenty-two, while winning a stunning 40 percent of
the vote. A local political scientist has observed, "the election results
constitute a recipe for delicate coalition politics that could easily border
on governmental immobility, instability or both." The problem was not
eased by the increased incidence of fraud and violence in the election
and the "unprincipled political opportunism" that dominated the subsequent maneuvers to form a coalition government.[49] Although Papua
New Guinea is in many respects unique, the experience of party fractionalization and government immobilism in dragging down democracy
elsewhere in Asia is certainly cause for concern. With public disenchantment with political corruption and opportunism growing, and
public confidence in the political system declining, the pressure is increasing on political leaders to produce effective, accountable government and to rejuvenate political parties.

Conclusion

If there is any common thread running through the democratic prospects
of all ten of the countries we examine in this volume, it is the crucial
importance of effective and democratically committed leadership. To
the extent that democracy is consolidated and deeply legitimated, it can
survive corrupt, abusive, and woefully incompetent leaders. In time,
they will be replaced. But when a prolonged period of undemocratic or
inept leadership is experienced, the system itself may begin to decay,
along with popular commitment to it. And when democratic institutions
do not enjoy deep, unquestioned legitimacy, and the protection of
complex and variegated checks and balances (both formal and informal),
the damage that can be done by even a few years of abuse may be
severe and lasting. Although the leadership variable tends to convey an
emphasis on the head of government or the few top leaders of the party
system, one should not ignore the damage that can be done by the
spread among political elites more generally of behavior and attitudes
that are corrupt, opportunistic, and contemptuous of democratic rules
and norms. While the structural constraints and possibilites vary
enormously among our ten cases, the scope for innovation or immobility, cooperation or confrontation, responsibility or greed, on the part

of the politicians is substantial, and will substantially affect the prospects for democracy in every one of them.

At the same time, it is useful to reiterate once more that while the truism that people get the leaders they deserve is overly simplistic, people, if they organize, can eventually get rid of leaders they do not want and achieve the kind of leadership they do. Deference to leadership has long been regarded as a quintessential feature of Asian political culture. But power that is too much deferred to can too easily be abused. From the evidence of our Asian cases, it would seem that the organization of the citizenry—autonomously, pluralistically, from the grassroots—both inside and outside the formal polity is an indispensable condition for the development and maintenance of a secure democracy.

• NOTES •

1. Juan J. Linz and Alfred Stepan, eds., *The Breakdown of Democratic Regimes* (Baltimore: The Johns Hopkins University Press, 1978).
2. Myron Weiner, "Institution Building in South Asia," in Robert A. Scalapino, Seizaburo Sato, and Jusuf Wanandi, eds., *Asian Political Institutionalization* (Berkeley: Institute of East Asian Studies, University of California, 1986), pp. 289–90.
3. Donald L. Horowitz, *Coup Theories and Officers' Motives: Sri Lanka in Comparative Perspective* (Princeton: Princeton University Press, 1980), p. 150.
4. For some characteristic and cogent interpretations, in addition to Das Gupta's in this volume, see Robert L. Hardgrave, Jr. and Stanley A. Kochanek, *India: Government and Politics in a Developing Nation*, 4th ed. (New York: Harcourt Brace Jovanovich, 1986), especially pages 121–22; James Manor, "Parties and the Party System," and Atul Kohli, "State-Society Relations in India's Changing Democracy," in Atul Kohli, ed., *India's Democracy: An Analysis of Changing State-Society Relations* (Princeton: Princeton University Press, 1988), pp. 62–98 and 305–18.
5. Paul Brass, "The Punjab Crisis and the Unity of India," in *India's Democracy*, p. 212.
6. Kohli, "State-Society Relations," p. 309.
7. Myron Weiner, "Empirical Democratic Theory," in Myron Weiner and Ergun Özbudun, eds., *Competitive Elections in Developing Countries* (Durham, N.C.: Duke University Press, 1987), pp. 18–20; Samuel P. Huntington, "Will More Countries Become Democratic?," *Political Science Quarterly* 99, no. 2 (Summer 1984): pp. 205–6; Richard L. Sklar, "Developmental Democracy," *Comparative Studies in Society and History* 29, no. 4 (October 1987): p. 695.
8. Weiner, "Empirical Democratic Theory," p. 18.
9. Ibid, p. 20.
10. Zakaria Haji Ahmad, "Malaysia," in this volume.
11. Lucian W. Pye, with Mary W. Pye, *Asian Power and Politics: The Cultural Dimensions of Authority* (Cambridge, MA: Harvard University Press, 1985), pp. 52–3.
12. Weiner, "Institution Building in South Asia," p. 290.
13. John L. S. Girling, *Thailand: Society and Politics* (Ithaca, N.Y.: Cornell University Press, 1981), p. 104.
14. For an early elaboration of the concept of political culture which influences its treatment here, see Gabriel A. Almond and Sidney Verba, *The Civic Culture* (Princeton: Princeton University Press, 1963), especially pages 11–16. See also Lucian W. Pye, "Introduction: Political Culture and Political Development," and Sidney Verba, "Conclusion: Comparative Political Culture," in Pye and Verba, eds., *Political Culture and Political Development* (Princeton: Princeton University Press, 1965), pp. 3–26 and 512–60;

and Gabriel A. Almond, "The Intellectual History of the Civic Culture Concept," in Gabriel A. Almond and Sidney Verba, eds., *The Civic Culture Revisited* (Boston: Little, Brown and Co., 1980).

15. Pye, *Asian Power and Politics*, especially pp. 339–41.

16. Myron Weiner, "India: Two Political Cultures," in Pye and Verba, *Political Culture and Political Development*, p. 214.

17. Sung-joo Han, "South Korea," in this volume.

18. Ulf Sundhaussen, "Indonesia," in this volume.

19. The misrepresentation of political culture theory as asserting only a unidirectional relationship between political culture and political structure has been effectively rebutted by Gabriel A. Almond. See "The Intellectual History of the Civic Culture Concept," in Almond and Verba, eds., *The Civic Culture Revisited*, especially page 29, and "The Study of Political Culture," published in German as "Politische Kultur-Forschung—Ruckblick und Ausblick," special number 18 of the *Politische Viertel-jahresheft, Politische Kultur in Deutschland*, Dirk Berg-Schlosser and Jakob Schissler, eds., (Westdeutscher Verlag, 1987), pp. 27–39.

20. Myron Weiner, "India: Two Political Cultures," pp. 235–37, and "Ancient Indian Political Theory and Contemporary Indian Politics," in S. N. Eisenstadt, Reuven Kahane, and David Shulman, eds., *Orthodoxy, Heterodoxy and Dissent in India* (New York: Mouton, 1984), pp. 123–24.

21. Gabriel A. Almond, "Introduction: A Functional Approach to Comparative Politics," in Gabriel A. Almond and James S. Coleman, eds., *The Politics of the Developing Areas* (Princeton: Princeton University Press, 1960), p. 23.

22. Almond, "The Study of Political Culture," (manuscript), p. 4.

23. Donald Horowitz, *Ethnic Groups in Conflict* (Berkeley: University of California Press, 1985), p. 39.

24. Ibid, p. 37.

25. Quoted from Das Gupta in this volume. See also the two essays in Kohli, ed., *India's Democracy*: Jyotirindra Das Gupta, "Ethnicity, Democracy and Development in India: Assam in a General Perspective," pp. 144–68, and Paul Brass, "The Punjab Crisis and the Unity of India," pp. 169–213.

26. For a fuller analysis of the role of electoral incentives in forming and maintaining multiethnic alliances, and a comparison of Malaysia and Sri Lanka, see Horowitz, *Ethnic Groups in Conflict*, especially pages 424–27.

27. Das Gupta, "Ethnicity, Democracy and Development in India," pp. 165, 167.

28. For a good overview with a case study of Assam, see Das Gupta, "Ethnicity, Democracy and Development in India."

29. Ghanshyam Shah, "Grass-Roots Mobilization in Indian Politics," in Kohli, ed., *India's Democracy*, pp. 262–304.

30. Barnett R. Rubin, "The Civil Liberties Movement in India: New Approaches to the State and Social Change," *Asian Survey* 27, no. 3 (March 1987): pp. 371–92.

31. Rajni Kothari, quoted in G. Shah, "Grassroots Mobilization," p. 302.

32. For a penetrating and detailed exposition of this thesis of development and decay in the party system, see James Manor, "Parties and the Party System," in Kholi, *India's Democracy*, pp. 62–98. Written just a year after Rajiv Gandhi's electoral triumph at the end of 1984, Manor's account could not definitely assess the prospect for institutional renewal of the Congress and the party system under the new prime minister. But the subsequent two years have done little to shake Manor's tentative conclusion that the young Mr. Gandhi had spurned and lost "a clear opportunity to make radical changes in the party" and to effect "a cleansing of corrupt, criminal or contentious elements" (pp. 93, 94).

33. Hardgrave and Kochanek, *India: Government and Politics*, pp. 94–95.

34. The formula used was Spearman's coefficient of rank-order correlation. For a description of the liberty measure and its source, see the notes to Table 1.1, in this volume.

35. For classic theoretical statements of this problem, see Samuel P. Huntington, *Political Order in Changing Societies* (New Haven: Yale University Press, 1968), and Samuel P. Huntington and Joan M. Nelson, *No Easy Choice: Political Participation in Developing Countries* (Cambridge: Harvard University Press, 1976).

36. Kohli, "State-Society Relations in India's Changing Democracy," pp. 309, 315; see also the other essays in his edited volume, *India's Democracy*.

37. In addition to the figures in Table 1.1, see also the data in The World Bank, *World Development Report 1987* (New York: Oxford University Press, 1987), Tables 1, 29, and 31.

38. To be sure, this is not to ignore the violence and repression that have surrounded these struggles. But much of the mobilization of the poor occurs within the political system, and even that by nonparty groups appears directed mainly to winning concessions from the democratic state and to enhancing the political capacities of the poor to pressure, compete for, and use democratic power. See, again, G. Shah, "Grass-Roots Mobilization in Indian Politics."

39. Sundhaussen, "Indonesia," in this volume.

40. See for example James Fallows, "The Bases Dilemma," *The Atlantic*, February 1988, pp. 18–30; for the contending views on this subject and broader issues surrounding Philippine-American relations, see Carl H. Landé, ed., *Rebuilding a Nation: Philippine Challenges and American Policy* (Washington, D.C.: The Washington Institute Press, 1987). On the other hand, termination of the U.S. bases might require a doubling of Philippine military expenditures while destabilizing aid and investment flows. From this perspective, the bases serve the security interests of the Philippines as much as those of the United States.

41. William J. Barnds, "Political and Security Relations," in John Bresnan, ed., *Crisis in the Philippines: the Marcos Era and Beyond* (Princeton: Princeton University Press, 1986), p. 257.

42. Guillermo O'Donnell and Philippe C. Schmitter, *Transitions from Authoritarian Rule: Tentative Conclusions about Uncertain Democracies* (Baltimore: The Johns Hopkins University Press, 1986); the quoted passages are from pages 11 and 43.

43. Ibid, pp. 48–56.

44. On these recent developments, see Rasul B. Rais, "Pakistan in 1987: Transition to Democracy," *Asian Survey* 28, no. 2 (February 1988): pp. 126–36. This section was written before the assassination of President Zia on August 17, 1988, and the electoral success of Benazir Bhutto's Pakistan People's Party in the subsequent mid-November National Assembly elections. However, the analysis remains essentially valid.

45. On recent developments and future prospects in the Philippines, see also Carolina G. Hernandez, "The Philippines in 1987: Challenges of Redemocratization," *Asian Survey* 28, no. 2 (February 1988): pp. 229–41; and Carl H. Landé, "Introduction: Retrospect and Prospect," in Landé, ed., *Rebuilding a Nation*, pp. 24–38.

46. Bharat Wariavwalla, "India in 1987: Democracy on Trial," *Asian Survey* 28, no. 2 (February 1988), p. 120.

47. Diane K. Mauzy, "Malaysia in 1987: Decline of 'The Malay Way,' " *Asian Survey* 28, no. 2, (February 1988): pp. 213–22. The most unwelcome of these court decisions was a High Court declaration early in 1988 that UMNO was illegal because some of its branches were improperly registered. As intra-party and intra-ethnic infighting intensified, the longstanding "Malay hegemony" in the polity was thrown into doubt, along with the capacity of the now-ravaged party system to contain future conflict.

48. Bryan Pfaffenberger, "Sri Lanka in 1987: Indian Intervention and Resurgence of the JVP," *Asian Survey* 28, no. 2 (February 1988): pp. 137–47.

49. Yaw Saffu, "Papua New Guinea in 1987: Wingti's Coalition in a Disabled System," *Asian Survey* 28, no. 2 (February 1988): pp. 244–45.

• CHAPTER TWO •
India:
Democratic Becoming and
Combined Development

JYOTIRINDRA DAS GUPTA

Developing countries are not supposed to offer conducive settings for democratic political systems. India's choice of democracy in a setting of poverty, ethnic diversity, and immense complexity of developmental problems must utterly puzzle any theorist of democratic politics. Anyone can imagine how precarious was the prospect of Indian democracy at the moment of its beginning. Four decades of continuous development of constitutional democratic government in India may then call for two kinds of interpretation. Either democracy in India is a misnomer and the pessimistic expectation did not go wrong, or the theorists of democracy were wrong in writing off the possibility of democracy's compatibility with the most stringent tasks of both economic development and political integration in developing countries.

Before we settle for one or the other interpretation, it would be more appropriate to examine the nature of the last four decades' development of democratic politics in India. This will call for, in the first place, an understanding of some of the basic ideas permeating the nationalist movement. The unfolding of these ideas through organizational practice in preindependence days covers a fairly long period. Indeed, the fact that the national ruling party is now more than a hundred years old may offer some solace to those theorists who worry about immature players taking chances with a sophisticated game like democratic politics in developing countries. For our purpose it is important to consider the inheritance of ideas and institutions that prepared the foundation of the new state. We will examine how a set of imported ideas were progressively indigenized to serve large-scale movements and enduring organizations that contributed to the subsequent development of democratic institutions. The second part of our discussion will examine the evolution of the major democratic institutions after independence. This will be followed by an examination of the performance of these institutions with respect to economic development, political participation, and national cohesion. Finally, an attempt will

INDIA

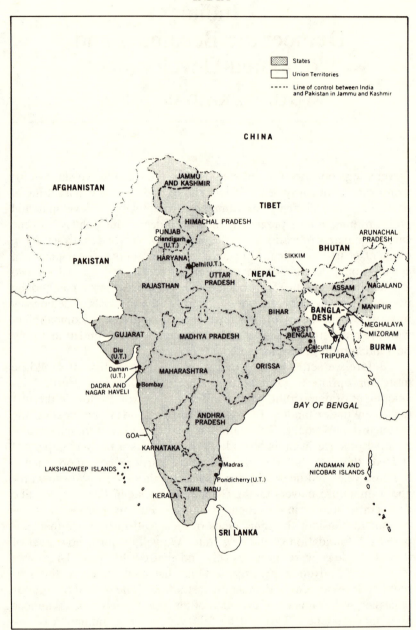

From Robert L. Hardgrave, Jr., and Stanley A. Kochanek, *India: Government and Politics in a Developing Nation* (New York: Harcourt Brace Jovanovich, 1986)

be made to analyze the significance of democratic development for India in terms of national and comparative implications.

• HISTORICAL REVIEW •

The Colonial Period

Nationalist fascination with liberal ideas and organized associations began in India by the first quarter of the nineteenth century. The initial stirrings were mainly directed to internal investigation of the working systems of religion, social organization, and education.[1] Colonial domination of the coastal areas had already enforced a new exposure to the ways of the victors. This was, however, a selective exposure. The terms of selection were largely determined by the rules of consolidation of the colonizing power. The imposed constraints may explain why early nationalist liberation in India chose to stay close to moderate reformism.

Modern nationalism in India began with the notion that Indians should reexamine the very foundation of their existing organization of religion, society, and education. The architects of modern reforms believed that grave weaknesses in these organizations had to be overcome before Indians could seriously strive for active opposition to the colonial rulers. Since the problem of nationalism was perceived to be primarily internal, the immediate target of nationalist action was to be their own society and not the foreign rulers'. The emphasis on internal decay was rather unusual for a nationalist ideal and it turned the focus of the reforms to several unspectacular but patient organizational constructions.

Rationalism and Liberalism

Ram Mohun Roy (1772–1833), and the intelligentsia of his generation, felt that the most impressive aspect of the strength of the West lay not in its hardware and firepower, but in its development of rational thought. In fact, Roy welcomed the British rule as a replacement of Moghul rule because it offered an opportunity for the Indians to challenge and reconstruct their superstitious modes of social order in favor of a rational reordering. He had no doubt that such a society should be based on "civil and political liberty."[2] But he did not leave this transformation to the chance that the colonial rulers might extend their domestic spirit of liberty to liberate the colonized people. Rather, he worked on the assumption that the window on the West would make possible an organized political education, which would enable Indians to recall their original, rational libertarian philosophy. A combination of indigenous and received principles would thus aid the construction of a politically free and socially transformed order.

Ram Mohun Roy's faith in liberal political education was impressed in a number of modern voluntary associations set up by him and his urban followers in the fields of religious renovation, social reform, and educational modernization. Their constructive initiative was directed toward language reform, legal reform, establishing a vernacular press, defending the freedom of the press, and articulating the rights of women, particularly widows.[3] The associational activities spread to different parts of India during the 1860s and 1870s. By this time railroad and telegraph lines had facilitated national communication, and the regional isolation of political consciousness was giving way to an expanding network of public associations concerned with social reform and political protest across the country.

These efforts, however, lacked popular appeal. The liberal appeal to reason and scientific discourse could expand more smoothly only if the pace of introduction of modern education was made faster than what the alien rulers cared for. This pace was dictated by the colonial need for a supply of educated servants of the regime. A unique opportunity for educating the public was missed because the colonial rulers felt educational expansion would threaten their own security.[4] In fact, the abysmally slow growth rates of literacy and education made it easier for the conservative nationalists to gain support from the less educated public on the basis of traditional symbols of solidarity derived from religion, caste, locality, and speech community.

Nationalist politics in India took a new direction following the extensive armed rebellion of 1857. This revolt was effectively suppressed but it left some deep scars on both the rulers and the ruled. Henceforth, India came directly under Crown rule. Strategies of selective favors and suspicions were now used by the regime to deliberately fragment the national perception of British action along religious lines. While this put a premium on religious solidarity for both the favored and the unfavored alike, it seriously damaged the prospects of rational and liberal national mobilization.

Setbacks for Liberalism

The original appeal of liberal ideas in underdeveloped countries consisted of an admiration for the value of the individual and his reasoned preferences unhindered by traditional ties. It is interesting that the historical timing and fascination with liberal ideas in Japan and India were not very far apart. Paradoxically, it was the perceived threat from the liberal West that moved Japanese nationalism toward preemptive militarist modernism, while the colonial rulers in India positively weakened the growth of liberalism by an intensified racialist policy. This hastened the development of reactive communalism, whereby each religious community increasingly came to depend on exclusive mobilization to defend its members' interests.[5]

It is easy to argue that the structural features of Indian society could account for the use of traditional symbols for exclusive mobilization in Indian politics of this time. This, however, would ignore the critical role of the political rewards, punishments, and prohibitions used by a newly centralizing effective power—Crown rule in India. For the strategists of Crown rule the need for Indian manpower offered an excellent opportunity to create a loyal base of support for the expanding colonial regime. Discriminatory preference seemed to offer a special dividend for the new rulers in a country where modern education and political consciousness was historically developing in an uneven spacial and ethnic distribution.

The strategy of selective preference deliberately encouraged the formation of particularistic organizations in Indian politics. The military component of this strategy was aided by a racial theory of graded competence—competence judged by loyalty and not by skill or achievement—whereby Sikhs, Rajputs, and Dogras were placed at the top of the scale of preference for recruitment and trust. The economic component of this preference meant a replacement of precolonial notables in the agrarian property structure by intermediaries drawn from groups promising loyalty to the regime. New revenue settlements (from the days of Permanent Settlement in eastern India to other types instituted in the rest of the country) created a rentier class innocent of productive needs but eager to strengthen the order and finance of the regime. The political component demonstrated, for example, a process of actively supporting the Aligarh movement for Muslim reformism against the antiforeignism of the Muslim fundamentalists and for Muslim exclusivism against non-Muslims. Similarly, exclusive ethnic politics was actively encouraged. Dravidian sentiments were promoted to drive a wedge between northern and southern Hindus and, at the same time, the less advantaged Hindus in all regions were encouraged to press their claims against their superiors in rank.

By the end of the nineteenth century, it seemed clear that the strategy of colonial security and the scramble for new economic opportunities would leave no chance for the growth of secular liberal nationalism. However, two elements came to the aid of the latter. One was the *ideological affirmation* that modernization necessarily calls for a larger political and economic coalition in order to attain both national advancement and individual enhancement. The other was the *pragmatic assessment* of the benefits of a nationally extended market for enterprise, commodities, and employment. What is more important to recognize is the linkage between the two. The promise of extended profitability may not melt all segmental coins but it can soften many for a strategic transition. Nationalist ideological affirmation was expected to facilitate such a transition.

Learning by Organizing

Mutual need more than abstract altruism provided the first major springboard for the construction of a national political platform. Thus when the Indian National Congress was created in 1885, it began as a platform of convenience. With various degrees of attachment to liberal principles, political associations that had grown up in the regional isolation of Bengal, Bombay, Madras, and other areas sought to build a coalition. Since the effective political authority in the country was centralized, it was natural to assume that a national bargaining instrument was necessary to augment the power of the constituents. Thus during the last quarter of the nineteenth century, the Indian Association of Calcutta, the Poona Sarvajanik Sabha, the Madras Mahajana Sabha, the Bombay Presidency Association, and a host of other active associations and individuals helped to form a national political organization that gradually evolved from pleas, petitions, and protest actions to one of the largest and most enduring mass organizations in human history.

During its formative decades, the Indian National Congress performed a number of important functions for democratic political development. It laid the foundation of a national political discourse that facilitated the formulation of political goals and demands in the public arena. It served as a forum for processing conflicting ideas regarding national goals and priorities. Democratic rules of procedure, tolerance of adversaries, and reconciliation of conflicting claims became part of the political education of the participants. From the very inception of the organization the founding leaders were eager to demonstrate their adherence to these democratic norms. Referring to the first phase of the Congress organization one perceptive historian writes that "even though the Congress's democratic procedures were more symbolic than substantive, they indicated a commitment both to representative institutions and to an accommodation of India's pluralism in a future Indian constitution. This commitment was enunciated clearly at the first session of the Congress in 1885, and it remained central in Congress thinking through the drafting of India's constitution after independence in 1947."[6] The founding leaders were highly successful professionals in their fields who did not have to live off politics. They were also aware of their distance from the Indian masses. In their attempt to speak for the people they recognized that their role was one of preparing the ground for popular self-expression and not one of formulating a corporate national will.

Their basic objective was to create a coherent national forum for representing what they perceived as nationalist interests. They were acutely aware of the social, regional, and religious diversities of the country, and the new organization was visualized as a medium for communication and coordination. That they demonstrated an eager commitment to representative institutions can perhaps be explained by a number of factors. Most of them were trained lawyers who were fascinated by the new legal culture and its linkages with liberal notions. Even those who were not in the new legal profession, including business professionals like Dadabhai Naoroji, appeared to be serious about preparing intellectually defensible cases for Indian representation based on empirical evidence. Thus the careful studies of the nature of Indian underdevelopment by scholars such as Naoroji, Ranade, Gokhale, and R. C. Dutt, using the modes of rational investigation normally employed by recognized intellectuals of the colonial home, set a rigorous standard of liberal discourse.[7] Few nationalist movements have yielded such a rich diversity of perspectives on the nature of underdevelopment and the sources of national misery. If Naoroji's work anticipated a dependence notion of underdevelopment, the others heavily emphasized the internal roots of mass poverty. No easy explanation was allowed to lend support to facile antiforeignism.

One positive result of these patient empirical investigations was the gradual evolution of a consensual strategy of democratic development during the early phase of Indian nationalism. Ever since Ranade's essay on Indian political economy insisted on separating political liberalism from orthodox notions of laissez faire, the nationalist leaders generally agreed about the crucial need for an active intervention of a democratic state for a coordinated development of agriculture, industry, and education.[8] It is not surprising that the continuity of this consensus has served as a basis for democratic economic planning since independence.

Repression and Radicalization

The turn of the century brought some major changes in the course of nationalism. Although the Congress leaders had succeeded in establishing a viable organ of national representation, the increasing repression and racial arrogance of the colonial regime had made it clear that it was in no mood to listen to voices of dissent or demand. The ruling lords felt secure enough by 1900 that the bureaucratic personnel and the armed forces could be relied upon to deliver the required goods—more revenue squeezed from an already famished country and the use of India as a springboard for mounting expansion of the empire.

If the immediate interests of the colonizer were realized, the long-term prospects of liberal nationalism in India and elsewhere also at the same time suffered a severe setback. The year 1905 marks a turning

point in Asian history. By this time more radical nationalists were
ascendant and the old liberal leadership was losing ground in the Congress and the nation. The arrogance and repression of the regime
offered a prize incentive to militant nationalism. In the ensuing struggle
between brutal imperialism and militant nationalism, whichever gained,
liberalism was the loser.

Japan's victory over Russia in 1905 created a new wave of self-
confidence all over Asia. This coincided with intensified repression in
India and enforced mobilization of Indian resources for British ex-
pansionism in Asia. Together these factors strengthened a radical
response. Desperation drove the new course of struggle to employ
emotional appeals based on highly evocative symbols of solidarity
derived from literature, religion, and selective recall of history. Often
the intensity of emotional activism erased the distinction between the
methods of peaceful resistance and violent adventure. As more people
joined the nationalist movement, with the attendant deepening of its
social base, the process also paid a high price of creeping cleavage in the
nascent nation.

Incentives for Diversion

Radical success using Hindu symbols and recalling the glory of the
Hindu heroes mobilized larger numbers but also increased the distance
between Hindus and Muslims. Muslim loyalists used this opportunity to
carve out a separate road for exclusive religious nationalism. Democratization of the national movement by social deepening through
popular mobilization, paradoxically, opened a wide opportunity for
attack on both secular mobilization and the principles of democratic
politics. The idea of a composite secular nationalism represented by the
Congress was challenged from 1906 onward by the exclusive claims to
representation based on religious community by the Muslim League and
Hindu revivalists. This diversion from the major secular movement for
national representation, of course, came in handy for the colonial rulers.
Henceforth the political system also actively encouraged a divided system
of representation, which reinforced incentives for segmental mobilization on ethnic lines. Beginning in 1909 and in a more elaborate form in
1935, a system of communal representation was introduced by colonial
legislation to institutionalize separate electorates for specified ethnic
groups.

Besides weakening the national challenge to colonial rule, official
encouragement to ethnic solidarity also devalued the case for democratic politics. If the Congress language of democratic politics was
embarrassing for some liberals in the administration, the open rejection
of democratic politics by the founders of Muslim nationalism must have

been a great relief for the regime as a whole. Sir Syed Ahmad Khan had struck the right note equally for the regime and minority religious separatism when he said that a democratic future for India would merely bring Hindu hegemony and oppression.[9]

Exclusive claims to represent a religious community were of course based on the idea that religious communities were homogeneous. The lines of division separating all religious communities in India among caste, language, socioeconomic class and regional groupings could not, however, be easily erased by the leaders' rhetoric. But religious nationalists were not entirely wrong in pointing out the appeal of religion in India. The timing was also appropriate for building separate constituencies in each religious community by intensifying their rivalry for economic opportunities within the colonial regime. The emphasis, however, was entirely on dividing whatever pie the colonial strategists were prepared to concede and not on strengthening the movement for expanding the size of the total pie.

Social Deepening and the Gandhian Phase

Secular nationalists were not unfamiliar with national heterogeneity. Their case for a secular movement seeking to represent people across ethnic boundaries was based on the notion that an individual is not exhaustively identified by his ethnic markers. They were also sensitive to the crosscutting nature of ethnic identities characterizing the Indians: major religious communities are split into many language communities, which in turn are stratified into caste and class formations. Thus Hindi speakers constituted only about a third of the Hindus, while among the Muslims, Bengali and Punjabi speakers outnumbered the Urdu speakers. Given plural identities, the politically interesting affiliations are rarely derivable from social affinities. In fact, an eagerness to utilize one affinity by a political leadership that seeks an easy constituency of popular support may encourage other leaders to exploit the other affinities of the same individual. Thus, for example, the easier course of exclusive Hindu mobilization, by seizing upon the Hindi language loyalty in northern India, created negative political reactions among Hindus who spoke other languages. Similarly, Muslim nationalists' mobilization using the symbols of Urdu language community often left the much larger number of Muslims cold and uncomfortable. Again, religion, language, caste, and other affinities have to compete with the economic affinities developing among people locked into similar stations of both disadvantage and advantage.[10]

It was the common cause of the greatest number that the secular nationalist leaders wanted to use as the foundation of national struggle. However, neither the moderate politics of protest nor sporadic radical movements in regions (as conducted until the end of World War I) had been able to generate mass participation in a common struggle on a nationally significant scale. To be sure, both the moderate and radical styles had helped build an organized arena for nationalist struggles. But it remained for the Gandhian leadership to generate and coordinate mass-based political movements into an effective threat to the colonial adversary.

Probably, the best-known contribution of the Gandhian leadership was to socially deepen the base of the national movement by active incorporation of support from peasantry, labor, and other occupational groups in rural and urban areas. Mass mobilization helped nationalist leaders build a political coalition of social groups to challenge alien rule by peaceful struggle. In doing so, these leaders recognized their mutual differences regarding the future issues of centrality of the state, domain of bureaucracy, role of industrialization, agrarian reorganization, control of production, and pattern of distribution. Gandhi's idealization of peasant production, for example, sharply contrasted with Nehru's idealization of centrally planned industrialism.[11] Moreover, significant support existed for more straightforward concepts of capitalist and socialist industrialization. In fact, during the three fateful decades of the ascendance of Gandhi's leadership, what kept the prominent leaders and groups together was a prudent sense of tolerance of fundamental disagreements rather than any significant agreement on specifics of ideology.

This pragmatic process of inclusion meant that from the second decade of this century the Congress organization increasingly drew sustenance from organized labor, peasantry, trading communities, nationalist business (big and small), students, and professionals. The initial impulse of unionizing labor or organizing peasants and other occupational groups did not always begin under the Congress leadership. However, Congress leaders in different regions gradually either joined the wave or brought the autonomous organizers into a close relationship with the Congress organization. Thus began an inclusionary process of linking mass participation in economic and political action into an institutionalized national organization.

Progressive success in incorporating interest groups called for a delicate task of balancing contradictory interests that was hardly easy for a political organization far from formal power. What made the task more difficult was the frequent need for complex conciliation of the conflicting interests of Indian owners and workers. When both the owners and the workers were aligned with the Congress, the latter could use its influence to mediate in cases of dispute. The joint pursuit of encouraging demands and containing demands by conciliation, in the larger interest of the national movement, helped train a leadership over decades in the art of managing conflicting interests in both the industrial and the agricultural sectors of the economy.[12]

Authority Formation and Coherence Creation

This transition from an elite-induced forum of protest to an institutionalized organization incorporating a broad spectrum of interests gradually endowed the Gandhian leadership with national authority long before it acquired state power. The readiness of this leadership to accommodate contending ideologies and interests, so long as their advocates were prepared to strengthen the common cause of national struggle and development, was a product of the conviction that consensus regarding national priorities is more important than either exclusive ideology or interest. For Gandhi this was much more than simply a matter of reiterating the primacy of the national collectivity over its smaller constituents. The way of accommodation was a part of his basic philosophy of *satyagraha* ("truth force"), or nonviolent resistance. In other words, this was not merely an issue of strategic prudence. Gandhi's strict philosophy of nonviolent resolution of disputes—where forsaking violence is never allowed to serve as a rationalization for acquiescence or submission to oppression—presupposed a theory of truth. According to this theory all that an advocate can claim for his case is incomplete knowledge. Arenas of contest enable rival advocates of incomplete knowledge to test their positions and to arrive at a new composition based on a creative resolution of dispute.[13]

While Gandhi's fellow Congress leaders were often uncomfortable with his strict adherence to nonviolence, they lost no time in recognizing the pragmatic value of consensus formation. The leaders close to Gandhi could use this consensus for strengthening their control of the growing organization, whereas others could at least hope to thrive on the assurance that dissenters would not be thrown out. Thus Gandhi's emphasis on nonviolence and peaceful resolution of conflict simultaneously served the purpose of generating organizational coherence and offering a novel technique of anticolonial resistance. His choice of targets and his capacity to channel isolated points of popular struggle toward a nationally converging course demonstrated an order of skill far superior to that of his colleagues. In addition, his detachment from office within the Congress not merely helped allocate a relatively smooth distribution of prized positions among his colleagues, but also impressed the importance of separation between power and authority.

Another aspect of the authority formation process actively pursued by Gandhi and his colleagues was the preemptive cooptation of outlying mass movements. This served both as a process of political education and a source of support. When Mohandas Gandhi began his political career in India in 1915, he had already earned a reputation for his political skill and moral saintliness during his two decades in South Africa. He used this reputation to gradually influence the Congress leadership, as well as to seek an entry into mass movements that were growing outside the Congress initiative. In fact, his successful conversion of local peasants' grievances against landlords in Champaran, Bihar, rural revenue agitation in Kaira, Gujarat, and a major industrial dispute in Ahmedabad into nationally significant resistance movements provided him with unique political capital from 1917 on.[14] These were followed by a succession of moves to enter, redirect, and nationally focus a diverse field of mass action that otherwise might have remained isolated efforts of limited import. Thus he succeeded in linking the national movement and religious demands of Muslim groups in the Khilafat movement, Sikh temple reforms, and Hindu lower-caste temple entry movements.[15] This process extended horizontally to areas that had never tasted an involvement in national movement and vertically to peasants, lower castes, and poor urban workers.

Although most successful in the practice of preemptive cooptation, Gandhi was not alone in its pursuit. Leaders like Nehru, although lacking Gandhi's rural insight, supplemented his moves by inducing the support of more urban-based groups that were fascinated by the Western idioms of socialism and industrial development. These contrasting styles and idioms held together the growing support groups with contradictory future interests and perspectives through a conciliatory system maintained by the Congress through the fateful three decades before independence. This is where the Gandhian transformation of earlier liberalism into a strategy of inclusionary participation, progressively channeled within a frame of rules of peaceful conflict and organized collaboration in and with the Congress, helped build an important historical foundation for future democratic development.

This mass incorporation, however, brought the challenge of providing national incentives sufficient to preserve new elements in an enduring structure of solidarity. While Gandhi appealed to the moral imperative, he also recognized that it calls for unusual dedication and patience. Most of his colleagues had more use for mundane power and interest. Organizational expansion also required attention to the issue of sustenance of different levels of leaders and workers. Increasing access to local governing institutions and legislatures, although strictly limited by colonial needs, opened new doors to Indian aspirants.

From 1919 on politics had to make room for these new temptations. The constitutional reforms of 1909 had conceded limited Indian representation, but the extension of the franchise and the responsibility of the elected members were severely circumscribed. The reforms of 1919 provided for a relatively large measure of responsibility at the local and provincial levels in subjects such as education, health, and public works that were not "reserved" or deemed crucial for colonial control.[16] However, even these limited concessions were immediately followed by utterly repressive laws known as the Rowlatt Acts of 1919. Growing nationalist resentment against such dubious packaging of reforms eventually led to another round of reforms encoded in the Government of India Act of 1935. While this package conceded an extended electorate based on property qualification to cover about one-sixth of the adult population, it offered no effective concessions for self-government at the center. But it did provide for responsible government in the provinces subject to the discretionary powers of the appointed governors.[17]

Although these hedged reforms evoked strong negative reactions from the nationalist leaders, the latter were at the same time reluctant to miss the opportunities offered by the new institutions and their promise of public and private power. Despite initial resistance by the Gandhian leaders to the temptations of limited power, pressures both within and without the Congress made them participate in the limited elections. In 1937 the Congress swept the provincial elections for general seats and formed ministries in seven (eight in 1938) of the eleven provinces.[18] Such electoral success during the preindependence decades helped the Congress organization accumulate valuable experience in constitutional, competitive politics and offered access to office and patronage.

Electoral reforms based on limited franchise were not, however, designed to offer instruction in democratic participation. The communal system of representation fashioned by these reforms put a premium on exclusive ethnic mobilization and collaboration with colonial rulers. The use of religious symbols in opposition to civic culture was now made doubly remunerative by the prospect of prizes for legislative access and colonial collaboration. The latter was made easier because of the bridge between the legislative and the executive arms of government in the British parliamentary system. The corrosive intent and effect of this colonial chemistry was not unanticipated by the Gandhian leadership, which tried to minimize these effects by several means. They scored impressive victories in Hindu as well as Muslim majority provinces and, at the same time, kept up the pace of mass movements in the form of active resistance and civil disobedience campaigns. Besides mass movements, they also extensively built up a network of constructive enterprises in the form of cooperative, small-scale industries and educational institutions and actively encouraged Indian initiative in large-scale industry and commerce. These constructive efforts provided sources of financial support both at individual and organizational levels and of productive engagement for organizational personnel during downswings of political agitation. But the taste of even limited parliamentary and executive access intensified an impatience for formal power. If Gandhi and a few other leaders could afford patience, most leaders found the decolonizing impulse following World War II to offer an opportune moment to settle for the prize of immediate power—even at the cost of a disastrous partition of the subcontinent.

• EVOLUTION OF THE DEMOCRATIC SYSTEM •

Political reconstruction in India since 1947 has been remarkable for its consistent and continuous use of constitutional methods for generating national coherence, political stability, and the development of economic resources and political freedom.

The special properties of democracy in developing countries call for an understanding of a complex process of combined political, social, and economic development. Unlike the historically established democracies, which benefited from a sequence of social mobilization and economic development preceding political democratization, democratic systems in developing countries have the unenviable task of simultaneously and rapidly developing the polity, economy, and society. The task gets all the more difficult because public assessment at home and abroad tends to concentrate on a partial development at any point in time without considering the set as a whole. Thus, for example, cursory examination of a slow pace of economic development in isolation may easily mislead one to a negative judgement when, in fact, this might be due to a transitional diversion of resources from efficient performers to under-privileged beginners in order to spread the process of social and political development in a more even manner.

Political Inheritance and Renovation

The initial moments of a new regime can be critical. Ironically, the timing of Indian independence earned largely by nonviolent popular movement coincided with an unusually violent moment in the country's history. The architects of the new state soon realized the complex legacy left in 1947 by the departed rulers. The nation was in disarray. Partition of the subcontinent brought mutual insecurity and suspicion between India and Pakistan. A large part of new India was under princely rule. The most important problems on the agenda of reconstruction were political order and territorial integration. One can imagine the severity of the test these imposed at the moment of Indian independence. It is no wonder that few observers writing in those early years could summon enough faith in democratic development to foresee that the Indian system would survive the test. Fortunately the Indian leadership was aided by three important factors. The peaceful transfer of power made for a continuity of leadership and institutional structures. A professional bureaucratic system, already manned mostly by Indians, was available for immediate use and required expansion. Above all, the development of the Congress organization into a nationwide political institution, reaching remote corners and incorporating major political segments of the population representing diverse occupational groups, made for a unified exercise of power. Fortunately as well, this power was already endowed with a sense of authority earned in the course of the nationalist movement. Evidently, the partition of the country and the formation of Pakistan appeared to strengthen the legitimation of power in new India by eliminating a major challenge to nationalism and helped establish a new linkage between the Congress party and the Muslim population. But the new leaders did not take their nationalist legitimation for granted. They sought to create a constitutional system that would institutionalize an authoritative democratic system of representation, competition, and exercise of power.

A comfortable Congress majority in the elected Constituent Assembly made for a largely consensual reiteration of some of the basic democratic principles enunciated in the earlier decades. The Constitution of India, operative since 1950, offered a complex coverage of elaborate legal and moral provisions, in the longest document of its kind, to a largely nonliterate people.[19] The basic principles enshrined in the justiciable part of the document provide for a parliamentary democratic system of government, fundamental rights, federalism tempered by a preeminent center, and secularism. The nonjusticiable part encodes a series of mild democratic socialist guidelines for the state. While codifying the rules of democratic government, the constitution carefully avoided the Gandhian principles of direct democracy, decentralized authority, and debureaucratization. The Gandhian leaders now needed Gandhi's mantle only for ceremonial legitimation.

In many ways the constitutional text could also be read as a developmental document, for it registered the basic aspirations of the members of a consensual intelligentsia to mold the country according to their tastes and preferences. An idealized blending of Western notions of liberal justice and indigenous notions of self-realization and social welfare had already become a part of nationalist culture that was widely shared by the educated classes. Constitutional encoding of these ideas satisfied their collective pride and reminded them of the social task ahead. Public responsibility was assumed to be mainly one of choosing the right legislators. The rest of the responsibility was now supposed to devolve on the state.

Accordingly, constitutional democracy in independent India cleared the way for an active state appropriate to the realization of simultaneous development on many fronts. A well-knit party, securing majorities in the national parliament and in a majority of state legislatures, on the basis of elections held every five years, can pursue extensive intervention in the social, economic, and political spheres to generate and direct resources for national development. The power of the government is subject to several limitations. The federal provisions of the constitution, the fundamental rights, judicial review, various statutory commissions and, of course, the legalized opposition may serve as sources of curbs, limits, and warnings. However, these provisions are subject to considerable muting in cases of overriding "public purpose," which can be invoked with fair ease if the government can obtain the required majority support, simple or complex as specified by the constitution.

Besides providing for cabinet-style authority armed with legislative support, the constitution also offers some directions and perspectives for national development. Part four of the constitution spells out the duties of the state, but these articles are not binding on the state. It says that the fundamental principle of governance shall include the duty of the Indian state to promote the welfare of the people by securing "as effectively as it may" a social order in which justice—social, economic, and political—shall inform all the national institutions. A following specification reads like a catalogue of objectives that would be congruent with an ideology of a socialistic welfare state that carefully steers clear of revolutionary socialism.[20]

What is left out, however, is any sense of priority or urgency among the preferred objectives. The basic law of the country, then, has authorized the state to adopt a course of moderate reforms, but at the same time its amendment procedures ensure that a confident popular mandate can enable a responsible executive to go ahead with more radical reforms. The crucial issue was not what the legal language expressed but rather what the nature of the democratic development in an inexperienced country would make of it.

Democratic Practice and Political Development

Between the first general election held on the basis of universal adult franchise in 1952 to the eighth held in 1984, the Indian electorate has demonstrated a growing capability that was hardly expected in the country and elsewhere. The turnout rate began with the relatively low figure of 45.7 percent in 1952 and moved fairly steadily to a 60.0 percent range in recent elections (see Table 2.1). Many observers had reservations regarding the capacity of largely nonliterate voters to exercise mature choice. In the course of all these elections, Indian voters have proved that they cannot be taken for granted either by the ruling or the opposition parties. At the national level the Congress party has been generally favored with substantial electoral pluralities, which (because of the single-member-district electoral system) have been translated into large, and sometimes overwhelming, parliamentary majorities (see Table 2.1). But when the same party was found to misuse the basic rules

Table 2.1   Summary Electoral Data: National Parliament and State Assembly Results from Eight Indian Elections, 1952–1985

	1952	1957	1962	1967	1971–72	1977–78	1980	1984–85
Electorate (in millions)	171.7	193.7	216.4	249.0	274.1	320.9	355.6	375:8
Voter turnout (in percent)	46	47	55	61	55	60	57	63
Congress party percentage share of popular vote								
Parliament	45	48	45	41	44	34	43	49
State Assembly	42	45	44	40	45	34	—	—
Congress party percentage share of legislative seats								
Parliament	74	75	73	55	68	28	67	79
State Assembly	68	65	60	49	60	16	48[a]	57[b]

Sources: Government of India, Press Information Bureau, *Lok Sabha Elections 1984*, 1984, pp. 1, 2; Lloyd I. Rudolph and Suzanne H. Rudolph, *In Pursuit of Lakshmi* (University of Chicago Press, 1987), pp. 130–131; Robert L. Hardgrave, Jr., and Stanley A. Kochanek, *India: Government and Politics in a Developing Nation* (New York: Harcourt, Brace, Jovanovich, 1986), p. 302; and others.

[a] Based on elections held at different times between 1979 and 1983.

[b] As of 1986; share reduced since the 1987 elections in five states.

of the constitutional system it was served with a crushing defeat in 1977.[21] The Janata party rule that followed also ended because of the electorate's dissatisfaction in 1980, and the Congress party was brought back to power. Dissatisfaction with the Congress party was seething on the eve of the eighth election when the intervening Punjab crisis and the assassination of the prime minister called for an unambiguous mandate for effective stewardship, and the electorate responded overwhelmingly in 1984. However, the same voters refused to give the Congress party a similar extent of support in the state-level elections that took place only a couple of months later. In fact, over the years, the dominance of the Congress party at the national level has not prevented the persistence of non-Congress parties in power in a number of states. The fragmentation and realignment of national opposition parties often persuade the voters to try them for ruling at the state level while refusing to support them at the national level. Since independence, and particularly in recent years, the Congress party has usually held a significantly smaller share of state assembly than national parliamentary seats (see Table 2.1).

By May 1987, when after a twenty-month rule the Akali party government was replaced by central rule in Punjab, the party distribution of state-level power was shifting away from the Congress party. Following the state elections in March and June 1987, the ruling party at the center lost control over about half of India's twenty-five states. The victory in Nagaland in November 1987 came as a poor consolation for the Congress. By that time the pattern of opposition party control of major states revealed this picture: the Communist Party (Marxist) and its allies ruling in Kerala, West Bengal, and Tripura; the Janata party in Karnataka; Assam Gana Parishad in Assam; Telugu Desam in Andhra Pradesh; All-India Anna Dravida Munnetra Kazhagam (AIADMK) in Tamilnadu; Lok Dal in Haryana; and the National Conference in coalition with the Congress party as junior partner in Jammu and Kashmir. As of early 1988 the Congress party did not command a single southern state but it did control the relatively larger states of northern, central, and western India, as well as Orissa in the east.[22]

The assured dominance of the Congress party during the first two decades following independence was rudely shaken by the results of the 1967 elections, when about half of the states chose to stay with the opposition parties.[23] When the Congress party split into two organizations in 1969, it was clear that the nationalist mantle was no longer sufficient to hold together a consensual organization for national reconciliation of dominant interests.[24] The subsequent realignment of the party signified a victory of the leadership that controlled formal power at the federal level of government. Indira Gandhi, the architect of this Congress party, increasingly transformed the nature of the organization from an institutional mode of accommodation to an electoral instrument beholden to a ruling leadership. The other Congress party, while continuing the older style, slowly disintegrated because of its distance from the state power and patronage. Neither the nature of the new dominance nor the pattern of the party system could ever be the same again.

When the vulnerability of the hegemonic role of the Congress party was demonstrated in the critical interlude between 1967 and 1970, political rivalry could no longer be contained within the old institutional structure of one dominant organization. A cynical game of changing allegiance and party alignment signified a transition toward a new mode of institutionalized party system. The Congress split of 1969 left Indira Gandhi's Congress without a majority and consequently dependent on the Communist Party of India and the regional party of Tamil nationalism, Dravida Munnetra Kazhagam (DMK), to continue in power. The other Congress led by the older organization men frantically sought help from opposition parties. This game of coalition politics put a premium on buying immediate support to stay in power, as against building support to win durable power. Indira Gandhi, as prime minister of the federal government, which controlled the strategic points of the economy, and as leader of the larger Congress party, could command larger resources to buy support than her opponents. She confidently went for new elections in 1971 and won the national vote on the basis of a populist rhetoric that enthused the disadvantaged groups without threatening the most advantaged groups in the society and the economy. Her party won a commanding majority in national parliament and in 1972 it won impressive victories in state-level elections. Meanwhile, she won widespread national admiration during the war in 1971 that led to the independence of Bangladesh.[25]

All this appeared to restore a pattern of Congress dominance, except that the institutional basis of this new dominance was different. This time the party was less a national institution of interest reconciliation than a central organization for mobilizing endorsement for the leadership and its hierarchical apparatus. Patronage resources at the top made sure that the successively lower echelon leadership was recruited on the basis of loyalty to the apparatus and capacity to cultivate demonstrative support for it. This plebiscitarian transformation left little scope for sustained building of interest-based support or systematic incorporation of diverse interests within the party. It resembled more a state-dominated party lacking an autonomous institutional authority of its own.[26] In fact, the old system of the Congress party, which had encouraged regional and local leaders to build sustained social bases of support, was now perceived as a threat to the plebescitarian organization. The old idea of a party-based state was now transformed into a state-based party.

This shift from relative autonomy of party to its dependence on the state obviously placed a new burden on the state. By emasculating the institutional system of interest incorporation previously performed by the party, it now had to assume the burden directly. By reducing the chief ministers of the states to a band of prime minister's men bereft of secure regional support and power the sites of regional conflict of interest were increasingly transferred to the national state. If the old structure could afford to reduce the intensity of disaffection by distributing its targets in a polycentric arrangement of institutions, the new system proceeded to concentrate the targets in a monocentric space. The conventional distinction between official and public authority was virtually erased. The prime minister's directorate now combined the official authority of the governing system with the public authority of the dominant party system.

Unfortunately for the new leaders, the problems of the early 1970s were too acute in terms of their depth, magnitude, and simultaneous demand on authority to make the new structure work. The refugee trail of the Bangladesh War, severe drought, energy crisis, and economic failures occurring together offered the most trying test for a newly reorganized authority. As resources were precariously depleted, mounting factional war within the ruling party and public protest against the government rocked the country. The opposition parties were aided by dissident factions within the ruling party and a convergence of nonparty political formations expressing popular disaffection. As the regionally initiated movements of unrest widened, the new ruling authority repressed them as an attack on the nation. This repression further polarized politics into a battle between an increasingly nervous ruling apparatus and an expanding coalition of opposition groups and parties.

Opposition Mobilization and the Emergency

History now presented an opportunity to the opposition that it had never tasted before. As we have seen, the single-member plurality system of electoral representation had discounted the electoral prospects of fragmented opposition parties. Extraelectoral politics of agitation now offered an incentive for these parties to mobilize popular discontent, form a coalition among them, and widen the scope of the coalition by inducting into it popular action groups from many regions, most notably Bihar and Gujarat.[27] The latter regions, in particular, could make use of the national prestige of leaders like Morarji Desai and especially Jayaprakash Narayan, whose Gandhian socialist credentials and continued ability to stay away from the small-time clash of economic and ethnic interests had won wide admiration. These ideologically diverse leadership resources helped forge a national unity of discontent although, inevitably, the nature of the coalition left a potential for rift. The goal of this national movement, as expressed in particular by Narayan, was to organize a popular initiative to replace a ruling leadership that was widely perceived as socially oppressive and politically authoritarian.[28]

While the pressure of the popular movements kept growing, the legal standing and the political stature of Prime Minister Indira Gandhi suffered a severe setback because of a conjunction of two critical events. Her own election of 1971 was invalidated in June 1975 by a high court decision on a case of electoral malpractice lodged by her socialist opponent.[29] Besides losing office, this conviction also entailed debarment from elected office for six years. The Supreme Court, however, awarded a conditional stay of the judgement that temporarily allowed her to retain office, without the right to vote or participate in the proceedings of Parliament, pending consideration of a full-scale appeal. Meanwhile, a coalition of opposition parties in Gujarat scored a decisive victory in the state elections in the same month. Her spirited campaign in the state was of no help to the sagging Congress party in the face of the widespread popular movement against her rule.

Indira Gandhi had a comfortable majority in Parliament. Her cabinet included several leaders of national stature and fairly impressive political and administrative record. She could wait for the conclusion of the legal proceedings and, meanwhile, let another leader of her party exercise formal power without much reasonable fear of losing long-term grounds. Ever since the Congress split, her faction-ridden colleagues had owed their political stature considerably to her populist appeal. However, she did not have confidence in a patiently drawn institutional strategy to utilize her populist appeal in a manner that would strengthen both her party and her democratic authority. Instead, she opted for a system of extraordinary powers by invoking the internal emergency provisions of the constitution.

The Indian constitutional system was designed to serve the country in normal and crisis situations. It was assumed during the making of the constitution that internal and external stresses faced by a newly developing country would require certain temporary deviations from normal procedures to tide the system over a crisis. Thus a complex set of emergency provisions permit comprehensive or partial use of special executive powers, depending on the specific situation.[30] External aggression or grave internal political disturbance permit comprehensive use, while political crises confined to state levels or financial crisis on a national level may warrant limited use of these abnormal provisions. Many of these provisions have been frequently used before and after Indira Gandhi's emergency phase. In fact, the possibilities of a constitutional dictatorship utilizing these provisions were discussed in the constitutional literature on India from the very beginning.[31] But until June 1975, the actual pattern of use of the enabling powers did not entail systematic subversion of constitutional, democratic government on a national scale. This is the crucial point that should help us distinguish between the use of specific emergency powers and an emergency regime that deliberately seeks a transformation of the basic democratic structure into an authoritarian mode of government.[32]

Indira Gandhi's choice of the emergency option was based on her claim that there was a deep conspiracy to destroy civil order and economic development processes in the country.[33] The equation between her own political crisis and national crisis was hardly convincing. In order to register her point she set out to dismantle the democratic system of persuasion and replace it with an authoritarian mode of creating and enforcing public assent. Thus the emergency episode was marked by mass arrests, suppression of civil rights and all opposition voices, elaborate censorship of the media, and a carefully orchestrated campaign to celebrate the virtues of collective discipline promoted by the leader, her son Sanjay, and their nominees. A meek majority in Parliament endorsed the executive orders issued by the prime minister's inner court and the judicial system was emasculated by amending the constitution. These amendments also ensured the supremacy of the prime minister's role, thus formalizing a system that, as we have discussed, was already in process since 1971.[34]

Much was made of the logic of disciplined economic development, which presumably called for a strong state to guide the economy to serve the nation and especially the poor masses. With all the fanfare surrounding the new regime's twenty-point program—later collapsed into five points—this strong state failed to deliver a rate of progress strikingly different from previous or subsequent regimes.[35] Some of the early gains in grain production were due more to climatic favor than organizational changes. Extensive labor repression and the favor shown to terms of discipline dictated by employers helped register some gains in industrial production, but the overall process of economic development served the rich better than the poor. In any event the populist appeal increasingly wore off as the regime stepped into its second year. By early 1977 Indira Gandhi was confident that her party could get a fresh mandate by appealing once again to the people through parliamentary elections.

Emergency measures were relaxed before the elections. The opposition parties accomplished a rare measure of unity in the form of the Janata party, based on the alliance brought about in the course of the Bihar and Gujarat movements. The March 1977 elections turned out to be a landmark event in the history of India's democratic becoming.[36] The Janata party and its allies won an overwhelming victory over Indira Gandhi's Congress party. That the Janata government did not endure beyond two years does not diminish the fact that the party system in India revealed a valuable reserve capacity to mobilize the political resources to replace the dominant system by a more competitive one in a time of democratic crisis.[37] This interesting case of institutional latency may reflect a deeper civic disposition to support a democratic system than what the manifest level of party competition would suggest.

Sources of Popular Mobilization

Political space in India has not been exhausted by the nationally or regionally organized parties or even interest groups of the conventional kind. At many critical moments of Indian politics, when these conventional formations failed to articulate popular grievances, the latter found their expression in relatively durable coalitions of public groups. Popularly known as "movements" in Indian politics, these serve as mobilizing platforms bringing together various parties, groups, and concerned publics.[38] These issue-oriented civic movements need to be distinguished from conventional social movements like labor, peasant, or student movements. While the latter represent persistent political formations organized for long-term interests of occupational or class groups, the short-term civic movements focus primarily on citizenship roles cutting across social groups.

Besides political parties, a wide variety of voluntary associations have offered durable organized vehicles for expressing popular interests and objectives. Industrial labor, organized in nationally extensive trade unions, and peasant associations have remained close to political parties.[39] The traditional dominance of the ruling, as well as the opposition, parties over these organized interests have been increasingly challenged by new leadership groups putting higher emphasis on economic issues, but their success has usually been limited to regional scales. Strong national combinations of industrial workers, white-collar employees and agrarian groups have provided Indian parties with bases of continuous support and stable manpower. Larger student associations have usually aligned themselves with political parties. Business associations have been more prominent in large-scale industry.[40] Their quiet pressures are usually more effective than many unquiet public agitations.

However, organizing rural peasants and workers, despite a long history predating independence, has not proved to be easy. Although the incidence of poverty is highest among agricultural labor and marginal income groups, including tenants and smallholder peasants, their mobilization into organized associations has been hampered by wide variations in agrarian property systems, ecological contexts, social authority patterns (mainly exemplified in caste systems), technological diffusions, and policy approaches.[41] Thus radical mobilization, although initially successful in the 1960s in a few southern districts in Tamilnadu and Kerala under the auspices of two Communist parties, gradually veered toward a wider, multiclass agrarian coalition, which lent an important base of support for the parliamentary radicalism of the dominant Communist party, the Communist Party (Marxist), or CPM. The frequent induction of the Communist parties into power at the state level in Kerala and, more durably, in West Bengal can be understood in terms of their ability to forge a still wider coalition between urban and rural groups with varied class interests.[42] The gains of democratic incorporation, not surprisingly, have also been the loss of rural and urban radical espousal of exclusive causes of the most deprived classes.[43] Access to democratic power, as it were, has served to highlight the compulsion for inclusive combination rather than exclusive mobilization of particular classes. Moreover, this same broadband combination has encouraged shifting reformist coalitions between middle- and lower-caste formations in north Indian states, whereby status-based mobilization has gained precedence over class-based mobilization.

Ethnic Affirmation

Representation or even politicized mobilization of functional interests occupies only part of the politics of participation in contemporary India. The right of association and its active pursuit has given rise to another system of pressures that often cuts across class or functional stations in the society. These associations succeed in recruiting intense loyalty of large segments of the population by seeking to promote exclusive interests based on language, religion, region, caste, and other cultural or ascriptive affiliations. Most observers have interpreted these forms of participation as expressions of primordial loyalty inconsistent with modern democratic politics. A developmental view of this participation may, however, offer a different picture. These are deliberately created political instruments of mobilization that freely utilize the logic of ethnic exclusiveness in order to bargain for certain advantages. How the symbols of ethnicity, to take one example, are used with strategic flexibility for competitive political advantage can be clearly seen in the Assamese movement that hit the headlines in the early 1980s.

Assam is one of the poorer states of eastern India, but it is also endowed with rich resources like oil, tea, and timber. Revenue from these resources, however, largely flows to other parts of India, including the central government. A keen sense of unjust deprivation of the Assamese people was initially enunciated by an Assamese literary association.[44] Poets, novelists, and musicians helped direct the resentment to the non-Assamese people and gradually articulated a notion of Assamese authenticity. College students sharpened the edge of the movement to the extent that it cut deep into the security and livelihood of the non-Assamese population in the state. Elected governments in Assam made use of the movement but increasingly failed to contain it.[45] The national government initially ignored it, and subsequently wanted to teach it a lesson by using the instruments of coercion, manipulation, and election. The forcing of an election in 1983 led to the eruption of mass violence of unprecedented proportion.[46] The massive scale of violence unnerved both the movement and the government. The internal contradictions of the movement were now more clearly exposed. Earlier Assamese authenticity had meant a language-based unity that was supposed to be shared by Hindu and Muslim members of the same speech community. Later the movement sought to rewrite the scope of Assameseness to exclude a substantial number of Muslim speakers of the language on the grounds that they were illegal immigrants from neighboring Bangladesh. Non-Hindi speakers drifted away from the movement and, after 1983, could be used by the elected government to its advantage. The convergence of an adroit leadership in state government and a more compromising national administration under Rajiv Gandhi facilitated a negotiated settlement in 1985.[47] The movement leaders also decided to convert themselves into a political party and to participate in the electoral process.

Clearly, the emergence of the Assamese movement and regional language movements in other parts of India including Punjab could have been avoided if the dominant party in the state and the nation had not written them off initially as irritants and, subsequently, as destructive. What is more important for our purpose is the lesson that an electoral mandate can mislead people in power to discount important sensitivities regarding issues of conspicuous disadvantage that, in the Indian case, have encouraged new political formations. The latter often began as small-scale associations outside the frame of conventional politics. These eventually widened into a mass base and led to large-scale associations, which grew stronger by increasingly establishing themselves as speakers for popular issues omitted from the agenda of normal democratic government. The expansion of popular participation encouraged by these populist ethnic movements could be consistent with democratic incorporation—as they had been in the course of two decades in most regions in India—if the inclusionary instincts of the dominant formal authority were not overcome in the early decades by Caesarist complacency. That the process of democratic inclusion need not be confused with incorporation in the dominant Congress party has been amply demonstrated in Tamilnadu, Andhra Pradesh, and elsewhere. The cases of the Tamil and Andhra movements also show how the displacement of Congress rule has enabled the democratic system to expand to incorporate new groups at the state level and also how the newly incorporated groups can be coordinated at the national level.[48]

When leaders like Nehru condemned their rivals as threats to modernity, democracy, and integration, they ignored the importance of progressive socialization of new forces to expand the political resources of a developing democracy. While they took roles ranging from disciplining schoolmasters to colonial policemen, they often lacked the political art of using a receptive state in a developing country to offer assurance to the new competition that it too is equally entitled to access and power. When the persistent hearing problems of these leaders were corrected by the shock treatment of violence, they discovered that accommodation helped to induct new groups with democratic schooling into the competition. The lessons of the 1960s in the Nehru phase were again ignored in the later years of the Indira phase when manipulative craft increasingly replaced the art of cultivating political support. Indira Gandhi's failure was dramatized by the fires that engulfed Assam in 1983 and Punjab in 1984. When her successor, Rajiv Gandhi, succeeded in bringing about workable accords in Punjab and Assam in 1985, it became evident once again that democratic institutions and behavior may be necessary to develop and manage a nation of India's size and complexity. However, the new prime minister has demonstrated greater skill in generating accords than in making them work, particularly in the case of Punjab as of early 1988.

• DEMOCRACY, PLANNING, AND DEVELOPMENT •

Strategy and Organization

Political democratization, in order to endure, requires a rapid development of economic and social resources so that expanding public demands can be effectively satisfied. But can a democracy in a developing country succeed in generating the required rate of development in a sustainable fashion? This is a question that should be distinguished from one that concerns ideal or spectacular rates of development. The difference in phrasing the question obviously stems from a difference in basic values. A concern for an ideal rate can ignore the issues of how it is brought about and with what cost to freedom, stability, and national autonomy. Those who cannot afford to ignore these issues may, however, opt for an optimum rate consistent with other valued accomplishments. But, it is not necessary to assume that such an optimum cannot approximate or even surpass the maximum attained elsewhere. The linkage problem simply reminds us that the crucial issues to consider with respect to comparative economic development are not, after all, simply economic.

The idea of democratically planned development was pursued by the nationalist leaders long before independence. Gandhian strictures on centralization, large-scale industrialization, and bureaucratic management of development did not prevent the emergence of a wide area of agreement among other leaders regarding the importance of centrally coordinated planning for rapid industrialization. In 1938 Subhas Chandra Bose, the only major leader in Congress history who openly admired fascist discipline, became the president of the Congress and Nehru became the chairman of the party's national planning committee. Immediately after independence the Congress, as the ruling party, appointed an advisory planning board. As the first prime minister, Nehru initiated the Planning Commission and became its first chairman; he encouraged a process of thinking that assumed that economic development was a matter of scientific problem solving.[49] Nehru's admiration for scientism was not shared by his party men.

How has planned development fared? The country experienced seven five-year and three one-year plans. During this period the economy registered a fairly steady, although unspectacular, rate of growth, experienced a partial renovation of agricultural production leading to self-sufficiency in food, developed a structure of industrialization that produces most of what the country needs, expanded the supply of educated and technical personnel able to execute all levels of sophisticated tasks, consistently held down the level of inflation to one of the lowest in the world, and in the process ensured a level of self-reliance and payment ability that kept it away from debt crisis. At the same time disturbing poverty persists, inequality hurts, technology languishes, the second economy thrives, and a number of shadows haunt the economic scene. And yet the popular report cards on the new government leadership in 1985, based on national polls, showed overall public confidence to be higher than expected.[50] But the polls can be misleading and confidence can erode. For a long-range perspective, it is more important to look at how development has prepared the required base for rapid enhancement of the people's capabilities to solve their problems. This will entail a wider view of development than the one that narrowly concentrates on material product alone.

The notion of people's capabilities, when applied to India, necessarily directs one to the rural situation. This is where the weight of decades of agricultural stagnation and technological obsolescence had dragged the largest segment of the nation's population to poverty and human incapacity. The most urgent task was to ensure a priority for rural development over everything else. Such a priority would have called for extensive intervention in the agrarian property structure in the form of land reform followed by investment in productive support, technological change, and improvement in human resources. And yet this is where the record of development has been discouraging. Land reform, initiated immediately after independence, still remains largely unrealized in terms of its redistributive goals. As late as 1984 Planning Commission documents giving an advance taste of the seventh five-year plan kept reminding the policy makers that a good part of the redistributive work of land reforms remains to be accomplished.[51] Drastic intervention in the rural property structure was, in fact, consciously avoided by leaving the reforms to the discretion of state-level legislation. The slow pace of land reform demonstrated a preference for a strategy of promoting production by offering financial and technical support to the relatively better-off segments of the rural population. The proportion of plan investment—implying mostly public investment—directed toward agriculture declined from the first through the second and third plans, the end period of which was accompanied by a severe crisis resulting from extensive drought.[52]

During this period public investment through planning was based on a preferred strategy of industrialization that encouraged considerably higher investment for developing organized industries, mining, power, and communications. A socialistic rhetoric was employed mainly to equate social progress with capital goods production under state control.[53] Scarce national resources were increasingly diverted to pursue import substitution under the leadership of the state. The use of foreign aid increased from a modest 10 percent of the first plan outlay to 28 percent in the third plan. At the same time the increasing self-empowerment of the national-level state through its expanding control of capital, strategic industries, power generation, communication networks, and employment created an impression that the ascendance of state capitalism was irresistible. Command over national, as well as external, resources and the apparatus of planned control of investment and enterprise by now had endowed the state with a degree of power that could be used to induce collaboration from larger private owners of resources in industry and agriculture. Indeed the prospect of such a collaboration could minimize the dependence of the ruling party on the poorer rural groups. Actually, as the ruling party's pursuit of industrialization strategy progressively intensified, its pursuit of the art of cultivation of mass support and its conciliatory coordination declined. A tired generation of Congress leaders appeared now to rely more on the formal instrument of the state, its tightly organized bureaucracy, its patronage powers, and its capacity to subsidize inefficient enterprise in order to consolidate and enjoy its power.

This was largely what one may call the Nehru phase of planned development. During his lifetime Nehru's influence welded the Congress party to a level of coherence sufficient to maintain a semblance of united pursuit of planned development. Nehru's death in 1964 was followed by Shastri's conciliatory style of coordination of major factions and regions. If his capacity for consensus generation ensured a stable transition in politics, the new phase simply succeeded in maintaining the earlier developmental policy frame. No major departures were expected either. The consensus style, however, increasingly emboldened the chief ministers at the state level to assert their role in national policy implementation. A process of regionalization of authority was already developing even during the Nehru phase, and during Shastri's brief tenure it grew stronger. The strength of the chief ministers of states within the party was dramatically revealed when, following Shastri's death in 1966, they helped elect Indira Gandhi as the third prime minister over the candidate of Congress organization leaders at the national level.

Indira Gandhi's style was inconsistent with a federalized system of authority within the party, but in 1966 consolidation was more important for her than anything else. The years 1966–1967 brought a severe crisis to the economy and the polity. Disastrous drought, legacies of wars with neighbors, economic debacle, and a close call in the 1967 elections appeared to offer the Congress party an impetus for rethinking. However, although five-year planning was temporarily dropped, no radical reorganization of the premises of planning came about. The only major innovation was intensive modernization of agriculture with stepped-up investment for selected crops and regions aimed at national self-sufficiency in foodgrain production.[54] Again, the major goal was immediate production promotion and not the wider objectives of raising the long-term capability of the rural poor who composed the majority of the country. Neither the subsequent consolidation of Indira Gandhi's power from 1971, including the phase of emergency, nor her recovery of the popular mandate in 1980 following a non-Congress interlude were used as occasions to question the earlier priorities. The Janata party rule, meanwhile, did raise some questions but its brevity of tenure weakened the effectiveness of its revision of priorities.

Human Base and Food Security

Indian planning began in a social context where nearly 85 percent of the population was rural, the national literacy rate was 12 percent, the majority of school-age children did not attend school, and for most people life was ruled by poverty, oppression, and morbidity. The state of the economy was equally dismal. Orderly management of the colonial economy during the five decades preceding 1950 had registered less than half-a-percent growth rate of per capita real output. Perhaps the only points of relief for the people were that life expectancy was short and the mortality rate was exceedingly high.[55] Clearly, something more than modest economic development was called for to make even a small step to alter such a nonhuman level of existence.

How does the record of democratic development stand as a response to that challenge? From the moment of independence in 1947 through the subsequent four decades, the people have lent an unexpectedly mature degree of support to the democratic process of economic development. What has this process yielded in terms of altering their level of living? How does it compare with the record of other developing countries following similar or different roads to development? Some basic indicators, despite their imperfection, can be revealing. Expectation of life at birth around 1940 was 32.1 years for Indian males and 31.4 years for females, and on the eve of planned development, around 1949, remained at 32.4 and 31.7 respectively. During the years of development, these figures rose to 41.9 and 40.6 in 1960, 46.4 and 44.7 in 1970, and 50.9 and 50.0 in 1980. A recent report puts the corresponding figures for 1985 at 57 and 56. By historical standards this rapid progress can be counted as encouraging. But by comparative contemporary standards, India's performance leaves room for considerable improvement because many other developing countries have done so much better during the same period. Sri Lanka, largely following a democratic path, succeeded in reaching respective figures of 68 and 72 by 1985, and China, following another path, scored 68 and 70. China's score is particularly interesting because twenty-five years earlier its base figures (41, 44) were close to India's and substantially lower than those for Sri Lanka (62, 62).[56]

Similarly, the mortality rate for infants (under age one) was 165 per thousand live births in 1960 for both India and China. By 1985 China had reduced the rate to 35 and Sri Lanka to 36, while India's rate was 89.[57] Sri Lanka's success dramatically showed that it does not take either a violent revolution or a high national income to bring about an unprecedented rate of improvement of human resources. India's average, of course, conceals the fact that within the same country there have been different rates of progress in different states. In Kerala both the life expectancy and infant mortality rates have registered improvements comparable to China's.

Food security, in the sense of general availability and the assurance of access to the stock of foodgrains, has been the most important issue facing the people. Indian planning began with the inherited base of production yielding barely fifty million tons. Production of foodgrains steadily rose until the crisis years of 1966–1967, when lower growth necessitated a sharp increase in imports, which in 1966 constituted 14.4 percent of total quantity available.[58] The drop in production and drag of foreign dependence pushed the state to begin a renewed effort to modernize agriculture, resulting in a big change on the food front. Production of foodgrains crossed the 100 million ton mark from 1971 and imports steadily declined. Dependence on imported food ended in 1978. In the subsequent three years, no food imports were needed. From 1980 to 1984 a small amount was imported mainly to augment the buffer stock. Production of foodgrains exceeded 150 million tons in 1983–1984—a big jump over the earlier peak of 133 million tons in 1981–1982. Net import of food from 1985 to 1987 was negative, and yet the size of the reserve stock of the state remained comfortable except for 1987 which turned out to be the worst year of drought since Independence. But the ability of the economy to cope with the drought was demonstrated by the fact that unlike the previous drought years of 1965 and 1979, this time the rate of growth of the national product was positive. Indeed, the capacity of the food security system and the general economy to resolutely tide over the crisis that usually accompanies droughts of this magnitude was a new experience for the country.[59]

Success in generating self-sufficiency in foodgrains was accompanied by extensive state action to ensure that demands from the deficit states of the federation were met by transferring the surplus stock of other states in a coordinated manner. The role of the federal government in procurement and public distribution of foodgrains can be crucial for ensuring food security. In the absence of it, there would be no assurance that nationally available food will actually reach the neediest regions and groups. The magnitude of state involvement in procurement and distribution is indicated by the fact that from the mid-1960s, on an average, close to 10 percent of foodgrains has been annually procured and distributed.[60] This has enabled the state to maintain price levels consistent with general planning needs and, at the same time, reasonable access for needy areas. And yet public ability to transfer food to deficit regions does not assure access to it at the lowest income levels in rural areas. This is a weakness that production promotion policies, without the benefit of deeper structural reorganization, will find hard to overcome.

A recent World Bank report on sub-Saharan Africa justifies optimism for Africa from the fact that, while contemporary despair about Africa was matched by a comparable feeling about India just two decades ago, the latter now "has emerged from despair to hope in the eyes of the world."[61] The elimination of famines in India since independence contrasts not merely with their catastrophic recurrence during the colonial years, but also with revolutionary China, where severe famine conditions claimed fifteen million lives during 1959–1961.[62] The experience of democratic planning has demonstrated that democratic instruments can be made to deliver impressive results by a mutual reinforcement of popular voice and prudent policy. But that experience also shows that the reactive type of prudence, as distinguished from anticipatory prudence, can extract a heavy price from the country and especially from the poorer population before a crisis shakes the policy planners.

Thus innovations on the food front should be judged also in the context of the fact that the per capita availability of food has registered only modest progress and that the actual access of the poorer people still remains lower than in many developing countries. The daily calorie supply per capita as a percentage of requirement for India in 1981 stood at 86, while the weighted average of thirty-four lowest income developing countries was 97. The corresponding figure for China was 107, Burma 113, and Sri Lanka 102. If the national average figures are disaggregated by income groups, lower-income groups in India will show worse scores than their counterparts in those three countries.

Nutritional deprivation in India does not stand alone. Progress in providing mass education has been discouraging despite tremendous strides at the higher and technical education levels. The adult literacy rate in India in the eighties has been less than 40 percent. In contrast, the developing countries of East Asia have exceeded 70 percent. The average rate for sub-Saharan Africa in 1970 was lower than that of India in the same period. Now India's rate lags behind that average. Primary school enrollment figures tell us an unexciting story.[63] If the premise of industrial priority explains the uneven emphasis on higher education and gross neglect of rural education at lower levels, it is difficult to imagine how comprehensive industrialization can be compatible with

poor quality of labor. Fortunately, this disparity in educational investment was reduced by the end of the 1970s, indicating a better sense of
balance among levels of schooling. India's earlier failure to coordinate
these components may deprive her industrialization of critical pace and
depth. If the human base is left weak, what will be the impact of such
weakness on overall economic and political development? We need to
examine the pattern of industrialization before we can seek answers to
this question.

Induced Industrialization

The dominant intellectual climate in the 1950s could leave no doubt in
the minds of any forward-looking leader of a developing country about
the virtues of state-induced industrialization.[64] Industrialization,
modernity, and efficient use of resources were universally equated, just
as agriculture, traditionalism, and inefficiency were believed to go
together. To imagine a situation of inefficient industry wasting resources
and modernized agriculture offering a better return on investment and a
sounder preparation for the future would have been a heresy unpardon-
able in the liberal, as well as revolutionary, West and, therefore, among
educated people in India. If the heresy has reversed in many sophisticated circles in the 1980s, we should not forget the charm of the original
equation.

Indian planning for industrialization was based on the assumption
that a rapid rate and a comprehensive pattern of industrial growth can
be obtained by assigning priority to the production of capital goods. If
this called for going slow on agriculture and consumption goods, it was
justified by the promise of future benefits for the nation as a whole.
Expanded capacity in the capital goods subsector was supposed to lay
the ideal foundation for subsequent production of consumption goods
and absorption of labor. Such an expansion was beyond the capability of
the private sector. Thus the logic of industrialization also provided a
logic of centralization, extensive regulation, and a strategic role for the
state in entering production, controlling supplies of inputs needed by
private enterprise, directing crucial financial resources, administering
key prices, and becoming the largest employer in the country. This logic
satisfied the educated middle classes' sense of national mission for a
number of reasons. It held a promise of national power and prosperity
at the same time that an expanded public control offered a moral
gratification. For here was an opportunity to use a socialistic language to
control resources in the name of long-run public interest. After about
thirty years, it is time to ask, where has industrialization arrived?

Judging in the 1980s, it is apparent that India has acquired a comprehensive structure of industrial production (see Table 2.2). It has pur-

Table 2.2   India: Selected Growth Indicators: 1950/51 to 1985/86

Item	Unit	1950–51	1960–61	1970–71	1980–81	1985–86	Annual percent increase 1950–51 to 1985–86
Population	Million	359	434	541	679	756	2.2
Literacy	percent total pop.	16.7	24.0	29.5	36.2	NA	NA
Real national income:	1950–51= 100						
aggregate		100	145	204.7	283.4	351.9	3.6
per capita		100	119.9	135.8	150.1	168.1	1.4
Gross domestic capital formation	percent of GDP	10.0	16.9	17.8	24.5	25.5	12.6
Foodgrain output	million tons	55.0	82.3	108.4	129.6	145.0	2.8[a]
Industrial production	1970–71= 100	29.7	54.3	100	150.7	206.8	5.7[b]
Village electricity	percent of total villages	0.5	3.8	18.5	47.3	66.0	15.2
Consumer price index (average)	1960=100	81	100	186	401	620	6.0
Government expenditure	percent of GNP	10	19.5	22.1	30.5	35.6	13.6
Foreign exchange reserves[c]	10 million rupees	755	245	438	4,822	7,384	6.7

Source: Center for Monitoring Indian Economy, Basic Statistics Relating to the Indian Economy (Bombay, August 1986), Table 8.1–4. For more details and annotation see the source.

[a] Compound annual growth rate between triennia centered on 1950–51, 1960–61, 1970–71 and 1983–84.

[b] Official calculation using a new base (1980–81=100 states that the growth rate accomplished by the industrial sector was 8.7 percent in 1985–86 and 9.1 percent in 1986–87. See Government of India, Economic Survey, 1987–88, (New Delhi: 1988).

[c] Excluding gold and SDRs; March to end of year.

sued a planned policy of import substitution that may be distinguished from the nonplanned variants followed by many other developing countries.[65] Unlike Brazil, to take one example, the planned variant in India made it possible to develop heavy and light industries simultaneously despite a higher emphasis on the former. The Latin American cases of gradual exhaustion of import substitution in light industries and then desperately scrambling for heavy industries, which led to political and economic crisis, involved a pattern that was not shared by the Indian case, spanning about the same period of history. In fact, India's policy of early emphasis on heavy industries may have allowed it to taste early and then to gradually cope with exchange crisis. Planned import substitution has also facilitated a pattern of industrialization that has endowed the Indian case with a degree of self-reliance rare among noncommunist developing countries acquiring a broad structure of industrialization during the same period of history. The structure of capital goods industries in India is comparable to that of China, but unlike China, a diversified base of consumption goods industries was allowed to develop. Yet a strict regulation of the latter left room for few luxury goods, so that the flood of durable consumption goods characterizing so many industrializing countries was not reproduced in India.

These gains in industrial development were balanced by significant disappointments, however. India's average annual percentage growth rate of industrial production during the period of 1960–1970 was 5.4 followed by 4.3 in 1970–1982.[66] China's rates were 11.2 and 8.3, Mexico's 9.4 and 7.2, and South Korea's 17.2 and 13.6 respectively. Neither self-reliance nor comprehensiveness can serve as factors inhibiting high rates. Can India's planners take the cover of democracy to explain their disappointment? That will not do because democratic developing countries like Malaysia and perhaps Sri Lanka have a better average record. They have to admit that, with all their devotion to industrialism as the key to rapid development, India's performance on many important counts has moved slower than the average rate for developing countries and for the world as a whole.[67]

The growth rate of industrial product may, however, be less important than the diversification of output indicating the creation of sophisticated capacity that makes an economy poised to move on its own. Between 1951 and 1960, sophisticated machinery and metal industries grew at a compound rate of 14.2 percent against the aggregate industrial rate of 6.4 percent, but during 1960–1970 the lead considerably narrowed, while between 1970 and 1983 the two converged around a low rate of 4.5 percent. The 1980–1985 figures actually indicate the former rate lagging behind the aggregate rate.[68]

Clearly something was wrong: India's industrialization was slowing down when other developing countries were moving faster. This was strikingly evidenced in the steel industry, where per capita production fell way behind that in many industrializing countries.[69]

At the same time, however, the national investment rate in India has not been so depressing. Gross domestic investment as a proportion of gross domestic product was about 10 percent in 1950–1951.[70] By 1980 India's percentage share of investment stood at 24, compared to 25 in middle income countries, 21 in low-income countries, and 27 in China. Whereas foreign financing of capital formation accounts for a quarter of the total in low-income countries and about a tenth in middle-income countries, it has substantially declined in India; since 1978 it has rarely exceeded 4 percent of the total.

So far Indian planning has tended more to raise savings than to make better use of capital resources. Persistent inefficiency of the public sector—the share of which in total capital formation rose to 50 percent in the mid-1960s and has remained close to 45 percent since then—largely accounts for the inefficient use. Lower capacity utilization, higher waste of capital and labor, and widespread subsidization of inefficient public sector enterprises have cost the process of industrialization so dearly that the original claims of national mission are now interpreted by the public as a euphemism for the private mission of groups in power to enrich themselves at the cost of national development.

No easy choice, however, awaits the democratic public in India. Not just the Congress party, but all major political parties in the country have misused the public enterprise. Public enterprises have rapidly expanded at the federal as well as state levels within the federation. The record at the latter level is much worse than at the federal level. A number of parties opposing the Congress party at the national level have ruled over these state-level public enterprises. These include regionalist parties in southern India and Communist parties in the south and the east. The paradox of public enterprise in India then can be understandable. Everybody knows their wastefulness and yet virtually no political group seriously asks for their immediate displacement.

Is this predicament a product of democratic development? Hardly so, since authoritarian China had been meanwhile stuck with a much more extensive public sector, which has recently been subjected to reform precisely on the ground that command from the top alone costs the nation efficiency and productivity.[71] Brazil's military regime rapidly expanded the public sector during the 1960s and 1970s, as the state encouraged and subsidized the largest expansion of durable luxury goods production in the developing world while plunging the country into massive foreign debt.[72] Democratic development in India has thus shared its inefficiency with socialist and capitalist authoritarian modes of development, but unlike them it established a pattern of parliamentary and public responsibility that has not merely kept open the channels of informed criticism, but also the possibility that public enterprises can be curbed and reformed, if not selectively displaced.

At least, public accountability has made sure over all these decades that the composition of commodities produced by these enterprises or through the encouragement of public sector as a whole remains compatible with the developmental needs of the nation rather than with the luxury demands of an exclusive class. For example, in the early 1980s—despite the attainment of one of the largest industrial and capital goods capacities in the developing world—India's ownership of passengers cars was only 1.3 per thousand population compared to an average of 14.3 for all developing countries and 15.0 for the Ivory Coast. Similarly, India had only 1.7 television sets per thousand population, whereas all developing countries in aggregate averaged 28.4 and the Ivory Coast 38.0.[73] Moreover, none of these products had to be imported to India, and most of the capacity created in automobile and communication industries were directed to serve production or defense needs.

Evidently democratic planning has enabled the country to develop an extensive structure of industrialization where quantitative expansion of capacity has not kept pace with qualitative increase in efficient utilization of productive resources. If this were consistent with the foundational logic of self-reliant industrialization in a large country well-endowed with natural resources and a potentially large internal market, a failure to make a timely transition to a more intensive system of industrialization could be self-defeating. This intensive phase would call for elaborate technological change, organizational improvements, and upgrading the quality of products to standards of international marketability. Obviously this would also require major political initiatives to renovate the old systems of planning, controls, management, and incentives. It would be too simple to subsume all these tasks under a blanket category of liberalization, for a mere dismantling of an inefficient system of regulation does not automatically make for an efficient system of resource utilization in a developing country. For example, if infrastructural investments have not paid the right dividends because of inefficient public enterprise management, the mere removal of the latter would not invite stepped-up efficiency and investment, presumably from private investors waiting in the wings for a liberal signal.[74]

The issue for India is more complex. Can democratic planning learn from its internal experience and external exemplars from developing countries well enough to make this crucial transition without violating the basic conditions that have historically sustained the democratic process? One can, of course, settle for simpler issues of industrial growth or efficiency and go for some ideal economic solutions while ignoring or condemning real political practice.[75] Since we are interested in democratic possibilities, the easier option in this case is obviously ruled out. India's experience suggests that industrial policy has not been a simple function of privileged pressures. If that were so, neither the capital goods emphasis nor the luxury goods deemphasis would have ruled for four decades. Rather, industrial policy has served as a democratic legitimating device that enables certain leadership groups to beat others.[76] Nehru's definition of national mission at least served him well in his leadership competition, just as Indira Gandhi's desperate spree of nationalization and imposition of control systems over organized industry were moves to outbid rivals inside and outside her party. If all these moves have inevitably strengthened the state, what will prevent another set of adventurous leaders from weakening selected groups of vested interests in and around the state by negotiating with foreign investors or donors or some internal radical publics to build new constituencies of support? After all, old constituencies of support may breed rivals while innovative new ones may have the virtue of preempting them.

All this is merely to indicate that multiple, although not unlimited, policy possibilities can exist within a democratic system, and these can be effectively utilized by creative or desperate state leaderships. Intensive industrialization would threaten a big chain of patronage but at the same time might open up opportunities for a larger chain of beneficiaries. In a democratic setup, where numbers count, and in a slowly developing country, where because of limited resources state-dispensed patronage soon threatens to peter out or close the routes of access, the promise of a shift of beneficiaries may yield appropriate support for new moves. Crisis in external relations, internal economy, or international alignments can make the moment of change more opportune. The point is that a democratic state need not be viewed as a passive system of receiving and reconciling vocal interests, it can also generate counter-interests to rival, if not beat, them. Particularly in a developing country like India, where privileged formations tend to be structurally, regionally, and ethnically fragmented, flexible support seeking by national political leaders seems to be all the more feasible. On the other hand, we should not underestimate the misgivings of the underprivileged economic or ethnic groups about policies that might diminish the subsidies and protections they have come to enjoy in the labor market.[77] A shift of industrial policy toward export substitution would naturally strengthen these concerns because of the imperatives of competition. But the increased income and employment opportunities can be used to allay such misgivings. Issues of welfare and justice need not necessarily contradict the case for intensive industrialization in the process of democratic development. When they do so, it signals more a poverty of leadership, mobilization, and policy than a poverty of democracy.

Welfare, Autonomy, and Justice

Democracy offers a unique opportunity to the disadvantaged groups in India to express their priorities regarding developmental values. This freedom of expression and the legitimation of appropriate popular mobilization have raised a number of interesting issues. National development priorities can be understood in terms of an abstract aggregation of collective aspirations imposed by the state, or in disaggregated terms, implying expanding access of less-advantaged groups to resources they need to enhance, if not to equalize, their social and economic opportunities.[78] Democratic states in developing countries cannot hope to arbitrarily impose priorities without violating their democratic nature. They have to work out a collective agreement from the welter of competing priorities expressed in the political arena by diverse disadvantaged groups. Not all of these groups are mobilized at once or in one convergent direction either to support or oppose the national state. This is what makes the linkage between development and justice difficult and yet possible in a developing democracy.

Demands for reversal of disadvantage have assumed a bewildering variety of forms. The nation itself was perceived as one disadvantaged community confronting the advanced states of the world, and thus poised for a prolonged struggle for self-reliance since the early years of the nationalist movement. But the very logic of autonomy also spilled over to subnational groups even before independence. As we have seen, Muslim separatism, leading to the partition of the subcontinent, was a prominent divisive expression of this sentiment. Political movements to reorganize states following independence, at times, began with secessionist threats. Soon, however, most of these threats proved to be strategies of bargaining for autonomy rights within the federal structure. The case for a southern separatism expressed by the Dravidistan movement gave way to several reorganized states in the region.[79] Cultural mobilization of the southern states had to compete with the language rivalry of each with the other, and when they peacefully settled for state-level autonomy, their language-based mobilization was substantially challenged by leaders who used caste- and class-based mobilization to gain access to power and privilege within each state.

Regional articulation of disadvantage or claims for autonomous rights have used horizontal mobilization of people who themselves are vertically divided into highly stratified social formations like castes or economic formations like classes. Whenever regional mobilization has confronted the national state, it has diverted attention from the deep structures of division underlying regional communities. Consequently, whenever the national state has refused to negotiate with regional leaders, it has strengthened the domination of the better-off regional elites over worse-off lower-status and class groups. Fortunately, sustained pressures from the regional mass movements have usually succeeded in realizing their autonomy, beginning with the creation of Andhra Pradesh in 1953 for Telugu-speaking people. This was followed by several phases of the states' reorganization leading to the creation of the twenty-fifth state in 1987.[80] In most cases the creation of autonomous states within the federation has facilitated a transfer of the targets of popular movements from the national state to the regional state. Mobilization at this stage has affirmed either subregional disaffection based on the disadvantages of the poorest areas of these states, as in the case of the Telangana movement in Andhra Pradesh, or wider lower-caste rights movement, as in Maharashtra.[81]

Federal accommodation of regional rights by inclusionary negotiation has in this way succeeded in incorporating into the national polity popular movements representing new political aspirants. By the early 1980s, however, the plebiscitarian mood of the populist leadership as described earlier in this chapter led to exclusionary responses played through manipulative or coercive craft, which drove the Assam and the Punjab regional movements to explosive proportions.[82] That the leadership was not beyond learning the lesson that such a strategy can destroy democratic rights and national cohesion at the same time was exemplified by the unprecedented Assam and Punjab accords signed by Prime Minister Rajiv Gandhi in 1985.[83] The following Assam and Punjab elections clearly demonstrated that the regional parties that came to power were less threatening to democracy and national cohesion than the national leadership that had earlier weakened both processes by their disjunction. If in Assam the accord had worked better, and in Punjab twenty months of the Akali Party rule has been succeeded by a dissolution of the legislative assembly, it certainly calls for a more imaginative implementation. If the Akali Party's pursuit of the accord was weak, it was not strengthened in any way by the sluggishness of the national leadership in implementing it.

Regional and ethnic justice issues inevitably bring in their trail the poverty and inequality issues that call for redistribution of resources among social and economic groups. Tamil, Telugu, or Sikh power often facilitates the case for internal social and economic competition. If the elites can use their communities against the central authority, the lower formations within them can use the same means to claim their share. The cascade effect of mobilization at successively lower layers of power and economic resources indicates how the class potential of ethnic struggles may be realized.

The limits of the ethnic movements to ensure a just sharing of developmental benefits are set by the fact that the major beneficiaries of successful incorporation have been the educated middle castes and classes. Democratic mobilization and incorporation have enabled them to displace the formerly privileged groups from political power without destroying their economic power. Expanded political mobility and access to state power have encouraged the new leaders to serve their constituencies by offering protected employment, preferential access to education and patronage, and expanded welfare provisions.[84] These measures have benefited the more advanced groups of the relatively backward castes and have only lightly touched the wider segments of the lowest castes and classes, including the scheduled castes and tribes. Yet it is interesting to note that the few states in India in which lower-status groups have registered discernible social advancements also happen to be the ones where ethnic politics has played a large part.[85] In fact the Hindi belt states closely associated with the national leadership, or for that matter the national average of all states in India, would reveal a generally poorer record of performance in economic growth or lower-caste or class advancement when compared with the major states where ethnic and regional mobilization have been salient.[86]

These gains, however, may be small consolation for the country as a whole where the shadow of absolute poverty haunts more than 40 percent of the population.[87] Statistical measures of income distribution in the mid-1970s indicate less inequality than in many developing countries. For example, the Gini coefficient for India was 0.38, showing slightly greater inequality than in China and Sri Lanka, which stood at 0.33.[88] However, income statistics can be notoriously misleading with respect to mass poverty and lower-class and status deprivation. Movements for social justice and redistribution of resources thus have a long way to go where demands for egalitarian and fair access suffer from the fact that caste, class, and regional stratification often compete for attention. Measures of protection and welfare, when extended to the lowest *castes*, may not take care of the lowest *classes*, or the worst-off region, or the most vulnerable ethnic groups. Competing and dispersed bases of deprivation and the consequent demands for competing norms of justice and equalization appear to strengthen the need for democratic political competition, for in the absence of it there may be little assurance that one issue of justice will not overwhelm other valid claims for justice. Plural justice thus requires combined pursuit of regional autonomy, progressive reduction of inequality of status, class and ethnic honor and security, and a pace of economic development consistent with but not overriding these objectives. Any fair assessment of democratic development in India has to wrestle with this stubborn complexity.

• THEORETICAL REVIEW •

Liberal democratic theories, as conventionally stated, are more preoccupied with political mechanisms for contestation and articulation than with what these mechanisms can accomplish for society. Such an emphasis on contest may be appropriate to societies where reasonable levels of living have been already accomplished or where crucial functions of development need not call for sustained collective endeavor. By excluding development from its charge, the state can simply be assigned some regulative and protective functions. But is this limited preoccupation justified by even the history of Western democracies? Perhaps the limited focus on *being* a democracy diverts our attention from the more complex historical issue of *becoming* democratic.[89] When the issue of active becoming is analyzed, it may show that there are more things in common between democratic evolution in the advanced and developing countries than is commonly assumed in the conventional literature.

Democracy in developing countries can hardly be appreciated merely in terms of degrees of contestation and expression, as many studies have sought to do.[90] A better way would be to focus on the gradual process of active cultivation of ideas and institutions contributing to the installation and strengthening of a democratic system, through a simultaneous development of social, economic, and political resources. This would imply an emphasis on the transformative role of the state as a collective instrument. The basic issues here, during a critical transition, would be less about formal mechanisms of checks and balances, rights and obligations, and more about the authority of political movements, the strength of operative (if not ideological) consensus, the weight and distribution of actual and latent opposition, and the ability of the system to evoke legitimating sentiments on the basis of performance. For, in a fragile moment of beginning, rules can be easily violated by a state that comes to control most resources in the name of the public. But the same state will more often respect the rules where the absence of such rules may deplete, if not defeat, the economic and social power of the ruling leaders.

The rules of democratic legitimation and incorporation have served the ruling groups rather well in India during their four decades of operation. Unlike in neighboring Pakistan, which emerged from exactly the same colonial experience, the Indian leaders benefited from an early process of converting nationalist support into electoral support. Continued electoral support allowed them to dominate the developing civil society through state control over economy, education, communication, coercion, and extensive systems of patronage and subsidy. The dominant economic classes in industry and agriculture generally found the system profitable and conducive to a stable set of expectations in a national market of vast potential. If occasionally, as in the staggered sequence of modest reforms of land tenure and private enterprise control, some threats were posed to the highest propertied classes, compensatory avenues of gains were maintained for them through formal or informal channels.

Moreover, new entrants to privileged formations were encouraged through the use of public sector financing, licensing, and tax policies in industries, and by promoting relatively affluent peasant entrepreneurs. At the same time, the promise of expansion of privilege offered a mobility incentive to a wider number in rural and urban areas who developed a sense of stake in the system more on the basis of aspiration

than accomplishment. The successful incorporation of regional aspirations in a federalized polity created another important constituency of
support for this legitimated democratic system. If all this was not enough to
impel the leaders to maintain the rules of the regime, the negative
reactions of wide segments of the public threatening the brief interlude
of rule violation during the emergency could make them fall in line.
Besides, the gains of abiding by the rules were also appreciated by the
opposition leaders when they realized—as in Kerala, West Bengal, and
other states—that access to power, and its prolonged use in cooperation
with other parties ruling in the center, would not be denied. When
leaders of capitalist and communist persuasion develop and sustain a
democratic system of rules with equal eagerness there must be something more to it than a mere veneer on class rule or a chance gift of
colonial history.

All these leadership sets have worked through fairly structured
organizational systems with relatively durable organizations and modes
of mutual interaction. This organizational system has worked best when
it has encouraged incorporation of multiple interests from civil society,
including ethnic expressions. Such voluntary associations have also
served as latent sectors of potential political leadership in moments of
crisis as, for example, discussed earlier in the context of plebiscitarian
adventures of central leadership. It is true that there have been occasions
when the organizational system in the country witnessed disturbing
challenges. These threats have always been limiited in time and territorial extension. Thus communist insurrectionary challenge in the early
1950s and late 1960s remained confined to a few districts, separatism of
the DMK or the hill peoples' secessionism failed to expand or converge,
and religion-using Sikh separatism in the 1980s had to contend with its
own rivals in a community that composes 2 percent of the nation's
population. All these widely dispersed threats were also widely staggered
over time, and in most cases yesterday's adversaries were turned into
next day's partners.[91]

This resilience or absorptive capacity has been considerably aided
by an ideological consensus (evolving since the nationalist period) regarding liberal means of resolving conflict, the basic premises of self-
reliant planned development, and the directive as well as responsive
functions of the state in society. Thus no matter which political party has
ruled at the center or at the state level, its functioning pattern has shared
a degree of similarity that would have been hard to anticipate from its
rhetoric before capturing power. This ideological consensus reinforces
the consensual readiness of political actors to play by mutually accepted
rules.

How deep is the foundation of support for the system? Studies of
advanced democracies show that basic agreements among articulate

groups seem to be more decisive than their wider penetration among the masses.[92] Empirical studies of Indian political perception indicate a degree of penetration that clearly goes beyond this minimal requirement. By 1967 70 percent of Indian adults identified with a party, compared to 60 percent in the United States in 1972. The attitudes of nonliterates and those with minimal education demonstrated strong commitment to parties, in fact considerably stronger than comparable U.S. cases. A high correspondence was demonstrated between party identification and party issue preference.[93] Another empirical study has found that partisanship is "not only associated with more [system] supportive attitudes, the attitudes themselves are richer and more basic to the viability of competitive institutions in India."[94] These studies also reveal that the perception of party differences among Indian partisans is informed by a remarkable tolerance of the ideologies of other partisans, who are rarely regarded as radical threats to the system.[95] Democratic political development has apparently not been constrained by the slow development of the so-called social and economic requisites of democratic being.[96]

Indian democracy can be understood as a deliberate act of political defiance of the social and economic constraints of underdevelopment. In fact it has been an adventure in creating a political system that would actively generate the social and economic development it lacked at its moment of foundation. This creative exercise in the autonomy of political initiative and inducement to reverse the expected sequence of democratic development called for a simultaneous treatment of multiple issues like national cohesion, economic development, social justice, citizen efficacy, and human development. The requirement of combination also presupposed that exclusive attention to one objective could be self-defeating. Rather, divided attention implied that the system could benefit from a plurality of expectations from various publics. For example, success in managing challenges to national cohesion and promoting agricultural development may reduce the intensity of adverse reaction to the slow implementation of land reform. Thus it is not surprising that aggregate public confidence in the democratic system has not depended on the performance of particular governments in exclusive issue areas. When the "sons of the soil" or the backward castes are enthused to support a regime that offers them special mobility through a protected job market or job reservations, the system obviously gains allegiance at the cost of economic efficiency.[97] But the consequent gains in the political efficacy of the system may allow it to promote efficiency in other areas of economic action.

Admittedly such balancing acts are favored by the nature of social divisions, structural diversities, and the ecological differences in a complex country like India. It is also clear that these acts have been performed well enough to sustain the regime so far. But the limits should not be ignored. Success in balancing requires an imaginative leadership, which no system ensures. Worse still, as one author had put it in a related context, it may be "a good net to catch allies, but one highly vulnerable to anyone with sharp teeth."[98] The art of balancing, even if forthcoming, may become vulnerable to resolute adversaries having independent access to crucial resources, particularly at a point when the resources of the state are dangerously depleted. Moments of economic crisis, international disturbance, tides of internal populism, or desperate actions by dominant classes to break a perceived stalemate may effectively challenge the hard-earned resilience of four decades.

Rapid development of the democratic state's resources of production, organization, distribution, communication, and legitimation can best preempt such danger. Unfortunately this art of balancing practiced in recent decades, by Congress as well as non-Congress leaders at federal and state levels, has thrived more on distributive skills—largely displayed in patronage, subsidy, and welfare promotions—than on rapid creation of resources.[99] It is tempting to believe that this is inherent in the process of democratic becoming in an inhospitable society. It is equally tempting to ask if the same society, with its compulsion for combined development, can be served better by alternatives to democracy, particularly at this point of development when the progressive taste of democratic becoming would scarcely make the people settle for anything less. However, neither logic nor the historical lessons discussed here would warrant a conclusion that democratic development in a context like India's must necessarily be more self-destructive than self-regenerating.

• FUTURE PROSPECTS •

Barely a decade after the launching of independent India's constitutional democracy, a major Western work on Indian politics confidently warned that "the odds are almost wholly against the survival of freedom and that...the issue is, in fact, whether any Indian state can survive at all."[100] Now that the structure of freedom and the state itself have survived such dire predictions for four decades, the issue can admit a somewhat different statement. The analysis in this chapter implies that the successful maintenance of democracy in India has ensured the stability of the new state and reasonably steady development, achieved with a degree of self-reliance and relative freedom from world economic oscillation that is rare in contemporary history. The processes of democratic becoming have crossed a threshold of reasonable success in a world which has witnessed, especially in the 1980s, a resurgence of interest in democratic development. As the appeal of the "glamorous" alternatives to democratic development wear off, more realistic assessments of the enterprise of what I have called the role of democracy in combined development will be possible.[101]

This is not to deny that the political accomplishments of Indian democracy can pose their own problems that can and should worry us. The mass mobilization in the late 1980s against the secular rules of the state on the part of Sikh, Muslim, and Hindu revivalists, to take one example from the ethnic agenda of Indian politics, indicates that democratic opportunities of expression do not rule out an attack on either secular rationality or democratic reason itself.[102] In fact, the social deepening of democracy can strengthen antidemocratic social and political forces in a manner even more threatening than the adventurous emergency regime of 1975–1976. After all, that adventure did not challenge the rationality of secular democracy. Neither did it create social dissension in the bureaucracy and the armed forces. And the adventure was short, shaky, and unsure of its own norm. Its continuity with some of the original elements of nationalist consensus may set it apart from the new moods of fundamentalism shared by a generation that can dispense with the basic values of the system as long as it can squeeze the system to its favor. Fortunately even the biggest potential danger to the system (i.e., Hindu revivalism) is likely to defeat itself if it chooses extreme courses, because of its own horizontal and vertical cleavages of region, language, caste, and class. The danger, however, cannot be minimized in view of the fact that a long evolution of Hindu inclination to avoid exclusivism has been the strongest pillar of secular rationality sustaining Indian democracy, as we have touched upon at the beginning of this chapter.

Although values alone cannot sustain a democracy in a developing country they need an emphasis in our story, in addition to that which we have given to structure, institutions, leadership, and performance. Democracy is about choice, and the citizens' choices are not inexorably determined by economic or social structural factors. As we have seen, many choices are made that cannot be explained by structural constraints alone, just as the advance creation of the political inclination to settle for some issue outcomes as opposed to others is a function of the art of creative and farsighted leadership. India has had its share of artful leadership and citizen choices consistent with democratic becoming. This is not simply a question of more visible national leaders enjoying or exploiting office—it refers to the larger issue of leadership at all levels of political life, including state and district levels. When the issue is posed whether the present state of democratic being can reproduce at least enough political and economic resources to continue the country's democratic becoming, we can do well to recall how the larger networks of political combination and leadership across parties and citizen groups have worked in recent years. This may afford us more optimism than by unreasonably locking our sight on those who, at the moment, happen to be in the limelight.

• NOTES •

1. For an early history of associations in India see, for example, B. B. Majumdar, *Indian Political Associations and Reform of Legislature (1818–1917)* (Calcutta: Firma K. L. Mukhopadhyay, 1965), ch. 2–5. See also S. Natarajan, *A Century of Social Reform in India* (Bombay: Asia Publishing House, 1962).

2. See Stephen Hay, "Western and Indigenous Elements in Modern Indian Thought: The Case of Ram Mohun Roy," in Marius B. Jansen, ed., *Changing Japanese Attitudes Toward Modernization* (Princeton: Princeton University Press, 1965), p. 318.

3. For details see J. Das Gupta, *Language Conflict and National Development* (Berkeley: University of California Press, 1970), pp. 78ff.

4. When the nationalists sought to persuade the ruling authority to introduce compulsory primary education, their move was turned down. As late as 1911 only 1 percent of Indians would be considered as literate in English and 6 percent in vernacular languages. According to high-ranking British administrators Indian "power to stir up discontent would be immensely increased if every cultivator could read." See Sumit Sarkar, *Modern India, 1885–1947* (Delhi: Macmillan, 1983), pp. 66–67.

5. For a discussion of preemptive militarism in Japan see Akira Iriya, "Imperialism in Asia," in James B. Crowley, ed., *Modern East Asia: Essays in Interpretation* (New York: Harcourt, Brace and World, 1970), pp. 122ff. Increasing racialism in colonial rule was typified in a comment like "we could only govern by maintaining the fact that we are the dominant race...," quoted in Sumit Sarkar, *Modern India*, p. 23.

6. John R. McLane, *Indian Nationalism and the Early Congress* (Princeton: Princeton University Press, 1977), pp. 94–95.

7. Dadabhai Naoroji, *Poverty and Un-British Rule in India* (Delhi: Publications Division, Government of India, 1969 [originally published in 1901]), p. 116. For a collection of others' writings see A. Appadorai, ed., *Documents on Political Thought in Modern India*, vol. 1 (Bombay: Oxford University Press, 1973).

8. See W. T. deBary, ed., *Sources of Indian Tradition*, vol. 2 (New York: Columbia University Press, 1963), p. 140, and A. Appadorai, *Documents on Political Thought*, vol. 1, p. 163.

9. See deBary, ed., *Sources of Indian Tradition*, vol. 2, pp. 194–195.

10. For a detailed discussion see Das Gupta, *Language Conflict and National Development*.

11. Gandhi's ideas are discussed in R. Iyer, *The Moral and Political Thought of Mahatma Gandhi* (New York: Oxford University Press, 1973). For Nehru's ideas see M. Brecher, *Nehru: A Political Biography* (New York: Oxford University Press, 1959). See also Ronald J. Terchek, "Gandhi and Democratic Theory," in T. Pantham and K. L. Deutsch, eds., *Political Thought in Modern India* (New Delhi: Sage, 1986), pp. 307–324, and B. Parekh, "Gandhi and the Logic of Reformist Discourse," in B. Parekh and T. Pantham, eds., *Political Discourse* (New Delhi: Sage, 1987), pp. 277–291.

12. The complexity of the job involved in keeping multiple interests together, and yet not exclusively serving a dominant interest due to populist compulsions of the movement, is discussed in C. Markovits, *Indian Business and Nationalist Politics, 1931–1939* (Cambridge: Cambridge University Press, 1985), pp. 180–181.

13. These ideas are analyzed in detail in Joan Bondurant, *Conquest of Violence* (Berkeley: University of California Press, 1965), esp. pp. 190ff.

14. See, for example, Judith M. Brown, *Gandhi's Rise to Power* (Cambridge: Cambridge University Press, 1972). For a detailed analysis of these movements, esp. pp. 52–122.

15. Ibid., especially pp. 190–249.

16. For a background of the 1919 reforms see S. R. Mehrotra, "The Politics Behind the Montagu Declaration of 1917," in C. H. Philips, ed., *Politics and Society in India* (New York: Praeger, 1962), pp. 71–96.

17. The Act of 1935 and its working is analyzed in A. Chatterji, *The Constitutional Development of India: 1937–1947* (Calcutta: Firma K. L. Mukhopadhyay, 1958), pp. 3–25.

18. The general seats were those that were not specifically designated for Muslims, Europeans, Anglo-Indians, Indian Christians, or Sikhs. For most purposes these would imply constituencies for Hindu candidates.

19. The official version of the constitution was in English. In late 1987 a Hindi translation of the document was approved by a constitutional amendment. Thus the fifty-sixth amendment relatively enlarged access in a country where most people cannot read English. Hindi reading ability extends to about one-third of the country's population.

20. See *The Constitution of India*, commemorative edition (New Delhi: Ministry of Law and Justice, Government of India, 1974), pp. 17–18.

21. For an analysis of the 1977 election see Myron Weiner, *India at the Polls: The Parliamentary Elections of 1977* (Washington, D.C.: American Enterprise Institute for Public Policy Research, 1978).

22. The first quarter of 1988 also witnessed the end of communist rule in Tripura, where a Congress-dominated coalition came to power. Meanwhile, the AIADMK rule in Tamilnadu failed to survive the succession crisis following the death of the party's most popular leader, M. G. Ramachandran.

23. This turning point and its aftermath is discussed in Richard Sisson, "Party Transformation in India: Development and Change in the Indian National Congress," in N. S. Bose, ed., *India in the Eighties* (Calcutta: Firma K. L. Mukhopadhyay, 1982), pp. 1–23; and Stanley A. Kochanek, *The Congress Party of India* (Princeton: Princeton University Press, 1968), especially pp. 407–447.

24. The idea of the Congress party as a national reconciler of interests has been extensively treated in many works, of which at least two may be noted: Myron Weiner, *Party Building in a New Nation: The Indian National Congress* (Chicago: University of Chicago Press, 1967); and Rajni Kothari, *Politics in India* (Boston: Little, Brown, 1970).

25. For details of the politics of the 1970s and its impact on the 1980s see Robert L. Hardgrave, Jr. and Stanley A. Kochanek, *India: Government and Politics in a Developing Nation*, 4th ed., (New York: Harcourt Brace Jovanovich, 1986), p. 204ff.

26. See Myron Weiner, "Political Evolution—Party Bureaucracy and Institutions," in John D. Mellor, ed., *India: A Rising Middle Power* (Boulder: Westview Press, 1979), especially p. 32f.

27. For the Bihar and Gujarat agitations see Ghanshyam Shah, *Protest Movements in Two Indian States: A Study of Gujarat and Bihar Movements* (Delhi: Ajanta, 1977). See also Geoffrey Ostergaard, "The Ambiguous Strategy of J. P.'s Last Phase," in David Selbourne, ed., *In Theory and Practice: Essays on the Politics of Jayaprakash Narayan* (Delhi: Oxford University Press, 1985), pp. 155–180.

28. Jayaprakash Narayan explained his position in these words: "I am aiming at a people's movement embracing the entire nation. A movement cannot have a clear-cut program. The main purpose of a movement is to articulate people's wishes." See his collected writings published under the title *Total Revolution* (Bombay: Popular Prakashan, 1978), vol. 4, p. 141. Positive programs favored by him and the core groups of this movement in Bihar are stated in pp. 165ff. These include political accountability of the elected legislators to their constituencies, devolution of decision making authority, and implementation of agrarian reforms through peoples' committees. See ibid., pp. 168–170.

29. The opponent was Raj Narain, who defeated Indira Gandhi in the election of 1977. The court case and the events following it are described in K. Nayar, *The Judgement: Inside Story of Emergency in India* (New Delhi: Vikas, 1977).

30. These provisions and their use in 1975 are discussed in Zubair Alam, *Emergency Powers and Indian Democracy* (New Delhi: S. K. Publishers, 1987), pp. 94–103. The 59th amendment of the constitution passed by parliament in March 1988 empowers the federal government to impose emergency in Punjab.

31. See, for example, A. Gledhill, *The Republic of India: The Development of its Laws and Constitution* (London: Stevens, 1951), pp. 107–109.

32. This distinction is discussed in detail in J. Das Gupta, "A Season of Ceasars: Emergency Regimes and Development Politics in Asia," *Asian Survey* 18, no. 4 (April 1978): pp. 315–349.

33. Why she ended up choosing this option has been subject to extensive speculation. A good analysis of possible reasons and explanations is in P. B. Mayer, "Congress [I], Emergency [I]: Interpreting Indira Gandhi's India," *Journal of Commonwealth and Comparative Policies* 22, no. 2 (1984), pp. 128–150. How the emergency leaders defended this case is exemplified in D. V. Gandhi, ed., *Era of Discipline: Documents on Contemporary Reality* (New Delhi: Samachar Bharati, 1976), p. 2 and passim.

34. The constitutional changes, as intended and executed, are discussed in detail in Lloyd I. Rudolph and Suzanne H. Rudolph, "To The Brink and Back: Representation and the State in India," *Asian Survey* 18, no. 4 (1978): especially pp. 392–399.

35. The developmental implications of emergency are analyzed in Das Gupta, "A Season of Caesars," pp. 332ff.

36. See Myron Weiner, *India at the Polls*, for a detailed analysis.

37. The political implication and the economic record of the Janata rule is analyzed in J. Das Gupta, "The Janata Phase: Reorganization and Redirection in Indian Politics," *Asian Survey* 19, no. 4 (1979): pp. 390–403.

38. Some of these mobilization processes are discussed by Ghanshyam Shah and J. Das Gupta in their papers included in Atul Kohli, ed., *India's Democracy* (Princeton: Princeton University Press, 1988): pp. 144–168 and 262–304. See also Barnett R. Rubin, "The Civil Liberties Movement in India," in *Asian Survey* 27, no. 3 (1987): pp. 371–392.

39. The literature on labor unions in India is extensive. For surveys of the role of trade unions in Indian politics, see S. Jawaid, *Trade Union Movement in India* (Delhi: Sundeep, 1982); and R. Chatterji, *Unions, Politics and the State* (New Delhi: South Asian Publishers, 1980), esp. pp. 27–86. For a survey of peasant associations see A. N. Seth, *Peasant Organizations in India* (Delhi: B. R. Publishing, 1984); and K. C. Alexander, *Peasant Organizations in South India* (New Delhi: Indian Social Institute, 1981).

40. See Stanley A. Kochanek, *Business and Politics in India* (Berkeley: University of California Press, 1974), especially part 3.

41. These are discussed in detail in an excellent analysis of the pertinent literature by Lloyd I. Rudolph and Susan H. Rudolph, "Determinants and Varieties of Agrarian Mobilization," in M. Desai et al., eds., *Agrarian Power and Agricultural Productivity in South Asia* (Berkeley: University of California Press, 1984), pp. 281–344.

42. The support bases in Kerala are discussed in T. J. Nossiter, *Communism in Kerala* (Berkeley: University of California Press, 1982); those in West Bengal are discussed in Atul Kohli, *The State and Poverty in India (Cambridge: Cambridge University Press, 1986)*, ch. 3.

43. As one study of Kerala points out, "It seems that the agricultural labor movement...has now been integrated into the existing system. The reduction in militant struggles, the increasing institutionalization of collective bargaining and parliamentary politics are all indicative of this." See Joseph Tharamangalam, *Agrarian Class Conflict: The Political Mobilization of Agricultural Laborers in Kuttanad, South India* (Vancouver: University of British Columbia Press, 1981), p. 98. Another more empirical survey conducted in Tamilnadu reaches a similar conclusion. See Marshall M. Bouton, *Agrarian Radicalism in South India* (Princeton: Princeton University Press, 1985), p. 310.

44. The role of a literary association like the Assam Sahitya Sabha in generating a popular movement was not unique to Assam. Similar cases of organized literary initiative in different states of India remind us of the political significance of nonpolitical associations. For a discussion of this association and its alliance with the All Assam Students' Union see my "Language, National Unity, and Shared Development in South Asia," in William R. Beer and James E. Jacobs, eds., *Language Policy and National Unity* (Totowa, N.J.: Rowman and Allanheld, 1985), pp. 208ff.

45. For a chronological survey see T. S. Murty, *Assam: The Difficult Years* (New Delhi: Himalayan Books, 1983).

46. On 18 February 1983 a mob of about 12,000 people killed 1,400 men, women, and children.

47. The Assam accord was announced by Prime Minister Rajiv Gandhi on 12 August 1986. It was described by newspapers as a balancing trick that left "no winners or losers." See, for example, *India Today*, 15 September 1985, international edition, p. 27.

48. The organizational durability of the DMK, and later of its breakaway part, the AIADMK (which ruled Tamilnadu until early 1988), and that of the Telugu Desam (which rules Andhra Pradesh), as well as their record of cooperation with national parties, were hardly anticipated at the time of their inception.

49. For a discussion of his ideas on planning see Bruce F. Johnston and William C. Clark, *Redesigning Rural Development* (Baltimore: Johns Hopkins University Press, 1982), p. 24.

50. For one example see *India Today*, international edition, 15 November 1985, pp. 8ff. This is actually an assessment of the prime minister's record. A reasonably discounted value can, however, be assigned to his government by implication. A similar positive result was recorded in another poll conducted by *The Telegraph*, Calcutta, 31 October 1985. By early 1988 the prime minister and his leadership continued to enjoy more public confidence than the national level alternative leadership despite the growing disappointment with his performance. See *India Today*, international edition, 29 February 1988, pp. 17–23.

51. See *The Approach to the Seventh Five-Year Plan, 1985–90* (Planning Commission, Government of India, July 1984). Center for Monitoring Indian Economy edition, p. 9.

52. The proportion of plan outlay devoted to agriculture was 14.8 percent in the first plan (1952–1956), 11.7 percent in the second plan (1955–1961) and 12.7 percent in the third plan (1961–1965). The corresponding figures for organized industry and mining were 2.8 percent, 20.1 percent, and 20.1 percent. See the *Statistical Outline of India, 1984* (Bombay: Tata Services, 1984).

53. For a critique of Indian plan strategies see John W. Mellor, *The New Economics of Growth: A Strategy for India and the Developing World* (Ithaca: Cornell University Press, 1976), especially pp. 274ff. For a sophisticated analysis defending the plan strategies see S. Chakravarty, *Development Planning* (Oxford: Clarendon Press, 1987), pp. 7–38.

54. This refers to the agricultural policies that have acquired the popular label of "green revolution."

55. For an account of this colonial legacy see Dharma Kumar, ed., *The Cambridge Economic History of India*, vol. 2 (Cambridge: Cambridge University Press, 1983), pp. 947ff.

56. See the *World Development Report, 1987* (New York: Oxford University Press, 1987), p. 258.

57. Ibid.

58. John Wall, "Foodgrain Management: Pricing, Procurement, Distribution, Import, and Storage Policy," in *India: Occasional Papers*, World Bank Staff Working Paper no. 279, May 1978 (Washington, D.C.: The World Bank, 1978), pp. 88–89.

59. See Government of India, *Economic Survey, 1986–87* (New Delhi, 1987), pp. 8 and S-7 through S-15, and *Economic Survey, 1987–88* (New Delhi, 1988), pp. S-23-24 and *passim.*

60. In 1985 and 1986 the procurement rates were 16 and 15 percent of new foodgrain production respectively. Even in the worst drought year of 1987, this rate exceeded 12 percent. *Economic Survey, 1987–88* (New Delhi, 1988), p. S-24.

61. *Toward Sustained Development in Sub-Saharan Africa* (Washington, D.C.: The World Bank, 1984), p. 2.

62. See Amartya Sen, *Resources, Values and Development* (Cambridge: Harvard University Press, 1984), p. 501ff, for an interesting comparison of the scale of famines in colonial India and socialist China.

63. Primary school enrollment as percent of age group for sub-Saharan Africa in the early 1980s was 77.6 percent, for East Asia 113.0, and for India 90.0. Compiled from The World Bank, *World Tables*, vol. 2 (Baltimore: Johns Hopkins University Press, 1984 edition), pp. 158–159, *World Development Report 1984* (New York: Oxford University Press, 1984), p. 226, and *World Development Report, 1987*, p. 262.

64. For an idea of how the leading economists of the 1950s thought about desirable strategies of development and how in the 1980s they assess their earlier thoughts, see Gerald M. Meier and Dudley Seers, eds., *Pioneers in Development* (New York: Oxford University Press, 1984).

65. Jagdish Bhagwati's distinction of several variants of import substitution would help one to place the Indian policy in a clearer perspective. See his "Comment" on Prebisch in ibid., pp. 201–202.

66. I have used total industrial growth rates because of easier availability, but growth rates in manufacturing are not very dissimilar. See The World Bank, *World Development Report 1984*, p. 220.

67. Thus one estimate suggests that the annual percentage rate of growth of industrial product in India was 4.1 compared to 6.3 for nonsocialist developing countries and 4.3 for the nonsocialist world. See S. J. Patel, "India's Regression in the World Economy," in *Economic and Political Weekly*, 28 September 1985, p. 1652. How seriously such estimates need to be taken is an issue that may be controversial. See, for instance, K. N. Raj, "Economic Growth in India, 1952–55 to 1982–83," in *Economic and Political Weekly*, 13 October 1984, p. 1804.

68. From *Basic Statistics Relating to Indian Economy* (Bombay: Center for Monitoring Indian Economy, August 1984), Table 14.9–2, and August 1986, Table 14.11–2.

69. With all the affection for steel, per capita steel consumption in India increased from five kilograms in 1952 only to seventeen in 1982, whereas in China it grew from two kilograms to forty-one. By 1982 per capita steel production in India and even China—two cases of relatively self-reliant planning—remained way behind compared to South Korea (339), Taiwan, Mexico (114), Argentina (121), and Brazil (105). *World Economy and India's Place in It* (Bombay: Center for Monitoring Indian Economy, October 1986), Table 8.8.

70. Data in this section has been compiled from sources cited in note 68 (including also Table 22.3) and World Bank, *China: Socialist Economic Development*, vol. 1 (Washington, D.C.: The World Bank, 1983), p. 120.

71. For some details of economic reforms in China, see W. Byrd, et al., *Recent Chinese Economic Reforms*, World Bank Staff Working Papers no. 652 (Washington, D.C.: The World Bank, 1984).

72. For an account of the Brazilian public sector's expansion and the attendant problems, see *Brazil: A World Bank Country Study* (Washington, D.C.: The World Bank, 1984), especially pp. 30ff. The strong preference for luxury goods production catering to the upper 20 percent of the population in a country of high inequality is discussed in Alain de Janvry, "Social Disarticulation in Latin American History," working paper for Giannini Foundation of Agricultural Economics, March 1984.

73. Compiled from The World Bank, *World Tables*, vol. 2.

74. Critical works on contemporary industrial policy discuss some of these issues. In spite of their different perspectives, they agree on the crucial public role in infrastructural investments. See Isher Judge Ahluwalia, *Industrial Policy in India* (Delhi: Oxford University Press, 1985), pp. 168–169; and Pranab Bardhan, *The Political Economy of Development in India* (Oxford: Basil Blackwell, 1984), p. 24.

75. Ahluwalia's *Industrial Policy in India* does not entirely ignore the contingency of compromising growth objectives (p. 172), but its detailed treatment is not included in the scope of this work. Pranab Bardhan seeks to account for the avoidance of "hard choices" by the current leadership in terms of its ties to proprietary classes. See especially pp. 73–74 of *The Political Economy of Development in India*.

76. The ideological issues are discussed in Myron Weiner, "The Political Economy of Industrial Growth in India," in *World Politics* 38, no. 4 (July 1986): pp. 604ff. For a discussion of room to effect policy change in the Indian context see John Toye, *Dilemmas of Development* (Oxford: Basil Blackwell, 1987), pp. 132–133.

77. See Barnett R. Rubin, "Economic Liberalization and the Indian State," in *Third World Quarterly* 7, no. 4 (October 1985): pp. 954–955.

78. We need not discuss in detail the implications of the different criteria proposed by various authors, e.g., primary goods (Rawls), basic capabilities (Sen), or resources (Dworkin). For our purpose it is enough to distinguish the aggregative from the disaggregative approaches to defining priorities. For a useful treatment of these criteria see John Roemer, "Exploitation, Property Rights, and Preferences," in Tibor R. Machan, ed., *The Main Debate* (New York: Random House, 1987), p. 365ff. See John Rawls, *A Theory of Justice* (Cambridge: Harvard University Press, 1971), p. 62ff, where the notion of primary goods includes basic rights, power, economic resources, and self-respect. See also Amartya Sen, *Resources, Values and Development*, p. 315ff and Ronald Dworkin, "Equality of Resources," in *Philosophy and Public Affairs*, Fall 1981, pp. 283–345.

79. See Robert L. Hardgrave, Jr., *The Dravidian Movement* (Bombay: Popular,

1965) for a general background of the movement in the south; and J. Das Gupta, *Language Conflict and National Development*, pp. 268ff for its linkage with democratic representation.

80. Maharashtra and Gujarat statehood followed in 1960 and that of Punjab and Haryana in 1966. The secessionist movement in Mizoram was transformed into an autonomy movement within the federal system and statehood was conceded in 1986. Earlier, in 1963 the state of Nagaland was created in response to secessionist threat. A decade later several new states were created in the northeastern region. The latest new state is Goa, promoted from the intermediate status of union territory to full statehood in 1987.

81. These processes are discussed in the context of a number of regions in A. Majeed, ed., *Regionalism: Developmental Tensions in India* (New Delhi: Cosmo, 1984), esp. pp. 89–114 for Maharashtra. See also G. Ram Reddy and B.A.V. Sharma, *Regionalism in India, A Study of Telangana* (New Delhi: Concept Publishing, 1979, pp. 24–35.

82. The Assam case has been discussed earlier. For a short account of the Punjab situation see D. Gupta, "The Communalizing of Punjab, 1980–1985," in *Economic and Political Weekly*, 13 July 1985, pp. 1185–1190. For details see A. Singh, ed., *Punjab in Indian Politics: Issues and Trends* (Delhi: Ajanta, 1985), and A. S. Narang, *Democracy, Development and Distortion: Punjab Politics in National Perspective* (New Delhi: Gitanjali, 1986), esp. pp. 136–189.

83. This was unprecedented because this was the first time that the prime minister signed a statement of accord with nonofficial political organizations. Even as of early 1987 the transfer of Chandigarh to Punjab, one of the elements of the 1985 accord, was not implemented by the national leadership. This obviously weakened the elected chief minister of the state and also the chances of peaceful solution in this area. See "The Bungled Accord," in *India Today*, international edition, 15 February 1986 for a discussion of the political problems of implementing the accord. See also Francine R. Frankel, "Politics: The Failure to Rebuild Consensus," in Marshall M. Bouton, *India Briefing, 1987* (Boulder: Westview Press, 1987), pp. 31–35.

84. Problems of preferential access are treated in Myron Weiner et al., *India's Preferential Policies* (Chicago: University of Chicago Press, 1981).

85. See Roderick Church, "The Pattern of State Politics in Indira Gandhi's India," in J. R. Wood, ed., *State Politics in Contemporary India* (Boulder: Westview Press, 1984), pp. 236–237.

86. Of the six major states gaining autonomy as a result of regional movements four have attained the highest per capita income level in the country. If we take the annual rate of percentage increase in per capita income at constant prices (1970–71) between 1971–72 to 1981–82, again (among fifteen major states) Punjab scores the highest rank, Maharashtra ranks third, Andhra Pradesh and Haryana rank fourth (tie), Gujarat ranks sixth, and Tamilnadu, seventh. Recent poverty level estimates show lower average poverty compared to the national rate in five of these six states. These comparative data are from *Basic Statistics Relating to the Indian Economy*, vol. 2 (Bombay: Center for Monitoring Indian Economy), September 1985, Tables 14.1 and 14.9.

87. The comparable figure for South Korea is 15 percent and Sri Lanka, 23 percent. See S. Mukhopadhyay, *The Poor in Asia* (Kuala Lumpur: Asian and Pacific Development Center, 1985), p. 8.

88. These comparative figures are from The World Bank, *China: Socialist Economic Development*, vol. 1, p. 94. In addition the share of income of the poorest 20 percent of households was greater in India (7.0 percent) than in any other developing country for which the World Bank reports data, while the share of the highest 20 percent is among the lowest. See The World Bank, *World Development Report 1986*, pp. 252–253.

89. Tocqueville's idea that Americans have come to democracy without having endured democratic revolution and that they are born equal, instead of becoming so, may have implications for impressing such bias. Some of these implications are discussed in another context in Albert O. Hirschman, "Rival Interpretations of Market Society: Civilizing, Destructive or Feeble?," in *Journal of Economic Literature* 20 (December 1982): pp. 350ff.

90. See G. Bingham Powell, Jr., *Contemporary Democracies* (Cambridge: Harvard University Press, n.d.), for some samples, pp. 3ff.

91. The taming of the leading Communist parties, the DMK, the Telugu Desam, the

Assam Movement, the National Conference of Kashmir, and the Mizo rebels are some examples.

92. See M. Mann, "The Social Cohesion of Liberal Democracy," in A. Giddens and D. Held, eds., *Classes, Power and Conflict* (Berkeley: University of California Press), pp. 388ff.

93. This congruence was revealed for all major parties and not just the Congress party. Samuel J. Eldersveld and Bashiruddin Ahmed, *Citizens and Politics: Mass Political Behavior in India* (Chicago: University of Chicago Press, 1978), especially pp. 80, 90, 104.

94. John Osgood Field, *Consolidating Democracy: Politicization and Partisanship in India* (New Delhi: Manohar, 1980), p. 288. This work is based on data collected in 1966 as part of a cross-national project.

95. Ibid., p. 292.

96. See, for example, Seymour Martin Lipset, "Some Social Requisites of Democracy: Economic Development and Political Legitimacy," in *American Political Science Review* 53, no. 2 (1959): pp. 69–105.

97. Backward caste demands usually benefit middle castes more than others. See Francine Frankel, "Middle Castes and Classes in Indian Politics: Prospects for Political Accommodation," in A. Kohli, ed., *India's Democracy*; and Myron Weiner, *Sons of the Soil*.

98. Adam Przeworski, "Some Problems in the Study of the Transition to Democracy," in Guillermo O'Donnell, Philippe C. Schmitter, and Laurence Whitehead, eds., *Transitions From Authoritarian Rule: Comparative Perspectives* (Baltimore: Johns Hopkins University Press, 1986), p. 63.

99. I have excluded the issue of corruption. It is a long story and most recently both the national and regional leaders have been involved. The issue of the Bofors arms deal in 1987 and N. T. Rama Rao's case in 1988 are just a few instances. But the corruption issue needs to be seen in the light of the fact that democracy has encouraged and, at the same time, exposed corruption. But exposure does not necessarily eliminate corrupt leaders from politics. Popular toleration of corruption is a problem that cannot be wished away. See, for example, K. S. Padhy, *Corruption in Politics* (Delhi: B.R. Publishing, 1986), esp. pp. 212–213.

100. Selig S. Harrison, *India: The Most Dangerous Decades* (Madras: Oxford University Press, 1960), p. 338.

101. Barrington Moore, Jr., who has inspired many scholars to defend "glamorous" options through his landmark work, *Social Origins of Dictatorship and Democracy* (Boston: Beacon Press, 1966), has recently observed: "political glamour can be a disaster that produces enormous amounts of suffering.... If humanity is to work its way out of its current plight...there will have to be leaders...who can turn their backs on political glamour and work hard for [barely] feasible goals rather than glamourous ones." *Authority and Inequality Under Capitalism and Socialism* (Oxford: Clarendon Press, 1987), p. 125. Not surprisingly, compared to his earlier work, *Social Origins*, Indian democracy comes out in a positive light in this new work (p. 123).

I have used the notion of *combined development* in the sense of the political compulsion to pursue simultaneous or at least multiple objectives in a multi-ethnic developing country interested in comprehensive national development. This use should not be confused with other uses of the term in the literature (notably, Leon Trotsky's use to convey the advantage of historic backwardness). For an elaboration of the latter use see J. Elster, "The Theory of Combined and Uneven Development: A Critique," in J. Roemer ed., *Analytical Marxism*, (Cambridge: Cambridge University Press, 1986), pp. 54–63.

102. The danger of recent Hindu mobilization can be appreciated if one follows the "*sati* incident," i.e., mass reactions in favor of the widow-burning case in Rajasthan in 1987. See I. Qadeer and Z. Hasan, "Deadly Politics of the State and its Apologists," *Economic and Political Weekly* 22, no. 46 (14 November 1987): pp. 1946–1949. The limits of Hindu confessional politics in the contemporary context are discussed in L. I. Rudolph and S. H. Rudolph, *In Pursuit of Lakshmi*, (Chicago: The University of Chicago Press, 1987), pp. 36–47.

CHAPTER THREE

Pakistan: Experiments with Democracy
LEO E. ROSE

Pakistan, as defined in this chapter, will be restricted in geographic terms to the state that has retained the name since the separation of the country into two national systems in 1971. Some references to East Pakistan, now Bangladesh, will be made in the analysis of pre-1971 political developments, but the primary focus will be on what was then called West Pakistan—the four provinces of Punjab, Sind, the Northwest Frontier Province (NWFP), and Baluchistan, plus some centrally administered adjacent areas.

Pakistan occupies a vital geostrategic frontier area in the section of southern Asia where three quite distinctive regions intertwine—South Asia, the West Asian societies of Iran and Afghanistan, and the Central Asian provinces in the Soviet Union and China. For more than four millenia, invading "hordes" from these adjacent regions have invaded South Asia—usually through Afghanistan, across the Khyber Pass on the Afghanistan-Pakistan border and then down through Pakistan into the great Indus and Gangetic heartland areas of the subcontinent. The political history of what is now Pakistan has, of course, been strongly affected by its highly strategic location and its vulnerability to invading forces from the east, west, and northwest. This is also true of Pakistan's contemporary history.

The impact of Pakistan's historical heritage on its post-1947 efforts to establish a democratic political system is a complex subject, as it is one of the many "new nations" in Asia and Africa in which there is a heterogeneous traditional political culture. Most Pakistanis prefer to define their country as an integral part of the Islamic heartland in West Asia, but that is only one small part of objective reality. There is a traditional Islamic political culture in the South Asian subcontinent, but in sociopolitical terms it is largely the product of the Turkic and Mongol (e.g., Moghul) invaders that dominated the northern half of the subcontinent for most of the period from the thirteenth to the eighteenth century.

PAKISTAN

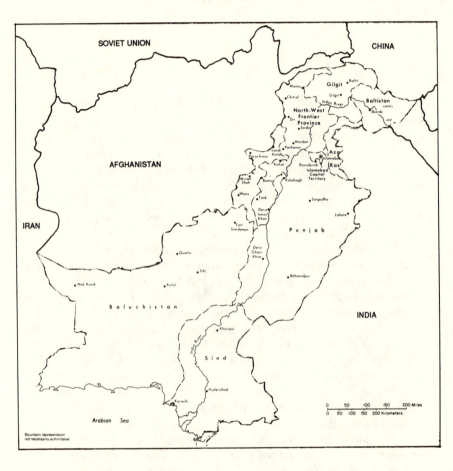

SOVIET UNION

CHINA

Gilgit
· Balti

· Mastej

· Chitral

Gilgit ·

Indus River

Baltistan

Jammu

· Skardu

North-West
Frontier
Province

· Dir

· Sadu

ind

· Mardan

· Peshawar

AFGHANISTAN

Land-
Kotol

Parachinar

· Kohat

Azo

· Islamabad

Islamabad
Capital
Territory

Kas·

Rawalpindi ·

Miram
Shah

· Bannu

Kalabagh

· Wana

· Tank

Sargodha ·

Dera
Ismail
Khan

IRAN

· Fort
Sandeman

Punjab

Lahore ·

Dera
Ghazi
Khan

· Quetta

· Sibi

· Bahawalpur

· Nak Kundi

· Kalat

INDIA

Baluchistan

· Khorpur

Indus River

Sind

Hyderabad ·

Karachi ·

Arabian   Sea

| 0 | 50 | 100 | 150 | 200 Miles |
| 0 | 50 | 100 | 150 | 200 Kilometers |

Boundary representation
not necessarily authoritative

68

These Muslim dynasties, moreover, imposed their rule over the existing Hindu political and social culture and, in the process, accommodated important aspects of the latter in their "Islamic" system. Such basic Hindu social institutions as the caste system are still readily evident, slightly disguised, in the heavily Muslim majority areas of what is now Pakistan.

From the mid-nineteenth century to 1947 Pakistan was part of the British "Raj" (Empire) in South Asia. The British colonial system retained much of the Moghul dynasty's formal bureaucratic superstructure while gradually changing the basic operational rules and procedures. By 1900 the Raj looked like a successor dynasty to the Moghuls, but in its governance principles functioned quite differently. Thus Pakistan's traditional sociopolitical culture is the remarkable hybrid of Islamic and Hindu cultures that evolved during several centuries of Islamic rule over a largely Hindu population—with a British colonial facade attached. Since 1947 both Pakistan and India have sought, in effect, to reject this eclectic cultural heritage and to concoct in its place a "purer" system—Islamic or Hindu as the case may be. The rhetoric employed is exuberant, but these purification campaigns have been of limited significance to date in the socialization and politicization of the public, as it is the composite cultural heritage system that has usually provided the operational framework.

• HISTORICAL REVIEW AND ANALYSIS •

Pakistan in the 1980s is the product of the dismemberment of two polities: the partition of the British Raj into India and Pakistan in 1947 and the separation of the eastern and western wings of Pakistan into two states, Bangladesh and Pakistan, in 1971. Both of these events had a major impact on the political systems and processes in Pakistan, and thus on the fate of its experiments with democratic forms of government.

The Colonial Period

While the British colonial system had retained a basically authoritarian character throughout the period of the Raj, a liberalization process was introduced slowly and gradually under which the local elites were absorbed into the governing process under carefully defined terms. The first reform program (1859) conceded representation on a few municipal councils, through a carefully restricted franchise, to only a few hundred "loyal" locals. The scope and powers of representative bodies were gradually expanded until, under the 1935 India Act, the provinces were governed by cabinets nominated by the state assemblies, most of whose members had been elected by locals on a greatly expanded but still restricted franchise. An elected national assembly was also established under the 1935 Act, but with much more limited powers than the state assemblies and no effective controls over the central government headed by the governor-general appointed by London.

The 1935 Act thus constituted only a partial and limited transfer of power. Ultimate decision-making authority was retained by the governor-general at the central level and, under prescribed conditions, by the appointed governors at the provincial level. Moreover, the basic operating principles of a highly authoritarian martial law regime were defined in precise legal terms by the British and imposed on the Raj in the 1939–1945 period. Thus, when the Pakistan military first moved into the uncertain world of a martial law regime in 1958, it could refer back to the extensive British experience with such a system in the subcontinent during World War II.

But while the governmental institutions of the British Raj were tilted toward an authoritarian system (despite the inclusion of the principles of representative government), this was less obviously the case for the education system the British introduced into the subcontinent. It was almost classically British in content and in the political socialization process implicit within it. This led to some basic contradictions, as the higher education system in India (as in England) tended to be (1) highly elitist in admittance patterns and social values espoused, but also (2) highly laudatory of the British (rather than the colonial) system of government, which by 1920 was becoming a populist democracy.

The local elite that became involved in politics in the British Raj was mostly educated in these British-style schools or, not infrequently (Gandhi, Nehru, Jinnah), in England itself. They were almost classically British in their political views, combining a highly elitist mind set with the verbal exposition of "radical" populist principles. Thus the political and intellectual elite that dominated Pakistani national politics during the first decade after independence could not be easily distinguished from the dominant elite in India's ruling Congress Party during that same period in socioeconomic class terms or in the democratic political philosophy they espoused. Most of the top leadership of the Muslim League (ML), the ruling party in Pakistan after 1947, was from Muslim urban elite families and had been educated in British-style schools rather than Islamic religious institutions in their place of origin. Some were from very prominent and wealthy rural elite families but had been educated in urban schools or abroad.

However, there were a couple of critical differences in the political capacities of the dominant Pakistani and Indian political elite in 1947. There was the unfortunate fact that most of the Muslim League leadership and much of the party's cadre were from sections of the British Raj that, in August 1947, became part of India rather than Pakistan. They were, in other words, *muhajirs* (refugees) in the country they dominated in the immediate postindependence period. And, as *muhajirs*, they lacked a solid political support base in Pakistan on which they could depend for mundane things like elections. A second difference was that the Muslim League lacked the three years' experience in governing provinces (1936–1939) that the Congress party had gained under the 1935 India Act. In 1947, therefore, the Congress party leadership was better trained for its awesome and novel tasks of organizing and administering a new democratic political system. In Pakistan the combination of an uncertain political base in most of the country and inexperience in governance by the ruling party had a negative impact on the democratic experiment.

There was a smaller contingent of the post-1947 Pakistani political and intellectual elite that had its home base in the Muslim majority area of northwest British India that became the western wing of Pakistan. They were concentrated in Lahore and Rawalpindi—the principal government, trade, and education centers in western Punjab—where they had been exposed to very similar educational and career experiences as the *muhajir* elite families. This largely Punjabi urban elite formed coalitions with the *muhajir* elite that dominated Pakistani politics in the 1947–1953 period through their control of the Muslim League, and into the 1960s through their near monopolization of the top posts in the bureaucracy. In the economic sphere, the Karachi-based *muhajirs* and the Lahore-based Punjabis dominated the private industrial sector—the "twenty-two families" that introduced industrial enterprises into Pakistan where none of any size had existed before 1947.

One very important social and economic elite group that was not fully accommodated into the national political system in the post-1947 period was the well-organized and powerful rural landowning elite in the Punjab, the "administered" (eastern) NWFP districts and some rural areas of Sind. These families, the dominant elite in most of rural Punjab in 1947, also contributed a high proportion of the Muslim army officers in the British military units that provided the basis for the Pakistani army in 1947. While they had dominated Punjabi provincial politics before 1939, they were newcomers into the Muslim League in the mid-1940s.[1]

The Punjabi/Pathan landowning families that dominated the officer corp in the Pakistan Army thus were virtually unrepresented in the core group of top leadership in the ruling Muslim League. By 1951 party politics in West Pakistan was evolving into an intraelite struggle between the largely *muhajir* and urban Punjabi Muslim League leadership, concentrated in Karachi, Rawalpindi, and Lahore, and the firmly established but fractionalized rural elites in the Punjab and eastern NWFP.

Given the familial connection between the army's officer corps and this rural elite there was a natural tendency for the military to tilt toward the latter group of leaders. Some of the problems the Muslim League government had with the army in the early days of independence grew out of this antagonistic sociopolitical environment.

The rural landowning elite in Sind and the tribal ethnic elites in the NWFP and Baluchistan, based on intricate kinship networks that extend into Afghanistan and Iran, shared the Punjabi rural elite's reservations about the Muslim League-dominated political system. The Sindhis objected to the *muhajir* domination of Karachi after 1947 as this allegedly provided these "outsiders" with an inordinate influence over Sind politics, to the perceived detriment of the Sindhi elite. Important elements in the Pathan (NWFP) and Baluchi "tribal" elite system had similar complaints but directed at different targets. They even demonstrated a lack of enthusiasm with the very concept of Pakistan because, in their view, such a political entity would inevitably be dominated by the principal threat to their traditional tribal system—the Punjabis, who constituted about 60 percent of the population in West Pakistan. While it took several years for these local elites to learn how to play politics at the national level, their dominance of politics at the provincial and local level in their areas was never seriously challenged by the Muslim League-based elite.

In West Pakistan in 1947 there was virtually no industrial labor class—as usually defined—for the simple reason that there were no industrial enterprises of any note. Some initial efforts at the organization of workers in communications or service enterprises met with only limited success, and thus the labor "movement" was an incidental factor in West Pakistani politics until the mid-1960s, by which time a few large factories were operative. Similarly, no peasant organizations of any significance had been formed in West Pakistan prior to 1947, and the few that had been established—almost entirely by Hindus and Sikhs—disappeared with the mass transfer of population that accompanied partition. Thus labor and peasant organizations were most notable for their absence in West Pakistan in the early postindependence period.

The Failure of Democratic Experiments: 1947–1958

There was a great deal of similarity between the political, economic, and intellectual elites at the national level in both India and Pakistan in 1947. The very different political histories of the two countries in the post-1947 period thus cannot be attributed to differences in the political values and objectives of the dominant groups in their respective national elites, but rather to the very different circumstances and conditions under which they sought to establish political institutions and processes in their country.

Pakistan's failure to establish and maintain a democratic political system has certainly not been from a lack of both elite and popular support for some form of democratic system. While some Pakistanis may have questioned the appropriateness of a democratic system for Pakistan in the 1960s and thereafter, they usually added either (1) "at this time [or stage] of our development," or (2) that the democratic system should be based on "Islamic" rather than "Western" principles. That all political leaders and all political parties and organizations, including the Islamic parties, proclaimed their dedication to some form of democracy is indicative of the broad popular support for democratic concepts, and this is reflected in the political history of Pakistan since 1947.

Few countries in the world have gone through as many experiments in as short a period in their efforts to formulate a constitutional and political system based on democratic principles. Since 1947 Pakistan has had five constitutions written and adopted (if the heavily amended versions of the British 1935 India Act and the 1973 Constitution are included), and there were three extended periods in which martial law emergency regimes replaced the civilian government. While there is no uniform pattern in either the constitution formation process or in the structure and operational modes of the martial law regimes, there have been several perceptible trends in the Pakistani political environment in which these developments occurred.

In the period from 1947 to 1956 the basic organic law under which Pakistan was governed was the 1935 India Act, as amended by Pakistan in 1947. There were several features of the 1935 Act (as amended) and of the political situation as it emerged in Pakistan that seriously complicated the task of formulating a democratic constitution and establishing a government based on this organic law. One of the more important was the decision of the "Father of Pakistan," M. A. Jinnah, to retain the position of governor-general, with the broad powers concentrated in that office, in the first Pakistan government. This proved to be a crucial decision, as it set the basic trend toward an authoritarian system (just as Jawaharlal Nehru's decision to serve as prime minister in India's first postindependence government set a trend toward democracy). Jinnah may not have intended for his decision to have this effect, but it did set the tone thereafter for the power relationships in Pakistan between the executive and the other branches of government. There has been an ongoing debate in Pakistan for three decades over the virtues of a presidential system versus a parliamentary system, but it is a meaningless exercise in real political terms. Except for the chaotic 1951–1958 period, when there was no strong leadership anywhere, the prime ministers (Liaquat Ali Khan, 1948–1951, and Zulfikar Bhutto, 1972–1977) have ruled just as much in the governor-general "colonial" tradition as the presidents who held office in other periods.[2]

Liaquat Ali Khan's assassination in 1951 proved to be particularly destabilizing, as the Muslim-League-managed political process under which a democratic constitutional system was being established fell apart—literally. The period from 1951 to 1956 was one in which there was no effective leadership from any source in Pakistan for other than very brief periods. National politics in these tumultuous years were characterized both by bitter factional strifes among "allied" political groups within the cabinets and national assembly and by highly publicized but rather meaningless contests for power—since they invariably lacked the requisite support base required—between the governor-generals and the prime ministers.

Another important factor in the politics of the 1947–1956 period was the fact that the *muhajir* leaders of the Muslim League had only distant and tenuous ties with the local elites in West Pakistan except in a few large urban areas like Karachi, Lahore, and Rawalpindi. After independence the Muslim League sought to accommodate some of the politicized local elites into the Muslim League and/or the government but only with limited and temporary success. Thus the apparent reluctance of some Muslim Leaguers to support the introduction of a functioning democratic system was due, in part, to their lacking a solid political base in Pakistan. While some of the local elite had been recruited into the Muslim League in or before 1947, their sense of identity with and loyalty to the party was limited. Once the party began a slow process of disintegration after Liaquat Ali Khan's assassination in 1951, a large proportion of these new recruits left the Muslim League for other parties.

Another serious deficiency of the Muslim League as a ruling party was its inability to establish itself as a dominant national party with some level of support within all ethnic and social groups in all regions of the country. This was evident in their retention, despite Jinnah's admonitions immediately after partition, of some policies that prevented the Muslim League from assuming the role of a national party—e.g., the "two nation theory" and the "separate electorate" system, under which the electorate was divided between Muslims and non-Muslims in the allocation of legislative seats. This may have made some sense when the Muslim League was portraying itself as the spokesman for what it defined as an "endangered species" under the British Raj, the Muslim minority. But it was an antinational, anti-integrationist policy in the postpartition period, when the Muslims constituted around 95 percent of the population in West Pakistan and about 80 percent in East Pakistan. The Muslim League, in other words, never became a national party for all Pakistanis, and even managed to alienate a majority of the Muslims in East Pakistan, the NWFP, and Baluchistan in what was widely interpreted as an effort to impose rule by *muhajirs* on the country.

With this failure to absorb key elites from large and important social groups in both wings of Pakistan, the Muslim League failed to assume the character that enabled the Congress party to play such a critical role in India—i.e., a political umbrella under which virtually all important social and economic groups could function politically and could hope to be suitably rewarded. The consequence was the extreme factionalization of Pakistani politics and political organizations in the early 1950s. There were almost as many political organizations as there were political leaders and/or social and ethnic groups. While these eventually coalesced into ten or twelve stable political factions with reasonably solid social/ regional bases, the coalitions of parties they organized on an ad hoc basis rarely had much longevity, and indeed could often be disrupted by the leader of one minor faction in one minor party.[3] Strong and stable governments capable of introducing and implementing basic political, economic, and social programs were not forthcoming—or at least such was the popular perception in Pakistan.

The Constituent Assembly, as reconstituted in 1954, reflected both the collapse of the Muslim League and the highly factionalized political party structure that had taken its place. The 1956 Constitution thus reflected a basic distrust of a strong central government intrinsic to a political system dominated by a large number of parties that represented local or regional interests, none of which had anything remotely re-sembling either a national base or an extensive organizational structure above the local level, with the exception of the small Islamic parties. The political system defined in the organic law was almost classically democratic, providing for broad freedoms for the people, political organizations, and the press, a responsible parliamentary system, and a federal structure that allocated responsibility to the states on the subjects that were most crucial to them. The 1956 Constitution, however, did not do two important things. First, it did not provide the basis for a reason-ably effective and stable government at the central level, and the popular view was that the central government was weak, ineffective, and incapable of providing strong leadership on domestic or international issues. The second deficiency in the 1956 Constitution was the failure to provide adequate checks on the emergency powers given to the presi-dent, including the power to suspend the constitution. From 1956 to 1958 there was a bitter contest between the president and the prime minister, both elected by the National Assembly, essentially over the leadership of the central government. As his ultimate weapon, President Iskandar Mirza declared a state of emergency in 1958, suspended the constitution, dissolved the cabinet, and assumed full powers himself. He retained these only for a month, however, as the army then stepped in and declared its own emergency, proclaimed martial law, outlawed political parties, and shortly thereafter, abolished the 1956 Constitution because of its supposed unsuitability for Pakistan.

The Ayub Khan Period: 1958–1969

The first martial law regime (1958–1962), headed by General Ayub Khan, borrowed extensively from the British martial law system. But General Ayub and the coterie of military officers and bureaucrats around him differed from the British in that there was no intention of reestablishing the 1956 constitutional system once the "crisis" was over. Retention of martial law for an extended period was not a likely proposition. While rule by the military had substantial support from the rural landed elite in the Punjab and the eastern NWFP districts that provided most of the officer corps, it was endured rather than supported by the more highly politicized public in Lahore, Rawalpindi and *muhajir*-dominated Karachi, as well as in Baluchistan, rural Sind, the western districts of the NWFP, and East Pakistan. A return to some form of *civilian* government in which the various component parts of the country would regain a voice in its governance was thus a political necessity. Ayub Khan displayed a remarkable talent in devising a system in the 1962 Constitution that preserved the central role of the presidency while conceding some powers and autonomy to representative institutions, the cabinet, and the courts. Moreover, this was disguised as an interim stage in a restoration, under more appropriate conditions, of a fully democratic system.

The 1962 Constitution was not the product of an elected Constituent Assembly but rather of a Constitution Commission appointed by and responsible to Ayub Khan. It has been called a de Gaullist type of constitution because of the way in which real political power was concentrated in the presidency. But perhaps its most distinctive features were what were termed the "Basic Democracy" principles, which ranged from a limited but real decentralization of powers to district level bodies (a very non-de-Gaullian concept) to an indirect elective system for the president and the National Assembly and state assemblies by the 100,000 Basic Democrats. This election system eliminated the concept of universal suffrage except at the very lowest (village) level of the Basic Democracies, but it was acceptable to most local elite families, particularly in the rural areas of West Pakistan.[4] The *muhajir* and urban elite families were less supportive of the 1962 political system, but only at the very last stage of the Ayub era did they initiate any serious protest movements.

Ayub's intention initially had been to establish a nonparty system but it quickly became clear that this would be counterproductive. Ayub then moved to the opposite extreme, legalized virtually all parties that applied, and formed his own party from an interesting combination of political factions. What was rather astonishing was that the 1962 constitution, Ayub Khan's rather cleverly disguised authoritarian system, went along from 1962 to 1969 with no serious political challenges. There were the recurrent troubles in East Pakistan (particularly after the 1965 Indo-Pakistani War), but these were handled with the usual combination of political repression followed by limited concessions to Bengali Muslim demands, and things returned to what passed for normal in this always difficult and potentially explosive relationship. Minor problems in Baluchistan and the NWFP were also handled through a careful application of carrot-and-stick measures. The rapid collapse of Ayub Khan and the Basic Democracy systems in 1969, therefore, came as rather a surprise to the Pakistani public. But there were several important political, social, and economic developments in Pakistan that contributed to Ayub's resignation and the restoration of a martial law regime.

The military had never been too enthusiastic about the "civilianization" of the martial law regime in 1962 and the reconstitution of the political system under Ayub into something close to a pure bureaucratic polity. The relatively balanced relationship that had emerged between the Punjabi-dominated military and the *muhajir*-dominated bureaucracy in the 1958–1962 period had been tilted distinctly in favor of the bureaucrats, who dominated both the Basic Democracy system at the district level and the central government as the "right arm of the president." Up until the 1965 Indo-Pakistani War, the military continued to be paid off in budgetary terms reasonably well and had few legitimate complaints. But with the total suspension of U.S. military assistance after the 1965 war, and the great pressure placed upon the budget merely for the replacement of equipment that had been destroyed in the conflict, the usual kinds of payoffs to the officer corps were now much more difficult to arrange.

The 1965 war had another impact on the Pakistani military. The poor quality of the generalship displayed by the army commanders on the battlefield was potentially embarrassing. The Pakistani public was, of course, not informed of this, but rather was told that the Pakistani army was on the verge of a major victory over the Indian Army when the cease-fire was declared. Then when Zulfikar Bhutto, who resigned (on request) as Ayub's foreign minister in 1966, denounced Ayub for accepting a cease-fire when "victory was in Pakistan's grasp," a large proportion of the higher levels of the officer corps at first quietly, and then more publicly, supported Bhutto's charges. This undermined a key support base for the Ayub Khan government—the military—when the political movement against him reached crisis proportions in the winter of 1968–1969.

The Ayub period was one of generally solid and impressive economic development in Pakistan—primarily in West Pakistan but in some significant respects in East Pakistan as well.[5] While this enhanced his reputation in the international aid community, it had at best mixed consequences for his political system. Ayub introduced a very moderate land reform program, usually described by foreign observers and Pakistani "progressives" as "token" since very little land became available for redistribution. It may have been token in terms of immediate economic benefits for most of the landless and tenant families in Punjab and Sind, but it did raise serious concerns among the landed interests in both states—previously reasonably solid supporters of Ayub.

Ayub also tried to introduce a more equitable distribution of administrative positions and of government revenues and foreign aid between East and West Pakistan, and with some success. There were still major imbalances between the two wings in 1969 when Ayub was forced out of office but these were much reduced over what they had been in 1962. But few .East Pakistanis gave Ayub any credit for what was accomplished, while the *muhajir* and Lahori families that had prospered from their near-monopoly on high bureaucratic positions were distressed by having to share the spoils, with East Pakistanis primarily, and thus were not inclined to support Ayub in 1969.

While the political parties had been legalized by Ayub Khan, they remained as badly factionalized on regional (ethnic), social, and personality lines as they had been before 1958. Some of the factions coalesced in Ayub's Conventional Muslim League (not a direct descendant of the original ML) in order to gain a few tawdry fruits of office. Others formed coalitions for major events, such as the 1965 presidential elections, but then went their own ways.

Probably the critical factor in the organization of a major political movement against the Ayub Khan government and the 1962 Constitution was an event that the system was ill-prepared to address. In late 1968 President Ayub had a serious stroke and the general expectation was that he did not have long to live or, in any case, would be incapacitated from continuing in office. The immediate effect was an upsurge in anti-Basic-Democracies political activity in both East and West Pakistan. To everyone's surprise Ayub Khan recovered enough to reassume his presidential duties, but by early 1969 he lacked any reliable support base. The military, referring to the broad-based party and regional demands for Ayub's overthrow, persuaded the president to resign, reinstalled a martial law regime under the commanding general, Yahya Khan, abrogated the 1962 Constitution, and called for national elections for a constituent assembly to prepare and approve yet another constitution.

The Second Martial Law Regime

The Yahya Khan martial law regime in the 1969–1970 period was a very different enterprise from the first martial law regime under Ayub Khan. While Yahya Khan held full powers as chief martial law administrator (CMLA), he defined his role in very different terms from those that Ayub had in 1958, as: (1) preparations for national elections to a new Constituent Assembly; and (2) encouragement of all political groups, including East Pakistani parties with broad autonomy demands (the Awami League), to participate in the political and electoral process. With the announcement that elections would be held by the end of 1970, the political protest movements in both East and West Pakistan were suspended and preparations for the elections commenced.

Yahya Khan also made two basic concessions to the East Pakistanis in 1969. First, he eliminated the fifty-fifty distribution of seats between East and West Pakistan and instead, using the "one man, one vote" principle, allocated a majority of seats in the new Constituent Assembly to East Pakistan. This was done despite the fact that, if only *Muslim* voters were counted, there was close to an even split between the two wings. This meant that the balance in the assembly was tipped toward East Pakistan because of its large Hindu minority. Second, Yahya Khan abolished the unified state in West Pakistan in response to regional demands and restored the four states of Punjab, Sind, NWFP, and Baluchistan, in the process providing East Pakistan with an advantageous bargaining position in the new assembly. Thus it was Yahya Khan's application of some basic democratic principles that, in 1971, proved a major complication in the complex politics that led to the Pakistan civil war and, eventually, the 1971 Indo-Pakistani war and the secession of the new state of Bangladesh, the former East Pakistan.

The December 1970 elections were held on schedule and were perhaps the only totally free, fair, and uninhibited national elections that Pakistan has held since independence. The election results were unexpected both in the eastern and western wings. The Awami League won all but two of the seats allocated to East Pakistan in the Constituent Assembly, thus gaining an absolute majority for the party despite the fact that it had not contested a single seat in the western wing. The new Pakistan People's Party (PPP), founded by Zulfikar Bhutto, won a majority of the seats in the west, but under rather curious circumstances.

In Punjab the PPP did quite well in Lahore and Rawalpindi in both seats won and votes. But in rural Punjab, where it won a large number of seats, its proportion of the vote generally ranged from 35 percent to 45 percent, and its victory was due to the division of the majority vote in each constituency. In rural Sind the situation was similar, while in *muhajir*-dominated Karachi the PPP did not do well. Nor was Bhutto's party able to make any real inroads into NWFP or Baluchistan against the dominant ethnic parties. Thus the PPP gained quite a few seats, but many of them from very insecure bases, and this became an important factor in determining the party's policy in the 1971 Bangladesh crisis.

The December 1970 elections had seemed to lay the groundwork for an orderly and coherent formulation of a new constitution. The Awami League, the East Pakistani majority party, had good relations with several of the smaller West Pakistani parties. The major obstacle, however, was the PPP, the majority party in West Pakistan, but which controlled only about one-third of seats in the National Assembly and was thus incapable of exercising any significant influence on policy matters. Bhutto, who was not prepared to accept the status of an opposition party leader, first demanded a coalition with the Awami League, with himself as deputy prime minister. When this was rejected by the Awami League, the PPP then sought to undermine the whole constitution-making process and, if necessary, to delay the organization of a national government. But given their own vulnerable position in the west and Bhutto's lack of confidence in the loyalty of some of his own MPs, this was a ticklish game.[6]

The economic, political, cultural, and strategic considerations that impelled the diverse but socially strongly based regional leadership in both wings of the country made cooperation on anything but very short-term and expedient conditions impossible. The Awami League and its leader, Mujibur Rahman (Mujib), had established the basis for such a coalition with several West Pakistani parties before March 1971; but this was an exercise in blatant expediency and there were doubts that these constituted a satisfactory basis for a viable long-term relationship between the two wings. Bhutto's demand for a coalition between the dominant parties in the eastern and western wings made good sense in the long-range development of a democratic system or, indeed, of any kind of political system. In the Pakistan of early 1971 any other basis for a democratic government was probably unworkable. On this issue then, in 1971, Bhutto was right and Mujib was wrong. But then much of the Awami League leadership was not particularly interested in a democratic system in a *unified* Pakistan.

The series of events leading to the crisis of 1971 were disastrous for Yahya Khan, the martial law regime, and for the military's reputation as interveners in and manipulators of Pakistan's political developments. This was not totally deserved, as Pakistani civilian politicians did little to prevent the series of crises that led to the dismemberment of Pakistan and meekly followed along or, as in Bhutto's case, made sure nothing obstructed dismemberment once the process had started. With the clearly evident defeat in the war with India, Yahya was forced to resign and the military made way for a remarkable oddity in any polity—a civilian head of a martial law regime, Zulfikar Bhutto. The Yahya Khan martial law regime is best known, of course, for the Bangladesh disaster and the ignominious defeat in the war with India. But on balance, it should also be noted for its liberal policies toward political parties, political activities, and elections in the 1969 to March 1971 period, and even for the rather restrained political controls exercised over West Pakistan in the March-to-December 1971 period, when a civil war was raging in East Pakistan. No parties were banned, very few people were imprisoned in the west for political activities, and Bhutto and the PPP were allowed to lay the foundations for what became Pakistan's first reasonably effective civilian government since the early 1950s.

The Bhutto Government (1972–1977) and the 1973 Constitution

Bhutto and his PPP government took office in January 1972 with a number of distinct political advantages. The military and, to a lesser extent, the bureaucracy were blamed by the Pakistani public for the 1971 disasters and were in no position to lock horns with a resolute prime minister who had a mind of his own and a well-defined political program. Indeed for the next three to four years, both the military and bureaucracy tended to shield themselves behind the vigorous Bhutto government. While this served their purposes at the time, it was an irritant and a blow to their pride and self-esteem—which may help explain their overreaction to a quite manageable political protest movement following the 1977 national elections.

Bhutto also used the distress with the 1971 events in what remained of Pakistan to appeal to a sense of dedication to the nation. This worked reasonably well until 1973, even in the NWFP and Baluchistan where the PPP had a weak political base and the state governments were dominated by opposition parties. Thereafter Bhutto had to shift to different tactics to maintain the PPP's dominant position throughout Pakistan. In rural Punjab, the political heartland of Pakistan after 1971, Bhutto initiated a concerted and, by 1974, an increasingly successful effort to entice the dominant landowning elite families in several key districts out of their affiliation to opposition parties and into the PPP on pragmatic terms. However, a price was paid by the PPP establishment, as some of the secondary elite families that had joined the party before 1970 and had won seats in the national or state assembly elections again found themselves relegated to a subordinate position in their local area. Some tried to fight this out within the party, while others denounced Bhutto and moved over to the opposition parties—but in a disorganized and incoherent fashion that did not particularly enhance the strength of the opposition in rural Punjab.[7]

Bhutto was much less successful in his efforts to absorb key elements of the dominant ethnic elite families in the NWFP and Baluchistan, and had to resort to more directly repressive tactics as well as more subtle programs of political organization in these two states. By 1974 he had declared illegal the ethnic-based political parties in the NWFP and Baluchistan that had formed a coalition called, rather ironically, the *National* Awami Party (NAP), and had replaced the NAP-led state governments—that still had majority support in the state assemblies—with "governor's rule." In both states Bhutto sent in the military to conduct a vigorous and rather bloody campaign against the protest movements organized by "dissident forces."

Potentially more important perhaps was Bhutto's concerted effort to enlist young, educated Pathans and Baluchis from secondary elite or nonelite families into the PPP organizational structure as a counterforce to the ethnic opposition parties that were still dominated by the traditional ethnic elite. This was a part of Bhutto's most important long-range political strategy throughout Pakistan—the creation of local party organizational structures recruited primarily among young educated Pakistanis. It was still a dominant characteristic of Pakistani political parties in the early 1970s that they consisted of "national" leaders with a few state and regional subordinates scattered around some areas of the country, but nothing resembling a real party organization or party cadre system.

After assuming the presidency in 1972, Bhutto placed a high priority on organizational programs, and this time with considerable success. The PPP used student organizations, labor unions, and welfare and rural development programs as the institutional base through which PPP cadres were recruited into the party. While the results were not particularly impressive when compared to party organizational activity in India, they were far more extensive than the cadre systems of the rest of the Pakistani parties combined and much more effective. The PPP was not a national party quite yet, as its organization in Baluchistan and the Western NWFP districts was still weak, but by the time of the 1977 elections its organizational capacities in the Punjab, Sind (other than Karachi), and some eastern NWFP districts were quite impressive.

The 1973 Constitution was an integral part of Bhutto's well-conceived political strategy designed to build up the PPP's political base at the expense of the opposition parties while still maintaining a non-confrontational relationship with these parties. The constitution represented a significant and pragmatic compromise between Bhutto and the widely divergent views (from each other as well as the PPP) held by the opposition parties. The 1973 Constitution restored a British style of parliamentary system similar in form to that of the 1956 Constitution, but with some critical modifications. Under the 1973 Constitution Bhutto became prime minister rather than CMLA/president. But in actual practice most of the essential features of the martial law regime were retained, if in a somewhat disguised formula.[8] While Pakistan now had a prime minister and cabinet that were formally responsible to the parliament, the 1973 Constitution actually operated more like Ayub's 1962 presidential system than the 1956 parliamentary constitution. Prime Minister Bhutto exercised very broad powers, virtually uninhibited by any sense of power sharing with his colleagues in the cabinet, the National Assembly, or the PPP executive.

The 1973 constitutional system thus was democratic in theory and format but no less authoritarian than the Ayub Khan and Yahya Khan governments in practice. Indeed Bhutto was far more skillful than either of his military predecessors in exploiting the various "emergency" clauses in the constitution to his own advantage. As Khalid B. Sayeed noted:

> Ever since Ayub seized power in 1958, Pakistan has been governed by a Bonapartist regime. By this is meant not just the rule of an arbitrary dictator but the rule of a leader who derived his power and authority from a well-established institution like the army, in the case of Ayub, or from a political movement, in the case of Bhutto.[9]

Bhutto's skill in handling politics in the key states of Punjab and Sind had, by 1975, made him somewhat overconfident of his capacity to do this on a continuing basis. He had a strong sense of disdain for virtually all of the leaders of the other political parties, whom he considered—not too inaccurately—as tired, old relics of the past, unqualified to serve in high governmental offices. Nor was Bhutto open to coalitions between the PPP and the opposition parties, or to the accommodation of opposition leaders into the PPP. The eventual consequences of this was a development unique in Pakistan's history—an effective coalition of all the major opposition parties in the four states. Nine parties—ranging from Islamic, conservative, and regional to moderate leftist—formed the Pakistan National Alliance (PNA) to fight the 1977 general elections together against the PPP. The PNA had some strong centers of support: in the NWFP and Baluchistan, where regional parties (united in the NAP) still dominated politics even though they had been declared illegal in 1973; in Karachi, where the *muhajirs* and large Pathan and Baluchi migratory communities supported different opposition parties; and in Lahore among the old Muslim League members. But in rural Punjab and Sind, the PPP had absorbed much of the landed elite and could expect to do very well in areas which elected about 60 percent of Pakistan's MPs.

It is probable that the PPP would have won a substantial majority in a fair and honest election. It had a much better organized party, a leader who was popular with the public (if less so with some elements of the elite), and plenty of money. But the election was rigged, at least in some of the urban constituencies in Lahore, Rawalpindi, and Karachi.

Whether this was on orders from Bhutto or by overconcerned party and government bureaucrats is unclear. The PNA protested and, to everyone's astonishment, maintained its coalition in the organization of a protest movement that demanded new elections under "impartial" (military?) supervision. The movement was largely confined to the urban areas where the PNA parties had some strength, with occasional scattered outbursts in NWFP and Baluchistan.

There is little doubt that the protest movement could have been controlled, but the cooperation of the army was required. This provided the military with the opportunity some of the top officers had been waiting for since 1972, when Bhutto had summarily dismissed a large number of the commanding officers and replaced them with officers whom Bhutto expected would be grateful to him for their promotion. Apparently what most impressed these officers, however, was the casual way in which Bhutto dealt with their careers for his own advantage, and the realization that they too could be dismissed at any time on the whim of the prime minister.

It was with some elation, therefore, that they accepted Bhutto's "temporary" resignation, reinstalled a "temporary" martial law regime, and then moved in to restore peace and stability, with virtually no effort on their part since the PNA cooperated throughout Pakistan in July–August 1977. As it turned out, however, this was the start of Pakistan's third and longest martial law regime, 1977–1985, under the leadership of CMLA/President Mohammad Zia-ul-Huq.

Political factors were the principal cause of the downfall of Bhutto and the elected civilian government, but economic issues played some role as well. Bhutto's nationalization of several key Pakistani private industrial firms was first introduced in the 1972–1973 period to mollify some of the middle-class urban leftists who had flocked to the PPP when it was founded in 1968. Bhutto's economic policies had shifted significantly by 1974-1975 because of the high priority he placed on absorbing the large landlord elite in the Punjab and Sind into the PPP—to the distress of the party's urban leftists, some of whom quit the party. But it was not possible to reverse the nationalization program quickly, even though it was a disaster in economic development terms and had not proved as rewarding to the labor union movement in economic payoffs as originally hoped.

Similarly, Bhutto's land reform program, somewhat more ambitious in real terms than the one introduced by Ayub Khan, had to be moderated in order to avoid alienating the landed elite. By 1977 the only group that was still supportive of Bhutto's economic policies was the traditional landed elite in Punjab and Sind and some of the technocrats in the economic ministries. Bhutto could still elicit responses from the public with his immense skills as a populist orator, but these were beginning to become counterproductive to a good part of the Pakistani public. This may help explain the lack of any very substantial public outburst in response to his removal from office in 1977 or even his execution in 1979.

Another factor that also played a modest role in Bhutto's fall in 1977 was his failure to provide the concept of "Islamic socialism" espoused by the PPP with any substance. Bhutto had tried to broaden the appeal of his moderately leftist—which he called "socialist"—program in 1970 by basing it on a very loose interpretation of certain egalitarian principles in Islamic theology. The reversal of his government's socialist economic policies in the 1973–1974 period did not, however, lead to an emphasis on more traditional Islamic principles. The 1973 Constitution, like its 1956 and 1962 (as amended) predecessors, paid lip service to the concept of Pakistan as an Islamic state and society, but in fact there was nothing in the functioning of any of these constitutions that would distinguish Pakistan from the non-Islamic states in South Asia. Any possibility that Bhutto and the PPP might elicit support from the Islamic political parties or, more important, from several powerful Islamic social and religious organizations, never emerged. Thus Bhutto's "Islamic socialism" ended up antagonizing both the professional leftists and the professional Muslim activists.

The Zia-ul-Huq "Islamic" Martial Law Regime

The first eighteen months of Zia's period as CMLA/president was marked by uncertainty and no very clear indications that he and his coterie of generals and bureaucrats had seriously considered an alternative system to the 1973 Constitution. Unlike Ayub Khan, who had moved early in the first martial law period to set the basis for the Basic Democracy institutions later incorporated into the 1962 Constitution, and unlike Yahya Khan, who quickly announced elections for a Constituent Assembly and then held them on schedule, Zia fluttered all over the place, promising elections, stressing the need for true islamization, and trying to find a reliable political base for a civilian government somewhere in Pakistan's party structure.

On taking office in July 1977, Zia promised elections within ninety days and the transfer of power to elected representatives. But with the gradual splintering of the PNA coalition and the probability that the PPP would win an election, Zia felt he had no option but to postpone elections and, most important, allow Bhutto to be placed on trial, allegedly for having ordered the murder of a minor political leader. Finally in early March 1979, two weeks before Bhutto's execution in April, Zia announced that elections would be held on 12 November 1979. However, Zia again had second thoughts on parliamentary elections, which he again postponed in September, while espousing true islam-ization and calling for local-body elections on a nonparty basis as a preliminary to national elections.

At this point Zia's credibility seemed to have worn thin with virtually everyone including, if reports are correct, some of the highest officers in the army and top bureaucrats. Several political parties went along with Zia but only on a few specific issues. No social, regional, or economic groups were supportive, again except on specific issues. Thus Zia's regime had no popular base despite his frantic efforts to exploit the islamization issue. But when things had reached a critical stage internally, it was the Soviet Union's military intervention in Afghanistan in late December 1979 that may have saved Zia. In these circumstances the military and a select group of bureaucrats considered it best to avoid the in-system coup that would have removed Zia and placed another general in the presidency. Instead, Zia was later able to carry out a wholesale purge of the top ranks of the military and replace them with officers who were, in some instances, from the same regional and social background as the president.

It was also in this international context that Zia finally began to demonstrate some political skills that benefited his regime domestically as well. He was able to revive the U.S. connection on fairly generous aid terms because of the U.S. government's concern over developments in Afghanistan and the perceived Soviet threat to Pakistan's security—a view that was shared by much of the Pakistani public, according to public opinion polls.

India also cooperated by at times seeming to threaten Pakistan, and thus arousing strong Pakistani nationalist reactions from almost all quarters, while on other occasions by responding to Zia's well-conceived "peace offensive" in ways that enhanced the president's reputation. China and most of the Islamic world also added their public endorse-ment of the Zia government, and this had a positive impact on Pakistani opinion.

By 1981 Zia appeared much more confident and directed in his leadership. In March he introduced a Provisional Constitutional Order that had two objectives in view: (1) the "islamization" of the judicial system; and (2) the establishment of a nominated national assembly as an advisory council (majlis-e-shoora) to the president.

Zia's first goal faced strong opposition from most judges and lawyers, while much of the public was not particularly enthusiastic about the substitution of Islamic (shariat) courts for the familiar British-style courts and the more informal judgments by consensus made by the village councils at the village level.[10] The majlis-e-shoora, while never a significant institution, was nevertheless broadly representative, with substantial political party (including PPP) membership. Zia was careful to heed its views on several important, if secondary, issues in which it differed from the reported position of the military and the civil bureaucracy.

A number of developments in 1983 made it clear to President Zia that something more than nominal concessions to the hodgepodge of opposition factions were needed if a domestic political crisis was to be avoided. Local-body elections were held on a nonparty basis in August-September 1983. Once again, party candidates, including a large number from the PPP, ran as "independents" but with their political affiliations well known, and won a high proportion of the seats. The PPP did quite well in both the administered and unadministered districts of the NWFP, a new area of strength for them, as well as in their old bases in rural Punjab and Sind.

Perhaps even more unsettling to the government were the major political disturbances that broke out in rural Sind in August 1983. These were different from any previous protest movement in Pakistan in that they were centered in rural areas and were not initially the products of any of the political parties, but rather of the local landowning elite and tenants, assisted by several very prominent Sindhi *pirs* (religious leaders) who helped organize the movement and provided a mass base for the demonstrations in some areas.

Coincidental with the outburst of the Sind movement in August 1983, President Zia had announced his plans for the establishment of a new political system in Pakistan that he hoped would elicit some support from political parties and the public. Under this program there would be phased elections, first for the provincial assemblies and then, by March 1985, for a national assembly, which would then be followed by the "transfer of power" to the elected representatives. Prior to the transfer of power, the 1973 Constitution would be amended, with Zia reportedly planning to substitute a presidential system for the parliamentary form.

Things did not work out quite as planned. The provincial and national assembly elections were held at the same time in March 1985, a few months after a rather dubious referendum in which the Pakistanti people (or the 20 to 25 percent that actually used their franchise) voted in support of a statement that endorsed the martial law regime's concept of Pakistan as an Islamic state. Zia then declared that the referendum constituted the public's endorsement of his program and, thus, support of him for a five-year term (1985–1989) as president.

The 1985 elections were initially run on a nonparty basis, although parties finally were allowed to set up "independent" candidates if they had registered properly. However, by the time this open door policy was adopted, most parties were already formally committed to boycotting the elections and it was too late for them to reverse their position. Nevertheless, a large number of party candidates (including some seventy PPP members) contested and won over a hundred of the 230 seats. The voter turnout in this election was about 57 percent, a striking contrast to the informal boycott of the referendum by most of the public, and the highest turnout in any election in Pakistan's history. A large number of candidates who held high positions in the martial law regime or who were identified as supporters of Zia were defeated. The PPP and several other parties publicly denounced the elections as contrived farces, but in private some of their leaders admitted that they had been conducted fairly, if under restrictive terms.[11]

Zia adjusted quickly to the election results and revised some of his earlier plans for systemic changes. The task of amending the 1973 Constitution—any consideration of a new constitution was dropped—was now passed on to the National Assembly, which met on 23 March 1985 and unanimously elected a civilian prime minister, Mohammad Khan Junejo, and his cabinet.

The martial law system, however, was retained for another nine months while President Zia and the largely inexperienced ministers and MNAs ("members, National Assembly") negotiated the terms of the "new" constitutional system. The critical ordinances in this political process in 1985 were: (1) the Revival of the Constitution Order (RCO) of March 1985; (2) the Eighth Constitutional Amendment, generally called the Indemnity Law, of October 1985; and (3) the Political Parties (Amendment) Act of December 1985. These set the basis for the termination of martial law and the reinstitution in January 1986 of the first fully civilian system of government since 1969.

The RCO amended sixty-seven of the 280 articles of the 1973 Constitution, and was described by opposition Pakistani sources as having expanded the powers of the executive in Pakistan. In fact, however, the most critical of these amendments, as proposed, concerned the broad powers already allocated to the prime minister in the 1973 Constitution and redirected these powers to the office of the president. An effort was made in the National Assembly to reword the amendments as proposed by Zia so as to attain an approximate balance in the distribution of powers between the president and the prime minister, and with some success. Legally, however, the tilt remained in favor of the former, as the president retained the legal authority to reassume an authoritarian position under the emergency clauses of the constitution, which he did in June 1988.

The Indemnity Law was primarily intended to protect Zia and his closest cohorts from legal responsibility for any actions taken during the martial law period. The discussion on this issue has been subdued, but it would seem to be intended primarily to protect Zia from retribution for his incredible decision to allow the execution of his predecessor, Zulfikar Bhutto. Zia must now face the grim prospect that he has set a precedent under which a case could be argued for bringing him to trial once he has left office. Whether the Indemnity Law would be honored by a successor government dominated by the PPP is certainly open to question, and this could serve as a deterrent to Zia's voluntary retirement from the presidency even if he should feel so inclined.

The Political Parties (Amendment) Act was submitted to the National Assembly by Zia and eventually passed with several changes. The act, similar to the party registration legislation in India and other South Asian states, requires a party to submit a statement of income and expenditure, a list of office bearers and registered members, and copies of the party's constitution and manifestoes. The law, which also provides for the disbarment of members of the National Assembly or a state assembly who defect from their party, is closely modeled after the antidefection amendment of the Indian constitution that Rajiv Gandhi pushed through in early 1985. While the Political Parties Act prohibits unregistered parties from participating in elections, it does not obstruct normal political activity by the unregistered parties.[12]

Since January 1986 Pakistan has been going through a transitional phase in systemic and organizational terms. The members of the National Assembly, elected on a nonparty basis, have virtually all joined either Prime Minister Junejo's Pakistan Muslim League (PML) or the Independent Parliamentary Group (IPG) organized by several opposition MNAs. The opposition parties, including the Pakistan People's Party, function freely and openly in most situations, with the government exercising restraint in using the rather stringent ordinances on the subject that are still in force. The parties have generally used peaceful and nonviolent tactics in organizing their public meetings and demonstrations, thus not giving the government a legitimate excuse to reimpose stricter political controls.[13]

The press, strictly regulated under both Zia and Bhutto, is probably freer and more open than at any time since the 1970 elections. The press uses its new freedom enthusiastically to editorialize critically on both domestic and international issues, but overall quite responsibly. The legal restrictions on the press were liberalized in July 1986 with the passage of the Criminal Law (Amendment) Bill 1986, which revoked the press curbs that had been imposed in 1979, but the broad legal power of the government to control the press based on pre-1977 legislation is still in force.

• THEORETICAL REVIEW •

The several efforts to establish democratic systems in Pakistan since 1947 were short-lived and never really operational long enough to test their "suitability." These democratic experiments were replaced by authoritarian regimes, usually dominated by the military, that were invariably identified as a transitional stage to a reformed and revised democratic system. In most instances these were not hard-line authoritarian regimes, for they permitted political, social, and regional organizations with differing views on basic issues to function openly, if on a restricted basis. Nor did these authoritarian regimes project alternatives to a democratic political system as their ultimate objective. Thus, while the efforts at democratization have not been successful, the advocacy of democratic principles by most of the political and general public has never wavered, and in the mid-1980s new experiments were again introduced.

There were several factors that contributed to the failure of the democratic experiments. The most commonly noted has been the highly fractionalized political leadership, regionally or ethnically based, that had a limited sense of identity with the "nation" and a predisposition against cooperating with other factions except on the most short-term and expedient basis. Indeed most coalitions of parties were organized as coalitions against other parties or regions rather than alignments based upon a broad consensus on policy.

This fractionalization of political organizations reflected, of course, the serious divisions within the Pakistani political elite in the 1950s. By the mid-1960s under Ayub Khan, the main contenders for a *national* elite status—the *muhajirs* and the Punjabi and Pathan landed interests (which included the military leadership)—had reached a reasonable accommodation on the sharing of power. But this working arrangement, usually described as a "bureaucratic-military polity," still excluded, in all but token ways, the newly emerging Bengali Muslim elite in East Pakistan as well as important ethnic and rural elites in Sind, NWFP, and Baluchistan.

The integration of ethnic communities into the national polity was a major problem and contributed to the political instability and the insertion of authoritarian regimes. A variety of strategies, both enticing and repressive, were used to further the integration process, but with only limited success: a referendum in the NWFP in 1947 that strained democratic credibility; the subordination of four ethnic regions into a single province (West Pakistan) in 1955; its redivision into four states in 1970; Bhutto's repressive measures against the Pathan and Baluchi tribal leadership combined with his efforts to organize a counterelite through the recruitment of young, educated Pathans and Baluchis into the PPP; and Zia's stress on "islamization" and the channeling of substantial resources into NWFP and Baluchistan for development purposes. Unfortunately, the periodic use of repressive force by the central government in these two states remains an integral part of their recent history, and there is as yet no great sense of confidence that the more moderate integrative policies introduced by Zia (e.g., the "affirmative action" principles now being applied for recruitment into the bureaucracy and military) will be retained.

Economic factors and the role of foreign powers are often assumed to have had a substantial impact on the fate of regimes, democratic or authoritarian, in Pakistan. This sounds reasonable, but it is very hard to document as the relationship is rarely clear and direct.

There is, for instance, no apparent correlation between the economic performance of a particular regime and its political fate. The Ayub Khan period (1958–1969) was one of impressive economic growth nationally, but this proved to be inconsequential, either for or against Ayub, in the complex politics of the 1968–1969 period that led to his removal from office.[14] Bhutto had a somewhat worse record in the 1972–1977 period, in part because of two drought-filled years. But the political movement that induced Bhutto to resign in 1977 virtually ignored economic issues and focused almost exclusively on the critical political issue—the charge that Bhutto had rigged the 1977 elections.[15] By 1977 much of the rural landowning elite in Punjab and Sind had been absorbed into the PPP and had been conceded, in essence, control over agricultural policy. While they had reservations about some of Bhutto's policies and rhetoric there was no need to work for his removal from office. The key opposition groups thus were the urban middle class, the Islamic parties, and the Establishment in other minor parties, some intellectuals, the military, and the bureaucracy. While economic factors may have influenced their political decisions, it would appear to be largely coincidental rather than deterministic.

The Zia period (1977–1987) has been one of solid economic growth and comparative prosperity for most Pakistanis. This may have tempered both the extent and the mood of opposition politics, but this is not readily evident. What is clear is that few Pakistanis credit Zia for the improvements in the economy and that his government has had little success in exploiting the economic issue against the opposition. There may be a general principle in Pakistani politics: a government can suffer marginally from a poor economic record but it receives few tangible benefits from a flourishing economy. But then this may be fair, as the Pakistan economy still is heavily dependent upon forces beyond the government's control—the weather, the affluence of the Islamic OPEC countries, and foreign aid.

With regard to the role of external powers, there is no doubt that a number of foreign powers—India, the United States, the Soviet Union, China, Iran, and the West Asian states—intrude into Pakistani politics, intentionally or otherwise, in various ways. What is less clear is that they have much of an impact on Pakistani domestic politics despite the vigorous rhetoric often used on the subject within the Pakistani elite.

s

Ayub Khan, for instance, could strengthen the alliance with the United States in 1959 and then, from 1961 to 1968, virtually abandon it in his effort to achieve a balanced relationship with the United States, China, and the Soviet Union—and all without paying any political price. Bhutto quietly sought to strengthen relations with the United States while, at the same time, resorting to anti-U.S. rhetoric in his appeals to select elements of the Pakistani elite—both to limited effect on his eventual fate.

It is interesting to note that the most vigorous "political" debate in Pakistan in the mid-1980s was not over democratization, but rather the policies of the United States and the Soviet Union on the Afghanistan issue. A substantial proportion of the political elite outside the government—but including some rather conservative Pakistanis with ties into the Zia/Junejo regime—favor an "accommodation with the Soviets" on the grounds that the United States is an unreliable external support force that will "abandon" Pakistan when Washington no longer considers it convenient or necessary to support the Afghanistani resistance through Pakistan. They charge the Zia government with following "U.S. policy"on Afghanistan, alleging that the United States has been the decisive influence on decision making in Pakistan on this issue.

The facts, however, are quite different. Pakistan had adopted its oppositionist policy on the Soviet intervention in Afghanistan, with the support of China and most Islamic states, about eighteen months before it came to terms with the United States on Afghanistan in the fall of 1981, after some tough bargaining. Zia's critics find it expedient to define his policy as "American" rather than "Pakistani," "Islamic," or even "Chinese." But what has been clear during this very difficult period is that Pakistan has not accepted advice, much less dictation, from the United States, the Soviet Union, or any other outside power that is perceived to be against its national or regime interests. Pakistan must pay attention to what the major powers say, but it has stubbornly refused to accept a subordinate role to any of them. The "accommodate-the-Soviets" faction among the Pakistani elite seems prepared to modify this staunchly independent approach to foreign policy, but as yet they lack substantial support among the broader political public.

Perhaps even more equivocal has been the role of Islam in the political process in Pakistan. This is surprising because Pakistan was founded in 1947 as an Islamic state and society. It was presumed that Islamic principles and concepts would provide the framework for the emergent political, social, and economic systems in the "new" state and serve as the integrating force for the heterogeneous and, in some cases, traditionally antagonistic social groups that became Pakistanis.

It has not worked out that way. Islam has generally been an incidental factor in decision making on basic issues since 1947, however effusive the rhetoric employed. It is, for instance, difficult to note any significant differences on economic, political, and even social issues between Pakistan and its non-Islamic South Asian neighbors that are attributable to the Islamic factor. Each Pakistani constitutional system has stipulated that all legislation and ordinances must conform to Islamic principles. But none of these regimes, including that of the ardent advocate of Islamization, Zia-ul-Huq, ever made anything more than perfunctory efforts to provide substance to the proclaimed objective,[16] at least through mid-1988.

There were good reasons for this. The urban, Western-educated Muslim leaders who founded Pakistan were modernists in their political-social views and were not inclined to concede a major role in the governance of Pakistan to the various Islamic fundamentalist factions. The military-bureaucratic oligarchy that emerged in the 1960s was equally insistent on (1) espousing Islam and (2) keeping Islamic organizations and leaders on the periphery of Pakistani politics. Moreover, the force of Islam as a factor in Pakistani politics was substantially limited by the basic division within the Islamic political community between the "populist" Islamic religious leaders and groups and those that identified as "purists," a conflict that dates back to the Moghul dynasty but is still critical to contemporary Islamic society in South Asia. Ayub Khan and Zia made tentative alliances with the "purists," while Bhutto, with his "Islamic socialism" slogan, sought a working arrangement with the "populists." But in none of these instances was there any substance or continuity to policies that, on all sides, were purely expedient.[17]

Islam thus has been a negligible factor in Pakistani politics since 1947, neither contributing to nor seriously obstructing the establishment of democratic institutions and systems to any significant extent. The Islamic parties call for an Islamic democratic system but they have been quite content operating under Western-style constitutions that assured them a broad range of freedom to function as political organizations. It is possible that the Iranian "model" for an Islamic system could emerge in Pakistan, but there is little evidence of this in the mid-1980s. On balance, in any case, the Islam factor appears somewhat more as a support force for democratization, as Zia's failure in his effort to use islamization in legitimating his particular form of authoritarian regime in the 1979–1983 period would seem to indicate.

The failure of the democratic experiments in Pakistan, therefore, is not attributable to the ideological opposition of the principal political, social, or economic elites in the country, but rather to the dissatisfaction of significant elements of the public with their perceived exclusion from the decision-making processes at the national level. These elites tend to be pragmatic and realistic on such matters, not expecting a dominant role but insisting on being involved. They respond positively to the concept of democratization even though some of them had strong reservations about previous experiments. The Zia system must adjust to this if it is to survive.

• FUTURE PROSPECTS •

The termination of martial law on 30 December 1985 and the limited but substantial liberalization policies introduced by President Zia and Prime Minister Junejo subsequently constituted significant steps toward the establishment of a fully democratic system in Pakistan. What are the key factors that persuaded President Zia that the time had come to commence the process of replacing a military-dominated regime with a broader-based civilian government? I would suggest that there are several important long-term social, economic, and political developments that make at least some concessions to a democratization process more difficult to resist in the late 1980s than at any time since independence. The political tactics and games that worked comparatively easily in the 1960s to sustain authoritarian systems no longer appear to be as effective. At least they elicit much more vigorous responses from both within the elite establishment and from a much more highly politicized and involved general public.

One critical factor is the military, and the concern of some high officers with what has happened to the Pakistan officer corps since 1977. Once lauded for its social homogeneity (90 percent from the Punjab and a few districts of eastern NWFP) and its capacity for reaching a consensus on vital issues, the officer corps is now seen to be divided into several groups with different interests and views.[18] Increasing numbers of Sindhis, Pathans from western NWFP, and Baluchis are being absorbed into the military under the government's national integration policy, while those from Punjab and eastern NWFP no longer come almost exclusively from landed elite families.[19] This may make good sense in national political terms, but it is beginning to have a significant, if still limited, impact on the military as a political institution. Moreover, there was increasing competition within the officer corps for assignment to the lucrative and politicized positions with Pakistani units conducting "training" missions in various oil-rich Middle Eastern countries, or to the only slightly less attractive positions in the central and state administrations that had become virtually the preserve of the officer corps since 1977. Zia has indulged in the militarization of the bureaucracy on a far broader scale than either the first or the second martial law regimes, leading to steadily increasing tension within the officer corps, as well as between the bureaucrats who previously held these positions and the officer corp.

There are reports of dissension within the officer corps between those assigned to civilian posts, who thus get access to "informal" sources of income (i.e., corruption), and those unfortunate officers still serving in military units. Some of those who are still military officers may be mollified for their sacrifices by some economic rewards—e.g., free land for homes in high-price urban areas—but at a much lower level than either of the other two categories of officers.

According to some sources there are important differences in the political views of these various categories of officers. Those that are still serving in military commands have doubts that their interests, or that of the military as an institution, are best served by a martial law regime and thus were not opposed to its termination in 1986. On the other hand, those officers holding civilian bureaucratic posts could well find their appointments reconsidered and their places eventually taken by civilian bureaucrats. Moreover, it would probably be difficult for them to work their way back into the regular military chain of command, and they might well end up without an appropriate appointment in either service. This group thus preferred a continuation of martial law or at least of the system in a disguised form under Zia or another military man.

On the other hand, some sources note that the Baluchi, Pathan, and Sindhi officers in the armed forces, and particularly in the air force, have reservations about martial law regimes in particular and excessive military intervention in politics in general. The result of all this is that there is no longer a solid support base for a martial law regime within the military. The military accepted the restoration of a civilian government and is not likely to demand the reinstitution of a martial law regime except under what they perceive to be compelling circumstances.

The bureaucray is also more divided institutionally than at any time in the past.[20] While the Zia regime has been a classic "bureaucratic polity" in basic operational terms since 1977, what is defined as the bureaucracy has changed substantially in the past decade. The intrusion of army officers in large numbers into many of the higher positions of the bureaucracy is a development that civilian bureaucrats consider unfortunate. The bureaucracy welcomed the restoration of a civilian government in 1986 as a step toward the recivilianization of the bureaucracy, although they may still prefer a civilian government of the Bhutto variety—i.e., democratic in form but semiauthoritarian in operation, and thus heavily dependent upon the cooperation of the bureaucrats for decision making and implementation of tasks. But what they do not want is the status quo, and some degree of democratization would now be acceptable to the bureaucracy.

There have been some interesting and potentially important economic developments in Pakistan that, over the next decade, could prove critical politically as well.[21] One is the emergence of a new class of small entrepreneurs in rural/small-town areas of Punjab, eastern NWFP, and more recently Sind, based initially on the large remittances from Pakistani migrant workers in the Middle East. Pakistan in the 1980s is beginning to go through the explosive rural economic transformation that adjacent areas of India experienced two decades earlier.[22] It is unlikely that this new entrepreneurial group will continue to accept unprotestingly the leadership of the large landowning families in their areas, and they are socially placed in their home communities to have some political mobilization capacities of their own. They are a new, still untested, but potentially very important factor in the rural/small-town politics of Pakistan.

At the same time Pakistan has been experiencing substantial shifts of population and employment from the rural to urban sectors, especially since 1960. In 1947, nearly 90 percent of (West) Pakistan's population lived in rural areas and was dependent on agriculture for its livelihood. By 1983, "nearly 30 percent of its population lived in urban areas and over 40 percent of its labor force was engaged in nonagricultural pursuits."[23]

In the urban areas the labor union movement has not grown very impressively in numbers since 1960, but it is now much better organized and is well integrated into the urban social and economic structure. During the Bhutto period, the unions were an active if, on balance, moderate political force, but from 1977 to 1985 they usually avoided an overt involvement in politics that might have brought the repressive power of the state down on their still vulnerable economic functions. With the return to a more open politics under a civilian government in 1986, however, there have been indications of a revival of union political activity, if still on a carefully monitored scale. Reportedly, a high proportion of the union leadership is affiliated with the PPP, but it is less certain that most of the members—a relatively privileged elite among Pakistan's "working classes"—share their enthusiasm for a party that preaches egalitarian principles.

The few tenuous efforts to organize the rural poor—small landholders, tenants, and the landless—during both the Bhutto and the Zia regimes never really got very far. There are a few "peasant organizations" in Sind, some the product of the 1983 agitation, as well as several elsewhere in Pakistan that are usually limited to a particular locality and not even integrated on a state level, much less nationally. Under Zia, the *kisan* (peasant) organizations have had to compete with the informal traditional social and economic networks (the *biradari*), usually dominated by the local landed elite, which often serve as the channels for the distribution of state resources for welfare, education, and development programs in their locality, and which have been more effective politically in the past. But a potentially important development in rural politics are the new, nonofficial social service, health, and education programs that have been established in several rural areas, primarily in the Punjab, financed by funds remitted by Pakistanis working abroad. It is now possible for those numerous rural families with one or more members employed outside Pakistan to assume a more independent posture to the local landed elite establishment inside Pakistan, and this is bound to have some political fallout eventually.

One curiously quiescent economic group has been the private industrialists and traders who are still largely organized along traditional familial lines. Heavily dependent upon government support and largess during the 1950s and 1960s, these industrial and trading firms never established a very strong sense of confidence in their own capabilities. Bhutto's nationalization policies in the 1972–1974 period, limited though they may have been, appeared to effectively intimidate the industrialists, most of whom went quietly along.[24] Zia's policies, on paper at least, have been directed toward "privatization" of the economy and the denationalization of some of the industries and firms seized by Bhutto, and the Junejo government had retained this as its economic policy. But the response of the entrepreneurial class since 1977 has been hesitant and restrained, probably as much for political as economic reasons.[25] Its reactions to the reintroduction of a liberalized polity reflect uncertainty about the political future in Pakistan and, in particular, the possible reemergence of the PPP, headed by Bhutto's daughter, Benazir Bhutto, as the dominant political force in the country. While they appreciate certain aspects of Zia's economic policies, in particular the somewhat more subdued role of the bureaucracy in economic decision making, there is an apparent perception that these are more in form than in operational substance, and thus a reluctance to take advantage of some of the opportunities offered by the privatization policies.

The ubiquitous student community may also be passing through another transitional period. Under Bhutto most of the organized student political groups had been strongly supportive of the PPP. During the Zia regime, however, there was an apparent shift in organized student group affiliation to various Islamic parties—so much so that by 1982 most of the student councils on university campuses were dominated by this faction. Zia's decision in 1984 to abolish *elected* student councils and replace them with appointive bodies was thus difficult to understand, as it tended to undermine the dominant position of the Islamic student groups that were supportive of the Zia government on some issues at least—probably the most his government could expect from the student community. In any case there were some signs of a renewal of student political activism by 1986. The PPP and the Islamic parties are likely to be the main beneficiaries of this development, while the ruling PML will probably find it difficult to attract a solid base of student support.

The integration of the Pathan and Baluchi communities into the broader Pakistani political and national system has been a major problem since independence, and in some respects an obstacle to a democratic system because of the proclivity of the central authorities to use force in repressing ethnic dissident forces. Since 1980, however, more sophisticated tactics have been employed. There has been the allocation of substantial foreign economic assistance and Pakistani development funds into the NWFP and Baluchistan in the context of the social upheavals that have accompanied the Soviet intervention in Afghanistan and the mass movement of Afghani refugees into Pakistan. These programs have had an impact on the tribal economy and on the ethnic-dominated politics of this area. Pakistan is now undergoing the kind of economic transformation at the rural level that neighboring areas of India have experienced since 1950—with major political consequences. The economic upsurge in the NWFP, Baluchistan, and some major urban centers in Sind and Punjab—the consequence in part of both the inflow of Afghani refugees and the greatly expanded input of financial and other resources, both legal and extralegal (e.g., the black markets in drugs and arms)—has led to sociopolitical movements and conflicts that are beyond the capacity of either the traditional ethnic elite or the central government to direct or easily control.

There is still concern in Pakistan over the prospect of the "balkanization" of the country, usually defined in terms of the separation of NWFP, Baluchistan, and/or Sind from a Punjabi-dominated polity. The Soviet intervention in Afghanistan had seriously complicated politics for dissident Sindhi, Pathan, and Baluchi factions. By 1987, however, the growing sentiment in Pakistan for a settlement in Afghanistan and an accommodation with the Soviets on almost any terms, added a spark of life to some of these ethnic dissident groups that had been comparatively quiescent since 1980. Abdul Wali Khan, the Awami National Party (ANP) leader in the NWFP, for instance, made a pilgrimage to Kabul in early November 1987—for the first time since the Soviet invasion of Afghanistan in December 1979.[26] This may have been an effort on his part to obtain funding for the local elections scheduled for late November, but it may also have been indicative of a new phase in Pakistani frontier politics in which an overtly pro-Soviet position is no longer political suicide. It may also have been a serious miscalculation on Wali Khan's part. While the opposition PPP did quite well in Peshawar and elsewhere in the NWFP local elections, the ANP was shut out in Peshawar and won only a few seats in its old rural Pathan strongholds in the "unadministered" districts in western NWFP.[27]

One important aspect of the financial side of the Pakistan federal system should be noted—namely, that the central government provides 65 to 70 percent of the funding for the state budgets. This is very similar to the situation in India and, for the same reason, the state governments are barred from collecting revenue in some of the most lucrative fields. The results are the same also—a massive dependence on the center and an equally strong resentment over the prevailing situation at the state level. An amendment to the constitution that would incorporate provisions for broader state autonomy on revenue collection within the federal system had been proposed by some of Junejo's supporters in the National Assembly. If this had been approved, most of the "separatist" factions in Pakistan may have had to come to terms with the system, since broader autonomy rather than independence is their real objective. This would mitigate the concern expressed in some quarters that the introduction of a democratic polity would be a step in the direction of the disintegration of Pakistan, for it would become evident that the result was in fact greater integration.

There have even been a few encouraging developments in the realm of political parties that may contribute to the democratization process. Factionalization is still the predominant characteristic of the party system, but the trend appears to be toward a tripartite structure, with the PPP and the PML as the major contending parties, around which most of the other parties will coalesce for both pragmatic and ideological reasons. A third important force in some areas, but not nationally, will be the more moderate and accommodative of the Islamic parties in Punjab and Sind and the ethnic-based coalition of parties in NWFP and Baluchistan.

The PPP-dominated coalition, organizationally based in the Movement for the Restoration of Democracy (MRD), has gone through some difficult times since mid-1986, when Benazir Bhutto tried to launch a mass movement against the Zia/Junejo regime—and failed. It became evident in this crisis that most of the leaders of the other parties in the MRD were reluctant to accept Benazir's leadership, as well as to attach themselves too closely organizationally to the PPP—probably because of their vivid memories of politics under her father, Zulfikar Bhutto. But the other MRD parties, counted either separately or together, do not have the political clout and organizational capacity of the PPP, nor is there any other political party leader with the public appeal of Benazir Bhutto. The other MRD parties thus will either have to work along with the PPP or come to terms with the PML in an election. They would probably divide up and do both, in the process further neutralizing their role in Pakistan's politics.

The Islamic parties and the avowedly Marxist parties have made only a limited impact on the Pakistani public and political process. The limits of the appeal of the Islamic parties have been reflected in the public's minimal response to Zia's islamization policy. The Islamic parties have also had a rather tenuous relationship with Zia, supporting the president on some issues while generally critical of his regime. And for good reason, since the military would never willingly accept the narrow, self-serving identification of an Islamic state and society that the Islamic parties espouse. The official Communist Party of Pakistan (CPP) is still largely the playhouse of some relatively affluent urban bourgeois who have no capacity for or interest in organizing a mass party that would soon shunt them aside. The CPP still retains the valuable support, financial and political, of the Soviet Union which is about the only thing that keeps it going. The more important leftist factions, potentially at least, are some groups such as the Sindhi Awami Tehrik (Sindhi People's Movement), which are usually defined as both Marxist and Maoist and have normally avoided a close relationship with the Soviets.

The political parties, like the government, find the federal structure in Pakistan a difficult problem since it often obstructs cooperation and coalition building between the parties. The MRD defined its position on center-state relations in May 1985, advocating: (1) that all powers be allocated to the states except in the very important fields of defense, currency, finance, communications, and foreign affairs; (2) that provincial representation in the bureaucracy and military be based on population percentages; and (3) that limits be imposed on the center's power to impose its direct rule over the states. These are reasonable, and the PML's position will probably not vary too much from this. But it was not sufficient for some of the more obdurate non-Punjabi politicians who, in April 1985, formed the Sind-Baluch-Paktoon Front (SBPF), which then called for the dissolution of the Pakistan federation into a loose confederation of sovereign units. The MRD publicly rejected the SBPF position and, in the context of the liberalization process, appeared to have the more solid popular support base even among the 40 percent of non-Punjabi Pakistanis.

What is clearly evident in Pakistan is that a new generation of political activists is finally emerging; what is less clear is where they are going. The old *muhajirs* who dominated Karachi, the bureaucracy, and private industry in the post-1947 period have now finally retired, and the young *muhajirs* or the "new" *muhajirs* from Bangladesh are a much more complex group with different views and perceived interests. This was also reflected in the 1985 "nonparty" election that brought a new collection of younger, educated, well-connected rural Pakistanis into politics. They all joined parties in 1986, either the PML or the official opposition group in the National Assembly, but some of them will end up in the PPP or one of the other opposition parties. Their entry into parties will have a considerable impact as, given their solid support base in rural areas, they would considerably broaden the social and economic ties of the political party leadership.

The growing tendency for young educated males from rural elite families to replace the older educated males from urban elite families who have long dominated most of the parties will thus be expedited. Pakistan may then go through the major change that India underwent in the 1970s—the transfer of the center of political power from urban to rural elites. And by and large, the rural political activists who will control two-thirds of the seats in an elected parliament will tend to be more supportive of a democratic system than the urban elites, who use the rhetoric of democracy enthusiastically but have reservations about any system based upon the "power-to-the-people" concept, given the rural-urban population ratios.

What then are the prospects for democracy in Pakistan—or, at least, for continuation of the process of liberalization that has already modified the basically authoritarian system in place in the mid-1980s? It is hard to be optimistic on this subject given Pakistan's rather dismal record on political systems since 1974. "Old Pakistan hands" usually insist that this kind of systemic change is really not feasible, but then we are no longer dealing with the Old Pakistan. Socioeconomic changes in Pakistan over the past decade have affected virtually all areas and groups in the country and are beginning to have an impact on the politics of the country.

How far this will go, and with what results, is still an open question. Certainly democracy is not the only option available, but is the one that has the broadest level of public support throughout Pakistan. In contrast, no political leader or group, including the Islamic parties, now advocates a nondemocratic polity; even President Zia, in his critique of "Western democracy" and his advocacy of "Islamic democracy," defines the latter in functional terms that make the distinction meaningless now that he has reluctantly accepted the inevitability of parties in *any* kind of democratic system.[28] Nor is there any confusion among the Pakistani public as to what a democracy is in institutional and operative terms, for they have been socialized through their educational system, the media, and political organizations on classic British concepts of representative government and popular sovereignty.

A process of gradual democratization of the political system thus is underway and will not be as easily reversed as it has been in the past. Pakistan is not yet another India, where virtually all major social, economic, regional, and ethnic communities are so effectively politicized that it is difficult to conceive of any system of government other than participatory democracy that could work for such a heterogeneous society. But politicization in Pakistan, largely restricted to a few elite groups in the past, has become much more broadly based both socially and regionally since 1970, and some form of participatory political system—in the public's perception—may now be necessary. This does not necessarily have to be a democratic sytem, as the leftists, the Islamic fundamentalists, and even the military (e.g., Ayub's Basic Democracy system) can provide options that are defined as participatory and representative, without being democratic.

There is no doubt, however, that politics have become much more complex in Pakistan and that the little games played within the elite establishment are no longer sufficient. By the late 1980s democracy appeared to be the best available option to a broad spectrum of political and institutional forces in Pakistan, so much so indeed that there seemed to be a consensus on the subject for the first time since 1958. Even more impressive were the careful, sensible tactics adopted by both the government and the opposition parties to avoid violent clashes that, in turn, could well have brought the democratic process to an end—for the time being at least. Some political elements on both sides have found this nonconfrontational approach unacceptable and have done their best to encourage and indulge in violence. But, for the first time, the balance may be against the advocates of conflict and represssion, thus making it possible for the process of gradual liberalization and democratization to continue through the first two years of the post-martial-law period.

• NOTES •

Note: This chapter was completed before the death of President Zia-ul-Huq on August 17, 1988.

1. Syed Nur Ahmad, *From Martial Law to Martial Law: Politics in the Punjab, 1919–1958*, ed. Craig Baxter (Boulder, Colo.: Westview Press, 1985), Pb. 2.

2. Khalid B. Sayeed, *The Political System of Pakistan* (Boston: Houghton Mifflin Co., 1967), pp. 101–126.

3. See M. Rafique Alzal, *Political Parties in Pakistan, 1947–1958*, and K. K. Azia, *Party Politics in Pakistan, 1947–1958*, both published in Islamabad by the National Commission on Historical and Cultural Research in 1976, for detailed but somewhat different analysis of political party developments prior to the first martial law regime.

4. Lawrence Ziring, *The Ayub Khan Era: Politics in Pakistan, 1958–1969* (Syracuse, N.Y.: Syracuse University Press, 1971).

5. Shahid Javed Burki, *Pakistan: A Nation in the Making* (Boulder, Colo.: Westview Press, 1986), pp. 57–62.

6. Richard Sisson and Leo E. Rose, *War and Secession: Crisis and Decision in South Asia, 1971* (Berkeley, Calif.: University of California Press, forthcoming in 1988).

7. Phillip E. Jones, "Changing Party Structures in Pakistan: From Muslim League to People's Party," in Manzooruddin Ahmed, ed., *Contemporary Pakistan: Politics, Economy, and Society* (Durham, N.C.: Carolina Academic Press, 1980), p. 134.

8. Shahid Javed Burki, *Pakistan Under Bhutto, 1971–1977* (New York: St. Martin's Press, 1980), pp. 90–92.

9. Khalid B. Sayeed, *Politics in Pakistan: The Nature and Direction of Change* (New York: Praeger, 1980), p. 89.

10. It should be noted, however, that members of the *shariat* bench of judges in each high court and the *shariat* appellate bench in the Supreme Court must be qualified common law judges, as well as learned in Islamic rules and principles, and that judges with these dual qualifications have been hard to find. Edward Mortimer, *Faith and Power: The Politics of Islam* (New York: Random House, 1982), p. 225.

11. Former PPP members won about forty seats despite the party's public "boycott" of the election. This led some observers to conclude that the PPP would have swept the elections in the Punjab and Sind if it had participated—not necessarily the case but a serious prospect for Zia. William L. Richter, "Pakistan in 1915: Testing Time for the New Order," *Asian Survey* 26, no. 2 (February 1986): pp. 208–212.

12. See President Zia's statement on this point in the *Pakistan Times*, 4 May 1986.

13. The one major exception was the PPP's decision to launch a broad-based political movement in August 1985 in which some party cadres and supporters used illegal tactics, some of them violent. The government responded equally forcefully. The PPP campaign subsided, though as much from the lack of support from the party's coalition partners in the Movement for the Restoration of Democracy as from the government's suppressive measures.

14. Shahid Javed Burki ascribes Ayub Khan's downfall in 1969 to popular dissatisfaction with (1) the inequities in the distribution of the substantial economic growth in the 1958–1968 period, and (2) the fact that the growth rate fell to a moderate level in 1966–1968 (*Pakistan: A Nation in the Making*, pp. 58–61). Perhaps, but most other analyses of the 1968–1969 developments attribute Ayub's problems to loss of support among the elite, little affected by a 2 percent drop in GNP, rather than to the popular demonstrations that, in other circumstances, would have been considered easily manageable.

15. It is interesting to note that in the 1977 demonstrations and counterdemonstrations, some economic groups such as the labor unions that had been the (unintentional) principal victims of Bhutto's disastrous economic policies were his most ardent supporters on the firing line.

16. Zia has been credited with introducing some "real" islamization, but much of this is more show than substance. Banks are barred from paying interest on saving accounts to conform with Islamic principles, for instance, but in the place of interest they now provide guaranteed profits at the same percentage. Islamization is more than changing the name for doing the same thing.

17. See Riaz Hassan, "Religion, Society and the State in Pakistan," *Asian Survey* 27, no. 5 (May 1987): pp. 552–565, for a useful analysis of the complexity of Islamic politics in Pakistan.

18. The best sociological analysis of the Pakistan military is Stephen P. Cohen, *The Pakistan Army* (Berkeley, Calif.: University of California Press, 1984).

19. Rodney W. Jones, "The Military and Security in Pakistan," in Craig Baxter, ed., *Zia's Pakistan: Politics and Stability in a Frontline State* (Boulder, Colo.: Westview Press, 1985), pp. 70–72.

20. Charles H. Kennedy, "Zia and the Civilian Bureaucrats: Pakistan's Bureaucracy in the 1980's" (paper prepared for the Columbia University Conference on Pakistan, 16–17 April 1987, forthcoming in a volume to be pulished by Columbia University Press in 1988).

21. John Adams, "Pakistan's Economic Performance in the 1980s: Implications for Political Balance," in Baxter, ed., *Zia's Pakistan*, pp. 47–62.

22. Holly Sims, "The State and Agricultural Productivity: Continuity vs. Change in the Indian and Pakistani Punjabs," *Asian Survey* 26, no. 4 (April 1986): pp. 483–500. See also Shahid Javed Burki on the substantial changes in the land ownership structure within the agricultural economy (*Pakistan: A Nation in the Making*, p. 108).

23. Ibid.

24. Asaf Hussain, *Elite Politics in an Ideological State* (London: Dawson, 1979), pp. 106–109.

25. Khalid Bin Sayed, "Pakistan in 1983: Internal Stresses More Serious than External Problems," *Asian Survey* 24, no. 2 (February 1984): pp. 225–226.

26. *Foreign Broadcast Information Service* (South Asia), 12 November 1987, p. 46.

27. *Foreign Broadcast Information Service* (South Asia), 1 December 1987, p. 71.

28. President Zia described the "new" political system in 1986 as more akin to a Western parliamentary form of government and noted that it was not Islamic. But he also said the elected government could bring about an Islamic system through an evolutionary and gradual process. (*Pakistan Times*, 4 May 1986). This was a novel view on this subject for Zia and possibly indicative of the political educational process he has gone through since 1977.

SRI LANKA

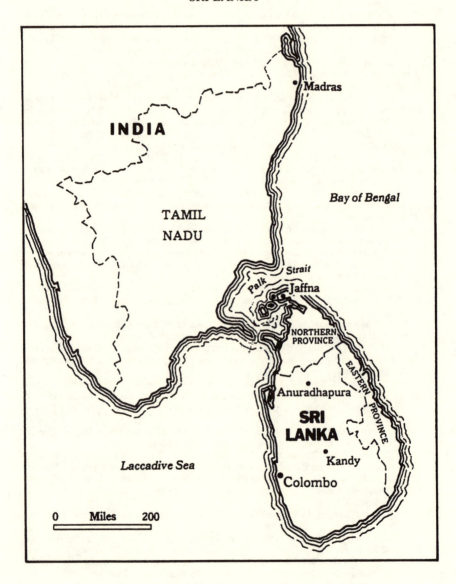

• CHAPTER FOUR •
Sri Lanka:
Crises of Legitimacy and Integration
URMILA PHADNIS

In general terms Sri Lanka is very much a part of the "developing" world: sparse in its resources, dependent on the global market mechanism for sheer survival, confronted with the rising expectations of its teeming youth population, and, last but not the least, attempting to cope with the simultaneous challenges of participation, distribution, and integration.[1]

And yet, within the developing world, not many countries have succeeded in building and sustaining a democratic order as Sri Lanka has. Even so, over the past decade, the stresses and strains on the democratic system have been severe. Sri Lanka has been in the throes of crises of legitimacy and integration, unprecedented in their intensity and magnitude in the history of the new state.

An appraisal of the causes as well as implications of the crises for the future of democracy in Sri Lanka necessitates an overview of: (a) the historical contexts of its sociopolitical order as evolved since independence; (b) the modalities of regime change as well as the catalysts of change therein; (c) social bases, ideological proclivities, policy options, and constraints of various regimes; (d) contending forces and lines of cleavage as manifested in the major challenges and conflicts; (e) the imperatives as much as the capabilities and will of the leadership of these regimes to steer through such conflicts without subverting the democratic norms and structures.

• HISTORICAL REVIEW •

The Plural Structure of the Island State

Covering an area of 25,232 square miles and a population of over fifteen million, Sri Lankan society represents the enmeshing of diversity in racial-religious, regional-linguistic terms. Spanning several centuries, the multiethnic configuration of Sri Lanka has been determined to a considerable extent by its proximity to India and its distance from any other landmass. In its early sociopolitical history Indian or India-derived elements figured prominently. Thus the ancestry of the Sinhalese, the majority community, as well as the Tamils, the second largest community, is traced to migrations from northern and southern India respectively. And so are their respective religions and languages.

Making up about three-fourths of the total population, the Sinhalese claim Aryan descent, speak Sinhala, and are predominantly Buddhists. The Tamils, about one-fifth of the population, speak Tamil, one of the major Dravidian languages of southern India, and are mainly followers of Hinduism. The Tamils are heavily concentrated in two out of nine provinces of Sri Lanka. According to the 1981 census, in the Northern and adjacent Eastern Provinces (which are in close proximity to the Tamil-dominant state of Tamilnadu in India), they account for 85 percent and 42 percent of the total population respectively.

The cumulative effect of racial, religious, and linguistic congruence has thus provided cultural referents to the ethnic identity and distinctiveness of both the Sinhalese and Tamil communities.

As for the rest, the Muslims, most of whom claim Moorish identity, account for 7 percent of the population, with the Eurasians, Burghers, and Malays—a legacy of the Western colonial era—constituting about 1 percent.[2]

The Colonial Context

Stretching to about four-and-a-half centuries, Western colonial domination began with the Portuguese and the Dutch. It was followed by the arrival of the British, who, unlike their predecessors, succeeded in bringing the whole island under their control.

The imperatives as well as exigencies of British colonialism led to the creation of a centralized authority structure, the bulwark of which were administrative, judicial, and communication systems encompassing the colony as a whole.

With the introduction of plantation agriculture the economy of the island underwent significant changes. To begin with, the plantation economy brought in its wake the import of labor as well as capital. The pioneer investors in coffee and, subsequently, tea were British civil servants and army officials. The labor was not indigenous but was imported from southern India to work on the plantations in the heart of the erstwhile Kandyan Kingdom, which retained its independence until 1815 when it was ceded to the British.

The large-scale immigration not only contributed to the rapid growth of population, but also led to the emergence of a class of landless laborers tied to its employers by a cash nexus alone. In view of its ethnic antecedents, the immigrant labor on the coffee and tea plantations added a new dimension to the Sinhalese-Tamil plurality.

Furthermore, encompassing the plantation culture, the money economy brought with it a consciousness of profits, wages, rent, and credit, besides leading to the establishment of such institutions as commercial houses, banks, etc. All this was alien to the barter-oriented, subsistence peasant system, which continued alongside but became organically linked in such a manner that, more often than not, the development of the former implied the underdevelopment of the latter.

The commercialization of agriculture led to the transformation of Ceylon into an export economy of primary products affecting the traditional power structure. There was, moreover, the emergence of an English-educated middle class, which was closely associated with colonial political and economic activities. This consisted mainly of the high-caste (*goyigama*) among the low country, upper-caste Jaffna Tamils and members of the three coastal castes who had risen to high status during this period. In the plantation of rubber and coconut, the other two export commodities (although not as substantial foreign exchange earners as tea), the members of these castes as well as the low-country *goyigama* families predominated. "Such kin-groups functioned both as nationally integrated units to further their collective class interests as well as regional factions competing against each other for power."[3]

Thus by community, caste, and religion the emergent middle class was varied in its composition. Even so, English education and socialization patterns, coupled with the interest convergence in the colonial power structure, imparted to it a certain amount of stability as well as homogeneity. And when Sri Lanka attained independence it was this class that held the monopoly of political power at the center. Nevertheless, the power elite was differentiated in horizontal as well as vertical terms.

During the British colonial period the revivalist movements had fairly distinct communal streams (Buddhists, Hindus, and Moors), despite their identification of a common adversary in the cultural as well as the political offensives of the British Raj. The politicoelectoral process, particularly after the reforms of 1931, reflected communal pressures and pulls in a somewhat more overt and organized form than ever before.

If the ethnic cleavages did not surface at the time of independence, it was because the power cake was big enough to accommodate the elite of the minority communities, among whom the Ceylon Tamils (as distinguished from the immigrants during the British period designated officially as "Indian Tamils") already held important positions in the bureaucracy and other professions like law and medicine. And yet, the Sinhalese manifested a strident political tone, reflected in the clauses on the political status of the Indian Tamils in the constitutional proposals of

1928. There were also subsequent wranglings between the Sinhalese and the Ceylon Tamil leadership over the weight to be given to the minority communities in the various proposals for constitutional reform of the 1940s.[4] These developments indicated that despite the homogeneity of the ruling elite in terms of its socioeconomic bases, ethnic cleavages had tremendous potential for political mobilization and competition. Within a decade after independence ethnic cleavage assumed a critical salience in the political processes of Sri Lanka.

The Transfer of Power

Unlike the transfers of power in other ex-British colonies like India and Burma, which followed agitational and turbulent movements, Sri Lanka's transition from a colony to a state was smooth, orderly, and peaceful. Besides, it was primarily through the modalities of constitutional reform that such a transition was brought about. Agitational politics, either of the left or of communal parties and groups, operated by and large within a constitutional mold.

The moderate tenor of the Ceylonese nationalist movement was facilitated to a great extent by the promulgation of the Donoughmore Constitution in 1931.[5] Under this constitution, a considerable degree of internal self-government was provided through the state council, comprising fifty members elected on the basis of universal adult franchise and a maximum of twelve nominated members. Sri Lanka was thus the first country in the colonial world to have universal suffrage. By the time the British withdrew in 1948 three general elections had already been held in 1931, 1936, and 1947. Besides, the executive committee system (as stipulated in the 1931 reforms) was replaced by the cabinet system of the Westminster type after the elections of 1947. Thus the political elite had worked in close collaboration with the colonial authorities in legislative, executive, bureaucratic, and economic spheres.

It was not surprising then that negotiations for the transfer of power were smooth and orderly. After agreeing to grant independence to India, the British in any case seemed to be reconciled and prepared to accede to similar demands in Sri Lanka. Continuities in certain crucial areas marked the transfer of power, as was evident from the continued preeminence of the British companies in the plantation sector, particularly tea, and arrangements regarding defense as spelt out in the Ceylon-United Kingdom Defence Agreement signed on the eve of the transfer of power.

Transition from "Notable" Politics to Mass Politics

As independence came to Sri Lanka without mass struggle, the nationalist

movement hardly made a direct contribution in evoking political consciousness at the mass level. Nonetheless, the cumulative effects of the
perennial demands for constitutional revison, the influence of the small
and vocal left leadership (mainly through vernacular media), coupled
with the dynamics of universal suffrage and election campaigns, had
facilitated greater politicization of the masses in the urban as well as the
rural areas.

A significant feature of the Sinhalese countryside was the increasing
influence of its lower middle stratum. Forming a broad social segment,
it comprised those who earned a major portion of their income from
nonagricultural sources but had a small piece of land too. In view of the
pyramid-like tenurial structure of Ceylon with big landlords controlling
a small percentage of landholdings, this class of petty landholders or
"proletarian landlords," had benefited from increasing commercial, as
well as educational, opportunities during the colonial and postcolonial
period.[6] If the commercial opportunities unfurled for them in their role
as petty traders, the educational reforms introduced in 1945, providing
for compulsory education until age fourteen and tuition free up to the
university level, had brought in its wake a large cadre of school teachers
in *swabhasha* (one's own language), i.e., Sinhala and Tamil. Added to
the vernacular-educated Sinhalese intelligentsia were the erstwhile
Buddhist clergy and the ayurvedic (indigenous medicine) physicians.

With the introduction of adult suffrage this social stratum played an
important role as intermediary in mobilizing votes for rural "notables."
However, the postindependence politics of the Western-oriented elite
of the United National Party (UNP) did not satisfy the aspirations for
socioeconomic advancement and status of this group. The preeminence
of English was perceived as a vestige of colonialism. In education as well
as employment the English-educated elite continued to predominate
over the Sinhalese- and Tamil-educated elite. Similar too was the case of
the indigenous medical practitioners vis-à-vis the others. Finally, the
Buddhist clergy and a segment of laity had hoped that after independence
greater state patronage for Buddhism would be provided. However,
when some of them approached the first prime minister, D. S. Senanayake (a devout Buddhist, but with a secular outlook) in 1951, he told
them that Buddhist canons had already provided for three "refuges" of
Buddha, Dharma, and the *sangha* (the congregation of Buddhist clergy).
Addition of a fourth "refuge" in the form of the state was therefore not
required except as a secular agency.[7]

Such an approach by the UNP leadership thus disillusioned the
Sinhalese-Buddhist enthusiasts, who found in S. W. R. D. Bandaranaike,
the leader of the Sri Lanka Freedom Party (SLFP), their articulate
spokesman in espousing the Sinhalese-Buddhist cause, promising to
make Sinhala the official language "within 48 hours."[8]

Until as late as 1954 both the UNP as well as the SLFP had adopted the policy of Sinhalese and Tamil as official languages replacing English. Thus Bandaranaike's *volte-face* reflected the stridency of forces for religio-cultural revivalism, particularly in the wake of Buddha Jayanti in 1954—the commemoration of 2,500 years of Buddha's death. Meanwhile, the UNP leadership too could feel the intensity of the popular mood. As a result it also decided to reverse its earlier policy of parity.

1956: A Watershed in Sri Lankan Politics

The elections, which were due in 1957, were advanced by a year in view of the UNP's policy change on the language issue and also presumably its ill-founded confidence in securing an electoral victory. In the 1952 elections it had won with a clear majority. The electoral verdict in 1956 showed that it had miscalculated heavily; it ended up with a derisory eight seats, with the Mahajana Eksath Peramuna (MEP—People's United Front) led by Bandaranaike winning fifty-one seats in an elected house of ninety-five members.

The MEP, referred to as "an assorted collection of sundry social and economic groups—a coalition of resentments against the UNP," had as its core the SLFP.[9] The other components were the Viplavakari Lanka Samasamaj party (VLSSP—Revolutionary Ceylon Equal Society party) led by Philip Gunawardena and the Sinhala Bhasha Peramuna (Sinhalese Language Front) led by W. Dahanayake. Although both Dahanayake and Gunawardena had at one time belonged to the Trotskyite Lanka Samasamaj party (LSSP), ideologically they had parted, with the former emerging as a right-winger and the latter heading the left group in the MEP. However, their common stand on the language issue had brought them together in the United Front.

In broad terms, the ideological planks of the SLFP-led MEP symbolized the resonance of Sinhalese Buddhist nationalism with a radical fervor. The translation of these policies into action, however, reflected the contradictions within the heterogeneous coalition, and also without, in class as well as ethnic terms.

The ideological package of the SLFP, for instance, had as its major components indigenization and socialization in domestic fields and nonalignment in foreign affairs. As regards indigenization, it had in the main an anticolonial, antiforeign stridency, with emphasis on indigenous values, norms, and institutions in the social spheres and autarky in the economic realm. However, the forms of such indigenous assertions were intertwined with a thrust of majoritarianism of the Sinhala-speaking Buddhists, who had suffered from a sense of past discrimination and neglect toward their culture. Such a thrust brought an ethnic division during the Sinhala Only Bill and communal violence thereafter.

Although Bandaranaike did try to work out a modus vivendi in this respect, his efforts were hamstrung by the militant Buddhist and opportunistic politicians. A glaring example of this was the pact that Bandaranaike signed in 1957 with S. J. V. Chelvanayagam, the leader of the Tamil Federal party (FP), formed in 1951 with the demand for a federal constitution (instead of the existing unitary framework) as one of its major objectives.[10] The Federal party leadership had succeeded in mobilizing the disillusionment of the Ceylon Tamils over the language policies of both the UNP and the SLFP and had emerged as the spokesmen of the Ceylon Tamils, winning ten out of seventeen seats in the Tamil-dominated Northern and Eastern provinces.

However, even before the ink was dry on the pact the UNP, although in tatters after its electoral defeat, was able to organize the Sinhalese Buddhists to a frenzy of such intensity that Bandaranaike decided to abrogate the pact. Although legislation providing for "reasonable use of Tamil" in the Tamil-speaking areas was enacted in 1958, it hardly met the approval of the Tamil leadership. Nor did it meet the approbation of a faction within the SLFP. The assassination of Bandaranaike by a monk in 1959 and the ties of the assassin to a segment of the SLFP reflected not only the factionalized character of the SLFP on a secular-communal continuum, but also in radical-conservative terms.

It is in this respect that the socialist measures of the Bandaranaike regime need to be appraised. Thus the nationalization of the port of Colombo and bus companies were measures that directly hit the affluent interests linked with the UNP. As such, they were welcomed by the stalwarts of the SLFP.

This was not so with the measures for land reform, as was obvious from the opposition within the ruling coalition on the Paddy Lands Act of 1958. The architect of this act was Philip Gunawardena, the radical minister of agriculture. As the act provided certain tenurial safeguards to the tenants and also provision for reduced rents, it was perceived by an influential group within the SLFP as inimical to its interests. Not only were certain changes made in the act, whittling down some of its substantive content, but the power tussle in the cabinet between its radical and conservative wings ultimately led to the expulsion of Gunawardena and a few others closely associated with him from the cabinet. The nonliberal and communal tendencies seemed to be on the ascendant at this stage in the Bandaranaike regime, which was brought to an abrupt end by his assassination in September 1959. Inheriting his charisma, his widow, Sirimavo Bandaranaike, succeeded to the leadership of the SLFP as a matter of course.

In the elections that followed in March 1960, no party could muster a majority. Although the UNP, as the largest major party, tried to form the government, it ended up with the shortest political inning in the island's history. Elections were held again in July 1960, bringing the SLFP back to power under the leadership of Mrs. Bandaranaike, who became the first woman prime minister in the world. Although the SLFP lost to the UNP in the 1965 elections, Mrs. Bandaranaike regained power in 1970 and governed for the next seven years, to be defeated once again by the UNP in 1977.

In sum, in the postindependence general elections, the SLFP and UNP alternated as victors and vanquished in a remarkably regular cycle, as evidenced in Table 4.1.

From One-Party Dominance to a System of Two Major Parties

Initially, after independence, the Sri Lankan party system had a brief spell of one-party domination under the UNP. However, the election of 1956 heralded the beginning of the system of two major parties, crystallizing in the Sinhalese-dominated areas in particular.

Table 4.1 Party Alternation in the Sri Lankan General Elections, 1952–1977

Election Year	Victorious Party or Front
1952	UNP
1956	MEP (Core Party SLFP)
March 1960	UNP
July 1960	SLFP
1965	UNP
1970	UF (Core Party SLFP)
1977	UNP

Source: A. Jeyaratnam Wilson, "General Elections in Sri Lanka 1947–1977" in K. M. de Silva ed., Universal Franchise, 1931–1981: The Sri Lankan Experience (Colombo: Department of Information, 1981), p. 105.

Under this system the UNP and the SLFP emerged as two major parties having more-or-less equally strong support bases. Both of them formed preelectoral alliances and/or postelection coalition governments with the minor parties. The electoral and political behavior of the minority parties reflected a consistency in such alignment patterns. The regional parties like the Tamil Congress (TC) or the FP preferred the UNP, perceiving it as relatively more secular and less chauvinist than the SLFP. The predominantly left-oriented parties like the Moscow-oriented Communist party (CP) as well as the LSSP and many of its breakaway groups chose the "centrist" SLFP. In the process, the imperatives of power sharing led to a diffusion of their radicalism and an endorsement of the majoritarian thrust of the SLFP, as was evident in the early 1960s when both the LSSP and the CP abjured their earlier stand on the parity of Sinhala and Tamil as official languages.

With the UNP and the SLFP governments alternating and having their major support bases in the Sinhalese areas, each competed to be more Sinhalese-Buddhist than the other and, in the process, increasingly alienated the Tamils. As regards the Indian Tamils, most of whom lived in the Sinhalese-dominated areas (mainly on plantations), many of them were disenfranchised by the Citizenship Acts of 1948–1949. Subsequently, the determination of their political status became a bilateral concern of the governments of India and Sri Lanka (as spelled out in the 1964 agreement signed between the late Indian Prime Minister Lal Bahadur Shastri and Sri Lankan Premier Mrs. Bandaranaike), but their political clout in electoral terms was far more inchoate and somewhat muted.[11] This was because of the continued uncertain political status of a large number of them. On the other hand the Ceylon Tamils, far more volatile politically and advanced in socioeconomic terms, had as their major spokesman regional Tamil parties that joined the coalition governments intermittently.

The coalitional nature of a number of regimes, although reflecting the diverse pressures and pulls of their respective ruling partners and leading at times to the edging out of one of them, did mark continuous efforts to evolve a consensus on many issues.[12] To this extent coalitional regimes symbolized aggregation and not fragmentation of politics, with the two major parties providing the core of the government or opposition in alliance or in concert with the numerically small parties and groups. In the event of the ruling party winning with a slender majority, the minor parties in coalition enjoyed a much greater maneuverability and bargaining power.

However, there was not merely the major-minor party syndrome; factionalism within the parties was of equal significance. On the one hand, the factional structure facilitated interparty dialogue; on the other, they provided ample leeway for floor crossing or change of party labels on the eve of the elections, thereby imparting a fluidity to the party system without disrupting it altogether.

Electoral Dynamics and the Party System

The development of the party system was facilitated by electoral laws that, by imposing certain qualifications for parties to be "recognized" to compete in elections and by putting the nomination fee for nonparty candidates much higher than those contesting on party tickets, checked the mushrooming of parties in the electoral arena. Sri Lanka's discriminating and highly politicized electorate also shaped the party system. This was evident in the continuous decline in the number of successful independent candidates. By 1952, for instance, eleven seats were won by the independents. By 1977 their number had been reduced to one.[13]

As for the political participation of the electorate, the election figures speak for themselves. In the first parliamentary election held on the eve of independence, the electoral turnout was 56.1 percent. In 1970 it had shot up to 85 percent and in 1977, 87 percent.[14] At the same time the number of invalid votes declined to less than 1 percent in the 1970 and 1977 elections.

Furthermore, in view of the increasing pyramidal age structure of the population (with about two-thirds being under twenty-five years of age) and also the lowering of the voting age from twenty-one to eighteen years since 1959, the electoral behavior of the numerically strong "new voters" (i.e., those qualified to vote for the first time) assumed a criticality in the highly competitive and politically volatile arena of the party system. In the 1965 elections, for instance, in a 4.7-million-strong electorate, the new voters accounted for 1.0 million and in 1970, 0.8 million out of a total electorate of 5.5 million. In 1977 they made up about 1.2 million, or 19 percent of the total electorate of 6.7 million.[15] By and large, it was believed that the new voters tended to be oppositionists.

Such an antiestablishment posture of the youth implied that the poor performance of successive governments on the economic front, leading to a soaring cost of living and increasing unemployment, failed to evoke in the "new" voters in particular either a vested interest or a stake in keeping the government for a further term—or for that matter, even in reaffirming their faith in the system as such. Their electoral choice thus underlined not so much their preference for an alternate party as their rejection of the ruling regime.

Such a negative stance, however, did help to facilitate a continuous turnover of the two major parties in successive elections. Nonetheless, it also reflected frustration, buttressed by the fact that while electoral politics opened (in theory) the avenues for all, in effect a considerably large number of the power wielders—whether they were in government or opposition—continued to be drawn from the upper strata of Sri Lankan society. The socioeconomic profile of the legislators demonstrates this aptly. The only major difference in the 1970 election from the earlier ones was a decrease of English-educated wealthy legislators and an increase of Sinhala-educated ones, few of whom had a humble rural background. The number of landowners, businessmen, and other professionals continued to be significant—a phenomenon that hardly changed in the 1967 legislature.[16]

Despite such a convergence among the parliamentary elites in socioeconomic terms, the pressures and pulls from their respective support bases, coupled with the divergence in their ethnic as well as ideological perspectives, pulled them in different directions. As for the predominantly Sinhalese UNP and SLFP, despite their divergent perspective on socioeconomic issues, the imperatives of ruling as successors to each other necessitated a certain degree of continuity within which policy changes occurred. Besides, a numerically strong opposition (implicit in such a competitive party system) provided checks on government's "bulldozing" in the promulgation of public policies, whether radical or conservative.

However, this political equilibrium was severely disturbed in 1970 and once again in 1977. Although the tradition of alternation of power between the ruling party and the major opposition party was maintained, the numerical balance between government and opposition changed drastically, with the United Front winning more than three-fourths of the parliamentary seats in the 1970 elections and the UNP winning a similar landslide in 1977. Consequently both attempted, in consonance with their respective ideological proclivities, to reorder if not totally overhaul the political edifice and economic direction of the civic society.

In many ways the innovations as well as the constraints on the SLFP during 1970 to 1977 and on the UNP since 1977 ramify the contradictions and dichotomies that have crystallized in Sri Lanka over the decades, particularly since 1956. Thus the support bases of the two administrations, coupled with their respective strategies and styles to cope with the development challenges since 1970, require a closer scrutiny.

The 1970 Elections: Socioeconomic Contexts of the UF Victory

As with the earlier elections the 1970 elections connoted a continuation in the two-major-party system. Save for two independents in an elected house of 151 members (to which six nominated members were added), the rest were nominees of the six parties. These parties had been in the electoral arena for quite some time, with the LSSP being the oldest (35 years), followed by the CP (27 years), the TC (26 years), the UNP (24 years), the FP (21 years), and the SLFP (19 years).

Since 1952, the LSSP and the CP had no-contest pacts with the SLFP in various elections. The LSSP had also been the coalition partner in the SLFP regime in 1964. In 1968 the SLFP-LSSP-CP Front emerged with a common program, and the 1970 elections were contested by the three parties as a United Front (UF) under a common manifesto. This coalescence of the UF furthered electoral polarization, as was evident from the fact that more than three-quarters of the electoral contests were directly between the UF and the UNP.

The electoral victory of the UF was unprecedented with the SLFP winning ninety-one seats and its partners, the LSSP and CP securing nineteen and six respectively, giving the UF 116 seats total. The UNP took only seventeen seats, as against the sixty-six it had won in 1965.

Table 4.2 Party Performance in the 1970 Sri Lankan Elections

Parties	Seats Won	Percent of Seats Won	Popular Vote	Percent of Vote
UNP	17	11.3	1,892,525	37.9
SLFP[a]	91	60.3	1,839,979	36.9
LSSP[a]	19	12.6	433,224	8.7
CP[a]	6	4.0	169,199	3.4
FP	13	8.6	245,727	4.9
TC	3	2.0	115,567	2.3
Independents	2	1.3	249,006	5.0
Others	0	—	46,571	0.9
Total	151[b]	100.0	4,672,656[c]	100.0
Total number of registered voters			5,505,028	
Voter turnout (percent)				85.2

Source: Report on the General Election to the Second National State Assembly of Sri Lanka, Sessional Paper 4, 1978 (Colombo: Department of Government Printing, 1978).

[a] United Front parties.

[b] The electoral constituency of Welimada was won by the SLFP without a contest.

[c] This total is less than the actual total of partywise popular votes (4,991,656). This is due to the multimember character of some of the constituencies. The same is the case with Table 4.3.

However, as illustrated by Table 4.2, the staggering defeat of the UNP in terms of seats (11.3 percent) was not commensurate to the percentage of votes (39.9 percent) secured. In fact the UNP actually won a higher proportion of the vote than the SLFP (36.9 percent).[17] The electoral system of first-past-the-pole (in both single-member and multimember constituencies) facilitated the massive victory of the coalition. In fact, according to one estimate, it was less than a 2 percent drop in the rural areas and less than a 1 percent drop in the urban areas of the UNP votes that accounted for the landslide victory of the UF.[18]

The UF's victory in the Sinhalese Buddhist areas was impressive without affecting the core of the UNP therein. The UNP's grow-more-paddy program had failed to relieve the problems of indebtedness, landlessness, and poverty of the lower sections of the peasantry and if at all, helped the relatively more affluent peasantry. Besides, its policy of giving one measure (about two pounds) of rice free and charging normal rates for the second measure, as against the earlier policy of providing a subsidized rate for two measures per person as part of the rationed commodities package, did not ameliorate the problems of the middle class. Rice being the staple diet, it was assumed that the housewife needed both the measures of rice for food consumption; therefore, the food budget had gone up. The UNP Premier Dudley Senanayake, it was quipped, had lost his election in the "kitchen." As in the past, food subsidies continued to be an important election issue.[19]

As regards the urban areas, the left parties had won twenty out of twenty-nine urban seats. The success of the left in these areas "not only reflected [its] traditional organizational advantage based in powerful trade unions in these areas, but also the response to the UF program by the growing SLFP base of smaller industrialists, handicraftsmen, and retail traders—the middle and petty bourgeoisie—which had found itself disadvantaged by the previous government's 'open-door' policy to foreign capital and aid."[20]

There is no doubt that the left parties contributed significantly to the public policies of the UF, by giving momentum to the socialist measures. However, their stand on issues pertaining to the language, religion, and culture of the majority community was perceived by the Tamils as partisan, thereby depriving them of the intermediary role between the two communities.

The 1970 elections thus brought in their wake the gradual crystallization of a dual-level polarization: (a) polarization at the center between the two major parties and their affiliates, and almost simultaneously, (b) polarization between the center and the regions. Until 1970, the major parties in the coalition governments were numerically not too strong, and this provided significant leverage both to the coalition partner within and the opposition without. The dismissal of one coalition partner (as in 1958) or crossing the floor by a group of MPs belonging to the ruling coalition (as happened to Mrs. Bandaranaike's regime in 1964) led to the fall of governments in some cases, but not always. The Federal party for instance, after being in coalition with the UNP for about four years (1965–1969), decided to quit the coalition but reserved for itself a stance of critical support. However, the important point regarding the clout of the minor parties vis-à-vis one of the major parties remained salient.

The Tamil Parties, The New Constitution and The UF Government

Such clout was virtually lost to the minor regional parties in 1970 and also 1977. As for the 1970 elections, the SLFP alone (not to mention the UF) had a near two-thirds majority in the Parliament. With its mammoth three-quarters majority, the UF could ride roughshod over the opposition, including the regional parties like the FP and the TC. And the extent to which such a majoritarian intransigence could prevail was evident from the proceedings of the Constituent Assembly during the 1970–1972 period, much to the chagrin of the Tamil community leadership.

Within a couple of months after taking over power, the UF proceeded to have the assembly of the elected representatives operate as a Constituent Assembly. The idea was met with aplomb, and an all-party consensus prevailed on the issue of promulgating the first postindependence constitution for the island. However, the consensus on the modalities of constitution making was seriously affected by the outbreak of insurgency in April 1971. Named as the Janatha Vimukthi Peramuna (JVP, or People's Liberation Front), it was spearheaded by a segment of radicalized rural Sinhalese Buddhist youth that, after voting the SLFP and its coalition allies into power, had planned to overthrow it. The JVP thus symbolized the aggregated aspirations of the younger and less-accommodated section of the Sinhalese masses—which perceived hardly any opportunity of benefiting from the existing socioeconomic and political arrangements—and, consequently, its disenchantment with the alleged "centrist" character of the government aided by the parties of the "established left."[21] The government quelled the insurgency with the assistance of six countries (India, Pakistan, the United Kingdom, the United States, the Soviet Union, and Yugoslavia). But in the Sinhalese-Buddhist thrust of the constitution—in the socialist rhetoric, and last but not least, in the incorporation of emergency provisions therein—its shadow seemed to haunt the ruling elite.

During the proceedings of the constitution making, the earlier consensus turned into dissensus on some of the substantive clauses of the constitution dealing with religion, language, fundamental rights, and regional autonomy. As for religion, the Tamil representatives objected to Buddhism being accorded a "foremost" place in the constitution. However, their major objections were related to the provisions pertaining to language, citizenship, and a federal framework. The Tamil members of Parliament wanted Tamil along with Sinhala to be accorded an official language status. This was not acceptable to the UF. Failing this, they wanted the Special Provisions Act of 1958 regarding the Tamil language to be incorporated in the constitution. This was not acceded to either. Finally the Tamil MPs, who by 1972 had been quite disillusioned with the constitutional safeguards pertaining to the minority community and had formed a Tamil United Front (TUF), presented a six-point proposal providing for the recognition of the Tamil language as a national language and also for greater autonomy of the Tamil-populated areas. The TUF also informed the government that in the event of noncompliance with these demands, it would launch a nonviolent direct action against the government.

It is noteworthy that during the 1960s, although the Tamil leadership had time and again complained of "broken promises" on the part of successive governments, it had struck to its demands within a federal framework. In fact as late as 1970, in its election manifesto, the Federal party (providing the core for the TUF in 1972) had categorically appealed to the Tamil-speaking people not to lend their support to "any political movement that advocated the bifurcation of our country." Division of the country in any form, it stated, "would be neither beneficial to the country nor to the Tamil-speaking people."[22]

And yet the end of the constitutional proceedings marked the beginning of a separatist movement among the Tamils. The very fact that the constitution was rejected by both the Tamil parties, as well as the UNP, deprived it of countrywide consensus as an all-party, all-community document.

As regards the UNP, its major disagreement with the UF lay on the broad parameters of the constitution in which the classical balance of powers between the various organs of the government was not maintained. The judiciary was given a back seat and the bureaucracy was politicized. The UNP also viewed with concern the exclusion of the right of private property from the list of fundamental rights, and feared that the constitutional framework would lead to a system of state capitalism by a "prime ministerial" government without adequate recourse and power to representative and participative channels. Finally, the UNP also charged the UF with adopting a parochial attitude and policies toward the Tamil community, and thereby alienating it.

The Tamil Sense of Grievance: Subjective-Objective Dimensions

The constitution catalyzed a Tamil sense of grievance that had been simmering for quite some time. Revolving around the issues of language and employment, land settlement or colonization, and regional autonomy, it had subjective as well as objective dimensions.[23] Alongside the concerns for status and self-prestige, it had strong economic aspects too.

Thus, on the issue of the official language, the Ceylon Tamils had feared that the provisions of the new constitution would restrict the access of the vernacular-educated Tamil youth to the employment market, particularly in the public sector and in certain professional fields in which earlier they had done well. This was evident from the fact that their share in these services was much higher in the 1950s than their share of the total population in the island. The Tamils also feared that with the state being the biggest employer, and with the center being Sinhalese-dominated, partisan considerations might prevail over merit.

Added to this was the issue of land settlement or colonization schemes, in the context of which Colombo was charged with turning the majority Tamil areas into Tamil-minority ones. Consequently, it was maintained by the Tamil leadership that the employment opportunities for the "sons of the soil" shrank further, not to mention the vitiation of the ethnic character of the Tamil homeland.

As regards the issue of regional autonomy, the abrogation of the Bandaranaike-Chelvanayagam pact of 1957, the nonratification of the Tamil Language Act of 1958 until 1967 on procedural grounds, and the abortive parliamentary debate on the district councils in the 1960s and early 1970s indicated that regional autonomy was viewed by some of the Sinhalese leaders as a step toward Tamil separatism and, consequently, a threat to national integrity.[24]

No doubt the UF did make efforts to give impetus to the processes of decentralization through the District Development Councils (DDC), the district decentralized budget and the District Political Authority (DPA), who was an elected member of the area. However, these could not really take off in view of their heavy dependence on the center and the partisan compulsions of the DPA. As regards the DDCs, they failed "in almost all their avowed objectives: in planning, implementation, and monitoring of programs no less than in ensuring genuine popular participation in such planning as they indulged in. Political considerations distorted the choice of projects and resource-allocation."[25] Finally, the tug-of-war between the bureaucracy and the legislators over demarcation of their respective jurisdictions robbed the institutional framework of its effectiveness in most of the districts. Needless to add, such an experience of regional autonomy, unless radically overhauled, did not evoke much confidence in the northern and eastern areas.

Furthermore, some of the measures adopted by the UF in higher education were perceived by the Tamils as an attack on them. In particular, their strong resentment was against "standardization" of marks obtained by the Sinhalese and Tamil students. "Standardization" implied that it was not possible to compare equitably the standards of students in Tamil and Sinhala languages. Instead arbitrary cut points were set up, which were higher for Tamil medium students than for Sinhala medium ones. Such a decision met with stiff opposition. Consequently, the government decided to "standardize" marks in 1973 and also brought in a scheme of district quotas that favored students from the "backward" districts. The ultimate result of such quotas and standardization was a progressive decline in the number of Tamil students in science and engineering faculties—the two coveted faculties in which they had previously done very well. In the engineering faculty, for instance, their number declined from 48 percent of the total in 1969 to 14 percent in 1975.[26]

In the Sinhalese perception the Official Language Act, as well as the standardization and quota system for university entrance, were "affirmative action" provisions designed to compensate for the earlier disadvantages of the Sinhalese. The Tamils, on the other hand, viewed them as discriminatory provisions adopted by the majority community, placing their language in an inferior position, restricting their chances for higher education, and blocking their access to government services. The progressive decline of the Tamil ratio in recruitment to various central government services lent credence to their feeling of relative deprivation.[27]

With the medium of instruction in Tamil areas having been the Tamil language at the school level since 1945 and de facto at the university level since 1956 (except for a few non-humanities facilities), the ranks of the frustrated Tamil youths swelled progressively. This was accentuated not only by the disabilities they suffered in finding employment, but by the political ethos in which they were bred, which alienated them from the other parts of the country.

Such a mood of the youth was captured by the Tamil leadership, which expressed symbolic defiance in the form of the octogenarian TUF leader Chelvanayagam resigning from his constituency to protest the imposition of the new constitution, and rewinning it by a thumping majority on the plank of the "Free, Sovereign, Secular State of Tamil Eelam."

The by-election, and following from it the resolution adopted by the TUF (rechristened as the Tamil United Liberation Front) in its 1976 meeting, symbolized a marked and a radical shift in the Tamil demand "from the struggle for fundamental rights to the assertion of self-determination, from the acceptance of a pluralistic experiment to the surfacing of a new corporate identity"—i.e., a separate Tamil state.[28]

The Economic Performance of the UF

The separatist response of the Tamil leadership underlined the pressures and pulls of a system becoming increasingly centralized in ethnic as well as secular terms. Herein lay the dichotomies of the predominantly Sinhalese-socialist overtones of the UF—the legacy of the Bandaranaike governments—which were deepened during the UF regime. Briefly stated, such an order envisaged a politicoeconomic framework blending economic growth with distributive justice. Alongside the dominant Sinhalese-Buddhist overtones therein, a set of interrelated premises could be discerned in this respect. First, as regards the constitutional framework, sovereignty resided with the elected representatives of the people—i.e., the legislature. In effect however, it was the cabinet that became the epicenter. Second, in ushering in the socioeconomic changes, increasing state control over the critical sectors of the economy— domestic as well as foreign—and consequently greater expansion of the public sector was envisaged. Third, a restructuring of land and property relationships were aimed at through ceilings on them. Fourth, more emphasis was placed on import substitution to impart a greater degree of self-sufficiency. Finally, increasing institutional innovations were made to evoke greater popular participation in developmental processes.

If the domestic compulsions made such a reordering of the economic structuring inordinately difficult, so did the external environment.[29] In 1970, along with the escalation of oil prices, there was also a worldwide shortage of food and fertilizers. Meanwhile, production on the export crop of tea had dropped and the prices had not gone up either. During the years 1970–1977 food imports accounted for about 40 percent of the budget, and a severe shortage of inputs in industrial as well as agricultural sectors assailed the economy.

The government enacted legislation that although radical, was tardily implemented and did not improve the health of the economy. To illustrate, the government took over private import-export trade, gem trade, and (later) agency houses. State corporations were created to administer these sectors, which in most cases ran at a loss. Under the Business Acquisition Act of 1971 the government could acquire the property of any undertaking it considered necessary for national purposes. Further, under the ceiling of the Housing Property Law of 1973, the construction and ownership of houses was restricted. As regards the rural sector, a series of land reform acts during the years 1970–1975 led to the ceiling of land ownership and also its nationalization. In fact, by the Act of 1975, the state had become the largest owner of plantations. However, in the management of the plantation sector partisan considerations outweighed economic concerns.

The UF policies thus led to the widening of the state sector with poor performance. Also, its efforts toward self-sufficiency in various commodities through rigid quotas and state controls led to scarcities and long queues. Nor could it accelerate economic activity on a large enough scale to generate greater surplus to extend the public sector and create employment opportunities. Added to inflation, unemployment, rise in the cost of living, and scarcity of foodstuffs were blighted crops as a result of drought, necessitating greater expenditure on food imports and subsidies. Finally, power struggles within the UF led to the ouster of the LSSP in 1975 and the breakaway of the CP on the eve of the 1977 elections.

The Character of UF Rule

During its tenure the UF, using its overwhelming majority in the Constituent Assembly, had contrived to extend its term from five to seven years, i.e., beginning its five years with the promulgation of the new constitution. Such an action, apart from eroding the legitimacy of its political authority, also flouted a democratic tradition. Besides, emergency regulations were invoked too often, limiting parliamentary scrutiny of executive acts, prohibiting judicial review, suspending the Bill of Rights, and thereby impairing normal democratic processes. A weak judiciary having hardly any jurisdiction on the validity of legislative enactments facilitated a greater arbitrariness on the part of the executive. Furthermore, the government's takeover of one newspaper group and closure of another indicated its scant regard for freedom of the media, a vital component in the democratic functioning of a political system. Operating most of the time as an "emergency regime," the UF government left behind an institutional edifice of a "centralized democracy," which was fairly elaborate but without functional equilibrium between its legislative, executive, and judicial organs.[30]

The 1977 Elections: Landslide Victory of the UNP and Its Aftermath

As in 1970, the 1977 elections had several surprises to offer. In terms of seats as well as votes, the UNP's victory was unprecedented. In the half-century-long electoral history of Sri Lanka, no party had secured such a large majority of seats (83.3 percent) and no party had ever polled a majority of votes (50.9 percent) (Table 4.3). However, the UNP's massive increase in seats from seventeen in 1970 to 140 was produced by an increase of just 13 percent in its votes.[31]

Table 4.3 Party Performance in the 1977 Sri Lankan Elections

Parties	Seats Won	Percent of Seats Won	Popular Vote	Percent of Vote
UNP	140	83.3	3,179,221	50.9
SLFP	8	4.8	1,855,331	29.7
LSSP	0	0.0	225,317	3.6
CP	0	0.0	123,856	2.0
TULF	18	10.7	399,043	6.4
CWC	1	0.6	62,707	1.0
Independents	1	0.6	353,014	5.6
Others	0	0.0	45,082	0.8
Total	168	100.0	5,780,283	100.0
Total Electorate			6,667,589	
Voter turnout (percent)				87.2

Source: Report on the General Election to the Second National State Assembly of Sri Lanka, Sessional Paper 4, 1978 (Colombo: Department of Government Printing, 1978).

Organizational as well as politicoeconomic reasons accounted for such a landslide victory of the UNP. To begin with, during the years 1970–1977 sustained efforts were made to organize and streamline the party by J. R. Jayewardene. After the death of Dudley Senanayake in 1973 he also assumed the party presidency. During this period sustained efforts were made to expand the support base of the party and reach the lower middle stratum in the rural as well as the urban areas. The leadership claimed the UNP as the party of the "common man," aiming to inaugurate a *dharmishta* ("just and righteous") society. Such a "new" society, promised the UNP, would foster the interests of the peasant, farmer, the small industrialist, and the petty trader.

With the benefits of the radicalization policies of the UF percolating to only a small section and with the economic situation becoming increasingly stringent, the voter seemed to be, true to tradition, willing to give a chance to the major party in opposition in response to its promise of employment and freedom.

Although the SLFP won a significant share of the vote (29.7 percent), its record in terms of seats was disastrous, falling from 91 to 8 percent. However, it was the "old" left that took the worst beating. For the first time in the electoral history of Sri Lanka, both the LSSP and the CP drew a blank. Such a total rout of the two parties could be ascribed to the fragmentation of the left forces, which contended with each other and the SLFP (with whom, for the first time, they did not have electoral alliances) in many constituencies. Added to this was their credibility crisis as the junior partners in the centrist UF regime and their limited ability to turn their promises into performance in the wake of the SLFP's dominance in decision making. In the process their image as "progressive" parties was tarnished. Their harsh criticism of the JVP insurrectionaries presumably made matters worse in this respect. That their support base was constricted further was evident from the low percentage of votes cast for them. The LSSP vote came down by more than half from 1970 and the CP percentage dropped almost as much (Table 4.3).

The breakup of the SLFP-LSSP-CP alliance and the total rout of the left parties in the election disturbed the polarized contexts of the two-major-party system. Complicating the situation was the electoral behavior in Sri Lanka's Tamil-dominated area, where the TULF won an impressive victory with the demand of a separate Tamil state as its rallying point. The distinction it won for the spokesman of the TULF, A. Amirthalingam, as the leader of opposition (as it won the second largest number of seats—eighteen—in the National Assembly) was quite incongruous with its separatist demands in as much as it imposed certain obligations on him in a parliamentary framework (turned presidential in 1978). In the prevailing Tamil ethos, acceptance of the leader-of-the-opposition role was fraught with imponderables: on the one hand, the front's electoral pledge implicitly required opting out of the system. On the other hand, it provided bargaining opportunity within and as part of the power structure to procure safeguards, substantive enough to assuage the Tamil sense of grievance. Unfortunately, the spiralling communal violence, as will be discussed later, did not seem to augur well in this respect.

• THE POLITICAL SYSTEM SINCE 1977 •

UNP Efforts to Recast the Political System into a New Mold

It must be stated at the outset that the UNP leadership, particularly its Prime Minister Jayewardene, had hoped that the plans of his regime to virtually cast the system into a new mold would reckon with ethnicity by producing political stability and rapid economic modernization. The logic of some of the policies and innovations ushered in after 1977, as well as the structural constraints and contradictions in the domestic realm, belied such an optimism. Finally, the external factors, to the extent they impinged on the issues of economic viability and political integration of the country, seemed to be equally salient during the UNP regime.

To begin with, soon after coming to power the UNP took steps to replace the 1972 Constitution by framing a new one, which was promulgated in 1978. As in 1972, the 1978 Constitution did not meet the approval of the opposition parties. Consequently the constitutional framework remained bereft of a national consensus.

The major innovations of the new constitution were an elected executive presidency, certain safeguards to the minorities, provision for a referendum on stipulated issues, and a radical change in the electoral system from the first-past-the-post system to that of proportional representation.

The changeover from the Westminster model of a parliamentary system to a de Gaullist type of presidential system was justified on the ground that, for the acceleration of economic development as envisaged by the new regime, a strong and stable government was required. A judicious balance between democratic participation and political stability for the speedy implementation of developmental policies would best be realized in such a system, because the president would not be subject to the "constituency" considerations that legislators were.

However, in effect the presidential system has led to an increasing centralization of power by an executive-centered government. The overarching powers of the president have also led to a de facto devaluation of power for the other governmental organs—the legislature and the judiciary—thereby diminishing the overall balance of a democratic framework.

Moreover, the combination of the chief executive of the governing

party and the state executive in one person has been a significant factor
in this respect, and the tendering of the undated resignation letters by all
the UNP MPs to the president is an indicator of what such a combined
role implies. Thus, ironically enough, if the tyranny of majority has
muted the protests of the numerically weak opposition, it has also
curbed an independent and critical stand by any government MP.

Notwithstanding its constitutionally supreme position, the extent to
which the Parliament has virtually turned into a rubber stamp institution
is evident in, among other things, the speed with which it has rushed
through legislation. Thus, according to one estimate, in the first four-
and-a-half years the UNP passed 415 acts of Parliament—an average of
one a week! When necessary the UNP used its tyrannical majority with
impunity, as in 1979, when it decided to amend the constitution in such a
manner as to make the crossover from the opposition to the government
legitimate and not vice versa.[32]

Moreover, about half of the government MPs have been ministers
of sorts, including cabinet ministers, deputy ministers, ministers without
portfolio, district ministers, etc. Thus nearly half the MPs wear two
hats, combining an executive as well as a legislative role. And in such a
combined role, the former has often supervened the latter. In such a
situation parliament—notwithstanding its so-called sovereign powers—
has become, in effect, an appendage of the executive.

The Weakness of the Judiciary

Moreover, through constitutional provisions, the executive has
endowed itself with powers to curb the judiciary in many ways—a
process started by the former SLFP regime and taken full advantage of
by the present government. To illustrate, in 1978 the UNP passed the
Special Presidential Commission of Enquiry Law, under which the
president can establish a Special Commission of Enquiry, the recommendation of which can not be questioned in any court of law. Any
commission appointed under this legislation thus bypassed all the powers
of the judicial framework.

The extent to which the judiciary has been subordinated to the
legislature is evident from the judicial twists and turns of the first
Presidential Commission of Enquiry, formed in March 1978 to investigate the excesses committed during the previous regime. When the
leader of the SLFP challenged the powers of the commission to investigate a matter from the period prior to the enactment of this legislation,
the Court of Appeal's verdict was in favor of Mrs. Bandaranaike.
Accordingly, it issued a writ of prohibition against the government.
Soon after, however, the government enacted legislation declaring the

judgement and order of the Appeals Court in Mrs. Bandaranaike's petition "null and void" and authorizing the commission to proceed.

It is noteworthy that the constitution does not provide for judicial review after Parliament enacts such legislation. However, while being debated in Parliament, a bill can be referred to the Supreme Court for its advice, and the court must give its opinion within three weeks. In the case of an "urgent" bill, the three-week period can be reduced to twenty-four hours, as happened, for instance, in the case of the Prevention of Terrorism Bill. Moreover, the judiciary's opinion can be waived through a two-thirds majority vote in Parliament. Thus in November 1978, when the Universities Bill was referred to the Supreme Court, the court found that three clauses in the bill contravened the constitution. The ruling party, however, decided to retain these clauses and, amid the protest of a numerically weak opposition, passed the bill.[33]

Finally, on some important bills, the majority-minority balance in the Supreme Court's decisions seem to be precarious. On the fourth constitutional amendment bill of 1982 (regarding the validity of referendum for extending the Parliament's tenure), for instance, the court's ruling was four in favor and three against. Added to the implications of such a slender majority is the issue of the "committed" character of a segment of the judiciary. Such an allegation does have some empirical evidence. Soon after the inauguration of the 1978 Constitution, the government, on the plea that the new constitutional framework required the reorganization of the judiciary, dropped a number of judges and appointed new ones. There was also "leapfrogging" and the ignoring of seniority, evident from a table prepared by the civil rights movement on this theme.[34] After that it was felt that the judiciary was gradually being "packed" with the "right type of people." In the process its credibility, as well as autonomy, eroded considerably.

In sum, the legislature in theory and the executive in effect, as with the previous SLFP regime, have a predominant position vis-à-vis the judiciary. Commenting on the relationship between the judiciary and the legislature during the SLFP regime, a British scholar concluded that in various cases "unconstitutional acts are permissible, but by two-thirds majority. A government with such a majority can therefore secure the passage of valid legislation inconsistent with the constitution."[35]

At the annual General Conference of the Judicial Service Association in December 1982, President Jayewardene's address reflected a somewhat similar trend in emphasizing the nature of the judiciary's relationship to other governmental organs. "However much a judiciary may be independent," he declared, "there are occasions when there is a conflict between the Executive, the Parliament, and the Judiciary . . . ultimately it is the President elected by the people—it is the sovereignty of the people that matters and is important."[36]

Use of Constitutional Devices for Political Status Quo

With its top-heavy system and tyrannical majority in the Parliament, the
UNP government has also harnessed the constitutional apparatus for
the continuance of the political status quo, which (although in consonance with the laws of the land) at times tampered with, if not
subverted, well-entrenched democratic norms and practices.

The mode by which the UNP government extended its tenure by
another term is illustrative of this. As stipulated in the constitution, the
government passed a constitutional amendment to this effect and then
sought the electorate's verdict on this subject through a referendum.
The UNP justified its action for tenure extension by maintaining that a
strong government was necessary to continue its development program.
It also claimed that if elections were held, the "antidemocratic" (Naxalite)
elements already in the opposition would enter the Parliament and
thereby threaten the stability of the system.

These were, however, only the apparent arguments of the UNP
leadership. In fact it was conceded by many that if the election had been
held as scheduled in 1983, the UNP would have won but by a reduced
majority quite possibly less than the two-thirds needed for amending the
constitution. Referendum thus was a convenient shortcut to maintain
the status quo in the Parliament for another six years.

The gains of the referendum move for the UNP were obviously
many. However, the manner in which such a well-recognized democratic device was employed did not strengthen the democratic processes
in the country. If at all, it smacked of political manipulation of the
democratic process and abnegation—at least for the time being—of
proportional representation at the parliamentary level. The very premise
of the proportional representation (PR) system was to provide the
various political forces with a wider and relatively more equitable
opportunity to obtain representation in the political system. By seeking
a mandate for extending the tenure of a Parliament that had not been
elected on the basis of PR, the PR system's founding fathers had dealt it
a virtual death knell at the central level and to some extent had severely
jolted the island's conventional electoral tradition.

Finally, ironical as it may seem, the holding of too many elections—
the local government elections (1979 and 1983), District Development
Councils elections (1982), presidential elections (1982), and a referendum (1982) followed by a minielection (1983)—seemed to make people
election-weary, as was reflected in a decline in voter turnout in the
referendum and local elections in 1983.[37] The referendum thus heralded
an increasing erosion of the competitive party system, ensuring the
continuation of the present regime until 1989. Consequently, sources of
protest and dissent which might have found expression in the electoral

arena in 1983 had the elections been held, increasingly resorted to extraconstitutional means, with the worst manifestations of this being in the ethnic realm.

Ethnic Conflict and Violence Under the UNP Government

As regards the ethnic issue, there is no doubt that the UNP has been a legatee to a problem which is deep-rooted and impregnated with a highly volatile ethos. And although the Jayewardene regime did adopt certain measures in the spheres of language and education to meet the Tamil demands, they seemed to come too late and were not considered adequate to assuage the Ceylon Tamils, particularly the Tamil-educated youth. Their socialization in a milieu emphasizing the minority status of their community vis-à-vis the "tyrannical" majority of the Sinhalese was a major factor in their political alienation. Added to this was the absence of an effective bilingual stream in education, which coupled with the impasse on the language issue, led to a widening communication gap between the northern-based Tamils and the rest, particularly the younger people. Also in their respective textbooks (in Sinhala and Tamil), the Sinhalese and the Tamils received different historical interpretations that at times conflicted, reinforcing cultural prejudice and racial distrust. Finally, as mentioned earlier, a progressive decline in the Tamil share in the government services and other professions since independence exacerbated the Tamil sense of discrimination and diminished stake in the center. Such diminishing stakes, emotional as well as material, coupled with their perception—whether real or exaggerated— of relative deprivation became the anchor for the demand of Eelam. A segment of the Tamil youth took to arms to achieve this objective, bringing with it the phase of insurgency and counterinsurgency.

During the UNP regime the enmeshing of three types of violence can be discerned: (a) violence perpetrated by the Tamil militants, popularly known as "Liberation Tigers"; (b) violence wrought by the coercive apparatus of the state—the police and the military; and (c) communal violence.[38]

Communal violence had erupted earlier—in 1956, 1958, and 1961. However, it is the magnitude and scale as well as the goal that differentiate the ethnic violence during the UNP regime (1977, 1981, 1983, and sporadically thereafter) in comparison to such outbreaks in the 1950s and 1960s.

Earlier the Tamil demands were intrasystemic—for greater autonomy within a federal framework—as against the extrasystemic demand for a separate state by a segment of the Tamil people. Second, while the earlier ethnic violence affected the Ceylon Tamil-dominated areas, as well as Colombo, the violent outburst during the UNP regime also encompassed the central and southern areas, where there is a strong concentration of Indian Tamils. Third, the ethnic turmoil has been far more intense than before, reflecting a siege mentality on the part of both communities. While the Tamils feel increasingly marginalized, the Sinhalese perceive the Tamil sessionist demands as a threat to their identity as the "chosen people" of the *Sinhala Dwipa* ("island of the Sinhalese"), the locus of their Sinhalese Buddhist culture and civilization. Fourth, the behavior of the Sinhalese-dominated security forces, pitted against the Tamil terrorists in the north, has assumed at times distinct communal overtones. Finally, the "internationalization" of the Tamil issue in various forms has further compounded the ethnic tangle.

July 1983: The Tidal Wave of Ethnic Violence

The worst blowup of ethnic violence was in July 1983.[39] Although the fuse that ignited the spark was the killing of thirteen soldiers by the terrorists in the north, tension had been building up for quite some time. The dialogue between the government and the TULF had almost reached a breaking point. The relationship between the military and the Tamil people in the Northern Province had gone from bad to worse. The hit-and-run activities of the "Tigers" were making headlines almost daily in the media. Meanwhile, the security operations were becoming increasingly harsh, leading to a sudden swoop on the citizens, arrest of young men, and at times indiscriminate burning of places and destruction of property, particularly when some of the security forces were incensed by the terrorist killings of their compatriots.

The violence reached its frenzy on the black Friday of 29 July when rumors of the Tigers attacking Colombo led some of the Sinhalese to go berserk and murder Tamils mercilessly in Colombo and other areas. In many instances the police and defense forces remained passive. In some they encouraged the marauders. Mob violence took insane forms with the killing and burning of the Tamils, young and old. Some of them found refuge in Sinhalese houses, but a large number of them huddled in refugee camps. The loss in terms of lives and property was bad enough, but even worse was the sense of insecurity among the Tamils. It was exacerbated further by the killings of Tamil political prisoners twice in the central Welikada Jail in the capital, following the July violence.

Since then, peace and normalcy have continued to elude the Northern and Eastern Provinces, with the spill-over effects of the violence encompassing, at times, the predominantly Sinhalese areas adjacent to these two provinces. Despite government efforts to quarantine violence, its impact has been much beyond the precincts of the Tamil-dominated areas. The emergency, for instance, which was imposed earlier in the Jaffna area, has also become a countrywide phenomenon since 1982.

Also, the Prevention of Terrorism Act (giving the government wide-ranging powers of interrogation), which was initially promulgated for three years in 1979, has acquired permanence since 1982, incurring the charge of the opposition that the "Draconian" law could be used with impunity against any political protests, not merely ethnic.

More so, the promulgation of the sixth constitutional amendment in 1983, which required all parliamentarians to take an oath renouncing support for a separate state, reflected the lack of political sagacity on the part of the government. Under the prevailing circumstances the TULF parliamentarians, as anticipated, did not take the oath. Consequently, the amendment in effect led to their removal from the Parliament, closing thereby the parliamentary avenue for discussion between the TULF and the government.

Although the UNP has made several efforts to evolve a consensus on an ethnic "formula" acceptable to the various groups, it has not made much headway. The All-Party Conference (APC) convened by the UNP in 1984 to discuss the ethnic issue illustrates this. Along with the representatives of various political parties, the conference also included spokesmen of ethnic and religious groups, apparently to directly involve the Buddhist clergy, sections of which had expressed strong objections to the Tamil demands in the past. Hence, although the APC was convened ostensibly to discuss a gamut of issues related to minority communities, some of its members raised the issues of Sinhalese disabilities too. The only consensus that could evolve at this stage was to place on the agenda the grievances of all communities.

Although several issues (e.g., official language, public employment, land settlement) were put on the agenda, the crux of the matter related to the proposals for devolution of powers to regional or local authorities. Devolution per se was agreed to. It was the form and substance on which divergence prevailed. Underlining the impasse were "two contradictory and apparently inflexible positions taken up by two sides—on the one hand, 'District Councils and no more' and on the other hand, 'Regional Councils and no less.' "[40] The Sinhalese Buddhist opinion, expressed most vociferously by a section of the clergy, opposed any unit of devolution larger than the district council, and suspected the regional councils as a step toward Tamil Eelam. The SLFP, the major opposition of the UNP, adopted an intransigent approach similar to that of the Buddhist clergy and objected to the Indian "connections" of the TULF. The impasse in the negotiations was further complicated by the hard-liners within the UNP, by the raising tempo of violence—as reflected between the "rounds" of both the terrorists, as well as the military during the year—and by the fact that some of the Tamil militant groups were operating from southern India, where they were provided not merely moral, but also material, support. Such a positioning of the

Tamils was perceived as constraining the government's efforts toward containing terrorism.

Although Delhi reiterated its commitment to the territorial inviolability and sovereignty of its neighbor, the activities of various political parties and groups in Tamil Nadu—including statewide closure of shops and offices in sympathy with the Tamil community across the Palk Strait, attempted self-immolation by a few Tamils in the state, participation in international forums on the Eelam question, and the demand by some of them that India should find a military solution to the Tamil problem—did little to build up the confidence of the Jayewardene government in its neighbor.

Nonetheless, as the only agency with leverage on both the government of Sri Lanka and the Tamil militants (based largely in India), India has continued its mediatory role since July 1983. Its diplomatic initiatives during the abortive APC parleys, and its efforts to help facilitate negotiations between the moderate TULF, as well as the militant groups and the representatives of Sri Lankan government at Thimphu during July-August 1985 and thereafter, reflect its concern to find mechanisms for the devolution of power as an alternative to the Tamil separatist demands.[41]

By the end of 1986 the Jayewardene government had evolved a set of proposals for provincial councils modeled very much on the Indian federal pattern. However, while some of the parties and groups gave qualified support to the proposals, the SLFP as well as the Tamil militants virtually rejected them. While the former viewed them as excessive, the latter regarded them as too little vis-à-vis the Tamil demands.[42]

Alongside these negotiations, the encounters between the military and the militants continued in the Northern and Eastern Provinces. By 1986 one of the militant groups, the Liberation Tigers of Tamil Eelam (LTTE), had virtually taken over part of the Jaffna Peninsula in the Northern Province. In the process it had waged its battle not only with the Sri Lankan military, but had also grounded some of its rival groups. Such offensives and counteroffensives caught the civilians in the cross fire as before. A "protracted war" situation thus continued to haunt the country. Meanwhile, defense expenditure escalated from Rs560 million in 1978 to Rs10 billion in 1986, impinging on the fledgling economy of the strife-torn country.[43]

Economic Performance of the UNP Government

Unlike the SLFP—the economic perspectives of which were somewhat inward looking as well as regulatory, and hinged on greater state control and foreign exchange restrictions, along with import substitution—the economic perspectives of the UNP revolved around the liberalization of the economy by allowing market forces and the private sector to play a major role. As such, its economic policy package provided for an open-door economy with accent on free enterprise. Foreign exchange controls were relaxed; incentives were offered to enhance investment and export; the import monopolies of the state were divested except in the case of certain basic food items; and greater free play to the private sector was permitted. Alongside a major devaluation of the rupee a unified exchange rate was introduced. The government also telescoped the span of the Mahaweli river project from thirty to six years to accelerate irrigation facilities, hydroelectric power generation, land settlement, and self-sufficiency in food, particularly rice. Finally a heavy cut in consumer services was made. Food subsidies for everyone were abolished. Instead, the government introduced "food stamps" for those earning less than Rs300 ($1 = Rs16) in order to cushion the economically depressed strata. In 1986 this amount was raised to Rs700 ($1 = Rs28). However, earlier, all the members of a family earning less than Rs300 had been entitled to food stamps. Under the new scheme the issue of food stamps was limited to a maximum of five in each such family.[44]

The cut in social services in the total budgetary expenditure was significant: from 43 percent in 1977 to an estimated 16 percent in 1984. This accentuated social inequalities, warping previous trends—such as they were—toward distributive justice.[45]

Although in the initial years, with massive foreign aid and loans, the UNP did succeed in generating an impressive record of economic growth and employment opportunities (cutting the rate of unemployment from 26 percent in 1977 to 13 percent in 1982), it has not been easy to sustain this rate. "We can not make progress on the employment front," commented Finance Minister Ronnie de Mel in 1986, "while so much of our scarce resources are being diverted to security-related expenditure. Furthermore, without peace the investment climate will not improve. A better climate for private sector investment is a *sine qua non* for sustained progress on the unemployment front."[46]

Alongside the negative effects of ethnic conflict, the downward plunge in the prices of primary commodities like tea and rubber—the traditional mainstays of Sri Lanka's exports—continued to reflect the country's economic vulnerability in its dependence on the world market for a couple of tree crops. Furthermore, the poor performance of most nontraditional agricultural exports and increases in import volumes led to large trade deficits and an increasingly adverse balance of payments.

Added to all of this has been an unprecedented foreign debt accumulation during the years 1977–1985. From 1977 to 1982, net receipts of foreign assistance from loans and grants accelerated from $151 million in 1977 to $403 million in 1982. Of the total resources mobilized during this period 40 percent were in the form of grants. However, since 1900 Sri Lanka had to resort increasingly to commercial borrowings from the European market, which had serious repercussions for its repayment obligations, and also for increasing debt service payments, which accounted for about one-fourth of its total exports in 1985.[47]

The further sustenance of the Sri Lankan economy thus increasingly hinges on external resources in the form of aid and investment. The future volume of aid (both multilateral and bilateral) is uncertain. This uncertainty only underscores the importance of a massive flow of foreign investment.

Earlier it was believed that, given the lease of life for another six years, the UNP would complete the Mahaweli Project, which will give an impetus to economic growth in many ways. In addition it was hoped that with the assurance of governmental continuity, greater foreign investment from countries like the United States, West Germany, and Japan would be forthcoming. With the induction of such foreign investment, the export-oriented economy might then reach its takeoff stage by the end of the 1980s.

However, such a hope has been shattered to a considerable extent. "A slowing down in the rate of economic growth," lamented the finance minister, "is expected in 1986. GDP is expected to grow by 4 percent in real terms compared to the average of 5 percent recorded in the previous 3 years. Our growth rate has declined in 1986 due to poor weather conditions, depressed commodity prices, reduced local and foreign investment, lower earnings from tourism, and above all, due to the ethnic troubles in the country. Investment, tourism, fisheries, agricultural production and transport were affected by the ethnic conflict."[48] The continuation of violence, leading to an escalation in military buildup and consequently defense expenditure, also contributed to economic strains, affecting in the process economic "growth, employment, and living standards."[49]

Under the circumstances, the chances of externally induced economic buoyancy reaching a takeoff stage by the end of the 1980s seem to be rather bleak. And if the political trends are any indication, the halfway-through Singaporean model of economic liberalism may not augur well for the prospects of democracy in Sri Lanka.

• THEORETICAL ANALYSIS •

Mixed Success With Democratic Governance

Structural constraints, coupled with the lag between the levels of political and economic development, account for the "mixed success" of the democratic experiment in Sri Lanka. Underlying such experiences are a number of contradictory pressures and pulls that besiege the democratic framework of the Sri Lankan state. If the regularly held elections and electoral mandate provided it legitimacy, the governmental processes have weakened the authority of such legitimacy. If the constitutional framework of a unitary state provided some leeway for power dispersal, the very mechanisms and public policies have rendered it increasingly centralized and narrowly based. Further, an adversarial concept of politics in a highly competitive and volatile ethos, coupled with an increasingly bland affirmation of majoritarian principles in a multiethnic society and maldeveloped economy, have brought in their wake the crisis of integration, particularly in the ethnic realm.

However, looking at the situation in a large number of Third World countries, what is striking in the Sri Lankan case is not just the challenges of legitimacy and integration assailing its political system, but the pertinent fact that so far it has managed to muddle through its democratic existence, which is becoming precariously unstable.

Social Mobilization, Economic Underdevelopment, and Politicization

The balance sheet of factors pertaining to the erosion and endurance of the democratic structure and norms is instructive in this respect. To begin with, democratic mechanisms originated in the colonial framework providing the opportunity to the Sri Lankan elite to acquire experience with democratic institutions prior to independence. In the postindependence period the Westminster model was followed with its usual checks and balances. A competitive party system emerged and an increasing number of people participated in electoral politics.

On the economic front, going by the general yardstick, economic inequality was limited, socioeconomic inequalities were dispersed, and class cleavages were not deep or polarized, not because of lack of poverty but because of lack of affluence. The economy continued to be dependent on the export of tree crops (tea, rubber, and to some extent, coconut) and did not gain the momentum for diversification. Such economic stagnation went along with welfare measures in the form of subsidized social services in health, education, and food. While on the one hand, these cushioned the economic conditions of the lower strata, on the other hand, they appeared to appropriate a lion's share in current budget expenditure. On one side, these welfare measures could be credited for the high physical quality of life indicators of Sri Lanka, which matched some of the countries having a much higher per capita income. On the other, the quantum of Sri Lanka's welfare expenditure was excessive, as reflected partly in its large balance-of-payments deficit.

Furthermore, the improvement of health services led to a population boom, not because of an increase in the birth rate (which in fact declined over decades) but as a result of declining infant mortality, leading to the phenomenon (often ignored in the context of many Third World countries) of persons below the age of twenty-five accounting for two-thirds of the Sri Lankan population in the 1970s. With literacy being 85 percent, thanks to the welfare services, this youth population has been literate and also fairly politicized. However, it perceived its opportunity structures as highly constricted in general terms because of the stagnant economy. More so, the imperatives of a competitive party system also brought the politics of patronage, with partisan considerations outweighing merit in an already stringent economy.

The Insurgency of 1971: Dichotomies of a Sprawling Middle Class

It is in this respect that the challenges to the democratic system posed by the 1971 insurgency become pertinent. Here was a segment of the youth of the rural lower middle strata, which had as its goal seizure of state power through violent means. Among other factors, this was a revolt of the "emerging elite" against the "established" ones. While the specter of unemployment was haunting, the rather narrow socioeconomic bases of the political elite did not leave much hope for this emergent group to make it in politics either. In other words, electoral participation gave the "emerging elite" an awareness of their political power, but without a share in power.

The Sinhalese insurgency of 1971 and the trials and tribulations of the Sri Lankan democracy thereafter indicate that if the political awareness of the masses is low and the economy is somewhat structurally differentiated, then the issues of credibility, legitimacy, and accountability may not assume a high salience and are thus easily handled by the power elite. However, with the processes of social transformation, the more the realization of the socioeconomic assumptions of democracy, the greater is the pressure on the ruling regimes to aggregate popular demands meaningfully. And the less the capability of the leadership to aggregate them, the more is its tendency to have recourse to populist slogans and to assume the traits of emergency regimes.

State Expansion, Centralization, and Emergency Regimes

In fact in Sri Lanka, the long track record to the United Front operating under emergency regulations was the beginning of the "constitutional dictatorship," with the country being governed under emergency regulations providing the government with power to suspend most basic freedoms with the concurrence of a majority in the Parliament.[50] These powers were incorporated in the 1972 Constitution, as well as 1978, and were frequently used by the leadership of the UF as well as the UNP. Emergency regimes, however, hardly succeeded in fostering development. If at all, they contributed to the trend of increased centralization.

Ironic as it may seem, an increasing centralization of state power in Sri Lanka occurred during the UF regime that had an unprecedented majority. Although sovereignty of the Parliament—the elective representative of the people—was enshrined in the new constitution, in effect, it led to executive-centered government, a trend further crystallized under the presidential system introduced by the UNP. Apart from vitiating the balance between various governmental organs, the centralization of state power also affected the dynamics of devolution of power—a significant component of a functioning democracy.

Alongside the trends of centralization, the efforts toward homogenization have also given a setback to the democratic process in Sri Lanka. This has been evident in the increasing tension between the Sinhalese and the Tamils, with its extreme manifestation being the enmeshing of the violence of the state apparatus and that of the militants espousing the cause of a separate Tamil state.

It may be noted that the expanding penetration of the state is not a phenomenon specific to a developing country like Sri Lanka but characterizes the state systems of the developed world too. This has been partly the result of the thrust of science and technology and partly its legitimation in ideological terms, particularly in the context of the liberal democratic concept of the modern state. Thus with the conception of state as a "social institution," not only have its activities widened but in the process a "territorial center" has emerged as the prime source of legitimacy around which identities have been built. Second, such a center has become the spokesman of the emergent political form everywhere, namely the "nation," defining both its internal and external boundaries. Third, as the state began to extend toward peripheries and the lives of the people in its attempt to deal with economic and social affairs and to manage diverse forms of conflict, this led to a continuing "expansion in the functions of the state and paved the way for its increasingly managerial and bureaucratic as well as mercantilist and welfare orientations."[51]

Implicit in the virtually irreversible process of state expansion is the issue of the nature and composition of its power elite. Equally significant are the issues of the consolidation of democratic institutions and of the strength of the democratic impulse, as reflected and cherished by the citizenry, which can provide the check to the trends of statism.

Such a consolidation of democratic institutions, reflecting as well as balancing the sociopolitical collectivities in Sri Lanka, have yet to go a long way. It seems that as long as its competitive party system remained coalitional, it had greater resilience in accommodating the interests of various groups. Besides, despite the change of parties alternating since 1956, not only was defeat accepted by the vanquished gracefully, but also with a certain degree of respect for the political opponent. Thus there was a widening of bipartisan areas and an acceptance of the imperatives of governance.

However, the election of 1970 changed significantly the coalitional and balanced nature of the party system. The constitution of 1972 crystallized this trend. An increasing ideological hiatus between the ruling UF and the UNP as also between the UF and the Tamil parties was brought into the open, followed by erosion of consensus among the major sociopolitical segments of the population.

As such, it was not the factionalization of parties but polarization of various parties and groups at two levels, central and central-local, that became critical. At the central level, the fact that in the highly volatile and competitive ethos of politics both the UNP and the SLFP had their base in the Sinhalese majority areas implied their partisan vulnerability on the ethnic question. Consensus on the issue of safeguards to the minority was not easy to evolve because both the parties, when out of power, tried to cash in on the Sinhalese Buddhist sentiments to the extent of getting the agreement between the government and the Tamil parties abrogated or abandoned. Herein lay the dilemma. The competitive party system as evolved in Sri Lanka vindicated the democratic principles through open and fair electoral competition. Almost simultaneously the majoritarian trends, inherent in such a competition, increasingly relegated the major minority to a peripheral position. The coalitional imperative had given the Tamil parties some leeway, but this diminished increasingly since the 1970s. As a result, interethnic cleavages intensified.

Ethnic Cleavages in an Ethnically Focused System

In contrast to India, which in terms of its ethnic group constellations has been rightly termed by Horowitz as an "ethnically dispersed system," the Sri Lankan system has been ethnically centralized. A major feature of such a system is that a few groups are large enough to have the issue and extent of their interaction be a "constant theme of politics at the center." Even when sharing power there is a competitive edge in their relationship with a felt, if not stated, premise that the claims of one group can only be made at the cost of the other. "In dispersed systems," observes Horowitz, "the relationship between group and group is mediated by the relationship between the locality and the center. In centralized systems, one group confronts another directly, generally in a competitive framework. . . . The center is not a neutral arbiter originating elsewhere. On the contrary the center itself is a focal point of competition. To the extent that contending groups succeed in controlling it, the center becomes an actor as much as arbiter in ethnic conflict."[52] In case of Sri Lanka the partisan vulnerability of the two major parties has not only been heightened by the electoral contests, but what is more, the pursuit of a tyrannical majority by both of them in succession has diminished possibilities of a durable Sinhalese-Tamil reconciliation.

On the Tamil side, in response to this situation, the moderate TULF finds itself compelled to adhere to its separatist demand. In the process, efforts to find a solution to the Tamil question have been caught in a vicious circle: the bullet of the army or the militants results in a situation of violence begetting violence, and a "protracted war" precludes not only political normalcy but also corrodes the democratic structure.

Moreover, the fact that the armed forces have been Sinhalese-dominated has provided a sharp communal edge to the majority-minority conflict. In due course, the Sinhalization of the military may be total—negating the plural character of Sri Lankan society.

Geopolitical Dimensions of the Ethnic Issue

In its effort to contain the militant edges of the Sinhalese-Tamil issue the government has to contend with its geopolitical dimension. In the past there was no doubt that the Jayewardene regime, despite seeking close links of cooperation with Mrs. Gandhi to contain Tamil Nadu's ambivalence toward separatism, felt rather uncertain about the extent to which Delhi would go to contain the activities of the militants in Tamil Nadu, and consequently perceived the major source of its security threat to be from India or via India. On the other hand the tilt in the Sri Lankan foreign policy toward the West, particularly the United States, and the considerable economic support that it received for developmental purposes, was at times linked to its geopolitical importance in the Indian Ocean. And despite the categorical denial of the United States, the prospect of a U.S. base in the excellent harbor of Trincomalee, in the Eastern Province, is regarded with seriousness in India. The possibility of this development has brought a divergence in the perception of the strategic interests of India and Sri Lanka, highlighting the geopolitical dimension of the ethnic tangle.

• SUMMARY •

In sum, over the decades the twists and turns of an "overheated" polity and a limping economy have operated in a manner that erodes the

consensus on basic issues among the various sociopolitical collectivities
and weakens the mechanisms—institutional as well as noninstitutional—
which mediated between the various social collectivities and the state in
order to manage conflict at various levels. The less effective their
initiative and clout for mediation, the greater has been the interlocking
of situations between the center and the various sociopolitical collectivities. And in situations leading to polarization and direct confrontation,
the more frequent the use of the state apparatus, the greater has been
the political vulnerability of the power wielders in terms of the legitimacy of their democratically elected regime.

In the process deep fissures can be discerned in the consensual mold
of politics as it evolved since 1948. Such fissures, related to a complex
web of factors and forces, domestic as well as external, reflect the
contradictory pressures and pulls of freedom, equity, and growth in a
civil society undergoing rapid social change in certain areas and virtual
stagnation in others.

• FUTURE PROSPECTS •

Sri Lanka stands at a crossroads today. Its present situation is essentially
a symptom of the aberration in participatory political culture (as the
country evolved since independence). At this juncture it is difficult to
foresee this aberration being corrected, and it is an open question as to
whether in the coming years the democratic framework of Sri Lanka will
survive the crises of state and nation building or will wither away.

If the challenges of integration and legitimacy confronting the
present regime as well as its predecessor and their performance in this
respect are viewed as pacesetters, then a further erosion of democratic
norms and structures seem a distinct possibility.

Even so, embedded in the system are also certain mechanisms that
do have the potential of containing such an erosion. The electoral
system and the dynamics of the ballot box, for instance, may operate as
cushioning factors in this respect. Thus in the event of general elections
being held in 1989 as scheduled, under a system of proportional representation, the electoral tradition of alternating governments may be
maintained, but not the massive majority of the ruling party as has
prevailed since 1970, partly because of the first-past-the-post system.

In the absence of the tyrannical majority, whether the context be
that of regime change or regime continuity, some of the distortions that
crept into the system under the 1972, as well as the 1978, Constitution
may not occur. But that may not adequately arrest the continuing trend
of centralization in political as well as economic spheres.

Prospects of the Free Market Economy

This seems to be implicit in the pattern of economic development initiated by the present government. In this respect the Singaporean model may have a modicum of success. However, it may not go very far for a variety of reasons. To begin with, it needs to be noted that if there are the success stories of South Korea, Taiwan, and Singapore to go by, there are also the not-so-successful experiences of countries like the Philippines and Thailand despite similar development strategies on the part of their power elites.

The experiences of these Southeast Asian states underscore the importance of (1) cultural factors, (2) an uninterrupted economic commitment, (3) the time span, and (4) the market availability as well as facilities for export of manufactured goods.

In the case of Singapore, for instance, it is a known fact that the linkage of its predominantly Chinese population with the Chinese overseas provided it with financial resources and, to some extent, technical know-how. As regards the South Koreans, their tradition of hard work and a somewhat disciplined ethos helped them considerably in comparison to, for instance, the Thai social ethos that, with its "rice bowl" culture, has been rather happy-go-lucky. The Sri Lankan social ethos seems to be closer to that of the Thais in this respect.

Besides, in both Singapore and South Korea, alongside an uninterrupted commitment of foreign economic flow (with economic and political repercussions) their respective economies needed almost two decades to gather a momentum of their own. In the case of Sri Lanka, it is difficult to determine whether it can be assured of such a flow for even a decade in the context of global recession and stagflation. The extent of aid from its donors, individually as well as collectively, is impressive. Even so, more economic assistance from these sources would be required in the 1980s and thereafter, and that too on a continuing basis, particularly in view of the inflow of foreign investment not being as big as expected because of civil strife. Consequently the Sri Lankan economy will have to go a long way to gather its own momentum. In any case, at least initially, economic liberalism and political liberalism may not go side by side.

The Challenge of Integration

With economic resources continuing to be somewhat constricted the ruling regime, then as now, will need to cope with the lingering issue of integration in elite-mass terms as well as ethnic terms.

The challenge of integration symbolizes the lag between policy and performance. More so, it focuses the issues related to participation at various levels and is ensconced in the dispersal of power and authority.

The Devolution Debate: Imperatives of a
National Consensus

As a principle, devolution of power has a universal acceptance in Sri Lanka as a bedrock of participatory democracy. And yet there has been a continuous expansion of the powers of the center. Moreover, the devolution debate has been going on without leading to a consensus among various parties and groups either regarding the focal unit or its powers and functions.

Generally speaking, a federal framework may be considered to be a device to cope with the demands of autonomy. However, in view of the Sinhalese-Buddhist susceptibilities, the devolution of power has to be provided for within the existing unitary framework but in a manner as to carry forward the devolution of authority principle vertically from the district to the provinces. And, on this point, not only have there been differences between the Tamil groups and the UNP, but also between the UNP and the SLFP. Thus the district development councils, as promulgated by the UNP, were not endorsed by the SLFP nor by the LSSP and the CP; nor did the latter three parties participate in the DDC elections of 1981. And in any issue pertaining to the minority community, only a bipartisan consensus can assure an enduring settlement.

In 1964 for instance, when the Sirimavo-Shastri pact was signed, Mrs. Bandaranaike had kept herself in continuous touch with the UNP leader, Dudley Senenayake, and had thereby procured his endorsement on the broad principles underlying the issue. Unless and until President Jayewardene succeeds in having an understanding with the SLFP leadership, any agreement with the Tamil leadership may not endure.

Restoration of Normalcy

Closely related to the issue of national consensus is that of cessation of hostilities. As on the framework of national reconciliation, and on the question of ceasefire, there have been charges and countercharges of breach of promise on both sides. A negotiated settlement cannot be worked out unless there is a truce, at least temporarily. It is in this respect that the "peace constituency" in both India and Sri Lanka needs to be strengthened. It is also not without significance that the individuals and organizations comprising such a constituency are virtually in unison in emphasizing the importance of the dimensions of human rights and freedom of the Tamils in particular and Sri Lankans in general.

At this juncture, although a negotiated settlement is not yet in sight, barring a very small segment on both the sides the imperative of political normalcy is recognized by all. However, the extent to which the domestic pressures and external persuasion tend to a negotiated formula will hinge considerably on the containment of violence.

Democracy, Political Credibility, and Accountability

Even if a negotiated settlement is arrived at, its credibility will depend on its implementation. Thus structural mechanisms may be significant but not sufficient requisites for conflict management. Their effectiveness in realizing the desired objective is equally important. And it is in this respect that the capabilities and will of the leadership assume a criticality.

In sum, the prospect of democracy in Sri Lanka will depend on the extent to which its leadership can cope with its partisan vulnerability, in fact rise above it, in evolving a consensual mold of politics that would enable the state to act as an arbiter and not as an agent of the dominant community.

• NOTES •

1. Until 1972 Sri Lanka was officially known as Ceylon. In the 1972 Constitution it was redesignated as Sri Lanka. In this chapter I have used both names interchangeably.
2. For statistical details on ethnic groups during the years 1881–1971 see Sri Lanka, Department of Census and Statistics, *The Population of Sri Lanka* (Colombo: CICERD, 1974), Table 3: 16, p. 44. For the census statistics of 1981 see Sri Lanka, Department of Census and Statistics, *Census of Population and Housing*, Sri Lanka, 1981: Preliminary Release No. 1 (Colombo: Department of Census and Statistics, 1981).
3. Amita Shastri, *Politics of Constitutional Development in South Asia in the Seventies: A Case Study of Sri Lanka* (Ph.D. thesis, School of International Studies, Jawaharlal Nehru University: New Delhi, 1984, mimeo), p. 132.
4. For details see Jane Russell, "Communal Politics Under the Donoughmore Constitution: 1931–1947," *Ceylon Historical Journal* 26 (1982) (Delhiwala, Sri Lanka: Tisara Prakasakayo). Also see Robert N. Kearney, *Communalism and Language in the Politics of Ceylon* (Durham, N.C.: Duke University Press, 1967), pp. 30–40.
5. The constitution was popularly named after the commission, appointed by the colonial office in 1927 to recommend the constitutional reforms. The commission submitted its report in 1928 and its recommendations were put into effect in 1931.
6. Shastri, *Politics of Constitutional Development*, pp. 103–109.
7. For details see Urmila Phadnis, *Religion and Politics in Sri Lanka* (Delhi: Manohar, 1976), pp. 121–122.
8. Bandaranaike was until 1951 a prominent member of the UNP, when he broke away from it and formed the Sri Lanka Freedom Party. For details see W. Howard Wriggins, *Ceylon: Dilemmas of a New Nation* (Princeton: Princeton University Press, 1960), pp. 106–124.
9. Denzil Peiris, *1956 and After: Background to Parties and Politics in Ceylon Today* (Colombo: Associated Newspapers of Ceylon, 1958), p. 10.
10. The Bandaranaike-Chelvanayagam Pact agreed to legislation providing the recognition of Tamil as the "language of the national minority." It also provided that the language of administration in the Northern and Eastern Provinces would be Tamil.

Furthermore, Regional Councils with powers relating to agriculture, education, and other matters (including the selection of colonists for government-sponsored colonization schemes) were to be established. Kearney, *Communalism and Language* p. 85.

11. Under this agreement, out of the estimated 975,000 "stateless" Indian Tamils, India and Sri Lanka agreed to grant citizenship to 525,000 and 300,000 in a 7:4 ratio over fifteen years. As regards the residue of 150,000, no agreement could be arrived at in 1964. Another agreement, signed a decade later, settled the residue with both the governments agreeing to share it equally. However, in early 1986, an estimated 94,000 "stateless" Tamils still remained, and Sri Lanka decided to absorb them, as most of those persons had not opted for Indian citizenship.

12. Of the eight parliamentary elections in Sri Lanka since 1947, two resulted in the formation of the coalition almost immediately after the elections (1947 and 1965). In the other two (1956 and 1970), an alliance was forged before the elections. Of the rest, in one (March 1960) the governing party the voted out of power almost immediately after the elections primarily because it had failed to obtain a coalitional consensus. In another, the ruling SLFP—after hanging onto a precariously slender majority for three-and-a-half years (1960–1964)—formed the coalition government with the LSSP.

13. Sri Lanka, *Report on the General Election to the Second National State Assembly of Sri Lanka (Eighth Parliamentary General Election 21 July 1977)*, Sessional Paper 4, 1978 (Colombo: Department of Government Printing, 1978). Also see G.P.S.H. de Silva, *A Statistical Survey of Elections to the Legislatures of Sri Lanka, 1911–1977* (Colombo: Marga, 1979).

14. Ibid.

15. Ibid.

16. For a socioeconomic profile of the MPs during the period 1947–1970, see Robert N. Kearney, *The Politics of Ceylon (Sri Lanka)* (London and Ithaca: Cornell University Press, 1973), pp. 48–50. Also see Shastri, *Politics of Constitutional Development in South Asia*, pp. 316–319.

17. Sri Lanka, *Report on the General Election.*

18. A. Jeyaratnam Wilson, *Electoral Politics in an Emergent State: The Ceylon General Elections of May 1970* (London: Cambridge University Press, 1975), p. 178.

19. For a brief account of the politics of rice see the author's "Sri Lanka Today," *Current History* 63 (November 1972): pp. 310–312.

20. Shastri, *Politics of Constitutional Development in South Asia*, p. 190.

21. Gananath Obeyesekere, "Some Comments on the Social Background of the April 1971 Insurgency in Sri Lanka [Ceylon]," *Journal of Asian Studies* 33 (May 1974): pp. 367–384. Also see Politicus, "The April Revolt in Ceylon," *Asian Survey* 12 (March 1972): pp. 259–274; and the author's, "Insurgency in Ceylon Politics: Problems and Prospects," *Institute of Defence Studies and Analyses Journal* 3 (April 1971): pp. 582–606.

22. For the text of the election manifesto of the FP see *Ceylon Daily News, Seventh Parliament of Ceylon, 1970* (Colombo: Associated Newspapers of Ceylon, 1970), pp. 190–195.

23. For an overview of the Sinhalese-Tamil cleavages, see Russell, *Communal Politics*. Also see various essays in Michael Roberts, ed., *Collective Identities: Nationalism and Protest in Modern Sri Lanka* (Colombo: Marga Institute, 1979); C. R. de Silva, "The Sinhalese-Tamil Rift in Sri Lanka," in A. J. Wilson and Dennis Dalton, eds., *The States of South Asia: Problems of National Integration* (Honolulu: University Press of Hawaii, 1982); and R. N. Kearney, "Language and the Rise of Separatism in Sri Lanka," *Asian Survey* 18 (May 1978): pp. 521–534.

24. Unlike the colonial period when the country had provinces as the highest administrative units, in the postcolonial period the district was recognized as the unit of administration. At present, there are nine provinces comprising twenty-five districts.

25. K. M. de Silva, *Sri Lanka: The Dilemmas of Decentralization* (Paper presented at the Ford Foundation Cross-National Workshop on Structural Management to East Ethnic Tension, Nairobi, September 1981, mimeo).

26. For details see C. R. de Silva, "Weightage in University Admissions: Standardization and District Quotas in Sri Lanka, 1970–1975," *Modern Ceylon Studies* 5 (July 1974): pp. 156–172; and "The Politics of University Admissions: A Review of Some of the Aspects of the Admission Policy in Sri Lanka: 1971–1978," *Sri Lanka Journal of Social Sciences* 1 (December 1978): pp. 88–123. Also see K. M. de Silva, "University Admissions

and Ethnic Tensions in Sri Lanka, 1977–1982," in Robert B. Goldman and A. Jeyaratnam
Wilson, eds., *From Independence to Statehood: Managing Ethnic Conflict in Five African
and Asian States* (London: Frances Printer, 1984), pp. 97–107.
  27. S. W. R. de A. Samarasinghe, "Ethnic Representation in Central Government
Employment in Sinhala-Tamil Relations in Sri Lanka, 1948–1981," in Goldman and
Wilson, eds., *From Independence to Statehood*, pp. 173–184.
  28. Neelan Tiruchelvam, "The Politics of Decentralization and Devolution: Competing Conceptions of District Development Councils in Sri Lanka," ibid., p. 198.
  29. For a succinct account of economic development during this period, see various
articles in two issues of *Logos* (published in Colombo) entitled "Insights into Sri Lankan
Economy" (vol. 19, no. 4, December 1980), and "Sri Lankan Economy in Crisis in the
Eighties" (vol. 20, no. 2, June 1981). For an overview of the Sri Lankan Economy until
1977, see N. Balakrishnan, "A Review of Economy," in Tissa Fernando and R. N.
Kearney, eds., *Modern Sri Lanka: A Society in Transition* (New York: Syracuse University,
1979), pp. 101–130. Also see Karl Jackson, *State, Policy, and the Economy with Case
Studies from Kenya and Sri Lanka, Research Series No. 12* (Hague: Institute of Social
Sciences, 1982).
  30. K. M. de Silva, *A History of Sri Lanka* (London: C. Hurst, 1981), p. 546.
  31. *Report on the General Election (1977)*. In writing this section, I have drawn
heavily from some of my recent writings, e.g., "The Political Order in Sri Lanka under the
UNP Regime: Emerging Trends in the 1980s." *Asian Survey* 24 (March 1984): pp.
279–294; "Sri Lanka: Stresses and Strains of Small State," in U. S. Bajpai, ed., *India and
Its Neighbourhood*, (Delhi: Lancer International, 1986), pp. 237–272; and *Ethnic Conflict
in Sri Lanka* (Report submitted to Gandhi Peace Foundation, New Delhi, July 1984,
mimeo).
  32. Article 161 of the constitution was enacted with a view to discouraging the
parliamentarians from defecting from one party to another. Section 161 (d) (ii) explicitly
stated that if a member ceased by resignation, expulsion, or otherwise to be member of the
political party under the label of which he had contested in the election, he was deemed to
have lost his seat. In the case of his expulsion, however, the Supreme Court was the final
arbiter in deciding the validity of such an expulsion. Two crossover cases prompted the
government to amend the constitution with retrospective effect. Section 161 (d) (ii) was
repealed and the amendment removed the provision relating to an individual vacating his
seat on his own volition and joining another party. As regards the issue of expulsion, even
if the Supreme Court recognized the validity of such an expulsion, the Parliament could
still appoint a select committee that could maintain that the member resigned from the
political party in the "national interest" and thus was not subject to expulsion. A resolution of the Parliament could decide the matter by majority vote. This implied that "under
normal conditions only the ruling party or coalition can provide this majority making the
crossover one-way traffic." W. A. Wiswavarnapala, "Sri Lanka's New Constitution,"
Asian Survey 20 (September, 1980): pp. 928–930.
  33. Ibid., p. 926.
  34. Civil Rights Movement, *The People's Rights* (Colombo: Civil Rights Group,
1979), pp. 132–133.
  35. Saul Rose, "The Constitution in South Asia: Westminster Remodelled," *Round
Table*, no. 252, October 1973, pp. 439–450.
  36. *Sunday Observer* (Colombo), 12 December 1982.
  37. In electorates where the UNP candidates had fared badly in both the presidential
election as well as referendum, by-elections were held. Out of eighteen such by-elections,
the UNP retained fourteen.
  38. Initially the "Tiger Movement" found its nucleus in the Tamil Students Federation," with its base in Jaffna in the early 1970s. According to a publication of the
Liberation Tigers of Tamil Eelam (LTTE), the Tiger Movement took birth in 1972 and
was called the "Tamil New Tigers." Subsequently it broke into two groups. The parent
group was renamed the LTTE, and the breakaway group called itself the People's
Liberation Organization of the Tamil Eelam (PLOT). Another group that came into being
around the late 1970s was called "Tamil Eelam Liberation Organization" (TELO). Apart
from them some groups had London as their operation base. Noteworthy among them are
the Eelam Revolutionary Organization of Students (EROS), tracing its origin to 1975 and
expounding Marxist-Leninist principles and the General Union of Eelam Students (GUES)

formed in 1977 as the student organization of EROS. Later these groups broke up, and the Eelam People's Revolutionary Liberation Front (EPRLF) came into being in 1979, taking GUES under its umbrella. A number of new groups have been added to those mentioned above. Most of them are breakaway groups reflecting the fragmented character of the Tamil militants. The need for unity among them has been a constant theme. In the Thimpu talks four major groups—the LTTE, EROS, EPRLF, and TELO—joined hands as the Eelam National Liberation Front (ENLF), with PLOT representatives participating as the fifth group and, also, representatives of the TULF. The differences in these organizations are in terms of ideology, cadre strength, local organizational base, international linkages, and personality differences at the leadership level. By 1986 the LTTE emerged as the strongest group among them.

39. For a succinct account of the factors and forces leading to the July violence see Virginia A. Leary, *Ethnic Conflict and Violence in Sri Lanka* (Geneva: International Commission of Jurists, 1983); Paul Sieghart, *Sri Lanka: A Mounting Tragedy of Errors* (Geneva: International Commission of Jurists, 1984); K. M. de Silva, *Managing Ethnic Tensions in Multi-Ethnic Societies: Sri Lanka 1880–1985*, (New York: University Press of America, 1986); and several articles, particularly that of Gananath Obeyesekere, in James Manor, ed., *Sri Lanka in Change and Crisis* (London: Croom and Helm, 1984).

40. All-Party Conference, *Memorandum Presented to the All-Party Conference by His Excellency the President, Chairman of the All-Party Conference* (Colombo: All-Party Conference Secretariat, 23 July 1984), p. 3.

41. For details see Silva, *Managing Ethnic Tensions*, pp. 342–358. Also see Robert N. Kearney, "Ethnic Conflict and the Tamil Separatist Movement in Sri Lanka," *Asian Survey* 25 (September 1985): pp. 906–917; and Umashanker Phadnis, "Indian Position: Sincere, Helpful," *World Focus* 5 (September 1984): pp. 23–25.

42. For the text of the letter of the SLFP leader Mrs. Bandaranaike to President Jayewardene on the devolution proposals, see *Island* (Colombo), 16 July 1986. For the text of the statement of the LTTE leader, V. Prabhakaran, see *Frontline* (Delhi) 15–28 November 1986, pp. 116–117.

43. For details of defense expenditure from 1941 to 1979 see Patrick Peebles, *Sri Lanka: A Handbook of Historical Statistics* (Boston, Mass., G. K. Hall and Co., 1982), Table 14, 1, p. 265. Also see the budget speech of Finance Minister Ronnie de Mel in Sri Lanka. *Parliamentary Debates* (Hansard) *Official Report* (uncorrected), vol. 43, no. 1 (12 November 1986), p. 138. It is necessary to note that in 1977 the Sri Lanka rupee was devalued and fixed at Rs16, after which it was allowed to float. In 1978 the exchange rate was $1 = Rs16. In 1986 it had shot up to $1 = Rs28.

44. *Weekend* (Colombo), 23 November 1986.

45. "Such a reduction," remarked a perceptive Sri Lankan administrator, "would inevitably have the effect of eroding the income support which the welfare programme provided for the poor . . . . The crucial issue would be whether the government will succeed in increasing the productivity and income opportunities for the poor through their growth policies for the diminuition and loss of welfare. In a strategy which diverts resources from present welfare to future growth, the inevitable lags between investment and output, between capital outlay and productive employment are certain to work against the poor, unless development strategies are consciously directed towards the poor." Godfrey Gunatilleke, "Reducing Poverty and Inequality in Sri Lanka," *Logos* 19 (December 1980); pp. 30–31.

46. Statement by the finance minister, (see note 43), p. 147.

47. For an overview of economy during the UNP regime see note 28, above. Also see Girejesh Pant, "New Economic Policy in Sri Lanka: Conflicts and Contradictions," in Urmila Phadnis, S. D. Muni, Kalim Bahadaur, eds., *Domestic Conflicts in South Asia: Economic and Ethnic Considerations*, vol. 2 (Delhi: South Asian Publishers, 1986), pp. 41–60, and I. N. Mukherjee, "Economy: Implications of Liberalism," *World Focus* 5 (September 1984): pp. 14–17. For a sharp critique of the 1986 budget see the speech of SLFP leader Lakshman Jayakody in the Parliament, *Ceylon Daily News*, 14 November 1986.

48. Statement by the finance minister, note 43, p. 178.

49. Ibid., p. 138.

50. For details see Arend Lijphart, "Emergency Powers and Emergency Regimes:

A Commentary," *Asian Survey* 18 (April 1978): pp. 401–407. As regards the developmental processes in emergency regimes, see Jyotirindra Das Gupta, "A Season of Caesars: Emergency Regimes and Development Politics in Asia," *Asian Survey* 18 (April 1978): pp. 315–349.

51. Rajni Kothari, "The Crisis of the Moderate State and the Decline of Democracy," in Peter Lyon and James Manor, eds., *Transfer and Transformation: Political Institutions in the New Commonwealth* (Leicester: Leicester University Press, 1983), pp. 29–30.

52. Donald L. Horowitz, *Ethnic Groups in Conflict* (Berkeley: University of California Press, 1985), pp. 39–40.

TURKEY

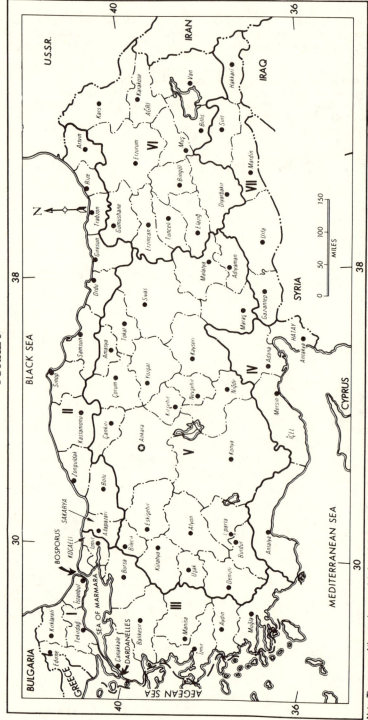

Note: The names of the provinces and their capitals are the same with the following exceptions: Kocaeli (İzmit), Sakarya (Adapazarı), İçel (Mersin), Hatay (Antakya), and Ağrı (Karaköse). The regions are defined by the heavier lines

I   European Region (separated from Region III by the Bosporus and
      Dardanelles straits and the Sea of Marmara)

II   Black Sea Region

III   Marmara and Aegean Region

IV   Mediterranean Sea Region

V   Anatolian Region (Anatolian Plateau)

VI   Eastern Highland Region (Eastern Anatolia)

VII   Southeastern Region (Southeastern Anatolia)

• CHAPTER FIVE •
Turkey: Crises, Interruptions, and Reequilibrations
ERGUN ÖZBUDUN

The record of democratic development in Turkey has been somewhat mixed. On the one hand, Turkey has remained committed to a democratic regime for the last forty years with only relatively brief interruptions. Presently it is the only democratic country in the entire Middle East (with the single exception of the very special case of Israel), as well as in all of Eastern and Southeastern Europe (with the single exception of Greece, whose post-World War II democratic record has not been appreciably brighter than Turkey's). By most socioeconomic indicators, Turkey is a middle-rank, developing country, with a per capita income of about $1,200. In view of the positive overall relationship between socioeconomic development and political democracy, Turkey is one of the few countries that are more democratic politically than they ought to have been according to the level of their socioeconomic development. However, Turkey's democratic process has been interrupted thrice in the last quarter of a century, which indicates a rather high degree of political instability. At best then, Turkey can be placed in the category of unstable democracies.

If the record of democratic development in Turkey is mixed, so are the factors that may have a bearing on Turkey's overall degree of success with democratic government. Culturally most Turks, elite and nonelite, seem to be committed to a democratic regime; yet this commitment does not always seem to be based on a set of profoundly felt concomitant democratic values, such as tolerance, compromise, and respect for individuality. The military shares the society's commitment to democracy, yet it also displays certain elitist attitudes and a tendency to see itself as the true guardian of the national interest. The major political parties have been nonideological and committed to democracy; yet their leaderships have not always shown a propensity for compromise and accommodation even in the face of a grave and imminent threat to the regime; furthermore, they have not been immune to polarizing influences, as was the case in the 1970s. The society is relatively homogeneous and well-integrated; yet ethnic or sectarian conflict can sometimes, if rarely, become violent. The rate of economic growth has on the whole been quite respectable; yet economic inequalities have also increased and are continuing to do so; moreover, there seem to exist serious obstacles to sustained economic growth in the future.

• THE DEVELOPMENT OF REPRESENTATIVE AND DEMOCRATIC GOVERNMENT •

The Ottoman Empire

Turkey differs from most of the developing countries of today in that it never experienced a colonial past. On the contrary, the Ottoman Empire—which at its zenith at the end of the sixteenth century comprised the entire Middle East (excluding Iran), North Africa, Southeastern Europe (including Hungary), and southern Russia—left a powerful legacy not only in the contemporary politics of its principal heir, the Republic of Turkey, but also upon those of other "successor states" to the empire.[1] A study of the development of democracy in Turkey cannot therefore be attempted without reference to its Ottoman past.

It is generally agreed that the Ottoman state conformed much more closely to a "bureaucratic empire" than to a European-style feudal system.[2] The Ottoman society was divided into two major classes. The *askeri*, literally the "military," included those to whom the sultan had delegated religious or executive power, namely officers of the court and the army, civil servants and *ulema* (religious functionaries). The *reaya*, on the other hand, comprised all Muslim and non-Muslim subjects who paid taxes but who had no part in the government. "It was a fundamental rule of the empire to exclude its subjects from the privileges of the 'military.' "[3] This accorded well with the fundamental concepts of state and society in the Ottoman Empire, which held that the social order was of divine origin and hence immutable. It was the sultan's duty to maintain this order, assisted by the members of the *askeri* class, by keeping everyone in his appropriate social position. Thus the state was above and independent of the society. Political power did not derive from the society, but was imposed upon it by the will of God (in effect, by conquest) from outside.[4] It was this primacy of politics over society that was to affect the nature of social and political changes in the Ottoman Empire for many centuries.

Two features of the Ottoman system reinforced the rigid dichotomy between the ruler and the ruled. One was the recruitment (*devsirme*) system, which was a periodic levy on the male children of Christian subjects, reducing them to the status of slaves and training them for service to the state. Since these slaves legally became the sultan's property, and he could take their lives and confiscate their wealth without legal process, they were in no position to challenge his authority. Furthermore, their removal from their former social environments prevented the development of locally entrenched, semiautonomous elements in the provinces.

A second feature, which was also instrumental in maintaining a strong central authority over the large territories of the empire, was the Ottoman land tenure system. This system vested in the state the original ownership of all the land, and limited the rights of the fief holders (*sipahi*) to the collection of taxes and the supervision of peasants under their jurisdiction. In return for the land grant, the *sipahi* were expected to recruit, train, and support a local contingent of soldiers; the fiefs were granted by the central government and could be taken away by it. Furthermore, the largest fiefs (*hass*) were perquisites of office. "The Ottoman feudal system seems to have differed from that of Western Europe chiefly in that the principal feudatories held their lands temporarily, in virtue of their offices. Hence the monarchy was exposed to little danger from the rivalry of this class of its tenants-in-chief."[5]

Two other significant social groups were the *ulema* (the class of religious scholars), and the merchants and artisans. Although part of the ruling class, the *ulema* differed from the "military" proper and the administrators in that it consisted of freeborn Muslims. However, the *ulema* did not constitute a hierarchy independent of government, since the most important among its members held appointive posts and hence were completely dependent on the state. As for merchants the Ottoman state, unlike its Western European counterparts, did not pursue mercantilist policies and did not favor the emergence of a powerful merchant class. Another factor that hindered the growth of a politically influential merchant class was the "ethnic division of labor." Non-Muslim minorities took the lead in mercantile activities, especially in international trade. But this group, so important in the development of early mercantile capitalism in Western Europe, was barred from the opportunity of converting such economic power into a significant political role because of the Islamic character of the state.

Thus, with no feudalism comparable to that of Western Europe, no hereditary aristocracy, no independent church hierarchy, no strong and independent merchant class, no powerful guilds, no self-governing cities, and with a ruling institution (i.e., the administration and the army) staffed with slaves, the Ottoman Empire represented a close approximation of an Oriental despotism. In the West, nongovernmental intermediary social structures operated relatively independently of government and played a cushioning role between the state and the individual. The Church was the foremost of these corporate structures such as the guilds, free cities, and the like. These had no parallels in the Ottoman Empire.

Islamic law does not as a rule recognize corporate entities. For all the theoretical supremacy of the *sharia* (Islamic law), even the religious class does not have a corporate identity. At least in Sunni (orthodox) Islam it forms part of the state bureaucracy, dependent upon the state for its appointments, promotions, and salaries. Similarly, in the Ottoman Empire, neither the cities nor the artisan guilds played any autonomous role comparable to their counterparts in Western Europe.[6] This dichotomy between the ruler and the ruled led to a class consciousness very different from that of the West, "that of *askeri* on the one hand and of their opponents on the other. . . . The saliency of these strata replaced the European saliency of strata connected with the production and distribution of goods and services."[7]

The bureaucratic nature of the Ottoman state and the concentration of political power in the hands of the sultan and his military and civilian bureaucrats explain the absence of representative institutions throughout the history of the empire until the last quarter of the nineteenth century. This contrasts sharply with the feudal tradition in Western Europe, which contained within itself the germs of representative and constitutional government. Western European feudalism implied a legally defined division of powers between a relatively weak central authority and local centers of power. It also implied some idea of representation for the estates, regardless of the frequency with which assemblies of estates were actually called. To this was added the corporate autonomy of the Church, the cities, and the guilds. From this medieval social and political pluralism and division of powers, it was a relatively easy step to modern constitutionalism, the rule of law, and modern representative institutions.

The Ottoman state, however, was not entirely devoid of the idea of "consultation" in the conduct of governmental affairs. It was an established custom for the Ottoman government to convene an assembly of leading civilian, military, and religious officials to discuss important matters of policy especially in times of stress. While it clearly had no representative character, this body nevertheless gave support to the notion that important policy decisions should be based on deliberations and consultations in a broader council. Such a consultative assembly was institutionalized in 1838 by Mahmud II, in the form of the "Grand Council of Justice." Mahmud's successor, Abdulmecid I, the council was given the responsibility of discussing and drafting new laws on matters of civil rights and taxation. In practice it "successfully operated as the principal Ottoman legislative organ. . . . All the important *Tanzimat* [Reform] decrees and regulations were prepared by it and over ninety percent of its recommendations were promulgated without change."[8]

In the next few decades, known as the "Reform" period in the Ottoman Empire, the development of representative institutions followed two different routes. One was the increasingly important role of the central legislative council and the effort to broaden its social base without, however, introducing the elective principle. The second was the establishment of local administrative councils based on limited elections. The elective principle in local administration was introduced in the Danube Province in 1864 and then extended in 1867 to the rest of the country. This provided for the election of only the lowest level of local officials (commune headmen) but attached semielected administrative councils to the centrally appointed governors of the each of the three tiers of local administration. A somewhat more representative institution was the "general assembly" created for each province. It was indirectly elected with largely advisory powers.[9]

The First Ottoman Parliament (1876–1878)

The next step was to be the linking of the effective principle adopted at the local level with the practice of nonelective legislative councils at the center. The first Ottoman legislature based on elections came into being with the constitution of 23 December 1876. Interestingly, Midhat Pasha, the leader of the constitutionalist faction, hoped to be able to convene a parliament even before the constitution was officially promulgated. Therefore, a Provisional Electoral Regulation was promulgated on 28 October while the constitution itself was still being debated in the drafting committee, which was composed of high-ranking civil servants.

Despite the limited and indirect nature of the suffrage and certain incidents of interference in the electoral process by provincial governors, it is generally agreed that the first legislative elections in the Ottoman Empire produced a Chamber of Deputies broadly representative (in a sociological sense) of various national and religious communities. While the Muslims, who outnumbered non-Muslims by a considerable ratio in the country, had a majority in the chamber, the Christians and the Jews were proportionally much better represented. The Turks as an ethnic group were a minority of the deputies as a whole, sharing the Muslims seats with Arabs, Albanians, Bosnians, and others. Although a large percentage of the deputies were former government officials, there were also many others representing other professions.[10]

The Chamber of Deputies had two sessions between 19 March 1877 and 14 February 1878, when it was indefinitely prorogued by Sultan Abdulhamid II. Although officially the fiction was maintained that the constitution was still in force, the Chamber of Deputies was not reconvened until the Young Turk revolution of 1908 forced Abdulhamid to do so. It is impossible to analyze here the full political context of the first experiment with constitutional government in the Ottoman Empire

or the reasons for its failure. Suffice it to say that the introduction of
constitutional and representative government was the work of a very
small group of reformist government officials and intellectuals; it was
based neither on broad support, nor on organized political parties.
Consequently, Abdulhamid's prorogation of the chamber did not lead
to any strong public reaction. On the contrary his absolutist rule, emphasizing the Islamic character of the state, seems to have been quite
popular with the conservative, anti-Western mood of public opinion.

The fundamental political cleavage in the Ottoman Empire until the
nineteenth century can be described as a center-periphery cleavage
between the political ins and outs. The ins were "the incumbents of the
Ottoman institutions. The outs were people who were excluded from
the state."[11] Beginning in the eighteenth century, this cleavage was
complicated by another one that resulted from the efforts of Westernization. The adoption of, first, Western military technology and, then,
Western laws and administrative practices was strongly opposed by the
old religious and military elites. This opposition was motivated not only
by religious grounds, but also by the fear that such reforms would
undermine their power and status in the society. In contrast to the older
center-periphery cleavage this one was located at the very center. The
Westernization movement undertaken by bureaucrats fractured the old
intraelite unity, and produced a conflict that remained for many years
one of the principal cleavages in Turkish political life. The political
implications of this culture change, first under the Ottoman reformers
and then under the leadership of Kemal Ataturk, will be discussed more
fully below.

The first Ottoman experiment with constitutional government reflects the emergence of yet another line of cleavage. This one pitted the
constitutionalists (called the "Young Ottomans") against the supporters
of monarchic autocracy. This was also an intraelite conflict, since both
the constitutionalists and the autocratic *tanzimat* reformers came from
the ranks of the Westernized, official elite. The Young Ottomans did
not represent either the local notables or urban merchants. However,
their advocacy of a parliament put them in a dilemma, one that was to
be faced by many generations of future modernizers: the modernizers
wanted to have a parliament as an alternative (and modern) source of
legitimacy. But they soon realized that when a parliament was convened, it "did not increase the power of modernizing officials vis-à-vis
the Sultan, but that it rather increased the power of notables against
state officials."[12] In fact, the Young Ottomans were often bitterly critical
of the abuses of local notables, and charged them with repressing the
countryside. The short life of the first Ottoman Parliament provided
clear manifestations of the deep conflict between the central bureaucratic
elite and the local (peripheral) forces.[13] It is also a good example of

unanticipated and undesired consequences democratization poses for modernizers in traditional or developing societies.

The Second Constitutionalist Period (1908–1918)

The electoral process was reinstated in 1908 after thirty years of absolutist monarchical rule when military-popular uprisings in Macedonia compelled Abdulhamid II to restore the constitution. This was a victory for the reformist-constitutionalist wing of the official bureaucratic elite organized in the underground Society for Union and Progress, which in time transformed itself into a political party. Indeed the second constitutionalist period witnessed, for the first time, the emergence of organized political parties and party competition. The 1908 elections gave the Society for Union and Progress a comfortable majority in the Chamber of Deputies. Of the other two elections held in this period, only that of 1912 was relatively competitive. Because of the administrative pressures exerted by the Unionist government and restrictions on opposition activities, this election came to be known as the "big stick election." The 1914 election was not contested by any opposition party.[14]

The democratic experiment of the second constitutionalist period is generally too easily dismissed as one that quickly degenerated into an internecine struggle poisoned by coups and countercoups, political assassinations and martial law courts, government manipulation of elections and repression of the opposition, becoming finally an outright party dictatorship. While this diagnosis contains a great deal of truth, the same period (especially until the Unionists' coup of 1913) also provided the first extended Turkish experiment with competitive elections, organized political parties, and the parliamentary process. The beginnings of mass politics in Turkey should also be sought in this period. Unlike the earlier military, bureaucratic, intellectual cliques, the Union and Progress, "had too broad a social base and too heterogeneous a class structure to be elitist. . . . The Committee was the first political organization in the Empire to have a mass following and this gave the politics of the day a populist basis."[15] Finally, under the crust of virulent and mutually destructive political struggles of the period, one can discern the beginnings of "issue-oriented politics," which pitted the modernizing, unifying, centralizing, standardizing, nationalist, authoritarian, and statist Union and Progress against three types of opposition: the liberals who favored parliamentary democracy, administrative decentralization, more reliance on private initiative, and a more Ottomanist policy (i.e., a policy aimed at creating an "Ottoman" identity around the common fatherland and dynasty, regardless of religion, language, and ethnicity); religious traditionalists who were opposed to the secularist aspects of the Unionist policies; and the non-Turkish minorities (whether Muslim or non-Muslim) who felt threatened by the nationalist and centralizing drive of the Union and Progress.[16]

The National Liberation Period (1918–1923)

With the defeat of the Ottoman Empire in World War I, the Ottoman government collapsed in fact, if not in theory. While the Istanbul government maintained a shaky existence during the Armistice years (1918–1922) under the control of the Allies' occupation armies, a new governmental structure was developed in Anatolia by the nationalists resisting the occupation.

The era of national liberation is a most interesting period in Turkey's constitutional history, and is full of constitutional innovations. Following the arrest and deportation of many deputies with nationalist sympathies by the Allied occupation forces and the consequent dissolution of the Chamber of Deputies on 18 March 1920, Mustafa Kemal, the leader of the nationalist forces in Anatolia, called for the election of a new assembly "with extraordinary powers" to convene in Ankara. This body, called the "Grand National Assembly," was fundamentally different from the Ottoman Parliament in that it combined legislative and executive powers in itself. It was a real constituent and revolutionary assembly, not bound by the Ottoman constitution.

The Grand National Assembly enacted a constitution in 1921. This was a short but very important document. For the first time it proclaimed the principle of national sovereignty, calling itself the "only and true representative of the nation." Legislative and executive powers were vested in the assembly. The ministers were to be chosen by the Assembly individually from among its own members. The Assembly could provide instructions to the ministers and, if deemed necessary, change them.

In the entire Turkish history, the political influence of the legislature reached its peak during the period of national liberation. The theory of legislative supremacy was also followed in practice. The Assembly closely supervised all aspects of administrative activity. Under the most difficult external and internal circumstances, Kemal and his ministers ruled the country in close cooperation with the Assembly and never attempted to ignore it.

In the months following the victorious termination of the War of Independence and the abolition of the sultanate in the fall of 1922, Mustafa Kemal formed a political party based on populist principles, which was named the People's Party (later the Republican People's Party, or RPP). In the 1923 elections it won almost all of the Assembly seats. However, the newly elected Assembly was also far from being an obedient instrument of the leadership. Disagreements on constitutional and other questions soon became manifest. In November 1924, twenty-nine deputies resigned from the People's Party and formed the Progressive Republican Party. The new opposition party was led by some prestigious generals closely associated with Kemal during the War of Independence. In its initial manifesto the party emphasized economic and particularly political liberalism, including a commitment to "respect religious feelings and beliefs." The manifesto stated its opposition to despotism, and stressed individual rights, judicial independence, and administrative decentralization. It promised not to change the constitution without a clear popular mandate. The Progressive Republican Party was strongly supported by the Istanbul press, and started to set up local organizations in big cities and in the eastern provinces.

Behind these publicly claimed policy differences also lay the personal estrangement of the Progressive leaders from Kemal, and their concern about his growing personal power. At a more fundamental level, however, their opposition reflected a more conservative mentality that Frey sees as typical of postindependence crises in developing countries. Behind all the ideas of the Progressive Republican Party, he argues that "there lay the conservative aim of making the new Turkey—if there was ever to be a *new* Turkey in any basic sense— conform as far as possible to the customs and traditions of the old. Change was to be gradual and evolutionary, not swift and revolutionary in the Kemalist mode."[17]

The Consolidation of the Republic

Justification for crushing the Progressive Republican Party was found in the Seyh Sait rebellion that erupted in eastern Anatolia in February 1925. The rebellion quickly reached serious dimensions. Consequently, the more moderate government of Fethi was replaced by a new one headed by Ismet Inönü, who favored more radical methods to deal with the rebellion. Legislation passed in March gave the government broad powers to ban all kinds of organization, propaganda, agitation, and publications that could lead to reaction and rebellion or undermine public order and security. Martial law was declared, and the Independence Tribunals (revolutionary courts created in 1920 to deal with treasonable activities) were reactivated. The Progressive Republican Party was shut down on 3 June 1925 by a decision of the Council of Ministers, which implicated it in the revolt, although no concrete proof of such connection was established. The suppression of the opposition party and much of the independent press marked the end of the first, semipluralistic phase of the Kemalist regime.

The following period can be characterized as the consolidation phase of the new republican regime. Between 1925 and 1945 the country was ruled by a single-party regime, with the exception of a brief and

unsuccessful attempt to introduce an opposition party, the Free Republican Party in 1930. This was a period of radical secularizing reforms
such as the banning of religious orders; the adoption of the Swiss civil
code to replace the *sharia*; acceptance of other Western codes in the
fields of penal, commercial, and procedural law; the closing of religious
schools; the outlawing of the fez; the adoption of a Latin alphabet and
the international calendar; the repeal of the constitutional provisions
that made Islam the official religion of the state, etc. This consolidation
of single-party rule, however, did not involve a doctrinal repudiation of
liberal democracy or of liberal values. Extraordinary measures were
justified by temporary needs to protect the state and the regime against
counterrevolutionaries.

Although the regime's authoritarian tendencies were somewhat
intensified after the failure of the Free Republican Party experiment in
1930, most of these tendencies were checked or arrested by the more
liberal or pluralistic countertendencies within the single party, the
Republican People's Party (RPP). Organizationally the RPP never
approached a totalitarian mobilizational party model. Ideologically, it
did not provide a permanent justification for an authoritarian regime.
Authoritarian practices and policies were defeated not on doctrinal, but
on purely pragmatic and temporary grounds. A liberal democratic state
remained the officially sanctioned ideal. Institutionally attempts were
made to partially open up the nomination and election processes starting
from the 1931 elections, such as leaving some parliamentary seats open
for independent candidates.[18]

As for its social bases, the RPP has often been described as a
coalition between the central military-bureaucratic elite and local notables, the former clearly being the dominant element especially at the
level of central government. This alliance was, at least partly, dictated
by the circumstances of the War of Independence. These two groups
were the only ones capable of mobilizing the peasant majority into a war
of national liberation. After the consolidation of the republican regime
this cooperation continued, since the Kemalists' emphasis on secularizing
reforms did not pose a threat to the interests of local notables. Thus the
RPP represented the old center, i.e., the world of officialdom, with
some local allies in the periphery. But in contrast to mobilizational
single parties, it did not attempt to broaden its social base or to mobilize
the periphery.

The Kemalist regime was highly successful, on the other hand, in
creating a set of new political institutions, among which the RPP itself
and the Turkish Grand National Assembly (TGNA) stand out as the
most important. Elections were also institutionalized and regularly held.
The forms, if not the substance, of constitutional government were
carefully maintained. All these political institutions survived with

minimal changes in the multiparty era once such a transition was made in the late 1940s. Indeed, political institutionalization under the aegis of a single party provided a kind of "democratic infrastructure" that eventually facilitated the transition to democratic politics.[19] In this sense, the RPP regime can be described as a case of low political participation (mobilization) and high political institutionalization.

Other features of the Kemalist regime in Turkey might have also provided facilitating conditions for eventual democratization. First, the loss of all Arabic-speaking provinces at the end of World War I and the exchange of populations with Greece following the termination of the War of Independence made the new Turkish republic a much more homogeneous state. It thus facilitated the basing of its corporate identity on Turkish nationalism instead of Islamic religion or loyalty to the Ottoman dynasty. Indeed, a reason for the relative failure (compared, for example, with the Meiji restoration in Japan) of Ottoman modernization reforms in the nineteenth century might well have been that such reforms could not possibly have produced sufficient social integration and social mobilization in a multinational and overextended empire. The second facilitating condition was the complete secularization of the governmental, legal, and educational systems under the Kemalist rule. By strictly separating religion from politics the Kemalists created at least a precondition for liberal democracy, i.e., a rationalist-relativistic, rather than an absolutist, notion of politics. Thus it should be no accident that Turkey is the only predominantly Muslim country that is both democratic and secular. Obviously there is a link between Kemalist reforms and those of the nineteenth-century Ottoman modernizers, especially the Young Turks. But the speed, intensity, and scope of the secularizing reforms of the republic clearly surpass those of the earlier eras.

Regarding the relationship between the Kemalist reforms and the development of democracy in Turkey, a counterargument can be made to the effect that the traumatic experience of such a momentous culture change, and the deep cleavage between radical secularists and Islamic traditionalists[20] would make a stable democracy very unlikely. It should be stressed, however, that despite the radical nature of Kemalist secularism, it never intended to eradicate Islam in Turkey. It was anticlerical, to be sure, but not antireligious. It aimed at individualization or privatization of Islam, attempting to make it a matter of individual conscience rather than the fundamental organizing principle of the society. Consistent with this, freedom of religion at the individual level was always respected, while organized political manifestations of Islam were strictly forbidden. Judged by these criteria, the ultimate aim of Kemalism seems to have been accomplished, since a majority of believing and practicing Turkish Muslims are now distinguishing between their religious beliefs and their public and political lives, as

evidenced by their voting behavior. Indeed, during the 1970s, fundamentalist Islamic political parties have been able to gain only a small
minority of votes.

Transition to Multiparty Politics and the Democratic Party Period

The transition from authoritarianism to competitive politics in Turkey is
highly exceptional in that it took place without a *ruptura*, i.e., a break
with the existing institutional arrangements. On the contrary, it is a rare
example of *reforma*, where the transition process was led and controlled
by the power holders of the previous authoritarian regime.[21] This transition started in 1945 when the RPP regime allowed the formation of an
opposition party, the Democratic Party (DP), by some of the dissident
members of its own parliamentary group. Despite some ups and downs
on the road, the process proceeded relatively smoothly and ended in the
electoral victory of the DP in the free parliamentary elections of 1950.

It is beyond the scope of the present study to give full account of the
transition or to assess its probable causes.[22] While such a momentous
change cannot be explained by a single factor, it appears that the
potentially democratic aspirations of the RPP regime and President
Inönü's firm personal commitment to democratization provided the
crucial impulse behind the move. In fact, whenever relations between
the RPP old guard (the "bunker") and the DP opposition grew tense,
Inönü intervened personally to soften the atmosphere and to reassure
the opposition. The most significant of these interventions was his
statement on 12 July 1947 after several rounds of talk with the hard-line
Prime Minister Recep Peker and the opposition leader Celâl Bayar. The
declaration included a promise by Inönü that the opposition party would
enjoy the same privileges as the party in power and that Inönü himself
would remain equally responsible to both parties as the head of the
state.

Inönü's commitment to democratization, in turn, has to be explained by the structural and doctrinal characteristics of the RPP regime.
The Kemalist regime evolved into a single-party model without, however,
having a single-party ideology. No component of the RPP doctrine
provided a permanent legitimation for the single-party system. On the
contrary liberal democracy remained the ideal, and authoritarianism
was justified only as a temporary measure arising out of the need to
defend the Kemalist revolution against counterrevolutionaries. Kemalism
as a doctrine was much closer to nineteenth-century liberalism than to
the authoritarian and totalitarian philosophies of the twentieth century.
Communism and fascism were never seen as models to be imitated. One
reason for this might have been that the Kemalist regime was born in the

immediate post-World War I period when democratic ideas and values were at the height of their appeal and legitimacy for the new nations.

The timing of the decision to democratize the Turkish system could have been influenced by favorable changes in the international environment. The victory of the democratic regimes in World War II, and Turkey's need for a rapprochement with the West in the face of the Soviet threat, no doubt provided an additional incentive for transition to democracy. Changes in the structure of Turkish society—notably the growth of commerical and industrial middle classes who favored a democratic regime in which their own party would have an excellent chance to win—on the other hand, do not seem to have played a decisive role in the transition. First, it is not clear why the commercial-industrial middle classes suddenly began to feel fettered under the RPP's statism, if statist policies really worked so much to their benefit. Second, assuming that this was indeed the case, there is no evidence that such internal pressures forced the RPP leadership into this decision. The experience of the Mexican PRI suggests that a pragmatic single party is capable of showing sufficient adaptability to accommodate newly emerging groups.

The DP came to power with a landslide electoral victory on 14 May 1950, also won the 1954 and 1957 national elections (Table 5.1), and remained in power for ten full years until it was ousted by the military coup of 27 May 1960. Socially the DP, led by a group of politicians who played fairly important roles in the single-party period, was a coalition of various types of oppositions to the RPP. It brought together urban liberals and religious conservatives, commercial middle classes and the urban poor, and more modern (mobilized) sections of the rural population. The RPP, on the other hand, retained the support of government officials, some large landowners, and a substantial portion of the more backward peasantry still under the influence of its local patrons. The heterogeneous character of the DP coalition suggests that the dominant social cleavage of the era was cultural rather than socioeconomic in nature. The common denominator of the DP supporters was their opposition to state officials. In this sense, the rise of the DP was a victory of the periphery over the center.

The ideological distance between the RPP and the DP was not great. They differed significantly from each other, however, in their underlying attitudes toward the proper role of the state, bureaucracy, private enterprise, local initiative, and toward peasant participation in politics. While the RPP-oriented central elite had a more tutelary concept of development, the provincial elites around the DP emphasized local initiative and the "immediate satisfaction of local expectations."[23]

Despite the nonideological nature of the partisan conflict relations between the two major parties quickly deteriorated. Especially after the

Table 5.1　Percentage of Votes (and Seats) in Turkish Parliamentary Elections (1950–1977)

Party	1950	1954	1957	Elections 1961	1965	1969	1973	1977
DP/JP	53.3	56.6	47.7	34.8	52.9	46.5	29.8	36.9
	(83.8)	(93.0)	(69.5)	(35.1)	(53.3)	(56.9)	(33.1)	(42.0)
RPP	39.8	34.8	40.8	36.7	28.7	27.4	33.3	41.4
	(14.2)	(5.7)	(29.2)	(38.4)	(29.8)	(31.8)	(41.1)	(47.3)
NP	3.0	4.7	7.2	14.0	6.3	3.2	1.0	—
	(0.2)	(0.9)	(0.7)	(12.0)	(6.9)	(1.3)	—	—
FP	—	—	3.8	—	—	—	—	—
	—	—	(0.7)	—	—	—	—	—
NTP	—	—	—	13.7	3.7	2.2	—	—
	—	—	—	(14.4)	(4.2)	(1.3)	—	—
TLP	—	—	—	—	3.0	2.7	—	0.1
	—	—	—	—	(3.3)	(0.4)	—	—
NAP	—	—	—	—	2.2	3.0	3.4	6.4
	—	—	—	—	(2.4)	(0.2)	(0.7)	(3.6)
UP	—	—	—	—	—	2.8	1.1	0.4
	—	—	—	—	—	(1.8)	(0.2)	—
RRP	—	—	—	—	—	6.6	5.3	1.9
	—	—	—	—	—	(3.3)	(2.9)	(0.7)
Dem. P	—	—	—	—	—	—	11.9	1.9
	—	—	—	—	—	—	(10.0)	(0.2)
NSP	—	—	—	—	—	—	11.8	8.6
	—	—	—	—	—	—	(10.7)	(5.3)

Note: In the first row of figures for each party are percentages of the popular vote and in the second row (in parentheses) are the percentages of seats won.
Abbreivations: DP, Democrat Party; JP, Justice Party; RPP, Republican People's Party; NP, Nation Party; FP, Freedom Party; NTP, New Turkey Party; TLP, Turkish Labor Party; NAP, Nationalist Action Party; UP, Unity Party; RRP, Republican Reliance Party; Dem. P., Democratic Party; NSP, National Salvation Party.

1957 elections the DP responded to its declining support by resorting to increasingly authoritarian measures against the opposition, which only made the opposition more uncompromising and vociferous. The last straw in this long chain of authoritarian measures was the establishment by the government party in April 1960 of a parliamentary committee of inquiry to investigate the "subversive" activities of the RPP and of a section of the press. With this, many opposition members were convinced that a point of no return had been reached and that the channels of democratic change had been clogged. The ensuing public unrest, student demonstrations in Istanbul and Ankara, and clashes between the students and the police led to the declaration of martial law. This put the armed forces in the unwanted position of suppressing the opposition on behalf of a government for whose policies they had little sympathy. Finally, the military intervened on 27 May 1960, with the welcome and support of the opposition. The National Unity Committee, formed by the revolutionary officers, dissolved the parliament, banned the DP, arrested and tried its leaders, and set out to prepare a new and more democratic constitution.

What is to be blamed for the failure of this first extended experiment of Turkey with democratic politics? One reason lay in the very nature of the DP, which was a coalition of diverse anti-RPP forces. This convinced the DP leadership that the party "could retain its unity only by keeping its ranks mobilized against the RPP. This was realized partly by accusing the RPP of subverting the government through its hold on the bureaucracy, and partly by raising the specter of a return of the RPP to power."[24] A second factor was that the DP leaders, having been socialized into politics under the RPP rule, had inherited many attitudes, norms, and orientations that were more in harmony with a single party than with a competitive party system. These included a belief that a popular mandate entitled the government party to the unrestricted use of political power. Coupled with the Ottoman-Turkish cultural legacy, which hardly distinguished between political opposition and treasonable activity, this attitude left little room for a legitimate opposition.

Perhaps an even more potent factor that eventually led to the breakdown of the democratic regime was the conflict between the DP and the public bureaucracy. The bureaucracy, which was the main pillar of the single-party regime, retained its RPP loyalties under multiparty politics, and resisted the DP's efforts to consolidate its political power. In the eyes of the DP leaders, this amounted to an unwarranted obstruction of the "national will." The bureaucrats, on the other hand, saw it as their duty to protect the "public interest" against efforts to use state funds for political patronage purposes. They were also deeply troubled by the DP government's careless attitude toward the "rule of law," as well as by its more permissive policies toward religious activities, which they considered a betrayal of the Kemalist legacy of secularism. These negative attitudes were shared by civilian officials and military officers alike.

Finally, all bureaucratic groups (again both civilian and military) not only experienced a loss of social status and political influence under the DP regime, but were also adversely affected in terms of their relative income. The DP's economic policies consisted of rapid import-substitution-based industrialization and the modernization of agriculture, largely through external borrowing and inflationary financing. Although a relatively high rate of economic growth was achieved in the 1950s, income distribution grew much more inequitable. Particularly badly hit because of the inflationary policies were the salaried groups. The 1960 coup found therefore an easy acceptance among military officers and civilian bureaucrats for economic as well as other reasons.

Turkey's Second Try at Democracy (1961–1980)

The 1960 coup was carried out by a group of middle rank officers who, upon assuming power, organized themselves into a revolutionary council named the "National Unity Committee" (NUC), under the chairmanship of General Cemal Gürsel, the former commander of the army. The NUC declared from the beginning its intention of making a new democratic constitution and returning power to a freely elected civilian government. In spite of the efforts by some NUC members to prolong military rule, the committee kept its promise and relinquished power in 1961 following the parliamentary elections held under the new Constitution and the Electoral Law.[25]

The constitution of 1961 was prepared by the NUC and a coopted Representative Assembly dominated by pro-RPP bureaucrats and intellectuals, reflecting the basic political values and interests of these groups. On the one hand, they created an effective system of checks and balances to limit the power of elected assemblies. Such checks included the introduction of judicial review of the constitutionality of laws; the strengthening of the Council of State, which functions as the highest administrative court with review powers over the acts of all executive agencies; effective independence for the judiciary; the creation of a second legislative chamber (Senate of the Republic); and the granting of substantial autonomy to certain public agencies such as the universities and the Radio and Television Corporation. On the other hand, the constitution expanded civil liberties and granted extensive social rights. Thus it was hoped that the power of the elected assemblies would be balanced by judicial and other agencies that represented the values of the bureaucratic elites, while the newly expanded civil liberties would ensure the development of a free and democratic society.

The 1961 elections, however, gave a majority to the heirs of the ousted Democrats (Table 5.1). The pro-DP vote was fragmented among the Justice Party (34.8 percent), the National Party (14.0 percent), and the New Turkey Party (13.7 percent), while the Republicans obtained only 36.7 percent of the vote. Following a period of unstable coalition governments, the Justice Party (JP) gradually established itself as the principal heir to the DP. In the 1965 elections, it gained about 53 percent of the popular vote and of the National Assembly seats. The JP repeated its success in 1969, when it won an absolute majority of the Assembly seats with a somewhat reduced popular vote (46.5 percent). Thus Turkey appeared to have achieved, once again, a popularly elected stable government.

Toward the end of the 1960s, however, the Turkish political system began to experience new problems. Partly as a result of the more liberal atmosphere provided by the 1961 Constitution, extreme left- and right-wing groups appeared on the political scene. This was followed by increasing acts of political violence, especially by extremist youth groups. The crisis was aggravated by the activities of various conspiratorial groups within the military. These radical officers, frustrated by the successive electoral victories of the conservative JP, aimed at establishing a longer-term military regime ostensibly to carry out radical social reforms. In fact the military memorandum of 12 March 1971, which forced the JP government to resign, was a last-minute move by the top military commanders to forestall a radical coup.

The so-called 12 March regime did not go as far as dissolving the Parliament and assuming power directly. Instead, it strongly encouraged the formation of an "above-party" or technocratic government under a veteran RPP politician, Professor Nihat Erim. The new government was expected to deal sternly with political violence with the help of martial law, to bring about certain constitutional amendments designed to strengthen the executive, and to carry out the social reforms (especially land reform) provided for by the 1961 Constitution. The interim government accomplished its first two objectives. Political violence was effectively stamped out. The constitution was extensively revised in 1971 and 1973, with a view to not only strengthening the executive authority, but also to limiting certain civil liberties that were seen as responsible for the emergence of political extremism and violence. The interim regime failed, however, in its third objective of carrying out social reforms, not only because of the conservative majority in the Parliament, but also because of the purge of the radical officers from the military in the months following the "12 March memorandum."

The 1971 military intervention can be characterized as a "half coup," in which the military chose to govern from behind the scenes instead of taking over directly. If one reason for the intervention was the failure of the Demirel government to cope with political terrorism, a more deep-seated cause was the distrust felt toward the JP by many military officers and civilian bureaucrats. Thus, in a sense, the 1971 intervention still reflected the old cleavage between the centralist bureaucratic elite and the forces of the periphery that commanded an electoral majority.

The interim period ended with the 1973 parliamentary elections, which produced a National Assembly with no governing majority. The RPP emerged, after many years of electoral impotence, as the largest party with a third of the popular vote and 41 percent of the Assembly seats (see Table 5.1). The RPP's rise was due on the one hand to the energetic leadership of Bülent Ecevit, who became the party leader replacing the octogenarian İnönü, and on the other to the new social democratic image of the party. As the 1973 voting patterns indicate, the new image of the RPP appealed to urban lower classes. This change signified a realignment in the Turkish party system, as the old center-periphery cleavage began to be replaced by a new functional cleavage. The RPP increased its vote particularly in the former strongholds of the

DP and the JP, and among those strata that up to that time loyally supported the DP and the JP.[26]

The Right, on the other hand, was badly split in the 1973 elections. The JP obtained only about 30 percent of the vote (Table 5.1). The Democratic Party, a splinter group of the JP, received just under 12 percent of the vote, as did the National Salvation Party (NSP). The NSP combined its defense of Islamic moral and cultural values with a defense of the interests of small merchants, artisans, and businessmen. Another new actor in Turkish politics in the 1970s was the Nationalist Action Party (NAP). Although it won only 3.4 percent of the vote in 1973, the NAP grew in the 1970s under the leadership of ex-revolutionary Alpaslan Türkes (one of the key figures in the 1960s coup) from an insignificant party into a highly dedicated, strictly disciplined, and hierarchically organized political force to be reckoned with. The NAP's ideology combined an ardent nationalism and anticommunism with strongly interventionist economic policies, and its tactics involved the use of militia-type youth organizations seemingly implicated in right-wing terror.

The composition of the 1973 National Assembly made coalition governments inevitable. First a coalition was formed, under the premiership of Bülent Ecevit, between the social-democratic RPP and the Islamic NSP. The coalition collapsed in the fall of 1974 and was eventually replaced by a "Nationalist Front" coalition under Süleyman Demirel, with the participation of the JP, NSP, NAP, and the RRP (Republican Reliance Party, a small moderate party led by Professor Turhan Feyzioglu, a former RPP member).

The 1977 elections did not significantly change this picture, although they did strengthen the two leading parties vis-à-vis most of the minor ones. The RPP, which increased its share of the popular vote by eight points, came close to an absolute parliamentary majority. The JP also improved its share of the vote and of the Assembly seats (Table 5.1). The NSP lost about one-quarter of its votes and half of its parliamentary contingent. The Democratic Party and the Republican Reliance Party were practically eliminated. The right-wing NAP grew considerably, however, almost doubling its popular vote while increasing its small contingent of Assembly seats fivefold.

Following the 1977 elections, a Nationalist Front government was formed again under Mr. Demirel, with the participation of the JP, NSP, and NAP. In a few months, however, the Front lost its parliamentary majority as a result of the defection of some JP deputies. Consequently, Mr. Ecevit was able to form a government with the help of these dissident JP members, who were rewarded with ministerial posts in the new government. The Ecevit government lasted about 22 months, resigning in November 1979, when the partial elections for one-third of the Senate and five vacant National Assembly seats revealed sharp gains by the JP, which won 47.8 percent of the vote while the RPP support declined dramatically (to 29.2 percent). Consequently, Mr. Demirel formed a minority JP government with the parliamentary support of its former partners, the NSP and the NAP. This government had been in office less than one year when it was ousted by the military coup of 12 September 1980.

How can we account for the failure of Turkey's second experiment with democracy? The immediate reason behind the military intervention was the growing political violence and terrorism that, between 1975 and 1980, left more than 5,000 people killed and three times as many wounded (the equivalent of Turkish losses in the War of Independence). Acts of violence, which became particularly acute between 1978 and 1980, also included armed assaults, sabotages, kidnappings, bank robberies, occupation and destruction of workplaces, and bombings. Some forty-nine radical leftist groups were involved in left-wing terror, while right-wing terror was concentrated in the "idealist" organizations with their unofficial links to the NAP. Thus, in a sense, the pattern that had led to the military intervention of 1971 was repeated, only this time on a much larger and more alarming scale. Just as in the early 1970s, the governments of the late 1970s were unable to cope with the problem even though martial law was in effect in much of the country. Martial law under the Turkish constitutional system entails the transfer of police functions to military authorities, the restriction or complete suspension of civil liberties, and the creation of military martial law courts to try offenses associated with the causes that led to the declaration of martial law. Thus it is a constitutional, albeit highly authoritarian and restrictive, procedure. In the crisis of the late 1970s, however, even martial law could not contain the violence. One reason for this was the infiltration of the police forces by right-wing and left-wing extremists. Another was the general erosion of the authority of the state as a result of growing political polarization in the country, as will be discussed below. It should be added here that a harmful side effect of martial law is the seemingly inevitable politicization of the armed forces, or the "militarization" of political conflict, which may pave the way for full-scale military intervention. Indeed, all three military interventions in recent Turkish history were preceded by martial law regimes instituted by civilian governments.

At a deeper level the incidence of political violence reflected a growing ideological polarization in the country. The polarizing forces were the NAP, and to a much lesser extent the NSP, on the right, and many small radical groups on the left. The NSP was not involved in violence, but its use of Islamic themes helped to undermine the regime's legitimacy among those committed to the Kemalist legacy of secularism, including the military. The parliamentary arithmetics and the inability and/or unwillingness of the two major parties (the RPP and the JP) to agree on a grand coalition or a minority government arrangement gave these two minor parties an enormous bargaining—more correctly blackmailing—power, which they effectively used to obtain important ministries and to colonize them with their own partisans. In fact this seems to be crucial for the crisis of the system. An accommodation between the two major parties would have been welcomed by most of the important political groups in Turkey, including the business community, the leading trade union confederation, the press, and the military, and would have been acceptable to a majority of the JP and the RPP deputies. A government based on their joint support would probably have been strong enough to deal effectively and evenhandedly with the political violence. However, the deep personal rivalry between Demirel and Ecevit, their tendency to see problems from a narrow partisan perspective, and perhaps their failure to appreciate the real gravity of the situation made such a democratic rescue operation impossible. As the experience of many countries has shown, antisystem parties can perhaps be tolerated in opposition, but their entry into government tends to put too heavy a load on the system to be handled by democratic means.

The radical left, unlike the radical right, was not represented in the Parliament, but extreme leftist ideologies found many supporters among students, teachers, and in some sectors of the industrial working class. Just as the JP was pulled to the right by its partnership with the NAP and the NSP, the RPP was pulled to the left by the radical groups to its left. Political polarization also affected and undermined the public bureaucracy. At no time in recent Turkish history had the public agencies been so divided and politicized as in the late 1970s. Changes of government were followed by extensive purges in all ministries, involving not only the top personnel, but also many middle- or lower-rank civil servants. Partisanship became a norm in the civil service, which had retained its essentially nonpolitical character until the mid-1970s.

A related phenomenon that contributed to a decline in the legitimacy of the political system was the *immobilisme* of the governments and parliaments in much of the 1970s. The very narrow majorities in the Parliament and the heterogeneous nature of the governing coalitions (be it the Nationalist Front governments or the Ecevit governments) meant that new policies could be initiated only with great difficulty. In the context of pressing economic troubles (such as high inflation, major deficits in the international trade balance, shortages of investment and consumer goods, unemployment, etc.), and international problems (such as the Cyprus crisis and the U.S. arms embargo), the inability of governments to take courageous policy decisions aggravated the legitimacy crisis. To put it differently this lack of efficacy and effectiveness served to delegitimate the regime. Perhaps the most telling example of such governmental failure of performance was the inability of the Turkish Grand National Assembly to elect a president of the republic in 1980. The six-month-old presidential deadlock ended only with the military coup of 12 September. Other examples of lesser deadlocks abounded particularly in matters of economic and foreign policy.

The 1980 Coup and the 1982 Constitution

From the moment it took over the government on 12 September 1980, the National Security Council (composed of the five highest-ranking generals in the Turkish armed forces) made it clear that it intended to eventually return power to democratically elected civilian authorities. It made it equally clear, however, by words and deeds that it did not intend a return to the *status quo ante*. Rather, the council aimed at a major restructuring of Turkish democracy to prevent a recurrence of the political polarization, violence, and crisis that had afflicted the country in the late 1970s, and thus to make the military's continued involvement in politics unnecessary. The new constitution, Political Parties Law, and Electoral Law prepared by the council-appointed Consultative Assembly—and made final by the council itself—reflect these objectives and concerns of the military and indicate the extent to which Turkey's new attempt at democracy is intended to be different from its earlier democratic experiments.

The constitution was submitted to a popular referendum on 7 November 1982. The extremely high rate of participation (91.27 percent) was, no doubt, partly due to the provision that those who did not participate would forfeit their right to vote in the next parliamentary elections. The constitution was approved by 91.37 percent of those who voted. The counting was honest, but the debate preceding it was extremely limited. The council limited debate only to those views expressed with the purpose of "improving the draft constitution" and banned all efforts to influence the direction of the vote. The constitution was "officially" explained to the public by President Kenan Evren in a series of speeches, and any criticism of these speeches was also banned. Another unusual feature of the constitutional referendum was its combination with the presidential elections. A "yes" vote for the constitution meant a vote for General Evren for a seven-year term as president of the Republic, and no other candidates were allowed. It is generally agreed that the personal popularity of General Evren helped increase affirmative votes for the constitution rather than the other way around.

The election of General Evren as president was one of the measures designed to ensure a smooth transition from the National Security Council regime to a democratic one. Another such transitional measure was the transformation of the National Security Council into a "Presidential Council"—with only advisory powers—for a period of six years, starting from the convening of the new Grand National Assembly. Also, during a six-year period, the president has the right to veto constitutional amendments, in which case the Grand National Assembly (GNA) can override the veto only by a three-fourths majority of its full membership. Finally, the constitution provides restrictions on political activities of former political leaders. The leaders, deputy leaders, secretaries-general, and the members of the central executive committees of former political parties are not allowed to establish or to become members in political parties, nor may they be nominated for the GNA or for local government bodies for a period of ten years. A less severe ban disqualifies the parliamentarians of former political parties from establishing political parties or becoming members of their central executive bodies (but not from running for and being elected to the GNA) for a period of five years. These bans were repealed by the constitutional referendum of 6 September 1987.

In addition to such transitional measures, the constitution introduces highly restrictive provisions on political activities of trade unions, associations, and cooperatives. Thus there can be no political links between such organizations and political parties, nor can they receive financial support from each other. Political parties are also banned from organizing in foreign countries (obviously, among the Turkish residents of those countries), creating women's and youth organizations, and establishing foundations. Also the 1982 Constitution transformed the office of the presidency from a largely ceremonial one, as it was under the 1961 Constitution, into a much more powerful one with effective autonomous powers. Although the political responsibility of the Council of Ministers before the GNA is maintained, the president is given important appointive powers (particularly, in regard to certain high-ranking judges) that he can exercise independently of the Council of Ministers. Also he can submit constitutional amendments to popular referenda and bring about a suit of unconstitutionality against any law passed by the GNA. The constitution did not go as far as the "French" 1958 Constitution, however, in strengthening the presidency. The system of government remained essentially parliamentary rather than presidential.

The National Security Council regime also adopted a new electoral law which retained the "d'Hondt" version of proportional representation with some important modifications. The d'Hondt formula is also known as the highest-average system. Briefly, it ensures that in a constituency no reallocation of additional seats would take place to increase proportionality. The "d'Hondt" system, in its classical version, slightly favors larger parties, but the modifications introduced by the new law made such effect much stronger. The most consequential novelty of the new law is a national quotient (threshold) such that political parties obtaining less than 10 percent of the total valid votes cast nationally will not be assigned any seats in the GNA. This provision is designed to prevent the excessive proliferation of political parties which, in the opinion of the council, contributed significantly to the crisis in the 1970s. The ruling council indicated on various occasions that it preferred a party system with two or three parties, which would ensure stable parliamentary majorities. Another novelty of the Electoral Law is the "constituency threshold," according to which the total number of valid votes cast in each constituency is divided by the number of seats in that constituency (which varies between two and six), and those parties or independent candidates that fail to exceed the quotient are not assigned any seats in that constituency. The combined effects of national and constituency thresholds favor larger parties.

Return to Competitive Politics and the 1983 Elections

The provisional article 4 of the Law on Political Parties gave the National Security Council the right to veto the founding members of new political parties (all former political parties had earlier been dissolved by a decree of the council). The council made use of this power in such a way that only three parties were able to complete their formation formalities before the beginning of the electoral process and, consequently, to compete in the GNA elections. Notably, two new parties that looked like credible successors to the two former major parties (namely, the True Path Party as a possible successor to the JP and the Social Democratic Party to the RPP) were thus eliminated from electoral competition, although both parties were allowed to complete their formation after the nomination process was over. Earlier, another successor party, the Grand Turkey Party, established or joined by a large number of former high-ranking JP figures, had been banned outright by the council. The provisional article 2 of the Electoral Law also required parties to have established their organizations in at least half of the provinces in order to qualify for electoral competition.

As a result of such qualifications, only three parties could contest the GNA elections held on 6 November 1983. These were the Motherland Party (MP), the Populist Party (PP), and the Nationalist Democratic Party (NDP). The MP is led by Turgut Özal, an engineer and economist who occupied high technocratic positions under Demirel, including the post of undersecretary in charge of the State Planning Organization. Özal became the deputy prime minister in charge of economic affairs in the Bülent Ulusu Government during the National Security Council rule. The PP was led by Necdet Calp, a former governor and undersecretary in the prime minister's office. The NDP leader, Turgut Sunalp, was a former general who served, after his retirement, as the Turkish ambassador in Canada.

The November 1983 elections resulted in a clear victory for Mr. Özal and his party. The MP won 45.2 percent of the total valid votes cast and 52.9 percent of the 400 assembly seats. Although a majority of the MP votes presumably came from former JP supporters, it appears that the MP also received votes from the supporters of the former NSP, NAP, and even the RPP. The PP came out as the second largest party with 30.5 percent of the vote and 29.3 percent of the seats, which was a better result than most observers expected. The PP appears to have gained the votes of a large majority of the former RPP voters. The main loser in the elections was the NDP. Despite the high expectations of its leadership, the NDP finished a poor third with 23.3 percent of the vote and only 17.8 percent of the seats. This seems to be related to the fact that most voters perceived the NDP as an extension of military rule, or as kind of a "state party," an image that the party leadership did not try to dispel. By contrast the MP was seen as the most spontaneous or the least artificial party of all three. In this sense, the election outcome can be interpreted as reflecting the desire of a majority of Turkish voters for a rapid normalization and civilianization.

The transition process proceeded smoothly following the elections. The legal existence of the National Security Council came to an end, the council members resigned their military posts and became members of the new Presidential Council. Mr. Özal was duly invited by President Evren to form the new government, and he received a comfortable vote of confidence from the GNA. Despite the speculations to the contrary, the new MP government did not include any independent ministers close to or favored by the military. Another MP deputy, Mr. Necmettin Karaduman, was easily elected speaker of the GNA, again disproving speculations that Mr. Ulusu (a former navy commander and the prime minister during council rule) was favored by the military for that prestigious post. Once in office, Özal started to put his economic liberalization program into effect with characteristic speed and boldness. One of the first laws passed by the GNA allowed all established parties (including the True Path and the Social Democratic parties) to contest the local government elections held in the spring of 1984. These elections confirmed the popularity of the MP. Thus, with the 1983 elections, civilian government has been restored and a new phase in Turkish politics has started.

An Appraisal

On the basis of the above historical analysis, Turkey's overall degree of success with democratic government can be described as "mixed" or "unstable." Democracy has been the rule in the last forty years, but has been interrupted thrice since 1960. Democratic rule is now in place, however, and there appears to be no immediate threat to its existence. A more positive evaluation is also suggested by the fact that of the three interruptions one was only partial, and the other two were of relatively short duration. Furthermore, in both cases, the military rulers declared from the beginning their intention to restore democracy. That they faithfully kept their promises is even more significant. Thus the democratic process was interrupted not by fully developed authoritarian regimes, but by interim military governments that aimed to effect a "reequilibration of democracy." The overall trend then has been *not away but toward* democratic government.

The transition in 1983 followed the pattern of *reforma* rather than *ruptura* or even *ruptura-pactada, reforma-pactada*, as did the transitions in the periods of 1946–1950 and 1960–1961. In fact it was even a purer case of *reforma* than the earlier ones. In the 1946–1950 transition the RPP government and the DP opposition at least agreed upon a new electoral law prior to the crucial elections of 1950. In 1960–1961 period the military government actively collaborated with the two opposition parties in making the new constitution and the electoral law. In the most recent transition, on the other hand, the National Security Council excluded all organized political groups from any meaningful role in the transition. The 1982 Constitution was prepared by the National Security Council itself in collaboration with an all-appointed, no-party Consultative Assembly, and the November 1983 elections were held under conditions carefully controlled by the council.

This process of transition and the new constitution as its product have been questioned by important sectors of Turkish public opinion. Of the three present major parties the MP is the strongest supporter of the new regime, although it has indicated that it was not against certain relatively minor constitutional amendments. The True Path Party of Mr. Demirel favors more substantial constitutional changes. The Social Democratic Party (which became the Social Democratic Populist Party after its merger with the Populist Party) strongly criticizes restrictions on civil liberties and union rights, and advocates a more rapid normalization. There is substantial agreement, however, that the transition to democracy is genuine (although to some, yet incomplete), and that the 1982 Constitution may serve as the basis of the new Turkish political regime with some (more or less important) modifications.

• THEORETICAL ANALYSIS •

What are the historical, cultural, social, economic, and political factors that favored or impeded the development of democratic government in Turkey? Since Turkey is a case of mixed success, it stands to reason that the following list is also a mixed one.

Political Culture

Two important features characterized the Ottoman political culture. One was the predominance of status-based values rather than market-derived values.[27] This was the outcome of the "bureaucratic" nature of the Ottoman Empire, which was described above. Briefly stated, the fundamental relationship under Ottoman rule between economic power and political power was essentially the reverse of the European historical experience: instead of economic power (i.e., ownership of the means of production) leading to political power (i.e., high office in the state bureaucracy), political power provided access to material wealth. However, the wealth thus accumulated could not be converted into more permanent economic assets because it was liable to confiscation by the state. Despite the growth of a substantial commercial and industrial middle class under the republic and especially in the last forty years, such status-based values still persist. The impact of this historical-cultural legacy on the development of democratic government in Turkey has been, on the whole, negative, since the predominance of status-derived values contributes to the strengthening of an all-powerful centralized state and hinders the development of a "civil society."

Another feature of the Ottoman cultural legacy has been the dichotomy resulting from the cultural division in Ottoman society between the palace (great) culture and the local or provincial (little) cultures.[28] They represented two very distinct ways of life, with different operational codes, different symbols (state versus village and tribe), different languages (highly literary and stylistic Ottoman versus simple spoken Turkish), different occupations (statecraft versus farming and artisanship), different types of settlement (urban versus rural), different literary and artistic traditions (*divan* literature and court music versus folk literature and music), and sometimes different versions of Islam (highly legalistic orthodox Islam versus often heterodox folk Islam). The nineteenth-century reforms and the Westernization movement did not eliminate, but perhaps further exacerbated, this cultural dualism by making the elite culture even more alien and inaccessible to the masses. Linguistic differences even among the Muslim subjects of the empire further contributed to this cultural fragmentation. Finally, the *millet* system that gave the ecclesiastical authorities of non-Muslim communities substantial control over their communal affairs without, however, granting them participatory rights meant that these communities maintained and developed their own cultures quite autonomously from the central or "great" culture. All this led to a low level of social and cultural integration of the Ottoman society.

To be sure, the republic made important strides in bridging the gap between elite and mass cultures. In particular, the last forty years of multiparty politics helped to integrate the mass electorate into national political life. "The distributive and the redistributive functions of government received increasing emphasis, while the prevalence of the extractive function began to decline. Second, as an outcome of the first point, the citizens became more interested in national political life and came to identify themselves more closely with national political institutions of which political parties were the main example."[29] Still, the lingering elitist attitudes within sectors of the centralist bureaucratic elite have produced tensions in the political system and remain dysfunctional for the development of democratic government.[30]

There are other features of the Ottoman-Turkish political culture that are also incongruent with a democratic political system. It has been argued, for example, that "there is an element in Turkish political culture to which the notion of opposition is deeply repugnant." Turks have shown a predilection for organic theories of the state and society, and solidarist doctrines found easy acceptance among the Young Turk and Kemalist elites. The Kemalist notion of "populism" meant a rejection of class conflict and a commitment to establish a "harmony of interests" through paternalistic government policies. This *gemeinschaft* outlook," present in both elite and mass cultures, finds perhaps its most poignant political expression in the excessive "fear of a national split." Indeed, one of the most frequent accusations party leaders hurl at each other is "splitting the nation."[31] Thus it appears that the notion of a loyal and legitimate opposition has not been fully institutionalized at the cultural level. The line separating opposition from treason is still rather thin compared to older and more stable democracies. The tendency to see politics in absolutist terms also explains the low capacity of political leaders for compromise and accommodation. Whether such low tolerance for opposition is comparable in the long run with the institutionalization of liberal democracy is open to question.

A related tendency is the low tolerance shown for individual deviance and heterodoxy within groups. In other words Turkish political culture attributes primacy not to the individual but to the collectivity, be it the nation, the state, or one of its subunits.[32] Individuality and deviance tend to be punished, conformity and orthodoxy rewarded in bureaucratic agencies, political parties, and even voluntary associations. Finally, most social institutions (families, schools, trade unions, local communities) display authoritarian patterns in their authority relations. This tends to create incongruences with the democratic authority patterns in the governmental sphere and to undermine stable democracy.[33]

On the more positive side, however, there seems to be a widespread consensus that the legitimacy of government derives from a popular mandate obtained in free, competitive elections. A democratic system is seen as the natural culmination of a century-old process of modernization and especially of the Kemalist reforms, the purpose of which was to create a Western type of secular, republican, modern state. In addition to this long-standing elite commitment to democracy, the peasants and the urban lower classes have come to see competitive elections as a powerful means to increase socioeconomic equality and to promote their material interests. A survey among some Istanbul squatters demonstrated, for example, that a substantial majority of them believed in the importance of voting and found political parties useful especially as channels of communication with government.[34] This attitude reflects a realization that a noncompetitive system would be less responsive to their group demands. Although there was a great deal of public anxiety over increasing political polarization and violence in the late 1970s, a majority of Turkish voters do not seem to hold the democratic system responsible for the crisis. Furthermore, in spite of such polarization, a centrist political orientation has remained strong among Turkish voters. In a 1977 preelection survey, 26.8 percent of the respondents placed themselves at the center, 27.7 percent at the left of center, and 24.6 percent at the right of center. About a fifth of the respondents (20.9 percent) claimed that they had no opinion on this question. If we assume that "don't knows" indicate a lack of interest in ideological politics, then close to half of all Turkish voters can be placed at the center.[35] While few people would like to go back to the circumstances that prevailed before the 1980 coup, there does not seem to be broad popular support for a prolonged authoritarian solution.

Historical Development

Certain historical factors favor the development of democratic government in Turkey. As the first part of this chapter demonstrates, the first movements toward representative and constitutional government started more than a century ago. Even if we discount the brief periods of

democratic government under the Ottoman Empire and the early republic, the present competitive political system has been in existence for forty years with relatively short interruptions. A generation born in the multiparty period and socialized into democratic values has already reached positions of authority in governmental as well as nongovernmental spheres. Following Huntington we may argue that such longevity, or "chronological age," has helped to institutionalize democratic organizations and procedures.[36]

That Turkey did not have a colonial past, unlike most of the Third

World countries, is also a favorable historical factor for democratic development. Democratic institutions were not imposed from outside, but are seen as a natural outgrowth of internal political processes, which tends to increase their legitimacy in the eyes of the elites and the masses.

One may argue that some sequences of political development favor the emergence of democratic institutions more than the others. It has been posited, for example, that the optimum sequence is to establish national unity (identity) first, then central government authority, and then political equality and participation.[37] Turkish political development followed this optimum course. Simultaneously with the creation of the Turkish Republic in place of the multinational Ottoman Empire, the question of identity was effectively solved in favor of a Turkish national identity. The already highly developed central governmental institutions of the Ottoman state were further strengthened under the republic and penetrated more deeply into the society. The expansion of political participation took place a generation later in the mid-1940s, and proceeded within the already existing institutional framework of elections, legislatures and parties.

Class Structure

The distribution of wealth and income appears to be highly unequal in Turkey. It is markedly so between the agricultural and nonagricultural sectors, within each of these sectors, between cities and rural settlements, and among geographic regions. A substantial proportion of the Turkish population has been, and remains, in a condition of low-end poverty. A study estimated that in 1973 38 percent of all Turkish households were below the subsistence level. Ownership of land is also highly unequal. Another 1973 study found that 22 percent of rural households were landless. About 42 percent of all rural households own very little land or no land at all, and the land owned by this 42 percent makes up less than 3 percent of total privately owned land. Conversely, households with 1,000 or more acres of land, constituting only 0.12 percent of all rural households, own 5.27 percent of total privately owned land. Land distribution is particularly unequal in the eastern and southeastern regions, which display markedly feudal features.[38] Overall income inequality seems to have further increased in the late 1970s and the early 1980s.

On the more positive side one may cite the existence of a rather substantial educated urban middle class of entrepreneurs, professionals, and bureaucrats, as well as a large group of middle-sized farmers. Under the liberal labor legislation that followed the 1961 Constitution, the number of unionized workers rose rapidly from less than 300,000 in 1963 to over 2.2 million in 1977. Thus the percentage of unionized workers reached 14.8 percent of the total economically active population and 39.8 percent of all wage earners.[39] Other alleviating factors ("dampening mechanisms") included the relatively high rate of economic growth (see below) and the availability of "exit" possibilities. Apart from more than a million Turkish workers (over 2 million together with their dependents) who have emigrated to Western Europe and to a much lesser extent to Middle Eastern countries, mass rural-to-urban migration helps to ease distributional problems in rural areas and reduces the propensity to resort to the "voice" option, that is, corrective political action.[40] Also contributing to the general lack of effective collective action aimed at income redistribution in rural areas are the strong in-group feelings and the absence of class-based politics among Turkish peasants who still compose roughly half the labor force. In some of the least developed regions (e.g., the east and the southeast), where land and income inequality is greatest and redistributive action is most needed, the low level of social mobilization and the strength of patron-client relationships tend to make peasant political participation more mobilized and deferential than autonomous and instrumental. In some areas (e.g., central Turkey), relative equality of landownership together with overall poverty also works against emergence of class cleavages among peasants by producing a "corporate village" pattern. This may explain why the social democratic RPP, which has based its appeal on the promise of a more egalitarian income distribution and has greatly increased its urban strength between 1969 and 1977, has not been able to achieve nearly the same degree of success in rural areas.[41]

National Structure (Ethnic and Religious Cleavages)

The breakup of the Ottoman Empire at the end of World War I made the present day Turkey an ethnically, linguistically, and religiously much more homogeneous country than its predecessor. Over 99 percent of its population profess Islam; an estimated 15 percent belong to the Alevi (Shiite) sect, the rest are Sunnis. The Alevis are concentrated in the east central region and have tended to support the RPP. The Unity party, formed in 1968 to represent the Alevis, has not fared well electorally. Its vote declined steadily from 2.8 percent in 1969, to 1.1 percent in 1973, and 0.4 percent in 1977. In the atmosphere of political polarization in the late 1970s, this sectarian cleavage led to violent clashes in several localities, the worst of which was the Kahramanmaras incident in which about 100 people lost their lives. The only large linguistic minority is the Kurdish-speaking minority (again an estimated 10 percent to 15 percent), which is concentrated in the eastern and southeastern regions. Although a few thousand separatist guerillas are currently active in the region, a very large majority of Kurdish speakers seem to be well integrated into Turkish society. There is no political party that specifically represents the interests of the Kurdish-speaking population. The voting patterns in these regions are not markedly different from the rest of the country except that personalistic and clientelistic influences are much stronger there because of economic underdevelopment and feudalistic social structure. Sectarian and linguistic cleavages do not coincide and mutually reinforce each other, however, since most of the (minority) Alevis are Turkish speakers, and a large majority of Kurdish speakers are Sunnis. Furthermore, neither of them coincide with class cleavages except that the eastern regions are in general much poorer than the rest of the country.

State Structure and Strength

One of the principal legacies of the Ottoman Empire is the strong and centralized state authority. The political center composed of the sultan and his military and civilian bureaucrats sought to eliminate all rival centers of power. The resulting situation has been referred to as the "absence of civil society," which means the weakness or absence of corporate, autonomous, intermediary social structures. The number of voluntary associations in Turkey rose tremendously in the multiparty era from a mere 802 in 1946 to 37,806 in 1968.[42] Yet organizational autonomy and the level of organizational participation in such associations are still much lower than in Western European and North American democracies. The relative ease with which interim military regimes abolished parties, restricted union rights, co-opted or neutralized professional associations, and curtailed the autonomy of universities testifies to the weakness of corporate structures.

The weakness of civil society is also evident in the weakness of local governments. The vast territories of the Ottoman Empire were ruled not by local bodies, but by centrally appointed governors. The first semielected, local administrative councils came into being, as we have already seen, only in the second half of the nineteenth century. As for the cities the Ottoman state had no tradition of independent, autonomous municipalities. Nor did the republic attempt to change this centralized system. Although a law passed in 1930 enabled local communities to establish municipal governments, the whole system of local administration remained highly centralized. Local governments, especially municipalities, gained some vitality in the multiparty era. Nevertheless, their autonomous powers have been very limited, central control over their activities (called "administrative tutelage") exceedingly strict, and their financial resources totally inadequate. In this sense both provincial administrations and municipalities have had to depend very heavily on the central government.[43]

Historically the state has also played a dominant role in the economy. This Ottoman legacy was further reinforced under the republic when the Kemalist regime initiated a policy of economic interventionism (statism) in the 1930s. Statism meant the direct entry of the state into the fields of production and distribution. Public economic enterprises started to be created in those years and grew rapidly. Despite the greater emphasis on the private sector in recent decades, such enterprises still produce about one-half of the total industrial output. Both under the Ottoman state and the early republic, private accumulation of wealth depended, in large measure, on position in or access to the state.

This combination of factors, namely the absence of powerful, economically dominant interests able to capture the state and use it to serve their own purposes, and the weakness or absence of corporate intermediary structures, had important consequences for subsequent modernization. First, it led to what is known as the "autonomy of the state," meaning that the state apparatus is not the captive or the handmaiden of any particular social class, but possesses sufficient autonomy to make decisions that can change, eliminate, or create class relationships. This autonomous state, unhampered by established class interests and strong corporate structures, has a high capacity to accumulate and expand political power and to use it for the economic and social modernization of society. The implications for the development of democratic government are not, however, nearly as positive. As has been argued above, an autonomous, bureaucratic state is much less likely to develop democratic political institutions than a postfeudal society in which feudalism and the system of representation of estates left a legacy of autonomous groups with corporate identity and rights.

The nature and autonomy of the state in Turkey also means that the costs of being out of power are extremely high. Because of the high degree of governmental centralization and the large role of the Turkish state in the economy, "those in government have access, directly or indirectly, to an immense amount of resources in relation to the resource base of society, which they can distribute."[44] Conversely, a party that is out of power tends to get weakened since it does not have access to political patronage resources.

The Turkish state, strong and centralized as it is, has generally been effective in maintaining public order. When it was faced with widespread terrorism and violence as in the late 1970s, however, it had to turn to the army by declaring martial law. This may be related to the fact that police forces, being within the direct jurisdiction of the Ministry of Interior, are more susceptible to political influences and, sometimes, even to infiltration by extremist groups, as was the case in the late 1970s. Especially in a politically charged atmosphere, therefore, police action is not considered as impartial and as legitimate by the public as military action.

Indeed the Turkish armed forces are broadly representative of the society as a whole. They are not dominated or controlled by any particular social group or political force. They are strongly committed to the legacy of Atatürk and to a modern, national, secular, republican state. More so than in many Latin American countries, they also have been committed to democratic principles, as attested by their voluntary and relatively rapid relinquishment of power to freely elected civilian authorities after each intervention. They display, however, certain ambivalent attitudes toward democracy, characteristic of the military in other developing nations. In the elitist tradition described above, they tend to see themselves as the true guardians of the national interest, as opposed to "partial" interests represented by political parties. They also consider themselves the protectors of national unity that, in their opinion, is often endangered by the divisive actions of political parties. These attitudes, which signify a deep distrust of parties and politicians, are clearly reflected in those provisions of the 1982 Constitution aiming to limit the power of political parties. Similarly, the constitution's numerous restrictions on trade unions and voluntary associations suggest that the military's conception of democracy is more plebiscitary than participatory. In short the military, reflecting the larger society's somewhat ambivalent values toward democracy, seem to share both a belief in its general appropriateness and desirability for Turkey, and some of the antiliberal, antideviationist, intolerant attitudes embedded in the Turkish political culture.

Political Structure

Some aspects of the political structure in Turkey have been positive in their implications for democracy but others have been negative. On the positive side the major political parties have been moderate and non-ideological. Despite the polarization in the late 1970s, the ideological and social distance between the two major parties has not been great. Major political parties have not sponsored or condoned acts of political violence, nor have they called for military intervention. However, the JP's coalition partnership with the NAP in the late 1970s forced it to be reticent about the right-wing terror.

Extremist parties, such as the NAP and NSP, have not had a significant electoral following. However, those parties played an important role in the 1970s because of the peculiar parliamentary arithmetic that resulted from the system of proportional representation. Although there were only four significant parties in the 1977 National Assembly, the system displayed the functional properties of extreme multipartism. Instead of the centripetal drive of moderate multipartism, the basic drive of the system seemed to be in a centrifugal direction. Standards of "fair competition" fell significantly and there was a corresponding increase in the "politics of outbidding."[45]

No major interest group is excluded from representation in the political system through a party or party faction. The constitution states, however, that the "constitutions and programs of political parties shall not be incompatible with the territorial and national integrity of the state, human rights, national sovereignty, and the principles of a democratic and secular Republic." To this is added a more specific provision banning parties that aim at establishing the sovereignty of a particular class or group, or a dictatorship of any sort. Thus the constitution excludes from political competition communist, fascist, religious, and separatist parties. Political parties that violate these bans shall be closed by the Constitutional Court. Trade unions are also prohibited from establishing political linkages with political parties. They cannot engage in political activities, nor can they support or receive support from political parties.

A strong and independent judiciary has developed, including a Constitutional Court with full powers to declare an act of parliament unconstitutional. The 1961 Constitution took special care to safeguard the judiciary vis-à-vis the legislature and the executive. The 1982 Constitution broadly maintained the same principle with some, relatively minor, modifications. Security of tenure for judges and public prosecutors has been recognized by the 1982 Constitution in identical terms as those of its predecessor, according to which "judges and public prosecutors shall not be dismissed or retired before the age prescribed by the Constitution; nor shall they be deprived of their salaries, allowances, or other personal rights, even as a result of the abolition of a court or a post." Personnel matters for judges and public prosecutors, such as appointments, promotions, transfers, and disciplinary actions are within the exclusive jurisdiction of the Supreme Council of Judges and Public Prosecutors, itself composed primarily of judges nominated by the two high courts in the country and appointed by the president of the republic.

A vigorously free and independent press strongly committed to democratic principles has developed. The press has, in general, maintained its independent attitude and commitment to democracy even in times of interim military governments, although martial law entailed severe restrictions on the freedom of the press. With the transition to a civilian regime in November 1983 and the subsequent lifting of martial law, the press has strongly reasserted itself. It has shown willingness to publicize domestic and foreign criticism of human rights practices.

On the basis of the preceding observations we may conclude that, of our set of variables, that which pertains to political structures is probably the most favorable one to democratic government in Turkey.

Political Leadership

Turkish political leaders have, in general, been committed to the democratic process, and have denounced acts of violence and disloyalty against it. They have also, in general, been reasonably effective and honest in governing. On the other hand, as our historical analysis has demonstrated, they have not, as a rule, shown a high capacity for accommodation and compromise in containing political conflict and managing political crises and strains. On the contrary their failure to do so seems directly responsible for both the 1960 and 1980 military interventions. In 1960, the deterioration of relations between the government and the opposition parties led to widespread public unrest that in turn triggered off the coup. Similarly, prior to the 1980 intervention, a coalition government based on the two major parties, or at least some broad understanding between them, would probably have satisfied the military and held off their intervention. This unwillingness to compromise seems partly a function of the political cultural characteristics and partly of the high costs of being out of power in Turkey.

Development Performance

The rate of economic growth in Turkey has been comparatively high, if somewhat uneven. In the 1950s and the 1960s the average annual rate of real GNP growth has been about 7 percent. Turkey was hard-hit, however, by the oil shock in 1974 and the subsequent "worldwide recession, concomitant with deteriorating terms of trade and continuation of trade policies geared more toward import substitution than export encouragement, including an exchange rate regime that discouraged inflows of capital and workers' remittances." Thus the GDP growth rate fell 2.4 percent in 1978, and declined further 0.9 percent in 1979, and 0.8 percent in 1980. Moreover, the rate of inflation reached 70 percent in 1979 and above 100 percent in 1980.[46] With the introduction of comprehensive reform measures in January 1980, whose chief architect was Turgut Özal (then the director of the State Planning Organization), economic growth has resumed at a modest rate of about 5 percent. These new policies aimed at greater reliance upon market forces and an easing of governmental interventions in the economy. They continued to be pursued by the military regime of 1980–1983, under which Özal was made the deputy prime minister in charge of economic affairs, and obviously since November 1983 when he came to power at the head of his new Motherland Party.

The relatively high rate of economic growth since the transition to competitive politics has been one of the "dampening mechanisms" that discouraged the political participation of low-income strata. It seems, however, that the benefits of growth have been quite unevenly distributed across regions, economic sectors, and social classes. Nevertheless, it is not the case that the rich got richer and the poor got poorer; rather they both got richer, but the rich got richer at a faster rate.[47] The implications for the future of democracy of this economic development performance will be discussed in the next section.

International Factors

Turkey's close alliance with the West since the end of the World War II has generally, but only indirectly, supported democratic developments in the country. Turkey has become a member of the NATO, of the Council of Europe, and an associate member of the European Community. These relations have meant linkages between Turkish political parties, parliaments, trade unions, business and professional associations, armed forces, and their Western European and North American counterparts. Over two million Turks living in Western Europe (a very large majority in the Federal Republic of Germany) provide another, and vitally important, link between Turkey and the West.

     While all these relations and linkages provide stimuli for democratic development, their effects have been far from decisive. Turks are proud and nationalistic people who do not like to be dictated to from abroad. A good example of this is that criticisms by the European Community, or the Council of Europe, or individual Western European governments of certain undemocratic practices during and after military rule usually create unfavorable reactions, even among those Turks who may be similarly critical of the same practices. The point is often made that Turkey will remain a democracy not to please its European allies, but because its people believe that this is the most appropriate form of government for their country. Nevertheless, the thought lingers no doubt in the minds of many Turkish leaders that an authoritarian Turkey, isolated and excluded from the club of European democracies, will probably experience greater difficulties in its international relations. The breakdown of authoritarian regimes in Greece, Portugal, and Spain in the 1970s makes the position of a pro-Western but authoritarian European country extremely lonely and uneasy.

• FUTURE PROSPECTS AND POLICY IMPLICATIONS •

Policies Promoting the Growth of Civil Society

In view of the positive and negative factors discussed above, what kinds of policies and political/economic developments would be most likely to support, nurture, and sustain democratic government? If one of the most serious obstacles to democratic development in Turkey is the historical legacy of an exceedingly centralized, overpowering state and the concomitant weakness of civil society, then policies that aim at establishing a healthier balance between the state and the society will clearly be functional for democratic development. One obvious area where the state's role can, and probably should, be reduced is the economy. The market-oriented economic policies of Mr. Özal are important steps in that direction. Greater reliance on market mechanisms, greater emphasis on expanding exports instead of an inward-turned, import substitution economic strategy, realistic exchange rates, and a sharp reduction in bureaucratic controls over private economic activities are the main ingredients of the new economic policy. Bold and far-reaching as these innovations are, one should not expect a sudden and radical diminution in the state's role in the economy. The state economic enterprises, which presently produce almost half of the entire industrial output, will be there to stay in the foreseeable future. If, however, their management is somehow given sufficient autonomy and left outside the scope of direct government intervention, this will help to lower the stakes of politics and reduce the winner-take-all, zero-sum character of political competition.

Another set of policies promoting the growth of civil society would be the strengthening of local governments. One recent positive development in this regard has been the substantial increase in their revenues after 1980 through the allocation of a greater share of public funds. If local governments are seen with less suspicion by the central government and given greater powers and responsibilities, they will no doubt play an important role in socializing people into democratic values. Such a development will also mean a more effective power sharing between the central and local bodies and, consequently, an effective check on the power of the central government. Finally, it will lower the stakes of political competition, since an opposition party that controls important municipalities will be able to render some patronage services to its constituents and thus maintain a certain level of political influence.

A third group of policies with the same overall effect would be those that would promote the growth of voluntary associations. As we have pointed out above, the number of voluntary associations increased very rapidly during the years of multiparty politics. The impact of this development on democratic government has not been entirely functional, however, since many associations displayed a propensity for overpoliticization. Instead of articulating the common interests of their members, many of them came to be dominated by small, politically motivated cliques, and became instruments of polarized political struggle. It was not a rare occurrence in the 1970s to see the members of the same professional group (including even the police forces) divided between extreme right and left-wing "professional" associations. Some of the restrictive provisions of the 1982 Constitution on voluntary associations, which may well seem excessive from a liberal democratic point of view, are understandable on the basis of this past experience. One may conclude, therefore, that the constitution aimed at a certain "depoliticization" of the society in general and associational activities in particular. Whether this aim can be accomplished without impeding democratic development remains to be seen. On the one hand, a vigorous life of voluntary associations and professional organizations is a prerequisite for democratic development. On the other, the overpoliticization of such associations has been a polarizing factor in recent Turkish politics. The optimum combination for democratic development would be some middle course between the two.

Policies Promoting Governmental Stability and Efficiency

It has been pointed out that the crisis of democracy in the late 1970s was due, at least in some measure, to the fragmentation of the party system and to the resulting fact that parliamentary balance was held by small antisystem parties. To this was added the incapacity of the political system to initiate new policies to meet new challenges, because of the narrow and heterogeneous governmental majorities in parliament. Two sets of institutional measures taken by the military regime of 1980–1983 may prove to be helpful in preventing the recurrence of a similar situation. One is the change in the electoral system. The adoption of a 10 percent national threshold for representation in the Grand National Assembly, together with various other features of the electoral system that favor major parties, make it extremely difficult for more than three significant parties to be represented in parliament. Given the tendency of the Turkish party system to coalesce around two major and non-ideological parties, this change is likely to remove one major polarizing factor.

The 1982 Constitution has also taken certain measures to increase governmental stability by strengthening the Council of Ministers vis-à-vis the Assembly. For example, while the vote of confidence taken following the formation of a new Council of Ministers does not require more than an ordinary majority, a vote of censure requires an absolute majority of the full membership of the Assembly. Furthermore, in a vote of confidence only negative (meaning no confidence) votes are counted (articles 99 and 111).

A much more consequential novelty of the constitution designed to increase governmental stability concerns the scope of the power of dissolution. The 1961 Constitution permitted the executive branch to call new elections for the National Assembly only under very exceptional circumstances. This limited right of dissolution did not offer any help in cases of protracted government crisis when no majority coalition could be formed. The 1982 Constitution empowers the president to call new elections when a government cannot be formed within forty-five days either at the beginning of a new legislative assembly or after the resignation of a government. The constitution has also adopted a new procedure in the selection of the president of the republic to prevent the kind of deadlock witnessed in 1980.[48]

Finally, the broadening under the 1982 Constitution of the law-making powers of the executive is designed to increase the efficiency of government. This power was given to the Council of Ministers for the first time by the 1971 amendment of the constitution, under which the Council of Ministers could issue ordinances or decrees that could amend existing laws. The 1982 Constitution further expanded the power to issue such ordinances. The enabling act of Parliament defines the purpose, scope, and principles of ordinances and prescribes the period during which they can be issued. In contrast to the 1961 Constitution, the enabling act does not have to specify which provisions of the existing legislation can be amended or repealed by ordinance. The 1982 Constitution also empowers the executive to issue a special kind of law-amending ordinances during periods of martial law or state of emergency. They differ from ordinary ordinances in that they do not require a prior enabling act and, even more important, they are outside the scope of review by the Constitutional Court. Both ordinary and emergency ordinances are subject, however, to review by the assembly.

Policies Promoting Economic Growth and Equity

It has already been mentioned that the relatively high rate of economic growth in the 1950s and the 1960s has been one of the positive factors supporting democratic development. However, the dominant economic development strategy of the era presents a close resemblance to the one pursued by some relatively developed Latin American countries, notably Brazil and Argentina, during the populist semiauthoritarian regimes of Vargas and Peron, with the same negative implications for democracy. In both cases, economic development strategies were based more on import substitution (of essentially consumer goods) than on export encouragement. One reason given for the emergence of military-bureaucratic-technocratic regimes in these countries in the 1960s and the 1970s is the economic difficulties and bottlenecks associated with this kind of development strategy (industrial dependence on imported inputs and government protection; inability to export, leading to foreign exchange shortages, and then to unemployment and economic stagnation).

As the economic pie got smaller, political conflict became more virulent, the populist coalition broke down, and the middle classes came to see the demands of the popular sector as excessive. The resultant military-technocratic regimes tended to restrict political participation by suppressing or deactivating the urban popular sector, and to follow growth policies that increased socioeconomic inequality.[49]

Thus similarities between the Turkish case on the one hand, and the Argentine and the Brazilian ones on the other are unmistakable, with the exception that the military regime was of much shorter duration in Turkey. The most appropriate policy to avoid a repetition of this vicious circle seems to be an economic growth strategy encouraging exports and export-oriented, internationally competitive industries, combined with an effort to increase equity. While Mr. Özal's economic policies have been highly successful on the first front, they have not been marked by a strong concern for equity. Thus the concluding remarks of an earlier study on the political economy of income distribution, still seems valid:

> With the equity tensions rising, it is abundantly clear that any optimistic scenario for distributional politics in the near and medium terms must be premised on a speedy, confident resumption of economic growth. Only with an expanding pie can the reslicing due to be demanded be reasonably peaceful and satisfying. An optimistic scenario, then, would posit such growth resumption . . . . But then it would also posit a leadership that would add to growth policies far more vigorous and sweeping redistributive reforms than have been yet accomplished. Failing this, the outlook appears to us bleak—along either of the two courses we see events branching. Either the forces favoring redistribution will strengthen their hold on political power and, lacking growth, will force a more equitable sharing of poverty. Or, alternatively, a more authoritarian regime [probably of a military variety] will intervene to repress both redistributive and participatory demands. The first of these less attractive cases, absent growth, would be very likely to induce a switch to the second. And whether the resort to it were immediate or delayed, it would thwart, for an uncertainly long time, Turkey's reach toward a more just and democratic system. Our profound hope is that both can be avoided—by a timely and bold adoption of the growth-with-equity alternative.[50]

Conclusion

As stated above, Turkey is one of the few countries that are more democratic politically than they ought to have been according to the level of their socioeconomic development.[51] This should be explained mainly by the strong elite commitment to democracy and the relatively favorable political structural factors, the elite commitment was the major factor in the crucial transition from authoritarian rule in 1946–1950 period. It was also instrumental in keeping the three military interventions either partial or of relatively short duration. Indeed, interruptions in the democratic process were more in the nature of reequilibrations of democracy than full-blown authoritarian interludes.⁵² Thus normalization proceeded more rapidly after the elections of November 1983 than most observers expected at the time. All four parties banned by the military regime have now been revived under new names, with the difference that the two old major parties have two competing heirs each (the Motherland and the True Path parties for the JP; the Social Democratic Populist and the Democratic Left parties for the RPP). The new electoral system with its high national threshold, however, is likely to force similar parties into merger in the long run. Given the fact that the pre-1980 polarization was the work mainly of small extremist parties and groups, their elimination from representation in Parliament may well turn out to be a stabilizing factor. The constitutional ban on the political activities of trade unions and on their establishing linkages with political parties, on the other hand, is not viewed as desirable or legitimate by the social democratic parties. It is to be expected that the most likely course of events in the next few years would be the consolidation of democracy, with the expansion of civil and union rights by means of relatively minor changes in the constitution.

• NOTES •

1. A comprehensive continuing study sponsored by the Center of International Studies of Princeton University attempts to analyze the legacy of the Ottoman Empire upon its successor states.

2. For the differences between bureaucratic and feudal states, and the implications for their developments, see Samuel P. Huntington, *Political Order in Changing Societies* (New Haven and London: Yale University Press, 1968), ch. 3.

3. Halil Inalcik, "The Nature of Traditional Society: Turkey," in Robert E. Ward and Dankwart A. Rustow, eds., *Political Modernization in Japan and Turkey* (Princeton: Princeton University Press, 1964), p. 44. The following analysis borrows extensively from my *Social Change and Political Participation in Turkey* (Princeton: Princeton University Press, 1976), pp. 25–29.

4. Niyazi Berkes, *Türkiye'de Cagdaslasma* (*The Development of Secularism in Turkey*) (Ankara: Bilgi Yayinevi, 1973), pp. 27–28.

5. H. A. R. Gibb and Harold Bowen, *Islamic Society and the West*, vol. 1, part 1 (London: Oxford University Press, 1950), p. 52.

6. Şerif Mardin, "Power, Civil Society and Culture in the Ottoman Empire," *Comparative Studies in Society and History* 2 (June 1969): passim; Clement Henry Moore, "Authoritarian Politics in Unincorporated Society: The Case of Nasser's Egypt," *Comparative Politics* 6 (January 1974): pp. 204–208.

7. Şerif Mardin, "Historical Determinants of Social Stratification: Social Class and Class Consciousness in Turkey," *A. Ü. Siyasal Bilgiler Fakültesi Dergisi* 22 (Aralik 1967): p. 127.

8. Stanford J. Shaw, "The Central Legislative Councils in the Nineteenth Century Ottoman Reform Movement before 1876," *International Journal of Middle East Studies* 1 (January 1970): pp. 57–62.

9. Roderic H. Davison, *Reform in the Ottoman Empire, 1856–1876* (Princeton, N.J.: Princeton University Press, 1963), pp. 147–149, 167.

10. Robert Devereux, *The First Ottoman Constitutional Period: A Study of the Midhat Constitution and Parliament* (Baltimore: The Johns Hopkins University Press, 1963), pp. 126–148.

11. Engin Deniz Akarli, "The State as a Socio-Cultural Phenomenon and Political Participation in Turkey," in Akarli and Gabriel Ben-Dor, eds., *Political Participation in Turkey: Historical Background and Present Problems* (Istanbul: Bogaziçi University Publications, 1975), p. 139. See also, Şerif Mardin, "Center-Periphery Relations: A Key to Turkish Politics?," *Daedalus* 102, no. 1 (Winter 1973): pp. 169–190; Metin Heper, "Center and Periphery in the Ottoman Empire, with Special Reference to the Nineteenth Century," *International Political Science Review* 1, no. 1 (1980): pp. 81–104.

12. Akarli, "The State as a Socio-Cultural Phenomenon," p. 143.

13. Kemal H. Karpat, "The Transformation of the Ottoman State, 1789–1908," *International Journal of Middle East Studies* 3 (July 1972): pp. 263, 268–270.

14. Feroz Ahmad, *The Young Turks: The Committee of Union and Progress in Turkish Politics, 1908–1914* (Oxford: Clarendon Press, 1969), pp. 143–144.

15. Ibid., pp. 161–162.

16. Özbudun, *Social Change and Political Participation*, pp. 38–41.

17. Frederick W. Frey, *The Turkish Political Elite* (Cambridge, Mass.: M.I.T. Press, 1965), p. 326.

18. For details, see my "Turkey," in Myron Weiner and Ergun Özbudun, eds., *Competitive Elections in Developing Countries* (Durham, N.C.: Duke University Press, 1987), pp. 328–368.

19. Ilter Turan, "Stages of Political Development in the Turkish Republic," (Paper presented to the Third International Congress on the Economic and Social History of Turkey, Princeton University, 24–26 August 1983), pp. 6–11.

20. Nur Yalman argues, for example, that the dispute between rationalism and tradition "happens to be especially bitter in Turkey. It is rare to see such virulent opposition to a country's own traditions and history." "Islamic Reform and the Mystic Tradition in Eastern Turkey," *Archive européene de sociologie* 10 (1969): p. 45.

21. Juan J. Linz, "The Transition from Authoritarian Regimes to Democratic Political Systems and the Problems of Consolidation of Political Democracy," (Paper presented to the IPSA Round Table, Tokyo, 29 March to 1 April 1982), pp. 23–41.

22. For details see my "Transition from Authoritarianism to Democracy in Turkey, 1945–1950," (Paper presented at the IPSA World Congress, Paris, 15–20 July 1985).

23. Frey, *The Turkish Political Elite*, pp. 196–197.

24. Turan, "Stages of Political Development," p. 17.

25. Ergun Özbudun, *The Role of the Military in Recent Turkish Politics*, (Cambridge, Mass.: Harvard University Center for International Affairs, Occasional Paper in International Affairs, 1966), pp. 30–39.

26. Özbudun, *Social Change and Political Participation*, passim; Özbudun, "Voting Behaviour: Turkey," in Jacob M. Landau, Ergun Özbudun, and Frank Tachau, eds., *Electoral Politics in the Middle East: Issues, Voters, and Elites* (London: Croom Helm, 1980), pp. 107–143.

27. Mardin, "Power, Civil Society and Culture," pp. 258–281.

28. Ibid., pp. 270–281.

29. Turan, "Stages of Political Development," p. 29.

30. Ibid., pp. 52–55.

31. Şerif Mardin, "Opposition and Control in Turkey," *Government and Opposition* 1 (May 1966): pp. 375–387.

32. Turan, "Stages of Political Development," pp. 46–47.

33. Harry H. Eckstein, *A Theory of Stable Democracy*, (Princeton: Center of International Studies, Princeton University, Monograph no. 10, 1961).

34. Kemal H. Karpat, *The Gecekondu: Rural Migration and Urbanization* (Cambridge: Cambridge University Press, 1976), pp. 205–211.

35. Üstün Ergüder, "Changing Patterns of Electoral Behavior in Turkey," (Paper presented at the IPSA World Congress, Moscow, 12–18 August 1979), pp. 13–15.

36. Huntington, *Political Order*, p. 13.

37. Eric A. Nordlinger, "Political Development: Time Sequences and Rates of Change," *World Politics* 20 (1968): pp. 494–520; Dankwart A. Rustow, *A World of Nations* (Washington, D.C.: The Brookings Institution, 1967), pp. 120–132; Robert A. Dahl, *Polyarchy: Participation and Opposition*, (New Haven and London: Yale University Press, 1971), ch. 3.

38. Ergun Özbudun and Aydin Ulusan, "Overview," in Özbudun and Ulusan, eds., *The Political Economy of Income Distribution in Turkey*, (New York: Holmes and Meier, 1980), pp. 10–12.

39. Maksut Mumcuoğlu, "Political Activities of Trade Unions and Income Distribution," in Özbudun and Ulusan, eds., *The Political Economy*, pp. 384, 404–405.

40. Albert Hirschman, *Exit, Voice, and Loyalty: Responses to Decline in Firms, Organizations, and States*, (Cambridge, Mass.: Harvard University Press, 1970).

41. Özbudun and Ulusan, "Overview," pp. 17–18.

42. Ahmet N. Yücekök, *Türkiye'de Örgütlenmis Dinin Sosyo-Ekonomik Tabani (The Socioeconomic Basis of Organized Religion in Turkey)* (Ankara: A. Ü. Siyasal Bilgiler Fakültesi, 1971), p. 119.

43. Michael N. Danielson and Ruşen Keleş, "Allocating Public Resources in Urban Turkey," in Özbudun and Ulusan, *The Political Economy*, p. 313 and passim.

44. Turan, "Stages of Political Development," pp. 55–60.

45. Giovanni Sartori, *Parties and Party Systems: A Framework for Analysis*, (Cambridge: Cambridge University Press, 1976), pp. 139–140; Ergun Özbudun, "The Turkish Party System: Institutionalization, Polarization, and Fragmentation," *Middle Eastern Studies* 17, no. 2 (April 1981): p. 233.

46. *Turkey: The Problems of Transition* (Bath: A Euromoney Special Study, 1982), pp. 49–50; Zvi Yehuda Hershlag, "Economic Policies," in Klaus-Detlev Grothusen, ed., *Türkei* (Göttingen, 1985: Vandenhoeck and Ruprecht), pp. 346–369.

47. Özbudun and Ulusan, *The Political Economy*, passim.

48. As under the 1961 Constitution, if no presidential candidate obtains a two-thirds majority of the full membership of the Grand National Assembly on the first two ballots, an absolute majority of the full membership will suffice on the third ballot. But under the new procedure, a fourth ballot, if necessary, will be held only between the two leading candidates, and if the fourth ballot does not produce an absolute majority, the Assembly will dissolve automatically and new general elections will be held immediately (article 102).

49. Especially Guillermo O'Donnell, *Modernization and Bureaucratic Authoritarianism: Studies in South American Politics* (Berkeley: Institute of International Studies, University of California, 1973); Samuel P. Huntington and Joan M. Nelson, *No Easy Choice: Political Participation in Developing Countries* (Cambridge, Mass.: Harvard University Press, 1976), pp. 23–24.

50. Özbudun and Ulusan, "Overview," p. 20.

51. See, for example, Tatu Vanhanen, "The State and Prospects of Democracy in the 1980's," (Paper presented at the IPSA World Congress, Paris, 15–20 July 1985). Vanhanen hypothesizes that "the fundamental factor affecting the nature of political systems is the relative distribution of economic, intellectual and other crucial power resources among various sectors of the population." He measures such distribution by a composite index called "Index of Power Resources" (IPR) and finds a strong correlation between the IPR score and political democracy. Turkey's calculated IPR score is 7.8, considerably lower than those for some South European and Latin American democracies: Greece (20.2). Spain (15.0), Argentina (15.7), Uruguay (17.0), Venezuela (11.0), etc. It should also be pointed out that the IPR score itself seems to be strongly correlated with the more conventional indicators of socioeconomic development.

52. See especially, Juan J. Linz, *The Breakdown of Democratic Regimes: Crisis, Breakdown, and Reequilibration*, (Baltimore and London: The Johns Hopkins University Press, 1978), pp. 87–97.

THE PHILIPPINES

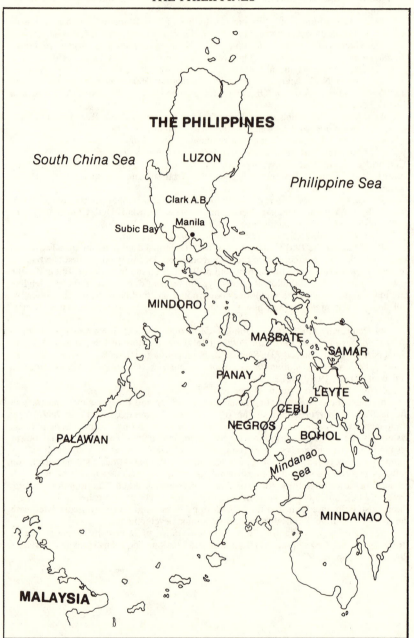

THE PHILIPPINES

South China Sea

LUZON

Clark A.B.

Subic Bay

Manila

Philippine Sea

MINDORO

MASBATE

SAMAR

PANAY

LEYTE

CEBU

NEGROS

BOHOL

PALAWAN

Mindanao Sea

MINDANAO

MALAYSIA

Reprinted from Carl H. Landé, ed., *Rebuilding a Nation: Philippine Challenges and American Policy*, by permission of the Washington Institute Press.

CHAPTER SIX

The Philippines: The Search for a Suitable Democratic Solution, 1946–1986

KARL D. JACKSON

All writers simplify reality to convey it; what separates description from insight is selecting the correct factors for modeling social reality. In government and the mass media there is a regrettable tendency to simplify by using the wrong factors, emphasizing the superficial to make the story comprehensible, even if the resulting stereotyped "explanations" bear scant resemblance to either real world problems or their solutions. This is particularly true with regard to conveying crises of political legitimacy in the Third World that are almost invariably reduced to stereotypes of good versus evil, the moral opponent versus the immoral leader, thereby transforming the analysis of complex events into a personal duel, a type of sporting event likely to catch the public's attention.

The Philippines has been in vogue since the dramatic events surrounding the fall from power of President Ferdinand Marcos and his replacement by Corazon Aquino. The tendency in government and popular media during the period 1983–1986 was to characterize problems as beginning and ending with Marcos and his family. He was seen as "the cause," just as the personality and actions of the shah of Iran were used "to explain" a revolution whose causes and complexity surely outran the limits of any man's personal perfidy. In the Philippines, as in Iran, the problems, in fact, are systemic, involving more than the faults or virtues of particular leaders. In both Iran and the Philippines, the political system had difficulty containing the strain produced by the collision of traditional mores with modern necessities; in both cases, programs that initially fostered relatively successful economic change led eventually to the growth of vocal minorities (often men of the book or the cloth) who redefined the moral standards to be applied to political figures in ways that contradicted the political traditions that brought the political leaders to power in the first place. In Manila the crisis that brought down the Marcos regime involved both the economy and the polity, but most fundamentally the critique of the regime was a negative

231

commentary on the way that politics has been conducted in the Philippines since it attained independence in 1946. It was not just Marcos's constitutional authoritarianism that was challenged and defeated by Corazon Aquino's presidential candidacy, but the Philippine political elite's *modus operandi* of politics for personal profit. The Aquino candidacy successfully challenged traditional pork barrel democracy, and the outstanding challenge of her presidency will be whether she can rule the Philippines effectively, solving its problems without resorting to the corrupt methods by which power has been garnered in the Philippines since independence. The essential challenge is whether President Aquino can permanently break with the corrupt practices while retaining the power necessary to solve the problems of the present.

• HISTORICAL REVIEW •

To explore the fall of Ferdinand Marcos and to understand why all solutions remain problematic, we must cast an eye backward over Philippine political history. In doing so we will discover that today's headlines are really yesterday's news, that is, military abuse, slow economic growth, personal corruption, and oligarchic control of enterprises have been "the problems" for most of the last four decades. Throughout the many changes that have transpired since independence crisis itself has been an enduring theme. In light of the current crisis concerning the New People's Army (NPA), it is instructive to note that there were more Huk guerillas per capita in 1950 than there are armed NPA today and that the Moro National Liberation Front at its zenith mustered almost as many soldiers as the present communist guerilla movement and yet was successfully contained through a combination of military and political pressure by the Marcos regime. Furthermore, every Philippine administration, with the exception of President Aquino and the late President Magsaysay, has been perceived as egregiously corrupt by its opposition, foreign observers, and probably any reasonable standard of measurement. Finally, with the exception of the first years of martial law under Marcos, the Philippines has uniformly manifested slow per capita economic growth rates and a yawning gap between promise and delivery, between high-flown populist rhetoric and inegalitarian reality.

None of the above excuses the decadence of the Marcos regime. However, the constant nature of the problems should shift our attention away from headlines—be they today's or yesterday's—to a concern for the underlying system and political culture that continually produce less than satisfactory outcomes—according to the people of the Philippines and international standards of good government.

In reality the Philippine experiment in government provides at least four distinctive phases: the period of free-swinging, somewhat chaotic democracy from independence in 1946 to the declaration of martial law in 1972; the martial law period (1972–1981) and its immediate aftermath 1981–1983); the twilight authoritarianism from the assassination of former Senator Benigno Aquino in August 1983 to the accession of power of Corazon Aquino in February 1986; and the reinstitutional-ization of democracy since February 1986. All four have certain shared characteristics: corruption, oligarchy, military abuse, internal insurrec-tion, and less than ideal rates of economic growth. However, there are also striking differences. The first period featured a degree of circula-tion of elites that was nearly unique in the post colonial world where "one man, one vote" has frequently been transformed into "one man, one vote, once" by postcolonial elites. In contrast, incumbent presidents in the Philippines were ousted in democratic elections in 1946, 1953, 1961, and 1965. Martial law in 1972 brought the circulation of elites to an abrupt halt but, at least in its initial phase, it proved remarkably successful in addressing some of the most important problems facing the nation: land reform, self-sufficiency in rice, breaking the hold of the landed oligarchs, collecting guns and dismantling private armies, and doubling the economic growth rate by harnessing technocrats in com-bination with foreign capital. Martial law had its obvious dark side: wholesale violation of the civil liberties through the imprisonment of political opponents; breaking the fragile institutions of the existing two-party system; the slow but steady resurgence of violence; chronic in-surgency; the First Family's greed; crony capitalism, and eventual national economic bankruptcy.

The twilight of authoritarian rule, from the Aquino assassination in the summer of 1983 through the February 1986 election, manifested opposite characteristics: an emboldened opposition, a resuscitated free press, international support for the rights of the democratic opposition, one fairly open and clean legislative election in May 1984, and the stunning election upset of February 1986. There were also negative trends in Marcos's twilight years. Growing tolerance for democratic opposition evolved simultaneously with a growing insurgency that threatened the Marcos administration and which has refused to dis-appear under the cleaner democratic government of President Aquino. Furthermore, rapid economic deterioration and the hollowing out of public and private institutions under Marcos may have undermined not only the Marcos regime, but also the problem solving capacity of the Philippine political system.

In all four periods what stands out is that the Philippines is almost never quiet or normal. Crisis is chronic, and yet the remedy, in all periods, is seen to be democracy. In spite of the fact that democracy in the earlier period did not yield meaningful solutions and the autocracy of martial law created new problems while solving others, the remarkable thing about the Philippines is that democracy is seen as the required medicine for curing the nation's ills.

Philippine Democracy: From Independence to Martial Law

The roots of twentieth-century Philippine politics grow from Spanish and U.S. colonial soil. The concept of being a Filipino grew out of social confrontation between the *mestizos* and the *peninsulares*, respectively those partly descended from Mexican, Iberian, and Chinese immigrants and those of pure caucasian background from Spain. The offspring of Philippine mothers and European, Chinese, or Creole fathers eventually became the font of Philippine nationalism and the eventual ruling elite of the nation. This pattern contrasts sharply with the evolution of Indonesia or Malaysia, where nationalists emphasized their wholly indigenous ethnic roots while rejecting the Eurasian and trading minorities as foreign collaborators with the colonial power. In the Philippines the new nationalist identity, being a Filipino, grew from a social community that in other Southeast Asian societies was disparaged and dismissed as antinationalist. The concept of being a Filipino was not based upon ethnic purity, but grew, in fact, from the lack of it. Those with wealth and connections, but no Creole, European, or Chinese blood were allowed to enter the *mestizo* social orbit. All were drawn together by dint of being rejected by the Iberian-born *peninsulares*.[1]

Another aspect of modern Philippine politics that descends from the Spanish period is the tradition of profiteering in government. Under Spanish rule everything was considered to be the property of the king of Castile. In sixteenth-century Spain no distinction existed between the king's personal household and the national treasury. Expeditions discovering and founding Spanish colonies were financed from the king's personal estate rather than flowing from impersonal government initiatives. The king's property in the colonies included "all colonial offices, privileges, and gainful positions in the colonies."[2] Many offices were bought and sold as investments, and it was assumed that the Spanish governor himself would grow immensely wealthy as a result of administering the colony. Because all governors were presumed to be corrupt, an institutional device called the *residencia* was developed that required all colonial officials departing the islands to undergo investigation and trial before a judge regarding their term in office. The arrangement was designed to enforce rectitude but in practice it increased malfeasance. The judges were always bribed and officials salted away extra sums to cover the cost inevitably involved in satisfying the *residencia*.[3]

In the case of early Indonesian nationalists, at least symbolically, the opportunity existed to calculate social status by reference to a precolonial lineage, connecting one's family, even if distantly or theoretically, with the sultans who ruled the Indies before the Dutch. In the Philippines the *mestizo* elite had no such "usable past," and status from early on in the Spanish era was reckoned in terms of wealth. As Steinberg has observed,

> Social status was not determined by ethnic purity, family tree, or caste. It is not surprising therefore, that the *mestizos* considered wealth and consumption to be the only available means by which a social hierarchy could be established. It did not matter who your parents or grandparents were if you had the funds to join, to intermarry, and to claim position.

In the Spanish era, government belonged to the *peninsulares* and therefore the *mestizos* concentrated on land ownership and moved rapidly into export-oriented crop production. From the wealth generated by various enterprises developed the *ilustrado* elite. The *ilustrados*, "the enlightened ones," attained language skills and educational levels far superior to most Asians in the nineteenth century. Jose Rizal, the greatest national hero, was a wealthy, fifth-generation Chinese *mestizo* and began the independence movement by writing a novel. The Spanish leadership had always been suspicious of the *ilustrado* leadership. Heavy-handed Spanish authoritarianism eventually united the wealthy *ilustrados* with other proponents of independence, such as Bonifacio and Aguinaldo, by publicly executing Jose Rizal, the most famous *ilustrado* of his time, in 1896.

U.S. colonial rule began by suppressing Aguinaldo's movement while simultaneously co-opting the most important *ilustrado* families into the colonial administration. Defection to the Americans occurred from the top rather than the bottom of the society, indicating a split between elite and mass political behavior that reappears in one form or another in political crises as diverse as the Japanese occupation, the advent of martial law under Marcos, and the elite maneuverings regarding the snap election of 1986.

The U.S. alliance with the *ilustrados* brought power and wealth to this social class while blunting the desire for nationalism and immediate independence. U.S. colonial rule confirmed the already substantial power of a small number of well-educated, landholding families who maintained oligarchic control of Philippine politics through the first six decades of the twentieth century. Although colonial administrators assumed that mass education would dilute oligarchic control, the result was in fact more ambiguous, a form of mass politics and a veneer of populist appeal disguising a traditional social structure whose real sources of power were networks of patron-client relations that also underpin politics in other Southeast Asian countries. The most progressive aspects of U.S. colonial rule never achieved the intended effect of leveling the hierarchical structure of the Philippine political elite. As elsewhere in Asia, egalitarianism succumbed to hierarchy and patron-client entourages predominated to the exclusion of a broader conception of the public interest. Paradoxically, the Nacionalistas, who always favored immediate independence, were opposed by some Filipinos who regarded immediate independence as a recipe for oligarchy rather than democracy, an oligarchy that would preserve its privileges rather than enact reforms.

The timing of Philippine independence was dictated by a combination of domestic U.S. politics and Philippine personal rivalries. Democratic administrations accelerated the independence process. Independence nearly became a reality before the 1920 election returned the Republicans to the White House. It eventually came about under Roosevelt who established the Philippine Commonwealth Government in 1935. According to the Philippine Independence Act of 1934, the Philippines became semiautonomous and was scheduled to receive full independence on 4 July 1946. From 1935 to the Japanese invasion, the Nacionalistas were the predominant political party although real sovereignty still emanated from the resident U.S. high commissioner. Factionalism manifested itself within the Partido Nacionalistas from its founding in 1907. Manuel Quezon's political rivalry with Sergio Osmena actually delayed the grant of independence in the 1930s because Quezon wanted to insure that he, rather than his rival Osmena, would receive credit for the achievement. The circumstances surrounding the approach to independence determined that an oligarchy of landed families would rule the Philippines rather than the type of revolutionary leaders who challenged colonialism in the rest of Asia. The *ilustrados* moved in gentlemanly fashion toward a sovereign and democratic future fashioned almost entirely out of a traditional oligarchic past.

The attack on Pearl Harbor was followed ten hours later by the Japanese attack on the Philippines. Uniquely in Asia, the Philippine common people fought valiantly on the side of the United States. The worst atrocities following the Japanese victory in 1942 were directed against Philippine officers and noncommissioned officers. In contrast to other colonial outposts in Southeast Asia, a massive anti-Japanese insurgency grew up in the Philippines, staffed almost entirely by Filipinos but giving wholehearted support to the United States. Japanese troops proved incapable of stifling this popular uprising in spite of savagely repressive tactics in the countryside and successful co-optation of the Manila political elite. The death toll, according to postwar leaders, exceeded 1 million, and the war resulted in the near total destruction of the cities and infrastructure built during colonial rule. Manila in 1945 had sustained almost as much physical damage as Warsaw, having been reduced virtually to rubble by the conflict between U.S. firepower and Japanese intransigence.

More potentially debilitating than the physical damage was the division between the Philippine elite and the masses. Although Quezon and Osmena and others had taken positions as a government-in-exile in Washington, and although some Philippine elite members (notably Ferdinand Marcos) had fought against the Japanese, most of the prewar leaders of the Partido Nacionalistas collaborated with the Japanese. The first president of the Philippines, Jose Laurel, was inaugurated during the Japanese occupation. Osmena, who orchestrated the anti-Japanese resistance from Washington, was beaten in the first postwar election by Manuel Roxas, who had served in Laurel's Japanese-sponsored government. Roxas founded the Liberal Party, by co-opting most of the elite of the Nacionalista Party, and became president in 1946.[4] In a remarkable display of syntactic and moral flexibility, Jose Laurel claimed that the collaborators were actually trying to shield the Philippines and that "everyone was a collaborationist; no one was a traitor."[5] The fact that those who collaborated gained power and further privilege after the war must certainly have been a school for cynicism among those who had sacrificed, that is, the Philippine masses. The most privileged and well-educated members of the society placed private comfort and position over the ideals for which the common people fought. In the end there were no trials, and amnesty for collaborators was declared in 1948. "Power evidently begot more power" as the ethical and national norms gave way to personal interests.[6]

The gulf between mass sacrifice and selfish elite behavior during the war seems to have set a pattern that was regularly repeated throughout the postwar era.

> Filipinos have seen public service used as a means to private gain. To be sure, the obligations of real and fictive kinship, the awareness of reciprocity in relationships, and the high social value placed on wealth as an arbiter of status have all contributed to the prevalence of nepotism and other anomalies. The collapse of law and order, the taint of collaboration, the confusion of allegiance, the starvation and deprivation, and the chance for quick profit . . . all played a role in shaping an independent Philippines, both before and after martial law.[7]

A final aspect of the postwar political era emerging directly from the Japanese occupation was the saturation of society with small arms and the rapid growth of violence in the country. Metropolitan Manila proved particularly susceptible to crime and violence throughout the 1950s and 1960s. Murders of political figures remained relatively common throughout the entire period. President Marcos himself gained national attention as a young lawyer when he defended himself successfully before the Philippine Supreme Court, thereby reversing his conviction in the murder of one of his father's political opponents. Below the level of persons of presidential stature, murder was the all too frequent fate of provincial politicians, and political figures throughout independence maintained body guards, arsenals, and private armies to protect themselves.

During the presidential election of 1946, Liberal party candidate Roxas campaigned to save the country from "chaos, corruption, and communism" while Osmena sought clean government and punishment for collaborators. Osmena allied with elements of the Left, including the Huk guerillas, who had not yet moved into armed opposition against the government. Osmena, who was the incumbent Philippine leader of the immediate postwar administration, was labeled as corrupt and inefficient. Roxas won by 200,000 votes and the Liberal-party-controlled Congress disallowed the seating of six Democratic Alliance congressmen (a group comprised of Huks, the Civil Liberties Union, and other elements of the Philippine Left).

One of the excluded leaders, Luis Taruc, later became the chief commander of the Huk rebellion. Exclusion from posts to which they had been elected was at least partly responsible for the Huk decision to withdraw from all legal political activity, resorting instead to guerrilla warfare.[8] Roxas refused to negotiate with the Huks, outlawing them in March 1948. The Huks then formed the Peoples' Liberation Army and launched a military campaign to take over the government. One month later President Roxas was felled by a heart attack and was succeeded by Elpidio Quirino. A power vacuum existed in the countryside, and Quirino expended virtually all of his energy on the upcoming 1949 election campaign. Quirino and the Liberal Party emerged victorious in what was perceived as the most corrupt election campaign to date. Squads of flying voters moved from one precinct to another and the deceased voted with regularity. Open warfare and violence also characterized the campaign.

Throughout the chaos the Huks prospered, and in 1950 they predicted they would take power during the year 1951. (In contrast to the present-day NPA, the Huks were concentrated within striking distance of Manila and mustered eight armed insurgents for every 10,000 people in the Philippine population, whereas the NPA are scattered throughout the archipelago and mobilize only 24,000 armed guerillas, or four combatants per 10,000.)[9] With Huk military raids threatening Manila itself the Philippines appealed to the United States for help, and President Quirino nominated as his secretary of defense Ramon Magsaysay.

With assistance and advice from the United States Magsaysay mobilized public support and galvanized a corrupt, abusive, and ineffectual Philippine Constabulary into action. Rural development programs were initiated, former Huks were given land in Mindanao, and the defense minister organized the army to guarantee free and clean elections in 1951. In addition a new organization, NAMFREL (The National Association for the Maintenance of Free Elections), designed by a U.S. diplomat, was organized in time for the 1951 congressional elections. The new, private organization policed the polling places to prevent fraud.

The party out of power, the Nacionalistas, gained heavily, and public confidence in the electoral process was substantially restored.[10] In 1953 the Nacionalistas offered the presidential nomination to Magsaysay, who resigned from the Liberal government to run for the office. By that point in time the Huk rebellion had largely been defeated and Magsaysay ran the first truly populist political campaign for the presidency. He toured the barrios in bare feet, promising land reform, government benefits for the masses, and an end to corruption. The incumbent was ousted in a massive landslide. However, even Magsaysay, with his enormous popularity and Nacionalista control of both houses of Congress, could not pass an effective land reform over the objections of landholding oligarchs who had always formed the core of the Nacionalista party.[11]

A new vacuum in Philippine politics was created by President Magsaysay's death in a plane crash in 1957. His vice-president, Carlos P. Garcia, was elected president with only 43 percent of the vote. (Diosdado Macapagal of the Liberal Party was elected to the vice-presidency, actually receiving more votes than Garcia). From the populist heights of Magsaysay, Philippine politics returned to its previous pattern, and by 1960 confidence in government was disastrously low and the taint of corruption enshrouded the Garcia administration.

Macapagal, a Liberal outsider in the Garcia administration, was elected president in 1961, pledging to eliminate corruption and to mount a massive program of socioeconomic reform. Delivering proved more difficult than promising. The agrarian reform law passed was too expensive to be implemented. Rice prices rose and the rice-rich Philippines imported ever greater portions of its most basic food commodity. The graft resulting from foreign exchange controls under previous administrations was replaced by smuggling to avoid tariffs designed to protect infant industries. Furthermore, the president himself was linked in the popular consciousness to a tobacco scandal. As had happened to so many before in Philippine politics, great expectations had been dashed and the Macapagal administration, like most before it, exited office having left the country with the traditional list of unresolved problems: agrarian reform, slow economic growth, rice shortages, and utilization of high public office for private gain.

During Macapagal's Liberal administration Senator Ferdinand Marcos defected to the Nacionalistas. In 1965, along with Senator

Fernando Lopez (who had served as Liberal vice-president under Quirion), Marcos was elected president, using populist rhetoric promising yet another new era. The Marcos-Lopez ticket, two Liberals born again as Nacionalistas, reflected the nonideological and basically unprogrammatic nature of both political parties before Marcos attained national political power.

> The founding Liberals came from the same social class as the Nacionalistas. The platforms of both parties throughout the postwar period were monotonously similar, all defending Christianity and Filipino traditions, all advocating enlightened foreign policies abroad, and land for the landless, social justice, and honesty in government at home.[12]

Marcos and the Coming of Martial Law

It is important to remember that the first two terms of President Marcos resulted from free elections, and he was the only president ever returned to office for a second term. Marcos's first election, like that of Macapagal, was touted as "a new beginning" and his first administration produced impressive results: a realistic development plan, improved tax collection, curbs on smuggling, centralization of police administration, and significant efforts to implement the 1963 Land Reform Act. The budget for land redistribution in 1967 was equal to that of the national military budget. Rice production reached self-sufficiency in 1968, and the infrastructure of the country was being improved with roads, schools, and airports.[13]

Marcos's first term was not without its blemishes. Although he assembled a team of technocrats who devised economic growth plans, implementation was imperiled by the reluctance of the Congress to pass tax measures and by the normal problems of bureaucratic inertia and nonimplementation. Violence was again on the rise especially as the country moved toward the 1969 presidential campaign. Marcos, in traditional fashion, emptied the national treasury in pursuit of reelection. The Liberal Party nominated Senator Sergio Osmena, Jr., but Marcos and Lopez were both reelected to unprecedented second terms in a landslide. In personal talents—both political savvy and oratorical skills—Marcos clearly outshown Osmena and he could justifiably point to physical manifestations of his first-term accomplishments. Furthermore, government checks were distributed in his name to barrio captains. Finally, his foreign policy statements put some space between the Philippines and the United States, thereby allowing him to adopt the mantle of an Asian nationalist.

The election victory, however, was purchased at a significant price. The relatively successful first-term reformer became a second-term political hack, espousing the rhetoric of reform and personal sacrifice.

Having emptied the treasury to maintain control of the Malacañang, retrenchment became the norm. Layoffs, expenditure curtailment, tight credit, etc. ended the second-term political honeymoon almost before it began. Student demonstrations left six dead in late January 1970 and the midterm elections were marred by new levels of violence. Vice-President Lopez switched to the Liberal Party in a murky episode that included assertions that Lopez or his supporters were financing extralegal activities to destabilize the regime or eliminate Marcos himself.[14]

In addition a remnant of the Huk rebellion, with some financial assistance from China, became the new Communist Party of the Philippines (CPP) and founded the New People's Army in 1969. Although it grew slowly, and was in fact overshadowed as a security threat by the Moro National Liberation Front, the NPA was spreading in central Luzon and beginning to reach out to other islands.[15] The most important motive force leading to the declaration of martial law was the sense that the center could not hold, that the entire system was about to disintegrate. The president and the Constitutional Convention could not agree on an alternative to the 1935 Constitution. The Liberal Party, under the leadership of Senator Benigno Aquino, seemed to be on the ascendandant in an atmosphere in which he and Marcos alternately accused one another of seditious acts. Political violence had risen even beyond Philippine norms with the 21 August 1971 Plaza Miranda bombing in which grenades were thrown at a Liberal Party rally, killing nine and injuring ninety.[16]

To this climate of fear one must add the overwhelming family ambition and developmental vision of Ferdinand Marcos and his wife Imelda (of the politically powerful Romualdez family from Leyte). Marcos was coming to the end of his second term. The Constitutional Convention refused to adopt a parliamentary system that would have allowed him to remain as chief executive. Family fortunes had always been bolstered in Philippine democratic politics. The Marcos family was exceptional chiefly in its unwillingness to allow the circulation of privileged access to other families within the elite; from 1965 to 1968 Marcos consistently sought to transform the temporary privileges of office into a permanent family emolument. As early as 1972 Ferdinand Marcos threatened to have his wife run against Aquino for the presidency, indicating a desire for a political dynasty. Marcos combined these motives with an intense belief that he knew how to lift the Philippines out of poverty, insurgency, corruption, and slow growth. If only he had the necessary power, the objectives that had eluded him in his first two terms would be attained.

On 23 September 1972 President Marcos declared martial law.[17] Without firing a single shot, and probably with the support of the vast majority of Filipinos, he overthrew the 1935 Constitution, assumed all powers of government, locked up 30,000 members of the opposition (including Senator Aquino), and embarked on a forced march toward economic modernization and social justice.

Before he declared martial law, Marcos detailed his view of Philippine society in a book called *Today's Revolution: Democracy*. He diagnosed the critical problems of Philippine society as being oligarchy and dependence, that is, oligarchic control of the heights of office in exchange for particularistic distribution of the fruits of office to a loyal mass entourage. Marcos called on the people to reject the old system in which "the aim of free and popular elections had been frustrated through the control, corruption, and manipulation of the political process . . . ." He specifically singled out abuses such as control of the mass media by the same families who controlled the political system. Marcos's remedy for precluding revolution from below was revolution from above, that is, drastic resort to authoritarian methods as the means to "democratize wealth," to "revolutionize society for the sake of man, not for the sake of the State." He stated that "the political culture abets the status quo, that too has to be radically changed." His "New Society" was designed to break the control over politics that the traditional families had maintained since the beginning of the century. In Marcos's vision the new system would concentrate power in the executive to do away with pork barrel democracy, which wasted both time and development resources. Decrees would bring reforms that the oligarchically controlled Congress had always refused to pass. Without the oligarchs of the Right, there would be no more meat on which the Left might feed, and the New Society sought to destroy both. A new discipline would also be required, and society would be guided to rapid modernization by technocrats and central bankers.[18]

What President Marcos sought in 1972 should be viewed in comparative perspective. He advised that by severely constraining the democratic process and adopting technocratic solutions he could achieve an economic breakthrough. Similar justification had been given by other Asian leaders when they dispensed with their squabbling, corrupt, and inefficient Western political forms. Sukarno's "Guided Democracy" was supposed to be more Indonesian and to bring prosperity to the masses that the democratic period, with its constant instability and patronage politics, had failed to do. Soeharto's "New Order" regime, with its disciplined amalgam of army officers, bureaucrats, and technocrats, produced a new surge of orderly development in what had been Southeast Asia's most obvious case of arrested development. What Marcos desired was the authority of powerful prime ministers, like Field Marshal Sarit of Thailand and Lee Kwan Yew of Singapore.

Essentially, Marcos sought to institute a bureaucratic polity, not unlike that found in Indonesia and Thailand, in which decision-making authority would be limited to the highest level of the state bureaucracy—the technocrats, bureaucrats, and key army officers. In Marcos's grand design, the state would sacrifice political participation in favor of efficiency and would use coercion, if necessary, to preclude interference from the corrupt political elite that had always stood in the way of progress. Direct democracy would be replaced by more controlled forms, citizen assemblies, and referenda by voice vote rather than secret ballot. What Marcos in 1972 was reflecting was an almost pan-Southeast Asian disgust with the outcomes produced by democratic politics. However, his design was doubly ambitious and probably doomed from the start because he was seeking to impose a much more authoritarian system on Southeast Asia's most educated and media-exposed mass public, a populace whose elite (no matter how corrupt) had absorbed democratic norms far more deeply than their Thai or Indonesian brethren. Marcos sought to roll back entrenched democratic traditions in the face of already well-advanced forces of social mobilization. Sukarno, Soeharto, and the Thai army institutionalized their departicipatory systems in time periods when the demand for democratic mass participation remained relatively low. Marcos's similar ambitions would ultimately fail because the traditions and social background of political participation were already firmly entrenched and the state lacked both the means and the will to adopt sustained coercion on the magnitude necessary to destroy all resistance from counter elites.

The power structure created by the New Society has been concisely described by Abueva:

> President Marcos . . . is the undisputed head of a new national power structure or grand coalition. It consists of: the military; cabinet members, technocrats and the bureaucracy under them; persons close to the president or Mrs. Marcos, whether relatives or loyal friends and former politicians; local officials, who also hold office by presidential appointment; and several big businessmen who enjoy the political stability and economic incentives which the administration provides. At the base of this political pyramid are the millions whose welfare is the avowed aim of the New Society, in whose name change and reform are being initiated, and whose support or acquiescence provide the regime with legitimacy . . . .[19]

This coalition was supported and maintained by despoiling the traditional oligarchs. Land reform, by which all tenants on rice and corn land were given rights to the land they worked, was the single most promising reform under the New Society. Not only did it help tenants by giving them an opportunity for security and upward mobility, but it had an additional political benefit, destroying the traditional, landlord-client relationship of Marcos's political enemies in central and south Luzon. Likewise, other reforms of the initial New Society period had political as well as social or economic implications.

Half-a-million weapons were collected and the private armies of the old society were disbanded. In the same breath, the size and well-being of the armed forces and police were increased. When martial law began there were 55,000 in the army, navy, and air force, but this rapidly increased to 113,000.[20] In addition, paramilitary forces consisted of 110,000 including 43,500 constabulary forces, 65,000 Civilian Home Defense Forces (CHDF), and 2,000 coast guard. The active duty military core of the Marcos regime consisted of at least 223,000, with another 124,000 troops in the reserves. The armed forces were woefully underpaid prior to martial law, and the defense budget rose from 608 million pesos in 1972 to 8.8 billion in 1984, an increase in the percentage of national resources devoted to the military. The functions of the military included combating insurgencies of the Left and Right as well as providing the regime with coercive power to use against its legitimate opponents. In any event, the growth of the military and police supplied the central government with a quantum of coercive power unprecedented in the history of the Philippines.

Cleansing the bureaucracy and the judiciary of corrupt and incompetent officials and reconstituting them as presidential appointments had a salutary impact on efficiency while simultaneously devastating the independence of the judiciary. Abolishing oligarchic control of the press may have been intended to give wider social elements access to the mass media; however, from Marcos's viewpoint, increasing access for others had the added benefit of denying media access to his opponents.

Finally, the industrial economy of the country was to be transformed. Whereas import substitution characterized the old society, under the new order the Philippines would adopt an export-oriented strategy, emphasizing industries in which the Philippines possessed comparative advantage vis-à-vis competing projects in the international market place. International loans were to be used to create these industries under a new industrial leadership. In a political sense this meant using state resources to favor industrialists handpicked by the president, a group that eventually became known as the "crony capitalists."

Two of the most disturbing aspects of the early martial law period were that it was accepted without mass protest and that it worked astonishingly well in the first few years. The broad masses of the Republic of the Philippines had always deferred systemic arrangements to the landed oligarchy of the Manila elite. Relief that something had at last been done to resolve the impasse was probably the predominant sentiment.[21] Opposition, even among the Manila middle class and at the university, was minimal. This is because the tens of thousands of persons most likely to lead agitation against the New Society were immediately locked up. The primary mobilization mechanism of politics had always been the patron-client coalition, and such networks are readily immobilized by detaining the key sources of both leadership and material patronage. This is precisely what Marcos did.

The initial years of martial law manifested fundamental reforms and a rapid acceleration of economic growth. The enforcement capacity of government immediately increased. Corrupt officials were fired and government tax collection efforts quickened. The government promised that tax revenues would be used for development and that those failing to pay their fair share would be penalized. The results were impressive. Tax revenues increased from 5.3 billion pesos in 1972 to 19.5 billion pesos in 1976.[22] Even after inflation this represented a significant increase. True to the president's word, a greater share of the GNP was invested in national infrastructure, especially roads, irrigation, and electrification. The first years of martial law were epitomized by rapid growth, declining underemployment, rising international reserves, and a surplus in the balance of payments. While real GNP per capita grew at only 2 percent per annum in the 1960s, this rate doubled in the early 1970s and the Philippines seemed to be headed for economic takeoff. Foreign investment as well as borrowing increased rapidly. In a single year, 1975, paid-in capital increased by 30 percent. Perhaps justifiably, in 1976 President Marcos claimed that more had been achieved in the previous three years than in all the years since independence combined.[23]

Land reform, above all else, was supposed to be the linchpin of the New Society. Martial law was declared in the closing days of September; on 21 October 1972, all tenant farmers on rice and corn land were given the right to obtain ownership of the land they were farming. The proclamation marked the first fundamental effort by any Philippine government to alter the underlying condition of tenancy and poverty in Philippine rural society.[24]

President Marcos and the technocrats, with their strategy of rice intensification, foreign investment, international borrowing, and export substitution, seemed to be steering the Philippines toward rapid modernization. The strategy went aground, however, on the shoals created by the oil shocks of the mid- and late 1970s, the long recession in commodity prices for sugar, copra, copper, and the nearly boundless greed of the First Family. Inflation grew to 40 percent in 1974, and by 1975 the Philippines were being whipsawed between rising oil and falling export prices. In combination these produced the first series of deficits in the balance of payments.[25] Real wages, especially in agriculture, declined substantially as they did in much of Asia. Those with land produced more rice, but employment opportunities could not keep pace with the rising labor supply. As oil bills escalated, so did foreign borrowing. Furthermore, the First Lady's show projects in Metro Manila required massive hard currency investments that never had much chance of producing the hard currency earnings necessary to pay off foreign loans. Foreign indebtedness, near zero at the advent of martial law, escalated rapidly as the Philippines borrowed its way into bankruptcy in the late 1970s. Finally, the regime's response to the oil crisis of the 1970s was to make multibillion dollar investments in geothermal and nuclear energy. As a result the Philippines managed to cut its foreign source energy dependence from 88 percent in 1972 to 57 percent in 1984. In fact the Philippines was well on its way to becoming the premier geothermal energy nation in the world. These investments, however, involved substantial cost overruns, graft and long delays. As a result the "wise" alternative energy investments of the 1970s became economically uncompetitive with oil in the 1980s.

Martial law altered the political structure at the local level by creating a system of *barangays*. These consisted of clusters of 500 or fewer families that were organized as citizens' assemblies to provide a uniquely Filipino institutional framework for representation. They were to be utilized for making community as well as national decisions and were also the unit of basic administration. After 1975 all *barangay* captains were appointed by the president, thereby ensuring that municipal and local government would be taken out of the hands of opposition elements. In the early years of martial law, the *barangay* councils, by voice vote, endorsed constitutional changes and the continuation of the president in office. The secret ballot had been replaced by a means of representation that was certain to produce results desired by the government in Manila.

The final structure created by Marcos was the Kilusang Bagong Lipuna (New Society Movement) or KBL. The KBL initially was not referred to as a political party, but was designed to select and elect candidates to local, provincial, and national offices. KBL candidates, in an atmosphere of restricted press and speech, triumphed in the 1978 interim assembly elections as well as in the 1980 local elections. The degree of limited participation is indicated by the fact that the 1978 opposition was led from a jail cell by former Senator Benigno Aquino. The interim assembly contained only fourteen non-KBL members out of 200 members. As time went on the KBL became an institution encompassing not only technocrats, bureaucrats, and army officers but also old-line politicians attracted to nascent participatory channels that might hold the balance of power in the post-Marcos era.

On 17 January 1981 President Marcos decreed an end to the martial law period he had begun eight years before. The National Assembly became a legislative body although the president retained the power to make laws by decree. Marcos submitted a new de Gaullist-style constitution. It featured an elected president who would appoint the prime minister. The new arrangement was approved by an April 1981 plebiscite. President Marcos ran for reelection in June 1981 but his logical opponent, former Senator Aquino, was excluded by the constitution, which required all nominees to be at least fifty years of age (Aquino was forty-eight). With virtually no opposition, President Marcos was reelected and Senator Aquino was released from prison for heart surgery in the United States.

Regime Disintegration, 1983–1986

By early 1983 an outside observer might have hypothesized that President Marcos was, as ever, firmly in control of a stable, if uneasy, political situation. Prompting his political demise and the consequent rise of democracy were a series of short-term factors (most involving excessive or erroneous political decisions) and long-term influences, such as the communist insurrection and the severe economic downturn that became apparent in 1983.

The Economic Crisis

The economic crisis of 1983–1984 supplied the backdrop for a legitimacy crisis that terminated the Marcos regime. The economic downturn both preceded the political crisis and continues into the presidency of Corazon Aquino.

It would be foolish to think that just any economic crisis can prompt the downfall of a bureaucratic polity, such as that existing under Marcos, not to mention similar regimes under Sukarno, Soeharto, and a succession of Thai governments. Departicipatory regimes are good at stifling the very outbursts that become prevalent when fully democratic societies are faced with widespread economic downturn. Bureaucratic polities are run by and for the benefit of narrow, capital city-centric elites, and economic distress only achieves political relevance when it begins to affect profoundly the lifestyle of the narrow ruling elite. Mere starvation on Java did not bring the downfall of the Sukarno regime although it provided part of the political tinder that eventually exploded into flames after 1 October 1965. Likewise in the Philippines, the lower classes had been suffering from declining real income since the late 1970s, but the economic crisis, which provided a necessary (but not sufficient) cause to drive Marcos from the political stage, was the crisis of 1983–1986, which affected the very narrow business elite that had previously backstopped Marcos's authoritarian rule. Although system-wide economic decline eroded mass support and supplied recruits to the NPA, the alienation of the Manila elite along with the middle class provided the vital organizational impetus that brought down the regime during the snap election of 1986. The economic crisis resulted from long-term weaknesses of the economy, which were exacerbated in late 1983 by capital flight and the inability of the technocrats to restore economic order. Even with the best possible economic and political management, the Philippines would have experienced serious economic problems in the early 1980s. The Philippines has neither the oil of Indonesia and Malaysia nor the industrial efficiency of Hong Kong, Taiwan, and Singapore. In addition, political and personal considerations of President Marcos and the First Lady had taken precedence over the technocrats' economic rationality after the first few years of martial law. The world recession in the early 1980s (with the attendant rapid decline in earnings from such key exports as coconut and sugar) brought the economy to the brink of rescheduling *before* the Aquino assassination (in August 1983) because the current account deficit was $1 to $2 billion and $9 billion of short-term debts were coming due. Capital flight in late 1983 provided an indicator of the elite's political alienation as well as its economic pessimism.

The extent of the economic crisis is illustrated by two figures. The GNP for 1983 (before the rapid devaluation of the peso) was $36.6 billion while foreign indebtedness totaled $25.6 billion. Foreign indebtedness as a percentage of GNP exceeded 60 percent—three times the level considered tolerable for a healthy economy. Second, the debt service ratio reached 40 percent at the end of 1982, meaning that 40 percent of the total export earnings was needed to meet interest payments on all debts, plus amortization on medium and long-term debts. Even assuming the Philippines had been able to roll over its entire short-term debt, the debt service ratio six months before Aquino's assassination clearly foreshadowed very serious cash flow problems. The business elite knew this and began shifting its money to safe havens abroad as well as casting about for new foci of political allegiance.

The peso was devalued repeatedly: from 9.4 pesos to the dollar (October 1982); to 11 pesos (July 1983); to 14 pesos (October 1983); to 18 pesos (June 1984). Inflation reached a zenith of 60 percent per annum in 1983–84 but declined rapidly in 1984–85 with the stagnation of the Philippine economy as a whole. In the first seven months of 1985 inflation was running at an annual rate of only 5.9 percent; however, this was a negative rather than a positive sign because it reflected the sharp decline in overall economic activity. According to official statistics unemployment in 1984 was approximately 6 percent, whereas an accurate figure was probably closer to 35 percent; austerity measures required by the IMF and the international banking community played a role by stimulating unemployment and adding to the already considerable amount of social tinder, especially in urban areas. Real GNP per capita declined steadily from 1983 to 1986. As the total population of the Philippines grew more than 2.5 percent per annum, GNP per capita fell from $776 in 1982 to $600 in 1985.

On 15 October 1983 the Philippines asked its creditors for a ninety-day moratorium on the payment of principal on the outstanding foreign debt. On 3 April 1985 the Philippines sought its seventh ninety-day moratorium because rescheduling agreements with private banks fell through repeatedly. This was because Marcos spent the last two-and-a-half years in power fighting a rear guard action, playing for time, trying to balance the needs of his dwindling elite supporters against the demands of the international institutions, his only source of "new money" for satisfying the appetites of an elite in the terminal stages of decline. Bankers contemplate current accounts but politicians pursue short-term survival; Marcos played his end game against long economic odds, always hoping that political advantage in the end would prevail, allowing him to retain power now and pick up the economic pieces later. During the end game Marcos, along with virtually every other Philippine political leader (prior to Corazon Aquino), calculated economic outcomes only within the context of short-term political gains.

One indication of the predominance of political reality over economic necessity during the decline of a bureaucratic polity is evinced by the dismal implementation record of the Marcos regime with the IMF and the World Bank. The pattern was one of protracted negotiation (partly in the Manila press) followed by reluctant acceptance of a compromise position and subsequent flagrant violation of the standby agreement. Reversing itself, the IMF refused to release the third *tranche* ($106 million, which would also have triggered the release of an additional $175 million in new foreign bank loans) out of the $615 million IMF credit facility in 1985. In a scene reminiscent of the systematic overreporting of Philippine foreign exchange reserves in 1983, the IMF had discovered that the budget deficit being run up by the Philippine government was three times the size originally agreed to and half again as large as the IMF's painfully negotiated fall-back position.[26] In addition, the IMF determined that Marcos's agreement to restructure the coconut and sugar industries had been worse than simply cosmetic. Rather than decreasing crony control of the Philippine rural economy, Marcos had continued to shape the implementation of agreements in ways enhancing de facto monopolistic control. For example, among the chief targets of reform had been Eduardo Cojuangco's control of the coconut industry along with Roberto Benedicto's hold on sugar production. However, the net effect of eleven months of strenuous negotiating with the IMF and World Bank had been that Cojuangco in 1985 was stronger than ever and moving into the sugar, wheat, and flour industries—in direct contradiction of the reforms that had been strenuously backed by the U.S. government through direct use of USAID appropriations as leverage. In addition, the peso had been allowed to appreciate in value, making export growth even more difficult and further contravening 1984 agreements with the IMF.

The political economy of Marcos's bureaucratic polity remained at the mercy of macroeconomic variables that were almost entirely beyond his control. Inflation fell but so did exports. In the first eight months of 1985 exports declined by 14.4 percent, compared with the already bleak situation in the first eight months of 1984. Falling coconut prices and a slackening U.S. demand for Philippine-produced electronic components contributed to this export decline. Electronic components, one of the country's leading export products, dropped 20 percent, and coconut, its premier traditional export, earned 40 percent less. Rather than a projected 10 percent growth in exports, the government facing a snap election was contemplating a decline of 15 percent for 1985.

The dismal economic equations derived at least as much from political as from macroeconomic trends. Stimulating economic growth would have required returning to the ideology of early martial law, opening up the channels to market forces rather than monopolistic economic practices. However, Marcos in his weakened condition could not afford to alienate the cronies. His wealthy and powerful friends constituted a fundamental impediment to the solution of Philippine economic problems, and yet President Marcos found it impossible to move against them because in doing so he would have severed one of his few remaining political lifelines. The IMF agreement, requiring full implementation of a plan for restructuring the coconut and sugar monopolies by October 1985, obviously would not be forthcoming for political reasons. If Marcos had broken the monopolies he would have lost the support of Eduardo Cojuangco and Roberto Benedicto. Without them political survival was problematic, and therefore economic reforms were largely irrelevant even though demanded by the IMF, the World Bank, private banks, and the U.S. and Japanese governments.

The New People's Army

The second fundamental facet of Ferdinand Marcos's crisis of legitimacy was the New People's Army (NPA). The rebellion's rapid growth became the focal point for Washington's public critique of the regime. Without the rebellion's existence, Washington's demand for reform and reinvigoration of the military would have been rejected as blatant interference. In the end the forces that finished Marcos were segments of his own military, elements that were most offended by military involvement in the assassination of former Senator Aquino, and groups perceiving military reform as the only way to defeat the communist insurgency.

In 1968, a group of young intellectuals from the University of the Philippines broke with the Moscow-oriented leadership of the Partido Kommunista ng Philipinas (PKP) to form the Communist Party of the Philippines (CPP). The NPA was formed in 1969 as the armed wing of the CCP. From a handful of middle-class radicals the organization had spread by late 1985 throughout most of the provinces of the Philippines and mustered approximately 16,500 guerillas. The NPA virtually doubled in size during the last year of the Marcos regime, setting off alarm bells in Washington and, more important, within Marcos's own defense establishment.[27] Before the regime fell, the NPA had gained influence or control in approximately 20 percent of the villages with an estimated mass base of several million. The major operational locale of the NPA was Mindanao, over 450 miles south of Manila, but the movement had both military and political presence in the majority of provinces of the Philippines. Areas of particularly rapid growth, in addition to Mindanao, were the poverty stricken, sugar-rich island of Negros and also Cebu and central Luzon. The virtual collapse of the world sugar market, crony monopolization of both the coconut and sugar industries, joblessness, and declining income levels threatened the traditional political and social structures of islands such as Negros. Communist insurgents were concentrated in several geographic pockets. The intensity of the conflict in these special locations was underlined by government statistics indicating that the chief cause of death in 1984 among adults in Davao (the provincial capital of Mindanao and the third largest city in the country) was armed violence, mostly knife and bullet wounds. Although some portion of the 854 violent deaths in 1984 was unrelated to the insurgency and its suppression, the figure provided a bench mark for how war-torn the Philippines could have become if the insurgency had spread with the same intensity to other provinces.

The number of mayors, policemen, and informers assassinated by the NPA "sparrow units" in 1984 grew to over 500. As in Vietnam, assassinating natural leaders at the village level fundamentally sapped the political structure of its resilience. As an additional similarity, the National Democratic Front's twelve-point program spoke of "blood debts" that must be settled if the revolution ever came to power. Within the church and the military the success of the NPA in the 1984–1985 period galvanized significant opposition to Marcos. Just as the economic collapse drove businessmen into opposition, the insurgency alienated elements that ultimately were vital to the regime's survival.

The CCP's National Democratic Front called for nationalization of most elements in the economy, termination of the U.S.-Philippines Mutual Defense Treaty and closing of the two main U.S. military bases—Clark Air Field and the naval base at Subic Bay. Its most important propaganda slogan derided the New Society as "the U.S.-Marcos dictatorship," thereby questioning Marcos's nationalism while simultaneously denigrating his importance. Furthermore, the NPA profited from the military abuses committed by the ill-trained, under-equipped, and frightened 65,000-member Civilian Home Defense Force

(CHDF). Finally, the rapid disintegration of both the economy and social structure of Mindanao and Negros generated recruits because the NPA provided youth with opportunities for leadership and social recognition.[28]

The Political Crisis

The Marcos regime would probably have endured if it had not created a *cause célèbre*, the assassination of Senator Aquino and the ensuing cover-up. The assassination was the critical event uniting moderate democratic forces throughout the Philippines as well as alienating the Reagan administration.

By early 1983 Senator Aquino had become restless in the United States, assuming that his last opportunity to become president would pass him by if he did not return to the Philippines while Marcos remained alive. When Aquino voiced his plan to return to the Philippines, numerous warnings flowed from the Marcos entourage. The First Lady met him in New York and warned him that if he returned he might be in danger from a communist plot. Senator Aquino, on the phone every night to Manila, became convinced that President Marcos was near death. Marcos was indeed gravely ill in August. There was panic in Malacañang Palace with cabinet ministers approaching the First Lady to assure her of their loyalty in the expected succession crisis. On 21 August 1983 Aquino returned to Manila, and was murdered while in the custody of the Aviation Security Command (AVSECOM). According to the official version, Senator Aquino's demise had been at the hand of a lone gunman, Reynaldo Galman, who in turn was immediately killed by the security forces. The assassination of Benigno Aquino mobilized opposition to President Marcos that was unprecedented in its size and social breadth. Opposition to his handling of the Aquino affair and the board of inquiry surfaced within Marcos's New Society Movement (KBL). In particular Prime Minister Cesar Virata, Foreign Minister Carlos Romulo, and his successor Arturo Tolentino, each took actions that undercut President Marcos's early efforts to sweep the crisis aside.[29] The Makati business community, which for years had suffered in silence, was brought out into the streets and into the election campaign by the Aquino assassination and the continuing economic crisis. Roman Catholic Cardinal Jaime Sin placed the church in direct opposition to the Marcos government and to Imelda Marcos in particular. The peaceful opposition was supplemented by the student radicals and protestors who became a "parliament of the streets" under the leadership of Benigno's brother, Agapito Aquino, and Senators Lorenzo Tanada and Jose Diokno.

The May 1984 elections marked a new beginning for the opposition.

After having been beaten and cheated repeatedly by the Marcos machine, UNIDO (United Nationalist Democratic Organization), under Salvador Laurel, and other parties fielded candidates for the Batasan (the legislature of the Marcos regime). In addition NAMFREL, founded during the 1951 election, was resuscitated by Makati business interests to police the polls. In spite of the fact that the Commission on Elections (COMELEC) disallowed NAMFREL activities in half of the districts just prior to election day, the poll watchers of NAMFREL were instrumental in preventing Marcos's political operatives from stealing votes after they had been cast. During the week prior to the May election President Marcos indicated he would be the most shocked person in the world if the opposition gained more than twenty seats.[30] When the votes had been cast the initial quick counts of NAMFREL indicated the opposition was leading in more than half of the seats. When all votes had been counted and the Marcos-controlled COMELEC had done its work the opposition still ended up with an astonishing fifty-nine seats. This was in spite of the fact that prominent politicians of the Left had urged a nationwide boycott. Eighty percent of the voters turned out to cast their ballots, indicating a continuing faith in the democratic process as a means for registering protest and forcing reform. As in all previous Philippine elections a great deal of money changed hands, votes were stolen, and political killings occurred; however, according to Cardinal Sin the May 1984 elections were among the cleanest postwar elections.

Prior to the Aquino assassination the Armed Forces of the Philippines (AFP) had been controlled by officers who were the proteges of General Fabian Ver, the one-time chauffeur and bodyguard of Ferdinand Marcos. One of Ver's sons commanded the Presidential Guard, a 15,000-man elite unit. Likewise, at the time of the assassination, Ver's loyalists controlled all important commands in and around Manila and had frozen out Lieutenant General Ramos (the commander of the Philippine Constabulary) and Juan Ponce Enrile (minister of defense). The trial of General Ver for Aquino's murder, and his temporary replacement as acting chief of staff during the trial by General Ramos, provided an atmosphere in which a reform movement grew up within the armed forces. The movement, operating through the 3,000-member Philippines Military Academy Alumni Association (PMAAA), grew rapidly during the period 1984–1985, increasing its influence among young graduates of the academy, and even some field and star ranks. The movement was privately endorsed by General Ramos and Defense Minister Enrile, who remained convinced that unless drastic reforms were instituted, the communist insurgency would escalate toward civil war and reach a point where the government might falter.[31] General Ver was reinstated as chief of staff of the AFP in December 1985 immediately after his acquittal, but the reform movement refused to disappear within the AFP. In the regime's final crisis, RAM officers (Reform the Armed Forces of the Philippines Movement) rallied to their early patrons, Enrile and Ramos, rather than accepting Ver's attempt to reassert control. What became known as the miracle at Edsa united an important part of the establishment (led by Enrile and Ramos) with the RAM colonels, the church, and the street crowds of "people power." This coalition in the end proved more powerful than all of the military commands whose control had been husbanded by Marcos and Ver.

Marcos's Last Hurrah

The final elements of the political crisis of 1985 were provided by Marcos's call for a snap election and the obviously rigged verdict of the Sandigan Bayan court, which exonerated all twenty-seven defendants in the Aquino murder trial. On 3 November 1985 President Marcos, on a U.S. television program, attempted to steal the thunder from his critics in the United States by offering to seek a new mandate from the electorate. Marcos's calculation probably went something like this. The urban intellectuals, the middle class, and the small segment of the peasantry supporting the NPA would obviously vote with the opposition; however, the patronage machinery of the KBL along with the coercive capability supplied by Ver would probably be able to deliver the vote one more time, at least as long as Marcos appeared healthy. The president's party was a patronage network that utilized large sums from the national treasury to bring in the votes. The competition for control of Malacañang had always emphasized "guns, goons, and gold," and Marcos counted upon his superior abilities in all three categories.

Calling the snap election proved to be the fatal misstep for four reasons. First, President Marcos assumed that the opposition would be weak and unable to unify around a single appealing candidate. He assumed that Salvador "Doy" Laurel and Corazon Aquino would not be able to convince their faction-ridden political followers to fight a united campaign. This prognostication was upset by the intervention of Cardinal Sin, who used his moral weight to enforce unity around the Aquino candidacy. The U.S. embassy also played a part by insuring that the two sides kept talking to one another. The result, in mid-December, was what Marcos most feared, the so called Coy-Doy ticket that united the appeal of a political innocent whose popular husband had been gunned down with the country's only significant opposition political organization, UNIDO, led by Salvador Laurel.

The second aspect of Marcos's election miscalculation was his assumption that the election would be fought according to "Philippine rules of the game." Philippine elections during the democratic period prior to martial law always featured rampant vote buying. Philippine elections had seen patronage democracy on a scale that would have made Chicago's Mayor Daley envious. In Philippine presidential elections in the 1960s, 10 to 20 percent of the voters exchanged their votes either for direct payments at the polling places on the day of the election or for jobs, special favors from government, and the like. Voting "early and often" had been more prominent in the Philippine democratic elections of 1965 and 1969 than it ever was in Mayor Curley's Boston. Hence in January 1986, Marcos's political operatives were confident, even though opinion polls in December showed the two candidates running neck and neck with more than 15 percent undecided. They assumed that the fence-sitters would be readily mobilized by the KBL election machine during the last seventy-two hours before the vote. Aquino had money for neither precinct workers nor bus transportation to the polls and had foresworn publicly the utilization of payments at the polling places on election day.

The third aspect that Marcos did not anticipate was that this would be the first mass media election in the history of the Philippines. As a U.S. embassy official remarked early in December, "There are three major stories in the world: South Africa, Khadafy, and the Philippine elections. South Africa is no longer news and covering Khadafy is either boring or dangerous. That leaves only the Philippines." By election day 1,000 employees of the U.S. mass media had descended on Manila. Many had never been to the country before, and Philippine history for most of them had begun in the summer of 1983 with the assassination of Senator Aquino. There was no appreciation of the fact that candidates from Ilocano (like Marcos) have always carried Ilocano districts in northern Luzon by thunderous majorities,[32] that the martial law administration initially had doubled the rate of growth of real per capita income, and that Marcos, with a handwritten 1972 proclamation, had given the right to land ownership to all tenants working rice and corn land. To the press Marcos was a tired, corrupt dictator who could not possibly be popular, and certainly not overwhelmingly so, even with his own ethnic group. As the election approached the press was primed to write one story, "How Marcos stole the election." Sticking to a "good" versus "evil" story line avoided complications such as explaining past voting patterns of northern Luzon, traditions of patron-client politics, and the peculiarities of Philippine pork barrel democracy.

The fourth aspect that President Marcos did not appreciate was the sincere determination of Washington to ensure a fair vote count. The U.S. government as part of a bipartisan policy pinned its hopes on NAMFREL, the citizens' poll-watching organization. When the policy was put in place there was no realization that NAMFREL itself would become relatively partisan during the course of the campaign. The assumption of the press and U.S. politicians was that NAMFREL would operate as it had in earlier elections, as the equivalent, if you will, of the League of Women Voters. For this reason, Senator Lugar, head of President Reagan's official panel of election observers, endorsed the NAMFREL count before the voting began. As the vote totals at NAMFREL indicated an early Aquino lead, cheers rang out from the "nonpartisan" vote tabulators.[33] Likewise, when NAMFREL refused (on grounds of fraud) to include any of the votes cast in the Marcos strongholds of northern Luzon, ignorance of the political past of northern Luzon combined with NAMFREL's League of Women Voters image to make the selective count acceptable to the international press and to wide segments of the U.S. government, especially on Capitol Hill.

When the government election commission (COMELEC) and NAMFREL showed different election results, the assumption was that NAMFREL was objectively nonpartisan and reliable. NAMFREL refused to count 30 percent of the total vote nationally in known pro-Marcos areas where there were no NAMFREL volunteers. NAMFREL informally reported (but did not include in its vote count) margins of 98 to 99 percent in favor of Marcos in some of these areas, particularly the Ilocano areas of northern Luzon. In the 1965 election, when Marcos won the presidency for the first time, Marcos as an Ilocano received 95 percent of the vote in purely Ilocano areas; however, NAMFREL in 1986 decided the high percentage favoring Marcos and turnout above the national average indicated massive fraud in northern Luzon and therefore refused to count any of the votes from these areas.

The election of 1986 was probably the most abuse-filled in Philippine history; however, what was unique was not the presence of government-sponsored abuses but the level of outrage expressed by the church as amplified by the mass media. In any case the true vote totals (which will never be known) probably showed the candidates within 5 percent of one another. Neither candidate achieved a clear mandate by numbers, but Aquino won. Both sides selectively tabulated returns, but Aquino's claims were given credibility by the church, U.S. politicians, and the international media.[34] For the first time in Philippine electoral history there had been a close vote, and neither side was willing to accept the outcome. Marcos's solution was to remove vote counting from the hands of COMELEC and NAMFREL, giving it to the constitutionally appropriate vote-certifying organization, the Batasan, the legislature that just happend to be two-thirds controlled by Marcos's own party. The legislature certified Marcos as the winner, but the certification did not increase the legitimacy of Marcos's claim, either inside or outside the Philippines.

At this point security was clearly beginning to disintegrate even in Manila. Cracks had begun to appear in the facade of the Philippine establishment. Defense Minister Enrile and Lieutenant General Ramos for two years had been quietly encouraging the military reform movement as part of their struggle to regain control of the military from General Fabian Ver. In the immediate postelection furor it became increasingly apparent that Marcos would be forced to reassert his control by using the armed forces to restore order. Such actions would be opposed by the military reform movement, and the logic of the situation required that Enrile and Ramos be pushed aside and Ver maintained in control in spite of the fact that Marcos had announced Ver's retirement. At this juncture Enrile and Ramos did something absolutely unprecedented in the history of the Philippine military. They went into open rebellion against the civilian authority of President Marcos, and they were given the wholehearted backing of Cardinal Sin. Their charges against the Marcos administration echoed those of the church, the opposition, and the foreign observers. With their statements, as well as their personally courageous stand, Enrile and Ramos irretrievably committed Washington to pushing President Marcos out of power. Official U.S. disenchantment with President Marcos had been growing steadily since August 1983 when the panicked inner circle of critically ill Marcos carried out the hamfisted assassination of former Senator Aquino. From the assassination onward the attitude of official Washington permanently soured. Officials who previously argued that there was no alternative to Marcos began discussing the post-Marcos era. The assumption was that Marcos had entered a twilight period in which the United States must push for internal reform and democratization while simultaneously distancing itself from the corrupt and crumbling power structure. The ever-rising tide of the communist New People's Army combined with the rapidly declining economic fortunes to create a growing sense in Washington that something simply had to be done about the Philippines. This sense of foreboding brought Senator Laxalt's October 1985 mission to Manila to urge President Marcos to undertake vital economic, military, and political reforms.

In the immediate postelection furor the Reagan administration seemed to hesitate in taking the final steps necessary to push Marcos from power. On 11 February President Reagan, at a press conference, suggested that fraud and violence had taken place on both sides. However, by 19 February the administration began to sever its connection with Marcos when Secretary of State George Shultz stated that "fraud and violence on a systematic widespread scale" had been the work of Marcos supporters. The final outcome became inevitable when Juan Ponce Enrile and Fidel Ramos went into open revolt. At that point Washington threatened to cut off all military aid to the Philippines, and messages were conveyed through diplomatic channels that an orderly transition of power required the immediate exit of President Marcos.

Theory and History in the Philippines

What does the Philippine case study tell us about the nature of politics and the prospects for democracy in the Philippines, Southeast Asia, or even the Third World? Does the February 1986 revolution provide us with more than a morality play with a happy ending in which a bereaved heroine overcomes a wicked authoritarian?

The saga through which the Philippines passed from democracy to dictatorship and back to democracy may be relatively unique for several reasons. First, the Philippine democracy destroyed by Ferdinand Marcos's declaration of martial law had been quite firmly established, with power routinely changing hands, from Roxas's defeat of Osmena to Marcos's victory over President Macapagal. Second, the Philippine people had been schooled for citizenship by a blatantly democratic colonial power that stressed the need to end colonialism long before such ideas became fashionable. The emphasis on universal education during the colonial era led to one of the highest literacy rates in Asia and to the development of an elite justly renowned for the polished nature of its political oratory and feistiness of its journalism. Third, as an Asian "showcase for democracy" in the 1950s and 1960s, the Philippines was repeatedly touted as a premier example of the successful transplantation of Western institutions to an alien political culture.

Many of the preconditions for democratic rule seemed permanently inscribed in the Philippine political cortex and yet in 1972 the entire system was overturned with remarkable ease, and a dictatorship maintained itself through fourteen long years in spite of its self-evident failures in economic growth and equity, order and justice, peace and stability. Given the Marcos regime's failure and its obvious shoddiness, why was it able to institute authoritarian rule and to endure so long in a political culture predisposed toward democracy?

Several different types of explanations are involved. First, most citizens in most polities most of the time are not as interested in politics as those of us who write about it. Most citizens, most of the time, do not care vitally about who governs. In democracy mass apathy is more typical than mass involvement.[35] Concerns such as earning a living and raising a family tend to predominate, for instance, over concerns about whether the legislature should be bicameral and whether the country should be ruled by a president or prime minister.

Second, democratic institutions had always existed as an overlay on traditional Philippine political culture. Patron-client coalitions had always been the chief mechanism of political mobilization. These networks have always been fragile and can be thoroughly disorganized and neutralized if opposition patrons can simultaneously be imprisoned and therefore neutralized. In 1972 Marcos had the opposing patrons picked up and immobilized the mechanism that the political opposition would have used to prevent him from assuming a third term.

Third, Marcos's martial law declaration was popular because it promised to make the Philippines both more dynamic economically and more Asian politically. Both of these were attractive goals in the Philippines in 1972, when disillusioned with the old society's slow growth, corruption, and incipient political radicalism, the democratic polity gave the impression that the society had lost its bearings and might be careening into chaos.

Fourth, at the time martial law was declared, Marcos found natural allies in the military (that perceived the nation as threatened by the Moro National Liberation Front and the fledgling NPA) and the technocrats (who perceived strong, centrally controlled planning as the only escape from the chronic slow growth). For both military and technocratic interests martial law provided power, prestige, and access to new resources.

But why did the long night of Philippine democratic politics last so long? First, in its initial years the New Society delivered the goods. The real growth rate per capita doubled, land reform was declared, violence decreased, and the MNLF was brought under control. Second, Marcos changed the entire character of Philippine politics by centralizing power in Manila, systematically hollowing out all potential rival institutions, be they the legislature, the judiciary, or local government. Power had previously grown up from the barrios, from which local power brokers controlled election to Congress, which in turn constituted the vital proving ground for all aspirants to the presidency. The political parties were patron-client groupings rather than issue-oriented or ideological organizations. When Marcos did away with the legislature and co-opted large numbers of local leaders into his movement, he disorganized the traditional means of expressing opposition. His reforms not only tinkered with the rules, they changed the entire shape of the game. Third, Marcos strengthened the internal security apparatus and used it on a scale (and with a ruthlessness) entirely unprecedented in Philippine politics. Fourth, Marcos's access to tens of billions in international loans gave him more patronage powers than any previous president ever imagined. Although it was clear that there would eventually be a day of reckoning, the showcase projects of the Marcos regime supplied a level of funds that dwarfed even the traditional power-holding families. This ability to attract resources from abroad in the form of loans and grant aid supplied his regime with slack resources that were spread widely enough within the elite to make up for the disenchantment that grew, especially when the initial burst of economic growth tailed off in the late 1970s.

Paradoxically enough, the very factors that allowed him to sustain himself in power in the mid-1970s became disadvantages in the mid-1980s. First, the rapid economic growth of early martial law was short-lived, discrediting the notion that centralized authoritarian rule would supply a panacea for the Philippine tradition of slow growth. Second, Marcos's tendency to concentrate power progressively in the hands of the Marcos-Romualdez clan meant that the coalition of interest supporting martial law inevitably shrank. Bureaucratic polities all seem to share one characteristic, that is, the founding coalition shrinks with time as power concentrates around the chief executive and his immediate associates.[36] In the Thai case power concentration and coalition shrinkage usually results in regime collapse. For example in 1973, conventional wisdom had it that Thanom Kittikachorn's regime had created an ironclad, family-reinforced monopoly on military and police power, and this, as in the case of Marcos, was in fact largely true. However, the regime virtually imploded because no one outside the extremely narrow elite circle surrounding the prime minister retained a vital interest in regime preservation. The invincible rulers retained the heights of power but little else; the state had become a nearly empty void that precious few were willing to defend. The rulers were abandoned by the very military apparatus over which they exercised formal power but little authority. Likewise in the Marcos case, from 1983 to the end all power was concentrated in the hands of a minuscule subelite composed of the Marcos-Romualdez clan, the immediate cronies, and the ever-loyal General Fabian Ver. Power concentration, and the disappearance of slack resources with the financial crunch, resulted in severe coalition shrinkage that ultimately led to the Enrile-Ramos defection and ensuing regime collapse.

In 1983 the cracks had already become apparent. The officer corps that had benefited from martial law was denied promotion because Ver superloyalists were kept beyond normal retirement limits. Likewise Ramos, the professional soldier, was repeatedly shunted aside in favor of Ver, the loyalist. Even Enrile, who with Marcos had initiated martial law, found himself frustrated and virtually powerless as minister of defense, while an increasingly embattled Marcos concentrated all control over promotions in his own hands or those of Ver. To almost the last days of Marcos, the regime commanders loyal to Marcos and Ver "controlled" all troops in greater Manila. However, when the crunch came in, as it had in 1973 in Bangkok, the regime's political base, even within its own armed forces, had become so narrow that middle-level officers were no longer willing to support the regime; formal power arrangements in the end were devoid of all authority. In the end the supposedly invincible security apparatus of Marcos and Ver was forced to give up without a fight. Having hollowed out all legal institutions by concentrating virtually all power in the security apparatus, when the security apparatus itself faltered Marcos had no fall-back position. The courts and legislature he had corrupted could provide no meaningful legitimacy once candidate Aquino refused to accept the flawed outcome of the election.

· THE PHILIPPINE FUTURE ·

When Corazon Aquino assumed office in February 1986, she faced a myriad of critical problems including political instability at the center, insurrection in the countryside, economic stagnation, and the tradition of government enriching the governors rather than serving the people. President Aquino has clearly made progress toward reinstituting democratic government—a constitution has been written, the people have confirmed it overwhelmingly in a plebiscite, and congressional elections have been held in which her slate of candidates triumphed. All of these have been seen as important milestones, setting in place new democratic institutions that should strengthen President Aquino's ability to deal with dissident elements within and without her own military establishment.

On the economic side the first year of the Aquino administration made limited but significant progress. The sugar and coconut monopolies of Benedicto and Cojuangco have been broken up and the crony enterprises have been sequestered by the state. State enterprises are being sold off to staunch the drain on state resources. Far higher levels of foreign economic assistance were forthcoming in the first year of the Aquino administration than under Marcos. In addition debt rescheduling was accomplished after protracted negotiation. Real economic growth of 1.5 percent was achieved in 1986 and respectable economists predict real growth in the 3.3 to 4.6 percent range for 1987. If this occurs the increase will result in the first growth of GNP per capita since 1982.

During 1986 foreign investors remained leary, but the government looks forward to increased interest in new undertakings once the entire elected constitutional framework is in place. Political legitimacy and the perception of stability are critical to the return of both domestic and foreign investor confidence. Without large-scale capital investment the resumption of real growth substantially exceeding the rapid rise in population will be unlikely. The Philippines should be one of the most attractive places to invest in Asia because of the breadth of the business elite, the English-speaking labor force, and the low wage rates resulting from the peso's devaluation. However, substantial impediments remain. The continued presence of corruption prompted Cardinal Sin to speak out, and foreign investors remain reluctant to assume the other risks inherent in investing in the Philippines if they must also contend with rapacious and unpredictable demands for graft.

Insurgency remains the final element of uncertainty.[37] President Aquino and her immediate entourage came to office convinced that the NPA resulted from Marcos and that it would collapse, perhaps spontaneously, once freedom and democratic rights were restored. President Aquino was personally committed to the search for national reconciliation that resulted in a sixty-day cease fire, 10 December 1986 to 9 February 1987. Many had hoped that large numbers of NPA members would abandon armed struggle after experiencing the new freedom of the post-Marcos era. Trends, however, remain contradictory. The NPA has refused to fade away and in fact the number of active operatives has increased in the first year of the Aquino administration. Furthermore, the CPP has been able to operate more openly than ever in the democratic space created by President Aquino's political reforms. Although it is reassuring that the legal arm of the extreme left, the Partido ng Bayan, failed to capture either Senate or House seats, it is important to remember that insurgent movements do not come to power in elections. By definition insurgents are disaffected minorities whose road to power is through bullets rather than ballots. In fact there is no firm evidence that NPA recruiting sources have dried up, and the political substructure of the movement may still be expanding. The limiting factor on NPA activity continues to be the shortage of weapons and supplies rather than an absence of recruits. Even if NPA recruiting stopped immediately, the amount of armed strength could still nearly double if the unarmed half of the approximately 24,000 communist rebel activists received guns.

Very substantial reforms have been undertaken by the AFP since the fall of President Marcos. The overstaying generals have almost all been retired. The Civilian Home Defense Forces (CHDF), which previously were responsible for the more egregious human rights violations, have decreased in number from 65,000 to 40,000 and have been placed under tighter disciplinary control. Retraining centers have been established for regular army units, and the human rights thrust of the Aquino administration has led to a marked decline in the types of human rights violations on which insurgency feeds. In addition, AFP forces received pay increases that should decrease the frequency of irresponsible behavior toward the civilian population. Finally, a start has been made on repairing the infrastructure of the AFP. Large numbers of trucks, radio sets, shoes, clothing, and a variety of spare parts have been provided since the February Revolution. Even though military assistance from the United States is now flowing much more rapidly than it had in the last five years of the Marcos regime, the size of the aid input remains relatively small in proportion to the underequipped and poorly maintained condition of the AFP inherited by President Aquino. By one estimate, the AFP's maintenance backlog could absorb $1 billion in spare parts and supplies.

Given the sharply constrained nature of worldwide U.S. military assistance resources, it remains unlikely that anything like that amount will be forthcoming. However, successful counterinsurgency campaigns in Indonesia in the 1950s and 1960s and Thailand in the 1980s have taught us that the role of armed force is secondary to that of coordinated social, economic, and political reform. Solutions emphasizing high-tech weapons and increased firepower have never worked except in combination with a willingness on the part of civil and military agencies to remain in rebel areas over time to undertake the painstakingly slow process of recreating loyalty bonds among those previously alienated from the government. In the counterinsurgency context, accurate information and effective local government is more important than firepower alone. For this reason, the task with highest priority for the Aquino government must be implementing a powerful, interagency counterinsurgency program simultaneously addressing needs for agrarian reform and social justice, as well as particular programs aimed at tempting guerrillas to lay down their arms and return to civil society. The quality of implementation of an overall civilian-military program will determine whether the NPA continues to expand. Much has been done in the first year to reconstitute the enervated institution that the AFP had become, and the NPA is no longer growing at nearly 100 percent per annum as it was in the last years of Marcos. That much still needs to be done is indicated by the 9 percent growth rate in NPA regulars in the first year of Aquino. Only an indigenous counterinsurgency strategy, in which military operations play a relatively subordinate role, has the prospect of containing and eventually reducing the NPA.

• CONCLUSION •

The chief policy problems of President Aquino are precisely those of her predecessors—slow growth, corruption, and insurgency. If anything, the problems have become more intractable with the passage of time, population growth, and the expansion of national indebtedness over the twenty years before she attained power. In some ways the excitement of the miracle of democratic deliverance provides a poor model for the future. Whereas the miracle at Edsa required short-term courage of thousands, solving the economic and social problems will require long-term sacrifices by millions. The outstanding question is whether President Aquino's personal popularity can be translated into coherent, pragmatic policies capable of eventually producing peace, prosperity, and justice in the Philippines.

• NOTES •

1. David Joel Steinberg, *The Philippines: A Singular and a Plural Place* (Boulder, Colo.: Westview Press, 1982), pp. 20–28.

2. Onofre D. Corpuz, *The Philippines* (Englewood Cliffs, N.J.: Prentice Hall, 1965), p. 79.

3. Corpuz, *The Philippines*, pp. 78–82; Steinberg, pp. 35–38.

4. See Jean Grossholtz, *The Philippines* (Boston: Little Brown, 1964), pp. 29–30.

5. Steinberg, *The Philippines*, p. 57.

6. Ibid., pp. 57–58.

7. Ibid., pp. 60–61.

8. See Grossholtz, *The Philippines*, pp. 33–36.

9. See Karl Jackson, "Post-Colonial Rebellion and Counter-Insurgency in Southeast Asia," in Chandran Jeshuran, ed., *Armed Communist and Separatist Movements in Southeast Asia* (Singapore: Institute of Southeast Asian Studies, 1985), p. 23.

10. See Office of the President, President's Center for Special Studies, *The Present State of the Opposition Parties*, (Quezon City: Eastchem Development Corporation, 1984).

11. Corpuz, *The Philippines*, p. 104; Grossholtz, *The Philippines*, pp. 43–44.

12. Corpuz, *The Philippines*, p. 94.

13. Lela Garner Noble, "Politics in the Marcos Era," in John Bresnan, ed., *Crisis in the Philippines: The Marcos Era and Beyond* (Princeton: Princeton University Press, 1986), pp. 73–74.

14. See Noble, "Politics in the Marcos Era," pp. 77–81.

15. On the NPA see Larry A. Niksch, "Insurgency and Counterinsurgency in the Philippines," (Washington, D.C.: Congressional Research Service, 1 July 1985); and Ross H. Munro, "The New Khmer Rouge," *Commentary*, December 1985.

16. Steinberg, *The Philippines*; pp. 111–112; and Jose Veloso Abueva, "Ideology and Practice in the 'New Society'," in David A. Rosenberg, ed., *Marcos and Martial Law in the Philippines* (Ithaca, N.Y.: Cornell University Press, 1979), pp. 32–36.

17. On the martial law period, see Abueva "Ideology and Practice;" and A. James Gregor, *Crisis in the Philippines: A Threat to U.S. Interests* (Washington, D.C.: Ethics and Public Policy Center, 1984), pp. 26–47.

18. See Noble, "Politics in the Marcos Era," p. 83; and Abueva, "Ideology and Practice."

19. Ibid., p. 55.

20. See Carolina G. Hernandez, "The Military and the Future of Civilian Rule in the Context of the Prevailing Philippine Crisis," in Alexander R. Magno, ed., *Nation In Crisis: A University Inquires into the Present* (Quezon City: University of Philippines Press, 1984), p. 95.

21. See Abueva, "Ideology and Practice," pp. 45–51; Noble, "Politics in the Marcos Era," pp. 84–86.

22. Abueva, "Ideology and Practice," p. 43.

23. Ibid., pp. 57–63.

24. For a variety of evaluations of the land reform effect see Steinberg, *The Philippines*, pp. 114–115; Benedict J. Kerkvliet, "Land Reform: Emancipation or Counterinsurgency," in David A. Rosenberg, ed., *Marcos and Martial Law in the Philippines* (Ithaca, N.Y.: Cornell University Press, 1979), pp. 113–144; Abueva, "Ideology and Practice," pp. 66–67.

25. Noble, pp. 92–96.

26. Whereas the deficit for the first half of 1984 constituted 12 percent of the total budget, in the first half of 1985 the deficit equalled 26 percent of the budget.

27. James A. Kelly, "Situation in the Philippines and Implications for U.S. Policy," Statement to the Committee on Foreign Relations, United States Senate, 18 September, 1984.

28. See Niksch, "Insurgency and Counterinsurgency in the Philippines."

29. Abby Tan, "Noted Manila Official Bitter at Handling of Aquino's Murder," the *Washington Post*, 17 December 1983, pp. A21, A32.

30. William Branigin, "Marcos is Confident of Victory," the *Washington Post*, 14 May 1984, p. A12.

31. "Backing Reform," *Asia Week*, 14 June 1985, pp. 17–19; Rodney Tasker, "The Hidden Hand," and "Power to the Reformer," *Far Eastern Economic Review*, 1 August 1985, pp. 10–13.

32. Harvey A. Averch, John E. Koehler, and Frank H. Denton, *The Matrix of Policy in the Philippines* (Princeton: Princeton University Press, 1971), p. 50.

33. See Rodney Tasker, "Marcos Fights Back to Stem the 'Cory' Tide," *Far Eastern Economic Review*, 20 February 1986, pp. 11–12.

34. Guy Sacerdoti, "Standing Polls Apart," *Far Eastern Economic Review*, 20 February 1986, pp. 10–11.

35. See the U.S. voting literature, particularly Bernard Berelson, Paul Lazarsfeld, and William Macphee, *Voting* (Chicago: University of Chicago Press, 1954).

36. See Fred Riggs, *Thailand: The Modernization of a Bureaucratic Polity* (Honolulu: University of Hawaii Press, 1966); and Karl D. Jackson and Lucian W. Pye, eds., *Political Power and Communications in Indonesia* (Berkeley: University of California Press, 1978).

37. On the insurgency, see Richard L. Armitage, Statement before the Subcommittee on Asia and the Pacific, Committee on Foreign Affairs, House of Representatives, 17 March 1987; and Karl D Jackson, Statement before the Subcommittee on Asia and the Pacific, Committee of Foreign Affairs, House of Representatives, 19 May 1987.

SOUTH KOREA

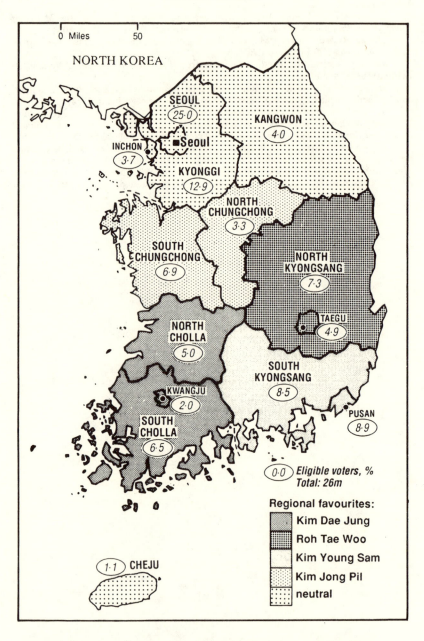

NORTH KOREA

0 Miles   50

SEOUL
25·0

KANGWON
4·0

INCHON
3·7

■Seoul

KYONGGI
12·9

NORTH
CHUNGCHONG
3·3

SOUTH
CHUNGCHONG
6·9

NORTH
KYONGSANG
7·3

NORTH
CHOLLA
5·0

TAEGU
4·9

SOUTH
KYONGSANG
8·5

KWANGJU
2·0

SOUTH
CHOLLA
6·5

PUSAN
8·9

0·0 Eligible voters, %
       Total: 26m

Regional favourites:
Kim Dae Jung
Roh Tae Woo
Kim Young Sam
Kim Jong Pil
neutral

1·1 CHEJU

Copyright © 1987 by the *Economist* magazine. Reprinted by permission.

• CHAPTER SEVEN •
South Korea: Politics in Transition
SUNG-JOO HAN

Since 1948, when an independent government was established, South Korea has gone through several stages of political evolution: (1) the "First Republic" (1948–1960) under the government of President Syngman Rhee, which became increasingly dictatorial; (2) the democratic period of the "Second Republic" (1960–1961), which was ousted by a military coup d'état; (3) the semiauthoritarian period (1961–1972) under President Park Chung Hee; (4) the highly authoritarian Yushin ("revitalizing reforms") period (1973–1979), which ended with the assassination of President Park; and (5) the authoritarian period (1980–1987) of the government of President Chun Doo Hwan. Throughout the entire postindependence period, there has always been a very strong and intense aspiration for democracy. Yet, except for.a brief interlude of nine months during the 1960–1961 period, South Korea did not enjoy democratic politics. Those in power resorted to undemocratic means to sustain their rule—rigging elections, oppressing the opposition, altering the constitution by illegitimate means, and restricting basic political freedoms. As the opposition to authoritarian rule—hence the demand for democracy—grew, successive governments had to resort to increasingly repressive and harsh, if sophisticated, measures. These in turn brought about even more intense opposition.

After four decades of predominantly authoritarian rule, South Korea is now undergoing a rapid political transition. Authoritarianism has generated so much opposition from all sectors of the society that, regardless of its possible merits for a developing society, it has been rejected as a viable system for South Korea. The demand and aspiration for democracy have been so intense and forceful that even the supporters of an authoritarian government have come to admit the inevitability of democratization. However, it is an open question as to whether there has been enough change in the substance and significance of those factors—political, social, cultural, economic, and international—that have supported an authoritarian system in South Korea in the past for them now to foster and sustain full-fledged democracy.

Contemporary South Korean politics can be characterized as semi-authoritarian, with strong democratic pressures and promises. Whether those promises will be fulfilled depends upon the answers to be given to a series of questions. What are the explanations for the failure of democracy to be instituted and take root in South Korea in the past? How strong and stable are the factors and forces for authoritarian politics? What are the factors and forces that would now work for or against democracy? What are the likely processes by which democratic development and consolidation would take place? These questions will be explored in the following pages.

• HISTORICAL REVIEW AND ANALYSIS •

Democratic Experiments

In May of 1961, a coup d'état by a group of military officers in South Korea put to an end the nine-month-old government of Prime Minister Chang Myon. It also meant the end of the Second Korean Republic, established in July 1960 after Syngman Rhee's ouster in the wake of student uprisings three months earlier. The relative ease with which the coup was carried out was matched by the absence of any overt sign of resistance to the military takeover on the part of the general population. The end of the "Second Republic," as the Chang period was to be called later, marked the second failure of the Koreans to create and preserve a democratic government.

Korea's first democratic experiment ended in failure during the Syngman Rhee period. The first Korean republic was established in 1948 after a thirty-five-year Japanese colonial rule followed by a U.S. military occupation government. It was the product, in large measure, of the determination and persistence of Syngman Rhee, a venerable leader of the independence movement, and his conservative nationalist supporters. They opposed the trusteeship plan of the allied powers (the United States, the Soviet Union, and the United Kingdom) for all of Korea—north and south—and insisted on the immediate establishment of an independent government in the south even if it meant the loss, perhaps permanently, of the northern half of the peninsula to rule under a communist government.

The new government was born with a democratic constitution and with the expectation that it would usher in democratic politics for South Korea. But the Rhee government became increasingly arbitrary and dictatorial. Above all, Rhee was determined to remain in power—for life—which required several constitutional changes, election rigging, and repression of the opposition. Rhee was able to establish his personal dictatorship by making use of the state power as exemplified by the national police.

Many factors contributed to the formidable power of the state and the police: the general proclivities of the great majority of the Korean people at the time for obedience to the state and conformity with others; the absence of strong social organizations that could challenge the prerogatives of the state; the highly centralized and well-disciplined nature of the police organizations; and the existence of a communist threat from the north, as well as from within South Korea itself. The absence of nationwide social organizations other than the police and the administrative bureaucracy greatly contributed to the supremacy of state power, and the prior existence of a well-organized police and bureaucratic apparatus presented a serious obstacle to the development of effective political parties in Korea. And all these gave an insurmountable advantage to the incumbent president and his supporters, who proceeded to undermine the democratic process to perpetuate their rule.

But Rhee's dictatorship, based primarily on coercive force and to some extent his personal charisma, was heading toward a confrontation with the political public, who were being increasingly alienated from his government. When the Korean government was established in 1948, belief in democratic values and practices was not widespread among the people at all levels of the society. However, increasingly large numbers began to demand "free and fair" elections as the actual performance of the government became increasingly less democratic. The rise in democratic consciousness among the public was largely the result of extensive democratic education and rapid urbanization following the Korean War. "Education in democracy" was taken very seriously in both the elementary and secondary schools. Extensive exposure of the highly literate urban and semiurban population to the mass media was instrumental in convincing many Koreans of the virtues of democracy. The positive results of this democratic political education are seen in the fact that in many surveys young people were found to be more "democratically oriented" than their elders.[1]

The polarization of political forces into the progovernment Liberal Party and antigovernment Democratic Party by the mid-1950s made it easier for voters to identify whom to vote for and whom against, depending upon the level of their political consciousness. For the relatively mobilized population the only easy and obvious way to uphold their newly acquired democratic values was to vote against the candidates and party of a government acting undemocratically, and for those opposing the government. Thus in a political setting in which ideological diversity was not tolerated and thus all major political parties were essentially conservative, the only choice for the voters was between a party that was against democracy and one that was for democracy. A large-scale election fraud in March 1960 resulted in massive student uprisings in April and ultimately the fall of the Rhee regime, as the military that had been mobilized to defend it refused to use violence against the demonstrators.

South Korea failed with its first democratic experiment because of the abuse of power by its leader, Syngman Rhee. The second experiment that followed the fall of the Rhee regime ended when a military coup d'état ousted the democratically elected government of Chang Myon only nine months after its inauguration. One obvious reason for the fall of the Chang Myon government (1960–1961) was its inability to detect and destroy a plot within the army. More important, however, the democratic government of Chang Myon was unable to deal with serious ideological and social cleavages effectively, and consequently lost much of the support with which it came to power and gained little new support or loyalty for the regime.

Two sets of conflicts stood out during this period: the social and ideological polarization between the conservative and radical political groups and that between the pro- and anti-Syngman Rhee groups. First, the Chang Myon government, with its indecisiveness and inconsistency regarding punishment of former leaders of the Rhee regime, alienated itself from both the supporters and opponents of the Rhee regime. Second, given the acuteness of the conflict between the anti-Communists and the radical groups within the country, any government committed to political toleration ultimately would have fallen victim to one of these conflicting groups. In this it was difficult to achieve liberal democracy in its true sense. A regime would have survived at the time only by means of alliance with one of these groups and suppression of the other.

Concerning the division between supporters and opponents of the Rhee regime, it can be stated that the first group consisted of Syngman Rhee's immediate subordinates in the Liberal Party, police and bureaucratic personnel, military officers (especially the top-ranking ones) and businessmen, while their opponents included the opposition politicians of the Democratic Party, the intellectuals in the "university-press nexus," and the students. Thus the April "revolution" could be understood as a successful challenge to and overthrow of the rule of the first group by the second.

The Chang Myon government, which owed its creation to a loose coalition of intellectuals, newspaper writers, liberal students, and anti-Rhee politicians, was expected to satisfy the immediate aspirations of the anti-Rhee forces—namely, the "revolutionary" punishment of former officials of the Rhee government. The Chang government's commitment to due process and liberal democracy was largely responsible for its initial failure to fulfill this task. This failure, however, alienated many of its coalition partners from the Democratic government. Subsequent punitive legislation against former Rhee supporters in turn served to alienate from the Chang government those conservative groups that had supported the Rhee regime and that could conceivably have been wooed to the side of the Democratic regime by offering them protection. As a result, the Chang government not only lost the support of its electoral and intellectual constituencies, but also succeeded in neutralizing the effectiveness of its administrative and law enforcement apparatus.

The dilemma of liberal democracy in South Korea was especially acute in the Second Republic because of the presence of powerful groups strongly committed to oppose any form of leftist radicalism. The division of the country between the communist-controlled north and anticommunist south was primarily responsible for the intolerant anti-communist attitude among key groups in South Korea, such as the armed forces, the police, the bureaucracy, and most party politicians. Communist agitation in South Korea during the immediate postliberation period, "red" and "white" terror during the Korean War, and the threat of North Korean subversion and attack accounted for the development of such a rigid anticommunist attitude in South Korea.

During the First Republic, Syngman Rhee and his regime dealt with the ideological conflict by ruthlessly suppressing any leftist movement as "communist-controlled" or "communist-inspired" conspiracies. Such a policy proved to be quite effective because of the support it received from the powerful anticommunist sectors, which feared the prospect of a real social revolution in South Korea in the event of a leftist takeover. The relatively liberal political atmosphere following the collapse of the Rhee regime provided leftist politicians and other political groups with an opportunity to organize and advocate their "radical" views without the same type of pressure they had felt in the past. The radical movement after the collapse of the Rhee government was supported not only by former leftist politicians, but also by many college students and school teachers who felt the need to correct what they considered to be socioeconomic injustice at home, and to achieve national unification, which they believed was being hindered by the presence of foreign powers on Korean territory. However, the leftist politicians and parties experienced a near complete defeat in the July 1960 election, perhaps the most open and fair one in South Korean history, revealing that a significant gap existed between them and a great majority of the voters. The ideologically conservative nature of the urban voters and culturally traditional nature of the rural voters made the electoral success of the leftist candidates almost impossible. As a result of its failure in electoral process, the leftist movement turned its emphasis from parliamentary to nonparliamentary politics.

The leftist agitation in turn helped to mobilize the anticommunist elements in the society, who discredited the Chang government because of its failure to firmly suppress the leftists. Furthermore, when the choice was between a radical leftism and a radical anticommunism, most supporters of liberal democracy, such as the leading members of the opposition New Democratic Party, chose the latter, as shown by their acquiescent attitude toward the military coup d'état.[2]

Throughout the Second Republic the military continued to be a key factor in Korean politics. Despite the pervasive factionalism among the top-ranking officers, the military constituted the only nationally effective organization with the capacity to exercise coercive force during the post-Rhee period. The military was thus capable of preventing a radical change in the status quo and suppressing the rise of any significant leftist or other revolutionary groups if necessary. When the conservative politicians appeared unable to carry out that task most of the military officers refused to commit themselves to defending them against their enemies, making it easier for organizers of the May coup d'état to accomplish their goal.

Obviously many factors contributed to the fall of the Chang Myon government. The failure of his liberal democratic government to survive and provide a foundation for democracy in South Korea can be explained by South Korea's socioeconomic "immaturity," its undemocratic authority patterns, and the constitution that provided for a weak cabinet government. Yet the most immediate source of the Chang Myon government's problems appears to have been the social and ideological cleavages. Because of its liberal character, these cleavages and conflicts were more visible during the Second Republic than at any other period after the establishment of the Korean republic in 1948. This visibility of conflicts, however, became one of the most important reasons for the government's downfall.

Given the acute nature of the social conflict, the government faced the necessity of allying itself with one of the antagonists and suppressing the other. This, however, would have been diametrically opposed to what a liberal democracy should stand for, and the Chang government was both unable and unwilling to abandon its commitment to liberal procedures and institutions to insure its own survival. Such was the tragedy of liberal democracy in South Korea in 1961.

The Authoritarian Legacy of South Korean Politics

South Korean politics during the twenty-six-year period between 1961 and 1987 can be characterized as basically authoritarian.[3] Even during the height of political oppression in South Korea, opposition parties, elections, policy debates, and the subsystem autonomy of various official and nonofficial groups and institutions have existed and have been meaningful, although only to a limited extent. Elections since 1963 have generated competition and debate mostly *within* the government and opposition parties, but not *between* them. Because of the built-in safeguards (for the incumbents) in the electoral system, the opposition parties have not won the presidency or a majority in the National Assembly. Serious and lively debates on public policy issues have been allowed to be conducted within and outside of the government and its party, but only as long as they did not question the nature of the governing system or of the top leadership. Yet social groups and institutions generally have been left free from intense ideological indoctrination or politicization. What the state has exercised in an effective way is a *negative* control aimed at preventing antigovernment activities rather than a *positive* control of the totalitarian type designed to elicit explicit and total support for the government or party in power.

Although there are both historical and sociological explanations for the authoritarian trends in Korea, much of the structural and practical applications of authoritarian politics can be traced to the eighteen-year rule of the Park Chung Hee government (1961–1979). Thus understanding the nature of the Park period is essential for an analysis of contemporary South Korean politics.

Major General Park Chung Hee came to power in May 1961 after toppling the constitutionally established government of Chang Myon, accusing the latter and the civilian leadership of being corrupt, incapable of defending the country from internal and external threats of communism, and incompetent to bring about economic and social transformations. Upon taking over power, General Park pledged to transfer the government to "fresh and conscientious politicians" when the tasks of the revolution had been completed. During the ensuing two years, Park made preparations to assume the leadership of the future "civilian" government by (1) banning for at least six years more than 4,000 politicians of the previous regime from political activities; (2) consolidating his own position within the ruling group of primarily military leaders by purging the recalcitrant elements and potential rivals; (3) having a new constitution providing for a strong presidential system with a weak legislature adopted by a national referendum; and (4) building a party (the Democratic-Republican Party) to aid him and his supporters in presidential and legislative elections.

Following a series of political crises that resulted from Park's reluctance to relinquish the military rule, a presidential election was held in November 1963 under pressure from the United States and political forces at home. Park, who had formally retired from the military at the end of August to participate in the campaign, won the election, considered to have been conducted in a reasonably fair atmosphere. Park received in the election 46.7 percent of the votes cast over his major civilian opponent's 45.0 percent. Park's support was weak in the urban areas; he also failed to receive strong support from the so-called military areas along the demilitarized zone.[4] In the legislative election that immediately followed, Park's party won a large majority, 110 seats out of the total of 175. Park was reelected in 1967 by a more comfortable plurality of 49 percent of the votes cast over his chief opponent's 39 percent (the anti-Park and antimilitary vote was split between two major civilian candidates). In the second half of the 1960s, all appeared to be going well for President Park's continued stay in office except for two elements. One was the agitation of the students who opposed the Park government for its "military" character and the "reactionary" nature of its foreign and economic policies; the other was the constitutional restriction on the presidency of two four-year terms.

The first major outbreak of student demonstrations since 1961 took place in 1964 against the proposed Korea-Japan normalization treaty. Many students believed that South Korea had made too many concessions to Japan and that it was negotiated in a "humiliating" manner. They were demonstrating not only against the treaty but also against what they considered were many failures of the Park government. The government initially attempted to mollify the students through postponement of the signing of the treaty and a cabinet reshuffle. However, as the protest grew in size and intensity, the government, well aware of the consequences of the April 1960 student uprising, sternly suppressed it by declaring a state of martial law and arresting several hundred students. Large-scale demonstrations occurred many times since then during the Park regime; in 1965 against the ratification of the Korea-Japan treaty; in 1967 against allegedly unfair National Assembly elections; in 1969 against the constitutional revision that permitted a third-term presidency for Park Chung Hee; and after 1972, against the Yushin (revitalizing reforms) Constitution. In the face of a mounting threat to the regime caused by student disturbances, President Park tightened the legal ban against student activism. In October 1971 the president ordered, among other things, the expulsion from school of the leaders of demonstrations, rallies, sit-ins, strikes, or other "disorderly activities," the disbandment of all nonacademic circles and groups in the campuses, and the prohibition of all "unauthorized" publications by students. A presidential decree of April 1974, later repealed, provided for punishment up to the death penalty against student protest activities.

When the 1969 constitutional amendment—achieved through a referendum—enabled the president to run for his third term in 1971, the move became another serious impetus for agitation by the students, which in turn necessitated further and heavier penalties for their antigovernment activities. The 1971 presidential election, in which Park's chief opposition candidate Kim Dae Jung received 46 percent of the votes cast, indicated to Park that his continued stay in office could be threatened under the existing electoral system despite enormous advantages he enjoyed in elections as the incumbent.

It seems that, except for the KCIA (Korean Central Intelligence Agency) activities and the suppression of student political activism, many of the oppressive features of the regime did not begin to appear in full force until 1972. There was relative freedom of the press, speech, and opposition activities. All three presidential elections held prior to 1972 were rather close ones that could have gone the other way with a little more unity, popular appeal, and astuteness of the opposition. The question arises as to what might have happened if Park had actually lost one of those elections. Kim Se Jin, a student of Korean military politics, pointed out the irony of Korean democracy: "Park's victory [in 1963] was in fact a blessing for the future of democracy in Korea. Had the military lost, it can be safely assumed that the military would have ignored the electoral outcome and continued to rule even though such rule would have meant a total destruction of constitutionalism."[5]

During the 1970s the restrictions on opposition activities and limitations to effective political competition were legally prescribed. Until 1979, when the Park government collapsed following his assassination, the key legal instrument for this purpose was the Yushin Constitution, which was adopted in a referendum held under martial law in November 1972. The Yushin Constitution had been proposed by the Park government, assertedly to facilitate national unification, to cope with the changing international situation, and to effectively carry out the country's socioeconomic development. It provided for an indirect election of the president by the locally elected (and thus more easily subjected to the influence of the government) National Conference for Unification; appointment by the president of one-third of the 219-member National Assembly (the rest of the membership being elected in seventy-three two-member districts); an unrestricted number of six-year terms for the president; reduction of the powers of the legislature and the judiciary; and curtailment of civil and political rights by presidential decrees.[6] In the face of mounting criticism and protest, the Park government promulgated a series of "emergency measures" in 1974 banning all criticism of the Yushin Constitution and demand for its revision. A March 1975 revision of the criminal code provided for heavy jail terms for any citizen at home and abroad who "insults, slanders or harms by rumors or other means the government or its agencies." Student demonstrations and rallies were strictly prohibited by law and presidential decrees under penalty of imprisonment and expulsion from school.[7]

An overall assessment of President Park's legacy and contribution to Korean political development would indicate both negative and positive aspects. One of the Park regime's negative contributions was its failure to provide for an institutional and political framework within which an orderly succession could take place following his departure from the political scene, voluntarily or otherwise. He left the nation with a constitution that was highly unpopular and unworkable after his death. Park needed the Yushin Constitution to prolong and strengthen his presidency. But it had been tailor-made only for him, making a major constitutional revision inevitable. When President Park died the country did not even have a legal framework within which a new leader or government could be chosen in an orderly way.

Second, the Park regime played a negative role in institutionalizing political parties and a party system within which a new generation of leaders could emerge and which could bring various forces and interests into the political process. Park was personally suspicious of both the progovernment and opposition parties and considered them as a necessary evil at best and a threat at worst. Neither his own Democratic-Republican Party nor the opposition New Democratic Party was given a proper opportunity to develop the necessary leadership structure and to cultivate grassroots support. Neither party could attract the participation of high-caliber individuals or induce strong identification with it by the electorate or major social groups. As a result, political parties failed to become the main medium by which struggles for power and influence could be carried out following Park's death.

Third, in the course of his prolonged rule, President Park had generated so much opposition to and alienation from not only his own rule, but also the sociopolitical system as a whole that, once he departed from the scene, piecemeal changes and peaceful transition became almost an impossibility. Various individuals and groups sought radical solutions and tried to "settle old scores" immediately. In addition, during President Park's tenure, much of the top elite circulation took place horizontally and within a limited circle of supporters, thus frustrating the power aspirations of ambitious individuals both within and outside of his own party. This intensified the intraparty, as well as interparty, power struggles following President Park's death in 1979.

Another negative legacy was the increased propensity and capability of the military to play a political role. In large part because of the way the Park government came to power and also because it depended heavily on the military for staying in power, the military became prone to intervening in politics when it would feel there was the need and the justification. Finally, as Park became increasingly unpopular, he made political use of the security issues with the unfortunate result of weakening its credibility. Many people, particularly the students, acquired the habit of showing cynicism toward South Korea's security problems, which were nonetheless genuine. At the same time, the political involvement of some of the government law enforcement and intelligence agencies compromised their effectiveness in performing their tasks and caused them to lose credibility.

Against the "negative" legacy discussed above, a few political consequences of a positive kind should also be mentioned. As a result of his persistent drive for rapid economic development, President Park succeeded in creating a substantial economic class that could become the mainstay of a democratic political system if and when it were established. A democratic government in power would be able to count on the support of this class as long as it could provide continued economic growth, social stability, and security from external threats. A related consequence of Park's rule was the regularization of government procedures and the institutionalization of executive power. It is true that these were accompanied by excessive bureaucratization of the government and the proliferation of authoritarian practices surrounding the presidency. However, they could also be seen as serving positive purposes by making the exercise of administrative power by the government and its leaders more economical, predictable, and effective. It could provide continuity and stability of the government even when democracy requires rather frequent changes of government.

Thus at the time of President Park's death, Korean society had a potential for acute polarization and power struggles, but the necessary leadership structure and institutional mechanisms by which such struggles could be managed without necessitating violence or social disorder were lacking. These were the very sociopolitical conditions that induced and enabled a group of military leaders to step in and take over the reins of power in the political vacuum that followed the death of President Park in October 1979. The restoration of democracy in South Korea thus had to be postponed until after another round of authoritarian politics was to complete its cycle.

Explaining the Authoritarian Trend in the 1970s

Concerning the authoritarian trend in Korea during the 1970s, various explanations have been offered by critics and apologists for the government, as well as observers purporting to be objective. Neo-Marxist writers argue that the South Korean government has had to resort to repressive measures in order to collaborate with and serve the economic interests of international capitalism led by the U.S. and Japanese multinational corporations.[8]

On a more general level, scholars have pointed out factors such as (1) the centralizing and hierarchical nature of Korea's social structure and political culture; (2) ideological cleavages between the "rightists" and the "leftists," as well as between the "authoritarians" and the "liberal democrats"; and (3) the unbalanced development of political institutions—i.e., the "overdevelopment" of the output institutions such as the bureaucracy and the military relative to the input institutions such as political parties and interest groups.[9] Other explanations include the political leaders' personal penchant for power and the legacy of Korea's recent history, especially the Korean War, which has left the society militarized and lacking in civil values.[10]

Comprehensive as the above listing of the explanations might appear, it is not quite adequate in two respects. First, it does not distinguish between what might be called the "permissive" factors that constitute the general background to authoritarianism on the one hand, and the "causal" factors that act as the direct moving force in what might be called an authoritarianizing process" on the other. Second, the explanations do not adequately address themselves to the question of why the process of authoritarianization was accelerated in South Korea from around the end of the 1960s.

It seems that the general-level explanation—sociocultural, ideological, institutional, and historical—provided a permissive environment for authoritarian rule. The "militarized" nature of the society—a large number of military personnel and veterans, diversion of huge amounts of resources to defense, priority given to military considerations in foreign and domestic policy making, and a permanent emergency atmosphere—as well as the support that the Park government received from the military, bureaucratic, and business sectors, also contributed to creating a political setting that permitted the authoritarianizing process to proceed.

The most important and immediate impetus for the emergence of an oppressive regime, however, came from the Park government's realization that elections under the existing system (pre-Yushin) would not guarantee continued victories for the DRP candidates and that, should a favorable outcome be engineered by illegal means to give the incumbent an election victory, it would provide the government's opponents with a rallying point against it, as such an action had provoked Syngman Rhee's opponents to collective action in 1960. The 1969 constitutional amendment, which enabled President Park to run for a third term, can be considered to have been a turning point in the government's ability to maintain the electoral support necessary to keep the president in office indefinitely. Many of those who had held a reasonably favorable attitude toward the Park government and had a high regard for its achievements were disappointed by its tampering with the constitution to prolong Park's presidency. Since the 1969 amendment only permitted a third term for the incumbent, a further stay in office beyond the term would have required another change in the constitution, which in turn would have cost the Park government more popular support.

It seems certain that during the several years following his narrow election victory in 1963, President Park succeeded in increasing his support levels, primarily because of the successful implementation of the government's economic development plans. In elections he and his party were also aided by the availability of disproportionately large amounts of campaign funds, which were of crucial importance in Korea.[11] However, as the situation was changing substantially after 1969, a significant restructuring of the legal and governing system was deemed necessary if a transition of power either within the government party itself or to the opposition were to be prevented from happening.

On its part the government argued that, by eliminating for practical purposes the interparty electoral competition, much "waste" of resource and energy that had been an indispensable part of electioneering by both parties could be eliminated; that the government, through its system of so-called administrative democracy—which places emphasis on identification, articulation, and representation of interests by administrative means and mechanisms—could more effectively concentrate on solidifying the nation's defense and achieving social and economic development without interference from "politics"; and that the country would not be turned over to a weak government that could easily be toppled by another military coup d'état. Apologists for the government also argued that an authoritarian, but humane and benevolent, government was not adverse to Korea's political-cultural tradition and was therefore not unacceptable to a great majority of the Korean people.[12] Regardless of the validity of these arguments, however, opposition to the authoritarian regime was growing at a rapid rate and the government was losing legitimacy as well as ability to maintain social stability and effective governance.

Politics in the 1980s: Democratization Postponed

The authoritarian system of Yushin collapsed in 1979 with the assassination of President Park Chung Hee by his chief intelligence aide, who claimed that his action against Park was motivated by his desire to spare the nation from a "bloodbath" that might have resulted from growing protest against the Park regime and its strong reactive measures. It is not certain if the Park regime would have collapsed soon by growing opposition to it had the assassination not taken place. It is clear, however, that serious strains began to appear in the regime, and the polity was heading toward instability and a major crisis. Its popularity was at an all-time low, measured even by the results of elections heavily interfered with by government power. For example, Park's Democratic-Republican Party had suffered a serious loss in December 1978 when it obtained only 31 percent of the popular vote in the National Assembly election.

Large-scale riots took place toward the end of his regime in such major cities as Pusan and Masan.

Park's death was greeted with the expectation that authoritarian rule would come to an end and full democracy be restored. However, a period of active anticipation and lively political activity by various groups and individuals was followed by the declaration of full martial law in 1980 and the assumption of power by General Chun Doo Hwan who had headed the Military Security Command under the Park government. Authoritarian rule in South Korea received another lease on life and democratization suffered another setback and postponement. With the support of key military leaders, Chun first took over the post of chief executive as acting president in August, after which the rubber stamp National Conference of Unification elected him as president. In October a new constitution, which retained many of the key features of the Yushin Constitution, was put to a national referendum that approved it by an overwhelming vote. Under the new constitution, Chun was elected president without competition for a seven-year term in January 1981.

Upon assuming power Chun disbanded all political parties of the previous regime, purged their leaders, and placed under political ban hundreds of politicians and other activists. In addition to his own Democratic Justice Party he allowed the formation of several parties by political personalities and organizations that could not challenge the ruling group in any effective way. Instruments of "power and control," such as the KCIA (renamed the National Security Planning Agency) and the Military Security Command were retained or strengthened. The new National Assembly and the interim Legislative Council that had preceded it in 1978 enacted laws that enabled effective control by the government of the press and labor movement. In short, another cycle of authoritarian rule devoid of political competition and civil rights had begun.[13]

There was nothing inevitable about the fact that in 1980 South Korea's democratization process would face another serious setback and authoritarian rule would be restored. It is possible, however, to offer a few explanations as to why the transition to democracy that had been so ardently and overwhelmingly aspired to by South Koreans after nearly two decades of authoritarian rule had to be postponed once again.

First, it may be pointed out that even though Park had died, the power structure—the military, the bureaucracy, and other groups that had a vested interest in the status quo—remained intact. Only the ruling Democratic-Republican Party was seriously weakened, although it did not collapse. This was in contrast with the post-Rhee period, when few organizations or groups remained supportive of the political or socio-economic system that the Rhee regime had left behind. Thus the remnants of the Park governments, as an organization if not as individuals, including the interim cabinet of Choi Kyu Hah (who had been Park's prime minister before his death and who had temporarily succeeded him), were able to hold off the pressures and demands of the anti-Park forces to implement the democratization process immediately. They bought enough time for those who had a stake in the authoritarian system to regroup among themselves and render support for a regime that was likely to be more favorable to their interests than a democratic one.

Second, the party politicians, particularly of the opposition, lacked effective leadership and unity. The chasm was especially evident between the incumbent leaders of the New Democratic Party, the principal opposition party during the Park period, and the forces represented by and supporting Kim Dae Jung, who had been imprisoned and deprived of the right to participate actively in politics. Being certain that their turn to assume power had come, and preoccupied with struggle and competition among themselves, the democratic politicians of the opposition allowed the antidemocratic forces outside of party politics to gain control of events and ultimately supersede party politics.

The radical and vengeful image of certain groups, particularly among dissident students, intellectuals, and progressive Christians, as well as the politicians who were supported by them, also contributed to a certain degree of acquiescence that the general public exhibited when authoritarian rule was restored by Chun. Even though riots broke out in certain cities such as Kwangju when martial law was extended throughout the nation in May 1980, citizens began to show as much concern about the social instability and disorder accompanying the democratization process as about its delay. Such concern became more poignant as student demonstrations intensified and after large-scale riots by miners and steel mill workers broke out in April. The "middle class," to the extent that their existence could be ascertained and delineated, had grown during the Park regime with its economic developmental efforts to the extent that it had a vested interest in socioeconomic stability and continuity. But it was still too insecure about its political and economic status to opt decisively for political freedom and democracy at the risk of sacrificing its country's continued economic growth and its own newly secured socioeconomic status.

A fourth explanation for the relative ease with which Chun and his military associates could take over power can be sought in the nature of the South Korean military itself. It was with General Park Chung Hee's military coup d'état in 1961 that the Korean military began directly intervening in politics. Until then President Syngman Rhee had skillfully kept the military under control and away from political involvement. It was only during the last few days of the Rhee government that the military played a decisive role in the political outcome when it refused to use violence against the anti-Rhee demonstrators. But by coming to power by a coup d'état, and by staying in power primarily through the support of the military, the Park government contributed greatly to politicizing the military. Top officers came to believe they had a claim, and indeed an obligation, to involve themselves in South Korea's politics by virtue of their position as defenders and protectors of a society under constant threat of external invasion and internal subversion. After all the military was getting a disproportionate share of the national budget and manpower, and the society had been highly militarized in terms not only of its resource priority, but also of the mentality and ways of life. Furthermore, although the Korean military had lacked cohesion among the high-ranking officers and between the higher and lower officers during the earlier (Rhee and Park) periods, by 1980 the core and mainstream of the South Korean military came to consist of regular graduates of the Korean Military Academy, among whom there was a strong sense of camaraderie, shared interest, and sense of responsibilities. Thus it is not a mere coincidence that General Chun represented Class One of South Korea's regular military academy and that his military colleagues were able to secure the acquiescence, if not support, of a substantial part of the middle- and lower-ranking officers (colonels and captains) in their takeover of the government.

Finally, a contributing factor in the collapse of the democratization process was the absence in South Korean society of individuals, groups, and institutions such as a monarch or respected political elders who could act as a mitigating, mediating, and moderating force among and between the contending political forces. Political conflicts therefore tended to be of a naked, confrontational and zero-sum nature. In this normative vacuum there was no one person or institution that could bestow upon or deprive a person or group of legitimacy. Neither could anyone authoritatively endorse or deny someone else's claim to power even when it was clear that fair and due process was ignored and popular aspirations betrayed.

Knowing that he had come to power without popular mandate Chun devised a novel definition of democracy, arguing that its most important ingredient was a "peaceful transfer of power" at the end of the president's prescribed term, something that had never happened in South Korea's post-World War II political history. Thus he repeatedly stressed his determination to step down at the end of his seven-year term in early 1988. Clearly, this gesture was far from adequate to mollify the anger and frustration of those who saw their democratic aspiration and struggle nullified by a group of ambitious military officers. The antigovernment, democratic movement in due course picked up where it had left off upon the death of President Park. Only this time it was to be better organized, more forceful, and more widely spread than before. As it became clear toward the end of the Chun government that his idea of "peaceful transfer of power" was to be within the "power group" rather than to the civilian opposition, antigovernment activities intensified to the extent that the Chun government came to have only the choice between total suppression by mobilizing all the coercive instruments of power, including the military, and making substantial concessions to the opposition to begin the democratization process.

The End of an Authoritarian Cycle

From the outset the government of President Chun Doo Hwan lacked legitimacy and was beset with opposition. He came to power after squelching the democratic hopes and expectations that had been aroused in the wake of President Park's death. His ascendance to power was accompanied by the tragedy of the Kwangju uprising in which several hundred citizens were killed. In addition his government inherited all the hostility and antagonism toward a military-authoritarian government that had been generated during the Park government. The mainstay of President Chun's power was the military. As such, he saw little need for and thus gave insufficient effort in becoming a popular leader. Even if he had, Chun probably would not have succeeded as his lack of prior experience in political life made him inept in mass politics. That Chun was not a good politician was perhaps a blessing in disguise for South Korean democracy, as it made authoritarian rule vulnerable and the democratic movement stronger.

Having secured the legal basis of power through the adoption of the new constitution, Chun and his supporters attempted to strengthen their basis of power by devising a party system that would give the government an overwhelming advantage over the opposition. They thus tried to establish a multiparty system in which the dominant (government) party would be opposed by several minor parties. Furthermore, in this plan there was to be scarcely any competition within the dominant party. Such a scheme seemed to be having some success as, in the first National Assembly election held after the establishment of the Chun government, the ruling Democratic Justice Party (DJP) received 36 percent of the votes cast while the rest was shared by twelve other parties, including the opposition Democratic Korea Party (DKP), which obtained 21 percent, and the National Party (which was formed by individuals with close connections with the defunct Park government) with 13 percent of the votes.

This was only a temporary phenomenon, however. As the political ban on former politicians was lifted for the most part, there was a coalescing of opposition forces into a single party. The parliamentary election of February 1985 brought about a basic realignment of political power and parties. In that election, the New Korea Democratic Party (NDP), formed largely by politicians who had been placed under political ban in 1980 by the Chun government, made an impressive showing, winning sixty-seven of the 184 elective seats. This compared with only thirty-five for the existing Democratic Korea Party that, even though it had acted as the main opposition party during the preceding four years, was seen by the electorate as being accommodating to the Chun government. The new opposition party's electoral success led to a mass defection of the KDP members to the NDP, with the result that a virtual two-party system emerged. Now the battle line was clearly drawn— between the government party, which insisted on the legitimacy of the government as well as the existing constitution by which it came to power, and the opposition party, which argued that the government lacked legitimacy and the system as it stood favored the incumbent party, because in an indirect election of the president the electoral college is susceptible to government influence.

As the government party had a clear majority in the National Assembly, however, the battle—with constitutional revision as the key symbolic as well as substantive issue—was waged in the streets and campuses and largely by the *chae-ya se-ryok* ("forces in the field"), consisting of dissident student leaders, intellectuals, and progressive Christians. Even Cardinal Stephen Kim, who headed the 3-million-strong Korean Catholics, joined those who called for a constitutional change. In the face of large-scale demonstrations, mostly by university students, continuing social instability and pressure from various groups including the church, intellectuals, and lawyers, as well as the United States, the Chun government decided in February 1986 that the constitution after all would be revised before the expected transfer of power in 1988. It was perhaps not a mere coincidence that only a few weeks earlier, the Marcos government was ousted by "people power" in the Philippines.

As the debate on constitutional revision continued through 1986, it became clear that the opposition was determined not to retreat one step from its demand for a presidential system of government in which the president was to be elected by a direct, popular vote. The government, on its part, proposed a parliamentary system of government in which the chief executive would be elected indirectly by the legislature.

Several reasons prevented the opposition from entertaining the idea of compromising with the government in the constitutional revision. First, there was so much distrust of the government by the opposition that any move, even apparently a conciliatory one, was seen as mere maneuvering by the ruling military group to perpetuate itself in power. It suspected that Chun was simply trying to buy time.

Second, the opposition was divided internally so that a leader could give the appearance of accepting a compromise solution only at the risk of being accused of selling out and betraying the cause of democracy. This was especially true in view of the fact that the opposition leader, Kim Dae Jung, who was technically still under political ban and therefore carried something of a moral authority within the opposition, remained adamant about the proposal for direct popular election of the president. Under these circumstances even an opposition leader with the stature of Kim Young Sam, who had previously advocated a parliamentary system for South Korea, could not even suggest the possibility of a compromise. In 1987 a leading proponent of compromise, NDP leader Lee Min Woo, would pay a heavy price for acting on his inclinations.

Finally, in the Korean political culture and under the existing rules of the game, compromise is not seen as a sign of rationality and good will but as a signal of weakness and lack of resolve not only by one's adversaries, but by one's allies as well. This leads the power players to chronically overestimate their own strength and underestimate that of their rivals. Any gesture toward compromise is likely to be met by further demands by the adversary, which tries to take advantage of the opponent's perceived feebleness. Politics in Korea usually takes the form of a zero-sum game in which winning is more important than keeping the game playable and productive. It was for this very reason that the government refused to entertain the idea of accepting the opposition proposal. It accepted the opposition proposal only when it was forced to do so in the face of a massive show of force by student demonstrations, which were often accompanied by violence.

1987—The Beginning of a Democratic Cycle?[14]

By any measure 1987 was a momentous year for South Korean democracy. Running against the political clock of the end of President Chun Doo Hwan's seven-year term in February 1988 and the international clock of the Seoul Olympics in the summer of 1988, events moved briskly—from massive protests in the spring to government capitulation in June and from the negotiation for and adoption in October of a new constitution, to the election of a president in December by a direct popular vote. The economic situation seemed to favor South Korea's difficult but inevitable transition to democracy.

The year began inauspiciously for President Chun Doo Hwan and his Democratic Justice Party. As the deadlock between the ruling party and the opposition New Korea Democratic Party on the issue of constitutional revision remained unresolved and antigovernment student demonstrations persisted, the country learned in mid-January that Park

Chong Chol, a Seoul National University student, had died of torture under police interrogation. The revelation of the incident, which was confirmed by the government, could not have come at a worse time for the DJP, as it was trying to persuade the opposition to accept its proposal for a parliamentary form of government in return for certain democratic reforms. The opposition on its part had been in disarray, split from within among those who were adamant about their proposal for a presidential system with a direct popular vote and those who were willing to compromise. The torture death of Park Chong Chol not only gave the antigovernment movement in and outside of party politics a rallying point, but also contributed to strengthening the position of hard-liners within the opposition who now regarded the government as weak and vulnerable.

The actual power and leadership within the opposition were held by Kim Young Sam and Kim Dae Jung. Kim Young Sam, on his part, insisted that the party's 1985 election pledge for direct presidential elections was the very basis of the party's existence. As noted above his political rival for leadership of the opposition, Kim Dae Jung, took an even more hard-line stand. The two Kims succeeded in quashing an initiative by nominal party leader Lee Min Woo, who offered to consider the DJP's constitutional formula in exchange for seven major political reforms, including the release of political prisoners, press freedom, and the restoration of Kim Dae Jung's political rights.[15] Nonetheless, the squabbling within the opposition did not subside, and in early April the two Kims split from the NDP to form a new party. Sixty-six of the NDP's ninety lawmakers followed the Kims' breakaway lead and, on 1 May formally inaugurated the Reunification Democratic Party (RDP) with Kim Young Sam as its president. The humiliated Lee Min Woo, on his part, merged the remnants of his party with the People's Democratic Party (PDP), which had split from the NDP in early 1986, to form a twenty-six-seat bloc in the National Assembly.

But the origin of political drama in 1987 can be traced directly to President Chun Doo Hwan's declaration on 13 April of his "grave" decision to suspend debate on constitutional reform. Only a few months earlier the Chun government had seemed quite capable of maintaining its authoritarian system with only modest concessions to the opposition and to democracy. The opposition was split between those who were, although silent for the most part, willing to accommodate and those who were not. Student protest, although continuing, was losing sympathy and support among the general public because of its radical and extremist tendencies. Thus, if it had wanted to, the government could have tried to pass a constitutional amendment embodying its own proposal. The opposition leadership could not and would not have accepted it. But if it had been accompanied by a program of genuine democratic reforms, the passage of a new constitutional draft as required by the existing constitution might have elicited, while not perhaps enthusiastic acceptance, at least a fair degree of acquiescence among the public.

In a classic case of miscalculation the Chun government decided to push its luck, and announced that constitutional revision, after all, would not take place and the next presidential election would be held under the existing—unpopular—constitution. In defending the measure the DJP argued that the opposition (badly splintered) could not act as a responsible negotiating partner and that time was running out; continuing political uncertainty and instability would hurt the chances for successfully crossing South Korea's twin hurdles of 1988: the change of government and the Seoul Olympics. Rather than bringing about certainty and stability, however, Chun's decision was met with near universal disapproval by the South Korean public, and provided new momentum to student protest, which was losing sympathy and support among the general public because of its radical and extremist tendencies. The government was placed in an even more embarrassing position following disclosures in mid-May of a cover-up in the Park Chong Chul incident. Chun's cabinet shake-up of May 26, dropping three of his closest aides (Prime Minister Lho Shin Yong, Home Minister Chung Ho Yong, and the director of the Agency for National Security Planning, Chang Se Dong) did little to cool the anger of the protesters.

Street violence reached its peak after 10 June when the DJP, in an audacious act of political insensitivity and imprudence, formally nominated Roh Tae Woo as the party's presidential candidate to become Chun's handpicked successor under the existing unpopular constitution, which provided for an indirect election of the president. Thousands of students poured into the streets, many hurling firebombs. The riot police, which responded mainly with massive tear gas attacks, was hopelessly outnumbered by the demonstrators, often joined in and cheered by middle-class citizens. Several hundred people were injured and one student died in the clashes. The central districts of Seoul, the capital city, were turning into what the *New York Times's* Clyde Haberman depicted as a "war zone."[16]

In the face of massive, prolonged, and often violent antigovernment demonstrations, the choice for the Chun government and the DJP was narrowed to one between, on the one hand, mobilizing the troops to quell the demonstration and risking large-scale violence and possibly a civil war and, on the other hand, making a wholesale concession to the forces of democracy and risking the loss of power. Chun tried to mollify the opposition by proposing a meeting with Kim Young Sam. At the meeting, which took place on 24 June, Chun indicated to Kim that he was willing to allow a resumption of parliamentary negotiations on constitutional reform. Sensing that Chun's position had weakened, however, Kim rejected Chun's offer, insisting instead that the government should agree to an immediate national referendum to choose between a parliamentary system and a presidential system with a direct popular vote, to release all political prisoners, and to restore the civil and political rights of Kim Dae Jung.

In a dramatic turn of events Roh Tae Woo, the DJP's presidential candidate and a former military colleague of President Chun's, surprised both the supporters and opponents of the government by announcing on 29 June a democratization plan that embodied a wholesale acceptance of the opposition's demands, effectively ending the "spring of discontent."[17] Roh's eight-point proposal, which was subsequently accepted and endorsed by President Chun, pledged "the speedy amendment" of the constitution, allowing for direct presidential elections, and amnesty for Kim Dae Jung and the restoration of his civil rights. The opposition in a rare show of approval welcomed Roh's action. A democratization process finally began.

The immediate results of the Roh declaration were the restoration of Kim Dae Jung's political rights, release of political prisoners, and the start of negotiations on constitutional amendments. Kim Dae Jung, the man who unsuccessfully ran against Park Chung Hee in the 1971 presidential election, was considered as a perennial anathema to the successive regimes of Park and Chun. He had been kidnapped from Japan by agents of the Park government in 1973 and incarcerated until 1979, when Park was assassinated. After a brief period of active politicking in the spring of 1980, Kim was arrested by the martial law command in May 1980 on charges of inciting riots. He was subsequently sentenced to death by the Chun government, which eventually commuted the sentence to a twenty-year prison term. Kim was then allowed to travel to the United States, where he stayed for two years before returning to Korea in February 1985. After the restoration of his political rights in July 1987, Kim Dae Jung officially became an adviser to the RDP while sharing on an equal basis effective power within the party with party president Kim Young Sam.

But no sooner did power seem to be within reaching distance than trouble started in the marriage of convenience between the two Kims. Each Kim saw himself as the hero of South Korea's political drama, and plainly thought the other was behaving unreasonably in refusing to pull out. Kim Young Sam claimed he appealed to a broad cross section of increasingly middle-class Koreans. This made him not only very electable, in his view, but also a much more suitable figure, once elected, to unite a politically fractious nation. Kim Dae Jung saw things differently; after exile in the United States and repeated jailings and house arrests in Korea over the years, he had suffered more in the cause of democracy, he claimed. His failure to run in the presidential election, he warned, could churn up anger and frustration among his many supporters and reignite the potentially dangerous regional antagonisms that had always bedeviled Korean politics. After meeting a few times, the two Kims failed to agree on a single candidacy, and both of them eventually decided to run, even at the risk of defeating themselves. After the formal adoption of the new constitution on 22 October, Kim Dae Jung formed a new party—the Peace and Democracy party—and declared himself a presidential candidate.

The new constitution, which was adopted by a national referendum following a series of negotiations between the government and opposition parties, was the fruit of a long struggle by the two Kims, who insisted on a direct popular election of the president. But it was also a product of political convenience and expediency. Working against the political clock, representatives of the two parties negotiated for a constitution that provided for a direct, popular election of the president. The most problematic aspect of the new constitution was that it allowed the election of the president by simple plurality. The three presidential aspirants, but particularly Kim Dae Jung and Roh Tae Woo, knew that they would have difficulty in obtaining a majority of the votes and thus their chances of winning would be maximized in a situation of multiple candidacy.[18] The constitution also failed to provide for a vice-presidency, making it even more difficult for power contenders within the same party to compromise and remain united.

Joining the three-way race of Roh Tae Woo (Democratic Justice Party), Kim Young Sam (Reunification Democratic Party), and Kim Dae Jung (Peace and Democracy Party), was Kim Jong Pil, former prime minister under President Park Chung Hee, who ostensibly wanted the people's vindication of the record of his defunct Democratic Republican Party (1963–1980). Since each candidate knew he could win by securing firm support from a minority, campaigns were conducted to maximize regional and partisan appeal. Roh Tae Woo, who promised political stability and continued economic growth, had his largest support in the southeastern provinces, among the middle-class voters, and in the rural areas. Kim Young Sam, who called for an end to decades of military rule in South Korea, also appealed to voters in the southeast and to the middle-class voters, although his support was particularly strong among the urban white-collar voters. Kim Dae Jung, who enjoyed solid support in his native southwest, tried to maximize this support among the underprivileged and young voters. The role of Kim Jong Pil, who was strong in his native Chungchongdo provinces, was essentially that of a spoiler, drawing votes from the upper middle classes, which could have gone to either Roh Tae Woo or Kim Young Sam. (See map at the front of this chapter.)

Regional rivalries, often expressed in violent disruption of campaign rallies by candidates from rival provinces, were most conspicuously manifested between the southeast and southwest. Many of Kim Dae Jung's supporters in the southwestern Chollado provinces felt that their region had been discriminated against by the successive regimes dominated by leaders from the southeastern Kyongsangdo provinces. Citizens of Kwangju, in particular, felt that their city had been the object of regional oppression in 1980 at the time of the "Kwangju uprising" in which more than 200 people were killed. Ultimately, the level of voting support for each of the candidates closely coincided with his regional background; Kim Dae Jung received more than 90 percent of the votes from his home provinces and less than 5 percent from the southeastern provinces.

Localism played an especially important role in the 1987 election because of the particular combination of candidates, which tended to magnify the rivalries and animosities between regions. The strong regional identification that the candidates, particularly Kim Dae Jung, fostered ensured that the campaign was to be divisive and emotional. The newly adopted electoral system allowed the election of a president by a mere plurality of votes, thus encouraging multiple candidacies. This in turn led the candidates to conduct a parochial campaign with the result that each of them alienated a large segment of the general population. By casting themselves as regional champions they also tended to promote regional rivalries. Although localism will continue to be a salient factor in South Korean politics, its importance will probably decrease in future elections with a change in the composition of the candidates and the emergence of new campaign issues. It is thus unlikely that regional rivalries will constitute a serious obstacle to Korea's future democratization process.

The 29 June declaration by Roh Tae Woo brought about a brief hiatus in student political activities. Soon, however, the activists went to work, demanding the release of all "political prisoners," and accusing the Chun government of scheming to rig the election. Small-scale demonstrations continued throughout the fall. As the election approached in December, however, the students decided to concentrate on working to ensure a fair election, having organized themselves in teams of election and ballot watchers.

One development that served as a key factor in the campaign was the controversy surrounding events on 12 December 1979. On that day several military leaders, including Generals Chun Doo Hwan and Roh Tae Woo, had mobilized troops, apparently without proper authorization, to overpower and arrest General Chung Sung Hwa, who was then the army chief of staff and martial law commander. General Chung, it had been argued, was suspected of complicity in Park's assassination. During the election campaign, General Chung joined the Kim Young Sam camp and publicly accused the Chun-Roh group of having carried out a "mutiny." The public revelation of details of the 12 December incident was a serious setback for Roh Tae Woo's effort to present a nonmilitary image of himself, although the extent of damage done to his election campaign was impossible to ascertain.[19]

Despite charges of irregularities, the voting took place as scheduled on 16 December and Roh Tae Woo, the DJP candidate, was elected with 36.6 percent of the votes cast. Kim Young Sam, the more moderate of the "two Kims," was second with 28.0 percent, while Kim Dae Jung came in third with 27.0 percent of the votes. Although the losing candidates charged the government with an unfair election campaign and "frauds" in ballot counting, it was clear that the main reason for the defeat of the opposition was that its vote was split almost evenly between the two major candidates. A divided opposition not only brought its own defeat, despite the fact that the two Kims together received a majority (55 percent) of the votes, it also produced a minority government that would face challenges to its legitimacy.

The December presidential election and the events of 1987 that led to it have contributed to resolving, at least in part, the thorny question of legitimacy that had loomed large throughout the period of the Chun Doo Hwan government. Although the DJP candidate won by a mere 37 percent of the vote and there were charges of serious election irregularities, most people accepted that the election of the president by a direct popular vote passed the test of due process, particularly in view of the fact that it was the opposition that defeated itself through its own internal divisions—specifically, its inability to agree on a single candidate. Furthermore, it seemed inevitable that, no matter who was elected, the democratization of Korean society would continue apace. The next government promised to be more democratic than any of its predecessors—if by democratic is meant a government chosen by an open and competitive election that respects the basic freedoms of expression, assembly, and organization. The candidates campaigned unhindered by government restrictions, and each of them, including the government candidate, was subjected to spirited debates and tough questioning. The government that was to emerge from this process would have no choice but to keep the momentum going, the alternative being popular opposition on a massive scale.

One of the most serious problems in the aftermath of the election was the continuing and worsening disarray within the opposition, which remained divided. It appeared incapable of reshaping itself into a political force that could compete effectively in future presidential elections. A majority of the voters, who supported the opposition candidates, were frustrated with the election results and angered by the opposition, which in effect threw the election away. In the absence of a strong, united opposition that could provide the necessary checks and balances on the government, there appeared to be no chance of early and complete democratization as the consequence of an electoral victory by political forces that fought against authoritarian rule. It appeared, instead, that continuing democratization of South Korea would have to depend on the good faith and sound judgement of a government party that would see its own interest to be in fulfilling the commitment to bring about democracy.

Why the Authoritarian Cycle Came to an End

It is impossible to tell whether South Korea's transition to democracy will be successfully completed and consolidated. There is one certainty, however: the latest cycle of authoritarian rule has come to an end. How did this come about? One obvious explanation is the persistence, strength, and determination of the opponents to the Chun government, including the opposition politicians, antigovernment students, and ideological dissenters. More important, however, authoritarianism lost whatever remained of its usefulness and mandate. In 1980 Chun's authoritarian government came to power out of turn, following an eighteen-year rule by Park's authoritarian rule. The Chun government inadvertently further helped the democratic cause with its ineptness in dealing with the opposition politicians and the constitutional revision issue. It helped to unite the opponents of the government with its indiscriminate policy of oppression and rigidity. It lacked logic and consistency in its approach concerning the constitution, and could not retain existing supporters or convert new ones. The personal unpopularity of the president also helped to strengthen antiauthoritarian movement. With a more popular and charismatic leader the authoritarian cycle might possibly have lasted longer.

It may also be argued that certain successes of the authoritarian regime actually contributed to limiting its options when it was confronted with a massive and widespread protest movement. Mobilization of troops, in addition to the uncertainty that it could actually restore order, was certain to have disastrous consequences for the South Korean economy, which was performing well, and for the hosting of the 1988 Olympic Games, for which the regime took so much credit and pride. In addition the urban "middle class," which in 1980 lacked confidence in its economic status and political position, became large and strong enough to assert political rights and expectations. Although its new attitude was not demonstrated by participation in antigovernment activities for the most part, its government was certain to lose its support and acquiescence; its endurance and patience simply wore too thin.

Finally, the pragmatic attitude and approach of South Korea's military leaders and military-turned-politicians should be pointed out. Faced with an overwhelming show of force by the demonstrators and political opponents, the military leadership—including President Chun and the DJP presidential nominee, Roh Tae Woo—decided to accommodate, rather than to mobilize troops and risk a breakdown of the political system and a resultant plunge in the country's economy and international standing. It is also possible that the United States, with which South Korea is allied and which counseled prudence and restraint, particularly on the part of the military, was instrumental in their decision to try the democratic route. Equally important, perhaps, was their assessment that, given the factional divisions with the opposition forces, the DJP had at least an even chance of winning the next presidential election even with a direct popular vote. In fact the DJP made every effort to boost the image of its nominee by giving him the sole credit for the democratization gestures of the DJP and the government. Indeed it is ironic that the ruling party of an authoritarian government, unless it is forcibly ousted, will agree to democratization measures only if it has a reasonable prospect of winning the next democratic election.

• THEORETICAL ANALYSIS •

What are the factors that promote democracy in South Korea on the one hand and those that hinder it on the other? The preceding analysis of political evolution in South Korea during the post-World War II period points to several factors that promote democratization in South Korea: democratic socialization among the highly literate populace; the growth of the "middle class," whose members are becoming increasingly confident with the economic achievement and political rights; the high cost of repression resulting from a rapidly growing democratic movement; the national desire to be accepted and recognized by the outside world as a modern democratic nation, a status that is becoming increasingly important in continued economic expansion; and the peculiar externality of South Korea as a nation closely allied with the United States for its acute security needs.

Underneath the social changes that have pushed for democratization is the rapid economic growth that South Korea has achieved during the past two decades. Between 1967 and 1987, the South Korean economy grew at an average annual rate of over 7 percent, moving it from an underdeveloped, low-income country to what has come to be called a newly industrializing country with a per capita income of nearly $3,000. The rapid economic growth has brought about social changes that not only increase the pressure for democratization but also facilitate that process. First of all, it meant an increase in the size of the middle-income group that is politically conscious, interested, and assertive. A 1987 survey showed that as much as 65 percent of Koreans identify themselves as members of the middle class, indicating the emergence of a social base upon which democratic politics can be built.[20]

Rapid economic development has also been accompanied by increasing complexity and pluralization of the society, in which social groups and organizations require, demand, are capable of, and become accustomed to autonomy in management and decision making. The result has been a social environment in which excessive state involvement in the private sector is resented and resisted. Furthermore, industrialization is accompanied by rapid expansion in the means and modes of communication and transportation, facilitating the exchange of information and people. This makes it difficult if not impossible to sustain a government that is weak in popular support and legitimacy. Finally, for a country such as South Korea, which has placed the utmost importance in the promotion of exports, expansion of external relations is an inevitable consequence as well as a requirement of economic growth. In due course the government and the people realize that democratization is the necessary ticket for membership in the club of advanced nations. This provides a strong incentive for political, as well as economic, liberalization at home.

On the other hand rapid industrialization and economic growth can also hinder or delay democratization, at least in the short to medium term. Successful economic development may serve as a useful justification for the continuation of an authoritarian regime, as was the case with the Park Chung Hee government in South Korea. By providing economic benefits and creating a class of people who depend on the government for their economic well-being and privileges, the government finds a useful *raison d'être* as well as an important support base. This enables it to forego or delay any measure that would hasten democratization. The increasing amount of economic means at the government's disposal also enables it to deal effectively with its potential opponents and critics both at home and abroad. Advanced communication and transportation, public relations skills, organizational capabilities, and other techniques of persuasion can work to the advantage of an authoritarian regime that tries to remain in power without having to resort to democratic elections. At the same time rapid industrial development often results in the problem of unequal distribution of wealth and privileges, both real and perceived, and is accompanied by socioeconomic dislocation. This creates the danger, at least in the minds of the middle and upper classes, of radical ideologies and movements, inclining them to support the authoritarian status quo rather than risk the uncertain future of democracy.

The democratization process in South Korea is also hindered by other factors, which include the following: the highly centralized socio-political structure with a minimum degree of social pluralism; uneven development of political institutions in favor of the "output" institutions; authoritarian social patterns and values; ideological polarization between the "authoritarians" and "democrats" on the one hand and between the "rightists" and the "leftists" on the other; and genuine security problems that require a large military establishment and a certain degree of social militarization in values and behavior patterns. More immediate obstacles to democratization have included such factors as the personal ambitions of those in the power game, which make accommodation and gradual evolution difficult; corporate (such as of the military) and regional interests as well as loyalties; the ideologically radical nature of significant parts of the opposition, which provides justification for the authoritarian reaction of the power holders; and the retribution factor, which has become more salient as rapid economic growth has provided opportunities of corruption for those in power.

Institutionally, the failure of a stable party system to take root presents one of the most serious problems for democratization in South Korea. There are several reasons for the weakness of political parties and party systems. First, a serious imbalance that exists between the bureaucracy (including the military) and political parties has hampered the development of the latter. Power holders in Korea generally tend to favor and depend more on the bureaucracy, which is readily available and generally dependable, than political parties, which are often hindrances to unquestioned and unchallenged power. The large and well-developed military bureaucracy magnifies the problem of bureaucratic supremacy, which is the result of a long Confucian tradition as well as Japanese colonial rule.

Second, parties have not been able to cultivate a stable following among the voters because, in the post-1948 period, there has been no room for ideological deviation from the officially accepted line on virtually all important issues, including unification, national defense, socioeconomic development, and management of wealth. This insistence on ideological consensus is the result not only of traditional preoccupation with orthodoxy under Confucianism but, since 1948, the physical and ideological confrontation with communist North Korea. Ideological uniformity has thus deprived the parties of opportunities to offer meaningful policy choices and to effectively reach and organize sectors of the society that are yet to be mobilized for electoral support and party activities. This is becoming an increasingly serious problem, as political challenge to the governmental and socioeconomic systems is growing among those who are opposed to the government on ideological grounds. Emphasis on economic development and export-led industrialization, it is argued, render social gaps and contradictions more serious—between the rich and the poor, the industrial and nonindustrial sectors, and the international and national orientations. "Socioeconomic justice" and "national identity" have become catch phrases with which dissenters who oppose the entire system join the antiauthoritarian "democrats" in their antigovernment activities.

A third reason for the weakness of the party system can be found in the many changes of regimes and constitutions that took place, usually through extraordinary measures by governments that came to power by nondemocratic means. No party—neither government nor opposition—has survived long enough to claim the loyalty and support of the public. Instead, parties and their leaders have often been purged and discredited after one or another of the uprisings, coups, or other upheavals South Korea has frequently experienced.

Still another obstacle to the development of a strong party system is the private nature of South Korean politics. Personal, factional, and regional rivalries are still deeply embedded in Korean political behavior. Factions and personal ties are often formed on the basis of provincial origins, school ties, the same graduating class (as in the case of the military ties), common experience in the past, or a common patron who had assisted the members in financial and other matters. Personal ties (*inmaek*) constitute an extremely important political factor even under circumstances of curtailed political activities. In contrast with political factions in Japan, which in some way contribute to stable party policies, Korean political factions and groupings tend to be fragmented, amorphous, and often lacking in strong personal leadership.

Finally, the government's occasional banning of existing leaders from active political participation, as happened during the early Park as well as the Chun periods, makes institutionalization of parties extremely difficult. Certain other legal measures, including regulations controlling political activities, have reduced the chances for party continuity and stability.

The Korean party system, for all its unstable and fragile nature, has exhibited an enduring tendency since the 1950s. It is partly due to the presidential system of government that the country has had for the most part the proclivity of the politicians to gather around two major parties—one for and the other against the government. This is exactly what happened in the wake of the February 1985 election. The ruling party had no choice but to accept the situation although its own preference was obviously a multiparty system in which the opposition would be divided among several parties. Until the two Kims went their separate ways in the 1987 presidential election, the two-party system survived in its basic form even when the opposition party split between the hard-liners and the "accommodationists," as most of the opposition members then joined the splinter Reunification Democratic Party.

Various social and political groups play important roles—both negative and positive—in the democratization of South Korea. What role the workers and farmers play in the democratic institutionalization depends very much upon the government's ability to sustain economic vitality and expansion and to channel their demands and aspirations through an orderly and legitimate process. The serious labor disturbances in the spring of 1980, as well as in the mid-1980s, indicate that there is a potential for further problems in case the workers' demands are not adequately responded to and/or there is a limit in the government's ability to control and establish order. With a very young population entering the labor market in large numbers workers will become increasingly assertive and susceptible to ideological mobilization. Since the early 1960s successive regimes have limited, through legal and extralegal means, the organizational activities of the workers. With political democratization the scope of their organization, activities, and demands is likely to expand radically. Unless institutional means (primarily parties) are found to represent their interests and channel political aspirations, worker participation will take place in large part outside of the regular political process, seriously straining the effort to consolidate democracy.

The farmers are not likely to resort to collective disorderly actions, but their continued positive support for the existing government—even if it is an authoritarian one—has been indispensable for any government party in sustaining an electoral majority in South Korea. For all the emphasis on economic growth and industrialization the Park Chung Hee government had a strongly agrarian orientation, emphasizing the need to provide benefits to the rural areas. Even under the Chun government, which has paid more attention to industrial and urban problems, rural areas have been the mainstay of political support for the ruling party. It is one of the many ironies of South Korean democracy that assurance of electoral success in the rural areas has been an important condition for the party in power to implement measures that enable meaningful political competition, the key element in political democracy.

Because of the large number and concentration of university students in major cities, their political role has been and will continue to be very important for some time to come. Their agitation has made the continuation of authoritarian rule difficult. Similarly, however, student activism will prove to be a major challenge to a democratic government in its consolidation, as their extrainstitutional political participation will not only immobilize the government but also give foes of democracy a justification to take over power through undemocratic means. A combination of political, social, psychological, and organizational factors makes and keeps the student situation in South Korea fluid. Student protest is becoming increasingly well organized, ideological, and violence-prone.

Generally speaking there are three ways of looking at student political activism in Korea. Some regard it as an essentially passing phenomenon at a certain stage in industrial development. According to this view student activism will run out of steam on its own accord and normalcy will be restored after a period of unrest, as it seems to have been the case, for example, in Japan. Others argue that student activism in Korea is a response to a particular combination of socioeconomic and international circumstances, so that no matter what kind of a government is in power it is likely to pose a serious political problem for a considerable period of time. An eclectic view would agree with the second view in that it regards as inevitable the existence of an ideologically committed minority of students who will seriously challenge the existing socioeconomic system under any kind of politics—authoritarian or democratic—as long as the basic socioeconomic structure is maintained. The third view differs from the second in arguing that these radical students are able to take advantage of antiauthoritarian sentiments and mobilize the support of a large number of students only when the political system is not democratic.

If the third view is accurate, with the passage of time and as the democratization process proceeds, radical and activist students will be deprived of the most important justification for mobilizing the support of other students. But this will be only a slow and gradual process that will involve many setbacks and detours, particularly in view of accumulation of the grievances of several generations of students who have opposed, and suffered under, successive authoritarian regimes. Nonetheless, in due course, and with improved situations in both economy and politics, the "student problem," as it is called in South Korea, will become far less serious than it has been so far.

The military plays a crucial role in politics, indirectly by providing or witholding support for a government and directly by taking over power. In a country that devotes a disproportionate amount of human and material resources to defense and security, the military can easily prevail upon the civilian sector in carrying out a political role for itself. The military may temporarily retreat from active involvement in politics, under pressures from the sentiments and forces against military-dominated authoritarian government. But it will always lurk over the shoulders of a civilian regime, either as a supportive force or a potential threat to its existence. As we have seen, the increased propensity and capability of the military to play a political role was a legacy left by the Park government. Thus the military became ready to intervene when it felt there was the need and opportunity. After several decades of direct and indirect intervention, however, the military is now acutely aware that a government cannot rule in South Korea without the consent of the governed. It is thus not likely that the military will intervene in politics without major provocation. Experience in other countries such as Brazil has shown that the military can agree to take a back seat on its own accord when the civilian sector offers a moderate alternative.

• CONCLUSION: SOUTH KOREAN DEMOCRACY AT A CROSSROADS •

With the rapid increases in social complexity and affluence, political awareness, and international involvement, South Korea faces growing pressure for more pluralistic and democratic politics. However, democratization and its consolidation will encounter many difficulties and take time.

Korea is a modernizing society undergoing rapid socioeconomic change. Thus one must consider the problem of democracy in Korea, above all, within the context of political consequences of social and economic modernization. Modernization entails social mobility, industrialization, rational and secularized thinking, and political awakening. On the negative side for political stability secularization undermines traditional bases of political authority. Furthermore, increased awareness creates demands and expectations that cannot be met by the government. Industrialization will tend to create new social and ideological cleavages and conflicts. Social mobility and urbanization would make people more susceptible to ideological agitation and disorderly mass action. On the positive side for democracy rational thinking will make more feasible and necessary electoral choice of the government. Improved communication and greater awareness will make it difficult to maintain an authoritarian government. Economic growth and social development will contribute to social groups such as the middle class, which would support a democratic system of government.

Given these general tendencies, what actually happens to the politics of a modernizing society during a particular period in its history will depend upon the following several factors: (1) the nature of the traditional society; (2) the ways in which social change (modernization) has come about—for example, whether it has taken place in a controlled or uncontrolled manner; (3) the timing of the period in question in the modernization process; (4) the external environment of the country; and (5) the ways in which benefits of socioeconomic change are distributed and such distribution perceived.

Turning first to the traditional legacy, before the process of modernization began in the late nineteenth century, Korea had been an authoritarian society ruled by a highly centralized bureaucracy under an autocratic monarch. This was in sharp contrast with such feudal societies as traditional Japan that, although equally authoritarian, had maintained a pluralistic and decentralized polity. The concentration of power in the central government in Korea was further heightened in the twentieth century during Japanese rule, which imposed on Korea a highly centralized colonial administration. Until the end of World War II, Koreans had experienced only a highly centralized executive power that was neither checked nor balanced by countervailing power groups such as regional lords or elected representatives. In South Korea today there is still a highly unbalanced development of political institutions—that is, the "overdevelopment" of the output institutions such as the bureaucracy and the military as opposed to the "underdevelopment" of input organizations such as political parties and interest groups.

Second, social change in Korea took place in an uncontrolled and indiscriminate way. During the colonial period the traditional elite lost its power and social status; much of its values were discredited, and its practices were discarded. Korea experienced a total dismantling of its political institutional and authority structures. Socioeconomic modernization was introduced to Korea by a foreign elite who had no interest in preserving its traditional institutions. Thus, when Koreans had the opportunity to form their own government after their liberation from Japanese colonial rule, they had to build their political structure from the very beginning. They had not preserved any traditional mechanisms by which loyalty to the new government could be generated; excessive burdens would be placed on new means of legitimacy such as elections, which are yet to be fully institutionalized.

What kind of politics a modernizing society is likely to experience at a given time period depends in part upon how much time has elapsed after the modernization process began. South Korea's experiments in modern politics had their beginning only four decades ago. It did not have satisfactory results with either the "charismatic" leadership of Syngman Rhee or parliamentary democracy during the 1960–1961 period. Such an unsatisfactory experience with other systems might be called "legitimacy by default"—that is, the acceptance, albeit without enthusiasm, by the people out of the feeling that other alternatives were not much more desirable. A governmental system that would have been rejected if it had been attempted before experiments with other systems were made might be deemed acceptable because of the unhappy experience with the earlier ones. Now authoritarianism has had its turn—a long one at that—and has been decidedly rejected as a suitable system for South Korea today.

As for the fourth factor, South Korea has been under constant and acute security threat since 1948, a devastating war having taken place in the 1950–1953 period. For this reason it has had to maintain a large military establishment, a government capable of mobilizing national resources for defense purposes, and a society oriented toward maximizing security against internal subversion and external attack. Such requirements have tended to favor the rise of a "firm" and strong state. Indeed a substantial portion of the people seem to feel that a "soft" state will not be able to cope with the security problem nor to handle the task of economic development that is deemed necessary for security. A corollary of this argument is that a strong state is not compatible with a democratic system of government.

Finally, the dilemma of liberal democracy has been especially acute in South Korea because of the serious social and ideological cleavage between the conservatives and the radical Left. The division of the country between the communist-controlled north and anticommunist south has been primarily responsible for the intolerant, anti-Left attitude among key groups in South Korea such as the armed forces, the police, the bureaucracy, and individuals in the "establishment." On the other hand radicalism has grown, particularly among the students and those who consider themselves belonging to the "deprived" groups, to the extent that it is seen by the conservatives as posing a genuine threat to the survival of the nation, not to mention to the existing socioeconomic order.

Radicalism in Korea exhibits traits of strong nationalistic and egalitarian beliefs.[21] The appeal of radicalism derives from the perception among many of an uneven distribution of the benefits of socioeconomic change and of the country's excessive dependence on foreign powers. Radical activists thus demand a complete overhaul of not only the political system but also the socioeconomic structure itself. This, however, hinders the democratization process. As the defenders of the socioeconomic status quo see it, the choice is between revolutionary change and defending the existing socioeconomic order rather than between liberal democracy and dictatorship. The result can be a vicious circle of oppressive measures and radical demands, leaving little room for democracy.

Nevertheless, Korea is at the threshold of an evolutionary process by which democracy is restored and takes root. The society's growing complexity and international involvement will result in increasing demand and pressure for pluralism, openness, and competition in politics. More important the political public, both in and out of the government, is anxious to achieve progress in democratization, even if it is a slow and sometimes a socioeconomically costly process. Whether the various factors that work against democratization can be successfully overcome by those factors that work for it will depend upon whether the polity as a whole can avoid confrontational politics and learn the necessary lessons from the unhappy experiences of the past.

• NOTES •

1. See, for example, Yun Ch'on-ju, *Han'guk chongch'i ch'egye* (*The Korean Political System*) (Seoul, 1981), pp. 189–248.

2. President Yun Po-son, who was a leading member of the New Democracy party, reportedly declared after learning about the coup: "The inevitable has come!" See Yun Po-son, *Kugugui kasibatkil (Thorny Road Toward National Salvation)* (Seoul, 1967), p. 110.

3. Juan Linz defines authoritarian regimes as "political systems with limited, not responsible, political pluralism; without elaborate guiding ideology (but with distinctive mentalities); without intensive or extensive political mobilization (except at some points in their development); and in which a leader (or occasionally a small group) exercises power within formally ill-defined but quite predictable limits." See Juan Linz, "Opposition in and Under an Authoritarian Regime," in Robert A. Dahl, ed., *Regimes and Oppositions* (New Haven: Yale University Press, 1973), p. 185.

4. Se-jin Kim, *The Politics of Military Revolution in Korea* (Chapel Hill, N.C.: University of North Carolina Press, 1971), p. 135.

5. Ibid., p. 136.

6. Chae-jin Lee, "South Korea: The Politics of Domestic-Foreign Linkage," *Asian Survey* (January 1973): pp. 99–101.

7. Sung-joo Han, "South Korea: The Political Economy of Dependency," *Asian Survey* 15 (January 1975): pp. 43–45; John K. C. Oh, "South Korea 1975: A Permanent Emergency," *Asian Survey* 16 (January 1976): pp. 74–75.

8. See, for example, Herbert P. Bix, "Regional Integration: Japan and South Korea in America's Asian Policy," in Frank Baldwin, ed., *Without Parallel: The American-Korean Relationship Since 1945* (New York: Pantheon Books, 1973), pp. 179–232; Gerhard Breidenstein, "Capitalism in South Korea," ibid., pp. 233–70.

9. Gregory Henderson, *Korea: The Politics of the Vortex* (Cambridge, Mass.: Harvard University Press, 1968); Edward Reynolds Wright, ed., *Korean Politics in Transition* (Seattle, Wash.: University of Washington Press, 1974); and Sung-joo Han, *The Failure of Democracy in South Korea* (Berkeley: University of California Press, 1974).

10. See U.S. House of Representatives, *Human Rights in South Korea: Implications for U.S. Policy*, Hearings before the Subcommittee on Asian and Pacific Affairs of the Committee of Foreign Affairs, 93rd Congress, 2nd Session (Washington, D.C., 1974).

11. Chang Won-jong, "Son'go Kyongje ron," ("Electoral Economics"), *Shin Dong-a* (June 1971): pp. 98–111.

12. Pyong-choon Hahm, "Toward a New Theory of Korean Politics: A Reexamination of Traditional Factors," in Wright, ed., *Korean Politics in Transition*, pp. 321–356.

13. For an excellent description of events in 1980, see Chong-Sik Lee, "South Korea in 1980: The Emergence of a New Authoritarian Order," *Asian Survey* 21 (January 1981): pp. 125–143.

14. This section borrows substantially from my article, "South Korea 1987: The Politics of Democratization," *Asian Survey* 28 (January 1988).

15. *Far Eastern Economic Review*, 5 February 1987, p. 16.

16. The *New York Times*, 22 June 1987, p. 1.

17. *Far Eastern Economic Review*, 9 July 1987, p. 8.

18. For example, Kim Dae Jung wrote after declaring candidacy that "the candidacy

of Kim Young Sam, my colleague in the opposition, increases the size of my lead."
International Herald Tribune, 11 November 1987.

    19. Wolgan Chosun, *Monthly* (December 1987): pp. 189–225.

    20. Ibid.

    21. For a definition of "radicalism" in Korea, see Sungjoo Han, *The Failure of Democracy in South Korea*, p. 5.

THAILAND

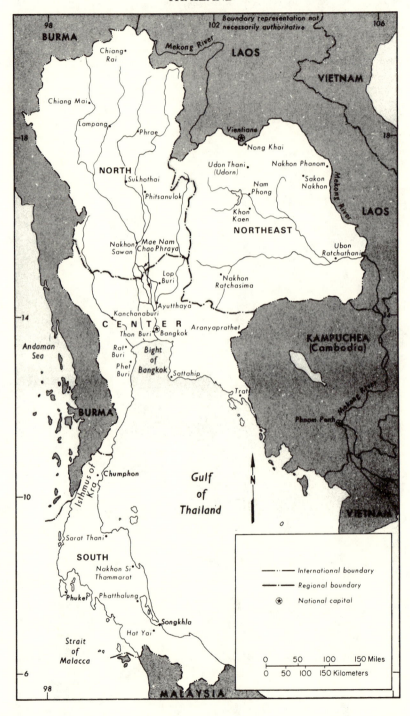

BURMA

Chiang Rai

Mekong River

LAOS

VIETNAM

Chiang Mai

Lampang

Phrae

Vientiane
Nong Khai

NORTH

Sukhothai

Udon Thani
(Udorn)

Nakhon Phanom

Sakon
Nakhon

Phitsanulok

Nam
Phong

Khon
Kaen

Mekong River

LAOS

Nakhon
Sawan

Mae Nam
Chao Phraya

NORTHEAST

Ubon
Ratchathani

Lop
Buri

Nakhon
Ratchasima

Ayutthaya

Kanchanaburi

C E N T E R

Aranyaprathet

Thon Buri Bangkok

KAMPUCHEA
(Cambodia)

Andaman
Sea

Rat
Buri

Bight
of
Bangkok

Phet
Buri

Sattahip

Trat

BURMA

Phnom Penh

Mekong River

Chumphon

Gulf
of
Thailand

N

VIETNAM

Sarat Thani

SOUTH

Nakhon Si
Thammarat

Phuket

Phatthalung

Songkhla

Hat Yai

Strait
of
Malacca

MALAYSIA

Boundary representation not
necessarily authoritative

————·—— International boundary

——·—— Regional boundary

⊛ National capital

0   50   100   150 Miles

0   50   100   150 Kilometers

• CHAPTER EIGHT •
Thailand: A Stable Semi-democracy
CHAI-ANAN SAMUDAVANIJA

• HISTORICAL REVIEW •

Alone in Southeast Asia Thailand was never colonized, maintaining its independence through the height of the Western imperial presence in the region. Traditionally the Thai political system has relied on the monarchy as the basis for its legitimacy. The monarchy reigned and ruled and was the focus for the loyalty, love, respect, and religious faith of the Buddhist populace. The king and the dynasty were central to both the ideology and reality of political rule. This was a classic centralized hierarchy, in which the entire focus of legitimacy and status emanated downward from the king through the royal elite to the ordinary citizen, and outward from the palace in Bangkok through the provincial towns to the villages.

Independence in Thailand means that it never experienced the imposition and transfer of institutions from the West that took place in many developing countries. The absence of colonialism also means that traditional structures, particularly the monarchy, the Buddhist Sangha (monastic order), and the military and civil bureaucracy were not disrupted. Although Thailand did not benefit from the process of democratization through the transfer of colonial institutions, neither did it suffer the kind of destruction of the social fabric that many European colonies in the Third World experienced. Because King Chulalongkorn (1868–1910) and his advisors were able to respond effectively to the colonial threat the country also escaped the necessity of overthrowing its colonial yoke. Since no independence movement was necessary the institutions and ideology concomitant with independence movements around the world—especially political parties and mobilized mass movements—never emerged. The Buddhist Sangha, which is the social and religious institution closest to the masses, was therefore not politicized like its counterparts in Burma, Sri Lanka, and Vietnam. Its traditional linkage with the monarchy was not disrupted, but instead has been fostered so that the two institutions have remained complementary to each other.[1] In this sense Thailand faced only a limited political challenge. This allowed the country to defer its true political development to the present.[2]

Democracy as a system of government was adopted in Thailand in June 1932 by a group of junior army, navy, and civilian officers calling themselves the People's Party. Prior to this, constitutionalism and democracy had been discussed among the Thai intelligentsia for a long time. In 1887, a group of princes and officials submitted a lengthy petition to King Chulalongkorn outlining the immediate problems facing Siam and suggested that a constitutional monarchy be instituted.[3] In the late 1880s Tienwan, a commoner and Buddhist scholar, argued in his magazine, *Tulawipak Pojanakit*, that the most effective way to promote justice was to institute a parliamentary form of government.[4] In the 1910s a group of lesser army officials attempted unsuccessfully to stage a coup to replace the absolute monarchy with a republican government. In 1917 Prince Chakrabongse submitted a memorandum to the king suggesting that it was time to grant some kind of constitution to the people. From the latter 1920s to May 1932—a month before the end of the absolute monarchy—the question of whether a democratic form of government was suitable for Siam was one of the major concerns of the regime. Starting from the reign of King Vajiravudh (1910–1925) the monarchy, as an institution, began to be questioned and criticized openly. With the increasing suffering from the Great Depression in the late 1920s, the desire for change was more pressing and resulted in growing awareness of the anachronism of the absolute monarchy.

The reactions of the kings to political reforms were quite similar.[5] Not all of them rejected constitutionalism and democracy as an ideal or a concept of governance, but the appropriateness of the model and practices were questioned. It had always been maintained by the old regime that while constitutional government might be desirable and even inevitable, it was still premature to establish such a system in Siam. The main reasons against the establishment of a constitutional government expressed by foreign advisors, the king, and senior princes were:[6]

1. There was no middle class in Siam. The Siamese peasants took little or no interest in public affairs. Most of the electorate were uneducated; hence to set up a parliament with real power without an educated electorate to control it would only invite trouble and corruption.
2. Parliamentary government was not suitable for the Siamese people, and it was even possible that there must also be certain racial qualities that the Anglo-Saxons possessed and the Siamese did not have to make democracy a successful form of government.
3. Not only was a real democracy very unlikely to succeed in Siam,

it might even be harmful to the interests of the people. The parliament would be entirely dominated by the Chinese.[7]

4. The great bulk of the people of Siam were as yet not trained in political or economic thought.[8] As for the students who returned from Britain, Europe, and the United States, their idea of democracy was half-baked, and their Western ideas were often superficial and misunderstood.

It is clear that the arguments against the adoption of a constitutional government were not so much concerned with democracy as a concept but rather as a form of government, especially its political implications.

Yet it was admitted that Siam would ultimately be forced by circumstances to adopt a democratic form of government, and hence the regime should be well prepared to direct this change gradually. King Prachatipok, however, cautioned that the main danger and the obstacle to this gradual experiment lay in impatience.[9]

Those who were impatient were the Western-educated military and civilian bureaucrats. In the absence of a sizable middle class, a large and strong bureaucracy became the locus of power in the new institutional arrangements. Thai politics after 1932 have therefore been dominated by the bureaucrats, as best described by David Wilson:

> Some 30 years ago the bureaucracy—much strengthened by the reorganization and development of the previous 40 years and by the new techniques of communications and control imported from the West—was cut free of the restraints of absolutism. As much as the leadership of the Thai revolution might have wished things to be otherwise, it was not able to muster much popular interest outside the bureaucracy upon which to base itself. As a result, politics has become a matter of competition between bureaucratic cliques for the benefits of government. In this competition the army—the best organized, most concentrated, and most powerful of the branches of the bureaucracy— has come out on top.[10]

It is ironical that soon after the success of the Westernized elites in their seizure of power from the monarchy, constitutional idealism gradually eroded into formalistic constitutionalism.[11] Since 1932 the bureaucratic elites have been the prime movers in political institutional arrangements under different constitutions. Because of periodic changes in the rules of the game, the scope of political competition, the level of political participation, and the extent to which civil and political liberties are guaranteed have varied according to the nature of the regime.

It should be noted that from 1932 to 1945 the only formal political institution in Thailand was a unicameral legislature composed of two categories of members—half elected and half appointed. The People's Party did not find it necessary to transform itself into a political party since its leading members and supporters were already appointed members of the National Assembly. Political parties in Thailand, therefore, emerged as late as 1946 and were only recognized as legal entities nine years later in 1955. What was institutionalized instead was the political role of the bureaucratic elites. The new leadership relied upon the bureaucracy to play a leading role in educating and mobilizing the mass to participate in elections, as well as to learn about democracy through the symbol of constitution.

Since half of the assembly members were mainly military and civilian officers, the legislative process became an extended arm of, and provided an additional function for, the bureaucracy. Although the new military-bureaucratic elites formed the only organized political group in society, they were not united. On the contrary, soon after June 1932 the young military faction within the People's Party emerged and was, by 1938, able to eliminate the senior members. And since the civilian faction of the People's Party did not develop itself into a broadbased political party, its power and influence gradually declined while that of the military faction rapidly increased, especially after its leader Luang Pibul became defense minister in late 1934 and prime minister in 1938.

From the beginning of constitutional rule, the role of the elected members of parliament was oriented toward internal legislative activities rather than to act as a major political institution for participation and competition for major positions of government power. Hence the electoral process in Thailand, which began as early as 1933, did not lead to the recruitment of political leadership at the top. It was only a tool to legitimate the political system and process in which competition for power was not linked with the electorate but with the factions in the military.

It seems that the objective of the constitution was to establish and strengthen the power position of the new regime rather than to develop a truly democratic political system. The constitution and constitutional symbols were utilized to distinguish between the *ancien* and the *new* regime. In 1933 the National Assembly passed a bill on the protection of the constitution. In the same year it passed another bill establishing a special court to deal with 238 persons who were involved in the Baworadej rebellion. The special court had no provision for appeals or petitions.

The passage of the Protection of the Constitution Act and the special court legislation reflected the ability of the People's Party to control the National Assembly, as well as to utilize it in legitimating their power. Although there was an effort to educate the masses in democratic rule, such an effort was highly formalistic and symbolic rather than substantive.

The 1932 Constitution, therefore, provided considerable stability for the regime, as evidenced by the fact that factional rivalry and competition for power among the military did not result in the abolishment of either the constitution or the parliament. Although there were eight cabinets in a period of six years (1932–1938), there were only two prime ministers, compared with the much more turbulent period three decades later (1969–1979) when there were ten cabinets with six prime ministers under four constitutions.

Political parties were not allowed to function in the first fifteen years of constitutional rule, and the voting method in the first election was indirect. (Each village elected its representatives; the village representatives chose those of the districts, who in turn chose the representatives of the province.) Political participation was a mobilized action in which officials of the Interior Ministry at the village and district levels played a significant role, a pattern not dissimilar to that existing in contemporary Thai politics. Hence early universal suffrage in Thailand did not lead to meaningful political participation or the emergence of political organizations, as happened in other societies. It should be pointed out also that universal suffrage was given to the people when they were not familiar with the principles and the workings of the new system. It is not surprising therefore that constitutional rule was finally replaced by an authoritarian military rule—first by Field Marshal Pibul, and later by Field Marshal Sarit and Field Marshal Thanom respectively.

Pibul's cabinets from 1938 to 1944 marked the high point of rule by the army. During this period, there were seven cabinets with a yearly average of 51 percent military men in the cabinets. Also in this same period, the yearly average of the percentage of military expenditure to total national spending increased to 33 percent, compared with 26 percent during the 1933–1937 period. With the rise to power of Pibul heroism and ultranationalism, with emphasis on leadership, began to develop. Such developments finally led to militarization, especially before the outbreak of World War II. In 1942 the government amended the constitution to extend the tenure of the parliament for two years, and in 1944 the tenure was extended for another two years.

Although Pibul's rise to power did not in any way affect the constitution, his leadership style and ultranationalistic policies greatly affected civil liberties. His *ratthaniyom* marked the first and most systematic intervention of the state into the lives of the Thai citizenry. The Thai people were told what to do and what not to do by their "great leader." The state assumed its role in remolding the values and behavior of the citizens by imposing several orders, rules, and regulations. The nationalist drive also resulted in a number of discriminatory policies against the Chinese minority. Strangely enough, there was no challenge to the government's policies as being unconstitutional, either by the parliament or by the press. This reflected the weakness of democratic values and the inherently autocratic traits in Thai society, which were utilized to a great extent by Pibul and his principal political adviser.

Before the outbreak of World War II the Pibul Government was mainly controlled by members of the 1932 junior clique, including

Pridi—a prominent civilian leader who was the chief ideologist of the
1932 coup group. World War II brought about a major conflict between
Pibul and Pridi. The former chose to ally with the Japanese and the Axis
Powers while the latter identified himself with the Allied Powers. When
Thailand declared war against the Allies Pridi formed an underground
movement against the Japanese and the Axis Powers. The defeat of the
Japanese and the Axis resulted in the collapse of Pibul's military gov-
ernment.

Postwar Politics

Postwar politics was largely a matter of struggle among three groups for
dominance. One was the military group that supported Pibul and was
based mainly in the army. The second group, at first centering on Pridi,
was rooted in parliament and the civil service. The third group, considerably smaller, was traditionalist and royalist in character. This group
was led by Khuang Aphaiwong and Seni Pramoj.[12]

After Pibul's resignation in July 1945, which coincided with the
Japanese surrender in the following month, the National Assembly
began to play a dominant role in the political system for the first time.
Political parties were formed in late 1945 and early 1946. A new constitution was drafted and promulgated to replace the 1932 Constitution in
May 1946. The new constitution was an attempt by the temporary
civilian coalition of Pridi and Khuang to establish new institutional
arrangements to minimize the power of the military. It provided for a
bicameral legislature: the House of Representatives, to be elected
directly, and the Senate to be elected indirectly by the House. At the
first election of the Senate, most of the candidates were the appointed
members of the former National Assembly who were Pridi's supporters.

Politics during this civilian interregnum was highly unstable. From
August 1945 to November 1947 there were eight cabinets and five
different prime ministers. Competition among civilian politicians,
together with charges of corruption, economic hardship as the result of
the war, and the mysterious death of King Ananda, led to a military
coup in November 1947. The coup group abolished the 1946 Constitution
and replaced it with an interim constitution, resulting in the January
1948 elections in which the Democrat Party won a majority. However,
after less than two months of his premiership the leader of the Democrat
Party, Khuang, was forced to resign by the army, and Field Marshal
Pibul was installed as the new Premier in April 1948.

In March 1949 a new constitution was promulgated. This constitution provided for a bicameral legislature like that of the 1946 version,
but with an appointed Senate instead of an elected one. The new
constitution barred officials from being members of the National

Assembly, thus separating the once-powerful military and civilian bureaucrats from active involvement in politics. Such arrangements antagonized the military and finally led to the "silent coup" in November 1951 by the same officers who organized the 1947 coup.

The coup group reinstated the 1932 Constitution, which provided for a unicameral legislature with two categories of members—half elected and half appointed. Ninety-one (or 74 percent) of the total 123 appointed in the 1951 parliament were military members, of whom 62 were army officers, 14 were navy, and 15 were air force officers. It is also noteworthy that 34 of them were the younger generation of middle-ranking officers (major to colonel). As David Wilson pointed out, with the reestablishment of the 1932 Constitution the principle of tutelage was again imposed on an assembly that had been free of it for six years. The government was therefore able to control the legislature through its appointed members and no longer faced serious difficulty in organizing a majority group to support it.[13] In February 1952 an Emergency Law providing the government with wide powers of arrest and press censorship was passed. In November of the same year an Anticommunist Law was approved by parliament by an almost unanimous vote.[14]

Following their consolidation of power in the 1951 "silent coup," the 1947 coup group became deeply involved in politics and commercial activities. They built up their economic base of power by setting up their own business firms, got control over state enterprises and semigovernment companies, and gained free shares from private firms mainly owned by Chinese merchants. This active involvement in business ventures resulted in the division of the group into two competing cliques—popularly known as the "Rajakru," under the leadership of Police General Phao Sriyanond, and Sisao Deves clique, under the leadership of Field Marshal Sarit Thanarat. Each controlled more than thirty companies in banking and finance, industry, and commerce.[15] This split between Phao, the police chief, and Sarit, the army chief, was seen as an attempt by Pibul to maintain his power by manipulating and balancing off these two factions. However, the events of 1955 to 1957 culminated in the coup of September 1957 in which Sarit ousted both Pibul and Phao. This coup mainly concerned a succession conflict; "When a situation of considerable tension had developed in the Bangkok political scene, the Sarit clique moved with the army to take over the government and 'clean up the mess.' "[16]

After the September 1957 coup the constitution was temporarily suspended, resulting in the dissolution of the parliament. The coup group appointed Pote Sarasin, the former Thai ambassador to the United States, as the premier of a caretaker government. A general election was held in December 1957 in which no party won a majority in the parliament. Lieutenant General Thanom Kittikachorn, a leading member of the coup group, was chosen as the prime minister in January 1958. However, as a result of the inability of the government to control the internal strife within its supported party as well as deteriorating economic conditions, Sarit staged another coup in October 1958. This time he abrogated the constitution, dissolved the parliament, banned political parties, arrested several politicians, journalists, writers, and labor leaders, declared martial law, and imposed censorship on newspapers. In 1959, an Interim Constitution was promulgated establishing an all-appointed constituent assembly whose main function was to draft a new "permanent constitution." The interim Constitution also gave tremendous power to the prime minister. From 1958 to 1963 Sarit used the power given by article 17 of that constitution to execute without trial eleven persons—five for arson, one for producing heroin, and four on charges of communism.[17]

Sarit's rule (1958–1963) has been characterized as a dictatorship, as a benevolent despotism, and as military rule. However, as a noted scholar of this period observed, Sarit's 1958 coup marked the beginning of a new political system that endured until at least the early 1970s. What Sarit did in effect was to overthrow a whole political system inherited from 1932, and to create one that could be termed more "Thai" in character.[18] Apart from his strongly anticommunist policy and his initiation of a National Development Plan that opened the way for the tremendous developmental activities of the following decades, the most significant change Sarit brought to the Thai political system was the activation of the role of the monarchy. As Thak rightly pointed out Sarit made it possible, without perhaps so intending, for the monarchy to grow strong enough to play an independent role after his death. The relative political weakness of Sarit's successors brought the throne even more clearly to the center of the political stage.[19]

After Sarit's death in 1963 Thanom became prime minister and commander of the army. In 1968 a new constitution was promulgated after ten years of drafting. The familiar vicious circle of Thai politics, evident in earlier periods, recurred. A semiparliamentary system was established with a two-house legislature. Two years after that conflicts developed within the government-supported party, leading to a military coup in November 1971. Another interim constitution was promulgated, providing for a single constituent assembly composed entirely of appointed members, most of whom were military and civil bureaucrats.

The Breakdown of Military Rule

After the 1971 coup a new and ambitious strongman emerged: Colonel Narong Kittikachorn, the prime minister's son and Deputy Prime Minister Praphat's son-in-law. Narong was appointed assistant secretary-general of the National Executive Council, the supreme body of government administration after the 1971 coup. Apart from being the commander of the powerful Bangkok-based Eleventh Infantry Regiment, he acted as head of a new Committee to Suppress Elements Detrimental to Society, and was also made deputy secretary-general of a new anti-corruption agency. Narong was seen as the heir apparent to the prime ministership. This kind of dynastic succession, never before seen in the Thai military, generated tremendous discontent and criticism from the general public.

Leaders of the student movement were well aware that the growing popular animosity to Narong and the military offered a potentially unique opportunity to put pressure on the military for political reforms, a new constitution, and an elected parliament. On 6 October 1973 student leaders and political activists were arrested while they were distributing leaflets demanding immediate promulgation of a new constitution. The government announced that the police had uncovered a communist plot to overthrow the administration.

From 6 October through 13 October hundreds of thousands of students and others gathered to support the cause of the jailed students. Although the government agreed to release the students and promised to quicken the drafting of the new constitution, riot police on the morning of 14 October clashed with a group of demonstrators in front of the royal palace, thereby sparking violence in other parts of the city. In the meantime a deep split was developing within the military's own leadership. General Krit Sivara, army commander-in-chief, began to adopt a position independent from the Thanom-Praphat group. General Krit's intervention rendered further military suppression untenable, leaving Thanon, Praphat, and Narong no alternative but to flee the country, after being personally ordered by the king to do so. The king appointed Professor Sanya Thammasak, former chief justice of the Supreme Court and rector of Thammasat University, as the prime minister.

The Failure of Democracy, 1974–1976[20]

The student-led uprising of 14 October 1973 brought back once again the period of open politics and democratic experimentation. The 1974 Constitution was patterned after the 1949 Constitution. It limited the number of senators to only 100, with much less power than the elected House of Representatives. Government officials elected to the House or appointed to the Senate had to resign their bureaucratic posts; votes of no confidence remained the sole prerogative of the House; and the prime minister had to be a member of the House of Representatives. These provisions set the stage for a more open political system based on party and pressure group politics.

From 1974 to 1976 the political climate in Thailand became highly

volatile. Pressure group politics, mobilization, polarization, and confrontation replaced the usual political acquiescence and the achievement of
consensus through bargaining between established patron-client factions.
The students, labor unions, and farmer groups were most active in
expressing grievances and making demands, which led them into conflict with government officials, business interests, and landowners.

Primarily because the previous governing elite (especially the army)
was discredited, and because the abrupt departure of Thanom, Praphat,
and Narong had damaged existing patron-client linkages, no single
government political party emerged. Several factional groups formed,
each composed of members of earlier government parties. Progressive
elements also were unable to coalesce into a coherent political party,
instead splintering into numerous competing groups. Fragmentation
and political polarization of both Left and Right characterized Thai
politics during this period. The Democrat Party, the nation's oldest, was
divided into three competing factions; each formed its own political
party to contest in the 1975 elections. The members of the defunct
government party were also split into several competing groups, which
subsequently led to the formation of four identifiable parties, namely,
the Thai Nation Party, the Social Nationalist Party, the Social Justice
Party, and the Social Agrarian Party. These parties were linked with the
business community and the military-bureaucratic factions. Apart from
these parties, there were two new parties in the center-left spectrum, the
Social Action Party and the New Force Party, and two leftist parties, the
United Socialist Front and the Socialist Party of Thailand. Although
forty-two parties contested the 1975 election, only twenty-two gained
seats in the House. The Democrat Party, which had the largest number
of seats in the House (72 out of 269), formed a ninety-one-seat minority
government in February 1975, but the House on 6 March voted no
confidence in the newly formed government. The Social Action Party
under the leadership of Kukrit Pramoj, with only eighteen seats in the
House, together with three other major parties and ten minor parties,
formed a new coalition government. However, this government had a
built-in instability because of the lack of trust among leaders of the
various parties. Each party, aware of the possible dissolution of the
House at almost any moment, focused on building its own small empire.
As 1975 progressed, the pace of political maneuvering accelerated. On
12 January 1975—two days before the Democrat Party's scheduled vote
of a no confidence motion—Kukrit dissolved the parliament. In the
April 1976 election four major parties—the Democrat, Thai Nation,
Social Justice, and Social Action—emerged as the dominant powers,
compared with the multiplicity of small parties in the House elected
fifteen months earlier.

The election results, shown in Table 8.1, demonstrated several
continuing features of Thai politics. The national average voter turnout

was slightly reduced, 46 percent compared with 47 percent in 1975. Only 29 percent voted in Bangkok, compared with the 33 percent that had voted fifteen months earlier. Leftist parties suffered a humiliating defeat as the electorate displayed a strong conservative tendency in its overall orientation, a preference for political safety over political development. The two socialist parties dropped from twenty-five to three seats, or in percentage terms from 10 to 1 percent of the House as a whole; the progressive New Force Party declined from twelve to three seats. Thus the perceived radical alternative so touted in the months after October 1973 was obliterated by the results of a free election. The Socialists won even fewer seats in April 1976 than in the House elected under military rule in February 1969.

These election results confirmed certain basic trends. One fact was clear: while conflict between the political forces committed to change and those committed to maintenance of the status quo was continuing to escalate, most citizens long for the stability and security of an earlier, easier era. As they reflected on the extremes of violence that had become commonplace over the preceding months, many Thais were seriously asking familiar questions: "Can representative political institutions really survive in Thailand under these pressures?" And, of course, "When will the Army finally intervene?"

The Democrat Party's leader, Seni Pramoj (brother of Kukrit), took over as prime minister on 20 April, at the head of a grand coalition comprising the Democrat, Thai Nation, Social Justice, and Social Nationalist parties. Together these four parties controlled 206 of the 279 seats in the new House of Representatives. However, due in large measure to the weak and vacillating leadership of its aging head, the Democrat Party had by 1976 become divided into two sharply opposing factions, one progressive and the other conservative. The conservative faction, in alliance with other rightist parties, ultrarightist groups, and the military, attacked the progressive faction as being leftist and communist. The factionalism and the weakness of civilian leadership coincided with the growth of leftist ideology and political polarization. Amid these situations came the fall of South Vietnam, Laos, and Cambodia to the Communists. Hence, when a crisis occurred in October 1976 following Field Marshal Thanom's return to Bangkok, the weak and faction-ridden civilian government was unable to control the violent and chaotic situation. On 6 October 1976 the military once again intervened.

The Resumption of Military Rule

The 1976 coup resulted in a familiar autocratic political pattern with even more extremist overtones. The 1974 consitution, parliament, and all political parties were abolished; martial law was proclaimed. The coup group appointed Thanin Kraivichien, a staunchly anticommunist judge, as the new prime minister. Over the months that followed, Thailand was immersed in intense reactionary rule. Several thousand students were arrested while others fled to join the Communist Party of Thailand in the hills.

The ultrarightist policies of the Thanin government—especially its stipulated twelve-year plan for political development, its obsession with communism, and unnecessary aggressiveness toward communist regimes in neighboring countries—resulted in increasing polarization of the Thai society.[21]

Thanin's anticommunist zeal brought about rigorous indoctrination of civil servants, repressive educational control, pressure on labor unions, severe press censorship, and a rigid foreign policy. The military leaders, especially the emerging "Young Turks" in the army, became convinced that Thanin was leading the country to disaster, that his extremist policies were having a most divisive effect and were indirectly strengthening the Communist Party of Thailand (CPT). On 20 October 1977 the Thanin government was overthrown by the same group that had staged the coup that brought Thanin to power one year earlier.

The coup group eased social conflicts and political tension by abolishing the 1977 Constitution and replacing it with a more liberal one. A bicameral legislature with an elected lower House was again introduced and a general election was held in April 1979. However, the new military regime, like its predecessors, maintained its control over the legislature through the appointed Senate to ensure political stability.

The new government adopted a liberal policy toward the problem of communism by granting amnesty to the students and others who were arrested in the 6 October incident as well as to those who had fled to join the CPT. This move, together with other subsequent political measures and reduced support of the CPT by China, led to a diminution of the insurgency in the mid-1980s.

A significant political development from 1977 to 1980 was the rise to political influence of the "Young Turks" within the military establishment. The emergence of these young colonels as a pressure group coincided with the fragmentation of power among army generals. Their political importance stemmed essentially from their strategically important positions within the army organization, which provided a power base for the coup group and the government formed after the coup. Since parliamentary politics after the 1979 election was still unstable because of the proliferation of political parties and interplay conflict in the coalition government, and the military was still deeply split at the higher echelons, the Young Turks were able to exert pressure for changes in leadership. In 1980 they withdrew support for General Kriengsak's government, forcing the prime minister to resign, and installed General Prem Tinsulanond in his place. However, the Young Turks became frustrated a year later with the premier's choice of certain ministers (in a cabinet reshuffle occasioned by interparty conflict in the coalition government). On 1 April 1981 the Young Turks tried and failed to capture state power, despite their overwhelming military forces. The failure of their coup attempt was due largely to their inability to get the tacit approval and support of the king, who openly supported Prem. The Young Turks' power and influence thus ended abruptly.

As a result of the failed coup thirty-eight officers were discharged, leaving a power vacuum in the army. At the same time Major General Arthit Kamlange—who was responsible for the suppression of the 1 April 1981 coup attempt—rose rapidly to the rank of full general and became commander of the army in October 1982. Although he attempted to prove himself as a new strongman and as a successor to Prem, General Arthit found it difficult to advance his political career in that direction. The military's failure to amend the constitution in 1983 to allow permanent officials to hold cabinet positions made it impossible for General Arthit to enjoy the status his predecessors had as commanders of the army. As the army suffered a big split after the 1 April 1981 coup attempt, and the dismissed officers still maintained considerable influence among their troops, there was deep concern and widespread fear of a possible countercoup if a coup was carried out.

In September 1985, while the prime minister was in Indonesia and General Arthit was in Europe, Colonel Manoon Roopkajorn, the leader of the Young Turks, and a group of officers in the Armored Cavalry Regiment still loyal to him, staged an unsuccessful coup. Two former commanders-in-chief of the armed forces (General Kriangsak Chommanan and General Serm Na Nakorn), two former deputy commanders-in-chief, and a serving deputy commander-in-chief of the armed forces (Air Chief Marshal Arun Promthep), were put on trial together with thirty low-ranking officers, while Colonel Manoon was allowed to leave the country. The September 1985 coup created a wider rift between the prime minister and General Arthit since the premier's advisers suspected that the latter was behind the unsuccessful bid for power. Subsequently relations between General Prem and General Arthit became increasingly strained. On 1 May 1986 the government decree on diesel-fueled vehicle registration was voted down in the House, leading the prime minister to dissolve the parliament.

The dissolution of the parliament led to the formation of new political parties that openly declared their hostility toward General Prem. The scheduled election on 27 July 1986 was four days before the retirement date of General Arthit, and it was speculated by the premier's aides that General Arthit could make use of his positions as commander-in-chief of the armed forces and commander-in-chief of the army to

318   SAMUDAVANIJA

influence the outcomes of the election. On 27 May 1986 the premier
removed General Arthit as army commander-in-chief and appointed his
former aide, General Chaovalit Yongchaiyuth, to the post.

Table 8.1 Comparative Elections Results, January 1975 and April 1976, for Largest Parties
in Thailand

	January 1975		April 1976	
	Percent of Popular Vote	Percent of Seats	Percent of Popular Vote	Percent of Seats
Democrat	18.0	26.8	25.4	40.9
Social Justice	14.8	16.7	10.7	10.0
Thai Nation	12.2	10.5	18.1	20.1
Social Action	11.4	6.7	17.8	16.1
Social Agrarian	7.7	7.1	4.3	3.2
Social Nationalist	7.1	6.0	3.3	2.9
New Force	5.9	4.5	7.0	1.1
Socialist	4.7	5.6	1.9	0.7
Socialist Front	3.8	3.7	1.0	0.4
Peace-Loving People	3.5	2.9	—	—
Thai Reformist	2.0	1.1	—	—
Thai	1.7	1.5	—	—
People's Justice	1.7	2.2	—	—
Democracy	1.7	0.8	0.3	0.4
Labor	0.9	0.4	0.8	0.4
Agriculturist	0.7	0.4	—	—
Sovereign	0.6	0.7	—	—
Thai Land	0.5	0.7	—	—
Free People	0.5	0.4	—	—
People's Force	0.4	0.7	4.0	1.1
Economist	0.3	0.4	—	—
Provincial Development	0.2	0.4	0.5	0.7
Dharmacracy	—	—	1.4	0.4
Protecting Thailand	—	—	1.2	0.4
Democratic Front	—	—	1.0	0.4
Thai Society	—	—	0.7	0.4
New Siam	—	—	0.4	0.4
Progressive Society	—	—	0.1	0.4
Total	100.3	100.2	99.9	100.4

Sources: Chai-Anan Samudavanija and Sethaporn Cusripituck, An Analysis of the 1975
Election Results (Kan wikrorh phon kan luak tang samachik sapha phu tan ratsadorn B.E.
2518) (Bangkok: National Research Council, February 1977); Rapin Tavornpun, "Popular Votes in 1976 Elections," The Nation Weekly, 15 July 1976).
Note: Popular votes totaled 17,983,892 in 1975 and 18,981,135 in 1976. Seats totaled 269
in 1975 and 279 in 1976.

The 27 July 1986 general election did not drastically change the
political situation prior to it. Although the Democrat Party won the
largest number of seats in the parliament (100 out of 374), there were
another fourteen parties elected with representation ranging from one
to sixty-three seats (Table 8.2). It was therefore inevitable that a coalition

government be formed, and it is interesting to note that this has been the pattern of government since 1975. The only difference is that coalition governments after 1983 have been more stable than their counterparts during 1975–1976 and 1979–1982.

Table 8.2   Results of the Thailand General Elections 1983, 1986

	1983		1986	
	Number of Seats Won	Percent of Seats	Number of Seats Won	Percent of Seats
Democrat	56	7.3	100	28.8
Chart Thai (Thai Nation)	73	22.5	63	18.2
Social Action	92	28.4	51	14.7
Prachakorn Thai (Thai Citizen)	36	11.1	24	6.9
United Democratic[a]	—	—	38	10.9
Rassadorn (People's party)[a]	—	—	18	5.2
Community Action[a]	—	—	15	4.3
Ruam Thai (United Thai)[a]	—	—	19	5.4
Progressive	3	1.0	9	2.6
National Democratic	15	4.6	3	0.9
Muan Chon (Mass party)[a]	—	—	3	0.9
Liberal[a]	—	—	1	0.3
New Force	—	—	1	0.3
Puang Chon Chao Thai (Thai people)	—	—	1	0.3
Democratic Labor	—	—	1	0.3
Independents[b]	49	15.1	—	—
Total	324	100.0	347	100.0

Notes: [a] Parties formed after 1983.
[b] In the 1986 election candidates had to belong to political parties in order to be qualified to contest.

The outcome of the 1986 election did not affect the pattern of leadership succession. General Prem, who did not run in the election and does not belong to any party, was invited by seven political parties (Democrat, Thai Nation, Social Action, People's Community Action, Thai Citizen, and United Thai) to head the government. It is clear that the support from the military was the key factor in the decisions of political parties to nominate him as the premier. This confirms our assertion (see below) that the semidemocratic system is still the most accepted political arrangement in Thailand.

The present Thai political system can be called neither a democracy nor an authoritarian system. It falls between the two political modes and has been termed a semidemocratic government in which the bureaucratic elite have made certain concessions to the nonbureaucratic forces to allow participation in the political process. The semidemocratic system is a political compromise—made possible through distinctive constitutional arrangements—between the bureaucratic and the nonbureaucratic forces.

• HISTORICAL ANALYSIS •

Constitutional Structure and Change

During the half century from 1932 to 1987, Thailand has had thirteen constitutions, thirteen general elections, sixteen coups (nine of which were successful), and forty-three cabinets. There have been sixteen prime ministers, of whom six were military officers and ten civilians. During this period military prime ministers have been in power altogether for forty-four years, while their civilian counterparts were in office for a total of only eleven years. Moreover, some civilian prime ministers were simply fronts for the military.

Successful military interventions usually resulted in the abrogation of constitutions, abolishment of parliaments, and suspension of participant political activity. Each time, however, the military reestablished parliamentary institutions of some kind. This reflects the concern for legitimacy of every military group that came to power after 1932. But because of the weakness of extrabureaucratic forces and the lack of broadbased support for political parties, what has occurred in Thailand since 1932 is referred to as factional constitutionalism.[22] This explains why there have been as many as thirteen constitutions and seven constitutional amendments in a period of fifty-five years. It also explains why democracy in Thailand has many versions and is still being interpreted differently by various groups.

In Thailand a constitution does not normally provide for the general and neutral rules of the game to regulate participation and competition between political groups. On the contrary, it has been used as a major tool in maintaining the power of the group that created it. What Thailand has experienced is not constitutionalism and constitutional government, but rather different kinds of regimes that adjusted and readjusted institutional relationships between the executive and the legislative branches according to their power position vis-à-vis their opponents.

Constitutional arrangements have basically presented three main patterns. One is the democratic pattern, which takes as its model the British parliamentary system, in which the elected legislature and political parties have dominant and active roles in the political process. Under such a system the prime minister must come from a major political party and is an elected MP. An upper house may be maintained but the number of its members is relatively small and its power minimal. In this model military leaders have no opportunity to become prime ministers and bureaucrats are not allowed to take political positions. The second, a semidemocratic pattern, favors a strong executive vis-à-vis the legislative branch. The prime minister does not have to be an elected member of the parliament; the upper house is composed mostly of military and civilian bureaucrats with more or less equal powers to the lower house; and the total number of senators is almost equal to the number of elected representatives.

The third, the undemocratic pattern, has no elected parliament. A legislature is maintained but its members are all appointed, and it acts as a mere rubber stamp on executive decisions that require enactment into laws. Under this system political parties are not allowed to function; hence no elections are held.

Table 8.3 shows the types of constitutions and the periods in which they were in effect.

The most important aspect of a Thai constitution is not the provision and protection of civil and political liberties, but the extent to which it allows the elected House of Representatives to participate in the political process. While, theoretically, the constitution is the highest law of the land, the constitution limits its own power by stating that citizens have political and civil rights and liberties "except where laws otherwise so stipulate." Thus laws, executive decrees, etc. have precedence over constitutional rights and liberties. Such laws limiting rights and freedoms are framed in terms of national security, public order, public morality. Seldom, if ever, is a law challenged on the basis of unconstitutionality. Even if a constitutional issue were to be raised, it would not be decided by an independent judiciary but by a Constitutional Tribunal composed of three ex officio officers (president of parliament, chief justice of the Supreme Court, and director-general of the Department of Prosecutions) and four jurists appointed by parliament. Thus, while the form and structure of constitutional government is visible, in reality the game is fixed; the political deck is stacked in favor of the executive.[23]

In other words constitutionalism was not designed so much to constrain the rulers as to facilitate their rule. The constitutions therefore did not prescribe the effective norms of political behavior, but were used to cast a cloak of legitimacy over the operations of succeeding rulers and to set the stage for a play to be enacted by the extrabureaucratic performers—parliaments, political parties, electors.[24]

Having an elected House of Representatives means that a mechanism must be devised and agreement reached between elected politicians and nonelected bureaucratic politicians (military included) on the sharing of power in the cabinet. Whenever this relationship is strained the tendency has always been to abolish the constitution so that the elected House of Representatives will be automatically terminated. Similarly, having an entirely appointed assembly means that such mechanism and agreement have to be arranged among the bureaucratic elites, especially among the military.

Out of 13 constitutions, only 3 can be classified as "democratic" while 6 have been "semidemocratic" and 4 have been "nondemocratic" (Table 8.3). From 1932 to 1987, "democratic" constitutions were in

Table 8.3   Constitutions in Thailand: June 1932–December 1987

Consti-tution	Types of constitution					
	Demo-cratic (number)	Years in effect	Semi-demo-cratic (number)	Years in effect	Undemo-cratic (number)	Years in effect
1932[a] (provisional)			✓	5 months 12 days		
1932[b]			✓	13 years 5 months		
1946[c]	✓	1 year 6 months				
1947[d]			✓	1 year 4 months 13 days		
1949[e]	✓	2 years 8 months 6 days				
1932[f] (amended 1952)			✓	6 years 7 months 12 days		
1959[g]					✓	9 years 4 months 23 days
1968[h]			✓	3 years 4 months 28 days		
1972[i]					✓	1 year 9 months 21 days
1974[j]	✓	2 years				
1976[k]					✓	363 days
1977[l]					✓	1 year 1 month 13 days
1978*[m]			✓	9 years		
Total[n]	3	6 years 2 months 6 days	6	34 years 3 months 5 days	4	13 years 3 months 25 days

*   Still in effect as of 21 December 1987
Notes:[a] 27 June 1932–10 December 1932; [b] 10 December 1932–9 May 1946; [c] 10 May 1946–8 November 1947; [d] 9 November 1947–22 March 1949; [e] 23 March 1949–29 November

effect for only 6 years and 2 months while the "semidemocratic" and "undemocratic" have been in effect (through December 1987) for 34 years, 3 months and 13 years, 4 months respectively. (No constitution was in effect for 1 year, 8 months.) In other words, during these fifty-five years there were only six years when political institutions could operate within the democratic rules of the game. Moreover, these six years were thinly spread out among three different short periods.

Political Institutionalization

The weakness of the democratic pattern of rule can be attributed to the low level of political institutionalization in Thailand, which is the consequence of three important factors: the frequency of coups d'état, the discontinuity of elected parliaments, and the weaknesses of political parties.

Military coups in Thailand are a means by which political leaders alternate in power. Therefore it is not necessary that political, social, and economic crises be preconditions for a military intervention, although they could facilitate the intervention, particularly when the civilian government's supporters are very strong and active. From 1932 through 1987 there have been altogether sixteen military interventions, nine of which were successful.

As military interventions have become more frequent the commitment of the military to democratic institutions has declined. This is indicated by the fact that in all the five coups during the 1932–1958 period the coup groups changed only the governments in power but did not abolish the constitution. Elections were held and political parties were allowed to function, although their roles in parliament were limited by the presence of the appointed members of the assembly. After 1958, however, military interventions usually resulted in the abolishment of the constitutions and the "freezing" of participant political activities. In the following period of twenty years (1958–1978) there were altogether seven constitutions, only one of which can be classified as "democratic" (1974 Constitution); the rest gave vast powers to an executive branch that was dominated by bureaucratic elites. The high frequency of military interventions in Thailand has had diverse negative effects upon democratic political institutions and has bred more instability within the political system as a whole.

While democratic political institutions suffered setbacks and

Notes to Table 8.3 *continued.*
1951; [f] 8 March 1952–20 October 1958; [g] 28 January 1959–20 June 1968; [h] 21 June 1968–17 November 1971; [i] 15 December 1972–6 October 1974; [j] 7 October 1974–6 October 1976; [k] 22 October 1976–20 October 1977; [l] 9 November 1977–21 December 1978; [m] 21 December 1978 to present. [n] Excludes a total of 1 year, 8 months, 22 days when no constitution was in effect.

discontinuity, the military has greatly strengthened its organizations and expanded its roles in several areas. During the 1976–1982 period the defense budget averaged about 20 percent of the total government expenditure. The military has also been granted each year a considerable secret fund, which could be used for intelligence operations but has also been widely used for internal security and political purposes. Several civic action programs, political education projects, and rightist movements have been financed from this fund.

Most of the mass communication media, particularly radio and television stations, are under the control of the military—which has undoubtedly reinforced its political potency. Out of 269 radio stations— all of which are government-owned—the military stations account for some 57 percent, while 33 percent are operated by the Public Relations Department and the rest by other ministries and educational institutions. The army also runs two television stations.[25] The military can utilize radio and television programs for psychological warfare and/or mobilizing mass movements in times of political crisis. For instance, the Armored School Radio played a very active role during 1975 and 1976 in mobilizing the rightist movement against the student demonstrators, which eventually led to the coup on 6 October 1976.

In recent years the military has adopted a standpoint that serves to strengthen its legitimate role in politics. It has been emphasized that the military as an institution (or "national armed forces") is the principle machine of the state; therefore when a government composed of political parties fails to solve national problems, the military is entitled to use its own policies to solve those problems.[26]

In a country where participant political institutions are weak, the military can effectively rally public support by pointing to the instability of government and ineffective administration of state affairs by party politics. In their thinking, politics and government administration are inseparable; hence government officials could hold political positions, such as cabinet offices, concurrently with their administrative positions in order to ensure national security.

Historically, therefore, the military and civilian bureaucratic elites represent the most dynamic political forces in Thai society. They were prime movers in most of the events and changes. They are the most powerful political machine in the country, and have been able to control the political game fairly well. The circulation of the military and the bureaucratic elites is also worth noting. The control and command of military positions, especially those at the top of the pyramid and also at the politically important posts, can be utilized for multipurpose activities ranging from getting themselves appointed to the National Assembly to the chairmanship or membership of the public enterprise boards.

Unlike Malaysia and Singapore, where tenures of parliaments last without interruption, only four parliaments in Thailand completed their tenures; the rest were disrupted by coups d'état. While discontinuity of elected parliaments is a fact of political life, the appointed assemblies have been continued without disruptions. It is therefore not surprising that some military officials, such as General Prem, have been members of the appointed assemblies since 1958, while the majority of members of elected parliament in 1980 served in the House of Representatives for the first time.

When parliaments could not complete their tenures several bills proposed by the members had to be resubmitted, thus delaying the process of socioeconomic reform in response to the rapidly changing condition of society during these interim periods. Legislative supporting organizations such as legislative reference and research units were only established in 1974 and could not function effectively because of the lack of support from the government. Members on parliamentary standing committees keep changing from one parliament to another, preventing MPs from developing expertise in their chosen fields.

These consequences of parliamentary discontinuity have weakened the power of the legislative branch vis-à-vis that of the executive and prevented the legislature from becoming a potent force in the Thai political system.

Discontinuity of elected parliaments has had adverse effects on political parties in several aspects. Party organizations could not be developed and political mobilization could only be at best ad hoc. From 1946 to 1981 143 parties were formed but only a few survived throughout these years. All of the parties are urban based with weak rural organization, and party branches are not very well organized.

When political parties were allowed to function they suffered from lack of discipline among their members, who pursued factional and individual interests rather than abiding by party policies. Usually political parties in Thailand are primarily groupings of individuals or networks of patrons and clients who are forced to be together by a political party law requiring candidates to contest elections under party banners. After elections almost all of the parties have no significant programs that would link them with the masses.

Unlike Singapore and Malaysia, which are one-party-dominant states, in Thailand no single party has ever dominated the political scene. When government parties won a majority in parliament, factionalism within them usually led to political crises, culminating in military interventions. From 1975 to 1976, parliamentary seats were shared by from eight to twenty-two parties, resulting in highly unstable coalition governments.

Apart from the above-mentioned factors inhibiting the strength of political parties in Thailand, the development of a party system is affected by the hostile attitude of bureaucratic elites toward the role of political parties. As Kramol Tongdhamachart observes, "the bureaucratic elites often perceived political parties as the cause of national disunity and political instability and also as the political entity that could threaten their power positions."[27] When political parties were allowed to function, the bureaucratic elites usually imposed obstacles on their formation and performance, making it difficult for the parties to mature at a natural rate of growth. The 1981 Political Party Law requires the potential party organizers to fulfill several requirements before their parties can be registered and legally perform their functions. For example, they must recruit a minimum of 5,000 members with residence in five provinces in each of the four regions of the country. In addition, each province must be represented in the potential party with a minimum of fifty persons.[28]

To encourage a strong party system, the present constitution requires that, in the general election, parties must field candidates numbering not less than half of the total number of members of the House of Representatives. Except for the Bangkok Metropolis, which is divided into three constituencies, every other province is regarded as one constituency. The method of voting is to be that of a party slate system; political parties are to submit lists of the candidates supported by them to stand in the constituencies, for the voters to decide on the whole slates.[29] All these measures were made in the hope that they would eliminate small parties so that a two-party system would finally emerge. Naturally such measures have created a tremendous need for major political parties to mobilize funds for their campaigns. It is estimated that to be able to support candidates in a general election, a political party would need at least 50 million baht for campaign funding (U.S. $1 = 25 baht in 1987).[30]

The need for campaign funds has led to a closer relationship between political parties and business interests. Some prominent businessmen have thus become either deputy leaders or executive members of political parties, whereas in the past these people maintained relatively distant relationships with leaders of political parties. At the provincial level local businessmen are also more actively involved in politics both as candidates and as financial supporters of political parties. At the national level most of the businessmen who are party financiers prefer not to run in the election. However, because of their financial contributions, they are given cabinet portfolios in the coalition governments. Conflicts, therefore, usually arise between the elected politicians and the party financiers who are executive members of the parties and are given cabinet posts. The elected politicians call these party financiers "political businessmen," distinguishing them from the "grassroots politicians." Hence, although there has been more involvement from the private sector in the Thai political system, this development has created especially destabilizing effects. This is because, apart from cabinet positions, political secretaries to ministers, and a limited number of executive positions in public enterprises, there are no other significant official positions to which party financiers could be appointed. The competition for limited positions between these two groups of people in various political parties has markedly contributed to the overall instability of the system.

It is fair to say that most of the businessmen still prefer not to be formally identified with any political party. This is because party politics are not yet institutionalized, while bureaucratic politics provides more certainty. However, if there is continuity in the parliamentary system it is natural that compromises would be made between "grassroots politicians," who claim to represent a broader spectrum of national interests, and the "political businessmen," whose interests are more parochial. At present only the privileged groups have access to the formal political institutions through their alliances with political parties and lobbying. The underprivileged groups, i.e., the workers and farmers, have no formal links with political parties and take political actions independently. In other words, while all groups articulate their interests, only the interests of privileged groups are effectively aggregated by political parties.

Major political parties in Thailand have more or less similar policies. They can be classified as moderate and nonideological. Political parties in Thailand have not yet reflected any clear-cut economic interest. Although every major political party has many prominent businessmen on its executive committee, these people became involved in party activities because of their personal relationships with leaders of the parties rather than because of their economic interests. Since parliamentary politics have suffered from lack of continuity, it has not been possible for different economic interest groups to identify their interests along party lines. Parliamentary politics, whenever they are allowed to function, have enabled politically minded businessmen to participate in the competition for power. Short-term parliamentary politics make political and economic alliances highly dynamic and fluid. It is too soon, therefore, to classify Thai political parties by using a criterion of specific economic interests they represent.

Like other problems concerning the weakness of political institutions, the impotence of parliament and political parties in Thailand is unextricably linked with the perennial issue of the conflict between bureaucratic power and that of participant political institutions. Problems facing political parties must therefore be analyzed in a broader perspective and not restricted to internal characteristics of party organizations. It is impossible for any political party to develop its organization and to effectively perform its functions in a political system where coups d'état have become more or less institutionalized.

In historical perspective, democratic development in Thailand suffered setbacks because of certain unique circumstances. In the pre-1973 period, when extrabureaucratic forces were weak and political competition was limited to a few personalities and their cliques, the commitment to democratic values among the political elite gradually declined. This is understandable because those who were committed to democratic principles had no effective base of support, and had to engage in the same game of power play. Hence in the 1930s, the leaders of the People's party sought support from the armed forces in their competition for power. After being drawn into politics new generations of army officers quickly realized their indispensable role. The army officers who staged the coup in 1947 and remained in power until 1973 were not only uncommitted to democratic ideals, they also had strongly antipolitical attitudes. Hence, when extrabureaucratic forces became strong and began to play active roles in politics, they were regarded as destabilizing factors in national development. The military perceived legitimate politics in a very limited sense, involving activities centered in the parliament and not outside. As General Lek Naeomalee (former interior minister) commented: "When people in our country want to have freedom or liberty, they are going to create confusion and disorder—in our democracy we have members of parliament, but what do we get from having a parliament. Can members of parliament help make our country stable?"[31]

It is evident that "democracy" perceived by military men is quite different from the liberal democratic tradition. Its scope begins with a general election and ends at the legislature that is not necessarily an entirely elected body. It is democracy without pressure groups and is conflict-free. In other words there are another set of values higher than liberal democratic values. These values are national security, stability, and order. The attachment to these values is still strong among military officers, and the increased activism of newly emergent groups has further convinced them that full-fledged democratic rule would be detrimental to national security.

Another factor that impeded political development is that rapid socioeconomic changes coincided with the growth of the Communist Party of Thailand. This contributed to the weakening of the overall political system, since any democratic movement that aimed at mobilizing and gaining support from the masses was usually suspected of being communist-inspired. It is therefore unfortunate that significant socioeconomic changes did not lead to a stable pluralist democracy. Ideological polarization during the 1973–1976 period was too extreme and intense. Moreover, political parties were unable to establish linkages to politically active groups such as student, labor, and farmer groups. As a result political participation under the full-fledged democratic rule in the mid-1970s was close to anarchy. The military was therefore able to exploit the situation, suppressing radical elements and co-opting the moderate and conservative sections of these pressure groups.

Economic Development and Social Change

Thailand's economy has grown rapidly over the past two decades, with an average per capita income growth of almost 5 percent per annum between 1960 and 1980. (In 1961 per capita income was 2,137 baht compared with 12,365 baht in 1980. U.S. \$1 = 22 baht in 1980). Over the same period there was a rapid transformation in the structure of production, with the share of agriculture in total value added declining from 40 percent in 1960 to 25 percent in 1980. However, it was estimated that 76 percent of the Thai population still remained in rural areas, a decline of only about 10 percent since 1960. This labor force and population distribution reflects the unusually extensive pattern of Thai agricultural growth and the pervasive rural nature of the Thai economy and society. After two decades of development Bangkok still remains the primary city. While about 9.7 percent of the Thai population lived in Bangkok in 1980, 32.7 percent of total GDP in Thailand originated in Bangkok. Although the overall incidence of poverty was reduced from 57 percent in the early 1960s to about 31 percent in the mid-1970s, poverty remains largely a rural phenomenon.[32] It is estimated that in 1980 11 million people in the rural areas were living in poverty. The benefit of growth was not evenly dispersed but has widened the gap between the rich and the poor, and between the rural and the urban sectors.

The manufacturing sector expanded rapidly as a result of the policy of import substitution. Its share in the GDP rose from 10.5 percent in 1960 to 18 percent in 1980. The number of factories increased fivefold between 1960 and 1980. Figures in 1980 show that there were 3.6 million workers in industrial and service sectors. Apart from workers in privately owned factories, there was also a rapid increase in the number of workers in state enterprises, which rose from 137,437 in 1973 to 433,649 in 1983. Labor unions in state enterprises have been more politically active than labor unions in the private sector. In 1983, there were 323 labor unions in the private sector while there were 91 state enterprise labor unions. However, the former had altogether only 81,465 members compared with 136,335 members in the latter. Public enterprise workers in the Electricity Authority, the railways, and the Water Supply Authority are the most organized; their political significance is due to their control of public utility services in metropolitian areas, which gives them considerable bargaining power. Hence socioeconomic changes in Thailand are marked by the highly urban character of the society, with major potent political forces concentrated in the capital city.

By far the most important change in the Thai economy since the 1960s has been the rapid expansion of the "big business enterprises" (those with assets of more than 500 million baht). According to a 1979 study the value of capital owned by the big business enterprises amounted to nearly 74 percent of the GNP that year.[33] This growth of monopolistic capital was made possible by government development policies during the authoritarian regimes in the late 1950s and throughout the 1960s that favored the development of industrial capital outside agriculture. Such policies were aimed at creating a production base capable of transforming agricultural surplus into manufacturing commodities. As a result, policies of import substitution and trade protection were implemented. During the same period government after government pursued the policy of price controls in favor of urban communities at the expense of the agricultural work force. Prices of rice paddy have been kept low for the sake of city dwellers and consumers while farmers have to purchase chemical fertilizers at extra high prices as a result of additional transportation costs.[34]

In sum, economic development in the past two decades has resulted in the concentration of economic power in the capital city and has created a large urban working class. At the same time this development witnessed the growth of the bureaucracy, which, while remaining highly centralized, penetrated more into the rural areas. By 1980 the number of government employees (excluding military forces) reached 1.4 million, making the ratio between population (46 million) and government employees 33 to 1. In the same year, government expenditure on personnel services accounted for 35% of total government expenditures.[35] Bureaucratic expansion also resulted in a rapid increase in the number of students during the late 1960s and throughout the 1970s. This expansion, unprecedented in Thai political history, resulted from the heavy stress placed on education by the first three national development plans (1961–1976) and provided more than 30 percent of the total government funds each year to education at all levels. Most significant politically was the rapid expansion in the number of university students, which rose from 15,000 in 1961 to 50,000 in 1972, and has since increased greatly.[36]

As discussed earlier, in the early 1970s latent demands for participation were escalating exponentially. The student-led unrest in October 1973 and its aftermath were direct results of the frustrations and unfulfilled aspirations associated with this large and growing gap between change in society at large and stagnation in its political institutions. Although new nonbureaucratic groups emerged, most of them were anomic entities while the better-organized ones, such as the students and workers, were either destroyed or infiltrated and finally controlled by the government.

The Consolidation of a Bureaucratic Polity

It is indisputable that socioeconomic changes led to the emergence of new groups in society, but whether the existence of these groups would lead to a pluralist democracy is another matter. In the case of Thailand socioeconomic changes occurred under situations of semi-imposed development. In this pattern of development political and administrative structures such as the military and the bureaucracy have been able to grow alongside the growth of the private sector. In fact, they have been able to create new institutional structures of their own or to adjust existing structures and functions (or even the "style") to cope with pressures coming from extrabureaucratic groups. The military and bureaucratic groups may "lose" the first battle, especially when intraelite conflicts are high. However, as they had more and more experiences with new environments and situations, their advantage in controlling political resources, especially the use of legitimate violence, made it possible for them to gradually gain control over extrabureaucratic forces.

Rapid socioeconomic changes often create uncertainties and sometimes instability and disorder. In fact, democratic values and norms brought about by these changes are the antithesis of and pose great challenges to traditional values of the military elites, who welcome modernization and development as long as stability and order can be simultaneously maintained.

In the past five decades military interventions in the political process has taken only one form—a coup d'état. But recently, the military has been more sophisticated in developing a national strategy that has helped to expand its legitimate role in the political system. It has adjusted its strategies and tactics in dealing with emergent social forces. Cooperation and co-optation have replaced intimidation and suppression. The experience the military has gained in the past two decades was not from its participation in conventional politics, but from its encounter with the Communist party of Thailand in rural areas. The new generation of military leadership in the 1980s has been politicized in a manner totally different from that of its predecessors. Their experience in organizing the masses in rural areas to counter political activities of the CPT convinced them that the most effective way in dealing with pressure groups is not to suppress them but to find ways and means to control them. This approach is evident in the prime minister's orders No. 66/2523 and No. 65/2525. The former was known as the policy to defeat the Communist party of Thailand, which stated that to destroy the CPT

332   SAMUDAVANIJA

it was necessary to establish a truly democratic regime. Individual rights and liberty should be guaranteed and democratic groups encouraged to actively participate in politics. The army's role in implementing this order is therefore not only to suppress the CPT, but also to act as an instrument to solve political and socioeconomic problems. In a 1983 lecture on "The Changed Situation of the CPT and the Strategy to Defeat the Communists in 1983" Lieutenant General Chaovalit Yongchaiyuth,[37] deputy chief of army staff and the brain behind Order No. 66/2523, stated:

> Nowadays, Thailand has two policies to solve national problems. There is the political party policy, proposed to the Parliament by the government, and the policy of the National Army, the policy to defeat the Communists. These two policies, however, have conflicting contents since one policy is formulated by the political parties but the other by the National Army. But facts, reasons and theory prove that the National Army can solve national problems, namely to win over the CPT, while the political party policy has not succeeded in solving any problems.[38]

From this statement it is clear that the military has taken another step in redefining and reinforcing its role in society. The open criticism of political parties reflected the attitudes of army leaders on the roles of participant political institutions. In fact the military leaders are raising some very important questions, for example, the legitimate role of political parties, whether they really represent the people, and the extent to which parties could successfully cope with national problems.

In mid-January 1983 Major General Pichit Kullavanijaya, First Division commander, warned on a television program that the new electoral system would only result in bringing the "capitalists" into parliament, and, if there was no change in the constitution, the military might well have to "exercise" (to step in) to protect the security of the nation and the interest of the people.[39] He also pointed out that the military has been an important force in society for 700 years and has to be given a proper role in politics.

Order No. 65/2525 reflects a tendency toward a limited pluralist system, especially points 2.3 and 2.4 of the order which state:

> 2.3 Popular participation in political activities must be promoted to enable the people to have more practical experience which can serve to strengthen their attachment to and understanding of the principles of sovereignty. This must be done by involving the *tambon* councils, village committees and cooperatives,... encouraging the use of political parties as a means of promoting their own interests at the national or local level in accordance with the principles of democracy....
> 2.4 Activities of pressure groups and interests groups must be regulated. Pressure and interest groups can act either to reinforce or to obstruct the development of democracy. Therefore, to ensure that their role be a constructive one and to deter any such group from hindering this development, their activities must be regulated....[40]

Order No. 65/2525 (1982) identified six major groups that ought to be regulated: economic groups, the masses, students, progressive groups, the mass media, and the armed forces. While the first five groups were treated at length, the last—the armed forces—was given a very short guideline: "They should have a correct understanding of democracy and preserve this system."

In the same order it is stated that the personnel who will be the main instrument for achieving democratic development are to be "*government* officials" in every agency, as well as ordinary people with idealism who are prepared to *cooperate* to bring about a model democracy (italics added). Hence the Thai military in the 1980s has gone one step further; that is, in the past it only criticized civilian regimes, but now it has set the framework for the development of democracy.

Both the military and the bureaucracy compete with political institutions in organizing and mobilizing the masses in several ways. Although there are several private and voluntary associations, and interest groups, they are mainly Bangkok-based while the great bulk of people in rural areas are organized into groups by the military and the bureaucracy. At the village level the Ministry of Interior is in control of the village councils through the offices of village headmen and district officers. The army, through its Civilian Affairs Department, has not only organized and mobilized masses into groups such as Village Defense Volunteers, but has also infiltrated and taken over certain initially legitimate pressure/interest groups—e.g., student groups, labor, farmers, the media—and created polarization within these movements, weakening them as effective political forces. It was pointed out earlier that political parties had weak links with pressure groups and the masses. With the military's stand and approach to the groups mentioned above, it is very difficult for political parties to establish a closer and more viable relationship with these groups. Political parties are thus reduced to ad hoc electoral organizations, rather than being a meaningful participant political institution.

The present political system is therefore a unique one, in which the leadership of the military has not formed or openly supported any political party as it did in the past. The military and the bureaucrats, however, have their "informal political party," which is the appointed Senate.

The Senate is dominated by military officers and civil servants, with a few businessmen and intellectuals. Military officers are appointed to the Senate according to their seniority and positions (for example, all commanders-in-chief of the army, navy, and air force, chiefs of staff, divisional commanders) as well as for their loyalty to the prime minister. As for civil servants, the undersecretary of every ministry and those of equivalent stature are members of the Senate. These senators have a military whip, the army chief of staff, and a civilian whip, the under-secretary of the prime minister's office. Through their coordinating Committee on Legislative Affairs senators get slips recommending how to vote on various issues both in the Senate and in the joint sessions with the House of Representatives.

The role of the House of Representatives has been constrained by several provisions and procedures of the 1978 Constitution and parliamentary rules. For example, until recently, members of parliament could not freely propose legislative bills unless the Committee on Legislative Bills endorsed the bills. This committee was composed of seventeen members—three appointed by the cabinet, six by the Senate and eight by the House of Representatives. This provision of the 1978 Constitution was lifted in 1983.

Senate control over the House is exercised through the requirement in the constitution that the following matters are considered by a joint session: consideration and passage of The Budget Bill, motion of the no confidence vote, and consideration and passage of legislative bills concerning national security and economic aspects. Under the same constitution, the president of the Senate is president of the National Assembly, the agenda of the meetings is prepared by him and he chairs the joint sessions. The Senate is therefore an instrument for control of the political process—the legislative arms of the bureaucracy.

The semidemocratic pattern of rule described above is the outgrowth of the interplay of social, economic, and political forces in Thai society. It evolved from the nation's unique conditions that have existed for centuries. This semidemocratic pattern is a compromise between two sets of forces that have coexisted since 1932. One set of forces emanates from military and bureaucratic institutions, and values and norms associated with them. The other originates from more recent nonbureaucratic political institutions. These two forces operate within and adjust themselves to changes in the socioeconomic environment. In the Thai situation, changes resulting from social and economic modernization have not automatically strengthened voluntary associations and political groups because the military-bureaucratic structures, rather than the party system, have been able to incorporate and co-opt these new social groups, which then have their interests represented through bureaucratically created and controlled mechanisms. In other words, socioeconomic changes in Thailand have enabled the nonbureaucratic groups to participate more in bureaucratic politics rather than to fundamentally change the nature of the Thai political system from that of a "bureaucratic polity" to that of a "bourgeois polity."

In recent years economic development has brought increased criticism of the bureaucratic polity and of military domination of politics.[41] Ansil Ramsay has observed that political participation in decision making in

Thailand has recently extended to "bourgeois middle-class groups," especially the business elite, who have begun to play a major role in Thai cabinets and in economic decision making. Other groups from middle-class backgrounds, such as leading academics and technocrats, also have increased their access to decision making.[42]

But it is too early to conclude that the bureaucratic polity has already evolved into a "bourgeois polity." One obstacle to this development is the reluctance of these emerging middle-class elements to be politically independent. Moreover, despite the optimism that there have been more businessmen serving in the cabinets than in the past, they make little impact in policy matters. Their participation in the executive branch is usually counterbalanced by the use of advisers and technocrats as practiced under General Prem's governments. Such limitations on the role of the private sector and its leadership are due to the distrust of businessmen's direct involvement in politics on the part of the military and bureaucratic elites. The military, as pointed out earlier, has expressed its concern about the danger of "capitalist interests." Businessmen who have served as cabinet ministers often complained that they could not implement their policies because the bureaucrats did not give enough support.

It seems that the most significant political change in the relationship between bureaucratic and nonbureaucratic groups is that in the 1980s the latter have found a workable partnership with the former through the leadership of a former army general who has an interest in maintaining a semidemocratic system. In the past military leaders formally engaged themselves in parliamentary politics by becoming leader or sponsors of political parties. When conflicts arose between military factions, they were carried over into the arena of parliamentary politics. Political parties and elected politicians were brought into the power play and consequently suffered when conflicts were heightened, which lead to military coups. Under the present system, however, the prime minister is not directly involved in party and parliamentary politics. Indeed General Prem does not consider himself a politician. Also, the leadership of the military has no formal links with political parties. A balance has thus been achieved under the semidemocratic institutional arrangements. Since election campaigns in recent years have involved tremendous funds, the elected members of parliament are naturally concerned with the preservation of the system so that their tenure can be completed. The four parties in the coalition government are satisfied with the portfolios they were given, but the prime minister also appointed former technocrats, retired senior military generals, and a few intellectuals to his cabinets. Hence political power is being shared between bureaucratic and nonbureaucratic forces both at the executive and legislative levels.

It is clear that the military-bureaucratic dominance in the Thai political system is not waning, although it is evident that new and more subtle strategies and tactics have had to have been adopted to cope with social change.

The present state of Thai politics can therefore be described as "politics of contentment" or "politics of satisfaction." Thus continuation of the Prem government in the interest of stability may be viewed as a triumph for the democratic process, but rather as satisfying interests of the bureaucracy, the army (or certain factions in it), political parties, and the monarchy. However, pressure groups, although increasingly more vocal and demanding over the past decade-and-a-half, have remained on the periphery of this political circle of contentment.

• THEORETICAL ANALYSIS •

Politics have taken the shape of a vicious circle in Thailand. A constitution is promulgated and elections are held for legislative seats. A crisis is precipitated, and this triggers a military coup; the military then promises a constitution. Thus the process of democratization in Thailand has been cyclical; authoritarian regimes alternate with democratic or semidemocratic ones. In this situation neither authoritarian nor democratic structures are institutionalized.

Why, despite the social and economic changes that have occurred, is democracy in Thailand still unstable and why has there been the institutionalization of only semidemocratic rule? This is because a differentiated socioeconomic structure does not necessarily lead to the control of the state by societal groups. In Thailand socioeconomic change has occurred under conditions of semi-imposed, forced development, rather than being led by an autonomous bourgeoisie. An activist bureaucratic state competes with participant or nonbureaucratic actors, and this leads to greater bureaucratization, rather than democratization, as the state expands its development role.

The ability of the state to expand and adapt its role to changing situations and environments explains why emergent autonomous forces have failed to challenge the power of the military and the bureaucracy. Although there exists a sizable middle class in Thailand, it is mainly composed of salaried officials and other nonbureaucratic professionals whose interests are not institutionally linked with any of the participant political institutions. The capitalist and commercial class, which is predominantly Sino-Thai, is just beginning to take an active but cautious role in party politics. Neither the farmers nor the laborers, who together compose the majority of the lower class, have yet developed into a class for itself. Although there were some peasant and worker groups that developed consciousness of class antagonisms, they were easily suppressed by the authorities. This underprivileged class is not effectively represented by any strong political party, and is therefore a rather impotent political force in society. Moreover, the military and the bureaucracy have provided an important ladder for social mobility in the past century for many middle-class and lower-class children. This explains why there has been little class antagonism in Thai society despite distinct class divisions. The bureaucracy has therefore been able to function not only as the state mechanism, but also as a social organization.

It should be pointed out that Thai authoritarianism is not very repressive. Authoritarian regimes that attempted to be too repressive usually met with strong opposition from various sections of society. Once an authoritarian regime extended its controls and suppression to the general populace, it was usually opposed by the press, which has been one of the freest in Asia. An independent and long-standing judiciary is another institution that has always been safeguarding the encroachment of civil liberties. It is an autonomous body not subjected to the control of the military and the bureaucracy, but has its own independent recruitment and appointment procedures. The independence and integrity of the judiciary branch is reflected in the appointment of a senior judge to head a government in times of crisis.

The existence of countervailing forces such as an independent judiciary, a free press, and some favorable social conditions such as relatively little class antagonism or ethnic and religious cleavage, are necessary but not sufficient conditions for a viable democracy in Thailand. These conditions do serve as important factors in preventing an authoritarian regime from becoming extreme in its rule. In other words they soften authoritarian rule and, to a large extent, contribute to the maintenance of semidemocratic rule.

The most legitimate institution, which has greatly contributed to social and political stability in Thailand, is the monarchy. It took the monarchy only three decades to slowly but firmly reestablish its prestige, charisma, power, and influence in the Thai political system. By 1985, after almost four decades of his reign, King Bhumibol Adulyadej has become the most powerful and respected symbol of the nation. This is not surprising. He has survived seven constitutions, nine general elections, and over thirty cabinets with eleven different prime ministers. While politicians, military leaders, and civilian prime ministers had come and gone, the king has remained the head of state, the focus of his people's loyalty and cohesion, the fount of legitimacy. Because of the continuity of this institution in contrast to others in Thailand—especially elected legislatures and political parties—the king has gained political experience and developed mature insights into the country's problems.

It has been overwhelmingly accepted, especially since 1973, that the king remains the final arbiter of a national crisis. In 1984, and once again in 1986, in the midst of the conflict between General Prem, the prime minister, and General Arthit, the commander-in-chief of the army, the monarchy played a decisive role in restraining many an ill-advised move by the military.[43]

In this sense, the monarchy performs a highly important substituting function for other political institutions in bringing together national consensus, especially when there is a crisis of legitimacy. It has increasingly played the role of legitimater of political power, supporter/legitimater of broad regime policies, promoter and sanctioner of intraelite solidarity, and symbolic focus of national unity.[44] The social stability of Thailand, despite its periodic coups d'état, can be explained by the existence and positive role of the monarchy. As long as the bureaucratic-military leadership is supported by the monarchy the problem of legitimacy is, to a large extent, solved. Hence it has been observed:

> If any significance emerged from the eventful and volatile political developments of 1984, it was perhaps that the highest institution in the land, the monarchy, revered as a symbol of justice and authority, is likely to be the single most important force capable of holding the country together during times of chaos and crisis and of assuring the viability of a democratic process in Thailand. With a clear commitment of the monarchy to a constitutional government, democracy Thai-style ultimately may have a chance to take root.[45]

This view merits further analysis. What kind of democracy is it that "may have a chance to take root" in Thai society? Democracy Thai-style has been identified in this chapter as a semidemocratic one. Is there any chance for a pluralist democracy or a polyarchy to take root in Thailand?

One of the most important conditions for the development of a pluralist democracy is the more or less neutral "umpire" role of the state. In the case of Thailand, however, the state and its machineries have always played an active and dominant role in society. It should also be noted that the state's principal machinery, the bureaucracy, has been able to adapt its role to changing conditions, most notably by utilizing the ideology of development to expand and legitimate its presence in society.

Although new forces have emerged as a result of socioeconomic changes in the past two decades, they have been under close surveillance by the bureaucratic elites. The privileged organized groups, such as the Bankers' Association, the Association of Industries, and the Chamber of Commerce, have been given access to the decision-making process in economic spheres, but their participation is of a consultative nature rather than as an equal partner. Likewise, labor unions have also been given a limited consultative role in labor relations, while the bureaucracy still firmly maintains its control over farmers' groups through the Ministries of Interior and Agriculture.

Although there were general elections again in 1983 and 1986, popular participation remains relatively low. Where turnouts were high the successes were due to active mobilization by officials of the Interior Ministry rather than to voters' interest in political issues.

The Thai military and bureaucratic elites are by no means united but, despite factional strife and rivalry, they share a common negative attitude toward elected politicians. They are willing to tolerate the elected politicians only to the extent that the latter do not pose a threat to their interests.

The Thai case is different from the U.S. situation where elites are committed to democratic values. In the United States democratic values have survived because the elites, not masses, govern; and it is the elites, not the common people who are the chief guardians of democratic values.[46] Numerous studies on Thai political culture confirm that anti-democratic tendencies have a positive correlation with a high level of education.[47] It has also been reported that people who have high socioeconomic status, high educational levels, and good access to political information tend to have a higher degree of political alienation than other groups of people.[48] Furthermore, there is no difference in attitudes toward elections among voters with lower socioeconomic status. Electoral participation by the masses is ritualistic or mobilized participation rather than voluntary political action.[49]

It is fair to conclude that a dynamic balance is currently maintained among various forces, each of which can not possibly afford to dominate the political process on its own strength alone. The semidemocratic model seems to work quite well because, on the one hand, it permits formal and ritualistic political participation through a general election that produces an elected parliament, but, on the other, the real center of power is in the executive branch, which is controlled by the military-bureaucratic elites who, in recent years, have begun to carefully select some business elites to join their regime on a limited basis.

A pluralist democracy is unlikely to develop from an entrenched bureaucratic polity, especially where that bureaucratic polity is not a static entity, but can utilize the ideology of development to redefine its role, and where it exploits traditionally powerful social institutions to further legitimate its dominance by evoking fears of communism and instability emanating from external threats (such as Vietnam and the Soviet Union). While socioeconomic changes have led to the growth of newly emergent forces, they could at best restrain the bureaucratic power rather than capture it and replace it with a group-based bargaining and mutual adjustment system. As for the masses, the persistence of the bureaucracy and lack of continuity in the functioning of political parties have greatly affected their socialization in the sense that they have been bureaucratically socialized rather than politically socialized. This is particularly true in the case of the rural population since they have to rely on the delivery of services from the bureaucracy, and therefore have to learn to survive or to get the most out of what is available from the bureaucracy and not from the parties. The politics of who gets what, when, and how in Thailand is in essence a bureaucratic allocation of values rather than a politically authoritative distribution of benefits.

In conclusion, it should be pointed out that the failures of the April 1981 and September 1985 coups do not mean that Thai politics has developed into a mature democratic system. Military leadership elements continue to view the coup—however difficult it may be to implement—as an acceptable technique to transfer political power. However circumscribed the power of the military may be (due to factionalism), and however expansive may be the growth of nonbureaucratic forces, the result can not be interpreted as signifying a steady development of parliamentary democracy. The major constituencies of government remain outside the arena of its citizenry at large. The balance of power has not shifted to the democratic party system, but to the monarchy, whose charisma and grace enables it to control political power allocation and balance and referee often conflicting political power interests.

• FUTURE PROSPECTS •

In the past, democratic development primarily involved changes in the constitution to make it more democratic by giving more powers to the legislative branch. Such efforts usually led to the instability of the constitutions and the governments because formal political arrangements did not reflect the real power relationships in society. The problem of politics in Thailand is not how to develop a democratic system, but how to maintain the semidemocratic system so that a more participatory system of government can evolve in the long run. In other words, under the semidemocratic system in which an elected parliament is allowed to function, political parties and parliament could utilize the continuity of the political system (which is very rare in Thai political history) to strengthen their organizations. One of the least controversial and most practical aspects of democratic development is the development of the research and information capabilities of political parties and the parliamentarians. The strengthening of the supporting staff of parliamentary committees, as well as research capabilities of political parties, would greatly enhance the role of the parliament in the long run. A well-informed parliament can act more effectively in exercising its countervailing force vis-à-vis that of the bureaucracy.

The continuity of participant political institutions will have great impact upon local politics in the sense that elections for local government bodies, such as the municipalities and the provincial and the village councils, could continue to be held and allowed to operate alongside national politics. In the long run, it would be possible for political parties to extend their infrastructure to rural areas and mobilize support not only in national elections, but also in local elections. It is expected that as long as the elected politicians are willing to make a compromise by not demanding the abolishment of the Senate or insisting that all ministers must be members of the elected parliament, there will be no major disruption in the overall political system. This means that to be able to survive, participant political institutions have to share power with the military and bureaucratic elite.

It seems that the most significant change in Thai politics since 1981 has been the absence of a coup d'état. Some observers regard this as a progressive movement toward a more democratic system because of the more pluralistic nature of society. This led one scholar to conclude that the present Thai polity's strength is its ability to accommodate the demands of a wider range of groups than could the bureaucratic polity.[50] However, the stability and the strength of the present polity might, on the other hand, be attributed to its ability to accommodate the demands of the military and technocratic elites. In this sense, any change in the institutional framework that would upset the existing power relationships would precipitate a coup, because however difficult it might be to implement, military leadership elements continue to view the coup as an acceptable technique to transfer political power. It is their decision not to use this instrument at a particular point in time. When their interests are no longer accommodated and if they overcome factionalism within the army itself, then a coup becomes possible.

This does not mean that the Thai polity will maintain its semi-democratic pattern of rule forever. On the contrary, in the long run, when participant political institutions have the chance to prove their usefulness to the people, their image and credibility will be gradually strengthened. In the meantime, elected politicians should concentrate on their efforts in developing party organizations (such as party branches), and on improving the capabilities of the parliamentary research unit and committee staff so that their already accepted roles could be institutionalized. The improvement of legislative research and reference sections of the parliament and the strengthening of parliamentary committee staff aids are less controversial than the proposal to reduce the number of senators. But such "internal" political reforms will have great effect in the long run. Another recommendation is state financing of political parties in order to reduce the dependency of elected politicians on nonelected party financiers. The German method of reimbursing political parties for their campaign expenses provided that they get more than 5 percent of the votes cast in the election should be adopted in Thailand.

Under the present political situation where there are many active voluntary associations and interest groups that seek to influence government decisions and policies, the parliament should create a new standing committee to act as a channel for the expression of interests and opinions of various pressure groups. In this way groups would operate within the framework of the legislative process, and would reduce their perceived activist role play, which is not acceptable to the military. Instead of putting pressure on the cabinet through strikes, demonstrations, and protests, which so far have not been very effective in redressing grievances, pressure-group politics could best be legitimated through the provision of an institutional mechanism for their interactions with the government and the legislators. In the long run viable relationships would develop between political parties and interest groups.

The above-mentioned recommendations are likely to be acceptable to the military and the bureaucratic elites because they do not directly threaten the existing power relationships. The idea of bringing group actions into the legislative arena is also likely to be welcomed by the military, which has been staunchly opposed to political activism outside formal political institutions and processes.

It is unrealistic to propose any drastic change in the constitution since such a move would induce a military coup. The most important issue in Thai politics is how to avoid the repetitive pattern of political change that I have described as the "vicious cycle of Thai politics." The main reason explaining the persistence of the semidemocratic system, or "authoritarian constitutionalism," is the nature of authoritarian rule in Thailand, which has often been characterized by moderation, flexibility, and careful avoidance of confrontation. As Somsakdi Xuto aptly observes,

> The general public, in particular, has been relatively little affected by exercise of authoritarian power. In short, Thai authoritarianism has been somewhat softened by the personal characteristics of pragmatism and accommodation. Thus harshness or extreme measures typically associated with authoritarian rule in other countries have remained relatively absent, particularly as applied to the general public.[51]

The idea of keeping the elected parliament viable within the semidemocratic system is, of course, a second-best alternative. In the past decade it was impossible for any government to effectively implement its programs because of its preoccupation with surviving. The absence of a coup in the 1980s has enabled the government and the elected parliament to perform their functions without disruption, which is very important in meeting the increasing challenges and uncertainties coming from international political and economic communities. Perhaps improvement of the Thai political process has to begin by accepting existing politics for what they are and not what they should be.[52] It may be worthwhile to accept the role of the military in Thai politics by recognizing its sphere of influence expecially in internal and external security matters. It also means that their participation in the legislative process through the Senate has to be tolerated by the elected politicians. Improvements of internal mechanisms of participant political institutions as suggested above would gradually strengthen these institutions and prepare them well for the more important tasks in the future. A viable and responsible government that would emerge in Thailand may not be exactly like the British parliamentary model that has been followed in form since 1932. It may be a mixed system in which the military-bureaucratic elites and the elected politicians share powers and each side competes for support from the masses in their responsible spheres of influence. The peculiarity of the Thai polity is that, apart from the institution of the monarchy, no other political institution can claim legitimacy on its own account.

It seems that accommodation and compromise, to preserve political stability at whatever the cost, has led to stagnation rather than development in both the political and economic spheres. It has become a question of stability for stability's sake rather than a foundation on which to build progressive reform.

This social stability has enabled Thailand to sustain its economic and social development despite periodic coups d'état. However, as Seymour Martin Lipset rightly pointed out, in the modern world the prolonged effectiveness that gives legitimacy to a political system means primarily constant economic development.[53] Thailand, like other ASEAN nations, has embarked upon the strategy of export-led development in order to minimize its economic dependency on the agricultural sector. The problem is that such efforts will be hampered by increasing trade protectionism, as currently practiced by the United States and Japan. If the effectiveness of a political regime depends upon its economic performance, the export-led development strategy will not be very helpful in furthering the pace of political development in Thailand because it will create economic instability that will lead directly to political instability. As long as the protectionist sentiment remains pervasive in major industrialized countries, there is less hope for Thailand to utilize its export-led development strategy to sustain its economic growth. This problem is aggravated where Thai exports such as textile goods compete with U.S. textile and garment-manufacturing interests.

Because of the increased openness of the Thai economy and its heavy dependence on imported oil, Thailand will continue to face economic problems such as balance of payments squeezes, serious exchange rate fluctuations, accelerating inflation, and increased reliance on foreign borrowing.[54] This would have adverse effects on the performance

SAMUDAVANIJA

and credibility of the political system. It is expected that the failure to successfully implement the export-led development strategy would finally lead to economic nationalism and the maintenance of the semi-democratic regime.[55] If economic problems emanating from fluctuations in the world economy worsen it is possible that the military may resort to the adoption of a new corporate state model in order to mediate conflicts among various groups in society. Judging from the past record of political behavior of the Thai military the Western type of pluralist democratic model will not be favored, for it not only threatens the power of the military technocratic elite alliance, but is highly unstable in a society where the economy is very much dependent upon external forces.

In the case of Thailand rapid development has expanded the private sector, but the strength and autonomy of the bourgeoisie have not grown correspondingly to the extent that it could counter the political weight of the military and bureaucracy. This is because the bourgeoisie is largely composed of Sino-Thais who have been under the control of the military bureaucracy for several generations. However, it is likely that the present generation has shown its desire to be more independent by joining political parties and by beginning to be in the forefront by running in the elections. It would, however, take some time before this generation of the bourgeoisie could become a leading political force in society. This is due to the fact that the military has also sponsored a number of political parties to counter the growing extrabureaucratic forces. No matter how rapid the rate of urbanization, political participation in Thailand can never be truly autonomous, but will remain partly bureaucratically mobilized. In conclusion, democracy in Thailand is not regarded as a purely political rule and process, but a political system in which the military and bureaucratic forces largely determine the role as well as the mode of participation of the nonbureaucratic forces. It should be remembered that the Thai parliament is not, and has never been, the center of power. In recent years, as there have been fewer disruptions in the political system, the parliament is only now becoming a new source of power, struggling very hard to institutionalize its legitimacy.

A stable political system—Thai-style—is therefore a semidemocratic system where the bureaucratic and nonbureaucratic forces share political power and continually engage in bargaining and adjusting their strategies to maximize their powers.

• NOTES •

1. On Buddhism and politics in Thailand see Somboon Suksamran, *Buddhism and Politics: A Study of Socio-Political Change and Political Activism of the Thai Sangha*

(Singapore: Institute of Southeast Asian Studies, 1982), and S. J. Tambiah, *World Conqueror and World Renouncer: A Study of Buddhism* (Cambridge: Cambridge University Press, 1976).

2. For more details on Thai political development before 1932 see Chai-Anan Samudavanija, "Political History," in Somsakdi Xuto, ed., *Government and Politics of Thailand* (Singapore: Oxford University Press, 1987) pp. 1–40.

3. Chai-Anan Samudavanija, *Thailand's First Political Development Plan* (Bangkok: Aksornsumphan Press, 1969) (in Thai).

4. On Tienwan see details in Chai-Anan Samudavanija, *Selected Works on Tienwan* (Bangkok: Posamton Press, 1974) (in Thai).

5. See Chai-Anan Samudavanija, *Politics and Political Change in Thailand* (Bangkok: Bannakit Press, 1980).

6. Benjamin Batson, *Siam's Political Future: Document from the End of the Absolute Monarchy* (Ithaca: Cornell University Southeast Asia Program, Data Paper no. 96, July, 1974).

7. Ibid., p. 45.

8. Ibid., p. 10.

9. Ibid., p. 49.

10. David Wilson, *Politics in Thailand* (Ithaca, New York: Cornell University Press, 1962), p. 277.

11. Toru Yano, "Political Structure of a 'Rice-Growing State' " in Yaneo Ishii, ed., *Thailand: A Rice-Growing Society* (Monographs of the Center for Southwest Asian Studies, Kyoto University, English-language Series no. 12. 1978), p. 127.

12. Wilson, *Politics in Thailand*, p. 22.

13. Ibid., p. 20.

14. Thak Chaleomtiarana, *Thailand: The Politics of Despotic Paternalism* (Bangkok: Social Science Association of Thailand, 1979), p. 102.

15. See details in Sungsidh Piriyarangsan, "Thai Bureaucratic Capitalism, 1932–1960" (Unpublished M.A. thesis, Faculty of Economics, Thammasat University, 1980).

16. Wilson, *Politics in Thailand*, p. 180.

17. Thak, *Thailand: The Politics of Despotic Paternalism*, p. 201.

18. Ibid., pp. 140–141.

19. Ibid., p. 334.

20. For more details on Thai politics in this period see David Morell and Chai-Anan Samudavanija, *Political Conflict in Thailand: Reform, Reaction, Revolution* (Cambridge, Mass.: Oelgeschlager, Gunn and Hain, Publishers, Inc., 1981).

21. J. L. S. Girling, *Thailand: Society and Politics* (Ithaca, N.Y.: Cornell University Press, 1981), pp. 215–219.

22. Wilson, *Politics in Thailand*, p. 262.

23. I am indebted to Dr. William Klausner for his observation on this point.

24. Fred W. Riggs, *Thailand: The Modernization of a Bureaucratic Policy* (Honolulu: East-West Center Press, 1966), pp. 152–153.

25. Sethaporn Cusripitak and others, "Communication Policies in Thailand," (A study report submitted to UNESCO, March 1985), p. 37.

26. See details in Lieutenant General Chaovalit Yongchaiyuth, *Lectures and Interviews by Lt. General Chaovalit Yongchaiyuth 1980–1985* (Bangkok: Sor. Sor. Press, 1985).

27. Kramol Tongdharmachart, "Toward a Political Theory in Thai Perspective," (Singapore: Institute of Southeast Asian Studies Occasional Paper no. 68, 1982), p. 37.

28. Ibid., pp. 37–38.

29. This electoral system and voting method were changed to that of multiple constituencies and individual candidacy in the constitutional amendment in 1985.

30. A candidate uses about 800,000 baht in an election campaign although the election law permits a candidate to spend not more than 350,000 baht. In highly competitive constituencies a candidate spends as much as 5 to 10 million baht to win a seat.

31. *Matichon*, 16 September 1979.

32. See details in *Thailand: Managing Public Resources for Structural Adjustment* (A World Bank Country Study, Washington, D.C.: The World Bank, 1984), pp. 1–13.

33. Krirkkiat Phipatseritham, "The World of Finance: The Push and Pull of Politics," (Paper prepared for the seminar on National Development of Thailand: Economic Rationality and Political Feasibility, Thammasat University, 6–7 September 1983), p. 21.

34. Saneh Chamarik, "Problems of Development in Thai Political Setting," (Paper prepared for the seminar on National Development of Thailand: Economic Rationality and Political Feasibility, Thammasat University, 6–7 September 1983), p. 38.

35. Chai-Anan Samudavanija, "Introduction," in the *Report of the Ad Hoc Committee to Study Major Problems of the Thai Administrative System* (Bangkok: National Administrative Reform Committee, 1980), pp. 6–7.

36. Frank C. Darling, "Student Protest and Political Change in Thailand," *Pacific Affairs* 47, no. 1 (Spring 1974): pp. 6–7.

37. Lieutenant General Chaovalit was promoted to chief of army staff and became a full general in October 1985. In May 1986 he was appointed to the position of army commander-in-chief.

38. Lieutenant General Chaovalit Yongchaiyuth, "Guidelines on Planning to Win Over the CPT in 1983," Royal Military Academy, 21 June 1983.

39. I.e., the party slate system requiring the electorate to choose the whole slate of candidates proposed by each political party.

40. Translated by M. R. Sukhumbhand Paribatra in *ISIS Bulletin* 1, no. 2 (October 1982): pp. 14–18.

41. Ansil Ramsay, "Thai Domestic Politics and Foreign Policy," (Paper presented at the Third U.S.-ASEAN Conference, Chiangmai, Thailand, 7–11 January 1985), p. 4.

42. Ibid.

43. Suchit Bunbongkarn and Sukhumbhand Paribatra, "Thai Politics and Foreign Policy in the 1980s," (Paper presented at the Third U.S.-ASEAN Conference, Chiangmai, Thailand, 7–11 January 1985), p. 18.

44. Thak, *Thailand: The Politics of Despotic Paternalism*, p. 334.

45. Juree Vichit-Vadakan, "Thailand in 1984: Year of Administering Rumors," *Asian Survey* 26, no. 2 (February 1985): p. 240.

46. Thomas R. Dye and L. Harmon Zeigler, *The Irony of Democracy: An Uncommon Introduction to American Politics* (Belmont, Calif.: Duxbury Press, 1971) pp. 18–19.

47. See, for example Suchit Bunbongkarn, "Higher Education and Political Development" (Unpublished Ph.D. diss., Fletcher School of Law and Diplomacy, 1968); and Surapas Tapaman R. T. N., "Political Attitudes of the Field Grade Officer of the Royal Thai Army, Navy and Air Force" (Thesis submitted for the Degree of Master of Political Science, Chulalongkorn University, 1976).

48. Pornsak Phongpaew, "Political Information of the Thai People," (Unpublished research report submitted to the National Research Council, Bangkok, 1980), p. 131.

49. Pornsak Phongpaew, *Voting Behavior: A Case Study of the General Election of B. E. 2526* (1983), Khon Kaen Region 3 (Bangkok: Chao Phya Press, December 1984), pp. 155–156.

50. Ansil Ramsay, op. cit., p. 9.

51. Somsakdi Xuto, "Conclusion" in Somsakdi Xuto, ed., *Government and Politics of Thailand*.

52. Ibid.

53. Seymour Martin Lipset, *Political Man*, (London: Mercury Books, 1963), p. 82.

54. Thailand's reliance on foreign capital has reached the unprecedented level of 6 to 7 percent of the Gross National Product in 1984.

55. Dr. Ammar Siamwalla, a leading economist, suggested that the government could transfer resources to the agricultural sector by diverting budgetary allocations from other sectors to improve agricultural productivity. He also observed that if there should emerge public opinion to the effect that Thailand should detach itself from the present world economy, the agricultural sector would be the first to be hard hit. See details in *The Nation* (Bangkok), 21 July 1985, p. 1.

CHAPTER NINE

Malaysia:
Quasi Democracy in a Divided Society

ZAKARIA HAJI AHMAD

For many participants and observers, both domestic and foreign, Malaysia's relatively successful experience of democratic process and political stability since *merdeka* ("independence") in 1957, and even before, was seen to be demolished in 1969. In that year, Parliament was suspended and an all-powerful cabal, known as the National Operations Council (NOC), was established to rule the country in the aftermath of the convulsive event of communal riots now known as the "May 13th incident." Old Malaya hand John Slimming was so compelled by the turn of the events then that he issued a book to dramatize it, titled provocatively, if in retrospect erroneously, *Malaysia: Death of a Democracy.*[1] But the turn for the worse that everyone thought had taken place was reversed when in February 1971—barely twenty-one months after the breakdown of the open political process—the NOC relinquished its extraordinary powers and restored parliamentary democratic rule. Since then Malaysia has enjoyed again competitive party and national elections on a regular basis, a relatively open political process with basic freedoms, and orderly transition in leadership succession, all of which when viewed on a long-term basis—irrespective of the NOC interregnum— provide a semblance of a democracy, or in Robert Dahl's formulation, a polyarchy.[2]

Except for the 13 May episode that serves as a hiatus in the short period of only three decades—from 1957 to 1987—of nationhood, ethnically heterogeneous Malaysia has had a remarkable and enviable record of political stability and general social peace marred only by isolated instances of political violence. The phasing out of colonial rule and transition to indigenous rule was achieved smoothly and amicably even as a communist insurrection was in progress. Within half-a-decade of fledgling independence, the original Federation of Malaya was re-constituted into a larger polity with the amalgamation of the Bornean states of Sabah (formerly British North Borneo), Sarawak, and Singapore in 1963.[3] In the postindependence era, there have been three conse-

PENINSULAR MALAYSIA

MALAYSIA

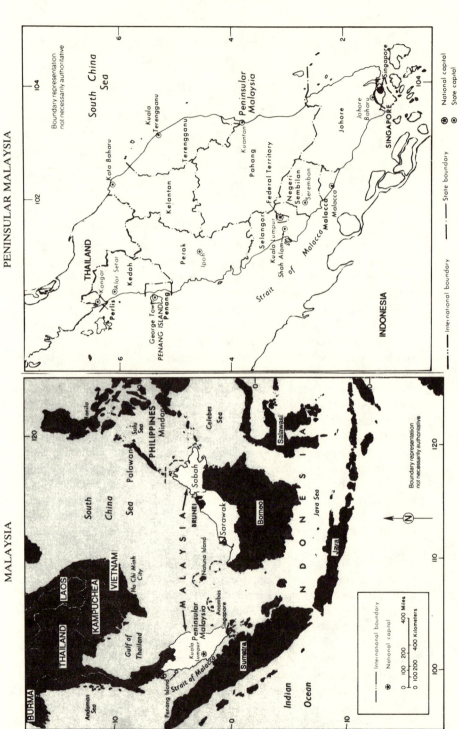

cutive changes of heads of government, seven general elections, and continuing institutionalization of the processes of government in which, *inter alia*, the supremacy of civilian authority has been unquestioned. At the same time economic growth has taken place and the standard of living has improved rather impressively.

However, in terms of democratic performance the record is mixed and its future less certain. Plural Malaysia *cannot* be characterized as nondemocratic if popular choice of government is a primary index of democratic performance. On the other hand, the dictates of and perceived need for a "strong" government able to deal effectively with the competing demands of an ethnically divided society, with strong laws that may even deny in specific instances habeas corpus (such as preventive detention without due process under the Internal Security Act or ISA), and other features present a cameo of antidemocratic elements.[4] Although elections at the national and state levels have been assiduously carried out, local-level polls were suspended in 1964 and subsequently abolished in 1971.[5] Emergency laws as defined under the constitution and effected in 1969 after the 13 May riots are yet to be repealed.[6]

Seen against these contradictions Malaysia is more of a "quasi democracy," its success in trying out a Westminster type of democracy having been a partial one, although certainly more successful than others of the genre. The pattern and style of democracy is more one of form than of substance, as noted by the country's second prime minister, Tun Abdul Razak, who heralded the return to parliamentary democracy after having wielded power in the NOC during the period of nondemocratic rule:

> The view we take is that democratic government is the best and most acceptable form of government. So long as the form is preserved, the substance can be changed to suit conditions of a particular country.[7]

If competitive politics through elections are a significant feature of Malaysian polyarchy, it is also useful to cite the observation of one analyst of Malaysian politics:

> Although Malaysia has many of the outward signs and some of the substance of democracy, to make the system of conflict regulation and elite accommodation viable there has also been substantial regulation of political competition and controls over popular participation, especially since 1969.[8]

In retrospect, the short period of nondemocratic rule in 1969 to 1971 is significant in that it provided for the adaptation of the Westminster model of parliamentary democracy to suit the exclusive demands of a polycommunal society in the postindependence era. The period of NOC rule was not therefore, as was hastily argued by Slimming, a "nonlearning" one but rather an interlude in the aftermath of a crisis whose impact is comparable to the Sputnik effect on the U.S. political system. Nonetheless, it is vitally important not to ignore the conditions under which parliamentary democracy had existed prior to 13 May and the underpinnings of Malaysian society as a consequence of both pre- and postindependence political developments, as these not only explain the continuities in the democratic experience but also the breakdown of the 1969–1971 period. Indeed, it may well be that the thrust of our enquiry should not be to ascertain the relative success, however partial, of democracy but rather why there has not been greater failure.

What then have been the factors that have allowed for a democratic and stable political process? What accounts for the successful functioning of democratic government and what undergirds it? Are there factors that inhibit the emergence of a nondemocratic alternative? Did the colonial experience have an impact? Why has there been continuity in the form of government in spite of a breakdown? Were and are there external factors that promote Malaysian parliamentary democracy? Is the Malaysian experience unique? These are the questions this chapter will attempt to unravel in evaluating Malaysia's democratic experience.

In order to facilitate discussion the chapter will focus on three major periods of political evolution, namely, the pre-1969 developments beginning from World War II; the 1969–1971 interlude of NOC rule; and the post-1971 period to the present. Although these three time periods are arbitrary in many senses, their division here essentially is based on the separation between the earlier and later phases of Malaysia's political evolution by the 13 May interregnum. The post-1969 period of democratic performance was only possible, it may be argued, because of the reordering of the "rules of the game" that had been in place before 1969.

The Context: Geography and Ethnicity

Malaysia is a country physically divided into two portions by the South China Sea. The "peninsular" (an official term replacing the former reference of "West Malaysia") portion comprises the former Federation of Malaya with the states of Perlis, Kedah, Penang, Kelantan, Terengganu, Pahang, Perak, Selangor, Negri Sembilan, Malacca, and Johore; and the other portion consists of the states of Sabah and Sarawak on the island of Borneo (formerly "East Malaysia"). Integration of the two portions is made difficult not only by physical separation and geographical distance, but also by differing histories and by certain state powers enjoyed by Sabah and Sarawak (such as immigration) that the peninsular states do not have. Suffice it to note as well that the very nature of the division of power between the federal and state governments presents peculiar problems in federal-state relations. Also, Sabah and Sarawak (and Singapore) joined the former Federation of Malaya to form Malaysia in 1963, whereas Malaya had gained independence in 1957.

The most important feature of the Malaysian sociopolitical context is the heterogeneous nature of the population and the tendency for every political issue to be transformed into a communal one. The Malays, who constitute only about 47 to 48 percent of the population regard their interests as more than primary because of their indigenous origins.[9] The other major peoples, namely the Chinese and the Indians (including Pakistanis), are migrants who have increasingly settled in the country but demand proportional powers as citizens who have rightfully placed their stake in the system. Malay-non-Malay (usually read "Chinese") political competition constitutes in effect the major parameter in Malaysian politics, accentuated by the prevailing conception that the latter dominates the economy and that politics is the preserve of the former. It is argued by some quarters that this compartmentalization is not necessarily an exclusive ordering, and that "Malay political supremacy" might be further ensured by the creation of opportunities and equity participation for the Malays in the business and economic sector, as spelled out in the New Economic Policy (NEP), promulgated as a result of official analysis of the 13 May riots.

But increased Malay participation in the economic sector does not necessarily connote that increased non-Malay (read "Chinese") participation in politics is welcome, indicating as such a lack of consensus on the "rules of the game." The notion exists among sections of the Malay elite that citizenship rights given to non-Malays prior to independence in 1957, seen as an exchange for Malay "special rights"—the so-called bargain—was in fact too much of a concession against Malay political dominance.[10] These conditions illustrate as such the primacy of the racial factor in Malaysia's political setting.

The ethnic parameter is further complicated by the existence and demands of other indigenous groups such as the Kadazans, Bajaus and others (in Sabah), and the Ibans (in Sarawak) who, together with the *orang asli* ("aborigines") in the peninsular and the Malays, are considered the *bumiputras* (literally "sons of the soil").[11] Indeed the ethnic cleavage problem is trichotomous: Malay versus non-Malay versus "natives" (i.e., the non-Malay indigenes). Of late the religious dimension has also become more salient, concomitant with global religious revivalism (both Islamic and non-Islamic) and the amplification of traditional ethnic cleavage as a Moslem Malay/non-Moslem non-Malay dichotomy in the political milieu.[12]

In terms of numbers the Malays and other indigenous groups compose about 58.6 percent of the population as compared to the non-*bumiputra* (Chinese about 32.1 percent, Indians 8.6 percent, and the remaining "nonindigenous" of about 0.7 percent), indicating the Malay/"indigenous"/"nonindigenous" proportions to be in slight favor of the former.[13] However, in terms of political representation the delineation of parliamentary constituencies is weighted heavily in favor of Malay-dominant rural ones. Hence there is less non-Malay representation, as there are fewer urban constituencies, where most of the non-Malays reside.

It should be noted that most of the following discussion is based primarily on peninsular Malaysia issues, as this sets the tenor of politics for the whole country, and hence the "Malay/non-Malay" distinction is especially relevant.

• HISTORICAL REVIEW •

The pre-1969 Period: "Democracy on Trial"

The period between 1957 and 1969 may appropriately be characterized as "democracy on trial," not because there was a conscious effort to test the democratic process but rather because the Westminster model was adopted without much modification, in spite of the realities of the society's communal nature and the naive understanding of freedom in a democracy, which meant few or no restrictions on the voicing of ethnic demands. In turn such ethnic demands only exacerbated the tensions in a highly communal society and culminated in the collapse of parliamentary democracy in 1969. If the "bargain" between Malay and non-Malay participation in the political and economic sectors, as has already been mentioned, was at least tacitly understood and downplayed so as to present a multiethnic front to gain independence from the British in 1957, the postindependence period that led to the breakdown in democracy in 1969 displayed how tenuous was the acceptance from *all* of these limits.

Given the argument that democracy can only flourish if the soil and climate are acceptable, it may be considered remarkable that within the short period of twelve years from independence, Malaysia experienced three general and *free* elections. In retrospect the period in question may not only have been too brief, but perhaps also there was too ready an acceptance of the British model of parliamentary democracy. Prime Minister Tunku Abdul Rahman, who held the post throughout the period under review and who also secured independence from the British, declared one year after *merdeka* the commitment to democracy:

> Whatever others may do, and however hard we may have to fight, we will stand by the ideals, and the principles of democracy. We are determined to

create a new nation evolving our own personality, maintaining our Malayan way of life and defending our Parliamentary democracy and upholding the principle that the state is made for men and not men for the state.[14]

Although the commitment to democracy—in whatever form—may be said to have been a priority principle of the Tunku and his successors, the principal challenge was and is whether such a system of government suits the communal basis of Malaysian society. The outstanding question throughout this period, starting from the end of World War II to 1969, was whether postcolonial Malaya, and later Malaysia, was to be a "Malay" or a multiracial entity, an issue at present seemingly subdued but probably not entirely resolved.

There was probably no question in the British scheme of things that their eventual legacy to the new indigenous regime of Malaya and Malaysia was that of a democratic system of government and a multi-racial polity. On the return of the British to Malaya in 1945, they set out to establish the Malayan Union Scheme (MUS), which would have abrogated the rights of the sultans of the various states and granted equal citizenship rights to both the Malays and the non-Malays (who then and hitherto had merely been seen as transients). In the event, Malay protests were so overwhelming that the proposal was replaced by the Federation of Malaya Agreement (1948), which allowed for a federal union of what had been before the war three separate entities under direct and indirect British tutelage.

As the basis for later constitutional developments the Federation of Malaya Agreement (1948) is important in that it provided for a strong central government in a federal setting—in other words, a strong central authority could impose its will in the context of democracy. Thus strong institutions of central state rule were evolved, as in the bureaucracy, the police, and the armed forces, and more important, the central government would also have strong constitutional powers. Also most of the symbols of power would have a decidedly Malay characteristic, and civilian authority was to be primary. Strong central government denoted that the federal government would have precedence over many areas of control. Given the lack of priority to local matters but a strong sense of linkage of any political event to *national* interests, federal-state relations have assumed a certain importance in a highly centralized polity. Who controls the state and federal governments becomes a serious matter. For the most part, federal and state governments have usually been in the hands of the intercommunal Alliance (later Barisan Nasional) government, and this has made democracy viable. When opposition parties have controlled state governments, this has often been viewed "seriously" by Kuala Lumpur—an indication of a "loss" of its control. In the Malaysian case the central government has not hesitated to resort to "emergency" powers to seize state governments run by opposition parties when it deemed a crisis in their authority existed, as in Sarawak in 1966 and Kelantan in 1978.

Because of the sudden "awakening" by the Malay masses and their leaders in protest against the MUS some observers portray the post-1945 period as the beginning of modern Malaysian political history, but more important was the eventual creation as a result of such mobilization of the United Malays National Organization (UMNO), a party that has become the central actor in Malaysian politics. On the other hand, however, UMNO's role could later be seen as a symbol of both *Malay* and *Malaysian* nationalism, although such a juxtaposition would often be viewed as anathema to the non-Malays. For the Malays, in the conception of a Malay-based Malay(si)an polity, UMNO is not only the vanguard of Malay aspirations but also the final arbiter of the ethnic question.

The armed challenge of the Malayan Communist Party (MCP) led the British to foster the creation of the Malay(si)an Chinese Association (MCA) in 1949, so as to enable the mass of Chinese in the country to seek a means of support in lieu of the largely Chinese MCP. In time, however, the MCA took on a political basis and "joined" up with UMNO in an electoral pact to contest the 1952 Kuala Lumpur municipal elections. Encouraged by the success of the electoral arrangement at the 1952 elections, in which they secured nine of twelve seats, the UMNO and the MCA teamed up with the Malay(si)an Indian Congress (MIC) and participated in the first countrywide legislative council elections of 1955 in which they won fifty-one of the fifty-two seats contested.

The important features of these developments were simply that politics was being mobilized on communal lines, and that the coalition that was created and proved a winning formula in mediating demands was the intercommunal Alliance Party, made up of the UMNO, the MCA, and the MIC.[15] The Alliance Party framework proved a useful device for sorting out the communal demands that each component party articulated but was also to prove a fragile arrangement, as compromises had to be worked out between the leaders of these parties in order to present a cohesive political front. This cohesive political front was deemed crucial to winning the struggle for independence, for the colonial power would only depart if a multiracial political formula was ready to take over the reins of power. The British in the meantime harbored the hope that postcolonial Malaya would be a homogenized polity, but finally accepted the Alliance formula both as a recognition of the realities and so as not to impede self-rule. In the struggle for independence, then, quite a number of critical ethnic demands became submerged, which only later surfaced to plague the legitimacy of the partners of the Alliance.

Malay primacy in politics was throughout this time paramount in the considerations of the postcolonial nation-state. The Federation of Malaya Agreement of 1948 entrenched the status of the Malay royal houses, the position of the Malays, and the Malay language. Citizenship rights were granted to the non-Malays as a compromise in return for their acceptance of the new nation-state and the "special rights" of the Malays. These ground rules, as it were, were written into the Malayan and Malaysian constitutions and were regarded by some as a "constitutional contract" (or more commonly, the "bargain") between the leaders of the intercommunal government. However, these provisions were never fully understood by those of the younger generation, and even those who had tacitly agreed to their necessity began to take issue with their implications in the 1960s. After Singapore, Sarawak, and Sabah joined Malaya to form Malaysia in 1963 a debate ensued on the status of the Malays and the non-Malays and the agitation for a "Malaysian Malaysia," rather than the acceptance of a "Malay Malaysia." Malaysia's creation was itself an exercise in "racial balancing"—ensuring the dominance of the Malays and their indigenous brethren of Sarawak and Sabah against the large influx of Chinese Singaporeans into the expanded population as a result of the merger between the four territories. Singapore's expulsion in 1965 had much to do with its role in questioning the primary position of the Malays in the Malaysian polity.

Within the Alliance itself, there arose demands for a reordering of the rights and obligations of the component parties. Before the 1959 general elections, the newly elected MCA leadership under Dr. Lim Chong Eu openly demanded more MCA candidates because of their numerical representation, as well as the preservation of "the Chinese way of life," the Chinese language, and Chinese schools. This precipitated a challenge to the Alliance formula that, according to one observer, "seemed to transgress the parameters of bargaining between the Alliance partners."[16] Bargaining on such issues was a common feature in the Alliance Party system, but its mode and resolution was to be an internal and nonpublicized matter. In any event, the Alliance leadership through the Tunku refused to accede to the demands and the Lim Chong Eu group lost their position in the MCA. Von Vorys concludes: "The lesson was clear: the top UMNO leadership had a virtual veto in the selection of the highest MCA leaders."[17] On the other hand though, the Alliance also protected its components from without, rebuffing for example the alternative to the MCA that Lee Kuan Yew offered when Singapore was part of Malaysia. Also the Alliance top leadership did not allow the advocacy of racial demands, those of the Malays included, to violate the intercommunal formula.

In essence, then, the Alliance formula worked well, for it allowed for an airing of views by its elites that would be settled within the inner circles of the coalition leadership. According to Karl von Vorys, what evolved was a democracy without consensus, which displayed the following features:

> First, the relationship of citizens with the same group would continue to be managed through a semi-autonomous communal hierarchy. Second, the relationship of citizens across communal boundaries or to the government would be regulated through terms agreed to by an inter-communal Directorate at the highest level. Third, the terms of inter-communal relations would be promulgated in a constitutional contract, then implemented and when necessary augmented by policies secretly negotiated. Fourth, the members of the Directorate would have to possess dual qualifications. They would have to be the leaders of the political organization [party] of their community most capable of mobilizing mass support behind the government in democratically controlled elections. No less important, they would also have to be men who could maintain the confidence of their colleagues by keeping negotiations within the Directorate secret and by refraining from *ever* mobilizing their external communal mass-support to bring pressure on the secret negotiations.[18]

The events leading up to 13 May 1969 of course only signified that this framework was unworkable, although in the post-1971 period the continued resort to the intercommunal formula only showed some of the ground rules had changed.

As has been noted, the British did not want to allow the continuation of ethnically based political parties in postcolonial Malaya, and hoped that the Independence of Malaya Party (IMP), led by Dato Onn bin Jaafar, would be a success after its formation in 1951. Dato Onn himself had led the Malay struggle against the MUS but had to voluntarily relinquish his position as president of UMNO when his party refused to follow his proposal to admit non-Malays into what he believed would be a nationalist party knowing no racial categories. As events were to prove, though, the IMP fared poorly in the Malaysian political area, as have other noncommunal parties.[19] The failure of noncommunal political parties is simply a consequence of the nature of the polity in which political mobilization has greatest success when it appeals to race. As noted by Khong, any single party that attempted to present a noncommunal framework had to contend with the challenge of attracting substantial amounts of both Malay and Chinese votes.[20] Similarly, the outlawed MCP, which chose the armed struggle to secure liberation from the British and to create a presumably noncommunal Malayan republic, never had much appeal. However, the MCP also had two other features that disqualified it, namely, that it refused to cooperate with the other nationalist groups for a peaceful struggle against the British and that it was always seen in Malay eyes as an alien movement.[21]

Because the struggle for independence was waged constitutionally, it was perhaps inevitable that the country adopted a political system based on constitutional democracy. The party system that came into being also meant that competition for power would be fought on party lines, although increasingly there emerged a view in some quarters, especially the bureaucracy, that party politics was a bane to the country's development.[22] The communal nature of politics produced parties that were communally based, and this led in effect to a fragmented political system, which made the working of democracy difficult. Rather than allow the continuation of a multiple-party system, in the post-1971 period the ruling elites in fact attempted a modified version of a two-party system, if not a one-party-dominant one.

The workability of democracy in Malaysia in a political environment so rife with ethnic demands had much to do with the personality of Tunku Abdul Rahman, who came across as a "father" of the nation not only because he led the struggle for independence, but also because he appeared to be above communal chauvinism. The British administration under Field Marshal Tun Sir Gerald Templer sought a figure with Tunku's attributes, and thus it was that the man who believed so much in British notions of popular government, including parliamentary democracy, appeared at the right moment in Malaysian history to lead the country to independence.[23] But the Tunku's retirement in 1970 was precipitated by the difficulty of playing the role of balancing ethnic demands; indeed, a section of Malay opinion saw him as having "sold" the country to the non-Malays, while non-Malay leaders close to the Tunku could no longer keep their followers in line in the face of greater demands for opportunities and access to the system.

For a time the Alliance formula seemed the best solution to the challenge of ethnic politics and one compatible with a framework of parliamentary democracy. After all, it led to resounding victories in 1952 and 1955 and did win independence from the British. In the 1959, 1964, and 1969 elections, it also held a majority of the seats and therefore was secure in its control of the government. However, a closer analysis (see Table 9.1) also shows that the opposition parties had begun to make inroads into the Alliance's margin of victory, especially when comparing the 1959 and 1969 election results. The 1964 election results did show the Alliance's massive strength, but this poll was conducted one year after the formation of Malaysia, and a show of unity with the government was not unexpected given the reality of an external threat from Indonesia. In the 1969 elections, although the Alliance still managed a majority of the seats, the better showing by the opposition caused a temporary loss of confidence and even the conclusion by some in the ruling party that it had lost its mandate. Indeed the Alliance formula could be seen as unacceptable to the voters since the opposition garnered 52.5 percent of the votes versus the Alliance's 47.5 percent. In fact, in the elections in Peninsular Malaysia, the percentages were 51.5 versus 48.5.

Table 9.1   Strength of Government and Opposition in the Malaysian Dewan Rakyat (Lower House), 1959–1986 by Seats and Percentage of Votes Won

Election Year	Government Number of Seats	Government Percent of Seats	Opposition Percent of Votes	Opposition Number[a] of Seats	Total Percent of Votes	Total Number of Seats
1959	74	71.2	51.7	30	48.3	104
1964[b] (Sabah)	89	85.6	58.5	15	41.5	
(Sarawak)	48	87.3	—[c]	7	—[c]	159
(Singapore)	92	63.9	47.5	52	52.5	144
1969 (Peninsular Malaysia)[d]	66	64.1	48.5	37	51.5	103
1974	135	87.7	60.7	19	39.3	154
1978	130	84.4	57.2	24	42.8	154
1982	132	85.7	60.5	22	39.5	154
1986[e]	148	83.6	55.8	29	41.5	177

Sources: Malaya. Election Commission. *Report on the Parliamentary (Dewan Ra'ayat) and State Legislative Assembly General Elections*, for the years 1959, 1964, 1969, 1974, 1978, and 1982. (Kuala Lumpur: Government Printer, 1960, 1965, 1970, 1975, 1979 and 1983); H. Crouch, *Malaysia's 1982 General Election* (Singapore: Institute of Southeast Asian Studies, Research Notes and Discussion Paper no. 34), p. 58; K. J. Ratnam and R. S. Milne, *The Malaysian Parliamentary Election of 1964* (Singapore: University of Malaya Press, 1967); and Karl von Vorys, *Democracy without Consensus: Communalism and Political Stability in Malaysia* (Princeton: Princeton University Press, 1975), p. 297. Office Automation Sdn. Bhd., *1986 Malaysian Parliamentary Elections Held on August 2nd & 3rd, 1986, Including Analysis of 1984 Electoral Delineation Exercise* (Petaling Jaya: Office Automation Sdn Bhd., 1986), [Tables ER1 and ER4].

Notes: [a] Includes "Independents."
[b] Parliamentary elections were only held in peninsular Malaysia. Seats for the whole country were calculated with the addition of state legislative seats for Sabah, Sarawak, and Singapore. (See Ratnam and Milne, as cited above).
[c] Not ascertainable.
[d] Excluding the result of the Melaka Selatan constituency where the election was delayed (see von Vorys, as cited above).
[e] There were 2.7 percent spoilt votes.

What is more interesting about the conduct of elections as part of the democratic process, however, was probably the unstated notion that losing an election meant virtually total political defeat. Therefore 1969 served notice to the Alliance leadership that it might have to one day face the prospect of an electoral defeat. Under "normal" circumstances such a prospect might be acceptable to the more democratic-minded Alliance elites; however, in a context of communal issues any such loss would be interpreted as the end of the primary rights of the Malays. The rules of the game of Malaysian democracy were therefore set for modification after 1969 because the prospect of a zero-sum electoral result would be unacceptable if Malay political supremacy was not to be assured.

Inasmuch as competitive politics denote that there must be ruling and opposition parties, it has been the intercommunal political party—the Alliance (later Barisan Nasional)—that has managed to be victorious at the various national elections that have been held. It must be noted as well that the Alliance framework allowed Malay political dominance through UMNO, even as the latter shares power with its other partners. In contrast, however, no opposition party has had the ability to present a power-sharing formula between the major ethnic groupings in the country. Opposition parties in Malaysia have at best only been regionally based or have appeared to be representative of one race even if they purport to be noncommunal (as the Democratic Action Party, DAP) or religious (as the Pan-Malaysian Islamic Party or PAS). Moreover, it can be noted that opposition parties have yet to be able to forge an alliance; they have thus often been fragmented or too sectarian to offer a real alternative to the Alliance formula in a political milieu in which racial representation is all-important.

It is often forgotten that competitive politics is possible only if the public order and national security situations provide the necessary conditions for their conduct. In the case of Malaysia, it is of course remarkable that parliamentary democracy before 1969 often operated in conditions of insurgency and even the threat of an external invasion. But what made possible the conduct of parliamentary democracy under such unfavorable conditions was that, to a large extent, the instruments for law and order and national security, being largely under Malay control and perceived so, ensured against a non-Malay seizure of power.[24] The high premium on law and order and Malay control of the forces of order and national security in this sense made democracy workable. Indeed democracy in Malaysia depends to some extent on faith in the ability of the police and national security agencies to uphold the law and maintain public order, as well as nonviolent political participation among the multiethnic public. One can attribute the government's inability to hold on to this faith to the apparent breakdown of law and order during the 13 May riots. On its eve, as noted by von Vorys:

> British example inspired the salience of democratic politics, but Malayan ingenuity adapted it to a polity dominated by communal cleavages. For twelve years the system appeared to be stable enough within expanding boundaries. It was able to control a variety of challenges: from the voters, from within the political leadership, from Communist insurgents, or from Indonesian military forces. It also managed inter-communal conflict. Although occasional clashes did take place, they were small and localized in scale. Order was quickly restored; communal violence was not permitted to become a widespread challenge.[25]

One other factor has a bearing on the country's generally pro-democratic stand. The challenge of the MCP, which resulted in a nationwide counterinsurgency effort known as the "Malayan Emergency" of 1948–1960 had led to a suspicion, if not phobia, about communism and even socialism.[26] This phobia about anything that smacks of the Left was most marked during the tenure of the Tunku, who saw communism in all things evil. The fact that the MCP's challenge was an armed attempt to overthrow legally constituted government meant that it was a real threat that had to be contained, if not eliminated—a situation that was not altered even after Malaya's independence and the formation of Malaysia.

The conception prevailed that communism was anathema to free or democratic politics. The impact of the communist challenge was so deep that the tendency arose to blame any problem such as the 13 May event on the influence or handiwork of Communists, as if any failure of democracy is simply because antidemocratic (read "communist") forces are at work.

Largely because the Communists, whether by subversion and/or through armed terrorism, were "controlled," there was perhaps the notion that the government did not have to exercise overwhelming curbs on the political process as to even inhibit choices or alternatives of government. "Strong laws" were and remain in force in order to provide the capacity to contain the communist challenge, but thanks to the personality and views of the Tunku and his followers, as well as the fact that the Alliance enjoyed political supremacy, the polity did not begin to have a more authoritarian government.

The 1969–1971 Period: Democracy Suspended

Whatever may be said of 13 May, it may well be that if it did not happen, it might have to have been invented. Up to 1969 the country's political system had allowed full vent to the airing of communal demands, which reached a crescendo in the campaign of the May general election. Ironically, perhaps, Malaysian democracy collapsed through a demo-cratic instrument, the elections, as succinctly described by one observer:

> On May 13, 1969, the delicate understandings and institutions which had maintained a tolerable equilibrium in this plural society broke down under the strain of a hard-fought election campaign.[27]

Why the 1969 election was so "special" that it led to a collapse of the system was perhaps because earlier elections had not marked the critical issues of the polity, in particular race; as noted by von Vorys, the 1959 and 1964 elections did not test the system in that the former was held in the "freshness of independence" and the latter "distracted" the electorate because of the external military threat of Indonesian confrontation.[28]

Seen in retrospect the 13 May episode was generally a breakdown that was localized in the federal capital of Kuala Lumpur, although the violence engulfed its whole population in a state of fear and panic. In terms of casualties there were only 196 deaths.[29] Although isolated incidents took place in other urban centers and there was a nationwide curfew, the impact was greatly felt because it was totally unexpected. So great was the perception of its severity that even the forces of law and order could not quite control the situation. Government as such was nonexistent, and public confidence plunged into an abyss.

The cause of the riots was largely the questioning of the racial "bargain" in the polity; in the heat of the communal passions that were generated, violence was perpetuated, although not as much by design as by emotive outburst. These outbursts were a result of a perception that the 1969 election results had showed that the Alliance formula, with UMNO's primacy, was no longer viable. The election results, showing such strong inroads by the opposition, aggravated the feeling amongst the Malays that they were no longer in control of their country and indeed would be pushed back to the *kampongs* (villages) by the non-Malays. In the first forty-eight hours of communal rioting that engulfed the capital, the first response of the Alliance government (which, although reduced in legislative seats, still commanded a majority, by a margin that most "Western" liberal democracies would consider a luxury) was to adopt a pacification approach to placate both Malays and non-Malays.

This was countermanded by the vigorous assertion of Tun Dr. Ismail's views. Tun Dr. Ismail had been an "anchor" in the ruling elite in the heyday of Alliance rule and had retired in 1967, but returned to the government's fold from retirement because of the crisis. He advocated tough measures and a declaration of "emergency rule." Indeed, he actually declared that "democracy is dead."[30]

Thus it was that the National Operations Council (NOC) was formed that would control the function of government with the suspension of parliamentary democracy. All this, significantly enough, was done under the rule of law, with the appropriate proclamation by the king as stipulated by the constitution.[31] As noted by von Vorys, "constitutional government was not being abandoned."[32] In fact the NOC functioned alongside the cabinet with the Tunku as the prime minister.[33] The decision to proclaim an emergency and form an emergency government (the NOC) seemed a matter-of-fact decision, according to von Vorys. According to this account the deputy prime minister, Tun Abdul Razak, had convened a few ministers along with Tun Dr. Ismail after the outbreak of the 13 May riots and they then decided to suspend parliamentary government.[34]

The period between 1969 and 1971 may be designated as the period of "suspended democracy," but its span was only temporary and actually a time for the country to pick up the pieces and start all over again, as it were. In the words of one of the NOC's members, their focus was on the restoration of law and order, the orderly system of government, and racial harmony.[35] In their deliberations, a choice had to be made as to

what the system of government would be after the end of NOC rule, as
to whether it would be a democratic or an authoritarian one. The choice
was the former. There was every opportunity that the NOC could be
arbitrary and, worse still, expropriate wealth with the powers at its
behest and even stage a coup within the government.[36] But these possibilities were safeguarded by "special measures," and the NOC concentrated its efforts on the restoration of parliamentary democracy.[37] There
was always the possibility that the NOC would prolong its power indefinitely, but it would appear that the leaders of the NOC had the
return to normalcy as a foremost goal in their minds. There is some oral
evidence to indicate that the NOC members debated extensively on the
merits of democratic versus nondemocratic models of government but
finally chose the former.[38]

It was clear, though, that the bases of the political system had to be
modified. The intercommunal formula would be retained somewhat and
the "constitutional contract" more or less left intact. As observed by von
Vorys:

> There was still room for bargaining and for a "give and take." But the final
> decision on cultural integration, the appropriate marginal rates of growth in
> the Malay access to the economy and Chinese access to government would
> not be resolved by a compromise among more or less equal parties. They
> would be decided by what the top UMNO leaders considered fair and in the
> interest of Malaysia. It was, of course, a very much simpler system.[39]

In going about this, the rationale rested in most part on the causes of the
13 May riots, and the steps were then taken to rectify the grievances that
had enveloped the system.[40] The Tunku stepped down (in part because
of exhortations by those in his party, in part because he had originally
wanted to do so) in 1970 and it was clear the country was poised for a
"new" era.

It was recognized that the basic rights of the communities as laid
down before 1969 would be maintained, but the need to continue with
democratic politics meant the imposition of restraints. Thus reforms,
bold and novel, were introduced in three areas.

First, a "national ideology" or *Rukunegara* was declared that provided
the basic ground rules of what was conceived as the quintessential Malaysian society. The parameters or *Rukunegara*, as set out, are best cited:

> Our Nation, Malaysia, being dedicated
>   to achieving a greater unity of all her peoples;
> to maintaining a democratic way of life;
> to creating a just society in which the wealth
>   of the nation shall be equitably shared;
> to ensuring a liberal approach to her rich and
>   diverse cultural traditions;
> to building a progressive society which shall be
>   oriented to modern science and technology;

> We, her people, pledged our united efforts to attain these ends guided by these principles:
> Belief in God
> Loyalty to King and Country
> Upholding the Constitution
> Rule of Law
> Good Behavior and Morality.[41]

Second, new educational and economic policies were introduced to redress the grievances of the economic imbalance so as to achieve national unity. Most prominent and expressly stated were the New Economic Policy (NEP) and the National Education Policy under which, among others, Malay would be vigorously implemented as the medium of instruction right through the university. The NEP, as an economic basis for the post-1969 political system, specified the ultimate goal of national unity through a two-pronged strategy of poverty eradication and of "restructuring," by which was meant the reduction, if not elimination, of the identification of race with vocation. Rather than accept the feature of Malaysian social structure in which non-Malays dominated the business and economic sectors and the Malays the agricultural and nonmodern sectors, a conscious effort was to be made to "urbanize" the Malays and assist them in gaining access to the more modern sector of the economy so that they could, at a minimum, be on par with the more advanced non-Malays.[42] In operational terms the Malay share of equity in the corporate sector was to be increased to 30 percent from the less than 1 percent proportion before 1969, and a percentage of posts in the business sector was to be created or reserved for Malays and other *bumiputras*. The major piece of legislation that governed the implementation of this policy was the Industrial Coordination Act.

However, given the NEP's twenty-year span (ending in 1990), its very achievements or lack of it are likely to generate political queries from both Malay and non-Malay sources in the future, as became evident in the years 1985–1986 when the country was affected by a severe recession. It is significant that the NEP was predicated on an assumption that economic growth would be dynamic (or that the economic pie would be expanding) and found tacit, if not ready, acceptance because of a general desire to remove the socioeconomic ills of the system that had erupted in the 13 May episode.

Finally, new legislation was passed in the reconvened Parliament of 1971 prohibiting public challenge of the constitution and the entrenched provisions—specifically Malay rights, citizenship (especially of the non-Malays), royalty, and Malay as the national language—and making it seditious to raise these "sensitive issues."

The NOC leaders were firm and forthright in setting the new rules of the game. But they also wanted their strategies for reform to be based on a majority of opinion. To this end there was the establishment of a National Consultative Council (NCC) with a wide range of representation from various groups in society and politics (save for two parties of the opposition, the Democratic Action party or DAP and the Labour party). A new department to oversee government's goals of national unity was set up—the Department of National Unity (DNU), which, at the initiative and under the leadership of Tan Sri Ghazali Shafie, drafted the *Rukunegara*.[43]

The mood of the country, given the shock and paralysis of 13 May, seemed "ready" for many of these innovative policies. It is difficult to analyze precisely what people's views, hopes, and fears were, but the yearning for a return to normalcy made it conducive to readily accept what appeared to be modest, however bold the prescription, and fair improvements to the system. The deliberations of the NCC were secret, but it is apparent that the persuasive powers of the ruling NOC and its prime actors such as Ghazali Shafie and Tun Dr. Ismail held the day in the midst of any argument. Thus when the then minister of education pushed for a national education policy, it was so quickly done that it could be considered a master stroke.

Powerful as the NOC was and could be, its role and position in the political system appeared twofold: one, to preserve law and order and ensure security of the larger regime so that there was normal functioning of government, and two, to use its extraordinary capacity to galvanize public-sector talent (especially in the government's central agencies such as the Economic Planning Unit) in the formulation of policies for the polity and economy. During its tenure, there was no open political activity but debate was allowed under wraps, as it were, within itself (the NOC) and the NCC. Several leaders of the opposition were incarcerated, such as V. David and Lim Kit Siang, and the NOC also took strong action against paramilitary groups capable of waging organized violence. Press freedom was initially curtailed but gradually there was a relaxation. If authoritarianism was the style of the NOC, it was benign, and its goal was not so much to wrest power but to achieve law and order.

Once the government was assured that it would have a two-thirds majority in Parliament—which it obtained after the elections were completed in Sabah and Sarawak—the stage was set for the government under Tun Razak to introduce legislation in the form of the Constitution (Amendment) Bill of 1971 that would establish the rules of the game whereby certain "sensitive" issues could no longer be raised and made a political issue, even in Parliament. The key concern was for national unity, which would set the succeeding stage of Malaysian politics. The rules of the game meant the entrenchment of the provisions of the constitution as already agreed to by the leaders of the intercommunal coalition during the fight for independence and the formation of Malaysia. These provisions would be the unquestioned basis of the post-1971 democratic regime.

Post-1971 Developments: Democracy Sustained

It might be argued of course that the constraints imposed on the system of parliamentary democracy after 1971 made difficult public discourse on issues that are central to the political system. However, those who instituted these restraints probably believed in the need to achieve such restraint not by fiat (which powers they had), but by the system of popular representation (the reconvened post-1971 Parliament and the NCC of 1969–1971).[44] The key, it was probably surmised, was to broaden the consensus.

Under Tun Razak, often seen as a leader with a penchant for action and dynamic administration, rather than the "father-like" qualities of his predecessor, Tunku Abdul Rahman, what mattered most was that there should not be excessive "politicking." Before 1969, the multiparty system only amplified the range of issues, which led to extremes because of the communal nature of politics. Now that curbs were imposed there was also a need to redefine the Alliance formula. There was, nevertheless, a streak of the paternalistic leadership style à la the Tunku, but certainly in a different form. In Tun Razak's words the Westminster form of democracy was not suitable for Malaysia:

> The Malaysian type of democracy is best suited to the needs of the country's unique multi-racial society. The Malaysian concept of democracy subscribes also to the need to balance individual interests against the general security of the State. The view we take is that democratic government is the best and most acceptable form of government.... We recognize that each nation must develop... its own chosen political and economic system and that the developing world has a special need of an articulated political system suitable to its own problems.[45]

Similarly, another prime architect of the "democracy of à la Malaysia" mode, Tan Sri Ghazali Shafie, maintained that the country needed a "native-based" system (meaning Malay primacy) but which at the same time also implied "cooperation with all the other races in the country." [46] In this period of democracy sustained the thrust has been on enlarging the intercommunal coalition, or in effect, the creation of "grand alliances."

Since Tun Razak the coalition builder passed away in 1976, it is not clear if the eventual objective was a grand coalition that encompassed all political groups, or if the party system should be simplified only to have ruling and opposition elements. On this, Razak's views seemed to indicate that the less opposition, the better:

> It is very well for some people to say that a strong opposition is essential to our democratic way of life.... But in our Malaysian society of today, where racial manifestations are very much in existence, any form of politicking is bound to follow along racial lines and will only enhance the divisive tendencies among our people.[47]

Accordingly, the strategy seemed to point to a process of co-opting the opposition as well.[48] The Alliance coalition formula became the Barisan Nasional or BN ("National Front") in 1974 and, as expected, did rather well at the 1974, 1978, 1982, and 1986 elections (see Table 9.1). In effect, the politics of the 1970s in the new democratic system meant that Barisan's opponents were mainly the Malay-based Party Islam or PAS which itself was in the BN between 1974 and 1978, and the Chinese-based Democratic Action party (DAP).

The process of coalition building in Malaysia after 1971 has resulted in several effects. First, the system is more stable and the government's strength no longer "fluctuating" as before 1969. In the last four elections (1976, 1978, 1982, 1986) the strength of the Barisan, both in terms of voting appeal and number of seats, has been just about constant and, as important, overwhelming. Its proportion of the vote has been between 55 and 60 percent, which—with the exaggerated parliamentary majority produced by the rural-weighted, single-member-district electoral system (see below)—has given it a commanding 83 to 88 percent of the seats in the lower house (Table 9.1). Second, given the awareness that racial conflagration benefits no one, there is an atmosphere of cooperation more readily available and that allows for a sense of being on the winning team for the members of the BN. In addition, such cooperation is not necessarily negative, as there is scope to discuss issues of *implementation* of policies over the accepted bases of the society. Third, the "grand coalition" success has probably meant that some critical issues have been subdued, presumably for the sake of racial harmony. Fourth, the "grand coalition" strategy, as contrasted with the earlier Alliance formula, enlarges the notion of participation in a ruling party that transcends the earlier Malay-Chinese-Indian configuration to be more representative of the various ethnic groups. Also, Sabah and Sarawak parties are involved in the sharing of power that allows for a greater sense of the national pursuit of stability and consensus. From a simple tripartite coalition as existed in the Alliance, the BN has enlarged to become a combination of eleven to thirteen components, its actual total being dependent on certain parties (especially in Sabah and Sarawak) which opt out at various times whenever state electoral contests are held.

More important, in terms of government and opposition, the fear of an electoral defeat has been diminished under the Barisan Nasional coalition concept. The parties that have not succumbed to the taste of power by joining the BN cannot pretend to be able to form the national government at any time in the foreseeable future. Because of its ability to incorporate diverse parties and additional components within its aegis, the BN can be confident that it will never "lose power." Even if its percentage of the popular vote cast now hovers between 55 and 60 percent, the BN's supremacy is determined by its ability to obtain two-thirds of the seats in the lower house, which is assured by the electoral system. This two-thirds majority is deemed crucial because it enables the BN to obtain passage of legislation, especially that pertaining to amendments to the constitution. Given its commanding majority in Parliament, the ruling Barisan government has been able to push into passage virtually every piece of legislation, and its two-thirds majority also provides an important ingredient of psychological advantage since it knows it can amend the constitution almost at will. During the 1986 election this "advantage" became the rallying point and battle cry of the opposition parties to deny the BN this "magical" two-thirds majority. Similarly, it can be noted that any feeling that the BN "does not have power" (as when at various times in the 1970s it did not have control of all state governments) is almost eliminated as a result of the BN's grand coalition mechanism.

Another aspect of the grand coalition formula of the BN is the implicit belief in a centralization of power by the dominant partner in the coalition, UMNO. The hesitation to recognize the victory of the Parti Bersatu Sabah (PBS) when it came to power in Sabah in mid-1985 (and which ratified its victory in yet another state election in 1986), and admit it to the BN was perhaps motivated by a fear in the center of an emergence at the periphery of a party that was non-Malay in character.[49] However, in view of the need to obtain the two-thirds majority in the August 1986 national elections, the PBS was admitted as a member of the BN coalition.

It has to be acknowledged, of course, that the internal and external conditions of Malaysia in the 1970s were conducive to the democratic format of an enlarged intercommunal coalition with entrenched Malay symbols of state rule. The resurgence of communist terrorist activities in the years 1974–1976 and the possible threat of an invasion from Vietnam only fortified the perceived need for a greater consensus on the stakes of the polity. One could argue as well that a more politically assertive ASEAN after 1976 has helped to foster better political development in Malaysia.[50]

On the other hand however, the government in power has found it increasingly necessary to impose restrictions on the conduct of democracy by using the majority it has garnered at the polls to enact legislation and measures that would often be viewed as "antidemocratic" by Western liberals. To some extent, the fears of the popularly elected

Barisan Nasional are founded on the challenges to the regime that are often viewed as a threat to both regime and national security: the 1974–1976 resurgence of communist insurgent attacks, the 1974 student and farmer demonstrations, and the aggravation of communal tensions as a result of its own policies of "restructuring." According to H. Crouch, all these "constituted a prospect of a further political upheaval" and "a turn to a more authoritarian form of government."[51] Crouch notes, as other examples, the strong if indirect influence over the press (most of which is now owned by the ruling political parties) and the 1975 Amendments to the Universities and Colleges Act that prevent students from taking part in political activity.[52] In the late 1970s there were also curbs placed on freedom of association by amendments made to the Societies Act.

The Mahathir Years

The death in 1976 of Tun Razak, the man who had presided over the transition into the post-1969 era, did not produce a national crisis nor did it lead to any significant changes, as his successor, Tun Hussein Onn, carried on and consolidated the BN style of government. In 1981 Tun Hussein resigned and was replaced by Dato' Seri Dr. Mahathir Mohamad, who then reaffirmed his position in general elections in which the BN secured the two-thirds majority it desired. Once again the smooth transfer of power demonstrated the stability of the Malaysian political system. The year before Tun Hussein stepped down from office, for example, could be characterized for Malaysia as one of "political consolidation and economic development, highlighting in fact a burgeoning political economy."[53] If any threat existed, it was merely from without, more precisely that of the expansionist nature of Vietnam after its invasion of Kampuchea.[54]

But with the advent of Dr. Mahathir, the country appeared poised for a "new beginning" through a man whose socialization was more indigenous in training (unlike his predecessors, he was not educated in Britain) and different in vocation (a medical practitioner as opposed to earlier premiers who were lawyers), and most significantly, was fired to bring forth a new "style" in Malaysian politics. Imploring his countrymen to turn away from the West, Dr. Mahathir initiated a "Look East" policy (to learn the work ethics of Japan and Korea). He set forth to pull the private and public sectors together as "Malaysia Incorporated," to leapfrog the country into modernization by heavy industrialization (including a "national car" project), to reassert the primacy of politics be reining in the growing power and role of the civil bureaucracy, and to manifest a "liberal" approach by releasing detainees under the Internal Security Act (ISA). As opposed to preceding administrations,

Dr. Mahathir's was forward-looking, dynamic, and action-oriented. Its legitimacy was given the seal of approval with the Barisan's win in the 1982 elections.

However, probably because he did not believe in the value of the Western type of democratic practices but claimed his writ to rule through majority support garnered at the polls, the Mahathir government (which soon began to be labeled by his critics as the "Mahathir shogunate") started to become less tolerant of those who opposed his policies. Most significantly, Dr. Mahathir's "confrontational" style appeared to open divisions within his own party and within the Malay community at large. In 1983, for example, he created a "constitutional crisis" when he proposed to reduce the role of royalty in the constitutional process (such as suggesting that the right to proclaim an "emergency" under article 150 of the constitution should rest with the prime minister and not, as stipulated, in the Yang di Pertuan Agong or supreme ruler). By 1986, in an unprecedented development, strife in UMNO's leadership led to the resignation of his deputy, Dato' Musa Hitam (who in the early days of the Mahathir government seemed to work so well with his chief—they had been the rebels against the Tunku in the heyday of 13 May 1969— that observers called the regime the "2–M government"), and the appearance of two factions in the party known as "Team A" and "Team B." Nevertheless, despite the divisions within UMNO and its major ally, the MCA, an economy hard-hit by recession and numerous scandals (*inter alia*, the failure of a government-backed venture in Hong Kong with a loss of U.S.$1 billion, an abortive attempt to corner the international tin market, and the arrest in Singapore of MCA leader Mr. Tan Koon Swan for criminal breach of trust), Dr. Mahathir's government won the 1986 national elections convincingly.

In April 1987 Dr. Mahathir's mantle was challenged by "Team B" in the UMNO leadership elections, but he narrowly beat his opposition. The outcome, observed an independent regional report, may have assured Dr. Mahathir's leadership, "but his party may have been weakened by the internal dissension."[55] In subsequent months criticism of the government began to escalate both within and without UMNO. This seemed to intensify the racial polarization in the country, exacerbated by several government policies (such as the collapse of deposit-taking cooperatives and the appointment of non-Mandarin-speaking administrators in the Chinese national-type schools), and created a tense atmosphere that some said resembled the conditions prior to the 13 May incident.

The outcome was a brake on the freedom of expression with the arrest of some 106 persons under the ISA beginning from late October 1987, and the closure of three local dailies.[56] In the wake of the arrests, which the authorities said were necessitated to prevent racial conflagration and maintain public order (but which critics said also included those who had been "antigovernment"), the government imposed further restrictions on the reportage in local and foreign publications, granted broader powers to the police to curb public gatherings, and "promised" to delineate more clearly the separation of powers between the executive, legislative, and judicial organs of government.[57] This latter element was seen as an expression of displeasure with the judiciary's decisions "that overturned executive actions."[58] Citing these steps as prophylactic, Dr. Mahathir justified the tough action as proving "that in our society, there are individuals and groups who aren't politically mature and don't know how to control themselves or how not to abuse our liberalism."[59]

The Nature of Democracy in Malaysia

If nonauthoritarian politics means that the public has a choice in selecting its government, it cannot be denied that ample opportunities have been made available since 1971 in the arena of political contestation. However, democracy sustained since 1971 has meant the imposition of curbs on the extent to which politicking can take place in Malaysia. These fears have been justified on the assumption that too much political articulation in an ethnically divided society like Malaysia is more likely to inflame passions and result in political violence. On the other hand, these curbs have resulted in what one observer has characterized as the "limiting of a limited democracy."[60]

The outward conditions of democracy are therefore visible in Malaysia, but at the same time the "rules of the game" are so tight that contenders for power have little room to maneuver in terms of pushing their issues too hard. Against a background of Malay political hegemony, ensured by the centralized nature of the BN coalition, it is therefore interesting that major issues since 1970 have been articulated by non-Malay parties, such as on the Merdeka University (a Chinese-language private tertiary institution) and the Bukit China (an ancient Chinese burial ground) development scheme. These have all been "rebuffed" by the Malay-dominant Barison Nasional.

For the past decade-and-a-half, from 1971 to the time of this writing in 1987, politics in Malaysia have been stable: although fully democratic conditions have not been allowed, nonetheless there has been a sense of political participation, as exemplified by four general elections, and of continuity, as evidenced in two instances of constitutional leadership succession. Although the later events of the continuing Mahathir period have been convulsive and a trying period, the major institutions and processes of Malaysian democracy are still intact and have shown a fair degree of resilience—in other words, there has not been a breakdown in the system. At the same time, however, the circumstances of economic performance (in this case a recession and the prospect of a diminishing "pie") and racial polarization (with religious revivalism rearing its head but not yet full-blown) have dogged the Malaysian political system. Democratic performance through regular electoral contestation has been counterbalanced by curbs on expression in order to prevent racial disaster. The "tight" rules of the game have maintained political stability while also ensuring Malay political hegemony through UMNO and a heavy hand of authority at the center. The result has been the persistence of a quasi democracy in Malaysia.

• MALAYSIAN DEMOCRACY: A THEORETICAL REVIEW •

Taking into account the divisive scenario of ethnic issues in Malaysia one participant-observer contended, in reflecting on the 1969 riots and their aftermath, that politics in the country was more akin to the "art of the possible."[61] It may well be of course that the ideals of Western liberal democracy, in particular the British parliamentary form, may hardly be possible in Malaysia's polycommunal setting. It can hardly be overstated as well that the cultural context, in which there is an amalgam of native, Malay, Indian, and Chinese civilizations and traditions, provides barriers to the unrestricted expression of dissent in the political process. Although Malaysia's record in holding regular and free elections over the past three decades is enviable for a country that still faces tremendous hurdles in socioeconomic modernization, it is possible to detect strong fears that too much democratization in terms of freedom of speech and association can only quickly and surely destroy the system. In large part these fears are based on the volatility of a context of competing communal demands, amply demonstrated by the eruption of the 13 May riots of 1969.

It is not surprising, then, to find a strong paternalistic element in the Malaysian democratic experience, itself not only an indigenous quality but related also to the impact of colonial rule characterized by the imperative need for strong government and a sense of "guidance." In this respect a sense of continuity exists in the pattern of authority from colonial to postcolonial times, in that it is felt any threat of disorder must be quelled quickly, if not already mitigated by deterrent measures. That is, political order as a hallmark of political stability is seen as an overriding goal. One significant feature of this dimension has been the virtual failure of left-wing nationalism to take root in Malaysia so that when independence came in 1957, the mantle of indigenous authority was carried by a set of Westernized, conservative elites led by Tunku Abdul Rahman.[62] That this was so, and was a tradition that continued at least up to the period of Tun Hussein Onn (1976–1981), has lent yet another sinew of stability and persistence to the mode of governing. Although Dr. Mahathir's style of governing since 1981 has been more "indigenous," nonetheless it is similarly paternalistic and perhaps even autocratic such that political order still remains a regime imperative.

The historical trend and style of leadership in Malaysia for the most part, then, did not allow for a serious imbalance between participatory and bureaucratic institutions that could have disrupted the political process.[63] Although the bureaucratic organs of government were built up under the British, consonant with a notion of the need for strong central state control, and buttressing the "custodial" nature of the colonial authority, nevertheless their inveterate status did not impede the growth of participatory entities such as political parties. Indeed, the fact that the leaders of the political elite were drawn from the administrative elite only smoothed the whole nexus of political and administrative functions in the postindependence state. Stable, democratic politics was and is workable for the most part because Malaysia is an "administrative state."[64]

Paternalism and the strong linkage between the bureaucracy and the top elites of the UMNO have only served to provide the sense of a need for conflict management in polycommunal Malaysia. Before 1969 the process was "loose" in that it relied mainly on the informal agreements hammered out within the Alliance intercommunal coalition (especially within the small circle of the top elite), but after 1971 it has become more specific and controlled. "Bargaining" between the components of the Barisan is still possible, but the rules of the game have been set to "satisfy" UMNO as the senior partner.

It can thus be theorized that democracy in a plural society like Malaysia's can only be workable if Malay political hegemony is assured. The coalition concept that is akin to a "consociational" form of democracy—in which the Alliance and later the Barisan Nasional parties make possible a sense of power sharing between communities as well as between the federal and state governments—engenders political harmony, but there can be no question that UMNO or Malay political values take ascendancy.[65] As such, as elaborated elsewhere, the post-1971 Malaysian political system is one in which there is political dominance by one communal group but also room for the accommodation of other communal interests.[66]

It can be said that Malay political hegemony and the unassailable political rights of the non-Malays present special problems of coalition formation and coalition building precisely because Malaysian society is not only plural but very divided. Donald Horowitz has noted that this divisiveness sets the tone for understanding race relations in Malaysia, which were exacerbated by the impact of the Japanese occupation in World War II.[67] In explaining later developments, he notes that the durability of the multiethnic coalition, the Alliance, and later the Barisan Nasional, was predicated on a single slate for electoral competition, which found permanence because of a mixture of electoral incentives and factors which abetted the coalition.[68] In addition, he explains that such a multiethnic coalition creates a situation in which "all the electoral opportunities are located on the ethnic flanks," since, "in an environment of ethnic conflict, there is room for only one multiethnic party or alliance."[69] After 1969 the broadening of the Alliance into the National Front was "motivated by the desire to neutralize threats on the flanks."[70]

Seen in these terms, the stability of the Malaysian political system through an interethnic coalition that receives its mandate through regular elections provides a safety valve in mediating ethnic demands that could easily disrupt the society. The primacy of the multiethnic coalition in this sense denotes that a degree of stability is present in the system because ethnic demands are accommodated within its structure. While the primacy of Malay rights is undeniable in a multiracial context, this provides for stability since neither multiracialism nor single-race politics provide avenues or alternatives to political power. The problem, though, is the proper balance between the two.

Since the beginning of nationwide elections, the system of representation in Malaysia has been based on the single-member constituency and not on proportional representation. In addition, the weightage of constituencies in favor of rural areas has further enhanced Malay representation, in effect almost guaranteeing Malay political power. In turn, despite such inequities in representation, this has assured the Malays of their political role and provides another aspect of the system's stability.[71] Given the parliamentary system as well, the single-member constituency and its allocation of seats under the BN (and its precursor the Alliance) formula provides for a parceling out of political rewards according to ethnic compromises worked within the coalition. As already explained, non-Malay partners of the coalition could still be assured of cabinet representation, sometimes even in a proportion greater than their electoral strength. Also, the discrepancy of virtual Malay political control may have been possible because of non-Malay domination of the economy, thus creating a trade-off of sorts.

The strategy of a "grand alliance" that was introduced after 1971 through the BN framework also had the important effect of accommodating state demands within the federal system in Malaysia, especially between the states of Sabah and Sarawak and Kuala Lumpur. It could be argued that greater state's rights in Sabah and Sarawak (as compared to those enjoyed by states on the peninsula) provide a level of autonomy for these two states, although the popular perception in these states is that it is being encroached upon by the center. In fact, because of the coalition formula, the seemingly inexorable centralizing authority of the federal government and certain built-in state legal provisions, state autonomy has not meant greater autonomy for ethnic groups. In Penang, for example, the non-Malays are more numerous than the Malays, but the sharing of power has always been a feature even with the fact of a Chinese chief minister. On the other hand, when non-Barisan parties have captured power (as in Kelantan), that they were Malay did not preclude the proclamation of emergency rule from the center as happened in 1978. The federal system, in other words, has kept intact the Barisan Nasional system of power sharing between its components and the various ethnic groups.

The problems of Sabah and Sarawak, even as their ruling political parties are part of the BN coalition, are that their ethnic configurations do not fit in neatly into the Malay-non-Malay division of Peninsular Malaysia. Thus, although the BN formula can be seen as fulfilling one of the conditions of Arend Lijphart's concept of consociational democracy, the Malaysian example does not exemplify all of the criteria associated with it.[72] It is possible that Lijphart's criteria for consociational democracy—grand coalition, proportional representation, mutual veto power, and autonomy over group affairs,[73]—were valid to an extent before 1969, but since 1971 Malay dominance in politics as well as the inexorable trend in centralization of the polity[74] would invalidate the relevance of the last three criteria.[75]

As has been explained, competing ethnic demands in Malaysia have been worked out within the context of bargaining and compromises in terms of Malay and non-Malay rights. After 1969 a more pronounced policy of preferences for the economically disadvantaged Malays was implemented, but its dynamic in itself seemed to provide another plank of stability to the system.[76] To some extent this has been possible with the high economic growth averaging 6 to 8 percent in the 1970s, and this also contributed to a sense of a "legitimate" political system in which the government has been able to "deliver the goods." However, increasing economic problems being experienced in the 1980s may call into question the arrangements forged under the BN framework.

It may well be, because conflict management is largely in "Malay" hands, that cultural values will act as a strong influence in thinking about politics and democracy. This proposition would seem to affect both the Malays and non-Malays. According to Pye, the strong curbs placed on open discussion of political issues is reflective of Malay cultural values, which assume that to do the contrary will only lead to disaster. On the other hand, non-Malay (read Chinese) political behavior that has to act in a situation where it is not dominant goes against the Confucian ideals of power, and hence the leadership in the MCA is always feuding internally and the Chinese are forever griping about their secondary status in Malaysian politics.[77]

In evaluating the cultural dimension of democracy, there is an apparent contradiction amongst the ruling elites: that while democracy as an ideal is sought, curbs are placed on the political process as a necessity of political survival. This may well be indicative of the perceived perils of politicking in an atmosphere rife with ethnic demands, but at the same time the danger is that it may actually lead to a less democratic system, as argued by several critics.[78] The seeming contradiction, however, may well be congruent with Asian political values in which strong authority is given a high premium and the forces of opposition merely tolerated. In a recent evaluation of democratic political performance in Asia, Lucian Pye notes that

> if democracy spreads in Asia it is likely to follow the Japanese pattern of a dominant party and fragmented weak opposition groupings . . . . The authoritarian traditions of Asia have in some cases been gradually eroded by the introduction of a controlled process of competitive politics in which a relatively secure dominant party commands the political scene and a diversity of fragmented opposition groups are around to give some life to the political process. In trying to establish the rules for this Asian form of semi-competitive politics the problem has been that of settling on what should be the boundaries of the dominant party and the degree of tolerance of an opposition.[79]

It cannot be overstated that Malay political power and dominance is the overriding theme in Malaysian politics, and in this regard, several attempts have already been made to provide alternative explanations by highlighting *class*, especially in terms of an alliance between Malay political elites and Chinese business interests. Although such explanations are important in themselves, their ideological slant provides little illumination on the whole context of stable democratic political performance.[80]

• FUTURE PROSPECTS •

As long as politics continues to be communal, it is less likely that the Malay political basis will be altered or challenged, notwithstanding any appeal that PAS, the other Malay political party, or even the Chinese-dominant DAP, may have. Indeed UNMO's supremacy is assured because its secular nature allows for an appreciation of non-Malay interests, which non-Malays fear would be "lost" in the theocratic state that PAS wants established. Neither is it clear that class will replace race as an issue in politics, and hence the DAP's appeal will always be short of Malay political support.[81] Given the Barisan coalition's assured dominance in the political system, the basis of democracy as set out after 1971 can be expected to persist for quite a while yet.

After the 1981–1982 period, with the advent of a new administration led by Dr. Mahathir Mohamad, new features have been emphasized in the priorities of government, such as the absorption of Islamic values and a "turning away from Western nations," but how these will affect democratic development in Malaysia is still too early to gauge. What is clear, though, is that there will be curbs on expression so as to preserve "racial peace." The democratic process of majority rule as determined by the vote is likely to be retained, and indeed in the first year of the Mahathir government the regime appeared to want to be more liberal so as to encourage comment, and also released several hundred persons detained under emergency preventive laws. However, Dr. Mahathir's stress on discipline and his priority on industrialization may brook less tolerance of dissent—as was demonstrated when he used the ISA in 1987. Thus, while the system is still open, the signs in recent years indicate a greater emphasis on "strong government" as an imperative of central state rule. This notion of strong government, while domestic in nature, finds a "ready" place in the setting of Southeast Asia.

If Malaysian politics can be understood to be generally elitist in nature, a lot depends on the democratic orientation of its ruling elites. For the most part, this orientation can be said to have existed among the leaders of postcolonial Malaysia, who in spite of the adversities of communal politics, have resisted the easy temptation to embark upon a nondemocratic version of government. One might add as well that the high growth rates of the 1970s have provided pause for the attempt at restructuring for national unity because of an expanding economic pie. Although a regime different in socialization and orientation has taken over the reins of power since 1981, it is not clear if more authoritarian measures will be implemented in this quest for rapid socioeconomic modernization, in which discipline (and as such less "politicking") has been heavily stressed. By and large, though, the outward form of democracy is likely to be maintained even if there will be strong curbs on the limits of civil and political liberties.

The workability of the political system and national security has been due in large part to the country's basis as a Malay-centric one, although inevitably this creates other problems that will loom larger as socioeconomic conditions are enhanced. As national security is in "Malay hands," the political underpinnings of the state are also perceived by the politically advantaged Malays as ensuring their political ascendancy. However, in some sense this indicates that the political and security problems in the next few years are likely to be "Malay" ones, such as the issue of Islamic religious extremism.

On the other hand, however, there is a high premium attached to the notion of "strong" government, not only in terms of having the police and military as well as other security organs safeguarding regime and national security, but being backed by powerful legislation as well, made possible by the ruling coalition's majority in Parliament. In this sense, the government in Malaysia has been able to exert its authority and also have the "will" to do so. This does not mean that it is repressive, but surely indicates a strong desire to maintain and protect its notion of national and state viability and survival. However, such bases of stability are more institutional in character and over time the polity will have to address the need to complement these with other measures.

In the long run, nevertheless, an enduring stability may not be due so much to the instruments of state but to the sense of well-being in the citizenry that will undergird the national consciousness. But for a while yet it is unlikely that race as a *leitmotif* of political consciousness and as a plank of political power will be overtaken by some other factor such as class. There has of course been a tendency for almost every issue to be seen in communalistic terms, even if it originated simply enough. This presents difficulties for the system, naturally, and while the case should not be overstated, it can also be remembered that race has provided for political identification and mobilization in Malaysia's politics. Integration, which includes territorial integration, is a daunting task. Even the attempt to demolish racial barriers via a national language has been viewed by some quarters as in fact having heightened ethnic awareness and tensions.[82]

Overall, therefore, Malaysia has a working form of parliamentary democracy that may lack the substance of more established democracies where the rules of the game are better accepted and understood, but it is not, relatively speaking, an illiberal society. The attempt to practice democracy has been a conscious one—despite a brief hiatus; the form adopted from the West has been restored at least in semblance. In addition, in spite of its divided society status, a formula for interethnic representation has been an important element in the country's stability and democratic performance. Indeed, the quest for political stability as precipitated by events in 1987 may also give impetus for highlighting national unity rather than democracy. Such an emphasis would feature "awareness of the historical background of the country; recognition of the institution of the monarchy and the local customs, taboos and religion; interracial harmony, and use of *Bahasa Malaysia* as the national language without obstructing the use of other languages.[83] Malaysia is as such a "quasi democracy," and even if there are strong limitations on the political process (making its politics semicompetitive), it is likely to persist in this mode, short of a drastic elite orientation to do otherwise.

• NOTES •

1. John Slimming, *Malaysia: Death of a Democracy* (London: John Murray, 1969). Nevertheless, a similar statement was made by Tun Dr. Ismail, who was then minister of

home affairs during NOC rule and who had reacted to the event somewhat despondently as like Slimming.

2. The term "polyarchy" is derived from Robert Dahl, *Polyarchy, Participation and Opposition* (New Haven and London: Yale University Press, 1971).

3. Singapore left the Malaysian federation in 1965.

4. See Zakaria Haji Ahmad, "Evolution and Political Development in Malaysia," in Robert Scalapino, Seizaburo Sato, and Jusuf Wanandi, eds., *Asian Political Institutionalization* (Berkeley, Calif.: Institute of East Asian Studies, University of California); and Zakaria Haji Ahmad, "Postscript: Continuity and Change," in Zakaria Haji Ahmad, ed., *Government and Politics of Malaysia* (Kuala Lumpur: Oxford University Press, 1987), p. 165

5. For details, see Zakaria Haji Ahmad and Mavis Puthucheary, "Malaysia," in Chung-Si Ahn, ed., *The Local Political System in Asia* (Honolulu: University of Hawaii Press, 1987).

6. The Malayan and Malaysian Constitution provide extraordinary powers to the government in power for "state survival." Article 149 gives Parliament special powers to deal with subversion and article 150 gives the executive and Parliament special powers to cope with an emergency. For a discussion of these powers, see Tun Mohamed Suffian Hashim, *An Introduction to the Constitution of Malaysia* (Kuala Lumpur: Government Printer, 1972), pp. 187–201. The country has undergone two explicitly declared states of emergency, the first to deal with the communist insurgency of 1948–1960, the second during the period of NOC rule.

7. Cited in Michael Ong, "Government and Opposition in Parliament: The Rules of the Game," in Zakaria Haji Ahmad, ed., *Government and Politics of Malaysia*.

8. D. Mauzy, *Barisan Nasional: Coalition Government in Malaysia* (Kuala Lumpur: Marican and Sons, 1983), p. 4.

9. Figures based on the 1980 census, cited by M. Ong, "Malaysia: The Limiting of a Limited Democracy," (Paper read at the workshop on "The Political System and Nation-building in ASEAN," Singapore, 23–25 January 1986).

10. For an elaboration see Gordon Means, "Special Rights as a Strategy for Development: The Case of Malaysia," *Comparative Politics* 1 (October 1972): pp. 29–61.

11. The "indigenous" elements in Sabah are sometimes referred to as *pribumis*.

12. For an elaboration see Chandra Muzaffar, *Islamic Resurgence in Malaysia* (Petaling Jaya, Malaysia: Fajar Bakti, 1987).

13. See Ong, "Malaysia: The Limiting of a Limited Democracy."

14. Tunku Abdul Rahman, *Contemporary Issues in Malaysian Politics* (Kuala Lumpur: Pelandok Publications, 1984), p. v.

15. K. J. Ratnam, *Communalism and the Political Process in Malaya* (Singapore: University of Malaya Press, 1965).

16. Karl von Vorys, *Democracy Without Consensus: Communalism and Political Stability in Malaysia* (Princeton: Princeton University Press, 1975), p. 164.

17. Ibid., p. 165.

18. Ibid., pp. 14–15.

19. For a study of noncommunal political parties before 1969, see R. K. Vasil, *Politics in a Plural Society* (Kuala Lumpur: Oxford University Press for the Australian Institute of International Affairs, 1971).

20. Khong Kim Hoong, "The Early Political Movements Before Independence," in Zakaria Haji Ahmad, ed., *Government and Politics of Malaysia*, p. 37.

21. See Zakaria Haji Ahmad and Zakaria Hamid, "Violence at the Periphery: A Survey of Armed Communism in Malaysia," in Lim Joo-Jock and S. Vani, eds., *Armed Communist Movements in Southeast Asia* (Singapore: Gower for the Institute of Southeast Asian Studies, 1984); and Khong, "The Early Political Movements," pp. 11–39.

22. This was the comment made by the central agency (now defunct), the Development Administration Unit (DAU), as to whether local government elections should be restored when it reviewed the report of the Royal Commission of Enquiry on Local Government. Development Administration Unit, *The New Local Government System for West Malaysia: Problems and Implications* (Appendix A) in *Report of the Committee to Study the Implications of the Report of the Royal Commission of Enquiry to Investigate into the Workings of Local Authorities in West Malaysia* (Kuala Lumpur: Government Printer, 1971).

23. Lucian Pye, "Five Years to Freedom: Sir Gerald Templer's Part in Building a Nation," *The Round Table* 278 (1980): pp. 149–153. Sir Gerald was the high commissioner and military commander in 1952–1954, during the period of the "emergency" (1974–1960) and is regarded as having had a lasting impact on Malaysian political history.

24. For an elaboration of this theme, see Zakaria Haji Ahmad, "The Police and Political Development in Malaysia: Institution Building of a 'Coercive' Apparatus in a Developing, Ethnically Divided Society," (Ph. D. diss., Massachusetts Institute of Technology, 1977); and "Malaysia," in Zakaria Haji Ahmad and H. Crouch, eds., *Military-Civilian Relations in Southeast Asia* (Kuala Lumpur: Oxford University Press).

25. Von Vorys, *Democracy Without Consensus*, p. 249.

26. Zakaria Haji Ahmad, "Political Violence in Malaysia: The Malayan Emergency and Its Impact," *7th International Association of Historians of Asia (IAHA) Proceedings*, vol. 1 (Bangkok: Chulalongkorn University, 1977), pp. 167–191.

27. M. Esman, *Administration and Development in Malaysia* (Ithaca, N. Y.: Cornell University Press, 1972), p. v.

28. Von Vorys, *Democracy Without Consensus*, p. 251.

29. Malaysia, National Operations Council, *The May 13 Tragedy: A Report* (Kuala Lumpur: National Operations Council, 1969), pp. 88–99.

30. See note 1.

31. The King or paramount ruler (*Yang di Pertuan Agong*) of Malaysia is a constitutional monarch who holds a fixed term of office. Together with the deputy paramount ruler, he is chosen for a five-year term by and from among the nine hereditary rulers of the Malay states, who, along with the heads of state of Malacca, Penang, Sabah, and Sarawak, constitute the Conference of Rulers (*Majlis Raja Raja*).

32. Von Vorys, *Democracy Without Consensus*, p. 249.

33. The NOC comprised the following:

Director of Operations—Tun Razak (also deputy prime minister)

Council Members

Tun Dr. Ismail	Minister of Home Affairs
Tun Tan Siew Sin	President of the MCA
Tun Sambanthan	Minister of Works, Posts, and Telecoms (and President of MIC)
Hamzah b Dato Abu Samah	Minister of Information and Broadcasting
Tengku Osman Jewa	Chief of Armed Forces Staff
Tan Sri Salleh Ismail	Inspector-General of Police
Tan Sri Ghazali Shafie	Permanent Secretary, Ministry of Foreign Affairs
Tan Sri Kadir Shamsuddin	Director of Public Services Dept.
Chief Executive Officer	Lieutenant General, Dato Ibrahim bin Ismail, Director of Operations, West Malaysia
Assistants	Abdul Rahman Hamidon Deputy Secretary, Ministry of Defence
	Lieutenant Colonel Ghazali Che Mat Ministry of Defence
	Superintendant Shariff b Omar Royal Malaysia Police
	Yusoff b Abdul Rashid Attorney General's Office

34. Von Vorys, *Democracy Without Consensus*, pp. 341–342.

35. Interview with Tan Sri Ghazali Shafie, September 1985.

36. Given the strong "coercive" instruments under its control, this was very possible. The "infighting" within UMNO at that time, especially between "old guard" and younger elements (such as Dr. Mahathir, Musa Hitam, etc.) lent credibility to rumors rife at that time.

37. Tan Sri Ghazali has clarified that an "outsider" with impartiality (who to this day cannot be identified) was given access to investigate the sources of income of all the NOC members.

38. Interview with Tan Sri Ghazali Shafie, September 1985. Some of the flavor of the debate within the inner sanctum of the NOC can be surmised from the speeches of Tan Sri Ghazali after 1969. See Ghazali Shafie, *Rukunegara, a Testament of Hope* (Kuala Lumpur: Creative Enterprise, 1985).

39. Von. Vorys, *Democracy Without Consensus*, p. 344.

40. The NOC report was of course the authoritative version of what was seen by the government as its causes, and the directions of reform. Malaysia, *The May 13 Tragedy: A Report* (Kuala Lumpur: National Operations Council, 1969). There were also other reports and analyses. *Inter alia*, see Tunku Abdul Rahman, *May 13, Before and After* (Kuala Lumpur: Utusan Melayu Press, 1969); Felix Gagliano, *Communal Violence in Malaysia, 1969: The Political Aftermath* (Athens, O.: Center for International Studies, 1970); John Slimming, *Malaysia: Death of a Democracy*; R. S. Milne and D. Mauzy, *Politics and Government in Malaysia* (Singapore: Federal Publications, 1978), pp. 77–100; and von Vorys, *Democracy Without Consensus*. The Tunku's version very much blamed the Communists.

41. Ghazali Shafie, "Nation Building and the Crisis of Values," in Tan Sri Ghazali Shafie, *Rukunegara, A Testament of Hope*, pp. 41–42.

42. The logic and arguments of this strategy are found in the various speeches of Tan Sri Ghazali Shafie, supra. Tan Sri Ghazali accordingly must be seen as a prime architect of the post-1969 system. Another architect, apart from Tun Razak, would be Tun Dr. Ismail. More evidence on his role would probably surface from his forthcoming biography/ memoirs, *Drifting into Politics and an Ambassador's Diary* (forthcoming).

43. For details see Milne and Mauzy, *Politics and Government in Malaysia*; von Vorys, *Democracy Without Consensus*, pp. 341–422; and Ghazali Shafie, *Rukunegara*, passim.

44. The form of the political system to be was discussed between Tun Razak, Tun Dr. Ismail, Tan Sri Ghazali Shafie and Khalil Akasah (as secretary) soon after 13 May. See D. Mauzy, *Barisan Nasional*, p. 46.

45. *New Straits Times*, 14 September 1971, as cited in Mauzy, ibid., p. 157.

46. "Leadership and a Motivated Society," *Development Forum* 2, no. 2 (December 1969): p. 5, as cited in Mauzy, ibid., p. 47.

47. *Malaysian Digest* 5, no. 1 (January 1973): p. 5.

48. For a comprehensive explanation of the process, see D. Mauzy, *Barisan Nasional*, pp. 75–150.

49. Khong Kim Hoong, "Leadership Crisis in Sabah," in The Asian-Pacific Political Science Association, *Political Leadership in A Changing Society* (Proceedings of the Second APPSA Conference, 16–18 October Seoul, Korea).

50. See Jusuf Wanandi, "Political Development and Regional Order," in L. Martin, ed., *The ASEAN Success Story* (Honolulu: East-West Center, 1987), pp. 143–165.

51. H. Crouch, "From Alliance to Barisan Nasional," in H. Crouch, Lee Kam Hing, and M. Ong, eds., *Malaysian Politics and the 1978 Election* (Kuala Lumpur: Oxford University Press, 1980), p. 5.

52. Ibid., p. 6.

53. Zakaria Haji Ahmad, "Malaysia in 1980, A Year of Political Consolidation and Economic Development," in *Southeast Asian Affairs 1981* (Singapore: Institute of Southeast Asian Studies, 1981), pp. 201–216.

54. Hans Indorf, "Malaysia in 1979: A Preoccupation with Security," *Asian Survey* 20, no. 22 (February 1980): pp. 135–143.

55. *Asia-Pacific Report 1987–88, Trends, Issues, Challenges* (Honolulu: East-West Center, 1987), p. 7.

56. At the time of writing, some forty-four persons had been unconditionally released.

57. For a running commentary see the various issues of the *Far Eastern Economic Review* and the *Asian Wall Street Journal* for the months in question.

58. "Malaysia Tightens Security, Press Bills," *Asian Wall Street Journal*, 7 December 1987, pp. 1 and 11.

59. Ibid., p. 1.

60. M. Ong, "Malaysia: . . . Limited Democracy."

61. Syed Hussein Alatas, "Trends in Politics: A Personal Interpretation," in Patrick Low, ed., *Proceedings and Background paper on Seminar on Trends in Malaysia, Trends in Southeast Asia No. 2* (Singapore: Institute of Southeast Asian Studies, 1971). Professor Syed Hussein was one of the founder members of the Gerakan party, which has been in power in the State of Penang for the last one-and-a-half decades. He is now in UMNO.

62. See W. Roff, *The Origins of Malay Nationalism* (Kuala Lumpur: University of Malaya Press, 1967).

63. For an elaboration of this thesis, see F. Riggs, "The Relationship between Administration and Politics," in J. LaPalombara, ed., *Bureaucracy and Political Development* (Princeton: Princeton University Press, 1964).

64. M. Esman, *Administration and Development in Malaysia*.

65. See the discussion in Milne and Mauzy, *Politics and Government in Malaysia*, pp. 352–356.

66. Zakaria Haji Ahmad, "Evolution and Development of the Political System in Malaysia."

67. Donald Horowitz, *Ethnic Groups in Conflict* (Berkeley: University of California Press, 1985), pp. 398–399.

68. Ibid., pp. 396–440.

69. Ibid., p. 410.

70. Ibid., p. 423. The durability of the Barisan coalition and the opposition's chances are systemic in nature. The number of seats given each member of the Barisan coalition is always "decided" before nomination (a factor not necessarily dependent on the component's electoral strength), but that cabinet posts are allocated on a form of ethnic balance, for example, has assured the workability of the coalition. As for the opposition, the non-Malay parties (in particular the DAP) can do well, as the DAP did in the 1986 elections when it increased its seats from nine to twenty-four. But its chances for power nevertheless rest on its being able to establish an electoral pact with a Malay party (such as PAS), an effort thus far unsuccessful.

71. S. Rachagan, "The Apportionment of Seats in the House of Representatives," in Zakaria Haji Ahmad, ed., *Government and Politics of Malaysia*, pp. 56–70 and p. 69.

72. Arend Lijphart, *Democracy in Plural Societies* (New Haven and London: Yale University Press, 1977).

73. Ibid., pp. 25–44.

74. R. Tilman, *The Centralization Theme in Malaysian Federal-State Relations, 1957–1975* (Singapore: Institute of Southeast Asian Affairs, Occasional Paper no. 39, 1976).

75. For an extended discussion, see Lijphart, *Democracy in Plural Societies*, pp. 150–176.

76. Horowitz, *Ethnic Groups in Conflict*, pp. 653–680.

77. Lucian Pye, *Asian Power and Politics: The Cultural Dimensions of Authority* (Cambridge, Mass.: The Belknap Press of Harvard University Press, 1985), pp. 248–265.

78. Foremost of which is Chandra Muzaffar. See his persuasive, if polemical, *Freedom in Fetters* (Penang: ALIRAN, 1986).

79. "Freedom '86: The Asian Experience", *Asian Wall Street Journal*, February 1987.

80. Zakaria Haji Ahmad, "Introduction," in Zakaria Haji Ahmad, ed., *Government and Politics of Malaysia*, pp. 1–10.

81. Zakaria Haji Ahmad, "The Political Structure," in E. K. Fisk and H. Osman-Rani, *The Political Economy of Malaysia* (Kuala Lumpur: Oxford University Press, 1982), pp. 88–103.

82. Zakaria Haji Ahmad, "Stability, Security and National Development in Malaysia: An Appraisal," in Kusuma Snitwongse and M. R. Sukhumbhand Paribatra, eds., *Durable Stability in Southeast Asia* (Singapore: Institute of Southeast Asian Suties, 1987), pp. 117–136.

83. As stated in a speech by Dr. Mahathir, reported in *New Straits Times*, 9 December 1987.

PAPUA NEW GUINEA

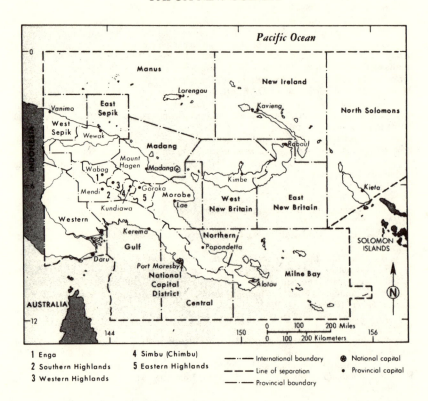

Pacific Ocean

1 Enga
2 Southern Highlands
3 Western Highlands

4 Simbu (Chimbu)
5 Eastern Highlands

----···---- International boundary
---- ---- Line of separation
----·---- Provincial boundary

⊕ National capital
• Provincial capital

CHAPTER TEN

Papua New Guinea: The Melanesian Ethic and the Spirit of Capitalism, 1975–1986

DAVID M. LIPSET

The huge, bird-shaped island of New Guinea, which lies 100 miles north of Australia, is one of the largest islands in the world. Today it is governed by two states: Irian Jaya, the western half, is a province of Indonesia, while the eastern half, the state of Papua New Guinea (PNG), was granted independence from Australia in 1975. Since that time there have been three changes of government in PNG, but all of them have occurred within a system of Westminster parliamentary democracy, led by a unicameral legislature. In the first eleven years of the postcolonial history of this Melanesian state, this democratic system has persisted without interruption. Although several very difficult and serious issues are challenging PNG, it still understates the case to say that democracy has merely persisted without interruption in this country—for it has thrived.

In attempting to explain the success of national democracy in PNG, this essay takes its title and analytic framework from Max Weber's discussion of the historical relationship of culture to Western capitalism.[1] Weber argued that capitalism in the West arose from a cultural contradiction between the longing for certain knowledge about salvation in the afterlife and the impossibility of possessing that knowledge. Examining and explaining democracy in postcolonial PNG primarily in cultural terms, I also argue that several important features of this political system have been shaped by a cultural contradiction between the meaning and use of wealth in primordial Melanesian politics and the meaning and use of wealth in the West. In PNG, national political ambition is at once constituted and driven by the pursuit of the common good, a Western virtue which is locally in terms of gaining development and wealth for one's constituency. But while these ambitions have their roots in the primordial culture, they are also limited by an insubordinate, yet engaged, constituency, which is no less rooted in an egalitarian political tradition, and which typically construes the pursuit of wealth as little more than thinly veiled greed. Often, such suspicions are corroborated by legal indictment. More often, they are translated into electoral defeat. In the early history of postcolonial democracy in Papua New Guinea which I represent below, a primordial system of meaning and value, an ideal type that I am calling a Melanesian ethic, conflicts with a Western one, and will thus be seen both to promote civil ties as well as to undermine them.[2]

A New Melanesian State

Excluding Hawaii, the state of Papua New Guinea comprises approximately half of the total population of the Pacific Islands (1983 estimate: 3.2 million). But 85 percent of the population still lives in rural villages, where political action still tries to rule over subsistence economics, which are organized in terms of the traditional idioms of gender, kinship, marriage, and ceremonial exchange, and where literacy, numeracy, and per capita income (1985: U.S.$680 per annum) have penetrated in an uneven way. To say the least, the nation is spread out, divided up and for geographical and cultural reasons, communication within it is quite difficult. The island of New Guinea has a backbone of volcanoes. The terrain is rugged and the flanks of the central mountain range are broken into secluded, high valleys and streams that run into deep ravines, much of the island is topographically fragmented, making lateral movement very difficult. Communication also became difficult for linguistic reasons: more than 700, or about one-third, of the known languages (not just dialects) in the world are spoken in PNG.[3] Two trade languages, Motu and Melanesian Pidgin English, are also spoken in addition to the many vernaculars, while to complicate matters yet further the national language is English.

Analytically and politically, the country is divisible between island and coastal provinces, on the one hand, and highland ones on the other. This division has many dimensions but for our purposes it is important to note that the island and coastal zones have had a lengthier colonial history than the highland regions. Some consequences of the earlier involvement in Western culture will become apparent in this discussion: the first set of national political leaders, for example, were coastals and islanders who have been opposed by rival highlanders.

The economy of PNG may be divided into two modes. The first, rural subsistence, consists of small-scale horticulture, animal husbandry, fishing, and intertribal trade and also the cash cropping of coffee, cocoa, copra, and fish. The second, large-scale commodity export through multinational projects, mainly involves the exploitation of minerals, such as one of the world's largest copper mines in Bougainville Island and several newly discovered gold deposits. For the most part then, PNG exports commodities and imports manufactures. But, in addition, nearly one-third of the (1984) annual budget is still provided by a yearly, no-strings-attached subvention from Australia, the excolonial power.

Thus while PNG has taken a leading position in the Pacific Basin, at the same time, it is still a deeply tribalized, fractious country in which the stratified divisions of modern, urban society—not to mention provinces, political ideologies, and parties—are still closely tied to a Melanesian ethic defined in terms of "clan membership, residence or locality, ego-centered kin relations, and a system of [gift] exchange."[4] In order to understand how this situation came about, the first step is to trace the country's historical relationship with the West.

· HISTORICAL REVIEW ·

The Colonial Background

Sporadic contacts with Europeans began from about 1512 and increased in frequency until, by the middle of the nineteenth century, people in the coastal and island regions were in regular contact with an expanding global system of manufactures and exchange. In 1828 the Dutch claimed part of New Guinea, settling Irian Jaya, the western half of the island, and laying the grounds for its Indonesian acquisition. From 1850 onward three developments began to change indigenous society on the eastern side. First, sugar plantations in northern Australia and elsewhere in the Pacific created a demand for cheap, indentured labor. Second, European currency and goods, such as metal tools, were introduced by trading companies. And third, the advent of German interests led to a more aggressive policy of land alienation and labor impressment centering on the establishment of coastal coconut plantations for copra (the dried endosperm of the coconut which yields oil). By 1889 New Guinea had become a German protectorate, a move which so alarmed Queenslanders that they annexed Papua, the land on the south coast of the New Guinea mainland. Formally, the Papuan region then became a colony of Britain; but by 1902 British lack of interest in this unhealthy, stone age backwater led to the reversion of rights in the area to Queensland and then, in 1906, to the newly formed Commonwealth of Australia. The German side of the island eventually came under Australian control in 1914, and except for the World War II years of Japanese occupation, the two territories of Papua and New Guinea remained under Australia until independence in 1975, although they were administered separately until 1946.

The early years of direct Australian administration involved the further development of the coastal plantation economy and some mining, entailing demands for cheap labor, which was indirectly coerced through the requirement that rural people pay taxes while being forbidden to raise cash crops.[5] The Australian colonial structure was based in the capital city of Port Moresby and regionally administered by a patrol system, in which young, multipurpose frontier officers and small groups of native attendants made periodic tours of the outlying areas.[6] This type of administration generated little by way of national political integration; regional districts remained weak, being responsible to the capital, while local policy was quite individualistic. Language policy, in addition, was divisive, with different lingua francas being in use in Papua and New Guinea. The outer islands, particularly the ones that later threatened secession, were neglected with respect to the provision of social services, which created antipathy toward taxation for what was seen as an administration favoring the mainland. The Papuan side, also reputed for its opposition to white settlement, was rather less developed than the New Guinea side, which had more plantations, a better road system, and more ports.[7] However, there was a uniform colonial commitment—implemented by patrol officers and missionaries, for the most part, via punishment rather than reward—to prohibit headhunting, cannibalism, and polygamy and thereby create a new legal-political order more consistent with European expectations and goals. The territory was split up into administrative districts, which became the model for the later provincial divisions.

Until World War II migration to urban centers was slow to develop in PNG. Native and expatriate living areas were carefully segregated by Australian colonial policy. In Port Moresby in the early 1950s a few Papua New Guineans did begin to find housing in suburbs constructed especially for them. With some education, a Western style of living, and skilled jobs, a proto-middle class was beginning to emerge. But except for markets where locally produced foodstuffs were sold, indigenous voluntary organizations or businesses were markedly missing in towns. The Papua New Guineans who did live in urban settings became urban villagers who continued to view the world in terms of kinship ties and ethnicity; the growth of large-scale, indigenous urban groups was minimal.

Pioneer missionaries, representing Catholic, Protestant, and a welter of small, evangelical sects, perhaps were more preoccupied with promoting a wider scope of social change than were colonial administrators. They were among the first to live and work with, as well as educate, Papua New Guineans and to then use them as evangelists. Although today PNG is for the most part a Catholic country, there was and is considerable competition for souls in rural areas, often leaving villagers to choose according to their own internal politics rather than sectarian doctrine.[8] "While the churches may have reinforced group loyalties based on traditional societies and administration areas, most of the units created by the churches are much larger than any units of pre-contact time."[9]

A general lack of financing and staff, the rough terrain, the small, isolated nature of the indigenous groups, the linguistic diversity, and a general reluctance to make reprisals even after attacks by natives prevented the quick opening and inhibited effective colonial control of much of the interior. The rate of change and development brought about by government and mission was thus very uneven throughout the country. By 1890, for example, pacification was well under way in coastal New Guinea,[10] while hundreds of thousands of highlanders remained insulated by high mountain ranges from experience with white people until 1933, and then the colonial process of pacification, etc. did not begin effectively until well after the end of World War II. In 1965, in addition, the decision was made to funnel government services, particularly agricultural support, to those who, by their evident economic success, had indicated that they were able recipients.[11] This strategy had the effect of concentrating wealth in the hands of rural entrepreneurs, largely local-level leaders in the highlands, which began a process of crystallizing them as a state-dependent class in a society that was beginning to approach the end of its colonial period.[12]

Following World War II Australian colonial authorities began to emphasize education. In addition to local-level economic and political development programs, more attention was paid to educating Papua New Guineans, a task which heretofore had been left to the missions. Still, by 1972, about half of all children of primary school age still had no school to go to, while about three quarters of the potential school population in the highlands had no space available to them in a classroom.[13] Political development, meanwhile, had begun in coastal and island areas before World War I when a system of government appointed headmen was introduced by the colonial administrators. Of these, village constables and councilors were often selected on the basis of their knowledge of Pidgin or Motu and potential as middlemen, and not for their local standing or legitimacy. The Australian administration did not attempt to amalgamate traditional political units under these leaders or to allocate judicial or taxing powers to them. More often than not these village authorities were powerless, lacking the attributes—a career in warfare, ritual, or ceremonial exchange—necessary for their status. During the early 1950s local government councils were introduced. In some areas they aroused resistance, but elsewhere, in other cases, they were accepted because they seemed to generate and distribute wealth or provide local leadership with a new arena to contest. Some councilors were able to collect taxes, and build schools and medical aid posts; others by contrast were poor, corrupt, inefficient, dazzled by heavy equipment, and in many cases dependent on the white advisor. By 1964, when the first general election for the House of Assembly was held, most people in the country still did not live in council-administered areas. "The top of the government pyramid had been completed before the base."[14]

Elections in the Preindependence Years: 1964–1975

Independence was not won by the violent overthrow of a colonial administration by a nationalist movement. Self-government was granted to PNG in 1973 by Australia and then two years later complete independence was attained. Indeed, Australia had even introduced national politics in 1964 and 1968 by holding elections under universal adult franchise for seats in a Westminster-style House of Assembly in Port Moresby. These first elections were a competition of individuals rather than political parties.[15] The first members of House of Assembly (MHAs) were subsistence farmers and small traders, who had been local-level leaders, long termed "bigmen" by social anthropologists.[16] They represented ethnic and regional groups rather than political parties or nationalistic ideologies. A few had been employed as interpreters or teachers and were literate English speakers, but most spoke only Pidgin English and found the legislative sessions incomprehensible.[17]

In the 1965–1967 period political parties first began to appear. One of them, which quickly collapsed, was composed of a small group of local-level leaders from the Sepik River region, and advocated adopting Melanesian Pidgin as the national language and statehood for PNG in Australia. A more viable party, formed in 1967, was composed of young public servants who had completed secondary schooling together and were galvanized by colonial wage discrimination. They founded the Pangu (an acronym for Papua and New Guinea) Pati. The following year, during the second House of Assembly elections, the Pangu Pati elected nine of eighty-four MHAs. They came from coastal and island districts, and were led by Michael Somare, a young Sepik River man, who had been a newsreader on a provincial radio station.[18] Although it was little publicized, the 1968 Pangu platform called for immediate home rule and eventual independence. Most candidates stressed local interests, but in many elections, such as around Port Moresby, the capital city, *no* issues were raised at all. The hope of increasing economic development attracted over 60 percent of registered voters to the polls.

By 1970, while the Australian government was beginning to concede independence to PNG, other political parties formed representing a continuum of views. Most conservative was the United Party, which was composed of wealthy white highlands businessmen (planters) and their anticoastal New Guinean sympathizers, which opposed independence altogether. Pangu was joined in its radical position against colonial rule by several parties, the National Party of the Highlands, the Mataungan Association of New Britain and the People's Progress Party, which was a faction of island independents with petty bourgeois backgrounds.

In the third national elections in 1972, the average number of candidates for each seat increased while voter turnout declined.[19] Some observers traced this contradiction to increased awareness that voting was voluntary, combined with the steady rise in educational levels among national candidates seeking the salary and perquisites of a position whose prestige they regarded quite highly. The 1972 elections also showed a distinct decline in white influence: the European proportion of elected members declined from 23 percent to 9 percent. This reduction also reflected a wider and more long-term trend of rapid turnover of incumbents in PNG parliamentary democracy. Of the 84 elected to membership in the second house, 73 stood again but only 52 percent were reelected. Through the sitting of the first three assemblies, only ten members served continuously. In 1972, only 40 percent of the candidates elected to serve in the third House of Assembly previously had sat in the legislature. The turnover had other significance. The average age of the third House was reduced from 41 to 35, with a substantial majority of members in their twenties and thirties. There was also a corresponding increase in the number of representatives with some form of postprimary education and a reduction in the number of members with no education at all. In addition, the number of members whose occupations were village centered had declined from 31 percent to 20 percent.[20]

Candidates in the 1968 elections generally avoided confronting rivals on policy or party matters.[21] Independent candidates fought on individual lines, by individual means, and largely through individual contacts. The Melanesian ethic, based on primordial ties, personality, and exchange, held sway over party organization. By contrast, the 1972 elections involved younger candidates throughout the country openly seeking party ties, while airing a number of basic national issues.[22] Nevertheless, beneath emergent ideology, Paypool concluded that in the southern highlands, candidates were continuing to rely on clan ties, ceremonial exchange, trading partnerships, and even war alliances for support.[23] One incumbent candidate, for example, distributed a sizable amount of his House of Assembly salary to his constituency. Andrew Strathern also saw the 1972 national election as an extension of primordial relationships but observed that, in addition, standing for national office did depend on a candidate's ability to show competence in modern government.[24]

Although by 1972 some substantial differences had emerged between parties in terms of occupational background of membership, regional bases of support, and, for the two largest parties, Pangu and United, on the issue of independence the level of organization and ideology of the four major parties was "extremely feeble."[25] There were no revolutionary fronts or congress parties as in Africa. Outside the legislature there were no mass movements of protest, and very little emerging nationalism. In the African context the political goal of confronting oppressive colonial powers was the dominant theme of leadership. In PNG, with a push from its colonial power toward independence, politics centered around the role of expatriate experts in the management of development. "The prevailing feeling at the time of self-government was one of doubt about the competence of the new nation's leaders in economic management and planning, as much as doubt about internal political problems."[26]

Only twenty Pangu-endorsed candidates were elected to the 100-member house in 1972. They were immediately joined by four more MHAs, which still left Pangu in a minority position in the House of Assembly, where the United Party held twenty-four seats, three small parties had a total of twenty seats and Independents had twelve. However, with the support of the smaller parties, Michael Somare, the Pangu leader, succeeded in forming a coalition government with himself as chief minister. "A vital key to...the...Coalition was a widespread... uneasiness [and]...fear...of a Highlands-dominated government... strongly influenced by expatriate business and plantation interests."[27] In December 1972 the Pangu Pati issued its Eight-Point Plan (later Aims), which called for (1) localization of the economy, (2) equal distribution of wealth, (3) economic decentralization, (4) national autonomy, (5) continued reliance on traditional modes of subsistence, (6) local revenues, (7) the increased political participation of women, and (8) government control of "those sectors of the economy where control is necessary."[28] However, by 1975, the Somare government was "preoccupied with a smooth transition to independence with as little change as possible in existing institutions. Political independence was its immediate objective, and it was not prepared to join the debate on ideological issues."[29]

While men armed with a model of plural, or segmentary, social structures may be quite ready to participate in Western democratic institutions as individuals, they fit less easily into the mold of long-term discipline and loyalty required by party membership. And certainly little cohesion had arisen under Australian administration.[30] Thus the consolidation of political parties in PNG may be seen as originating within the 1972 legislature, where four parties became divided between government and opposition and were in Dahl's terminology "highly competitive."[31] Between elections, parliament was preoccupied by internal politics, in which it played out issues of little moment to its constituencies.

Self-Government: 1973–1975

During the two years of self-government prior to independence, tension between the Somare government and the opposition United Party over the timing of constitutional changes, localization of the public service, a new lands policy, and other issues was complicated by disputes within the Pangu Pati itself. Relations between the parliamentary and the executive wings of the party deteriorated as the Somare government viewed the latter's involvement in the Constitutional Planning Committee (CPC) as threatening its authority. The CPC wanted to confine citizenship to those of Melanesian descent, create provincial governments and restrict foreign investment. Although the CPC favored a "first-past-the-post," simple plurality electoral system, the Australian preferential ballot was adopted with two important modifications. Universal adult suffrage was to be permitted but voters were not to be required to exercise the franchise (voting in Australia is mandatory). Papua New Guineans were also not to be required to indicate all their preferences (a ballot is declared "informal" in Australia if all preferences are not ranked). There was little dispute, however, about the decision to make PNG into a monarchy nominally led by Her Majesty's representative, a governor-general who would be elected by Parliament. PNG was "proud," said Somare, "of its links with the Queen."[32] Neither were rights to liberty, freedom of expression, conscience, thought, religion, and privacy subjected to dispute. A two-tier system of "open" and "regional" electorates was also continued, although the CPC recommended the elimination of the regional electorates, which had originally been devised—and allocated on the basis of one per province in 1964—to ensure short-run expatriate experience in the first House of Assembly. The plan had then been to eliminate them when more educated Papua New Guineans became available to hold office.[33]

Perhaps the most difficult and important problems confronting the chief minister prior to independence were disputes in the islands between pro- and anticolonial factions. In copper-rich Bougainville, and in the Papuan region immediately around the national capital, secessionist movements had actually developed.[34] The latter, the Papua Besena independence movement, was neutralized through skilled maneuvering by Somare in which development funds were allocated to the region. The Bougainville secessionist movement proved more intractable and led to a policy of "decentralization," and eventually to the establishment of nineteen provincial governments.[35]

The building of one of the world's largest copper mines from 1969 to 1973 gave rise to the espousal of ethnic ideology by a strong well-educated elite among the 80,000 Bougainvillean people to whom the mine had been presented as a *fait accompli*. In 1973 under the leadership of Father John Momis, Bougainvilleans demanded that they be immediately granted a system of elected government, with an executive, which would be codified as part of the national constitution and the CPC agreed. Nearly one-third of PNG's export income was derived from copper. "Partly from resentment," however, Somare's cabinet decided that if Bougainville should have provincial government, so should all of them.[36] An interim government was appointed for Bougainville in 1974. But while endorsing the principle of decentralization when areas were ready, Somare would not concede that their powers be delegated under the constitution.

Independence, Secession, and Provincial Government: 1975–1977

Father Momis was dissatisfied over the funding for Bougainville in the 1975–1976 budget and about the Somare position vis-à-vis the constitutional position of provincial government. On 1 September 1975, two weeks before national independence was to occur, Bougainville unilaterally declared itself the independent Republic of the North Solomons. Confrontations followed; the interim government was suspended and secessionists attacked government outposts. But by the end of January 1976, Momis and Somare were negotiating an agreement in which Bougainville would rejoin the nation in exchange for the establishment of a nationwide system of provincial governments that would be constitutionally entrenched. From 1977, nineteen interim provincial governments were created, consisting of fifteen to thirty constituencies, each with an electorate of about 10,000 people. Although the division of jurisdiction—e.g., police and the courts, roads, and hospitals—tilted toward the national government, by 1979 75 percent of the Public Service was responsible to the provinces.[37]

As in national politics, ideology and policy debate in provincial government have been secondary to personal factionalism, pork barrel allocation of funds, and disputes over the spoils of office. And in some cases, the concern of provincial leadership for the trappings of office, such as the automobile and the overseas study tour, rather than rural development, has even undermined village-level government. Electoral competition has been as high as ten candidates per seat in some provinces: a winner need rely on the backing of only a few clans in his language group, thus restricting access to regional leadership, for the most part, to candidates with relatively large networks of kin.[38] Provincial campaigning was not far removed from primordialism—one useful tactic for mobilizing such support has been throwing parties. Several outbreaks of interclan warfare marked the results of the 1980 elections in Simbu Province such that some provincial representatives could not move through their electorates and were forced to stay in the capital.

Relations between provincial and national government have also been volatile and competitive. Some national parliamentarians have used their superior resources to create factions of clients in their home provinces so as to control the provincial executive. Other MPs have blamed provincial governments for siphoning funds away from their control. Decentralization in many instances has led to waste, scandal, corruption, and rivalry rather than to the local autonomy envisioned by the Constitutional Planning Committee. At the same time, since provincial government is being undertaken together with the localization of administrative staffing, which has meant that untrained Papua New Guineans are learning their duties while on the job, conclusive evaluation is premature. Since 1976, however, the state has not been seriously threatened by secessionist movements, so to this extent one of the intended purposes of decentralization has been served.

A Businessmen's State

Although it had provided a constant moral frame of reference in the years preceding independence, the self-sufficient, egalitarian, and communalist rhetoric of the Pangu Pati's Eight Aims had become quite obsolete by 1976. During a period of divestment by foreign business just prior to independence, each of the four major political parties formed business arms—ostensibly to finance election campaigns. Despite regional or ideological differences, that is, each party was "committed to capitalism...[a] convergence of...policy [which] coincided to a large extent with an increase in the private business interests of parliamentarians."[39] The continuing relationship to Australia was clearly affecting national policy; the most important contradiction of the self-reliant rhetoric of the original Eight Aims, the dependence of PNG on an Australian subsidy for more than 30 percent of its budget, was not questioned by any party. In 1976, moreover, Australia made a five-year commitment of A$930 million to PNG. Not surprisingly, that same year Charles Lepani, then associate director of PNG's Central Planning Office, announced the abandonment of the goal of national self-sufficiency.[40]

With this shift also came a subtler one downgrading support for rural development in favor of urban areas and resource centers. From 1976 PNG Development Bank loans increased roughly ten times more for industrial purposes than for agriculture. Provinces with larger cities and resources were also allocated more than double the funds of poorer, less urbanized ones. Neither the state, nor the educated urban elite, nor the rural peasant groups were willing to develop enterprises that would advance the self-sufficiency of the country. "Overwhelmingly...[PNG nationals] buy into existing businesses [owned] by Europeans, or found new ventures in partnership with foreign capital—usually low-risk ventures in the major urban centers and predominantly of a service nature."[41]

The single most powerful pressure group in the country, the Public Service, also proved intractable to initial attempts at reform. The cost of paying this massive bureaucracy (70,000 employees in 1976) consumed two-thirds of the annual budget. Based on the centralized Canberra model in which initiatives are not permitted without reference to the capital, the Public Service is a hierarchical, conservative body, short on policy initiative but long on expensive salary structures, adorned by amenities and perquisites. The partnership between national politicians and bureaucrats in PNG has been attacked by neo-Marxist analysts[42] as an "emerging class structure" in a "neo-colonialist order" that is dominated by a "financially comfortable...middle class...[which is] psychologically dependent upon the Australian connection, and politically unabrasive."[43] Somare and his colleagues had little choice, given the sort of infrastructure they had inherited from Australia, but to settle upon a parliamentary alliance with the Public Service, the conservative bureaucratic system. Neither Pangu nor the other parties had been immediately able to construct a politics beyond that of management, Melanesian primordialism, and business.

The Elections of 1977

For 1977 changes were enacted that further modified the Australian preferential ballot system in use during the past three elections. A first-past-the-post, plurality system was adopted because it was simpler and because informal balloting, which had held to about 3 percent in the past elections, had only rarely affected the outcomes of balloting. The results were that 85 percent of candidates won their seats with less than a majority of votes cast while 45 percent of the victorious candidates won with 30 percent or less. The new electoral system seemed to have further encouraged candidates with the largest block of primordial backing to concentrate exclusively on this basis and not seek "outside" support, which previously took the form of cooperative exchanges for second or third preferences, with candidates representing other groups.

Of the 879 candidates who stood in the 109 electorates, (19 provincewide seats and 90 single-member constituency seats), the three major parties—Pangu, the People's Progress party, and the United party—endorsed 295 candidates, and many more direct contests emerged between endorsed candidates than had in 1972, when fear of party attachment had been greater. Campaign spending was higher than in the past; party labels were more widely known throughout the country, although they remained less recognized at the village level. Selection of candidates tended to be ad hoc and an important criterion still being the size of ascriptive (such as clan or *wantok*—i.e., ethnic) bases of support. And recruitment of candidates to accept party endorsement still had to be made through various financial and political inducements.

Each platform called for rural development, foreign investment to stimulate mineral resource projects and industry, the extension of infrastructure, increased educational opportunities, law enforcement, and government stability. Parties and candidates tended to appeal to voters on the basis of personalities of leadership. Somare and Pangu, the governing party, stressed its achievements, the smooth transition through self-government to independence, the introduction of a national currency (the PNG kina) and the renaming of the national airlines. The opposition criticized ministerial extravagance. The primary local issue was economic development, which every candidate promised to promote in all sorts of forms, from raising coffee prices and building schools to creating jobs. Although regional rivalries between the highlanders and the coastal/island peoples surfaced again, the major dissatisfaction of villagers was lack of contact with incumbents following elections.[44] To the extent that MPs enclaved themselves in the national capital and ceased to appear and maintain exchange relations with their constituents, they ceased to be moral persons, and thus became subjected to accusations of corruption and lining their own pockets. Except for a wealthy key elite who could go and come from the capital city regularly, the significance of this enclavement had contributed to the high rate of defeating incumbents.

The elections had been preceded by a by-election the year before in which Pangu lost the two seats contested (including the defeat of its party president). A number of policy-reviewing committees apparently had not met, and its countrywide branches were also rather inactive. No national policy existed apart from ad hoc positions adopted by ministerial members in daily cabinet discussion. "It...[was]...therefore quite impossible to portray Pangu as an independent force in national affairs, even if it was becoming a significant force in the national economy."[45] Nonetheless, Pangu had a much greater impact on the 1977 elections than it had had five years earlier, in large measure because of its link to Somare's positive image, which its opposition was unable to counter.[46]

The fourth general election in the history of the country, but the first unsupervised one following independence, showed an increase in the number of candidates per electorate from the 1972 election by an average of nearly 20 percent (see Table 10.1). Although this figure would seem to indicate a general rise in political participation in PNG, it must be assessed in light of the greater number of electorates, the creation of several new provinces, and a population increase from two to three million people between 1964 and 1977. The number of educated

Papua New Guineans had also risen. In conjunction with this expanding talent pool the prestige of becoming a national politician was high, and the association of business and politics throughout the country was pervasive.

Table 10.1   Participation in the First Four National Elections in Papua New Guinea

Year	Number of Electorates	Number of Candidates	Average Number of Candidates per Electorate	Percentage of Voter Turnout
1964	54	298	5.5	72
1968	84	484	5.8	63
1972	100	609	6.1	60
1977	109	877	8.0	59
1982	108	1025	10.3	60

Source: Compiled from R. R. Premdas: "Papua New Guinea: The First General Elections after Independence," *The Journal of Pacific History* 13 (1978): p. 78; and R. R. Premdas and J. S. Steves, "National Elections in Papua New Guinea: The Return of Pangu to Power," *Asian Survey* 23 (1983): p. 993.

In coalition with Julius Chan's Progress Party (PPP) the Somare government retained power in 1977. Winning sixty of 109 seats, the two parties then managed to expand their total numbers in Parliament to sixty-nine with the support of independents from island provinces. Despite charges by the highland parties—the National and the United— that the Pangu-PPP coalition was only a coastal party, the new Somare government had in fact mustered nationwide support. As a result of the 1977 elections, Pangu drew nearly a third of its parliamentary support from the highlands provinces, and the PPP, which was based in the New Ireland Province, had also gained a measure of national support from both coastal and inland provinces (see Table 10.2).

Table 10.2   Regional Distribution of MPs by Party Affiliation in 1977 in Papua New Guinea

Region	Party				
	Pangu/ Independent	PPP	UP	Other/ Independent	Total
Islands	8	4	2	3	17
Coastal	20	5	4	0	29
Highlands	15	4	18	2	39
Papua	6	6	3	9	24
Totals:	49	19	27	13	109

Source: Compiled from R. R. Premdas, "Papua New Guinea: The First General Elections after Independence," *The Journal of Pacific History* 13 (1978): pp. 82–84.

If nothing else, the 1977 elections demonstrated that party affiliation in PNG had become an important component of candidacy. Out of 109 elected MPs, all but ten had party affiliations. The parties played a role in candidate nomination and each spent freely on vehicles, insignia, media, and advertising throughout the country. But incumbents were still being defeated at a rate of nearly 50 percent, and party organization was incapable of overcoming an opposing candidate who came from a numerically superior ethnic group unless the latter's record was seen as questionable. Some analysts thus remained skeptical of the impact of party ties on actual voting behavior, which they still viewed as primarily determined by primordial loyalties.[47]

The No Confidence Vote: Parliamentary Politics: 1977–1980

The proportion of parliamentary executive positions with large budgets and associated extension duties that can be utilized for patronage purposes by the prime minister is quite high. In 1977, Somare immediately increased the number of ministries by four to twenty-two and announced the creation of eight new secretary positions. Spreading these positions among the provinces, while trying to defer to seniority, he then sought to stifle regionally based criticism and give a national appearance to his new government: the island and the coastal provinces each got five posts while the highlands and the Papuan provinces each received six.

Although left in disarray by the defeat, the highlands-based United Party formed the opposition in coalition with an awkward group of independents and small, regionally based, ex-secessionist parties. The opposition leadership, officially in the hands of Dr. John Guise, lacked cohesion; both highlands and islands politicians opposed Guise while opposing each other. But the same might be said of the victors. At the level of ideology Pangu and the PPP, its chief coalition partner, were in disagreement about economic issues. Although there was clearly no unanimity even within Pangu itself, Somare led the more moderate wing, while the PPP, led by Julius Chan, was more conservative, pro-capitalist, pro-foreign investment. In fact both parties appeared equally ready to support continued reliance on private enterprise and foreign investment.

In 1978, the first full year of the new Somare government, Iambakey Okuk, a maverick western highlands MP, revived the opposition. To guard against corruption and overly close alignment with foreign business interests, the prime minister had proposed a leadership code requiring that national leaders divest themselves of and pledge not to pursue business interests while in office, placing their assets in public trusts to be administered by the state. Somare stressed the moral commitment and obligation of leaders to the people's welfare in terms of the ideals of traditional Melanesian leadership, which he termed custodial and distributive of wealth rather than simply acquisitive.[48] The major objection to the new code came from Julius Chan, Somare's coalition partner, whose PPP faction had substantial business interests. Annoyed at not having been consulted by Somare, Chan argued that the leadership code was not only unworkable, but ran counter to national, rather than Melanesian, values, the most important of which being an individual's right to accumulate wealth. The flow of talent into politics would be blocked, he said, and the patronage-based consolidation of party loyalty would also be inhibited. The compromise PPP proposals, for strengthening an ombudsman's office and establishing a parliamentary register of assets were rejected by Pangu. Iambakey Okuk, the leader of the opposition, sided with Chan. "We believe in a private enterprise system," he asserted. "The present government, despite all its fancy talk, does not."[49] Several months of vitriolic debate ensued that threatened the unity of the governing coalition. Somare finally decided to shelve the code until a later session of parliament.

Okuk tried to take advantage of the tension by luring Chan's PPP into a new government. In August 1978, for the first time in the history of PNG, a no confidence motion was moved in an elected government. It was defeated sixty-eight to thirty-five, but Okuk went on attacking what he presented as socialist tendencies of the government. Three months later Somare reshuffled his cabinet, decreasing PPP power; the following week Chan withdrew his party from the government, again complaining about lack of consultation. The United Party immediately joined Somare and received five portfolios while Chan wondered publicly if the PPP withdrawal had been ill-considered. Okuk had also secretly, it was later revealed, approached the prime minister about joining a coalition. A second no confidence motion was then defeated by the new government, and the affair concluded.

Despite anxiety in the Australian press about the stability of democracy in PNG, the incident had taken place entirely within the constitutional framework and certainly reflected no sort of popular disaffection with the government. Indeed the central position of Michael Somare in PNG government and politics had been confirmed. Of the underlying pattern in postcolonial politics revealed by the episode, an expatriate writer observed:

> The "shake-out"...occurred but its consequences...do not appear to be particularly far-reaching. The economy remains aid and trade dependent. State power is in the hands of a political and administrative elite, or in class terms, shared by a loose alliance of an educated petty bourgeoisie and a rich peasantry. The rhetoric of redistribution is still current but the essentially accommodative political and governmental style ultimately works in the interests of those with the most economic and political clout. Internal crises are managed in an ad hoc fashion, the key to their resolution being political expediency and the dispensation of patronage. Despite the emergence of

tentative and often confused ideological positions the "pole" of political attention remains the center.[50]

The last year of the decade was certainly one of the most turbulent in the postcolonial history of PNG. Events in 1979 led to the country's first change of government—peacefully and constitutionally on the floor of parliament, rather than through military coup, or in the streets of Port Moresby, as some anxious Western observers had predicted.[51] Strikes, or threats of strikes, were mounted by national doctors, electricity commission employees, bus drivers, dock workers, airline pilots, teachers, nurses, mine workers, and university students. Further moves of no confidence by the opposition were tabled. Rural criticism of government neglect and accusations of poor administration by government officers were widespread. Rapid urbanization, unemployment, and general lawlessness in certain regions combined with policy inefficiency. Food imports were increasing. The economy was stagnating. The Public Service was ineffective. There was rivalry between the parliament and the provincial governments. The Somare government was itself divided by ministerial insubordination, and, worse, by a constitutional crisis. The prime minister was seen as incapable of handling the events, tired, short-tempered, and beset by malaise. He suffered from several bouts of illness that year and was widely expected to resign.

In June 1979 Somare declared a two-month state of emergency in the five highlands provinces because of an increase in interclan warfare.[52] The unprecedented act curbed civil liberties and affected the economy of a part of the country with nearly half the population and a disproportionately high share of the productive resources. But questions were being raised about whether tribal warfare was even a problem to be controlled by the legal apparatus of the state. Public reactions varied: some saw the state of emergency as victimizing the highlands people; a few highlands women evidently supported the move and initiated steps to reconcile the conflicting clans. In parliament, where the state of emergency had been declared without its approval, bills were first passed to authorize it and then to lift it.

Undoubtedly, however, the most serious problem to beset the Somare government was the Rooney affair, a judicial crisis that began with the deportation order of Ralph Premdas, the head of the Politics Department at the University of Papua New Guinea, who had been meddling in government. The Supreme Court granted Premdas a stay to enable him to appeal further. Without consulting the prime minister, the then-minister of justice, Mrs. Nahau Rooney, disputed the right of the wholly expatriate court to make decisions contrary to what she viewed as the national aspirations of Melanesians. The expatriate chief justice treated her public letter to him as an attempt to interfere with the independent operation of the judiciary. The public prosecutor then disclosed another communication from the minister of justice to the chief justice regarding another case. As the affair escalated, Premdas was deported.

Mrs. Rooney, the justice minister, was then tried by the Supreme Court, although its members were party to the conflict, and was sentenced to serve eight months in jail. The government responded by invoking the power of license vested in the Ministry for Justice—which by then had been assumed by the prime minister—to release the imprisoned former justice minister. Four of seven supreme court judges promptly resigned. The government took the opportunity to appoint a new expatriate chief justice, and also to appoint the first Papua New Guinean judge. Meantime, riots broke out in the nation's prisons while university students were staging demonstrations accusing the government of administering the law preferentially.

The crisis of law, the unprecedented suspension of civil liberties, the confrontation of the judiciary and the executive, and the expectation that the prime minister would resign aroused the opposition—still led by Okuk, now as leader of the newly formed National Party—to take every parliamentary opportunity to defeat the government. But the opposition (consisting of the PPP, the National Party, and Papua Besena) was still divided, being little more than a marriage of political convenience. Julius Chan's PPP was neither committed to the leadership of Okuk nor to his tactics. In 1979, Okuk tabled a third motion of no confidence unsuccessfully, which failure a national analyst attributed to Okuk's "impatient and blind push for political power."[53]

In October 1979 John Kaputin, minister for national planning, was jailed for ten weeks for omitting to file tax returns. Somare did not intervene, but reshuffled his cabinet a second time, later sacking two ministers (including Kaputin). Another resigned and a fourth was then charged for disturbing the peace. In the past Somare had beaten back parliamentary challenges by politicking. But by March 1980, his latest cabinet reshuffles, in which fifteen of twenty-three ministers were moved to different portfolios, had exhausted his best gambit, which was offering a ministry. A new political party, the Melanesian Alliance, formed by dissident ex-ministers, began negotiations with opposition parties to form a new government. Finally, that same month, Okuk succeeded: a motion of no confidence in the prime minister was passed fifty-seven to forty-nine. Having wider parliamentary support than Okuk, Julius Chan was nominated to replace Somare as prime minister. Aged forty-one, Catholic, of mixed race descent, and quite wealthy, Chan had held the Finance Ministry for what were perhaps the five most successful years of the Somare government during which he had had responsibility for the economy, widely regarded as well-off.[54]

The Chan Interlude: 1980–1982

The new coalition government, which consisted of five parties (Chan's own PPP, Okuk's National Party, Papua Besena, the Melanesian Alliance, the United Party) and a group of independents was nevertheless an unstable alliance. As 1980 progressed, members of the United Party and a small number of pro-Pangu MPs switched to the new government while a small number of coalition MPs drifted into the opposition, now led by Somare. With little other than discontent with the previous government uniting them, the new coalition members were divided over many of the major issues of the day: decentralization, foreign investment, the leadership code, and credentials for citizenship. And the initial coalition agreement, which was to allocate ministry portfolios collectively, further indicated the decentralized sort of power the new prime minister might wield.

The oversized Public Service, lawlessness, and tension between provincial and the national governments were all quite unresolvable problems. Chan's expressed concern was to regain control of the economy at a time of rising inflation and create a favorable climate for investment. However, his actual initiatives were relatively minor, and the 1981 and 1982 budgets introduced little change in the previous government's hard kina strategy (1982: K1 = U.S. $1.10), including wage restraint, steady growth in public spending, and continuing high levels of Australian aid (supplying 32 percent of the total budget in 1980). The Bank of PNG warned that severe damage was being done to the export sector by undisciplined spending and increased international borrowing.[55] In response, although it increased funds for primary education and social services, the Chan government retreated from its commitment to rural development.

In foreign affairs the new government did make a number of changes that won recognition. Until 1980 PNG had maintained a stance of universal amity. The new government shifted to a policy of "selective engagement" stressing relations with immediate neighbors and major trading partners; the objective being to take an increased role in South Pacific regionalism. In August 1980, at the request of the prime minister of the about-to-be independent state in Vanuatu (formerly the New Hebrides), Chan sent 350 PNG troops for peace-keeping purposes. In a month's work, the troops took over from a combined British and French commando unit, arrested numerous rebels, captured the leader of the anti-independence movement, and defeated the last outpost of French colons at Port Orly. The troops quickly returned home to an enthusiastic welcome.

But apart from the success of his foreign policy experiments, Chan's two-year tenure in government showed more differences in style than policy. While Chan maintained a low profile, Okuk, his deputy prime minister, drove his action-oriented image forward. Intolerant of what he considered bureaucratic interference, he offered well-publicized solutions to airlines management, energy planning, and education in pursuit of becoming the first highlands prime minister. He dealt provincial government and the process of decentralization its worst defeat by persuading the National Executive Council to allot sectorial program money to MPs rather than to the provincial work departments. But Okuk's aggressiveness was offensive to the consensual pattern of leadership that had come to characterize politics in PNG, and some held that Chan's seeming impassivity to Okuk's behavior was simply an attempt to allow him sufficient rope with which to hang himself before the 1982 elections. Actually, the governing coalition had so fragmented that Okuk's behavior was symptomatic of how little control Chan had over his minister. Allegations of petty corruption against national politicians were as frequent as they had been in the last months of the Somare government; coalition partners were pork barreling development funds and several ministers were forced to resign for indictable behavior or disloyalty. The ruling coalition was in a shambles.

While debate about urban violence and clan warfare continued, the cost of new airplanes that Okuk had illegally purchased for the government, local economic spin-off from a new gold and copper mine at Ok Tedi, in the Western province, and other suspiciously made resource deals in forestry and fish were also the subject of controversy in parliament. The misuse of sectoral funds by MPs, and the explicit attack on provincial government autonomy, fueled not only by criticism from Somare and his Pangu opposition but also from within the ruling coalition itself, gave rise to open conflict between Okuk and Father Momis, the Bougainvillean decentralization minister. Momis contended that PNG had become a neocolony that was floundering in a moral, economic, and political morass, against which the provincial decentralization process was crucial for revitalizing the nation and controlling its leaders. Okuk condemned the expense and mediocrity of provincial government and wished Father Momis an early return to the Catholic church. Grounds for the campaign of 1982 were being laid: commodity markets were depressed, mineral revenues were declining, and the government— seemingly fascinated by new airplanes, ill-conceived resource agreements, and television—appeared to be drifting away from the society.

The 1982 Elections

Eight major political parties in PNG endorsed approximately 60 percent of the 1,125 candidates who stood for parliament, although in some cases more than one party endorsed the same candidate. Except for that

of one small-scale party, the idealistic Melanesian Alliance, most platforms were again quite similar, calling for rural development, more and
better infrastructure, increased exploitation of natural resources, and
more foreign capital to stimulate economic growth. The parties varied in
resources and scale of organization with Pangu still the wealthiest and
most widespread, followed by the National Party of Okuk and the PPP
led by Chan. Pangu endorsed the most candidates, spent the most
money, and did not change its message, which emphasized the unabated
popularity of the ex-prime minister. "Somare," said the slogan in 1982,
"knows the way."

Candidates supplemented parties with primordial support and made
attempts to extend these ties through various church, local political, or
workplace associations. They toured electorates, demonstrating their
prestige and control of wealth through patronage gifts in the form of
beer parties, gasoline, trucks, pigs, and cash. The major issue to
emerge—which favored Pangu—was the economy. In the period from
1979 to mid-1982 the price of PNG's four major exports—copper,
coffee, cocoa, and copra—had dropped by as much as half. Stabilization
fund reserves for agricultural exports were nearly exhausted. For the
first time the quantity of retail goods sold in the country began to fall.
Foreign exchange reserves decreased and government expenditure even
in the 1981 austerity budget exceeded revenue by as much as 10 percent.
Private sector employment had fallen and there had been almost no new
foreign investment. Although the Chan government had few economic
levers available to it—except to appeal to Canberra to suspend cuts in
aid (still supplying 25 percent of government revenue)—and therefore
could not be held accountable for the situation, voters and Pangu
candidates nevertheless made explicit comparisons between the Somare
years of high prices and the lean years of Chan. The comparison,
although mistaken, marked "an important step in the 'nationalization' "
of party politics in the country even though the parties had essentially
been dormant during the interelection periods.[56]

Results dealt a harsh blow to incumbents. Of the 103 incumbent
MPs who stood for reelection, only 50 retained their seats; nearly half of
the 27 ministers in the outgoing government were defeated. The plurality-
only voting system, together with the large number of candidates, gave
victories to many candidates who received but a small percentage of the
vote cast. Only 14 seats were won by absolute majority, while 62 seats
were won with less than 30 percent of the vote. The plurality-only
system was criticized for seeming to discourage candidates from seeking
support beyond kin and village ties. Pangu then broached plans to
reintroduce the preferential ballot, but the attempt to require a U.S.
$1,200 entry fee for candidates created so much antagonism that it was
quickly withdrawn.

With substantial finances, two years out of power to plan its campaign, a Somare nostalgia sweeping the country, and the coalition
partners each fielding their own rival slates, Pangu won an unprecedented 50 of 108 seats (one election was deferred due to the death of a
candidate), receiving 34 percent of the vote (Table 10.3). With the
exception of the small Melanesian Alliance Party, Chan's coalition
partners each lost ground to Pangu. The 1982 elections saw the effective
dissolution of a highlands-based United Party, which had no platform
and was badly split by infighting. However its successor, Okuk's
National Party, also polled weakly and Okuk himself was defeated by a
Pangu candidate.

Table 10.3   1982 Election Results in Papua New Guinea: Parliamentary Seats Won, by Region

Region				Party		
	Pangu	PPP	National	Melanesian Alliance	PNG/ Independent Other	Total
Islands	8	2	1	8	3	22
Coastal	24	0	2	0	3	29
Highlands	13	8	8	0	6	35
Papua	6	4	2	0	11	23
Totals:	51	14	13	8	23	109

Source: Compiled from R. R. Premdas and J. S. Steves, "National Elections in Papua
New Guinea: The Return of Pangu to Power," *Asian Survey* 23 (1983): pp. 997, 999, 1001;
and D. Hegarty and Peter King, "Papua New Guinea in 1982: The Election Brings
Change," *Asian Survey* 23 (1983): p. 222.

Pangu consolidated its traditional coastal strength in 1982, continued at the same limited level in Papua, lost two seats in the highlands
(although it maintained the largest single party bloc in the region), and
lost support in the islands (see Table 10.3). The PPP, the incumbent
party of Prime Minister Chan, slipped badly, its size reduced by six
seats, with losses both in the coastal and island regions. The only
significant new group to emerge was the PNG Independent Group, led
by a former defense force commander whose electoral message had
consisted solely of an appeal for "new blood" in the country's leadership.
Of approximately 500 candidates who stood as independents, only ten
won election and most of them quickly declared party affiliation.

The Third Somare Coalition: 1982–1985

In a parliamentary democracy built on a mercurial, rather undisciplined,
multiparty system, the election of a ruling government in PNG had
become a two-step process. The second round of politicking—consisting
of a numbers game to assemble a majority coalition—follows in the five

weeks after the polls close when new or incumbent MPs are courted and lobbied, whether or not they have campaign commitments to honor, with tactics such as "reimbursing" candidates for their election expenses, denying access to other parties' persuasion, and making promises of portfolios, perks and privileges. Of course, little is gained from being a backbencher, so the party with the greatest numbers has the advantage of pulling independents into its circle. Somare wanted an all-Pangu government, or at least a government with an impotent partner. After each party was considered the emasculated remnants of the United Party and a gaggle of independents were selected to join the new Pangu coalition. In the end, Somare did not need the UP since eleven MPs switched to Pangu from other parties immediately after the poll or just prior to the parliamentary ballot, but in the interests of a more secure working majority he invited its six members to join his coalition. The opposition consisted of the National Party, the Melanesian Alliance, and Papua Besena. Chan preferred to take minority party status for his PPP rather than go with the official opposition.

In August 1982, after thirty months out of office, at the age of forty-seven, Michael Somare triumphantly returned to power. Despite earlier promises to trim the overall size of his ministry and instigate a general belt tightening, and despite strong parliamentary numbers, Somare announced a cabinet just one short of the maximum, and distributed a disproportionately large number of ministries to his United Party partners. The pressures to maximize patronage, to appease coalition members, and indebt potentially wavering independents and party swappers were apparently too great. The allocation of ministries favored the islands and the Papuan regions over the more populous and more Pangu highlands and coastal regions. Although nearly half of the new cabinet was made up of novice MPs, at least several of the new Somare appointments had made strong reputations for themselves in the Public Service.

The new government had to face old problems—the deepening economic recession, obstacles to major foreign investments, highly inflated land compensation claims throughout the country, corruption in national and provincial government, relations with Indonesia, the opposition—and oddly, the question of Somare's successor was being raised within Pangu itself. The new budget, which represented an overall cut of 5 percent in real terms, attempted to retrench 10 percent of the Public Service, but assumed that Australia would meet the former government's request to defer aid cuts. The new Labour government in Australia did announce an increase in PNG aid for 1982–83, as well as a new formula for lowered aid reduction that was to be tied to mineral revenues. The Australian bequest, which still constituted nearly 30 percent of the national budget, thus saved the Somare government from having to make further cuts in the inflated Public Service but certainly did not provide enough aid to support evening out its dual salary structure. The Public Employees Association called for a twenty-four-hour strike in February 1982 to protest expatriate salaries being more than double national ones (plus various perquisites). Although the threat by the Somare government to fire striking public servants was not carried out, the attempt to find a way to abolish the dual salary structure, while protecting incentives for skilled foreign workers to employ themselves in the country, was confounded by the impossibility of expanding the wages budget. Related issues of Western privilege, interests, and influence in the ex-colony thus seemed to be reemerging as a central issue in the country; although the money required to begin rolling back the dual salary structure would necessitate having to expand dependence on Australian aid.

Somare was also challenged by the return of Iambakey Okuk, his defeated archrival, who had won a by-election in his wife's district, and had returned to parliament. Okuk immediately announced plans to defeat the Pangu government in parliament, where he was acclaimed, rather than reelected, leader of the opposition. After intricate attempts to split the ruling coalition—without offering any policy alternatives—he tabled a vote of no confidence in November, and then withdrew it, realizing that the ensuing vote would humiliate him. Pangu seized the moment and moved a vote of *confidence* in itself, which was carried seventy to zero, as most of the opposition walked out of the chamber.

A border problem with Indonesia, which Pangu had studiously avoided debating during the elections of 1982, was also festering. Indonesian "transmigration" plans to replace indigenous Melanesians in Irian Jaya with a massive Javanese population crystallized fears in PNG about Indonesia's aggressive approach to the land and customs of the West Papuan peoples, as well as suspicions about ultimate designs on PNG itself. The conciliatory policy of the Somare government toward Indonesia, which at least tacitly was delimited by Australian interests in buffering themselves from that massive country, was nonetheless strained. In a radio program broadcast in Australia, the Pangu defense minister openly broke ranks with Somare and his foreign affairs minister by calling for increased military spending. The defense minister was subjected to an immediate portfolio transfer for his efforts—but not sacked. The government, however, did reject calls for deep personnel cuts in its 3,000-man defense force, while committing itself to re-equip and boost border patrols, which belied its optimistic approach toward the huge Asian neighbor.

In December 1986, Indonesian pursuit of West Papuan resistance groups (OPM) had led to several accidental border violations. Rabbie Namaliu, the foreign affairs and trade minister, went to Jakarta, where he took a strong position against the border incursions, which he later reiterated at the United Nations General Assembly. In Port Moresby a revision of the 1979 border agreement between the two countries was to be concluded, for which the Indonesian foreign minister, Mochtar Kusumaatmadja, came to PNG. Although the new agreement was ultimately signed, amid tensions and diplomatic slights, it almost immediately gave rise to differing interpretations of its joint border security provisions; with the PNG government resisting Indonesian pressure to mound joint patrols against the OPM.

While foreign relations were disputed within the cabinet, economic problems further unraveled Somare's remarkable return to power. In 1984 the government signaled the official end of its original distributional goals as it embarked on a growth oriented strategy. State-supported industrial development based on domestic and foreign sector investment was to be the new policy.[57] Past emphases on equity were criticized for stagnating the economy and leaving PNG behind other developing countries in Southeast Asia. The limitation of annual wage increases to 5 percent had meant that real wages declined from 1982 to 1984. When national parliamentarians voted themselves a 30 percent salary increase unions were incensed. At the same time, the mining sector was also presenting the government with reduced dividends, labor unrest, and huge unforeseen development expenditures. On the positive side, however, commodity prices were high, economic growth was solid, and a new five-year Australian commitment to PNG was announced in July 1985 with a smaller aid reduction than had been originally proposed.

Provincial governments were also tangling with the Pangu coalition, which suspended Enga, one of the highlands provinces, and Manus, an islands province, for financial irregularities. In addition, among the several provincial elections held in 1984, none produced results favorable to the Pangu Pati. Somare announced the beginning of a review of the nineteen provincial governments, the first step of which was to be a national referendum on discontinuing them. This aroused the ire of the island provincial premiers, who raised the specter of succession for the first time in several years.

By far, however, the gravest dilemma for the government was growing violence and crime in Port Moresby, the national capital, by "rascals," as gangs of urban youth are called in PNG. Responding in late 1984 to a wave of brutal gang rapes of young women, and the largest expression of public outrage ever seen in the capital, Somare called for a stronger campaign for law. The increase of crime had created serious effects on public confidence in law enforcement that, he argued, had also diminished business confidence. He proposed publicly flogging convicted rapists, hiring expatriate prosecutors, enlarging the largely demoralized police force, and giving the commissioner the power to call out the defense force for assistance in maintaining order.[58] In May 1985 Somare took more procrustean measures. Declaring that violence and crime threatened the state, he instituted a state of emergency, which imposed a six-month nightly curfew on Port Moresby, provided police wider search and arrest powers, and prohibited demonstrations of all sorts. Then he introduced bills in cabinet to provide for the castration of rapists and hanging for gang rapists where murder was involved. Four months later, a parliamentary committee reported that the temporary measures had improved the situation, reducing sexual assaults and robbery by more than half.

But politically Somare and his Pangu Pati had lost their hold on the 1982 coalition. With the partial withdrawal of United Party support, several more no confidence votes were tabled in 1984 and 1985 and Paias Wingti, Somare's deputy prime minister, resigned late in 1984 after demanding that three of Somare's strongest and most powerful supporters be sacked for being corrupt, uncaring, and too business-minded.[59] One of them, Tony Siaguru, did resign and then countered by demanding that Somare dismiss Wingti. Tense meetings filled back rooms of the posh new parliament building in Waigani and it was momentarily unclear whether Somare would be able to withstand another no confidence motion. The confrontation was avoided when Somare, having won the support of Chan, reinstated Wingti as deputy prime minister while assigning him charge over a lesser ministry. The vulnerability of the government was now obvious. In March 1985, taking thirteen other staunch Pangu members into the opposition, Wingti resigned again, attacking the government for lack of discipline and direction and vowing to form a new political party that would be dedicated to winning the government. The new coalition and ministry, which Somare then reformed, had Father Momis, the leader of the ideologically opposed Melanesian Alliance, as deputy prime minister.

Parliament wound up four days early without passing any of the government's legislative program, which contained two rather important constitutional amendments: one to force a by-election of any member who switched party affiliation after being elected, and the other enabling a prime minister to call for early national elections if he lost the confidence of parliament. The intent of both bills was to consolidate party unity, given the reticence of members to go to election, in light of the high rate at which incumbents tend to be defeated. Against heavy lobbying by his own coalition, Somare had blinked.[60]

At the next sitting of parliament Chan himself began to threaten further no confidence votes. Criticism of Somare's handling of the still deteriorating situation in the capital was mounting and accusations, made by Paias Wingti, the former deputy prime minister, of shady business dealings with a suspicious Australian airline, cast a pall of corruption for the first time in Somare's career. A commission of inquiry instigated by Somare himself was appointed to investigate the charges. The quagmire into which he was sinking at home, however, did not lessen Somare's characteristic ebullience for his state (and implicitly his own statecraft). For the tenth anniversary of the independence of PNG, which was also being celebrated in September 1985, Somare visited Sydney to launch two projects bearing his name. One, the Michael Somare Foundation, would provide funds to promote the principles of service to the cause of democracy in PNG. Praising the vitality of democracy in his country, Somare enthusiastically stressed its links to local-level political culture.

> During our first ten years we have overcome strong secession movements... without the use of force.... We are a democratic people.... The institutions which existed in our traditional societies were, almost invariably, based on democratic consensus decision-making.... Democracy in Papua New Guinea is not a new flower rooted in shallow soil.... We have molded our own distinctive democracy from the Melanesian traditions of our forefathers and the Western institutions bequeathed to us by Australia.... We have made democracy survive.[61]

Two months later, in November 1985, Somare lost a no confidence vote and was replaced by the thirty-five-year-old Wingti, who thereby became PNG's first highlands prime minister, having assembled a five-party coalition that centered around his new People's Democratic Movement. Somare congratulated Wingti, but allowed that he was planning and expecting to return to power following the national elections of June 1987.

• THEORETICAL ANALYSIS •

A Highly Successful Democracy

The first decade of statehood in PNG certainly fulfill Dahl's three, albeit crude, criteria that define a democratic system. A competitive level of participation for the major leadership governmental positions is seen in the high turnover rate of MPs in parliament. Fair national, provincial, and district elections have regularly occurred since 1964, and participation has been very inclusive. Civil and political liberties—except for the two states of emergency declared to control intertribal warfare in several highlands provinces in 1979 and to control crime in the capital city in 1985—have been unrestricted in the country: The media are little censored, political parties and labor unions organize without state interference, universal adult suffrage obtains. In all, then, the democratic system in PNG has been "highly successful" in terms of our, or any, comparative scale. Relatively stable, it has endured both parliamentary and electoral changes of government, without suspending the basic freedoms associated with democracy.

This is not, however, to endorse either Dahl's criteria or the evaluative scale, because neither offers indicators of what democracy *means* qualitatively. The history of PNG provides a vivid example of liberal democratic rule with a framework of regular elections, high voter turnouts, competitive party activity, high turnover rates of incumbents, parliamentary procedures, an independent judiciary, not to mention guaranteeing basic freedoms of expression, while still being oligarchic and rent by inequality, if not vaguely corrupt and occasionally authoritarian. How could and why should this be the case?

The history of postcolonial PNG seems to be one of form with minimal content (as it might be construed in the West)—of a democracy born without strong ideology, either against colonial oppression or for nationalism, either against various guises of the West or for a Melanesian way. PNG was born not in struggle but in caesarean section—brought out into the world by surgical incision with only the least of its own initiative and then protected by its Australian mother with massive annual grants. As a result primordial political idioms have held sway in national politics. The strongest elements in the first years of democracy in PNG are quite uniform. The normative rules are construed in Western terms: e.g., winning office through the electoral process and holding power in parliament through the consensual leadership of multiparty coalitions, undefined by ideology or class, but largely through the lure of a ministry.[62] The pragmatic rules of politics are more syncretic: Candidates recruit electoral support through primordial ties that are sustained through exchange, patronage, and pork barrelism; they must pursue wealth and assembly power in parliament, not in their constituencies.

Democracy in Papua New Guinea has not been denuded of its cultural background. Class formation is very much in process. The classes are still "related" today: an educated, urban bourgeoisie still has primordial, that is to say moral, ties, based on kinship and belief in supernatural sanctions, to what is very much a preliterate, rural, landed peasantry. The radical deculturation that was, for example, the result of French colonization of New Caledonia did not occur in PNG. When Australia left it had provided its ex-colonials with only the barest of tools with which to administer themselves. But there was some virtue in this; it had also left PNG more or less materially and socially intact, with most of its cultural and material resources remaining to be exploited by Papua New Guineans. More positively, Australia had also left PNG with more or less an end to internal warfare. PNG had been left with a strong model of democratic politics and with a citizenry that had learned, approximately, to expect that their point of view would be heard in local councils if not in national assemblies. The government was minimally corrupt and without international enemies. The press was free and active and had no tradition of political harassment. The judiciary was independent; the health service innovative. And Australia left PNG on good terms; with a readiness to continue to provide subsidy and support with no strings attached.

In order to understand the strengths of and threats to democratic culture in PNG—in which success in electoral politics depends on personality, compromise, consensus, patronage, and sustaining electoral support through exchange relations rather than ideology—it is necessary to examine cultural meanings, especially the meaning of democracy in traditional Melanesian cultures, which the politicians themselves acknowledge underlies their system.

The Melanesian Ethic

Papua New Guineans began to filter into their island from Australia and Indonesia some 40,000 years ago and developed societies closely linked to and divided by the rugged, mountainous environments they occupied.[63] However, environment does not explain political organization;[64] the terrain in lower altitudes and along the coast is perhaps less difficult than in the highlands, but a high degree of atomism prevailed in both regions, e.g., chronic warfare in which small groups of migrants displaced or absorbed earlier settlers. The most frequently cited consequence of this highly particularistic form of sociopolitical integration is the incredible number of languages spoken in PNG. But this linguistic diversity obscures a certain underlying, albeit schismatic, cultural and political homogeneity, an ideal type which I am terming a Melanesian ethic and which consists of four major features. First, language was not a salient social and moral category. If there are 700 languages spoken, then there are many, many more polities than that, for the village, hamlet, lineage, or clan, rather than the language/tribal group, was the politically autonomous unit holding corporate property and jointly defending itself in warfare. Second, not only was the language group subdivided; the ethos of warfare—egalitarian competition, hostility, and suspicion—pervaded the clan, village, and even the household.[65] Third, although it too was subject to the ethos of strife, the household was the fundamental economic and political unit and therefore relations of production, which were construed in terms of intimate, face-to-face kinship relations, were often organized by male-female categories. Women comprised the everyday work force while men were largely responsible for politics and warfare. Fourth, power was primarily won and lost by men engaged in small, sociodomestic rivalries. In many areas succession to traditional leadership, whether defined in terms of birth or merit, was in neither case automatic and depended on the competitive distribution of wealth, which often took the form of pigs and shell valuables during feasts or the display of special competencies during ritual or war. The accumulation and redistribution of goods and services created followers who were then obliged to reciprocate their labor and loyalty.

Traditional Melanesian polities thus consisted of kinship-based factions divided by a state of suspended warfare. Communities were small, fluid, and prone to schism. Networks of influence depended fundamentally on personal contacts. Oratorical skill was often critical to maintaining this form of consensual power. In public debate Melanesian men might perform with pride and verve, but with the purpose of reconciling opinion within their factions, and thus "the most successful orators...take a great deal of time before committing themselves to a definite position."[66] While assertive, in some cases ferociously despotic,[67] the bigman might also possess considerable self-control, patiently waiting for repayment, and able to defer to consensus.[68] Stratification, where it occurred, was rudimentary; the rise and fall of leaders was relentless. Local-level leaders were *primus inter pares*.[69] They had to reconcile a contradiction between their own strength and a pervasive cultural valuation of equivalence.[70]

Support was conditional and voluntary. Perhaps one of the most problematic aspects of the Melanesian ethic was the high level of personal autonomy to which leadership had to accommodate. The assertive male personality, given to intensive activity in warfare and exchange, only won influence over and deference from those people who needed his wealth or services. Such egalitarian leadership asserted itself in the whole range of community affairs, and consisted of cultural specialists who did what everyone did, but with more industry, skill, and frequency. The Melanesian leader was an intermediary, a middleman whose leadership depended in large measure on his ability to extend a network of influence: from household to clan, to other clans in his district.[71] The accumulation and circulation of value through them—in the form of goods, currencies, or ritual services—was key to their power.[72] When interest flagged or age set in, and a leader's level of activity declined; or when he was outdone by a rival, his prestige and power diminished too. The political situation, amid prepacification warfare, was thus intrinsically fissile. The Melanesian polity was "constantly subject to particularistic relapse...and the threat of secession was always a sanction against the operation of leadership as an 'office' with automatic powers and prerogatives."[73]

The divisive side of the Melanesian ethic is on the one hand the ethos of warfare and the value of personal autonomy, while, on the other, its integrative capacities center around surplus production assembled for competitive ceremonial exchanges staged by leaders engaged in zero-sum games. Little given to hierarchy, title, or noblesse oblige, then, this ethic involved reigning in a pattern of rampant individualism through manipulating a system of exchange within a rhetoric of kinship.[74]

Regime Legitimacy and Instability

By contrast to colonial experiences elsewhere in the Pacific, the manner in which a Western infrastructure was brought to PNG by Australia in the course of its colonial half-century seems relatively benign and laissez faire. For, in large part, one major criticism that may be leveled against the Australian administration is that it exploited social and material resources in the country while failing to alter or resolve the fragmented traditional setting. It made only the most minimal efforts to prepare Papua New Guineans for self-government. The different lingua francas, the competitive Western religions, the uneven economic development fostering regional jealousies, the urban enclavement, the small, weak army and police force, the nearly embryonic political and judiciary institutions, the huge public service, the very minimal education system, and a limited system of roads that made the country more dependent on an expensive system of air transportation all did little to introduce integrative infrastructure or any sort of national political symbolism and rhetoric to PNG.

However, a relatively benign colonial history did allow the democratic features of traditional Melanesian polities to perdure into the postcolonial context. The first eleven years of democracy in PNG may not have been informed by Western standards of ideological competition, but they have been informed by distinctively Melanesian forms of competition: the individual pursuit of prestige through the accumulation and redistribution of wealth within a fluid framework of political alliance. Apart from the obvious importance of primordial ties in electoral campaigning, the high degree of competitiveness, the extensive circulation of elites, the *personal* quality of power, the loose solidarity of the political parties, the ad hoc quality of policy, the insubordination of the electorate, the importance of exchange in the guise of patronage and pork barrelism, and the consensual nature of leadership and state power, each manifests the egalitarian, factionalized, exchange-based ethic of the traditional setting.

But in addition to indigenous and colonial history, the Melanesian ethic is today able to express itself within the framework of Westminster democracy, which is, I argue, quite appropriate and conducive to it. The three-tiered system of national, provincial, and local assemblies, based upon universal adult suffrage, is inclusive and itself decentralized. The division of the political system into four (now six) major parties enables regional loyalties to be both ventilated and crosscut in a way, given their weak cohesion, which facilitates compromise and inhibits polarization. Parliamentary leadership within this sort of system, with its perpetual emphasis on coalition assembly through a numbers game based in ministerial patronage and the no confidence motion, has also limited the accumulation of power, dividing the key elite rather than consolidating it. Despite the prominence of Michael Somare, the first prime minister, this post has become a pragmatic and mediating, rather than autocratic, office. The PNG case thus confirms Juan Linz's somewhat tautological argument that parliamentary leadership, being structurally less differentiated from its legislative basis, must rely more on consensus building than presidential leadership and must therefore be more responsive to legislative pressure.[75] Further, no confidence votes and lack of party cohesion minimize the zero-sum implications of elections so that the system is rather flexible.

As traditional power in Melanesia was for the most part personal rather than institutional, the electoral process today is highly competitive, resulting in impressive rates of incumbent turnover. Campaigning depends less on political party affiliation than on the size and solidarity of one's primordial backing, the perceived extent of exchange, either in the form of direct gifts or development projects, and only lastly on Western political skills. MPs are viewed by their constituents "as in...exchange relation[s] with...electors," and to the degree that they confine themselves to provincial or national capitals, they generate discontent among the electorate who begin to view them as acultural, immoral, and thus akin to distant, self-seeking white men.[76] So the Melanesian ethic may also undermine incumbents' support between elections and thereby increase grassroots participation in the democratic process.

Both constituency and candidate envision politics as a means of obtaining wealth and prestige. Other means exist, however. There are other employment options for educated, able Papua New Guineans, both in government and private sectors for those who fail in electoral politics. Class formation in the country is as yet relatively unbounded. The history of the state, as I have presented it, shows neither the private sector nor the Public Service under governmental reign. While ministerial-level jobs regularly change hands with a change of power, job tenure in the bureaucracy is more or less secure. Moreover, in addition to small-scale entrepreneurial opportunities, largely in coffee and cocoa growing, the economy benefits from enormous natural resources, of which tremendously valuable new mineral deposits are continuing to be discovered and exploited.[77] Although unemployment is high at lower levels of skill and ability, there are many more opportunities than skilled people to seize them at the upper levels. Standing for office is thus only one of several options in which highly educated, Westernized Papua New Guineans may try and make their fortunes. The continuing controversy in PNG about protecting the free market and the equitable distribution of wealth and the proper relationship of business to political conduct reflect both the open-endedness of the economy and two essential features of the Melanesian ethic that are the valuation of individual autonomy and the pursuit of wealth.

At the national level, but much less so at the local and the provincial levels, the judiciary has been independent and relatively effective policing the conduct of political life. As the Rooney affair illustrated, the consequences of tampering with, or entirely ignoring, the face of legal impártiality are very serious. But on a more mundane level, there is always a trickle of court cases making their way through the newspapers involving MPs whose careers are interrupted or terminated for repeated drunkenness or giving business advantages to kin. Although perceived with an understandable ambivalence, the respect for constitutional law derives in part from the strong model of Australian democracy. But a second, more general source of regime legitimacy has been the Christian missions, in which so many of the national politicians received primary and secondary education. Only a few ordained priests, such as the Bougainvillean Momis, have held elected office, but the vast majority of politicians consider themselves very Christian men. The relationship between mission and politics is quite complicated and one would be hard-pressed to define precisely how political-legal life has been influenced, and possibly stabilized, by them, but certainly a common biblical rhetoric infuses all levels of speechmaking. The churches, moreover, speak out critically on the foibles of political conduct, although to uncertain effect.

The army, the Pacific Defence Force, is an elite, well-to-do, well-educated, proud organization, but poses little threat to the state. The possibility of a military coup in PNG is limited although not impossible. Civilian and army elites do not consider each other rivals, being bound by informal ties, such as common experience in the national high schools. Lacking resources both in numbers and in administrative outposts outside of its few barracks, the army also lacks the vehicles to move troops throughout the far-flung country.[78] Moreover, although the army is respected throughout the country, the idea of a military dictatorship runs counter to indigenous notions of political authority and to a colonial experience in which Papua New Guineans learned to expect that their point of view could be heard at least locally if not nationally.

Moreover, the international climate of relations in which PNG has found itself has neither demanded a strong army nor threatened state sovereignty. Indeed the major problem, relations between PNG and

Indonesia, may have been resolved by a 1986 treaty calling for mutual recognition and dispute arbitration between the two countries. The government has also benefited in no small way, of course, from the large Australian subsidy. This aid has permitted it, for example to pay for an exorbitant public service, whose size the government has found impossible to reduce if it is to proceed with the process of indigenizing its bureaucracy.

The potential for primordial loyalties to destabilize the political system has been somewhat neutralized by their extreme atomization. Thus the larger political parties, at least, have been able to crosscut regional loyalties. National political leadership has also been effective in this regard by being pragmatic and disposed toward compromise—as evidenced in the creation of the provincial tier of government—and by being strongly committed to democratic ideals. But the neutralization of Melanesian primordialism is fundamentally achieved through parliamentary enclavement. The state is separated from its constituents between elections. This has both generated participation in elections just as well as it has weakened civil power.

"Law and order, or more to the point, lawlessness and lack of order, are fast becoming the Achilles' heel of PNG, the outstanding threat to the practice of humane government that has characterized the first ten years of her independent existence."[79] Although the incidence of rape and other forms of violence among unemployed urban men has been curtailed by the state, the tensions precipitating it, namely deculturalization and identity loss resulting from the frantic pace of social change, will not prove to be as simply and quickly resolvable. The resumption of interclan warfare in the highlands provinces is related to a quite different set of causes from those of urban crime but it too suggests that outside the national capital the state does not monopolize force. Indeed far worse, it does not even yet appear as a credible, much less institutionalized, form of social control to villagers. In 1986, following the death of Okuk of liver cancer at the age of forty-three, riots and looting broke out in Port Moresby during his state funeral, as they did in the highlands where men felt slighted that a national day of mourning had not been declared in his honor.

Part of the failure of the state to monopolize force results from the very Melanesian ethic that we have argued is so conducive to democracy: the traditional construction of legitimate authority for the most part excluded youth and women. Rather than being universalist, age- and gender-neutral, political power accrued exclusively to middle-aged or senior men. So the state is run today by illegitimate nonpersons, young men, and even a few women, whom it defines as the political equals of senior men through universal suffrage. But the crisis of authority has been compounded by the removal of the state from the problems of its rural constituency, and by a leadership that is seen as corrupt, or at least too business-minded. The state is seen as distant, but also, to the extent that it is visible, its performance is poorly evaluated, and seen as administratively inept in contrast to the colonial predecessor. Rural health services—for example in the area of malaria control—have declined sharply since Independence. Localization has created an expertise gap and the recent collapse of the Australian dollar has limited the extent to which this gap may be closed.

The death of the young Okuk is no anomaly. The premature mortality of many young, educated Papua New Guineans, employed full-time in Western jobs, reveals the very difficult toll that rapid social change is taking on political actors, whose diets change and whose stress levels increase. But there is also a civil implication to this mortality rate that is less explicit: sudden death is universally interpreted by Papua New Guineans to result from sorcery, that is, to result from malevolent human agency. Therefore the death of a politician is a murder that must have been committed by some rival, usually local or regional, which ought to be avenged. The level of suspicion of public life as a whole is confirmed and the state, as a viable concept, is undermined.

Thus a Melanesian ethic both stimulates and inhibits the development of democracy in Papua New Guinea in gross and subtle ways. For the most part I believe that the impetus provided far outweighs the constraints imposed on it. At the same time, however, the success of the democracy has been enabled by several other variables: a benign colonial history that set in train an appropriate parliamentary system, an independent judiciary and media, a committed and astute leadership, vast resources and a relatively healthy economy, an inchoate class structure, and minimal military or international threat.

Conclusion

To explain the quality and early success of democracy in PNG, I have relied heavily on an argument abstracted from *The Protestant Ethic*. In that book Weber makes three major claims with respect to explaining the process of development of rationality in the West. At the most general level he asserts that endogenous systems of meaning—culture—explain the initial impetus of, in that case, a new attitude about economic life. So it is the pursuit of the *meaning* of wealth, in terms of what it reflects about the possibility of eternal grace, rather than wealth itself, which engages Protestants and stimulates the process of economic change. Second, at a more specific level, he urges us to attend to gaps in meaning systems—cultural contradictions—in seeking to explain this motivation. Election is unknowable and the elect are ultimately invisible: uncertainty breeds the ascetic, systematic pursuit of wealth. Third,

Weber points to the unintentioned consequences of the attempt to resolve this contradiction: the dominance of Western rationality over Western primordialism, which is to him a tragic outcome.

In examining the particularities of democracy in PNG, obviously we are dealing with a non-Western set of meaning systems and with a process of change stimulated by exogenous rather than endogenous contradictions. But it is still analytically useful to look to Weber's framework for insight because, as I have tried to show, the democracy has both been driven forward and made vulnerable by the interplay of contradictory meanings of political participation, wealth, and person-hood. Melanesian conceptions have simultaneously complemented and contradicted Western ones. Whereas wealth is ideally valued and accu-mulated in the West for apolitical purposes, in order to reproduce persons who are independent of the constraints of society, in Melanesia wealth is still valued by bigmen for political purposes, in order to reproduce a network of relations in which persons are embedded through the tactic of exchange.[80]

When Papua New Guineans try to enter the national political arena, they are often motivated by a meld of Western and Melanesian valuation of wealth. The norms and rules of the arena they enter are nominally Western, while their electorate has expectations which are decidedly Melanesian. If they obey Western rules, and amass personal wealth, they will be repudiated by their constituency for being self-interested or for favoring their own kin groups. If they obey Melanesian rules and spread wealth or opportunity among their constituency, they will be indicted for corruption and condemned for ignoring the common good. But the damage done to political careers by this web of contradictory meanings does not seem to devalue the Westminster system to the electorate or to its potential leadership. Voting levels remain high and the number of candidates who stand for parliament has steadily risen at every election. The hope for wealth, e.g., for development projects and business opportunities, keeps both voter and leader attentive to and involved in the democracy. So, in light of the other variables cited above, we explain the outcome of democracy in PNG in terms of the contradiction between two systems of meaning that meet in this political culture. It is far too soon in the history of this country to evaluate the consequences, partly intended, likely tragic, of this outcome.

• NOTES •

    1. Max Weber, *The Protestant Ethic and the Spirit of Capitalism* (New York: Charles Scribner's Sons, 1958).
    2. Clifford Geertz, "The Integrative Revolution: Primordial Sentiments and Civil Politics in the New States," reprinted in C. Geertz, *The Interpretation of Culture* (New York: Basic Books, 1973), pp. 309–310.

3. William A. Foley, *The Papuan Languages of New Guinea* (Cambridge: Cambridge University Press, 1986).

4. Eugene Ogan, "Nasioi Land Tenure: an Extended Case Study," *Oceania* 42 (1971): p. 82.

5. The most important indigenous response to colonialism and capitalism were millenarian movements called "cargo cults." See Theodore Schwartz, "The Paliau Movement in the Admiralty Islands, 1946–54," *Anthropological Papers of the American Museum of Natural History* 49 (1962): pp. 211–421; Peter Lawrence, *Road Belong Cargo* (Atlantic Highlands, N.J.: Humanities Press, 1979); Peter Worsley, *The Trumpet Shall Sound* (New York: Schocken, 1970).

6. Robert J. Gordon and Mervyn J. Meggitt, *Law and Order in the New Guinea Highlands* (Hanover, Mass.: University Press of New England, 1985), pp. 39–70.

7. R. Joyce, *Sir William MacGregor* (Melbourne: Oxford University Press, 1971).

8. It should be pointed out, however, that this direct engagement of Melanesian culture was pragmatic rather than canonical. See M. F. Huber, "The Bishop's Progress: Ecclesiastical Integration and Socioeconomic Development in the Sepik Frontier," in N. Lutkehaus et al., eds., *Sepik Research Today* (Durham: North Carolina University Press, 1988).

9. Hank Nelson, *Papua New Guinea: Black Unity or Black Chaos?* (Victoria, Australia: Penguin Books, 1972), pp. 189–190.

10. M. Rodman, "Introduction," in Margaret Rodman and Matthew Cooper, eds., *The Pacification of Melanesia* (Ann Arbor: University of Michigan Press, 1979), pp. 1–23.

11. T. Barnett, "Politics and Planning Rhetoric in Papua New Guinea," *Economic Development and Cultural Change* 27 (1979): pp. 769–784.

12. Kenneth Good, *Papua New Guinea: A False Economy* (London: Anti-Slavery Society, 1986), p. 26.

13. H. Nelson, *Papua New Guinea*, p. 24.

14. Ibid., p. 119.

15. D. G. Bettison, C. A. Hughes, and P. W. van der Veur, *The Papua-New Guinea Elections of 1964* (Canberra: Australian National University Press, 1965), p. 388.

16. Lamont Lindstrom, " 'Big Man': A Short Terminological History," *American Anthropologist* 83 (1981): pp. 900–905.

17. R. S. Parker and E. P. Wolfers, "From Dependence to Autonomy," in A. L. Epstein, R. S. Parker, and M. Reay, eds., *The Politics of Dependence* (Canberra: Australian National University, 1971), pp. 24–25.

18. Michael Somare, *Sana: An Autobiography* (Hong Kong: Niugini Press, 1975).

19. D. Stone, "An Overview," in D. Stone, ed., *Prelude to Self-Government* (Canberra: Australian National University Press, 1976), p. 529.

20. Ibid., p. 533.

21. M. Groves, R. M. S. Hamilton, and M. MacArthur, "A Town and Its Hinterland," in A. L. Epstein et al., eds., *The Politics of Dependence*, p. 298.

22. T. Anis, E. Makis, T. Miriung, and E. Ogan, "Towards a New Politics?—the Elections in Bougainville," in D. Stone, ed., *Prelude*, p. 442.

23. P. Paypool, "Ialibu-Pangia Electorate," in D. Stone, ed., *Prelude*.

24. A. Strathern, "Seven Good Men: The Dei Open Electorate," in D. Stone, ed., *Prelude*, p. 283.

25. P. Loveday, "Voting and Parties in the Third House 1972–1975," in P. Loveday and E. P. Wolfers, *Parties and Parliament in Papua New Guinea* (Boroko PNG: Institute for Applied Social and Economic Research 4, 1976), p. 103.

26. R. E. Young, "Elite Ideology in Papua New Guinea," *Journal of Commonwealth and Comparative Politics* 16 (1978): p. 275.

27. D. Stone, "An Overview," p. 537.

28. Michael Somare, *Sana*, p. 109.

29. David Hegarty, "Issues and Conflict in Post-colonial Papua New Guinea," *World Review* 18 (1979): p. 198.

30. P. Hastings, *New Guinea: Problems and Prospects* (Melbourne, Australia: Cheshire Press, 1973), p. 124–125.

31. P. Loveday, "Voting and Parties," p. 104.

32. M. Somare cited in J.G., "Australian Political Chronicle: Papua New Guinea," *Australian Journal of Politics and History* 21 (1975): p. 126.

33. D. G. Bettison, et al., *The Papua-New Guinea Elections of 1964*.

34. M. Somare, *Sana*, pp. 111–139.

35. J. A. Ballard, "Policy-making as Trauma: the Provincial Government Issue," in J. A. Ballard, ed., *Policy-making in a New State: Papua New Guinea, 1972–77* (St. Lucia: University of Queensland Press, 1981), pp. 95–132; R. J. May, "The Micronationalists: Problems of Fragmentation," *New Guinea* 10 (1976): pp. 38–53; B. Standish, "Power to the People? Decentralization in Papua New Guinea," *Public Administration and Development* 3 (1983): pp. 223–238.

36. B. Standish, "Power to the People?," p. 227.

37. Ibid., p. 230.

38. Ibid., pp. 231–232.

39. Hegarty, "Issues and Conflict," p. 199.

40. C. Lepani, cited in ibid., p. 198.

41. Rex Mortimer, "The Evolution of the Post-colonial state," in A. Amarshi, K. Good, and R. Mortimer, eds., *Development and Dependency* (Oxford: Oxford University Press, 1979), pp. 224–225.

42. Ibid., pp. 232, 239.

43. D.D., "Australian Political Chronicle: Papua New Guinea," *Australian Journal of Politics and History* 22 (1976): p. 443.

44. D. O'Rourke and G. Kildea, *World: Getting Elected in Papua New Guinea* (Boston: WGBH TV, 1977), p. 13.

45. D.D., "Australian Political Chronicle," p. 438.

46. Ralph Premdas, "Papua New Guinea: 1979: A Regime Under Seige," *Asian Survey* 20 (1980): p. 89.

47. Ibid., p. 88.

48. M. Somare cited in D. W. Hegarty, "Australian Political Chronicle: Papua New Guinea," *Australian Journal of Politics and History* 24 (1979): p. 406.

49. I. Okuk cited in D. Hegarty, "Australian Political Chronicle: Papua New Guinea," *Australian Journal of Politics and History* 23 (1979): p. 107.

50. Ibid., p. 110.

51. Premdas, "Papua New Guinea: 1979."

52. R. Gordon and M. Meggitt, *Law and Order*, pp. 1–2.

53. Stephan Pokawin, "Papua New Guinea: Aftermath of Colonialism," in *Politics in Melanesia* (Fiji: University of the South Pacific, 1980), p. 407.

54. Raymond Goodman, C. Lepani, and D. Morawetz, *The Economy of Papua New Guinea*, (Canberra: Australian National University, 1985).

55. Cited by D. W. Hegarty, "Australian Political Chronicle: Papua New Guinea," *Australian Journal of Politics and History* 28 (1982): p. 464.

56. David Hegarty and P. King, "Papua New Guinea in 1982: the Election Brings Change," *Asian Survey* 23 (1983): p. 223.

57. K. Hewison, "Papua New Guinea in 1984: Consensus Crumbles," *Asian Survey* 24 (1985): pp. 249–256.

58. *Pacific Islands Monthly* (56), December 1984, p. 7.

59. "Having come so far in such a short time within Pangu, Wingti wanted to clinch the post-Somare succession in advance by clipping the wings of [his rival] Siaguru, by securing the promotion of backbenchers whose allegiance to himself he was assiduously cultivating, ... by enticing suitable opposition members to defect to Pangu...and, above all, by seeking to wrest control of...Pangu's business arm, and hence control over party funds." Y. S., "Political Chronicle: Papua New Guinea," *Australian Journal of Politics and History* 31 (1985): p. 331.

60. "In the debate on the issue in Parliament one MP actually opined that party stability is one of the dangerous policies we are trying to establish in this country." Ibid., p. 332.

61. Michael Somare quoted in *Pacific Islands Monthly*, October 1985, p. 23.

62. F. G. Bailey, *Strategems and Spoils* (New York: Schocken Books, 1969).

63. Peter Bellwood, *Man's Conquest of the Pacific: The Prehistory of Southeast Asia and Oceania* (New York: Oxford University Press, 1979), p. 275; William Foley, *Papuan Languages*, pp. 270–271; and P. Swadling, *Papua New Guinea's Prehistory: An Introduction* (Port Moresby: Papua New Guinea National Museum, 1981).

64. M. Fortes and E. E. Evans-Pritchard, "Introduction," in M. Fortes and E. E.

Evans-Pritchard, eds., *African Political Systems* (Oxford: Oxford University Press, 1940).

65. Theodore Schwartz, "Cult and Context: The Paranoid Ethos in Melanesia," *Ethos* (1973): pp. 153–174.

66. K. E. Read, "Leadership and Consensus in a New Guinea Society," *American Anthropologist* 61 (1959): p. 431.

67. J. B. Watson, "Tairora: The Politics of Despotism in a Small Society," in R. M. Berndt and P. Lawrence, eds., *Politics in New Guinea* (Seattle: University of Washington Press, 1971), pp. 224–276.

68. K. O. L. Burridge, "The Melanesian Manager," in J. H. M. Beattie and R. G. Lienhardt, eds., *Studies in Social Anthropology, Essays in Honor of E. E. Evans-Pritchard* (Oxford: Oxford University Press, 1971), p. 103.

69. M. Meggitt, "The Pattern of Leadership among the Mae-Enga of New Guinea," in Berndt and Lawrence, *Politics in New Guinea* (Seattle: University of Washington Press, 1971), pp. 194–195.

70. K. Read, "Leadership and Consensus."

71. L. Langness, "Bena Bena Political Organization," in Berndt and Lawrence, *Politics in New Guinea*, p. 313.

72. A. Strathern, *Ongka* (London: Gerald Duckworth, 1979), pp. 68–69.

73. Theodore Schwartz, "Systems of Areal Integration: Some Considerations Based on the Admiralty Islands of Northern Melanesia," *Anthropological Forum* 1 (1963): p. 67.

74. Marshall Sahlins, "Rich Man, Poor Man, Big Man, Chief: Political Types in Melanesia and Polynesia," *Comparative Studies in Society and History* 5 (1963).

75. See Juan Linz, "Democracy: Presidential or Parliamentary. Does It Make a Difference?" (Paper presented to the workshop on "Political Parties in the Southern Cone," Woodrow Wilson International Center, Washington, D.C.:1984).

76. A. Strathern, *A Line of Power* (London: Tavistock, 1984), p. 104.

77. In 1985 and 1986 the exploitation of two gold deposits, considered to be the largest postwar finds in the world, were in full force and the prospects of major oil discovery seemed imminent.

78. Hank Nelson, *Papua New Guinea*, p. 203.

79. Y. S., "Political Chronicle: Papua New Guinea," *Australian Journal of Politics and History* 31 (1985): p. 335.

80. E. Shils, *Tradition* (Chicago: University of Chicago Press, 1981), pp. 213–262.

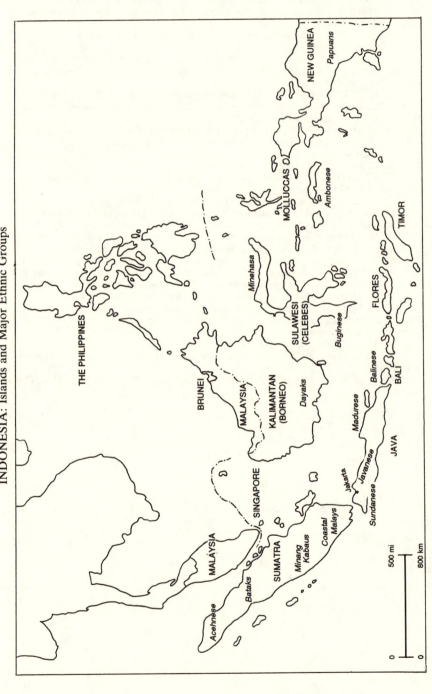

INDONESIA: Islands and Major Ethnic Groups

CHAPTER ELEVEN

Indonesia:
Past and Present Encounters
with Democracy

ULF SUNDHAUSSEN

Indonesia is rarely included in comparative surveys. This is mainly because of three reasons. Most Indonesianists have been exclusively parochial, preferring to look at events in Indonesia in a strictly non-comparative way.[1] Second, the subdiscipline of Indonesia watching had been extraordinarily politicized, making it quite unsuitable for cross-national research. And third, Indonesia has been unique in ways that most Third World countries cannot claim for themselves. This uniqueness will force the author to expand his analysis beyond the framework of this comparative project. This chapter begins with a brief survey of Indonesia's geographic, religious, and ethnic complexity. The historical review will be structured along the four distinct eras that have characterized Indonesian postwar history, with a brief account of the later colonial period preceding them. The third part will analyze these events within an Indonesian context, followed by an analysis based on the theoretical framework of the comparative study. A fifth part will consider past and likely future trends.

• THE LAND AND THE PEOPLE •

Geography

The Republic of Indonesia, until World War II The Netherlands East Indies, is an archipelago stretching almost 5,000 kilometers in a west to east direction from the Andaman Sea to the middle of New Guinea. It contains 13,611 islands, 990 of which are inhabited; its total land area amounts to 1,919,443 square kilometers.

The largest land masses in the republic are Kalimantan (Borneo; the northern quarter forms eastern Malaysia), Sumatra, West Irian (West New Guinea; the eastern part of the island is the heartland of Papua New Guinea), Sulawesi (Celebes), and Java. Particularly the volcanic areas of the archipelago, from the west coast of Sumatra to

423

Java, Bali, Sulawesi and the Moluccas, are very fertile, while the rest of the country is often either swampy or deficient in rain.

Indonesia has substantial oil fields in Kalimantan, Sumatra, and in the Java Sea. Also in various parts of the country are found copper, tin, and some gold.

Population

Indonesia has a population of approximately 170 million people, making it the fifth largest nation in the world. Annual population growth rate in the 1970–1980 period was 2.3 percent despite increasing efforts by the government to introduce the idea of family planning. Average population density approaches ninety people per square kilometer; but in Java, which supports almost two-thirds of the total population, there are rural areas with up to 2,000 people per square kilometer.

Most of the major cities including the capital, Jakarta (7 million), are located in Java. Java is the political, administrative, educational, industrial, and cultural center of Indonesia; in fact, a remnant of the colonial era is to refer to all of the archipelago except Java (and nearby Madura) as the "Outer Islands."

The great majority of the population is of Malay origin, having immigrated from mainland Asia in several waves since 2500 B.C. In the east the Papuans of West New Guinea are Melanesians, and some Melanesian influence extends farther west. There are four to five million Chinese scattered over the archipelago, as well as some Indians and Arabs.

The Malay majority is, however, by no means homogeneous. There are 366 different ethnic groups, with indigenous languages so different that communication between the communities is impossible[2] (an "artificial" language was developed as part of the drive for national independence, *Bahasa Indonesia*, based largely on the lingua franca of the region's trading communities).

In this context it will have to suffice to introduce only the thirteen largest ethnic groups. Since ethnic affiliation has been excluded from census figures for some time now we have to rely on guestimates for the numerical strength of ethnic groups. By far the largest group are the Javanese, inhabiting East and Central Java, and the northern plain of West Java. (See map). They account for approximately 45 percent of the total population; with the culturally similar Madurese of nearby Madura and the northern shore of East Java they constitute about 51 to 52 percent of the population. The second largest ethnic group are the Sundanese of West Java, traditional rivals of the Javanese, accounting for 14 percent of the population. The "Coastal Malays" of southern Sumatra may account for approximately 7 percent, the Minangkabaus of western Sumatra for 4 percent, the Batak groups of central north

Sumatra for 2 percent, and the Acehnese of the northern tip of that island for less than 2 percent. In the east of the archipelago the Buginese and the related Macassarese account for 4 percent of the population, and the Minehasa of northern Sulawesi for less than 2 percent, the Balinese constitute 2 percent, while the Dayaks of thinly populated Kalimantan, the Ambonese of the South Moluccas, and the Papuans of West New Guinea constitute even smaller minorities, yet in one way or another are of political significance.

Religion

Apart from geographic/regional and ethnic/racial differences Indonesia is also plagued by religious lines of division, with enormous implications for the politics of the republic. Indonesia is often described as the largest Muslim nation, with 90 percent of the population adhering to Islam. Such statements ignore the fact that less than half of all the so-called Muslims in the only free election of 1955 cast their vote with parties that advocated an Islamic state; the other half, the so-called *abangan*, adhere to the "Javanese religion," an amalgam of animism, elements of Buddhism and Hinduism, with Islam only the last layer. The *abangan* have resisted Islamization of society with as much determination as Christian, Hindu, and Buddhist minorities. Even the "good" Muslims, the *santri*, are divided into an orthodox and a modernizing yet devout wing, competing with each other through different parties and organizations.

Given the fact that primordial loyalties are weakening, that intranational migration is happening, ethnic purity is eroding because of marriages across ethnic boundaries, and religious affiliations are in flux, Table 11.1 should be seen as giving only a very rough overview:

Table 11.1 Ethnic Groups, Percentages, Location, and Major Religions in Indonesia

Ethnic Group	Percentage	Location	Major Religion
Javanese	45	Java	Orthodox *santri, abangan*
Madurese	7	Madura/Java	Orthodox *santri*
Sundanese	14	Java	Modernizing *santri*
Coastal Malay	7	Sumatra	Modernizing *santri*
Minangkabau	4	Sumatra	Modernizing *santri*
Batak	2	Sumatra	Christianity, modernizing *santri*
Acehnese	2	Sumatra	Modernizing *santri*
Buginese	4	Sulawesi	Modernizing *santri*
Minehasa	2	Sulawesi	Christianity
Balinese	2	Bali	Hindu
Dayak	1	Kalimantan	Animism, Islam, Christianity
Ambonese	1	Moluccas	Christianity, Islam
Papuan	1	New Guinea	Christianity, animism
Chinese	3		Confucianism, Christianity, Buddhism

• HISTORICAL REVIEW •

The Preindependence Period

The beginning of Indonesian nationalism can be dated back to the early twentieth century when Islamic traders founded the *Syarekat Dagang Islam* in defense against encroachment by Dutch and Chinese business-men into traditionally indigenous areas of economic activity. Member-ship was soon extended to a wider, nonbusiness constituency, and political demands added to the original concerns with economic matters.[3] While membership expanded rapidly in the early 1920s, the Communist Party infiltrated whole branches of the *Syarekat Islam* causing a split in the organization over ideological issues before it could become fully effective.

In 1926 and 1927 the Communist Party made a premature bid for power. Strikes by railway workers in West Java and Sumatra were to spearhead the revolution and the overthrow of the colonial administra-tion of the Netherlands East Indies. But the badly coordinated insurrec-tion was no match for the KNIL (Royal Netherlands Indies Army); the revolution was crushed and its ringleaders jailed or exiled.

Also in 1927, Sukarno, a graduate in architecture, set up the PNI (Indonesian Nationalist Party). A man of formidable oratorical skills, he advocated an independent Republic of Indonesia. But before he could become a real threat to the colonial regime he was arrested, tried for subversion, and exiled.

With his arrest the PNI disintegrated. The lesson of this sudden collapse of organized nationalism was not lost on Indonesian nationalists studying in the Netherlands. Upon their return to the colony, Mohammad Hatta and Sutan Sjahrir endeavored to rebuild nationalist organizations by concentrating on cadre training so that the demands for national independence could not be silenced by the authorities by simply arresting the chief spokesmen. But before their efforts could bear fruit they too were arrested and exiled.

Sukarno drew his own conclusions from the failures of the infant nationalist movement. Over a short period of time three distinct ideo-logical forces had emerged, each pursuing the goals of national inde-pendence by different means. The Muslims followed a strategy of economic assault on the colonial system, the Communists staged a pre-mature revolution, and Sukarno's nationalists had engaged in agitational politics. Each had drawn its supporters from a comparatively narrow constituency, and each had failed miserably. Obviously, then, the only possible path to success was to recognize as well as reconcile the different ideologies so that Islam, Marxism, and Nationalism would combine in achieving their common goal, the creation of an independent Indonesian republic.

Simultanesouly, the colonial authorities had come to realize that to stem the tide of nationalism required more finesse than just an iron fist. Thus the *Volksraad*, a largely advisory, at best semilegislative assembly was expanded to include those Indonesians who were willing to co-operate with the authorities in return for only modest political concessions. In fact the 1930s saw a host of political organizations emerging that endlessly debated whether, and to what extent, Indonesians ought to cooperate with the Dutch for what kind of purpose. When Nazi Germany overran the Netherlands and forced the Dutch government into exile, Indonesian factions in the *Volksraad* offered full Indonesian backing for any efforts to stem the forseeable Japanese invasion of the colony, in return for the promise of national independence once the war was concluded. But the government-in-exile declined the offer, and before it could reconsider its ill-conceived decision the Japanese invaded the colony in February 1942.

The Japanese occupation turned out to be an enormous boost for the cause of Indonesian independence. Not only did the rapid Japanese advance demonstrate that the whites were not invincible, but the interned Dutch administrators were largely replaced by Indonesian officials who thereby acquired skills and confidence. The exiled political leaders were released and allowed to mobilize the masses for nationalist goals as long as they also supported the Japanese war effort. Indonesian youths were given paramilitary training and recruited into either Japanese-officered auxiliary units or an Indonesian home army, the PETA.[4]

Independence was promised by Tokyo but, at the same time, Muslim nationalists were encouraged to organize themselves separately from the mainstream secular nationalists led by Sukarno and Hatta. With the end of the war in sight, the Japanese in early 1945 finally allowed the Indonesian leaders to prepare for national independence. In June Sukarno promulgated the *Pancasila* (Five Pillars), the state ideology of the republic to come, consisting of Belief in One God, Nationalism, International Cooperation, Democracy, and Social Justice.[5] These principles were deliberately formulated in a vague fashion so that they would be acceptable to each of the existing groups and factions. But before the nationalists could proceed with working out a constitution and proclaiming an independent republic, the Japanese surrendered.

The Period of the Struggle for Independence: 1945–1949

The Japanese surrender on 14 August 1945 presented the nationalist leaders Sukarno and Hatta with a dilemma: if they did nothing their youthful supporters were likely to take actions by themselves; and if they proclaimed independence, the Japanese (charged under the terms of surrender to maintain order in the occupied territories) might use force to quell all nationalist activities. Disenchanted by their indecision, nationalist zealots kidnapped them in order to force them into action but released them when they refused to bend to pressure. But on 17 August in a brief ceremony, Sukarno and Hatta proclaimed the unitary Republic of Indonesia. Within the promulgated presidential system of government, Sukarno without much controversy assumed the presidency, with Hatta as his vice-president.

The central question was how to deal with the Dutch intention to reestablish the colonial regime.[6] The older generation of nationalist leaders were inclined to negotiate with the Netherlands on the transfer of sovereignty. Sukarno and Hatta, although recognized by most Indonesians as the only legitimate leaders, were unsuited to enter into negotiations with the Dutch, who accused them of collaboration with the Japanese. But Sutan Sjahrir, who had had no part in the wartime Indonesian-Japanese cooperation and even claimed to have led an underground movement, was acceptable to the Netherlands as a negotiator. Both Sukarno and Hatta stood back when, on 14 November 1945, through threats and intimidation Sjahrir executed a constitutional coup in the infant, appointed parliament, maneuvering himself into the (unconstitutional) position of prime minister, and setting up a minority government based on his essentially social democratic Indonesian Socialist Party (PSI).[7]

While Sjahrir had the backing of Sukarno and Hatta on his policy of negotiation with the Dutch, forces determined to oppose the Dutch by whatever means necessary gathered around Tan Malaka, a veteran Trotskyist whose *Persatuan Perdjuangan* (Fighting Front) rapidly attracted a huge following. Faced with growing opposition inside and outside parliament, the Sjahrir cabinet resigned in February 1946. But the diverse elements within the Fighting Front were unable to agree on the composition of a new cabinet, whereupon the president invited Sjahrir to form another cabinet based on wider parliamentary support.

One of the first actions of the second Sjahrir cabinet was to eliminate the opposition by summarily arresting Tan Malaka and the leadership of the Fighting Front and jailing them without trial. In retaliation, elements of the Third Regular Army Division in late June arrested the prime minister; in return Sukarno had some of the conspirators arrested while troops loyal to the PSI freed Sjahrir, who then formed his third, more representative cabinet in October 1946.[8]

By November Sjahrir concluded the so-called Linggajati Agreement with the Dutch in which the latter recognized the republic's de facto authority over Java and Sumatra. The agreement also stipulated that a United States of Indonesia was to be formed, consisting of the republic, Kalimantan (Borneo), and East Indonesia; moreover, a Netherlands-Indonesian union under the Dutch crown was to maintain a link between the metropolitan power and its former colony.

But what first could have been taken as a victory for the strategy of diplomacy soon turned out to be an illusion. The colonial administration without consulting the republican leadership, surged ahead in creating federal states in areas under its control, which all were to have equal representation with the republic in the senate to be created.

On 27 May 1947 the Dutch issued an ultimatum in which they demanded to be recognized as the de jure authority over the whole of Indonesia, until the formation of the United States of Indonesia on 1 January 1949. Sjahrir was prepared to accept these terms but members of his own party, led by Minister of Defense Amir Sjarifuddin, refused to endorse his policies. On 27 June Sjahrir resigned to be succeeded by Amir Sjarifuddin.

Although, in the end, the new prime minister was prepared to offer even further concessions to the Netherlands, the Dutch on 21 July launched what they euphemistically called a police action, overrunning the republic's defenses in East and West Java and parts of Sumatra.

Under pressure from the United Nations the Netherlands was forced to agree to a cease-fire on 5 August. The Dutch were allowed to keep control over the recently occupied territories while a UN committee comprising Australia, Belgium, and the United States was to supervise the peace in the archipelago.[9] After Amir Sjarifuddin had signed an agreement recognizing the new realities, he found himself deserted by his coalition partners and on 23 January 1948 tendered his resignation.

With no parliamentary leader able to assemble a new coalition willing to take political responsibility under the existing circumstances, President Sukarno appointed his vice-president, Hatta, to form a "business cabinet."

Hatta immediately addressed himself to reforming the economic and administrative structures of the rump republic, and particularly supported a reform of the bloated defense apparatus. In these efforts Hatta had the willing cooperation of the army leadership under General Sudirman and Major General Nasution. Since another Dutch "police action" was seen to be more than likely, Nasution set out to prepare the army to fight a prolonged guerilla war.

But before those reforms could be fully implemented the republic erupted in violence. Under the leadership of old-time Communists and Amir Sjarifuddin, who now revealed that he had been a Communist himself for a long time, plans had been made for a people's revolution. On 13 September 1948 troops about to be discharged under Nasution's reform plans, and loyal to the Indonesian Communist Party (PKI), seized the city of Solo while the leader of the PKI, Musso, in nearby Madiun called for the overthrow of Sukarno and the Hatta cabinet.[10] But by the end of the month loyalist troops had recaptured all the strongholds of the rebels.

While the republic erupted in civil war, the Dutch stood by. But as soon as the revolution had been smashed they demanded special veto powers in the creation of the United States of Indonesia. Hatta had no choice but to accept these demands, but requested that guidelines be laid down. On 17 December the Dutch issued another ultimatum demanding that their terms be accepted within eighteen hours. Before the cabinet could formulate a reply the Dutch attacked the provisional capital, Jogjakarta, in the early hours of 19 December 1948.

The Dutch attack came as no great surprise. Nasution had made plans for the army to conduct guerilla warfare, and Sukarno had publicly promised to "lead his troops into the mountains" if the Dutch attacked again. But when the attack came Sukarno refused to vacate Jogjakarta immediately and instead gave himself up to the enemy.[11] While General Sudirman (by now terminally ill) joined his troops in the hills, Sukarno, Hatta, Sjahrir, and all cabinet ministers present in Jogjakarta allowed themselves to be captured by the advancing Dutch troops, who rapidly conquered all cities and towns still in republican hands.[12] However, the surrender of the government did not deter the republican army,[13] which maintained control of the countryside and harassed the Dutch in true guerrilla style.

By mid-1949 it had become abundantly clear that the Netherlands could not hope for a military solution to the conflict, as the republican army had also created a functioning military government in liberated areas, and had even begun to attack Dutch-held cities.[14] Moreover, international opinion had decidedly turned against the Netherlands. But for the Dutch to negotiate with the leaders of the republican army or even a nominal, provisional civilian government in the wilderness of Sumatra smacked too much of defeat. Instead, negotiations were begun with second-rank nationalists interned by the Dutch who were only too eager to reach an accommodation with the colonial power. Negotiations first led to a cease-fire and, on 27 December 1949, to the transfer of sovereignty over the archipelago (minus West New Guinea) from the Dutch Crown to a federated United States of Indonesia, with Sukarno as figurehead president and Vice-President Hatta as leader of a "business" cabinet in a parliamentary system of government.

The Era of Parliamentary Democracy: 1950–1957

The federal order was not to last long. It gave the wartime republic equal status along with another fifteen states represented in the federal Senate, many of which were hardly viable, had contributed little to the struggle for independence, and were seen by the republicans as little more than a "time bomb" planted by the Dutch to secure their lasting influence in the newly created nation. Some of these states dissolved themselves immediately after the transfer of sovereignty and merged with the republic. But other states were determined to maintain the federalist order, which was seen by many non-Javanese as an ideal constitutional means to preserve their cultural autonomy.

A test case for the survival or collapse of federalism was the state of Pasundan, situated in the western third of Java and enveloping the federal capital Jakarta. It was mainly populated by the Sundanese, who had been active supporters of the struggle for independence. Faced with constant acts of intimidation by the local military garrison, which was committed to the republican ideal of a unitary state, the government of Pasundan allied itself to a bunch of adventurers under the retired Dutch captain "Turk" Westerling. Westerling's forces temporarily occupied Bandung, the capital of Pasundan, but were defeated by loyalist troops. Now the leaders of Pasundan had no option but to dissolve their state. Other states succumbed to intimidation, but in the case of East Indonesia a full-scale military invasion was necessary, causing the Ambonese to declare an independent Republic of the South Moluccas. The resistance of the Ambonese was only broken in the early 1960s, but the federalist order had essentially collapsed by August 1950,[15] and Hatta, a Sumatran who—ironically—was sympathetic to the idea of federalism, resigned the prime ministership.

In the new unitary state a parliamentary system of government was retained, vesting power primarily in parliament and the cabinet although the president held important reserve powers. For the next five years the main feature of Indonesian politics was a constant change of cabinets and government coalitions. In September 1950 Mohammad Natsir, a leader of the progressive Muslim party Masyumi, assembled a coalition based mainly on ethnic minorities, Christian parties, and the PSI. His cabinet was toppled by his own party, and in April 1951 another Masyumi politician, Sukiman Wirjosandjojo, formed another cabinet excluding the PSI but including the (mainly Javanese) Nationalist Party (PNI). By February of the following year the Sukiman cabinet had resigned, to be replaced by a government led by the PNI politician Wilopo. The enemies of Wilopo, many from his own party, worked toward his downfall immediately after the formation of his cabinet. Using defense policy as the main lever to unseat Wilopo, they questioned every aspect of the military from the streamlining of the oversized ragtag army into a professional force as proposed by Nasution (who became army chief of staff after Sudirman died in January 1950) to the way the soldiers marched and saluted. When politicians used disgruntled officers to undermine the minister of defence and Colonel Nasution, the military leaders with the permission of the cabinet petitioned the president on 17 October 1952 to dissolve the incumbent appointed parliament and schedule elections for a new parliament. Sukarno refused this request and provoked open mutiny in three of the army's seven divisions against the headquarters. In an effort to hang on to office, Wilopo in early 1953 sacked Nasution and some of his closest associates, but this did not save his cabinet. Faced with a motion of no confidence that he was certain to lose, Wilopo resigned on 2 July 1953.[16]

He was succeeded by another PNI politician, Ali Sastroamidjojo, who based his coalition on the PNI, the conservative Muslim Nahdatul Ulama (NU), minor nationalist and leftist parties, and the Communists, who had promised parliamentary support and were represented in the cabinet indirectly through the communist Peasant Front.

The Ali cabinet was primarily concerned with organizing elections, an issue that after the "17th October Affair" could no longer be pigeonholed. In order to deny the military any further embarrassing input into politics, officers of the pro-Nasution faction were played off against the mutineers with such devastating effect on the cohesiveness and morale of the army that both factions held a unity congress in early 1955 in which guidelines for professional conduct and objective criteria for promotions and assignments were worked out and promulgated in the presence of the president and prime minister. However, Ali chose to ignore these guidelines when he appointed a relatively junior officer as the new army chief of staff. The army refused to accept this appointment and the coalition partners, disenchanted with both Ali's defense policy and his general highhandedness in cabinet deliberations, deserted the coalition, forcing Ali to tender his resignation on 24 July 1955.[17]

In the absence of Sukarno, Vice-President Hatta appointed the Masyumi politician Burhanuddin Harahap as prime minister, who formed a coalition based on his own party, the NU, and the PSI. Its immediate task was to hold the parliamentary elections scheduled for 29 September and, in December, elections for a constituent assembly charged with working out a new constitution. In the parliamentary elections the PNI turned out to be the largest party. The four major Muslim parties—Masyumi, NU, Partai Syarekat Islam Indonesia (PSII), and Perti—received jointly 43.5 percent of the votes. The PSI finished eighth after the Catholic Party and the Protestant Parkindo, while IP-KI, a party founded by Nasution after his forced retirement, achieved a respectable result with more than half a million votes. The Communist Party (PKI), devastated in the "Madiun Affair", had rebuilt itself to gain more than 6 million votes (Table 11.2).

The results of the elections for the constituent assembly were not markedly different. Although the coalition had received enough electoral backing to continue in office, the NU decided to pull out to enable new coalition negotiations on the basis of the election results. But before the cabinet resigned, the crisis over the army leadership was settled. After consultation with senior officers, Burhanuddin and Sukarno reappointed Nasution as army chief of staff.

Table 11.2   The Results of the Indonesian Parliamentary Elections of 1955

Parties	Number of Votes	Percentage of Votes	Number of Seats
PNI	8,434,653	22.3	57
Masyumi	7,903,886	20.9	57
NU	6,955,141	18.4	45
PKI	6,176,913	16.4	39
PSII	1,091,160	2.9	8
Parkindo	1,003,325	2.6	8
P. Katolik	770,740	2.0	6
PSI	753,191	2.0	5
IP-KI	541,306	1.4	4
Perti	483,014	1.3	4
18 other parties	—	—	24
Total	—	100.0	257

Source: H. Feith, The Decline of Constitutional Democracy in Indonesia (Ithaca, N.Y.: Cornell University Press, 1962), pp. 434–435.

The politician the president asked to form a new cabinet was none other than Ali Sastroamidjojo, who introduced his second cabinet based on the PNI, the Masyumi, and the NU on 20 March 1956. Many army officers were disillusioned with his reappointment as prime minister, and his assumption of the defense portfolio was especially seen as a provocation. Also, the reappointment of Nasution had not healed old wounds; rather, his efforts to professionalize the army and particularly to break the warlord-like powers of military commanders outside Java intensified conflict. But the major problems of the second Ali cabinet were that it soon lost credibility through corruption scandals and that it accelerated ethnic conflict.

Accusations that import-consuming Java was "milking" the export-producing "Outer Islands" had been made by the minorities ever since the federalist order had been suppressed by the leaders of the Java-oriented wartime republic.[18] Ali himself as well as his party, the PNI, were regarded as representing Javanese interests; and the manipulations of the foreign exchange rates in favor of Javanese interests as well as an excessive trade-licensing system to the disadvantage of business in the Outer Islands during the Ali cabinets seemed to bear out the anti-Jakarta charges of the minorities. After weathering a military conspiracy in West Java, Ali in December 1956 faced a revolt in West Sumatra that quickly spread to the rest of Sumatra, Kalimantan, and Sulawesi (Celebes). These so far nonviolent revolts were headed by regional army commanders but had the backing of the civil population, and were directed not only against the cabinet but also against Nasution—seen to be collaborating with the cabinet—and increasingly, the president, who had come to back communist participation in government (anathema to the religious Outer Islands) and to attack Western, liberal democracy in which "50 percent plus one are always right." In an effort to restructure the political system Sukarno came to advocate Indonesian forms of democracy, based on cooperation and consensus.[19] Faced with revolts everywhere outside Java, hostile coalition partners incensed by the resignation of Hatta from the vice-presidency in December 1956 (in protest against both the increasingly antiliberal utterances of Sukarno and the discriminatory policies of the cabinet vis-à-vis the Outer Islands) and a president critical of the political system that had brought his government into power, Ali—after declaring a state of war and siege—handed in his resignation on 14 March 1957.[20]

The Era of Guided Democracy: 1957–1966

In itself the fall of the second Ali cabinet was nothing extraordinary, and like most of the fourteen cabinets preceding it during the previous twelve years it fell from coalition partners deserting the government. However, two things distinguished this cabinet from all others: it was the first and only Indonesian cabinet ever to be assembled on the basis of free elections, and the divisions in society it had allowed to develop were so grave that no coalition could be formed in its wake.[21] After lengthy but fruitless negotiations Sukarno appointed Djuanda, a Sundanese politician without party affiliations, to form a "business cabinet" that was to govern through martial law, with the direct support of an increasingly active president and the army headquarters.

The most important task of the Djuanda cabinet was to bring the regional unrest under control. Negotiations between central authorities and the regional dissenters continued throughout the year, but a grand meeting between civil and military leaders of both sides in November 1957 yielded few tangible results, particularly since the rebels were incensed by provincial elections in Java in which the PKI had emerged as the strongest party with 27.4 percent of the popular vote. In December, nationalist and communist youths seized Dutch enterprises in Jakarta in protest against the Netherlands' refusal to relinquish the remaining part of the former Dutch East Indies, West New Guinea, to Indonesian control. These takeovers, condoned by Sukarno and the PKI but opposed by Djuanda, Nasution, the Masyumi, and the PSI because they were bound to further harm the Outer Islands' economy, brought the conflict to new heights. On 10 February 1958, while Sukarno was out of the country, the regional dissenters issued an ultimatum that Djuanda resign within five days, and that a new business cabinet be formed by Hatta and the PSI-leaning Sultan of Jogjakarta. When Djuanda refused to comply, a Revolutionary Government was formed in Sumatra by rebellious army officers and politicians of the Masyumi and the PSI.

But only three army regiments (in North Sulawesi, and West and Central Sumatra) were prepared to participate in the escalation of the

conflict to an extent where Indonesians might have to shoot at Indonesians. This possibility soon became reality when loyalist troops
attacked the hard-line rebel provinces. But with only some 5 percent of
the military in open revolt the outcome of the ensuing civil war was
predictable, despite the logistical support provided the rebels by the
United States and its allies in Southeast Asia. While rebel cities were
swiftly conquered, the last insurgent troops surrendered only as late as
August 1962.[22]

At the same time the fundamentalist *Darul Islam* rebellion, which
had been smoldering in West Java since 1948, was brought under
control, together with other Muslim uprisings in Aceh and South Sulawesi.

In the realm of constitutional politics Sukarno argued vigorously for
a new political system based on Indonesian traditions. He maintained
that the traditional concept of *gotong rojong* ("mutual cooperation")
should be interpreted as excluding no major political grouping—and
particularly not the PKI—from the processes of decision making, and
that voting on issues as practiced in Western democracy should be
replaced by *musyawarah* ("deliberation") until *mufakat* ("consensus")
was reached. If no consensus emerged in time decisions should be taken
under the guidance of the elder statesman, Sukarno himself.[23]

In the drive for a new, more viable political system Sukarno had the
close cooperation of Nasution, who argued that given the divisions in
Indonesian society, the army had a vital role to play in keeping the
nation together. During 1958 Nasution postulated what came to be
known as the army's "middle way": the military would not assume
political power but would play a political role as one of the forces
deciding the fate of the nation.[24]

The political parties had practically no input into the debate except
for the PKI, which, ostensibly on the path to power by electoral means,
ironically emerged as the most eloquent defender of parliamentary
democracy. But the parliament refused to take any initiatives, while the
constituent assembly remained deadlocked over the issue of just how
Islamic a new constitutional and legal order ought to be. On the initiative of Nasution, Sukarno on 5 July 1959 repromulgated the "revolutionary" 1945 Constitution and discharged the constituent assembly.[25]

Under the new political system known as "Guided Democracy" the
party system was drastically revised. The Masyumi and the PSI were
outlawed, ostensibly because they had backed the regional rebellion,
although the real issues were their continuing support for democracy
and minority rights and their opposition to any communist participation
in government. Only ten parties survived: the PKI and the Trotskyist
Murba Party; the PNI and a radical breakaway group, the Partindo, as
well as the IP-KI; the three Muslim parties NU, PSII, Perti; and the two
Christian parties. But political parties were denied the monopoly in

political representation: half of the seats in the new *gotong rojong* parliament were allocated to so-called functional groups formed on the basis of occupations and special status. The military came to occupy seats in the legislative assemblies as such a functional group. A (provisional) People's Deliberative Congress, or MPR(S), was created in accordance with the provisions of the 1945 Constitution, made up of parties, functional groups, and regional delegates, which was to elect the president, lay down the broad guidelines of state policy, and generally function as the highest constitutional authority in the land.

The government consisted of Sukarno, later elected by the MPR(S) as president-for-life, Djuanda as "first minister" (the 1945 Constitution did not provide for the position of prime minister), and a presidential, mainly civilian cabinet in which Nasution served (as minister of defense) along with eleven other military men.

In the years to follow, the cabinet came to be rivaled by an increasing number of institutions and government agencies with overlapping functions. Such a chaotic structure readily offered Sukarno the opportunity to play off one group against another and thereby remain at the helm of the political system.

Essentially, Guided Democracy was dominated by Sukarno, whose charisma made him the unchallenged leader of Indonesia. The army under Nasution was the junior partner in government, occasionally challenging particular views of the president but never questioning his standing as the supreme authority and "Great Leader of the Revolution." The PKI existed as a third center of power. Although in the first years not represented in cabinet, and every now and then persecuted by the army, it was clearly the most energetic party capable of rallying the masses.[26]

Until 1962 Nasution was obviously the second most powerful figure in the new political system. Being a sober tactician he increasingly abhorred Sukarno's reckless policies and flamboyant style of government. The disagreements between the two leaders developed into a confrontation when Sukarno embarked on "liberating" West New Guinea by whatever means that would require, while Nasution argued publicly that the scarce resources of the country ought to be used first to rehabilitate the ailing economy. When Sukarno's policies succeeded and West New Guinea fell to Indonesia, his prestige had risen to such an extent that he was able to relieve Nasution of his army command and power base. A last initiative in 1963 to rescue the economy failed when Djuanda, at one with Nasution over this issue, suddenly died. From 1963 Sukarno reigned supreme, supported by the PKI, which became the most important force in Indonesia, second only to the president.

In the following years Sukarno lost himself in daydreaming, seeing himself as the leader of the Third World, fighting NECOLIM, i.e., "neocolonialism, colonialism, and imperialism," and OLDEFO, the "old established forces," wherever they reared their ugly heads. He set out to "smash Malaysia," which he considered a mere tool of the West, created to "encircle" Indonesia. He dreamed of a Jakarta-Peking-Pnom Penh-Pyongyang axis and pulled Indonesia out of the United Nations. And while he strutted the international stage, Indonesia's economy collapsed and its politics became increasingly confrontational.

At the instigation of the PKI the Murba Party was banned, communist front organizations came forcefully to seize larger landholdings, while a "special bureau" of the Central Committee built communist cells in the armed forces. The Communists demanded that political commissars be attached to the military, accused the army headquarters of planning a coup, and suggested that workers and peasants be armed. The climax came in the early hours of 1 October 1965 when disgruntled officers of the Presidential Guard Regiment, and elements of the army and the air force who had been in contact with the PKI leaders, reinforced by communist and nationalist youths, kidnapped and killed the army commander, General Yani, and five of his closest associates. Nasution, still minister of defense, narrowly escaped the same fate.[27]

Within hours Major General Soeharto, by standing order deputizing for Yani whenever the latter was out of town, had rallied loyalist troops. Ignoring orders from the president, who had taken refuge near the rebels' headquaters, and confining all troops to their barracks, Soeharto first cleared Jakarta of rebels and, after Sukarno had left for his summer palace in the hills, took the rebel headquarters as well. Putting down a supporting uprising in Central Java required several more weeks.

Sukarno's attempts to shield the rebels by declaring that the murder of the army headquarters officers "was a mere ripple in the ocean of the Indonesian Revolution" was not appreciated by Soeharto and the army. When he continued to refuse to bring to justice those seen to be involved in the planning of the murders, the army and anticommunist civilian groupings took the law into their own hands. Before the year was out hundreds of thousands of Communists had been slaughtered, mainly by Muslims who had threatened *djihad* (holy war) on the PKI earlier in 1965; but depending on the area, nationalist, Christian, or Hindu youths also participated in the rampage. Where the army was firmly in control the bloodbath was less extensive but still substantial.

Sukarno's attempts to regain the initiative were largely unsuccessful, mainly because the economic suffering of the people had reached intolerable proportions and started to affect his charismatic hold over the masses. Continuous street demonstrations and the harassment of cabinet ministers by students and anticommunist activists, as well as the sighting of unidentified troops near the palace on 11 March 1966, frightened Sukarno into signing an edict that gave the power to restore order to

General Soeharto, who immediately banned the PKI officially, arrested leftist ministers, and put together an anticommunist cabinet.[28]

Sukarno was still president and formally the head of the government. Both Sukarno and Soeharto were interested in clearly establishing their respective prerogatives, and agreed to call a special session of the MPR(S) to sort out their powers. Sukarno believed that he still could count—even after purges of its communist representatives—on the congress that, after all, had not so long ago elected him president-for-life, while Soeharto relied on the support of Nasution who had been elected chairman of the congress. When the MPR(S) assembled on 20 June 1966, it turned its back on Sukarno and his anachronistic policies and ordered Sukarno and Soeharto to jointly form a cabinet that would end the costly confrontation with Malaysia, rehabilitate the economy, hold elections, and simplify the party system. The 11 March order of authorization of Soeharto's powers was confirmed and the PKI banned; Sukarno was forbidden to propagate Marxism in any form and asked to account for his role in the events of 1 October 1965.

But Sukarno was not willing to conform with the policies laid down by the Congress. After several public trials of Sukarno confidants in late 1966, which revealed not only the corruption of his administration but also his possible involvement in the murder of the generals on 1 October 1965, an increasing number of organizations demanded his removal from office and trial by military court. Even people who had remained loyal to him personally realized that he could not be saved after the parliament demanded his dismissal as well. A special MPR(S) meeting convened for March 1967 dealt exclusively with Sukarno. Its chairman, General Nasution, made it a demand of the "New Order" in Indonesia that the president not be exempted from the stipulations of the law, and that if he was involved in any way in the events of 1 October 1965, he be tried like any other person. After lengthy negotiations between all factions General Soeharto was appointed acting president, Sukarno was forbidden to engage in any political activities for some time to come, and the issue of his being tried was left to the acting president. But Soeharto made it clear that while Sukarno's involvement in the murder of the generals would continue to be investigated, it was unlikely that he would be made to stand trial. Sukarno died on 21 June 1970, at the age sixty-nine, still under house arrest.

The New Order: 1967–

Essentially, Soeharto faced three problems when he assumed full control: to strengthen his own position in the political system; to decide on a political format for the New Order; and, above all, to rehabilitate the economy, which was the issue that would legitimate or break his regime.

The first problem was solved very quickly. First of all, his formal standing in the community was enhanced when another MPR(S) session in March 1968 made him full president. An astute move of his was to win the cooperation of the Sultan of Jogjakarta—enormously popular among the ethnic Javanese who had also been the major ethnic source of support for Sukarno—who came to serve as vice-president. But most important was to make the military the loyal, unquestioning pillar of his power.[29] This required purging it of all officers of a leftist or Sukarnoist leaning. Moreover, in a series of reforms he brought the minor services (air force, navy, and police) more firmly under his control and reduced regional division commanders to little more than administrators stripped of operational command over large units of combat troops, thereby denying them a potentially forceful input into national decision making. A special Operations Command for the Restoration of Security and Order (KOPKAMTIB) became the political and intelligence watchdog of the New Order and a powerful instrument in the hands of Soeharto to suppress all enemies.

To reach a decision on the political format of the New Order to come was a far more difficult problem. Soeharto's quest for legitimacy required that he accept certain restraints on his choice of political systems. Part of the justification for the overthrow of Sukarno was that he had violated the 1945 Constitution as well as the stipulations of the *Pancasila*; so the New Order had to be seen to be based on the values contained in both. Moreover, there were the MPR(S) guidelines of 1966 that, for the same reasons, had to be adhered to, and these included the holding of elections and a "simplification" of the party system.

As stipulated by the constitution Indonesia would remain a unitary republic with a presidential system of government. Such a system enabled the president to choose his ministers from outside parliament, for instance, from among military officers, intellectuals, and technocrats.

While a fierce debate ensued during the 1967–1968 period over the electoral and party systems, factions of the undergound PSI and circles close to it argued that as a one- or no-party system was undemocratic, and a multiparty system was demonstrably unsuitable to Indonesia, the only choice left was to set up a two-party system consisting of a government party and a loyal opposition. Although unacceptable to most parties, the army command in West Java unilaterally and without the approval of Soeharto set out to enforce the two-party system in its provincial and district parliaments,[30] but before it could be fully implemented its proponents were relieved of their commands and exiled to overseas ambassadorships or other positions from where they could not interfere in Jakarta politics.[31]

The electoral and party systems as they emerged after lengthy debate retained the functional groups side by side with the political parties as stipulated in the 1945 Constitution. However, they were now to be centrally coordinated by New Order activists and military officers and, for all practical purposes, became the government "party" under the name of GOLKAR.[32] The PKI and the radical-nationalist Partindo, as well as the PSI, remained banned, and while the Masyumi in its old form and with its traditional leaders remained unacceptable because of its involvement in the regional rebellion of 1958, a new party, PARMUSI, was formed to cater for the former Masyumi electorate, the modernizing *santri* community of West Java and the Outer Islands. The Murba Party was not only resurrected but represented prominently in the cabinet through Adam Malik as minister of foreign affairs (and later vice-president). The high-level representation of the tiny Murba Party in the cabinet served several purposes. It was meant to demonstrate that the New Order was not rabidly antisocialist; it rewarded the party for two decades of incessant hostility to the PKI; and in giving the suave Malik a high profile, the Soeharto regime was bound to gain international credibility. In order to maintain military representation in legislative assemblies and have people in parliament who normally would be disinclined to go to the hustings, the president was granted the right to appoint 100 parliamentarians (75 military and 25 civilian) in addition to the 360 to be chosen in general elections.

In the 1971 elections, the first to be held since 1955, GOLKAR achieved a resounding victory with 62.8 percent of the vote, partly, but not only, because of government interference in the nomination process of party candidates and intimidation tactics.[33] Yet the NU, appealing to a clearly defined Moslem electorate, was able not only to maintain its following but even slightly to increase it (see Table 11.3).

With the danger in sight that in future elections the secular parties might be wiped out altogether, essentially leaving GOLKAR to face the Muslim parties in a two-way contest, the government decided to implement the 1966 MPR(S) stipulation to "simplify the party system." Not without considerable resistance were the four Muslim parties merged into a Development Unity Party (PPP), while the three secular parties and the two Christian parties formed the Indonesian Democratic Party (PDI). While the merger saved particularly the smaller parties from total oblivion it did not check further electoral advances by GOLKAR.

As envisaged already for Sukarno's Guided Democracy, decisions in parliament were not to be taken by majority voting, but by *musyawarah*. This has saved the non-GOLKAR groupings from being outvoted on every issue. There have been instances where the government has withdrawn bills because no *mufakat* was emerging. It is said that over 650 bills have been shelved in parliamentary committees (where the real discussions take place) before they even reached the plenum simply because the opposition refused to give its assent.

Table 11.3 Indonesian General Election Results, 1955–1987 (Percentage of Votes Cast, by Party)

	1955	1971	1977	1982	1987
Muslim Parties					
Masyumi/Parmusi	20.9	5.4			
Nahdatul Ulama (NU)	18.4	18.7			
PSII	2.9	2.4			
Perti	1.3	0.7			
PPP			29.3	28.0	16
Non-Muslim Parties					
PNI	22.3	6.9			
Parkindo	2.6	1.3			
P. Katolik	2.0	1.1			
IP-KI	1.4	0.6			
Murba	0.5	0.1			
PDI			8.6	7.9	11
PKI	16.3				
Functional Groups/GOLKAR		62.8	62.1	64.1	73

Source: Ulf Sundhaussen and Barry R. Green, "Slow March into an Uncertain Future," in Christopher Clapham and George Philip, eds., *The Political Dilemmas of Military Regimes* (London: Croom Helm, 1985), p. 106. The approximate figures of the 1987 elections are taken from U. Sundhaussen, "The Problem of Succession in Indonesia," *Third World Annual 1988*, (Third World Foundation for Social and Economic Studies: London, 1988), pp. 272ff.

Soeharto's economic rehabilitation program achieved some impressive results. Drastically cutting government and defense spending, it reduced within a couple of years the rate of annual inflation from 650 percent to 12 percent. Foreign debts—which at the end of the Sukarno era demanded more than the total foreign exchange earnings of the nation to service—were rescheduled, and new loans were obtained from Western nations while internal revenue was increased. The subsequent two decades saw a rapid pace of economic growth and social change.

However, the hallmark of the New Order and its political system, "*Pancasila* Democracy," has been order and political calm—although many critics would regard it as the calmness of a cemetery, stifling political debate through press censorship, control of the electronic media, and, when necessary, massive intimidation and even arrests of opponents or mere critics. While all these allegations are true, the press at times can also be extraordinarily free to criticize the government; civil rights groups are active in Jakarta and do win cases against the government in court, where an increasingly independent-minded judiciary may refuse to play the government's game.

Yet dissent from government policies has occasionally reached crisis proportions. In early 1974 the poor of Jakarta rioted in protest against corruption in government circles and an economic strategy that did not bring them immediate relief from economic misery. Until the early

1980s university students remained a constant irritant with protests against corruption, violation of democratic norms, and the suppression of civil rights. By 1980 retired military officers had formed organizations criticizing government policies, development strategies, and individual shortcomings. In the forefront of these officers was Nasution, who came to criticize *Pancasila* Democracy as a severe aberration from both the original *Pancasila* and democracy as stipulated in the 1945 Constitution. Moreover, *dwi-fungsi*, the "dual function" doctrine of the present regime—which serves to justify the presence of military men in virtually all positions of power—has been attacked by Nasution as an unacceptable, essentially undemocratic acceleration of his initial middle-way concept.

But Soeharto has withstood all internal criticism with political astuteness; also he has weathered international criticism directed particularly at the civil rights record of his regime, and the 1975 takeover of the formerly Portuguese possession of East Timor. As long as he is able to remain at the helm of the nation substantial change is not very likely to occur in the political system.[34] But his is a personalized system of government in which he, like Sukarno during Guided Democracy, reigns supreme,[35] and it may not survive his demise from the center stage of politics exactly as it exists today.

• HISTORICAL ANALYSIS •

Current Sets of Explanations

The space made available for this study requires us to limit analysis to what may be considered the two most important aspects of Indonesia's experience with democracy; namely, the reasons for the collapse of parliamentary democracy in 1957, and the extent to which there are democratic elements in the present political system headed by General Soeharto.

Four main arguments (no claims are made that this list is conclusive) have emerged to explain the demise of parliamentary democracy. According to Daniel Lev, "More than any other immediate factor, it was the army which brought down parliamentary government—a system in which it had no stake and to which it had no commitment."[36] This is a popular view among Indonesianists, which coincides with many analyses regarding civil-military relations in other developing countries. But in the case of Indonesia it is so inconclusively supported by evidence that in this context it does not warrant any further discussion.

A more sophisticated view is that democracy as a political system simply did not have enough proponents in Indonesia, an assessment that is supported by reference to other Asian countries. According to

W. Levi, the idea of popular sovereignty "has not found any support for hundreds of years in any major creed" in South and Southeast Asia.[37] Herbert Feith's influential study essentially argues that more democratically inclined so-called administrators headed by Hatta and Sutan Sjahrir lost out in the struggle for power to less democratic—or even undemocratic—"solidarity makers" led by a President Sukarno who professed to pursue the aims of a revolution promised in 1945, which more than a decade later were still unfulfilled.[38]

Third, it has been argued that the liberal constitution artificially grafted onto the political system did not reflect the political realities or even the aspirations of the populace, and excluded from the processes of decision making significant centers of real power: i.e., an excessively ambitious president who was allocated little more than ceremonial powers, the ethnic minorities—together almost half of the total population—who were in favor of federalism, cultural autonomy, and economic decentralization, and an army that was dragged into political controversies without having its nonmilitary functions sufficiently clarified.[39] According to this view, parliamentary democracy collapsed from within as a result of inept and selfish politicians being unable to cope with what Samuel Huntington has described as insufficient "institutionalization" of political processes.[40]

A fourth way of analysis has been to look at the demise of parliamentary democracy in Indonesia not from an ethnocentric point of view, asking the "intrinsically mistaken, or irrelevant" question of "what went wrong with Indonesia" but to see the collapse of the old political order in conjunction with the system of Guided Democracy, which at least initially appeared to be based on traditional concepts of village democracy, highlighting *musyawarah* until *mufakat* is established. In adopting an approach prominently featuring political culture, the above question would have to be reformulated into, "Why did parliamentary democracy last as long as it did?"[41]

The analysis regarding the Soeharto regime has a wider scope. The far left has advanced the familiar argument that Soeharto's New Order, being essentially a military regime, must have been hatched by the CIA.[42] Alternatively, a more daring and excessively Machiavellian argument advanced is that Soeharto himself masterminded the murder of his fellow generals on 1 October 1965 in order to be able to take over the army leadership and, ultimately, the leadership of the country.[43] For these writers democracy in the post-Sukarno era is not an issue at all; rather, Soeharto's rule is described as "terror" from above.[44]

The main body of the literature on the New Order is only marginally less critical, and primarily concerned with detailing every instance of political behavior contravening Western standards of democracy. This list would range from the suppression of civil rights to interference in internal party affairs, intimidation of the electorate before elections, curtailmentt of press freedom, and heavy-handed indoctrination, as well as the corruption of regime leaders and the growing impoverishment of certain sections of society. Most of the listed allegations would be based on indisputable facts, but what is wrong with this type of chronicling is that it leaves out the positive aspects of Soeharto's policies that undoubtedly also exist. The proponents of this writing of history share a fervent belief in the imminent downfall of the Soeharto regime. Although this article of faith is only rarely expressed in writing,[45] it has lost none of its appeal among the believers, although the fact of twenty years of consistently wrong prediction ought to have given cause for reconsideration.

Although the concept of political culture as an approach to the study of non-Western societies has lost currency, presumably because it may possibly be seen as the bedeviled "orientalism" in new clothes,[46] it has rendered excellent insights into the value system and, consequently, political behavior in Third World countries, including Indonesia.[47] Such an approach, when applied to the Soeharto regime, not only provides a clearer perception of the way of thinking and goals of the New Order leaders, but also obliges the observer to chronicle those policies—like saving the smaller parties from total collapse[48]—which ought to earn the New Order a pat on the back from proponents of democratic government.

Finally, a novel approach to political economy deserves to be highlighted here, in which worn-out dependency theories have been largely discarded and class analysis used to point out that the "most important revolutionary force at work in the Third World today is not communism or socialism but capitalism," and that a capitalist class is emerging in Soeharto's New Order, which in time is bound to have important ramifications for the political system in Indonesia.[49]

A Framework of Analysis

The approaches, analyses, and findings in the study of Indonesia are more diverse and mutually contradictory than the disagreements common to most academic pursuits. A newcomer to Indonesian studies may well be tempted to ask whether Indonesianists most of the time are indeed talking about one and the same country.

These sharp disagreements may in specific cases be of an ideological nature. But more fundamental is the disinclination of Indonesianists to employ comparative and theoretical frameworks in their analyses, which has impaired a better understanding of Indonesia.[50] Only in the last few years has there been a growing disposition among particularly the newer generation of researchers to see Indonesia in a wider context.

To inquire into the support for, and potential of, democracy in Indonesia, an unambiguous perception of what constitutes democracy and which groups or classes are normally inclined to support and maintain it is indispensable. Obviously democracy can take different shapes, and is desired by different people for different purposes.

The following classification of democratic forms of government is only an abbreviated version of a more detailed concept.[51] It excludes so-called "non-liberal democracies"[52] of the communist or Third World one-party varieties, and essentially differentiates among those democratic systems that qualify in Dahl's terms as polyarchies.[53]

Four basic models can be distinguished, each created and supported by different groups and classes for different purposes, and maintained by different structures and procedures. The most familiar to the reader of English-language literature is the Anglo-Saxon variant, established by a trading and manufacturing middle class whose members are intent on enlarging their freedom to create wealth for themselves, a political culture leading ultimately to capitalism.

A second variant is that of continental Western Europe, where for a variety of historic and geopolitical reasons, the trading and manufacturing middle class had been weakened since the Middle Ages, leaving the struggle for liberty and democracy against absolute monarchies primarily to intellectuals, jurists, and civil servants. With such an intellectual and salaried, instead of a trading, middle class in the forefront of the fight for civil liberties, the result was a more dogmatic concern with the principle of equality rather than the more practical notion of economic freedom; moreover, the planning of political as well as economic and social strategies is regarded with much more sympathy on the Continent.

A third kind of democracy has evolved without either the trading and manufacturing or the intellectual and salaried middle classes; if they did exist at all they did not play a significant part. In many parts of Europe, from the southern Urals to Iceland, egalitarian peasant democracies emerged, many of which perished not because they failed to become politically, structurally, or economically viable, but because they were overrun by disproportionately more powerful empire builders.

The fourth variant of democracy is rooted outside Europe. It is supported not by individuals but by whole communities. Middle-class elements may exist but are politically extremely weak, and economically often almost destitute, or salaried and in state employ. This kind of democracy is the result not of a victory in class warfare, but of inherent weakness: none of the component groups are strong enough to assert themselves over others, and each is determined to maintain a degree of autonomy for itself. A state consisting of a variety of such primordial units will either have to break up, decline into chaos, or function with all units accepting each other as fully recognized partners in a dialogue aimed at a democratically organized, essentially confederated polity.

Having made these distinctions of models and motivating forces, it is now possible to assess more accurately the support for democracy in Indonesia, which in turn will provide a closer insight into why parliamentary democracy collapsed, what the democratic contents of the New Order are, and what the chances are for a return to forms of democracy more closely resembling Dahl's polyarchy.

The Democratic Potential

The notions that parliamentary democracy generally "failed" because democratic values were not—or not sufficiently—supported in the communities of Southeast Asia or, particularly, that the more revolutionary elite group of "solidarity makers" won the struggle for power in Indonesia against the more democratic "administrators" are of limited heuristic value since they only beget another question; namely, why were democratic values not supported? A fresh approach to this question, based on the notion that there exists more than one model or concept of democracy and several (possibly contradictory) democratic goals, will reveal that there was, potentially at least, substantial support for democracy, and that the crucial failure was that of democratically inclined leaders to articulate and aggregate the interests of such electoral groups,[54] and to propagate in word and deed the advantages of democratic government.

As Herbert Feith has convincingly demonstrated, party leaders and ideologies at the time of the transfer of sovereignty (1949) and thereafter had great difficulties in articulating what they actually stood for.[55] "Democracy" was as naturally acclaimed as motherhood, with very little thought wasted on its meaning and purposes or its constitutional, legal, and political implications. There were expressions of ideological hostility to "liberalism" emanating from such diverse forces as the ultraconservative and traditionalist Javanese parties, Greater Indonesian Union (PIR), Greater Indonesia Party (Parindra), President Sukarno, the PNI, and (for different reasons) the Catholic Party. But democracy as such, in one form or another, was not even opposed by the Communists.

Initially at least there had been support by trading and manufacturing middle classes for more political freedom that would enable them to pursue more profitably their economic interests, the kind of political movement that in Anglo-Saxon societies ultimately led to capitalist democracy. The *Partai Syarekat Islam Indonesia* (PSII) initially started as a traders' association. During the Ali cabinets the political importance of this class was recognized, although measures devised in its support were soon subordinated to party interests, with state aid flowing to loyal government supporters rather than bona fide entrepreneurs. Even during the more socialistically inclined Guided Democracy period privately owned business still enjoyed a degree of preferential treatment over public-sector enterprises.[56]

The New Order, at least theoretically, recognized from the beginning the importance of indigenous entrepreneurs for its policies of economic rehabilitation and political stabilization. Yet, in their efforts to effect economic improvements quickly, New Order leaders have preferred to turn to the more efficient transnational corporations and resident Chinese businessmen with more capital and international market connections. The resulting alienation between the "rising Moslem commercial bourgeoisie" and the regime leaders have assumed such proportions that, in the estimation of Professor Utrecht, the former are now financing the opposition against the regime.[57] On the other hand, it has been argued that the "Muslim merchant bourgeoisie" is not on the rise but definitely on the decline, "overtaken by history"[58] and by a new, secular class of entrepreneurs.

But the stronger democratic culture in Indonesia in any case has been that reflecting Continental European democracy. The new intellectual elite was brought up both at home and in the Netherlands on a diet of Continental rather than Anglo-Saxon thought. More importantly, coming from a petty aristocratic, bureaucratic rather than trading bourgeois, background and trained to become civil servants, jurists, and intellectuals, the majority of this new elite came to perceive their role as similar to that of their equivalent in Continental Europe, with similar concerns for social equality rather than economic freedom and—given the fact that most Indonesians were impoverished peasants—for state intervention in the economy and economic planning.[59]

It could even be argued that there was support in Indonesia for a form of peasant democracy. Although traditional society is usually described as feudal and hierarchical, it appears that at least on a village level there was a developed sense of equality, social justice, and accountability.[60] If this egalitarian harmony was disturbed the result has often been messianic rebellions in which economic issues, rather than religious ones, were the prime movers.[61] There are even instances where egalitarian peasant "republics" existed—or still exist—in Indonesia: the self-insulated Badui community in West Java is a case in point. Moreover, in some localities, particularly in Aceh, noncommunist revolutionary actions took place during the wars of independence aimed, ostensibly, at establishing an egalitarian peasant society.

But the most important democratic thrust in Indonesia was that toward what can be described as "confederate democracy," involving primarily not individuals, but whole minority groups intent on seeking a degree of autonomy within the larger framework of the state, with a system of democratic dialogue as the means to achieve and maintain that autonomy. Almost all significant ethnic minorities as well as the Catholics and Protestants were strongly in support of such a democratic order, and the major parties representing their interests—the Masyumi, the Protestant Party, and soon after the Catholic Party as well—were all staunch defenders of parliamentary democracy. When their political rights appeared to be threatened they were prepared to oppose the essentially Javanese and increasingly authoritarian government, sometimes even to the extent of taking up arms in defense of their perception of democracy.

In some cases motivations overlapped. For instance, the Masyumi largely represented certain ethnic interests as well as the interests of much of the trading and manufacturing middle classes throughout Java, and at times could be seen to support the principles of social equality too.[62]

Crucial for the course of Indonesian democracy were the attitudes of Sukarno, who influenced Indonesian politics until 1966 more than any other individual, and those of the army leaders who have controlled the fate of the country ever since. Sukarno was influenced by traditional Javanese thought as well as Marxism, Western European social democracy, and Islam without being totally committed to any of them. Rather, he attempted to synthesize them and thereby become acceptable to all major streams of thought as the great unifier of this diverse society. Yet, at the beginning of his Guided Democracy, he practically disenfranchised most ethnic minorities as well as the intellectual community by banning the Masyumi and the PSI. During the following years he argued for a continuing revolution and the unity of nationalist, religious, and communist parties for this common cause, only to see his dream collapse in a huge bloodbath.

Future generations are unlikely to see him as the "great unifier" he purported to be, but may hail him as the founder of a viable form of Indonesian democracy. His criticism of liberal democracy had started in 1949, culminating in a number of speeches he made at the end of 1956 and the beginning of 1957, when he stressed that he was a democrat; however, "I don't desire democratic liberalism. On the contrary I want a guided democracy."[63]

Sukarno opposed Western parliamentary practices and majority decisions—"50 percent plus one are always right"—as essentially enhancing rather than solving conflict, putting minorities forever in the position of permanent losers. Rather, he felt Indonesia ought to return to the age-old form of democracy practiced in the villages, where deliberations were held until consensus emerged, in the spirit of mutual cooperation. This, in his view, was true democracy, brought about under the guidance of a trusted elder who could summarize and aggregate all expressed sentiments and pronounce the decisions of the assembled.[64]

Musyawarah became the apparent practice in the legislative assemblies of his Guided Democracy. Yet this kind of democracy must be pronounced a failure not so much because it had proven unworkable, but because these assemblies were unrepresentative, with no elections ever held during Guided Democracy, and large groups excluded from the process of decision making, which increasingly came to rest solely in the hands of the president.

The army's attitudes toward democracy have been no less ambivalent. Although alienated by the early socialist cabinets and the conduct of parliament between 1952 and 1956, army leaders have in the main supported or at least tolerated the system of parliamentary democracy as long as parliamentarians were able and willing to put together government coalitions. Only when parliament ceased to function did they seek to involve themselves in the processes of decision making, not as usurpers of all power but as one of the forces determining the fate of the nation.

Of particular importance are the views of Nasution, who has had by far the greatest impact on the evolving ideological platform of the army. As a Batak from North Sumatra he was well aware of the ethnic problems of the country, and while he abetted the smashing of the federalist order he has also continued to call for adequate preservation of the rights of the Outer Islands. Making the *Pancasila* the centerpiece of the army's ideology, he committed himself implicitly, and often enough explicitly as well,[65] to maintaining some form of democracy.

With guerrilla warfare the major defense strategy until well into the 1980s, and the army's involvement in antiguerrilla warfare to smash the numerous internal uprisings, Nasution was keenly concerned with keeping the civil population on the government's side by respecting their aspirations and preventing their total impoverishment.[66] His insistence that social policies ought to have priority over foreign policy goals provided Sukarno with the means to relieve him of the command over the army. As chairman of the (provisional) People's Deliberative Council, MPR(S), he enhanced the legislative role of this body and became a vocal critic of the Soeharto regime when, after an initial "liberal" period that saw open debate on the future of the political system and a strengthening of political parties in parliament at the expense of the functional groups,[67] it became increasingly authoritarian.[68]

We now can summarize the strength of democratic forces in Indonesia and assess their potential. At the general elections of 1955 the "hard-line" democratic parties—the Masyumi, PSI, the two Christian parties, and possibly the PSII—received over 30 percent of the popular vote. This of course is far short of a majority, but it ought to be remembered that democracy itself was not an election issue, and none of the major parties explicitly rejected parliamentary democracy. Yet, barely eighteen months later, parliament had lost the will and the capacity to form another coalition and thereby surrendered its prerogative to select the executive branch of government, bringing parliamentary rule effectively to an end.

Clearly, this rather sudden turnabout cannot primarily be blamed on society at large and its reportedly low level of affection for democracy: the masses had little, if any, direct impact on what was substantially politics among a very small elite. It is the actions and attitudes of this elite—and especially those sections of the elite that purportedly stood for democracy—which must be scrutinized.

The explanation for the demise of parliamentary democracy lies in a number of ideological, structural, tactical, and personal errors and shortcomings of the democratic elite, and a lack of concern and farsightedness on the part of the less democratic politicians. First, the goals of the parties committed to Western forms of democracy were diverse, focusing on the principle of equality in the PSI, on economic freedom in sections of the Masyumi and the PSII constituencies, and on the concern for minority rights in the Christian parties as well as in the Masyumi. Yet this did not prevent these parties from cooperting closely with each other, probably because their goals remained so ill-defined, papering over differences but also hindering the emergence of a long-term common strategy.

Second, the fact that Indonesia had a multistructured minority problem was not sufficiently recognized. The parties of the wartime republic, including all the "hard-line" democratic parties, were opposed to the (democratic) federal order that obviously would have been the most promising constitutional arrangement to contain the evident anxieties of the ethnic minorities.[69] Just browbeating or even clobbering ethnic minorities into submission did not solve the problem at all; rather, it led to protracted internal warfare for more than a decade and only heightened the tensions between the Javanese majority and the non-Javanese minorities. Had the Masyumi, as well as republican leaders hailing from the Outer Islands, such as Vice-President Hatta, Sutan Sjahrir, and General Nasution, stood up for a possibly somewhat revised federal order, the history of Indonesia would have taken an entirely different course.

Third, the general elections of 1955 were fought mainly on the issue of Islam versus secularism. It was a grave tactical error to assume that the future of democratic government was not an issue worthy of attention during the election campaign, particularly in view of the fact that the constant overthrow of cabinets pointed to a serious malfunction and increasingly came under public questioning. Another tactical error of consequence was for the Masyumi to desert the second Ali cabinet in early 1957 and, a year later, to be a leading partner in the anti-Jakarta revolutionary government in Sumatra. The interests of the Outer Islands, of Indonesia as a whole, and of the cause of democracy would have been better served if it had stayed in the coalition and worked diligently toward an alleviation of the grievances of the non-Javanese regions.

Fourth, the democratic parties and leaders commonly seen to be associated with them were far from setting high standards of democratic behavior or democratic commitment. The Socialists, often seen as the most Westernized and democratic party in Indonesia's history, usurped power in November 1945 and attempted—rather undemocratically—to govern without majority support in parliament. Their intellectual exclusiveness and arrogance prevented them from building a mass base, with devastating consequences at the 1955 elections. Sutan Sjahrir, for all practical purposes, dropped out of active politics after the demise of his third cabinet; the Sultan of Jogjakarta, a democrat loosely connected to the PSI, remained muted in the last years of parliamentary democracy; and Vice-President Hatta, the Outer Islands' counterweight to Sukarno, even deserted his office in 1956 while the ethnic crisis came to boiling point.

Evidently, these failures and personal shortcomings did enormous damage to the cause of democracy. But considerable blame also has to be allocated to the other parties who professed to be democratic in one form or another. All happily participated in the game of toppling cabinets, thereby preventing urgently needed, fundamental policies from being devised and implemented, as well as giving parliamentary democracy a bad name. Their unwillingness to form another coalition after Ali's second resignation, and their inability to take any major political initiative in the following two years before Guided Democracy was promulgated, represent one of the least explicable features of Indonesian history, particularly when seen against the background of Sukarno's frequent threats of a government by a "youth junta" or possibly a military regime.

The self-inflicted impotence of the parties carried over into Guided Democracy and the New Order. During the years 1967–1969 the parties were provided with another chance of playing a significant role. With a return to liberal, parliamentary democracy absolutely out of the question because of its perceived instability and unimpressive track record, the two-party system proposed by the West Java army leadership and its allies could have been a way back to political prominence for party politicians. But only the Catholic Party realized that this might be the last opportunity for a long time to come to create a truly democratic order, and offered to merge itself into such an order; all other national party organizations declined, only to find themselves a few years later in a three-"party" system in which the traditional parties command some influence only by virtue of the *musyawarah*-type of parliamentary debate, without which they would jointly be outvoted on every single issue.

In summary, there are many ways and approaches to explain the demise of parliamentary democracy, most with some intrinsic value. The approach developed here has been to look not at the lack of support for democratic values, but to search for both the actual and the potential support and to find an answer to the question of why this potential was not fully harnessed. While recognizing that Javanese society in particular is culturally not well disposed toward democratic thought, this approach suggests that the structure of Indonesian society as a whole, and the interests of existing and emerging groups and classes, are such that democracy ought not to be regarded as a necessarily lost cause. A greater intellectual effort on the part of those committed to democracy, identifying the problems of democracy, aggregating the political aspirations of those sections of society explicitly or implicitly in support of one or the other model of democratic government outlined above, and devising suitable strategies and behavior patterns might have saved the parliamentary system or might, in the future, create an order more democratic than the present regime.

• THEORETICAL ANALYSIS •

Overall Trends and Dependent Variables

Indonesia's checkered history does not allow us to conclude that the country is—or ever was with the exception of an eighteen month period in 1955–1957—democratic within the confines of Dahl's definition of polyarchy. But, as will be argued in the concluding section, the possibility of Indonesia becoming a more democratic polity—probably along lines beyond the definitions of democracy used in this comparative study—cannot be ruled out.

We may gain a better understanding of the fate of democracy in Indonesia if we apply the three democracy variables and the two stability variables set for this study, to the four major periods of Indonesian history and their subcategories, and use a three-tier marking system to evaluate the prominence of each variable at any one time (see Table 11.4).

The variable of inclusive popular participation in the selection of top office bearers through fair and free general elections was lacking during the struggle for independence: the composition of parliaments

Table 11.4 Democracy and Stability in the Indonesian Polity, 1945–1987

Period	Democracy Variables			Stability Variables	
	Competition	Inclusiveness	Liberties	Persistence	Legitimacy
Struggle for Independence, 1945–1949	medium	low	high	low	low
Federalist Order, 1950	medium	low	medium (declining)	low	low
Parliamentary Democracy, 1950–1954	medium	low	high	low	medium
Parliamentary Democracy, 1955–1957	medium (improving)	medium	high	low	medium (declining)
Martial Law Rule, 1957–1959	low	low	medium (declining)	medium	low
Guided Democracy, 1959–1966	medium (declining)	low	low	high (declining)	medium (declining)
Early New Order, 1966–1973	low	low (improving)	low	medium (improving)	low (improving)
Late New Order, 1974–1987	low	low (improving)	low (improving)	high	medium

was the result of the guesswork and political sympathies of President Sukarno and his advisors, as well as the lobbying of political forces dissatisifed with their share of the spoils. During parliamentary democracy, general elections were held in 1955 that had some bearing on coalition politics within parliament; two years later, in 1957, provincial elections took place in Java, with the major result of Sukarno becoming increasingly sympathetic to including the winning PKI in national government. At no stage has a president been elected directly by the people. According to the 1945 Constitution in force between 1945 and 1949, and since 1959, the Deliberative People's Congress elects the president. Sukarno was for the first time "elected" by congress in 1963—after eighteen years in office—and not for a particular term, but for life (reversed three years later)! And the congress that "elected" him had not been the result of an electoral process but had been handpicked by Sukarno himself. In the New Order four parliaments were popularly elected, but with the government "party" GOLKAR so strongly winning that this had little impact on the tenure of General Soeharto. With choices limited to three parties, and with "extremists" of both the Left and the Right denied the right to be elected to any leadership positions (including a seat in parliament), "inclusiveness" has remained essentially low although it now is an improvement over the degree of inclusiveness of Guided Democracy.

Similarly, the variable of legitimacy does not reveal a significant movement up or down in a consistent pattern. Legitimacy has been at no stage high since some significant sections of society were always denied an input into the political system. The result was significant authority deficits and levels of alienation, which in the early decades of Indonesian history, moved people to take up arms against the central authorities, and of late have prompted demonstrations, protests, and riots.

The three remaining variables form a clear pattern, with the year 1957 as the major watershed, but not one that portends well for democracy. Competition was at a medium level in the earlier stages: while the offices of president and vice-president were not up for grabs, the position of prime minister changed hands so frequently that it seriously imperiled the stability of the nation. Since the introduction of martial law rule and the abolition of the prime ministership competition has drastically declined. The most horrible result of the lack of properly institutionalized competition was the events between 1 October 1965 and the end of that year. Admittedly Sukarno was relieved of his office, but only under extraordinary circumstances. And while Soeharto has been challenged more than once during the late 1970s, these challenges were, more typically, met by forceful responses in the form of jail sentences. At the same time civil liberties have been eroded from a "high" in pre-1957 periods to a "low" in 1959, with the only signs of improvement being the barely tolerated activities of human rights advocates in the New Order, the occasional finding by a court against the state, or the provision for defendants in political trials to turn court sessions into an arena for political debate and agitation,[70] signaling a possible increase in political autonomy on the part of the judiciary. Conversely, the persistence of governments has significantly improved from very low standards in the pre-1957 periods to a situation where toppling a government by legal means has become virtually impossible.

Thus the only conclusion one is allowed to draw from this tabulation of variables is that, over the decades, Indonesia has moved from a highly unstable, less-than-perfect democracy (somewhere at the bottom end of the given category 3 of "mixed success: democratic but unstable") to a system that is basically stable but democratic largely in name only, but that features traces of an indigenous form of democracy and also contains prospects for a more democratic polity in the future (a combination of category 4, "mixed success: partial democracy" and category 5, "failure but promise"). These findings can be further sustained by examining a number of independent variables.

Political Culture

While we can assume that some kind of deliberative democracy may have existed on the lower administrative levels of many societies in the archipelago, on state and district levels the predominant political culture in the past resembled an essentially feudal and authoritarian order. In the Javanese value system power derives from the cosmos and is neither good nor evil. It is bestowed on one person, the sultan, and anyone acquiring any power independent of that of the sultan will do so at the expense of the power of the sovereign.[71] The implications of such a belief system are clear: a political order that is not based on some form of political morality is unlikely to evolve into a democratic polity. Second, the central authorities cannot tolerate an opposition or anybody gathering power resources independently because this will endanger the political potency of the state. These ideas are not just matters of the past. Traditional values are constantly transmitted through the enormously popular Javanese shadow play, the *wayang*,[72] socializing youths into a political culture that modern elites have recognized to be advantageous for their retention of office.

But Javanese values are not necessarily those of all minorities, and national leaders have from the beginning of the emergence of nationalism attempted to establish a national political culture. While Sukarno tried to create unity by introducing Guided Democracy and propagating NASAKOM, the unity of secular nationalists, religious forces, and Communists, Soeharto has fostered the *Pancasila* as the uniting symbol. Building a new national culture has involved running *Pancasila* indoctrination courses, confining all parties and organizations to publicly state their adherence to the *Pancasila*, and even dubbing his political order "*Pancasila* Democracy." With one of the *silas* being a commitment to democracy, and another one a commitment to social justice, there is at least verbally a shift from traditional authoritarianism to more progressive values that may, over time, lead to a more democratic system of government. But whether all minorities will accept the *Pancasila*ization program is a different matter altogether: their suspicions of the Javanese still linger on, and such fiercely independent-minded groups as the Acehnese may well regard the *Pancasila* as just another device to subdue the minorities.

Legitimacy and Effectiveness

Legitimacy in Indonesia has been based on a mixture of traditional concepts, "revolutionary" credentials, and political as well as economic effectiveness. Sukarno was hailed by many Javanese as the messianic *Ratu Adil*, the Just Prince, who would turn the "mad ages" (of colonialism, occupation, and struggle) into the "golden ages" (of peace and popular well-being). He was accepted, also by the minorities, as the most outstanding nationalist leader, notwithstanding the facts that his leadership during the "revolution" against the Dutch was more often than not indecisive and his strategies questionable. The lack of effectiveness of the government did not affect his standing since he had started early to criticize the system of parliamentary democracy, but it affected the political parties that had operated it. It may well be said that, with the exception of the PKI, the parties never regained the prestige they gambled away during the era of parliamentary democracy.

But even the charismatic Sukarno could not forever escape public judgment regarding his effectiveness as a leader, and his downfall during the period 1966–1967 has to be largely attributed to the collapse of his political vision, the malfunctioning of his political institutions, and the breakdown of the economy. Soeharto, who has "revolutionary" credentials as one of the more successful military commanders during the guerilla war[73] but absolutely no charisma, realizes that his legitimacy rests solely on his capacity to provide "good government." From the beginning his regime has aimed primarily at achieving internal rather than external goals—the rehabilitation of the economy as "the center of its attention" and securing political stability, a policy for which it had a mandate from the people who helped topple Sukarno, as well as from the People's Deliberative Congress.[74]

Until now, except for a rather bizarre incident in 1976 in which a mystic sought the transfer of presidential office from Soeharto to the former Vice-President Hatta—and ultimately to himself—hardly anyone has openly challenged Soeharto's authority to govern. There has been severe criticism of the regime, though, particularly by students[75] and, lately, by retired military officers questioning the regime's legitimacy on the basis of its corruption, the excessively large role of the military in civilian roles, the character of its economic policies, and its unsatisfactory lack of democratic procedures.[76] But it appears that as long as a growing proportion of the population enjoys the fruits of Soeharto's economic policies and remembers the economic and political chaos of the pre-Soeharto days, his legitimacy may be questioned but his critics will not gain enough elite and popular support to endanger his tenure of office.

But it is by no means certain whether Soeharto can maintain such a degree of legitimacy. A significant downturn in the economy, a fading in the memory of what pre-Soeharto Indonesia was like, and popular dissatisifaction with too much stability at the expense of participation may dent his legitimacy.

Historical Development of Democracy

While colonial rule was indeed very oppressive during most of Dutch domination, it allowed during the early half of the twentieth century the emergence of very different political forces. In fact nationalist forces were sharply divided along ideological lines, burdening the republic with a degree of divisiveness and excessive competition long before participatory, democratic procedures could be established. The struggle for independence, including the wars in 1947 and 1948–1949, did little to overcome this divisiveness. Under these circumstances democratic procedures emerged less from a popular will for democratic government than from the need of divided elites to establish the means of communicating with each other.

The Round Table Conference of 1949 between Indonesian nationalists and the Dutch, which created the short-lived federalist order, doubtlessly helped to institutionalize democracy in Indonesia. Yet concepts of democracy current among Indonesians at the time of the transfer of sovereignty bore little resemblance to Western—and particularly Anglo-Saxon—concepts of democracy: there was little concern for the rule of law, the idea of a system of checks and balances, or minority rights; democracy was seen, rather, as a means of nation building. In some of the advocates of democracy the idea of *musyawarah*-style village democracy was still alive; others sponsored democracy because they had learned to operate the parliamentary system, and because their power depended on maintaining parliament as an institution. Furthermore, democracy was seen as a means to demonstrate to the world that Indonesia was a politically mature nation.[77]

Last, there simply was no alternative to some form of democracy. A return of absolute monarchy would have been an anachronism. Military rule was no alternative either, although the prestige of the army had risen considerably as a result of its waging war on the Dutch while the civilian leadership had surrendered. The charismatic General Sudirman, the only military man commanding sufficient prestige to assume government, died in January 1950 and, moreover, the ideological platform of the armed forces at that time simply did not allow for a seizure of power.[78] With the capacity for other possible constitutional innovations sharply limited by the lack of appropriately skilled intellectuals at that stage of development, Indonesia had no choice but to settle for democratic rule. Democracy in Indonesia was thus not the result of a struggle between ruling and ruled classes, and the commitment to its values was therefore at best rudimentary. Not surprisingly, when democracy collapsed few stood up in defense of it, or tried to rally the potential democratic forces which undoubtedly existed in this country.

Class Structure

Until fairly recently class analysis—in the classic Marxian sense—was rarely applied to Indonesian society by either Indonesian politicians or observers and commentators. Virtually the only exception were communist leaders who were ideologically obliged to do so, although this caused considerable analytical and definitional problems.[79]

With very little industry in Indonesia, the industrial proletariat in the pre-Soeharto era has been estimated to have numbered no more than 500,000; their numbers have disproportionately increased since. In the rural areas where two-thirds of the national population earns a living from agricultural activities, peasants with landholdings too tiny to support a family, or with no land at all, are on the increase. Population growth was about 30 percent between 1961 and 1976,[80] and there is a lack of additional arable land, although the governments since colonial times have tried to alleviate the pressure on the land in densely populated Java by essentially insufficient and very expensive transmigration schemes to underpopulated islands.

Apart from relatively few plantations there has been no large landholding pattern. What could be described as a class of landowners, often devout Muslims, consists of farmers with only some more land than can be worked by the owners' families and absentee landlords who have salaried positions in the towns and cities. Until the campaign for the 1955 elections took politics into the villages, rural communities lived largely in harmony, and social relationships were determined by a sense of social responsibility of the richer for the poorer.

A petty bourgeoisie existed in the form of small traders, artisans, and independent craftsmen, and an upper bourgeoisie consisted mainly of salaried middle-class elements drawn from the former petty aristocracy. The richest people were, and are, Chinese and other alien businessmen, while political power has always been held by a very small, Jakarta-based elite of professional politicians both in mufti and in uniform.

The introduction of capitalist values and attitudes by the New Order—propagated in the late 1960s as "mental investment"—had profound consequences. Old social relationships of interdependence in closely knit communities had already been severely damaged ever since the 1955 elections and particularly since the PKI's so-called unilateral actions of land seizure during the 1963–1965 period, but the new drives for economic development, profitability, and efficiency led to further erosions of these relationships and ultimately to greater class differences. In the rural areas land ownership has become more concentrated, and the introduction of more technology has endangered the livelihood of the landless rural workers. In the cities the new economic order has changed the social fabric of society as well, and increased national wealth has also increased income differentials. It now has become more feasible to analyze Indonesian politics in terms of class structure, and especially the emergence of a clearly definable middle class is enjoying scholarly attention,[81] while the study of urban labor is still lagging behind.

Potentially, the shaping of a class society could have enormous consequences. An emergent middle class—as well as an industrial proletariat—could in due time demand political rights for itself and thereby pave the way for a democratic society. However, important here is that such a middle class will not speak with one voice. The trading and manufacturing element of the middle class will, as long as it remains relatively small and comparatively rich in a sea of poverty, not endanger its position of privilege and is more likely to ally itself to the political elite, while the much stronger salaried middle class has a vested interest in maintaining its own power in what is essentially a bureaucratic polity. Equally, the industrial proletariat is unlikely to gear itself for radical action as long as holding down a relatively secure, well-paid job is in itself a privilege. Moreover, the mass slaughter of Communists in late 1965 will not fade from memory for sometime to come and will caution against what may be seen as revolutionary activities. Thus we are dealing here with a phenomenon that may have significant implications for the formation of a democratic society but one that, at best, will require decades before it may come to fruition.

National Structure

Apart from class distinctions, or the divisions between rich and poor, Indonesian society is characterized by an additional four, major, partly crosscutting lines of cleavages (see Table 11.5). Because of the low capacity of politicians to solve or at least contain conflict, each of these divisions have led to hostilities, riots, uprisings, or even outright civil war.

As has been briefly pointed out already, there is a profound disagreement between orthodox and modernizing, yet devout Muslims on the one hand (*santris*), and "statistical Moslems" (*abangans*) on the other.[82] The *abangan* community is largely religious too, but its religion consists of a syncretic amalgam of Javanese animism and mysticism, Buddhism, Hinduism, and—only as a last layer—Islam. In order to resist complete Islamization the *abangans* have pursued policies that on the surface appear to be secular, backing the PNI or, if poor, the PKI rather than the Masyumi, the NU, or other explicitly Islamic parties. Going by the results of the relatively free 1955 general elections, it seems that the *santri* community constitutes a minority in Indonesia. Extremist stances in this struggle between *santri* and *abangan* communities have led to

Table 11.5 Lines of Cleavage in Indonesian Society

Field of Cleavage	
Religious	Santri -----> Abangan[a] <----- Muslim -------------> Christians (Buddhists, Hindus, animists) <-------------
Ethnic	Javanese -----> Minorities <----- Indonesians (1962) -----> East Timorese <-----
Racial	-----> Chinese Indonesians <----- <----- Papuans
Regional	Jakarta <----- Java <-------Outer Islands

Note: [a] Arrows reflect direction of antagonism; double arrows mutual antagonism.

Muslim uprisings in West Java (1948–1963), South Sulawesi, and Aceh, and wider-spread threats of *djihad* (holy war) against the PKI during the latter's policy of "unilateral action" in which Muslim landowners were labeled "village devils."

Clashes between Muslims and Christians have occurred occasionally, usually as a direct result of especially aggressive missionary activities on the part of Protestant churches in particular. The Buddhists and Hindus, inoffensive minorities that keep to themselves, are not involved in large-scale animosities.

Another major line of cleavage is between the dominant Javanese and the ethnic minorities of the Outer Islands and West Java; this, as has been pointed out already, has been a major source of unrest from 1947 onwards. Its latest violent manifestation is the rejection of all Indonesians by the majority of the recently, and violently, incorporated East Timorese.[83]

Racial tensions have taken two forms. There is widespread intense dislike of the Chinese minority, which constitutes approximately 4 percent of the total population, dispersed over all urban centers throughout the archipelago. The dislike, expressed in almost regular anti-Chinese riots, owes more to the fact that the Chinese are also a class than it does to their different customs and values: popular wisdom has it that this 4 percent of the population controls 75 percent of the cash flow. The other form of racial strife concerns the rejection of Indonesian overlordship by the Papuans of West New Guinea, which has led to violent uprisings ever since this province was absorbed into Indonesia in 1963.[84]

The last line of division is between the center and the periphery. All of Indonesia resents high-living Jakarta, where political power and economic wealth are concentrated. While Java's resentment of Jakarta is significant, the sharpest cleavage has been between the entrepreneurial culture of the Outer Islands and that of aristocratic-administrative Java, with the former the export-oriented net earner of national income and the latter the net consumer of the wealth created in the Outer Islands.[85] The regional rebellions of 1956 to 1958 ultimately led to civil war.

Some of these cleavages overlap but they are never identical. For instance, the rebellions of 1956–1958 were mainly regional in character but also reflected ethnic conflict; or, given the strong and active roles Christian churches play in West New Guinea and East Timor, these conflicts are not only ethnic and racial, but religious as well.

Conflict has been managed by the state on four levels, with only mixed success. Naked force has been employed where necessary but, by and large, on a comparatively low level in accordance with the anti-guerrilla warfare doctrines developed in the Indonesian army, which advocates the application of political, economic, social, and psychological means before military actions are launched.[86] Also important, potentially troublesome groups may be appeased by buying their support, thereby forestalling violent discontent. For example, during Guided Democracy Sukarno bought Muslim support by appointing more *ulama* than initially planned to sit in parliament, and by building the largest mosque in the world. Soeharto has bought the support of the Outer Islands by creating an economic climate favorable to entrepreneurial aspirations.

The obvious constitutional solution for solving ethnic and regional conflict, federalism, was discarded for ideological reasons, but the twenty-seven provinces (and, on a lower level, the districts) have their own parliaments that propose candidates for the post of provincial governor to the president.[87] Provincial governments have not only administrative tasks but formulate their own development plans. The central government maintains close control over the provinces, though by selecting the governors and through fiscal control since the direct income of provinces is minimal. Finally, while recognizing the fact of social diversity the state has engaged in large-scale propaganda campaigns highlighting unifying slogans and symbols: during Guided Democracy NASAKOM was (unsuccessfully) employed to serve this purpose, while the New Order has resurrected the *Pancasila* as the unifying symbol of Indonesia.

State Structure and Strength

One of the many weaknesses of the Indonesian state apparatus has been that the bureaucracy has never been really free from penetration by political parties and forces. In the period of parliamentary democracy the civil service was infiltrated and dominated by the PNI: part of the outstanding success of the PNI at the 1955 general elections was that the regional civil service could be employed to cajole villagers into voting for this party. At the beginning of Guided Democracy civil servants as well as cabinet ministers had to choose between party membership and their jobs, and their promotions and assignments became dependent on their allegiance to the president and his policies. The military, under its concept of the "dual function"—both as an agency in charge of external defense and internal security, and as one of the sociopolitical forces of the land—had started to penetrate all state branches and services from 1958 onward. But with the ascendency of the New Order many, if not most, of the top jobs in the civil service came to be occupied by military officers.[88]

These different penetration patterns have prohibited the bureaucracy from becoming an autonomous, truly professional service. Equally damaging has been the fact that Sukarno allowed civil service salaries to decline to such an extent that state employees could not possibly feed their families on their official income and were thus forced into succumbing to the temptation of corruption. It is only due to the widespread suffering of the masses as well, and the existing feudal values with their inbuilt respect for authority, that the bureaucratic arm of the state did not suffer irreparable damage.

Almost the same maladies affected the armed forces. From 1945 onward, party politicians have tried to use the military for their own particular purposes in total disregard of the need to keep officers out of politics if the military was to abstain from intervention. The relationship between the officer corps and the politicians was so tense that one of the earliest goals of the army was to remain free from party ideologies, and to serve the nation rather than the ever-changing "government of the day." The army headquarters had loyally served the democratic order and ceaselessly attempted to inject into civil-military relations a rational and professional system of prerogatives until parliamentary rule was abandoned by the politicians in early 1957.

The army has not increased its political power by coups against legitimate governments, but rather has stepped in whenever vacuums needed to be filled, especially in 1957 and 1966. It has come to see itself as the savior of the nation from rapacious and incompetent politicians as well as rightist and leftist extremists endangering the unity of the country, a role that has become enshrined in military doctrine.[89]

During Guided Democracy, and increasingly so under the army-supported New Order, the life of autonomous social, occupational, and cultural organizations, trade unions, and business associations has been gradually strangled. Only in the last ten years or so have new forces striven to attain a degree of autonomy like, for instance, KADIN (the Chamber of Trade and Commerce). But with the state still the major investor and main proprietor of banks, mines, industries, and trading houses, even potentially independent-minded businessmen can rarely afford to lose government contracts by exhibiting too much autonomy. While private fortunes are being made, though, they are often made by Chinese businessmen who depend on the government and the army for their personal safety, the myriads of licences and concessions required to do business in Indonesia, and the truly lucrative connections. The trade union movement remains firmly under state control, with the former head of the military security and intelligence organization KOPKAMTIB, Admiral Sudomo, as minister for labor and manpower, although wildcat strikes are becoming a more frequent feature of the industrial scene.

Political Structure

The "revolutionary" 1945 Constitution stipulates a bicameral, presidential system in a unitary state, in which political parties compete with functional groups to represent the electorate in both the lower-house parliament and the upper-house People's Deliberative Congress, consisting of the lower house and an equal number of additional members, including regional representatives. According to the constitution, the Congress elects the president and the vice-president and determines the broad guidelines of state policy. Yet this constitution was largely ignored as soon as it was promulgated: elections were not even attempted; the upper house was never formed and, obviously, the president not elected by this body; and within three months of its promulgation a parliamentary system evolved, complete with prime minister, in total disregard of constitutional stipulations.

The negotiations with the Dutch during 1949 leading to the transfer of official sovereignty to Indonesian leaders created a federal constitution that, however, was abandoned in the following year, replaced by a "provisional" constitution that was to last until 1959. In 1955 general elections were held on the basis of a proportional representation system for both a parliament and a constituent assembly. When the assembly declared itself unable to table a permanent constitution the 1945 Constitution was repromulgated in 1959 by presidential edict; it is still in force.

During Guided Democracy the Congress was established, as well as the kind of parliament stipulated in the constitution, with *musyawarah* as its working principle and functional groups sharing representation with traditional political parties. A Supreme Advisory Council rivaled both houses in policy initiatives, while executive power was dispersed between cabinet, two "operations commands," and a variety of semiautonomous state agencies. But with all institutions handpicked by Sukarno, all power and authority rested with the president and, to a lesser degree, with the army headquarters.

The legal profession, following the Dutch example from which it still derives its principles, procedures, and structures, had been independent and even politically prominent during the parliamentary era.[90] But in the Guided Democracy period jurists came under considerable pressure for being too bourgeois and Western-oriented. Their fortunes have been revived with the New Order, though: their expertise—and a working legal system—are needed for modern economic structures.

The party system underwent considerable change too. When the idea of a one-party system fancied by Sukarno died quickly after the proclamation of independence in August 1945, a multiparty system sprang up based on modern ideologies, religions,[91] and regional, ethnic, or simply personalistic loyalties. The more popular parties often created their own trade unions, scout movements, women's organizations, newspapers, and even armed militias. The "simplification" of the party system in 1960 reduced the number of political parties from around 100 to a mere ten; a second "simplification" in 1973 outlawed all parties except the government-controlled functional group "party," GOLKAR, the union of Muslim parties, PPP (Development Unity Party), and the even more artificial federation of all non-Muslim parties, PDI (Indonesian Democratic Party). Party politicians have been unable to grasp the opportunities a unification of weak parties may afford, and have preferred to continue with the bickering and infighting that had been the hallmark of coalition politics in the 1950s. Since the introduction of martial law rule in 1957 political parties—in this order—progressively lost their political will, the capacity for innovative action, and ultimately their political freedom.

Press freedom has declined analogously. The electronic media have always been state-controlled, while the press, either private or party-owned, initially enjoyed privileges practically unlimited by libel laws. Excessively lively, and more concerned with arguments than with facts, the press contributed to bringing liberal democracy into disrepute. During Guided Democracy many newspapers were banned on the insistence of the PKI while others survived only under the protective umbrella of the army. After the 1965 "coup" the situation reversed, with the radical left papers being banned while for the next eight years or so press freedom for noncommunist papers reached new heights. By now, of the quality press only one daily, the Catholic *Kompas*, and one weekly, *Tempo*, have survived waves of closure of newspapers too independent for the tastes of the regime.

Development Performance

During the early years of the republic economic policies and problems held little attraction for the politicians: except for Hatta and his "business cabinet" of 1948, ideological questions and the sheer survival of the republic were the overriding issues pursued to the almost total exclusion of economic policy.

In the era of parliamentary democracy politicians, even those of nonradical persuasions, engaged in expounding philosophical treatises on the desirable nature of the Indonesian economy. As Wilopo, a former "administrative-minded" prime minister, asserted in 1955, "Economic activity has no longer the motive of personal gain but rather the motive of serving the community for the common good."[92] This was seconded by the "PSI-leaning" eminent economist Widjojo Nitisastro, who argued that "the raising of per capita income without an accompanying redistribution of income would ultimately inhibit a rise in per capita income, . . ."[93] in other words, dividing up the cake had priority over baking it.

But what was most damaging to the cause of liberal democracy was neither the preoccupation of politicians with lofty economic models nor the generally rather poor economic performance of "liberal" cabinets. With large-scale and powerful enterprises firmly linked to Dutch and other overseas and resident Chinese interests, the market economy came to be denounced as alien, exploitative, and—ultimately—undesirable. Most important, capitalism came to be seen as inextricably linked to political liberalism, thereby contributing to undermining the rapidly diminishing legitimacy democracy enjoyed in Indonesia.

Not surprisingly Guided Economy, Sukarno's "revolutionary" economic system during Guided Democracy, was in character xenophobic and isolationist: foreign enterprises were nationalized and—in accordance with Sukarno's proudly professed ignorance of economic matters—allowed to run down. Only the army and First Minister Djuanda showed any concern for economic policy until their last initiative to rehabilitate the economy was overruled by Sukarno in 1963, setting the country on a rapid spin into an economic abyss that in the end cost Sukarno his political office.

As has been pointed out already, the New Order of General Soeharto has made economic development the yardstick by which it likes its legitimacy to be measured,[94] and has embarked on a series of five-year development plans started in April 1969. Most foreign observers have given Soeharto the thumb down on this economic performance; some were so keen to do so that they were not prepared even to wait for the first five-year plan to run its course.[95] While the regime has undoubtedly failed on many accounts—income disparity is increasing, corruption is widespread, the country's oil company, Pertamina, went through phases of severe mismanagement, economic development is given absolute priority over political development—it also has its achievements. As noted earlier, it brought down the annual rate of inflation from over 600 percent to 12 percent within two years of taking over from Sukarno. In addition, per capita income has increased sixfold since 1969; the percentage of the population living below the recognized poverty line has dramatically decreased and literacy and life expectancy have improved (see Table 1.1).[96] Indonesia is developing an industrial base and in the agricultural field has reached self-sufficiency in food supplies.

These achievements, which outweigh the economic shortcomings of the regime, strengthen the notion that only "strong government" can deliver the economic goods. Conversely, economic failure is associated with civilian government, which bodes ill for any hope of a return to liberal democracy.

International Factors

From its inception Indonesia recognized that, at least in the economic sense, it would be in the orbit of the West. But this ought not to be interpreted as Indonesia being, or ever having been, pro-Western. Indonesia's foreign policy, at least theoretically, is one of equidistance from both the East and the West, a policy described as *bebas dan aktip* ("independent but active"), probably best formulated by Vice-President Hatta in 1953.[97] Indonesia hosted the Afro-Asian Conference in 1955, and has been one of the founding members of the Non-Aligned Movement.

Attempts by the Truman administration to bind Indonesia firmly to the Western camp forced the resignation of the mildly pro-Western Sukiman cabinet in 1952.[98] In 1958 the United States intervened in Indonesian politics by supplying money, arms, airplanes, and pilots to the countergovernment set up by regional rebels. While Sukarno from 1960 moved cautiously toward better cooperation with the Soviet Union and, later, China and North Korea, the Kennedy administration tried to improve relations with Indonesia by persuading the Netherlands to evacuate West New Guinea and by offering economic aid. The anti-Western stance of Sukarno reached a new height when he denounced the formation of Malaysia as a Western, neocolonialist plot and, in 1965, pulled Indonesia out the United Nations.

The Soeharto regime has often been labeled pro-Western. Obviously it is excessively anticommunist internally, and it has "frozen" diplomatic relations with China, which it considers to have been involved in the 1965 "coup." Moreover, economic rehabilitation, which requires an inflow of capital, has depended on economic cooperation with the West.

But while it has maintained close economic links with the United States and Japan it has never agreed to a formal alliance. .

Indonesians are fully aware that theirs is the fifth largest nation in the world, and that they deserve respect for that fact alone. Any attempts to meddle in the internal affairs of the country, or any pressure exerted on its external policies, have been—and still are—strongly resented and resisted, whether they orginate in the East or the West. For instance, attempts by Australian politicians, academics, and journalists to impose Western values and political behavior patterns on the Indonesians have reduced a once almost intimate neighborly relationship to one that nearly constantly requires some crisis management to stem further deterioration of this relationship into open hostility.

• CONCLUSIONS AND PROSPECTS •

The main purpose of this chapter has been to argue that, contrary to most expressed views, there has been a potential for democratic government in Indonesia, and that the embryonic democratic system once in existence in Indonesia was, essentially, not destroyed by all sorts of sinister antidemocratic forces but, in the first place, gambled away by indecisive, selfish, narrow-minded, and incompetent politicians unable to give the democratic potential of the country leadership and direction. Yet, while democracy was allowed to be gradually eroded it has not vanished without trace, even after twenty years of military rule. The ideological pillars of the state, admittedly all too often overruled by political practicalities and expediency, are focused on democratic ideals, although these ideals may contain indigenous notions difficult to reconcile with Western, liberal norms. The central question in this context is, can the existing democratic potential of Indonesian society become revitalized, and its democratic ideals made operational and institutional?

The starting point for such speculations—and no considerations of future long-term trends ought to be seen as anything else—would be the question of whether the present regime can survive much longer. Provided President Soeharto, now in his mid-sixties, continues to enjoy good health he can be expected to run, basically unopposed, for one more term of office. But then changes appear to be inevitable.

It has to be remembered that military regimes are the results of crises: they are not "normal." They are, almost by definition, not meant to be permanent. I think it was Talleyrand who pointed out to Napoleon that one "can do almost anything with a bayonet except sit on it." History reveals that military regimes face an inevitable legitimacy crisis: they either solve the problems that provided them with the opportunity to intervene in politics, in which case they have brought about their own redundancy; or they fail to do so, in which case there is no point in having them around. Thus, no matter whether they perform well or badly, they, in time, face demands for change.

The Indonesian military is well aware of this dilemma, and therefore has elevated its intervention in politics to something to be enshrined in state doctrine, in which *dwi-fungsi* has been declared a permanent feature of the political system. But doctrines, regardless of how solemnly they have been postulated, have the tendency to wither away under the pressure of changing public moods and political realities.

As has been pointed out the New Order is a political system in which all power rests with one man, Soeharto, and not with a junta or any other clearly defined leadership group that could provide continuity once Soeharto leaves the center stage. It is likely that his successor will come from the senior ranks of the military, but so far no crown prince is in sight. Moreover, the military officers likely to vie for power in the future belong to a different generation, one which cannot claim to have given birth to the republic, and hence cannot derive from that a right to determine the fate of the country. Moreover, this younger generation of officers will have different political experiences and, unlike the "1945 generation" of officers, will be professionally trained men with necessarily different values and attitudes from those of the unprofessional freedom fighters of the late 1940s.

Thus there are general indicators, as well as those specific to Indonesia, signaling that change in the long run is highly likely, if not inevitable. The next question then is change in what direction? Basically, following Huntington, there are four options.[99]

First, a new generation of professional officers lacking the political values and skills of the founding generations of the Indonesian military may choose not only to retain power firmly in their hands, but also to restrict further popular participation if declining economic conditions and the resulting political problems endanger the overall development of the nation as chartered by the military. In some ways, particularly in regard to civil rights restrictions, this option is increasingly implemented already. But such a policy is bound to cause resentment requiring more oppression that in turn of course causes further resentment. It solves no problems and, more often than not, is a sure sign that the regime is already in the middle of a legitimacy crisis and under siege.

Second, a post-Soeharto military regime may follow the example of the early New Order period and expand participation by recruiting new social groups into the ruling elite, while basically retaining power. The new trading and manufacturing middle class emerging—ironically—as a result of the regime's economic policies, as well as a middle class of salaried officials better educated than the average officer, provide the opportunity for such a policy without immediate threats to *dwi-fungsi* and the power of the military. In the longer perspective, however, this may lead to real power sharing with civilian groupings and, ultimately, to demands for the military to return to the barracks.

The professionalism that may tempt the new military leadership group to impose an even more restrictive regime on Indonesia may also work the other way around: respect for professionalism may cause military men to restrict themselves to do what they are trained for, i.e., national defense and, probably, internal security, while providing an opening for the professional politician—provided, of course, he adopts professional standards as well. Thus the military may retreat from government responsibility, while either still restricting participation or allowing a completely open political system to emerge.

Which option will be chosen will depend not only on what the officers deem to be the appropriate choice, but also on the mix of reasons for withdrawal and the preconditions to do so at the time when choices have to be made.[100] If, for instance, opposition against the regime increases dramatically, a military regime will have to offer significant concessions if it does not want to behave like an occupation army; on the other hand, one of the most important preconditions for a return to the barracks is that an alternative elite exist to which power can be handed to.

Given the lack of inherent legitimacy of the new generation of officers, the costs of an excessively oppressive state apparatus (the Indonesian army being extraordinarily small in relation to the population, and very cost-conscious), and the military's professionalism, it is unlikely that a post-Soeharto military leadership group will opt for a more oppressive political system unless external threats or internal unrest make such a choice plausible. Equally unlikely is the fourth option of a complete retreat from political power while allowing unrestricted politicking. Such a choice would allow a return to liberal democracy, a system so discredited not only in the eyes of the military but many civilian circles as well that its reemergence would not be tolerated. Moreover, the military would not entertain the possibility of the radical left or radical Islam to assert themselves in an open political arena. If the military would surrender political control at all it would certainly place restrictions on who could contest general elections in order to bar the PKI, secessionists and separatists, and Islamic fundamentalists from positions of power.

The most likely option then is a gradual expansion of the power elite under military leadership, incorporating the new middle classes, granting more autonomy to GOLKAR, keeping the PDI alive by increased state subsidies, and encouraging the PPP to play a more active role, and, on the outside, strengthening organized labor in order to achieve a better functioning neocorporatist economic order. In the long run, GOLKAR may travel the road of Mexico's Institutional Revolutionary party (PRI), which, although tolerating opposition parties, remained the hegemonic party by whatever means required. Yet, over the last five decades or so the political influence of the military, once a cofounder of the PRI, gradually receded within the party as well as within the state while its corporatist interests were well protected.

Such a system ought to be less oppressive, while allowing more time for primordial loyalties to be superseded by secular loyalties to the state. Also, such a system would allow further experiments with *Pancasila* democracy, i.e., *musyawarah* and *mufakat*, a political system that, given the many diverse minorities in Indonesia and the protection it at least potentially affords them, is increasingly seen to be a more appropriate—and more democratic—system than any of the Western models of democracy. Most important, this gradualist, open-ended option would, for the time being, circumvent the thorny question of whom to hand power to: neither the PPP, nor of course the PDI, would be able to muster majority support in the electorate and thereby be able to promise stable government, a prerequisite for economic development. And such a system would be a step closer to the undertakings given more than forty years ago when the promulgation of the *Pancasila* promised to the people democracy and a "just and prosperous society."

• NOTES •

I am greatly obliged to Barry R. Green for his assistance in writing this essay, and especially for his critical comments on the final draft of this study.

1. Ulf Sundhaussen, "Comparative Analysis and the Study of Indonesian Current History and Politics," in David P. Chandler and Merle C. Ricklefs, eds., *Nineteenth and Twentieth-Century Indonesia: Essays in Honour of Professor J. D. Legge* (Clayton, Victoria: Centre of Southeast Asian Studies, Monash University, 1986), pp. 225–242.

2. See M. A. Jaspan, *Daftar Sementara dari Sukubangsa-bangsa di Indonesia* (Jogjakarta, 1958). See also Guy J. Pauker, "The Role of Political Organisations in Indonesia," *Far Eastern Survey* 27 (1958): p. 135; and Frank M. Lebar, *Ethnic Groups of Insular Southeast Asia* (New Haven: Human Relations Area Files Press, 1972).

3. George McTurnan Kahin, *Nationalism and Revolution in Indonesia* (Ithaca, N.Y.: Cornell University Press, 1952), pp. 65–72; Bernhard Dahm, *History of Indonesia in the Twentieth Century* (London: Praeger, 1971), pp. 38–56.

4. Nugroho Notosusanto, *The PETA-Army in Indonesia, 1943–1945* (Jakarta: Centre for Armed Forces History, 1971); Joyce C. Lebra, *Japanese-Trained Armies in Southeast Asia* (Hongkong: Heinemann, 1977), pp. 75–112.

5. Sukarno, "The Pantja Sila," in Herbert Feith and Lance Castles, eds., *Indonesian Political Thinking* (Ithaca: Cornell University Press, 1970), pp. 40–49.

6. Robert Cribb, "A Revolution Delayed: The Indonesian Republic and the Netherlands Indies, August-November 1945," *Australian Journal of Politics and History* 32 (1986): pp. 72–85.

7. Sutan Sjahrir, *Out of Exile* (New York: John Day, 1949), p. 20.

8. Kahin, *Nationalism and Revolution*, pp. 187–192; Ulf Sundhaussen, *The Road to Power: Indonesian Military Politics, 1945–1967* (Kuala Lumpur: Oxford University Press, 1982), pp. 28–30.

9. For the texts of agreements between the Dutch and the republic, see P. S. Gerbrandy, *Indonesia* (London: Hutchinson, 1950), pp. 195–198, 199–205.

10. For a critical evaluation, see D. C. Anderson, "The Military Aspects of the Madiun Affair," *Indonesia* 21 (1976): particularly p. 19.

11. John D. Legge, *Sukarno. A Political Biography* 2nd rev. ed. (Sydney: Allen and Unwin, 1985), p. 233.

12. Sundhaussen, *Road to Power*, p. 41.

13. T. B. Simatupang, *Laporan dari Benaran* (Report from Benaran), (Jakarta: P. T. Pembangunan, 1960), p. 168.

14. A. H. Nasution, *Fundamentals of Guerrilla Warfare* (London: Pall Mall, 1965), pp. 105–324.

15. Sundhaussen, *Road of Power*, pp. 54–57.

16. Ibid., pp. 64–76.

17. Herbert Feith, *The Decline of Constitutional Democracy in Indonesia* (Ithaca: Cornell University Press, 1962), pp. 406–409; Guy Pauker, "The Role of the Military in Indonesia," in John J. Johnson, ed., *The Role of the Military in Underdeveloped Countries* (Princeton, N. J.: Princeton University Press, 1962), p. 211; J. R. W. Smail, "The June 27th Affair" (Unpublished paper, Ithaca: Cornell University Modern Indonesia Project, 1957). For a dissenting view, see Sundhaussen, *Road to Power*, pp. 86–88.

18. Gerald S. Maryanov, *Decentralization in Indonesia as a Political Problem* (Ithaca: Cornell University Modern Indonesia Project, 1958), pp. 38–42.

19. Feith, *Decline of Constitutional Democracy*, pp. 541–542.

20. Daniel S. Lev, *The Transition to Guided Democracy: Indonesian Politics, 1957–59* (Ithaca: Cornell University Modern Indonesia Project, 1966), p. 15.

21. For a detailed account of the second Ali cabinet, see Feith, *Decline of Constitutional Democracy*, pp. 462–555.

22. Sundhaussen, *Road to Power*, pp. 107–111.

23. Feith, *Decline of Constitutional Democracy*, pp. 515–518.

24. C. L. M. Penders and Ulf Sundhaussen, *Abdul Haris Nasution, A Political Biography* (Brisbane: University of Queensland Press, 1985), pp. 130–133.

25. Ibid., pp. 132–136.

26. The most enlightening study of the relationship between the president and the PKI in the early Guided Democracy period is Donald Hindley, "President Sukarno and the Communists: The Politics of Domestication," *American Political Science Review* 56 (1962).

27. For the actions on 30 September and 1 October 1965, as well as the various interpretations of these actions, see Sundhaussen, *Road to Power*, pp. 194–210.

28. Ibid., pp. 235–236.

29. Ulf Sundhaussen, "The Military: Structure, Procedures, and Effects on Indonesian Society," in Karl D. Jackson and Lucian W. Pye, eds., *Political Power and Communications in Indonesia* (Berkeley: University of California Press, 1978), pp. 66–79.

30. Formally, at least, all parties and most functional groups, mass organizations, and religious leaders in West Java had consented to the introduction of a two-party system. See (no author) *Kubulatan Tekad Rakjat Djawa-Barat untuk Meningkatkan Perdjuangan Orde Baru (The Firm Determination of the People of West Java to Advance the Struggle of the New Order)* (n.p., n.d.), pp. 40–77.

31. Harold Crouch, *The Army and Politics in Indonesia* (Ithaca: Cornell University Press, 1978), pp. 251–252; Brian May, *Indonesian Tragedy* (London: Routledge and Kegan Paul, 1978), pp. 235–236.

32. For the history of GOLKAR see Julian M. Boileau, *GOLKAR, Functional Group Politics in Indonesia* (Jakarta: Centre of Strategic and International Studies, 1983); David Reeve, *Golkar of Indonesia, An Alternative to the Party System* (Singapore: Oxford University Press, 1985).

33. Masashi Nishihara, *Golkar and the Indonesian Elections of 1971* (Ithaca: Cornell University Modern Indonesia Project, 1972), p. 42.

34. At the time of writing Soeharto appears highly likely to seek another five-year term in 1988, when he will be sixty-six years old. For an in-depth discussion see Ulf Sundhaussen, "The Problem of Succession in Indonesia," *Third World Annual 1988*, forthcoming.

35. Sundhaussen, "The Military: Structure, Procedures, and Effects," pp. 45–81.

36. Lev, *Transition to Guided Democracy*, p. 4.

37. W. Levi, "The Fate of Democracy in South and Southeast Asia", *Far Eastern Survey* 28 (1959): p. 26.

38. Feith, *Decline of Constitutional Democracy*, pp. 606–608.

39. Sundhaussen, *Road to Power*, pp. 120–122.

40. Samuel P. Huntington, *Political Order in Changing Societies* (New Haven and London: Yale University Press, 1968), pp. 12–13.

41. Harry J. Benda, "Democracy in Indonesia," *Journal of Asian Studies* 23 (1964): pp. 450–453.

42. Peter D. Scott, "The United States and the Overthrow of Sukarno, 1965–1967," *Pacific Affairs* 58 (1985): pp. 239–264.

43. W. F. Wertheim, "The Missing Link—Soeharto and the Untung Coup," *Information on Indonesia Quarterly* 1 (no. 3).

44. Malcolm Caldwell, ed., *Ten Years' Military Terror in Indonesia* (Nottingham: Spokesman Books, 1975).

45. Ben Anderson, "Last Days of Indonesia's Soeharto?", *Southeast Asia Chronicle* 63 (1978).

46. Sundhaussen, "Comparative Analysis and the Study of Indonesian Current History," p. 228.

47. Benedict R. O'G. Anderson, "The Idea of Power in Javanese Culture," in C. Holt, ed., *Culture and Politics in Indonesia* (Ithaca: Cornell University Press, 1972).

48. Sundhaussen, "The Military: Structure, Procedures, and Effects," p. 49; see also *Far Eastern Economic Review*, 2 April 1982.

49. Richard Robison, *Indonesia, The Rise of Capital* (Sydney: Allen and Unwin, 1986), p. vii.

50. Sundhaussen, "Comparative Analysis and the Study of Indonesian Current History," p. 234.

51. Ulf Sundhaussen, "Democracy and the Middle Classes, Reflections on Political Development" (Unpublished conference paper, June 1986).

52. C. B. Macpherson, *The Real World of Democracy* (New York: Oxford University Press, 1972), pp. 12–34.

53. Robert A. Dahl, *Polyarchy: Participation and Opposition* (New Haven and London: Yale University Press, 1971), pp. 1–16.

54. Gabriel A. Almond and G. Bingham Powell, *Comparative Politics: A Developmental Approach* (Boston and Toronto: Little, Brown and Co., 1966), pp. 73–127.

55. Feith, *Decline of Constitutional Democracy*, pp. 38–45.

56. Peter McCawley, *Industrialization in Indonesia, Developments and Prospects* (Canberra: Australian National University Development Studies Centre, 1979), p. 5.

57. Ernst Utrecht, *The Military and the 1977 Elections*, occasional paper no. 3 (Townsville: South East Asian Studies Committee, James Cook University of North Queensland, 1980), p. 19.

58. Richard Robison, "Towards a Class Analysis of the Indonesian Military Bureaucratic State," *Indonesia* 25 (1978): pp. 18–23.

59. John D. Legge, *Indonesia*, 2nd ed. (Sydney: Prentice-Hall, 1977), pp. 10–11, 131; H. W. Dick, "The Rise of a Middle Class and the Changing Concept of Equity in Indonesia, An Interpretation", *Indonesia* 39 (1985): pp. 85–86.

60. Supomo, "An Integralistic State," in Feith and Castles, *Indonesian Political Thinking*, p. 190.

61. Sartono Kartodirdjo, *Protest Movements in Rural Java* (Singapore: Oxford University Press, 1973), pp. 65–80; Dick, "Rise of a Middle Class," p. 82.

62. Masjumi of North Sumatra, "Welcoming the Social Revolution," in Feith and Castles, *Indonesian Political Thinking*, pp. 56–57.

63. Legge, *Sukarno*, p. 280.

64. Ibid., p. 283.

65. Penders and Sundhaussen, *Nasution*, p. 101.

66. Ulf Sundhaussen, *Social Policy Aspects in Defence and Security Planning in Indonesia, 1947–1977*, occasional paper no. 2 (Townsville: South East Asian Studies Committee, James Cook University of North Queensland, 1980).

67. Nishihara, *Golkar and the Indonesian Election*, p. 57.

68. Ulf Sundhaussen, "Regime Crisis in Indonesia: Facts, Fiction, Predictions," *Asian Survey* 21 (1981): pp. 815–837.

69. Feith alternatively suggests that the antifederalist movement had "enormous popular support." Feith, *Decline of Constitutional Democracy*, p. 71.

70. See, for instance, Heri Akhmadi, *Breaking the Chains of Oppression of the Indonesian People, Defence Statement at his Trial on Charges of Insulting the Head of State* (Ithaca: Cornell University Modern Indonesia Project, 1981); and David Bourchier, *Dynamics of Dissent in Indonesia, Sawito and the Phantom Coup* (Ithaca: Cornell University Modern Indonesia Project, 1984).

71. Anderson, "Idea of Power," passim.

72. Soedarsono, "Wayang Kulit, A Javanese Shadow Theatre," *East Asian Cultural Studies* 15 (1976): p. 94.

73. O. G. Roeder, *The Smiling General, President Soeharto of Indonesia* (Jakarta: Gunung Agung, 1969), pp. 120–121.

74. Department of Information, *Laporan Presiden Republik Indonesia pada Achir Tahun 1968 kepada Seluruh Rakjat Indonesia (Report of the President of the Republic of Indonesia at the End of 1968 to the Indonesia People)* (Jakarta, 1969), p. 12.

75. For instance, Heri Akhmadi, *Breaking the Chains of Oppression*, passim.

76. Sundhaussen, "Regime Crisis in Indonesia," passim; H. Ali Sadikin et al., *Menegakkan Hukum, Keadilan dan Kedaulatan Rakyat sesuai dengan Tekad Orde Baru (Establishing Law, Justice and People's Sovereignty to Fit a Determined New Order)* (Jakarta, 1981).

77. Feith, *Decline of Constitutional Democracy*, pp. 38–45.

78. Sundhaussen, *Road to Power*, pp. 52–53.

79. Rex Mortimer, *Indonesian Communism Under Sukarno* (Ithaca and London: Cornell University Press, 1974), pp. 141–174.

80. Gavin Jones, "Population Growth in Java," in James J. Fox et al., eds., *Indonesia: Australian Perspectives* (Canberra: Research School of Pacific Studies, Australian National University, 1980), p. 516.

81. See Robison, "Towards a Class Analysis"; Dick, "The Rise of a Middle Class"; and Richard Robison, "Class, Capital and the State in New Order Indonesia," in Richard Higgott and Richard Robison, eds., *Southeast Asia, Essays in the Political Economy of Structural Change* (London, Boston, Melbourne, and Henley: Routledge and Kegan Paul, 1985).

82. The key to understanding the differences between *santri* and *abangan* is Clifford Geertz, *The Religion of Java* (New York: Free Press of Glencoe, 1964).

83. See, for instance, Carmel Budiardjo and Liem Soei Liong, *The War Against East Timor* (London: Zed Books, 1984).

84. Robin Osborne, "OPM and the Quest for West Papua Unity," in R. J. May, ed., *Between Two Nations: The Indonesia—Papua New Guinea Border and West Papuan Nationalism* (Bathurst, NSW: Robert Brown, 1986), pp. 49–64.

85. Feith, *Decline of Constitutional Democracy*, p. 31.

86. A. H. Nasution, *Fundamentals of Guerrilla Warfare*.

87. In the eyes of the wartime republic, federalism was discredited because it was seen to be a Dutch design for weakening independent Indonesia and preserving as far as possible the influence of the Netherlands posing as the protector of minority rights. This antagonism toward the federalist order was strongest among Javanese leaders, while republican leaders from the minorities were often more apprehensive. The outbreak of the 1957–1958 regional rebellions verified the fact that the desire of the minorities for a degree of autonomy had been more than a mischievous Dutch invention, although from the perspective of Jakarta it further descredited federalism. Whether federalism would have worked in Indonesia is difficult to say, with one dominant but impoverished ethnic group and many smaller but richer minorities.

88. J. A. MacDougall, "Patterns of Military Control in the Indonesian Higher Central Bureaucracy," *Indonesia* 33 (1982).

89. Nugroho Notosusanto, ed., *Pejuang dan Prajurit, Konsepsi dan Implementasi Dwifungsi ABRI (Fighter and Soldier, the Concept and Implementation of the Dual Function of the Armed Forces)* (Jakarata: Sinar Harapan, 1984), pp. 149–363.

90. Daniel S. Lev, "Origins of the Indonesian Advocacy," *Indonesia* 21 (1976): p. 160.

91. J. Kristiadi, "Sejarah Perkembangan Organisasi Sosial dan Partai Politik di Indonesia" ("The History of Development of Social Organizations and Political Parties in Indonesia") *Analisa* 8 (1984): pp. 602–608.

92. Wilopo, "The Principle of the Family Relationship," in Feith and Castles, eds., *Indonesian Political Thinking*, p. 380.

93. Widjojo Nitisastro, "Raising Per Capita Income," ibid., p. 382.

94. (Major General) Ali Murtopo, *Some Basic Thoughts on the Acceleration and Modernization of 25 Years Development* (Jakarta: Center for Strategic and International Studies, 1973).

95. See, for instance, Rex Mortimer, ed., *Showcase State: The Illusion of Indonesia's "Accelerated Modernization"* (Sydney and London: Angus and Robertson, 1973).

96. R. M. Sundrum and A. E. Booth, "Income Distribution in Indonesia: Trends and Determinants," in Fox, *Indonesia: Australian Perspectives*, p. 462.

97. Mohammad Hatta, "An Independent Active Policy," in Feith and Castles, *Indonesian Political Thinking*, pp. 449–453.

98. Feith, *Decline of Constitutional Democracy*, pp. 198–205.

99. Ulf Sundhaussen, "Military Withdrawal from Government Responsibility," *Armed Forces and Society* 10 (1984): p. 547.

100. Ibid., pp. 548–554.

• The Contributors •

LARRY DIAMOND is senior research fellow at the Hoover Institution, Stanford University. He is the author of *Class, Ethnicity and Democracy in Nigeria: The Failure of the First Republic*, and numerous articles on Nigerian politics and development, and on ethnicity, class formation, and democracy in Africa. During 1982–1983 he was a Fulbright Visiting Lecturer in Nigeria at Bayero University, Kano.

JUAN J. LINZ is Pelatiah Perit Professor of Political and Social Science at Yale University. He has written dozens of articles and book chapters on authoritarianism and totalitarianism, fascism, political parties and elites, democratic breakdowns, and transitions to democracy both in Spain and in comparative perspective. His English-language publications include *Crisis, Breakdown and Reequilibration*—volume one of the four-volume work, *The Breakdown of Democratic Regimes*, which he edited with Alfred Stepan—and "Totalitarian and Authoritarian Regimes" in the *Handbook of Political Science*. From 1971 to 1979 he chaired the joint Committee on Political Sociology of the International Sociology and Political Science Associations. In 1987 he was awarded in Spain the Premio Principe de Asturias in the social sciences.

SEYMOUR MARTIN LIPSET is senior fellow at the Hoover Institution and Caroline S. G. Munro Professor of Political Science and Sociology at Stanford University. He has published widely on various themes in comparative political sociology. His many books include *Political Man, The First New Nation, Revolution and Counterrevolution, The Confidence Gap* (with William Schneider), and *Consensus and Conflict*. He has served as president of a number of academic bodies, including the American Political Science Association, the Sociological Research Association, the International Society of Political Psychology, and the World Association for Public Opinion Research.

JYOTIRINDRA DAS GUPTA is professor of political science at the University of California, Berkeley, where he has also served as chairman of the Center for South and Southeast Asian Studies and coordinator of the Program in Development Studies. His work has focused on politics, language planning, ethnic mobilization, and socioeconomic development, both in India and in comparative perspective. His publications include *Language Conflict and National Development, Authority, Priority and Human Development*, and numerous journal articles and book chapters.

LEO ROSE is co-editor of *Asian Survey* and an adjunct professor of political science at UC Berkeley. He is the author of more than a dozen books and monographs, and numerous articles, on the politics and foreign relations of Nepal, India, and Pakistan, and related problems of conflict and security in South Asia. Among his books are *Democratic Innovations in Nepal, U.S.-Pakistan Relations*, and (with Richard Sisson) *War and Secession: Crisis Decision-Making in South Asia, 1971*. During 1984–1985, he was a member of the Policy Planning Staff for South Asia of the U.S. Department of State, and has served for many years as a consultant to it.

URMILA PHADNIS is professor of south asian studies at Jawaharlal Nehru University in New Delhi, India, and has been a Commonwealth Senior Fellow at the University of Sussex and a Fulbright Scholar at the University of California, Berkeley. A native of India, her field work has also taken her to Sri Lanka, Nepal, Bangladesh, Pakistan, Maldives, and Bhutan. Among her four books and numerous articles on the politics of South Asia are *Religion and Politics in Sri Lanka* and *Maldives: Winds of Change in an Atoll State* (with Ela Dutt Luithui). She has also co-edited (with Indira Malani) *Women of the World: Illusion and Reality* and (with S. D. Muni and Kalim Bahadur) *Domestic Conflicts in South Asian States*. Currently she is writing a comparative study of ethnicity and politics in South Asia.

ERGUN ÖZBUDUN is professor of constitutional law and comparative politics at Ankara University Law School in Turkey. Currently he is also president of the Turkish Political Science Association and vice-president of the Turkish Democracy Foundation. He has been a visiting professor at numerous other institutions, including Columbia University and the Woodrow Wilson School at Princeton. He has written widely on democratic politics both in Turkey and in comparative perspective. He is the author of three books, including *Social Change and Political Participation in Turkey*. Among his edited works are *The Political Economy of Income Distribution in Turkey* (with Aydin Ulasan), *Ataturk: Founder of a Modern State*, and *Competitive Elections in Developing Countries* (with Myron Weiner).

KARL D. JACKSON is associate professor of political science at the University of California, Berkeley. He has written extensively on the politics, national security, and economic development of Southeast Asia. He is the author of *Traditional Authority, Islam and Rebellion*. He is also editor of *Cambodia, 1975–1978: Rendezvous with Death, Political Power and Communication in Indonesia* (with Lucian Pye), *ASEAN Security and Economic Development* (with Hadi Soesastro), *ASEAN in Regional and Global Context*, and *United States-Thailand Relations*. In June 1986, after completing his contribution to this volume, he took an assignment in Washington as deputy assistant secretary of defense for East Asia and the Pacific.

SUNG-JOO HAN is professor of political science at Korea University, where he has also served as director of the Asiatic Research Center. He has written extensively about South Korean politics, development, and foreign relations. Among his English-language publications are *The Failure of Democracy in South Korea* and several edited works, including *The U.S.-South Korean Alliance* (with Gerald L. Curtis) and *Foreign Policy of the Republic of Korea* (with Youngnok Koo). Professor Han is also a columnist for *Newsweek International* and a director of the Korean Political Science Association, and has been a visiting professor at Columbia University.

CHAI-ANAN SAMUDAVANIJA is professor of political science and a Royal Scholar at Chulalongkorn University in Bangkok, Thailand. In addition to his 30 books in Thai on Thai politics, he is the author of many articles in English, and two books, *Political Conflict in Thailand* (with David Morell) and *The Thai Young Turk*. He was a member of the 1974 Constitutional Drafting Committee, secretary of the Thai Legislative Reform Committee (1974), and adviser to the Prime Minister (1980–1981), in addition to numerous other positions of government and academic service. In 1986 he was honored as the most outstanding researcher in political science by the Thai National Research Council. Currently he is project adviser, Management of Economic and Social Development Project, Thailand Development Research Institute.

ZAKARIA HAJI AHMAD is coordinator of the Strategic and Security Studies Unit at the Universiti Kebangsaan (National University of) Malaysia, where he previously headed the Department of Political Science and edited the journal, *Akademika*. He is the author of numerous scholarly articles, book chapters, and reports on politics, administration, social change, the military, and national security in Malaysia, and on ASEAN international affairs. His recent publications include *Military-Civilian Relations in Southeast Asia* (co-edited with H. Crouch) and *Government and Politics in Malaysia*.

DAVID LIPSET is assistant professor of anthropology at the University of Minnesota. He has done extensive field research on politics, culture, and social structure in Papua New Guinea, and has published several articles on these themes. He is also the author of *Gregory Bateson: A Biography*.

ULF SUNDHAUSSEN is senior lecturer in political science at the University of Queensland in Australia, where he specializes in Asian and comparative politics. Among his many works on the military and politics in Indonesia is his book, *The Road to Power: Indonesian Military Politics, 1945–67*. He is also writing about problems of military intervention and withdrawal and democratic evolution and development in comparative and theoretical perspective.

· Index ·